Criminal Litigation In Practice

An integrated guide to the law and practice of criminal litigation

Judith Gowland
Senior Lecturer in Law
LLB (Hons), Solicitor

Joanne Clough
Senior Lecturer in Law
LLB (Hons) Solicitor-Advocate
(Higher Courts Criminal Proceedings)

NORTHUMBRIA
LAW • PRESS

Note:

The case study is a work of fiction and any resemblance to actual events or persons, living or dead, is unintentional and purely coincidental.

First edition	1999
Second edition	2000
Third edition	2001
Fourth edition	2002
Fifth edition	2003
Sixth edition	2004
Seventh edition	2005
Eighth edition	2006
Ninth edition	2007
Tenth edition	2008
Eleventh edition	2009
Twelfth edition	2010
Thirteenth edition	2011
Fourteenth edition	2012

Published in 2012 by Northumbria Law Press
Sutherland Building, Newcastle upon Tyne NE1 8ST

© Northumbria University 2012

ISBN 978 1 906596 16 3

All rights reserved. No part of this publication may be reproduced or transmitted, in any form, or by any means, electronic, mechanical, photocopying, recording, or otherwise, or stored in any retrieval system of any nature, without the written permission of the publisher.

Printed by Northumbria Graphics, Northumbria University.

PREFACE

All legal aid lawyers live in interesting times. The current coalition government has consulted on significant cuts to the scope of civil legal aid, and criminal legal aid awaits decisions on how reductions in the Criminal Defence Service budget can best be achieved, and whether there will be a continuing push to implement a new system of bulk tendering for criminal work. This lull is accompanied by a massive series of court closures, which themselves will impact on the ability of all parties to access the criminal courts.

It is unsurprising that over the last decade more and more firms have taken the decision that they cannot afford to do publicly funded criminal defence work. And yet for many lawyers criminal defence work remains both the most demanding and the most rewarding work that they undertake. Arrayed against the accused are all the resources of the State – the police, the prosecution services, the forensic service – and only the defence lawyer exists to protect the rights of the accused individual, to force the State to prove its case to the satisfaction of a court or of a jury, to ensure that rights of even the least deserving person are properly protected.

Well over 90% of criminal cases are dealt with in the magistrates' courts, and solicitors will deal with the majority of those cases. Solicitors in criminal practice, or their representatives, will undertake all representation at the police station stage of the criminal process. Solicitors are on the front line the criminal litigation process and yet the emphasis of almost all criminal litigation texts remains on those rare cases which are heard in the Crown Court, and which are dealt with by barristers and solicitor advocates with higher rights.

What happens at the police station will fundamentally affect the case against your client – and you, as a trainee solicitor will be giving that advice. What happens with defence disclosure is crucial to the way that a case is presented at trial – and as a trainee you will be responsible for this work. Case preparation is more than simply the planning of your advocacy, taking statements from your client, negotiating with the CPS, obtaining further evidence – all of this will be your responsibility.

In this book, we have tried to focus on the work that you will be doing as a solicitor and as a trainee. We have used cases – often very recent cases – to show how the increasingly complex legal framework is actually applied in practice. It is easier and more entertaining to learn the law by looking at cases rather than simply at statutes. We have also provided a case study, so that you can see how a typical case would be run in practice.

Recent and forthcoming developments

One welcome innovation from the coalition government has been a substantial decrease in the amount of criminal legislation that is currently being considered. This is not to overlook some significant and worrying changes particularly the continuing tension between the case management imperative of the courts and the duty of defence practitioners to uphold their client's rights within an adversarial process. However there has not, this year, been the kind of substantial change to procedural law that we had grown accustomed to.

Significant changes: PACE continues to be subject of regular review, and recently has seen the substantial rewriting of much of Code D on identification evidence. Changes have also been made to Codes A and B on stop and search, given Government expressions of concern about the impact of bureaucracy on the police.

Video technology and criminal justice: The virtual courts pilot - a small scale pilot in which suspects "attend" court via the video room at a police station - seems to be rumbling on, and it may be that this will be seen as quick, convenient and efficient (although the pilot arguably does not support this), notwithstanding some obvious concerns about the ability of defendants (in particular) to engage with the process. Not dissimilar projects that would enable police witnesses to give evidence by live link are likely to become more common. If this is the case, then the priority has to be to ensure that the quality of justice is maintained – and that courts and those who "appear" before them are able to engage effectively with the trial process.

Digital Case Files: The CPS are moving towards a digital system of case work and defence practitioners will have to work alongside this initiative by signing up to a secure email system through which electronic versions of case documents will be sent. Prisons and court cells will permit the use of laptops and mobile devices where solicitors need to use these in order to take instructions from their clients.

Regulation of solicitors: This has also been overhauled and October 2011 saw the new SRA Handbook being introduced, along with the Solicitor's Code of Conduct 2011. The new Code of Conduct is very different from the previous rules and rather than containing prescriptive rules and regulations, it will set out key principles and a list of outcomes to be met by practitioners. The outcomes describe what is expected of you in order to comply with the principles. They are supported by non-mandatory indicative behaviours which illustrate the types of conduct which might indicate whether the outcomes are being achieved. This is a completely new regulatory regime for solicitors and it will be interesting to see how this rather innovative approach develops.

Caselaw: Character evidence continues to make most of the running – Criminal Law Week lists about fifteen appellate judgments in the last twelve months as compared with around four judgments addressing inferences from silence. The Court of Appeal has handed down a particular full and useful analysis of the CJA hearsay provisions in the case of *Twist and others* [2011] EWCA Crim 1143. The court looks in detail at the position in respect of "implied assertions", in this case mainly in the form of text messages, and concludes that in most instances these will not be statements made by a person wishing the recipient "to act upon the basis that a matter stated … is as stated", and thus fall outside the hearsay rules. There will be continuing academic debate, but the judgment is a useful guide.

Case of the Year:

At 1220hrs on 7th November 2010, Paul Hookway was arrested on suspicion of murder. He arrived at the police station at 1240hrs that day and his detention was authorised at 1301hrs. Before the expiration of the initial 36 hour detention period, the investigating officers successfully applied for a warrant of further detention which extended his detention for a further period of 36 hours. Before the expiry time on the warrant, Mr Hookway was released on police bail, returning to the station on five occasions to be re-bailed pending the outcome of further enquiries. He finally answered police bail on 5th April 2011 at 1006hrs with what the police believed to be just over 7 hours remaining on the extended detention clock. Before the expiry of this 36 hour period, the police applied for an extension of the warrant of further detention but this application was dismissed by the District Judge at Salford Magistrates' Court, as the expiry time stated on the original warrant had in fact long since expired. The police challenged the decision by way of judicial review. The question for the High Court was whether it had power under s.44 PACE to extend the warrant of further detention when the original detention of 96 hours from the "relevant time" had expired but due to the suspect's release on bail, he had not spent all of those 96 hours in police detention. The decision of the District Judge was confirmed by the High Court, Mr Justice McCombe pointing out that PACE expresses the limits of detention as being for a period calculated from a "relevant time". In the Hookway case, the relevant time to calculate detention clock was from 1240hours on 7 November 2010 (i.e. the time he arrived at the police station). Despite the provision in s.47(6) that "any time during which [the suspect] was in police detention prior to being granted bail shall be included as part of any period which falls to be calculated under this Part of this Act", it was decided that where a period of time has expired, it does not fall to be counted at all. The application was dismissed. *R (oao Chief Constable of Greater Manchester Police) v. Salford Magistrates' Court and Hookway* [2011] EWHC 1578 (Admin).

This decision left police practice in a situation where police had to arrest, bail and charge suspects within a complete 36 hour period - not an easy task in a murder enquiry for example! Since PACE came into force, police interpreted the detention time limits as relating to a period of hours in detention. There is no express provision in the Act which deals with time spent on police bail pending further enquiries; only a provision confirming that time spent in custody counts (s.47(6)). The Hookway ruling highlighted that a detailed reading of PACE, shows that detention time limits are in fact calculated from a specific time (the relevant time), therefore by implication, time spent on police bail must count towards that time limit. As a consequence of the ruling, any attempt by police to authorise detention where a suspect answers bail for example, three weeks after the initial arrest, would be unlawful. On 5th July 2011, the Home Office introduced the Police (Detention and Bail) Bill. The subsequent Act, comprising a mere two sections, came into force on 12th July 2011, some three weeks after the publication of the High Court ruling. It gave clear legislative authority to the police practice of treating detention in terms of a number of hours and to the notion that the detention clock stops while a suspect is on bail. The Hookway decision caused an instant media furore and instigated the passing of emergency legislation. Irrespective of the huge fuss the case caused, the law on detention time has remained as it always has, and we can effectively continue our practice as if the Hookway case had never happened.

Authors:

The original idea for this book came from Professor Philip Plowden who, in 1999, decided to write a concise and accessible guide to the criminal justice system for LPC students. Professor Plowden is a qualified solicitor and barrister specialising in criminal litigation and human rights. He taught for many years at Nothumbria Law School and became Dean in 2008. Philip was the sole author of the first ten editions of this book, bringing senior lecturers Joanne Cough and Judith Gowland on board for the eleventh and subsequent editions. In 2011, Philip Plowden left Northumbria to become Deputy Vice Chancellor at Derby University and the book is now written and edited by Judith and Joanne. They remain indebted to Philip for creating this book which will continue to be an invaluable resource for budding criminal lawyers.

Feedback:

We continue to be very grateful for the very positive feedback from students, lecturers and practitioners. As ever we are very happy to receive your feedback and if you would like to contact us to suggest improvements, or to correct errors, we can be e-mailed on judith.gowland@northumbria.ac.uk or joanne.clough@northumbria.ac.uk.

This book is, to the best of our ability, up-to-date as of June 2012.

CONTENTS

Preface
Contents
Table of Cases
Table of Statutes and Codes of Practice
Table of Statutory Instruments, Practice Directions, International Conventions and Professional Conduct Rules

1 Introduction

1.1 What is in the book
1.2 Research sources
1.3 Criminal Litigation – an overview
1.4 The Criminal Procedure Rules

Flowchart: Criminal Litigation - overview

2 An introduction to PACE

2.1 The power to stop and search
2.2 The power of arrest
2.3 Cautions
2.4 Powers after arrest
2.5 Search under other powers
2.6 Human Rights Issues

Flowchart: Stop, search and arrest

Self Test questions

3 In the police station

3.1 Detention
3.2 Access to a solicitor
3.3 Advising your client
3.4 The interview
3.5 Fingerprints, footwear impressions and samples
3.6 Identification issues
3.7 The charge and after

Flowchart: Detention and Questioning

Self Test questions

4 Funding the case

4.1 Funding criminal cases: Legal Aid
4.2 Defendants and Costs

Flowchart: Legal Aid

Self Test questions

5 First Hearings

5.1 Getting the defendant to court
5.2 The first hearing
5.3 Procedure on summary only offences
5.4 Procedure on either way offences
5.5 Procedure on indictable only offences
5.6 Committal for sentence
5.7 Transferring linked summary offences to Crown Court

Flowchart: First Hearings

Self Test questions

6 Bail and Bail Advocacy

6.1 Remands and adjournments
6.2 The right to bail
6.3 Refusal of bail: imprisonable offences
6.4 Bail for summary and non-imprisonable offences
6.5 Bail conditions
6.6 How do you apply for bail?
6.7 Refusal of bail – "appeals"
6.8 Human Rights Issues

Flowchart: Bail

Self Test questions

7 Interim Hearings & Disclosure

7.1 Case management by the courts
7.2 Summary trial: Pre-trial hearings and case management
7.3 Trial on Indictment: Pre trial hearings and case management
7.4 Briefing Counsel
7.5 Disclosure
7.6 Human Rights Issues

Flowchart: Disclosure

Self Test questions

8 Advocacy

- 8.1 Advocacy - the basics
- 8.2 Examination in chief
- 8.3 Cross-examination
- 8.4 Re-examination
- 8.5 Speeches
- 8.6 Trial within a trial: voir dire hearings
- 8.7 Conduct

Self Test questions

9 Trial preparation and Trial Procedure

- 9.1 Case analysis
- 9.2 Witnesses and statements
- 9.3 Summary trial procedure
- 9.4 Trial procedure in the Crown Court

Flowchart: Trial Procedure

Self Test questions

10 Sentencing

- 10.1 Sentencing principles
- 10.2 Procedure post-conviction
- 10.3 Custodial sentences
- 10.4 The Community order
- 10.5 Fines
- 10.6 Other Sentences
- 10.7 Ancillary Orders
- 10.8 Road Traffic cases
- 10.9 Sentencing in Regulatory matters
- 10.10 Advocacy – speeches in mitigation

Flowchart: Sentencing outcomes

Self Test questions

11 Appeals

- 11.1 Appeals from the magistrates' court
- 11.2 Appeals from the Crown Court
- 11.3 Further appeals
- 11.4 Human Rights Issues

Flowchart: Appeals

Self Test questions

12 Juveniles and Mentally Disordered Offenders

- 12.1 Principal Aim
- 12.2 Juveniles at the police station
- 12.3 Juveniles and Youth Courts
- 12.4 Sentencing and Juveniles
- 12.5 17–20 year olds
- 12.6 Crime and Anti Social Behaviour
- 12.7 Mentally Disordered Offenders
- 12.8 Mentally disordered offenders at the police station
- 12.9 Mentally disordered offenders at court
- 12.10 Sentencing of Mentally Disordered Offenders

Flowchart: Fitness to Plead Procedure

13 White Collar Crime and Regulatory Offences

- 13.1 The investigation and prosecution of white collar crime
- 13.2 The investigation and prosecution of regulatory offences
- 13.3 Sentencing

14 Introduction to Evidence

- 14.1 What is evidence?
- 14.2 Admissibility
- 14.3 Competence and compellability
- 14.4 Burden and standard of proof
- 14.5 Human Rights Issues

Flowchart: Evidence – the basics

Self Test questions

15 Silence and Inferences

- 15.1 Silence at common law
- 15.2 Failure to put forward defence facts: s.34 CJPOA
- 15.3 Failure to explain objects, substances, marks or presence: s.36 and s.37 CJPOA
- 15.4 Failure to testify: s.35 CJPOA
- 15.5 Human Rights Issues

Flowchart: Silence and inferences

Self Test questions

16 Confessions and the exclusion of evidence

- 16.1 The common law
- 16.2 What is a confession?

16.3 Oppression and unreliability: s.76(2)
16.4 Unfairness: s.78
16.5 Human Rights Issues

Flowchart: Excluding evidence

Self Test questions

17 Character and Disposition

17.1 The basic rules
17.2 Bad character and the defendant
17.3 Admitting the bad character of others
17.4 Other provisions
17.5 Good character

Flowchart: Character

Self Test questions

18 Hearsay Evidence

18.1 The general rule
18.2 Common law exceptions
18.3 The Criminal Justice Act 2003
18.4 Human Rights Issues

Flowchart: Hearsay and the exceptions

Self Test questions

19 Reliability Issues

19.1 Corroboration
19.2 Collateral questions and cross-examination
19.3 Memory refreshing documents
19.4 Opinions and experts

Flowchart: Reliability

Self Test questions

20 Privilege

20.1 Privilege – the basic principles
20.2 Self incrimination
20.3 Lawyer-client privilege
20.4 Public policy immunity
20.5 Human Rights Issues

Self Test questions

Appendix A   Answers to the Self Test questions

Appendix B   *R v Butcher*: a criminal case study

    Document 1   *Custody Record*
    Document 2   *Transcript of Interview*
    Document 3   *Charge Sheet*
    Document 4   *Criminal Record: Peter Butcher*
    Document 5   *Application for Representation Order: Form CDS 14*
    Document 6   *Application for Bail*
    Document 7   *Letter to client: client care and other matters*
    Document 8A–H   *Advance Information*
    Document 9   *Attendance Note: Character evidence*
    Document 10   *Proof and Comments: Peter Butcher*
    Document 11   *Letter to client: Mode of trial*
    Document 12A–B   *Statements: defence witnesses*
    Document 13A–C   *CPS letter and draft indictment*
    Document 14   *Magistrates' court case directions*
    Document 15   *CDS 11: report*
    Document 16A–B   *Prosecution Disclosure letter (A) and Schedule of Unused Material (B)*
    Document 17A–B   *Prosecution bad character application; Defence response*
    Document 18A–C   *Letter enclosing Defence statement (B) and Defence Witness Notice (C)*
    Document 19A–B   *Prosecution Disclosure of witness convictions*
    Document 20   *Plea and Case Management Hearing questionnaire*
    Document 21   *Brief to Counsel*
    Document 22   *Cross-examination of Arthur King (extract)*
    Document 23   *Pre Sentence Report*
    Document 24   *Mitigation speech*
    Document 25   *Form NG 2 & 3: appeal to Court of Appeal*

Table of Cases

A (cross-examination in rape cases) (HL) [2002] 1 A.C. 45	**14.3.4**
Ackinlose [1996] Crim LR 747	**15.4.2**
Agis (2009 Newcastle Crown Court, unreported)	**13.2.2**
Al-Khawya and Tahery v United Kingdon [2009] ECHR 26766/05	**18.4.1**
Alladice, (1988) 87 Cr App R 380	**16.4.3**
Allen v United Kingdom 18837/06 [2010] ECHR 420 (30th March 2010)	**5.8.2**
Argent [1997] 2 Cr App R 27	**3.3.4, 15.2.2**
Attorney General's Reference (No.3 of 2000) [2001] 4 All ER 897	**16.4.4**
Attorney General's Reference (No 2 of 2001) [2004] 2 W.L.R. 1	**16.5.3**
B [2008] EWCA Crim 1524	**16.4.3**
Barnes v DPP [1997] 2 Cr App R 505	**3.6.7**
Barker [2010] EWCA Crim 4	**14.3.3**
Barton v D.P.P. [2001] EWHC Admin 223, [2001] All ER (D)141 (Mar)	**5.1.2**
Baskerville [1916] 2 KB 658	**19.1**
Beckles (R v Beckles) [2004] EWCA Crim 2766	**15.2.2**
Beckles v United Kingdom (2003) 36 EHRR 13	**15.2.2, 15.5**
Betts and Hall (2001) 2 Cr App R 16	**15.2.2**
Birch [1989] 11 Cr App R (S) 202	**12.10**
Blenkinsop [1995] 1 Cr App R 7	**19.1.3**
Blunt v Park Lane Hotel [1942] 2 All ER 187	**20.2**
Boardman [1975] AC 421	**17.2.1**
Bovell [2005] EWCA Crim 1091	**17.3.2**
Bowden [2000] *2 All ER 418*	**3.4.1, 20.1.2**
Braithwaite [2010] EWCA Crim 1082	**17.1.1**
Britzman [1983] 1 WLR 350	**17.2.7**
Brogan v United Kingdom (1989) 11 EHRR 117	**2.6.3**
Brown [1991] Crim LR 835	**18.1.1**
Brown v Stott [2001] 2 WLR 817	**15.5, 20.2**
Carter v Eastbourne Borough Council 164 J.P. 273	**14.1.1**
Chandler [1976] 1 WLR 585	**15.1**
Charles v CPS [2009] EWHC 3521	**16.4.3, 3.1.9**
Christie v Leachinsky [1947] AC 573	**2.2.1**
Christou (1992) 95 Cr App R 264	**16.4.4**
Clarius [2000] All ER (D) 951	**17.5**
Clark (Joan) The Times 27th January 1999	**10.10.2**
Clarke v Chief Constable of North Wales Police, The Independent (C.S.), May 22, 2000	**2.2.1**
Clayton, Re [1983] 2 AC 473	**5.1.2**
Compton (2003) 147 SJ 24	**15.3.2**

Condron [1997] 1 Cr App R 185	**15.2.2, 20.1.2**
Condron v United Kingdom (2000) 31 E.H.R.R. 1	**3.2.1, 11.4.1, 14.5, 15.2.2, 15.5, 20.5.1**
Cowan [1995] 4 All ER 939	**15.4.2**
CPS v Picton [2006] EWHC 1108 (Admin)	**5.1**
Cumming v Chief Constable of Northumbria Police [2003] EWCA Civ 1844	**2.2.2**
Davies [2002] EWCA Crim 85	**20.3**
Davies (Anita) [2006] EWCA Crim 2643	**18.3.2**
Davis [2008] EWCA Crim 1156	**17.2.3, 17.2.7**
Delaney (1988) 88 Cr App R 338	**16.4.3**
Delcourt v Belgium (1979-80) 1 EHRR 355	**11.4.1**
Devas & Co, Re [2002] EWCA Crim 1689	**4.2.2**
Doherty [2006] EWCA Crim 2716	**18.3.2**
Doldur [2000] Crim.L.R. 178	**15.2.2**
D.P.P v Ara [2001] EWHC Admin 493	**3.7.2**
DPP v Bury Magistrates' Court [2007] EWHC 3256	**4.2.2**
DPP v Kilbourne [1973] AC 729	**14.2.5**
DPP v Wood [2006] EWHC 32	**7.5.2**
Dunn (1990) 91 Cr App R 237	**3.4.2, 16.4.3**
Edwards [1975] QB 27	**14.4.1**
Edwards [1991] 1 WLR 207	**19.2.1**
Edwards [1998] 2 Cr App R (S) 213	**13.3.2**
Edwards [2001] EWCA Crim 2185	**19.4.2**
Edwards and others [2005] EWCA Crim 1813	**17.2.3**
Edwards and others (No. 2) [2005] EWCA Crim 3244	**17.2.5**
Edwards and Lewis v United Kingdom [2003] 1 WLR 3006	**7.6, 20.5.2**
Effik (1992) 95 Cr App R 427	**16.3.2**
Elliott [2002] EWCA Crim 931	**15.2.3**
Ferrous Protection Ltd. v Health and Safety Executive [2000] C.O.D. 273	**13.3.4**
Fiak [2005] EWCA Crim 2381	**2.2.1**
Fitt v United Kingdom (2000) 30 E.H.R.R. 480	**7.6**
Fitzgerald [1998] 4 Archbold News 2	**15.2.3**
Forbes [2001] 1 AC 473	**11.4.2**
Fox, Campbell and Hartley v United Kingdom (1990) 13 EHRR 157	**2.2.1, 2.6.3**
Foxley [1995] Crim LR 636	**18.1.3**
Friend [1997] Crim LR 817	**15.4.2**
Friskies Petcare (UK) Ltd. [2000] 2 Cr. App. R (S) 401	**13.3.4**
Fulling [1987] QB 426	**16.3.1**
Galbraith [1981] 1 WLR 1039	**5.4.1, 9.3**
Gillan and Quinton v United Kingdom (2010) 50 E.H.R.R 45	**2.1.7**

Glaves [1993] Crim. L. R. 685	**16.3.3**
Goldenberg (1988) 88 Cr App R 285	**16.3.2**
Goodsir [2006] EWCA Crim 852	**15.2.2**
Goodyear [2005] EWCA Crim 888	**9.4.1**
Grant [2005] EWCA Crim 1089	**3.3.5, 16.4.2**
Great Atlantic Insurance v Home Insurance [1981] 1 WLR 529	**20.1.2**
Gourlay v H.M. Advocate 2000 J.C. 93	**3.2.1**
H and C [2004] UKHL 3	**7.5.1, 7.6, 20.4.2, 20.5.2**
Hadley [2006] EWCA Crim 2544	**7.5.1**
Halsall [2002] 9 Archbold News 3	**9.2.3**
Hall [1971] 1 WLR 298	**15.1**
Hanson, Gilmore, Pickstone [2005] EWCA Crim 824	**17.2, 17.2.4, 17.2.7, 17.2.8, 17.2.9**
Hart and others [2006] EWCA Crim 3239	**11.2.1**
Harvey [1988] Crim LR 241	**16.3.2**
Hasan [2005] UKHL 22	**16.2.2**
Haynes [2004] 148 SJ 181	**3.6.3**
Hennessey (1978) 68 Cr App R 419	**20.4.1**
Hickin [1996] Crim. L.R. 584	**16.4.3**
Highton and others [2005] EWCA Crim 1985	**17.2.4, 17.2.7**
Hillard [2004] EWCA Crim 837	**15.2.2**
Holgate-Mohammed v Duke (HL) [1984] AC 437	**2.2.2**
Horseferry Road Magistrates court, ex parte K [1977] QB 23	**12.9.3**
Horncastle [2009] UKSC 14	**18.4.1**
F Howe & Sons (Engineers) Ltd [1999] 2 All ER 249	**13.3.3**
Howell (1982) QB 416	**2.2**
Howell (2003) Crim LR 405	**15.2.2**
Imran and Hussain [1997] Crim LR 754	**3.3.6, 15.2.2**
Ingram [2004] EWCA Crim 1841	**10.5.2**
James [1996] Crim. L.R. 650	**2.3.1**
Jasper v United Kingdom (2000) 30 E.H.R.R. 441	**7.6**
Jeffrey [2004] 1 Cr App R (S) 179	**10.1.3**
Jones v Whalley [2006] UKHL 41	**3.7.2**
Joshil Thakrar [2001] EWCA Crim 1096	**7.6**
Joyce and Joyce [2005] EWCA Crim 1785	**19.2.2**
Kamuhuza 173 JP 55	**18.3.3**
Karia v DPP 166 JP 753	**3.6.7**
Kavanagh [2005] EWHC 820	**15.4.2**
Keenan (1990) 90 Cr.App.R. 1	**16.4.3**

Khan (1987) 84 Cr App R 44	**14.3.2**
Khan [1993] Crim LR54	**2.4.4**
Khan (Sultan) [1996] 3 WLR 162	**16.5.1**
Khan (Sultan) v United Kingdom, [2000] Crim.L.R. 684	**16.5.1**
Kidd [1998] 1 Cr App R (S) 243	**10.2.4**
Knight (1980) 2 Cr App R (S) 82	**10.5.2**
Knight [2004] 1 Cr App R 117	**3.3.7, 15.2.2**
Kostovi v Netherlands [1990] 12 EHRR 434	**18.4.1**
Kuruma [1955] AC 197	**16.1**
Lambert [2001] 2 Cr. App. R. 28	**11.4.2, 14.5.2**
Lasseur [1991] Crim LR 53	**17.2.7**
Leatham (1861) 3 E&E 658	**14.2.4**
Lewis [2005] EWCA Crim 859	**11.4.2**
Loosely; Attorney General's Reference No.3 of 2000 [2001] 4 All ER 897	**16.4.4**
Loveridge (2001) 2 CAR 591	**16.5.1**
MacPherson [2006] 1 Cr App R 459 (30)	**14.3.3**
Makanjuola [1995] 1 WLR 1348	**19.1.2**
Malcolm v DPP [2007] EWHC 363	**7.1.2**
Mangena [2009] EWCA Crim 2535	**19.3**
Martin (Paul David) The Times 20 December 1999	**17.5**
Mason 86 Cr App R 349	**3.3.4**
Mason [1988] 1 WLR 139	**16.4.2**
Mason [2002] Cr App R 38	**3.3.4, 3.3.5**
Massey, CA, unreported, 13th October 2000	**14.2.5**
McAllister [2009] 1 Cr App R 129 (10) CA	**17.2.4**
McGarry [1999] 1 Cr. App. R. 377	**15.2.3**
McGovern (1990) 92 Cr App R 229	**16.3.2, 16.3.3**
McGowan [1975] Crim LR 113	**10.5.1**
McInness (Paul) v H.M Advocate [2010] H.R.L.R 17	**11.4.2**
McNally v Chief Constable of Greater Manchester Police [2002] EWCA Civ 14	**20.4.1**
McNeill [2007] EWCA Crim 2927	**17.1.2**
Miles [2006] EWCA Crim 256	**10.2.4**
Mills v DPP 173 JP 157, DC	**14.4.3**
Moulding [1996] Crim LR 440	**14.4.2**
Murray v United Kingdom (1996) 22 EHRR 29	**15.2.2, 15.5**
Mushtaq [2005] UKHL 25	**16.3.4**
Nelson [2006] EWCA Crim 3412	**17.2.7**
Newton (1982) 77 Cr App R 13	**10.2.5**
Ngyuen [2008] EWCA Crim 585	**17.1.1**
Norbrook Laboratories (GB) v Health and Safety Executive, [1998] The Times February 23	**14.1.1**

O'Connell v Adams [1973] Crim LR 113	**8.3.1**
O'Halloran and Francis v United Kingdom (ECtHR, 29th June 2007)	**15.5**
O'Hara v Chief Constable RUC [1997] Crim LR 432	**2.1.3**
O'Hara v United Kingdom (2002) 34 EHRR 32	**2.1.3**
O'Hare [2006] EWCA Crim 471	**9.3.1**
Oladimeji v DPP [2006] EWHC 1199	**11.1.2**
Olliver (1989) 11 Cr App R (S) 10	**10.5.2**
Oosthuizen [2005] EWCA Crim 1978	**10.3.2**
Orrell [1972] RTR 14	**18.1.1**
Osborne [2005] EWCA Crim 3082	**16.2.1**
Osman v DPP (1999)163 J.P. 725	**2.1.4**
Page [2004] EWCA Crim 3358	**10.3.2**
Paris and others (1993) 97 Cr App R 99	**16.3.1**
Park [1994] Crim LR 285	**16.2.2**
Parkes [1976] 1 WLR 1251	**15.1**
Patel [1965] 3 All ER 593	**18.1.1**
Patterson, Jamie (2000) 165 J.P.N. 225	**10.3.4**
Pearce [2001] EWCA Crim 2834	**14.3.2**
Pedley & others [2009] EWCA Crim 840	**10.3.8**
Perks, [2001] 1 Cr.App.R.(S.)	**10.3.3**
Porter v Magill [2002] 2 WLR 37	**16.5.3**
Pritchard [1836] 7 C&P 303	**12.9.1, 12.9.2**
R v Benjafield [2002] UKHL	**13.3.1**
R v Boakye [2012] EWCA Crim 838	**10.1**
R v Bryant [2005] EWCA Crim 2079	**7.5.2**
R v Calder Justices ex parte Kennedy (1992) 156 JP 716	**5.6.2**
R v Camberwell Green Youth Court ex parte D, [2005] UKHL 5	**14.3.4**
R v Canavan & others [1998] 1 Cr App R (S) 243	**5.4.1**
R v Chief Constable of South Yorkshire ex parte Marper [2004] 4 All ER 193	**3.1.4**
R v Clark [1996] 2 CR App R (S) 351	**5.4.1**
R v Cundell [2008] EWCA Crim 1420	**5.4.1**
R v Cooper [1969] 1 Q.B. 267	**11.2.1**
R v Cotswold Geotechnical Holdings Ltd (unreported)	**13.1.4**
R v Crown Court sitting at Inner London ex parte LB Lambeth [2000] Crim L R 303	**11.1.1**
R v D [2006] EWCA Crim 1354	**9.4.4**
R v Derby Magistrates' Court, ex parte B [1996] AC 487	**20.3**
R v Elicin & Moore [2009] 1 Cr.App.R.(S)	**10.2.5**
R v Essa [2009] EWCA Crim 43	**7.5.1**
R v H & C (2004) 2 AC 134	**7.5.1, 7.6**

R v Jones [2003] 1 AC 1	**9.3.1**
R v Kefford [2002] EWCA Crim 519	**10.3.2**
R v Manchester Crown Court, ex parte McDonald [1999] 1 All ER 805	**5.1.3**
R v New Look Retailers Ltd [2011] 1 Cr.App.R (S) 57	**13.3.3**
R v Newell [2012] EWCA Crim 650	**19.2.2**
R v Northallerton Magistrates' Court, ex p. Dove [2000] 1 Cr.App.R.(S.)	**10.7.2**
R v Penner [2010] EWCA Crim 1155	**7.1.2**
R v Registrar for Births, Deaths and Marriages ex p. CPS [2003] 1 All ER 540	**14.3.2**
R v Rezvi [2002] UKHL	**13.3.1**
R v Rochford [2010] WLR (D) 220	**7.5.1**
R v Special Commissioner ex p Morgan Grenfell & Co Ltd [2002] UKHL 21	**20.3**
R v Stratford Youth Court ex parte DPP [2001] EWHC Admin 615	**12.2.1**
R v SVS Solicitors [2012] EWCA Crim 828	**4.2.2**
R v Thames Magistrates' Court, ex parte Polemis [1974] 1 WLR 1371	**5.1**
R v Underwood [2005] 1 Cr.App.R.13	**10.2.5**
R (on the application of DPP) v Havering Magistrates Court [2001] 2 Cr App R 2	**5.8.2**
R (on the application of DPP) v Havering Magistrates Court [2001] 2 Cr App R 2	**5.8.2**
R (oao Michaels) v Highbury Corner Magistrates' Court [2009] EWHC 2921 (Admin)	**2.1.4**
R and D [2006] EWCA Crim 1354	**9.4.4**
R (oao Fergus) v Southampton Crown Court [2008] EWHC 3273 (Admin)	**5.6.1**
R (on the application of H) v London Bus Services, Lawtel, 17/01/02	**13.2**
R (oao Jane Laporte) v Chief Constable of Gloucestershire Constabulary and others [2006] UKHL 55	**2.1.7**
R (oao Kelly) v Warley Magistrates Court [2007] EWHC 1836	**7.1.2**
R (oao M) v Isleworth Crown Court [2005] EWHC Admin 363	**5.7.4**
R (oao O) v Crown Court at Harrow [2006] UKHL 42	**5.2.1**
R (oao Punatar) v Horseferry Road Magistrates Court [2002] EWHC 1196	**4.1.3**
R (oao Robinson) v Sutton Coldfield Magistrates' Court [2006] EWHC 307	**17.2.9**
R (on the application of Sonn & Co.) v West London Magistrates' Court DC, unreported, 30/10/2000)	**4.1.3**
R (Marper) v Chief Constable of South Yorkshire [2004] 4 All ER 193	**3.1.4**
Rafferty [1998] Crim LR 433	**5.4.1**
Randall [1998] 6 Archbold News 1	**15.2.2**
Raphaie [1996] Crim LR 812	**2.4.4**
Renda and others [2005] EWCA Crim 2826	**17.2.6**
Re Alexander [2009] NIQB 20	**2.2.2**
Richardson v CC of West Midlands Police [2011] EWHC 773 QB	**2.2.2**
Roberts v Chief Constable of the Cheshire Police [1999] All ER (D) 63	**3.1.7**
Roble [1997] Crim LR 449	**3.3.4, 15.2.2**
Rosenberg [2006] EWCA Crim 6	**3.3.5**

Rowe and Davis v United Kingdom (2000) 30 E.H.R.R. 1	**7.6, 11.4.2**
Rowton (1865) L & C 520	**17.5**
S and Marper v United Kingdom [2008] All ER (D) 56 Dec	**3.1.4**
Salabiaku v France (1988) 13 E.H.R.R 379	**14.5.1**
Samuel [2005] EWCA Crim 704	**16.3.2**
Sang [1980] AC 402	**14.2.1, 14.2.4, 16.1**
Sat-Bhambra (1988) 88 Cr App R 55	**16.2.2**
Saunders v United Kingdom (1997) 23 EHRR 313	**14.5, 15.5, 20.1.1, 20.2**
Sekhon [2002] EWCA Crim 2954	**13.3.1**
Self [1992] 3 All ER 476	**2.2.3**
Senior [2004] EWCA Crim 454	**2.3.1**
Sharp [1988] 1 WLR 7	**16.2.1**
Sheldrake v DPP [2004] UKHL 43	**14.5.2**
Sheikh (Hafeez), Sheikh (Saqeb), Sheikh (Junaid) [2004] EWCA Crim 492	**10.7.3**
Slater [1995] Crim. L R 244	**19.1.3**
Smurthwaite [1994] 1 All ER 898	**16.4.4**
Spiby (1990) 91 Cr App R 186	**18.1.5**
Stevens (1986) 8 Cr App R (S) 291	**10.2.5**
Subramaniam v Public Prosecutor [1956] 1 WLR 965	**18.1.2**
T [2008] EWCA Crim 8.1.5	**12.1**
T and V v United Kingdom [2000] Crim L R 187	**12.3.2**
Teixeira v Portugal (1999) 28 EHRR 101	**16.4.4**
Thomas and Flannagan (1998) Crim LR 887	**18.4.1**
Tompkins (1977) Cr App R 181	**20.1.2**
Turnbull [1977] QB 224	**19.1.3**
Twist [2011] EWCA Crim 1143	**18.1.4**
Vasiliou [2000] 4 Archbold News 1	**7.5.1**
Vye [1993] 1 WLR 471	**17.5**
Wahab [2003] 1 Cr App R 15	**16.3.2**
Wandsworth London Borough Council v Rashid [2009] EWHC 1844	**13.2**
Walker [1996] Crim LR 742	**19.1.2**
Walsh (1989) 91 Cr App R 161	**16.4.3**
Walters [1969] 2 AC 26	**14.4.2**
Webber (2004) 1 WLR 404	**15.2.3**
Weir and others [2005] EWCA Crim 2866	**17.1.2, 17.3.2**
Wildman v DPP [2001] Crim LR 565	**5.8.2**
Woolmington v DPP [1935] AC 462	**14.4.1**
Z [2009] EWCA Crim 20	**18.3.1**

Table of Statutes and Codes of Practice

Access to Justice Act 1999	**4.1.3**	s.52	**5.5**
Anti Social Behaviour Act 2003	**12.6.4**	s.65	**12.2.2, 12.4.1**
Bail Act 1976			
s.3	**5.2, 5.2.2, 5.5.5**	s.66	**12.2.2, 12.4.1**
s.3(6)(d)	**10.2.2**	Criminal Appeal Act 1968	
s.4	**5.2, 5.3**	s.1	**11.2.1**
s.4(2)	**5.2**	s.2	**11.2.1**
s.4(4)	**5.2**	s.9	**11.2.2**
s.5(2)A	**5.2**	s.29	**11.2.1**
s.5B	**5.7.5**	Criminal Justice Act 1967	
s.6	**5.2, 5.5.6**	s.8	**14.4.2**
Sched.1	**5.2.1, 5.3, 5.3.1, 5.3.2, 5.4, 5.6.2**	s.9	**7.3.3, 9.3, 18.1.2, 18.3.8**
Children and Young Persons Act 1963		s.10	**9.3, 14.1.2**
s.29	**12.5**	Criminal Justice Act 1987	
Company Directors Disqualification Act 1986	**13.3.2**	s.2	**13.1**
		s.4	**5.5.1**
Companies Act 1985		Criminal Justice Act 1988	**13.3.1**
s.458	**13.1.2**	s.30	**19.4.4**
Coroners & Justice Act 2008	**14.3.4**	s.40	**5.7**
s.54	**9.3.1**	s.139B	**2.1.7**
s.114	**5.2.1**	Criminal Justice Act 2003	
s.115	**5.2.1**	See also specific CJA 2003 sections in chapters.	
Part 4	**10.1**	s.4	**2.4.5**
Corporate Manslaughter and Corporate Homicide Act 2007		s.11	**3.1.4**
s.10	**13.1.4**	s.13	**5.5**
Courts Act 2003	**7.2**	s.14	**5.2.1**
Crime and Disorder Act 1998	**5.2.1, 10.6.4, 12.1**	s.15	**5.2.1**
		s.19	**5.2.2**
S.1C	**10.6.4**	s.29	**5.1**
s.34	**12.1**	s.34	**7.5.1**
s.37	**12.1**	s.41	**5.4, 5.4.2**
s.51	**5.7.2, 5.5, 7.3.2**	s.51	**9.3, 14.3.4**
		s.98	**17.1, 17.1.1**
s.51 (E)	**5.5**	s.100	**7.5.1, 17.3**

s.101	**17.2**	s.143	**10.1.2, 10.1.3**
s.101(1)(a)	**17.2.1**	s.144	**3.3.5, 5.4.1, 10.1.4**
s.101(1)(b)	**17.2.2**		
s.101(1)(c)	**17.2.3**		
s.101(1)(d)	**17.2.4, 17.2.8**	s.145	**10.1.3**
		s.146	**10.1.3**
s.101(1)(e)	**17.2.5**	s.148	**10.4.1**
s.101(1)(f)	**3.3.6, 17.2.6**	s.149	**10.4.3**
s.101(1)(g)	**3.3.6**	s.150A	**10.4**
s.101(3)	**17.2.4, 17.2.8**	s.151	**10.4.1**
		s.152(2)	**10.3.1**
s.101(4)	**17.2.8**	s.153	**10.3.5, 12.4.1**
s.103(3)	**17.2.4, 17.2.8**		
		s.156	**10.2.1**
s.104	**17.2.5**	s.157(1)	**12.10**
s.105	**17.2.6**	s.162	**10.5.2**
s.106	**17.2.7**	s.172	**10.1, 12.4**
s.107	**17.4**	s.174	**10.1**
s.108	**17.4**	s.177	**10.4.1**
s.110	**17.4**	ss.181-182	**10.3.7**
s.112	**17.1.1**	ss.183-186	**10.3.7**
s.114	**18.1.1, 18.3.1**	ss.189-194	**10.3.6**
		s.224	**10.3.5, 12.3.2**
s.115	**18.1.4**		
s.116	**18.3.2**	Part 10	**5.1.2, 9.4.4**
s.117	**18.3.3**		
s.118	**18.2.2, 18.2.3, 18.3.4**	s.240	**10.3.5**
		s.240A	**10.3.5**
		Sched.3	**5.4**
s.119	**19.2.2**	Sched.5	**5.1.2**
s.120	**19.2.8**	Sched 15	**10.3.8**
s.121	**18.3.5**	Sched 15A	**10.3.8**
s.123	**18.3.6**	Chapter V	**10.3.8**
s.124	**18.3.7**	Criminal Justice and Court Services Act 2000	**5.6.1, 12.5**
s.126	**18.3.8**		
s.127	**19.4.3**		
s.129	**18.1.5**	Criminal Justice & Immigration Act 2008	
s.139	**8.2.2, 19.2.2, 19.3**	s.1	**12.4.1**
		s.21(4)	**10.3.5**
		s.51	**5.5, 5.5.3**
s.142	**10.1.1**	s.98	**10.6.4**

s.99	**10.6.4**	s.3(1)	**7.5.1**
Part 7	**10.6.4**	s.5	**7.5.1**
Schedule 1	**12.4.1**	s.6C	**7.5.1**
Schedule 11	**5.5, 5.5.3**	s.6	**7.5.1, 7.5.2**
Criminal Justice and Police Act 2001	**2.5.3**	s.6A	**7.5.1, 7.5.2**
Criminal Justice and Public Order Act 1994		s.6C	**7.5.1, 7.5.2**
s.25	**5.2.1**	s.6E	**7.5.2**
s.26	**5.2.1**	s.7A	**7.5.1**
s.32	**19.1.2**	s.8	**7.5.1**
s.34	**15.2, 15.2.1, 15.2.2, 15.2.3**	s.11	**7.5.2**
		s.11(2)	**7.5.1**
s.35	**14.3.1, 15.4.1, 15.4.2**	s.12	**7.5.1**
		s.13(1)	**7.5.1**
s.36	**15.3, 15.3.1, 15.3.2**	s.40	**7.3**
		Domestic Violence Crime and Victims Act 2004	
s.37	**15.3, 15.3.1, 15.3.2**	s.17	**9.4.3**
		Drugs Act 2005	**3.5**
s.60	**2.1.7**	Drug Trafficking Offences Act 1986	
s.60AA	**2.1.4**		**13.3.1**
Criminal Law Act 1967		Firearms Act 1968	**2.1.2**
s.3	**2.2.1**	Fraud Act 2006	
s.4	**3.3.5**	s.4	**13.1**
s.6(3)	**9.4.3**	Health and Safety at Work Act 1974	
Criminal Procedure Act 1865			**13.2.2**
s.3	**17.1.2, 19.2.2**	s.33	**13.2.2**
		s.37	**13.2.2**
s.4	**19.2.2**	Human Rights Act 1998	**5.8.1, 5.8.2, 15.5**
s.5	**19.2.2**		
Criminal Procedure (Insanity) Act 1964		s.3	**5.2.1**
s.4	**12.9.1, 12.9.2**	Justices of the Peace Act 1361	**10.6.2**
		Knives Act 1997	**2.1.7**
s.4A	**12.9.1, 12.9.2**	Legal Aid, Sentencing and Punishment of Offenders Act 2012	**4.1, 6.7.5, 10.3.8, 10.4.2, 12.4.1**
s.5	**12.9.1, 12.9.2**		
Criminal Procedure and Investigations Act 1996	**7.5.1, 7.3.2, 20.4.2**	Magistrates' Courts Act 1980	
		s.1	**2.2**

s.5	**6.1**	s.1(7)	**2.1.2**
s.6(1)	**5.4.1, 7.3.2**	s.2(2)	**2.1.4**
		s.2(3)	**2.1.4**
s.6(2)	**5.4.1**	s.8	**2.5.1**
s.8A & S.8B	**7.2**	s.10	**20.3**
s.10	**6.1**	s.10(2)	**2.5.3, 20.3**
s.11	**9.3.1**	s.17	**2.5.2**
s.12	**9.3.1**	s.18	**2.4.3, 2.4.4**
s.17	**5.4**		
s.19	**5.4.1**	s.19	**2.5.3**
s.24(1)(a)	**12.3.2, 12.4.3**	s.24	**2.2, 2.2.2**
		s.24(1)	**2.2.2**
s.101	**14.4.1**	s.24(4)	**2.2.2**
s.108	**11.1.1**	s.24(5)	**2.2.2**
s.111(1)	**11.1.2**	s.24A	**2.2.3**
s.115	**4.1.2**	s.28	**2.2.1**
s.123	**5.1.2**	s.28(2)	**2.2.1**
s.127	**5.1.1**	s.28(4)	**2.2.1**
s.128	**6.6.2**	s.30	**2.4.4, 2.4**
s.128A	**6.1.2**	s.30(10)	**2.4.4**
s.111(1)	**11.1.2**	s.30A	**2.4.5**
s.142	**11.1**	s.32	**2.4.1, 2.4.2**
Mental Health Act 1983			
s.1(2)	**12.8.1**	s.32(1)	**2.4.1**
s.12	**12.10**	s.32(2)	**2.4.1**
s.37	**12.10**	s.37	**3.7.3, 3.1.1**
s.37(3)	**12.9.3**		
s.37	**12.10**	s.37(1)	**3.1.3**
s.41	**12.9.2, 12.10**	s.37(7)	**3.7.3**
		ss.37A-37D	**3.1.3, 3.7.1**
s.136	**12.8.2**	s.38	**3.7.3, 12.2.1**
Misuse of Drugs Act 1971			
s.5	**6.2.2**	s.40	**3.1.7**
s.23	**2.1.7**	s.40A	**3.1.7**
Police and Criminal Evidence Act 1984		ss41-44	**3.1.8**
ss.1-7	**2.1.1**	s.43(1)	**3.1.8**
s.1(1)	**2.1.4**	s.47	**3.7.3**
s.1(2)	**2.1.2**	s.55	**3.1.4**
s.1(3)	**2.1.3**	s.56	**3.1.3, 3.1.5, 12.2.1**
s.1(4)	**2.1.4**		
s.1(5)	**2.1.4**		

s.58	**3.1.3, 3.2.1**	A3.4	**2.1.4**
		A3.5	**2.1.4**
s.60A	**3.3.7**	A3.6	**2.1.4**
s.63	**3.1.4**	A3.8	**2.1.4**
s.63B	**3.5**	A4	**2.1.4**
s.64A	**3.5**	A, Notes for Guidance 2, 3	**2.1.5**
s.67(11)	**16.4.1**	A, Notes for Guidance 4	**2.1.4**
s.76	**14.2.1, 16.2.4, 16.4.1, 16.4.3**	PACE Code of Practice C	
		C 1.7	**12.2.1,**
		C1.7B	**12.8.2**
s.76(1)	**16.2.3**	C 2	**3.1.2**
s.76(2)(a)	**16.3, 16.3.1**	C 2.4	**3.1.2, 3.3.4**
s.76(2)(b)	**16.3.2**	C 3	**3.1.3**
s.76(4)	**16.3.3**	C.3.2	**3.1.3**
s.76(8)	**16.3.1**	C3.6-10	**3.1.3**
s.76A	**16.3.2**	C3.6	**3.1.2**
s.78	**2.4.4, 14.2.1, 14.2.4, 16.2.4, 16.3, 16.4, 16.4.1, 16.4.2, 16.4.3, 20.1.2**	C3.19	**12.8.2**
		C3.21	**3.1.3**
		C 4	**3.1.4**
		C 4.4	**3.1.4**
		C 5	**3.1.5**
		C 5.1	**3.1.5**
		C5.6	**3.1.5**
s.79	**8.7**	C 6.1	**3.2.1**
s.80	**14.3.2**	C 6.4	**3.2.1**
s.80(3)	**14.3.2**	C 6.5	**3.2.1**
s.80(4)	**14.3.2**	C6.6	**3.2.2**
s.80(5)	**14.3.2**	C6.6(d)	**3.2.2**
s.82(1)	**16.2.1**	C 6.9	**3.4.2**
s.82(3)	**16.1**	C 6.12	**3.2.1**
s.117	**2.2.1**	C 6.15	**3.3.1**
PACE Code of Practice A	**2.1.1**	C 6D	**3.4, 3.4.1, 3.4.2**
A1.1	**2.1.1**		
A1.5	**2.1.6**	C 8	**3.1.6**
A2.2-2.11	**2.1.3**	C 9	**3.1.6**
A2.6	**2.1.3**	C 9.2	**3.1.6**
A2.9	**2.1.5**	C 10.5	**2.3**
A2.11	**2.1.6**	C 10.1	**15.2.2**
A2.18-26	**2.1.7**	C 10.11	**15.3.2**
A3.2	**2.1.4**	C 11.1A	**2.4.4**
		C 11.1	**2.4.4**

C 11.5	**16.3.2**	1.13	**12.8.2**
C 11.6	**3.4.3**	3.5-3.10	**12.8.1**
C11.17	**12.2.1**	3.20	**12.8.2**
C Note 11B	**3.4.2**	Annex G	**12.8.2**
C Note 11C	**12.2.1**	Police and Justice Act 2006	**3.7.1**
C12.2	**3.4.3**	Police Reform Act 2002	
C 12.8	**3.4.3**	s.50	**2.1.5**
C 15	**3.1.7**	Powers of Criminal Courts (Sentencing) Act 2000	
C 16.5	**3.7.1**		
Annex A	**3.1.4**	generally see	**Ch. 10**
Annex B	**3.1.5, 3.2.2**	s.1	**10.2.6**
		s.3	**5.4.1, 5.6**
Annex C, para 2	**2.3**	s.4	**5.4, 5.6**
Annex E	**12.8**	s.8	**12.3.1, 12.4.3**
PACE Code of Practice D	**3.6, 3.6.2, 16.4.3**		
		s.12(1)	**10.6.1**
D1.2	**3.6.1**	s.16–32	**12.4.1**
D 2.6	**12.8.2**	s.73	**12.4.1**
D3.1	**3.3.4, 3.6.2**	s.79	**12.4.1**
		s.91	**12.4.3**
D3.3	**3.6.4**	s.91	**12.3.2**
D 3.4	**3.6.4**	s.100, 101	**12.4.1**
D3.12	**3.6.3**	s.111	**10.3.5**
D3.13	**3.6.3**	s.126–129	**10.5**
D3.14	**3.6.5**	s.130	**10.7.1**
D3.16	**3.6.5**	s.143	**10.7.3**
D 3.17	**3.6.5**	s.146	**10.6.3**
D3.21	**3.6.5**	s.161	**10.3.4**
D 3.28-29	**3.6.6**	Proceeds of Crime Act 2002	**10.7.3**
Annex A	**3.6.5**	s.6.	**13.3.1**
Annex B	**3.6.5**	s.11	**13.3.1**
Annex C	**3.6.5**	s.23–24	**13.3.1**
PACE Code of Practice E	**3.3.7**	s.40–49	**13.3.1**
PACE Code of Practice F	**3.3.7**	s.50–51	**13.3.1**
PACE Code of Practice G		s.75	**13.3.1**
1.2	**2.2.2**	s.340	**13.1.1**
1.3	**2.2.2**	s.327–329	**13.1.1**
Note 3	**2.2.1**	Part 8	**13.3.1**
PACE Code of Practice H	**3.1.8**	Proceeds of Crime Act 2005	**13.3.1**
Note 1G	**12.8.1**	Prosecution of Offences Act 1985	
Note 11C	**12.2.1**	s.18(1)	**4.2.1**

s.19A	**4.2.2**
s.22	**6.1.3**
Protection of Freedoms Act 2012	**2.1.7**
Road Traffic Offenders Act 1988	
ss.1 and 2	**4.1.1**
Sexual Offences (Amendment) Act 1976	
s.2	**14.3.4**
Sexual Offences Act 2003	
Sched 3	**10.6.4**
Serious Organised Crime and Police Act 2005	**3.1.1**
Supreme Court Act 1981	
s.81	**6.7.2**
Terrorism Act 2000	
ss.44–47	**2.1.7,**
Terrorism Act 2006	**3.1.8**
Code of Practice	**3.1.8**
Violent Crime Reduction Act 2006	
s.6	**10.6.4**
Youth Justice and Criminal Evidence Act 1999	**14.3, 14.3.3, 14.3.4**
s.41	**14.3.4**
s.53	**14.3.1, 14.3.3**
s.55	**14.3.3**
s.56	**14.3.3**
s.59	**20.1.1**
Sched. 3	**20.1.1**

Table of Statutory Instruments, Practice Directions, International Conventions and Professional Conduct Rules

Attorney-General's Guidelines on the Acceptance of Pleas [2001] 1 Cr.App.R. 425
 9.4.1

Attorney-General's Guidelines on the Acceptance of Pleas and the Prosecutor's Role in the Sentencing Exercise 1 December 2009
 10.10

Attorney-General's Guidelines on Disclosure, unreported;
 see generally **Chapters 7 and 9**

Civil Procedure Rules, R52	**11.1.2**
Part 54	**11.1.3**
Code for Crown Prosecutors	**5.1.2, 13.2, 13.2.1**

Consolidated Criminal Practice Direction: (http://www.justice.gov.uk/criminal/procrules_fin/contents/practice_direction/pd_consolidated.htm)

Acceptance of plea	**10.2.5**
Bail: I.13	**6.5.6, 9.3.1**
Clerks: V.55	**9.3**
Mode of Trial	**5.4.1**
Newton Hearing IV	**45.10 45.14 10.2.5**
Plea and Directions hearings: IV.41	**7.3.2, 7.3**
Post transfer	**7.3.2**
Preliminary hearings	**7.3**
Spent convictions: I.6	**17.3**
Trial in absence	**9.3.1**
Trial of young persons: III.30	**12.3.2, 12.9, 14.3.4**
Victim personal statements: III.28	**10.3.3**

Crime and Disorder Act (Service of Prosecution Evidence) Regulations 2005
 7.5.1

Criminal Procedure Rules 2010

Rule 1	**7.1.1**
Rule 1.1	**7.1.1**
Rule 3	**7.1.2**
Rule 3.2	**7.1.2, 8.1.1**
Rule 3.3	**7.1.2, 7.2**
Rule 3.4	**7.2**
Rule 3.5	**7.1.2, 7.2**
Rule 3.8	**5.2.1**
Rule 9	**5.4.2**
Rule 9.7	**5.5**
Rule 21	**5.2**
Rule 33	**7.1.2**
Rule 34	**18.3.9**
Rule 35	**17.2.9, 17.3.4**
Rule 35.3	**17.3.3**
Rule 35.6	**17.2.9**
Rule 37.3	**9.3**
Rule 37.10	**7.1.2, 9.3.1**
Rule 42.4(3)	**11.1**
Rule 64	**11.1.2**
Rule 76.8	**4.2.2**
Part 3	**5.2.1, 7.3.2**
Part 15	**7.3**
Part 19	**6.6.2, 6.7.1, 6.7.5**
Part 21	**7.5.1**
Part 28	**7.3.2**
Part 63	**11.1.1**

European Convention on Human Rights Chapter 11		Solicitor's Code of Conduct 2011	
Article 3	**10.3.8**	Principle 1	**3.3.5**
Article 5	**2.6.1, 2.6.2, 6.1.3, 6.2.1**	Principle 2	**6.5.1**
		Principle 3	**6.5.1**
		Chapter 3	**3.3.5**
	6.8, 10.3.8	Chapter 4	**3.3.5**
		Chapter 5	**8**
Article 6	**6.1, 7.5.1, 11.2.1, 11.4.1 11.4.2, 14.5, 14.5.1, 15.4, 16.4.4, 16.5.1, 17.6, 18.4.1, 20.5.1, 20.5.2**	Outcome 3.4	**6.5.1**
		Outcome 4.1	**6.5.1**
		Outcome 5.1	**8.1.4, 8.7**
		Outcome 5.2	**9.2.2, 8.1.4, 8.2.2, 8.7**
		Outcome 5.3	**8.7**
		Outcome 5.6	**8.7**
Article 8	**16.5.1**		

National Mode of Trial Guidelines 1995   **5.4.1**

Practice Direction (Consolidated: Crime) see Consolidated Criminal Practice Direction

Practice Direction (Crime: costs in Criminal Proceedings) 18th May 2004, (2004) 2 All ER 1070   **4.2.1**

Regulators Compliance Code   **13.2.1**

Sentencing Guidelines Council guidance

    <u>New Sentences</u>   **10.4.1, 10.4.3, 10.4.4, 10.4.5**

    <u>Overarching principles: Seriousness</u>   **10.1.2, 10.1.3, 10.3.2**

    <u>Reduction in Sentence for a Guilty Plea</u>   **3.3.5, 6.5.5, 5.6, 10.10.2**

Solicitors' Code of Conduct 2007 (2009 edn)

    Guidance 13(f)   **9.2.3**

CHAPTER 1

INTRODUCTION

When studying criminal litigation in the classroom, it never made any sense at all. When the time came to do it in a training contract, everything fitted together however what was learnt in the classroom rarely reflected that later experience in the police station and in court. This book aims to ensure that you understand not just criminal litigation, but how criminal litigation works in the real world.

Criminal Litigation is only a small part of the Legal Practice Course and there is very limited time available for its teaching. Within that time, you have to learn enough to be able to go to the police station alone and in the middle of the night and to make decisions about whether to exercise the right to silence or to consent to identification and other forensic procedures – decisions which will later be picked over by judges and advocates at trial. You have to learn enough to be able to prepare a case, to interview and advise your client, to obtain funding, sort out bail, and make decisions on where and how the case should be tried. You have to know enough to be able to advise your client on potential sentencing outcomes, and on rights of appeal. Above all you will need to be able to identify Human Rights issues, and to use the Human Rights Act to protect your client's rights. Because, of course, if you get it wrong, it won't simply be a matter of your client paying more tax for his company, or finding that a footpath crosses his garden. If you get it wrong, your client could be sent to prison for a long time. It is a testing area of work, and one that you have to be able to do competently from the word go.

[1.1] WHAT IS IN THE BOOK?

1.1.1 Why Criminal Litigation *"in practice"*?

This book is about the way that criminal litigation works in practice. It looks at how that law is applied every day in police stations, in magistrates' and Crown courts. As a purely academic subject criminal litigation makes little sense. Why are there restrictions on any party raising evidence of previous misconduct, whether by the defendant or anyone else? How can your client be said to have a right to silence if exercising it could help to prove the case against him? How do the courts decide whether an offence is "so serious" that only custody can be justified? Criminal litigation only makes sense if you see it in its practical context. For this reason we have used summaries of relevant cases to show how the courts have actually applied the law. If you see how the courts use the law, much of the subject will become clearer.

1.1.2 Why does this book deal with "skills"?

Of all the compulsory subjects on the Legal Practice Course criminal litigation benefits most from being able to draw on all the practical skills that you develop on the course. The legal skills don't exist in a vacuum. You may be assessed on Research or Drafting or Interviewing or even Advocacy in the context of other LPC subject areas, but all of these are skills that you will have to use in your criminal litigation work.

This book draws on all the LPC skills: it looks at drafting letters and briefs, at interviewing and advising your client and taking statements, at researching the case and at developing case analysis powers, and above all, at advocacy. Throughout the book you will find examples of how the skills of Drafting, Research, Interviewing and Advocacy are used in the criminal context. In the case study, you will find a fully annotated case file, which should let you follow a case in practice from its beginnings in the police station to the final stages of an appeal.

1.1.3 Why does this book deal with professional conduct?

It is no accident that lay people's first question to lawyers is often, "How can you represent a person you know to be guilty?" Criminal lawyers are seen as a touchstone of all that is morally ambiguous in the lawyer's role. As a criminal lawyer, it is not simply your duty to represent those who are often guilty; it is your duty to do the best that you can for them.

It can be a corrupting area of work, particularly for those who don't ever question their role. The familiar line: "It's not a question whether I believe my client to be guilty; it is for the court to make that decision" can lead to an abdication of responsibility. The work is often distressing. Much of it is conducted at anti social hours in police stations, in anti social places like prison cells, and without support of colleagues. It is work that can be insidiously corrupting. Your role in protecting your client's rights can lead to a Them and Us attitude to the police. The desire to win the case can displace the proper duty to do your best for your client. You have to know not just the rules of professional conduct but also how to apply them. The professional conduct rules changed in October 2011 so that solicitors are now regulated on an outcomes based approach rather than under a strict set of rules and guidelines. We have tried to highlight likely issues, as they arise during the litigation process and we have set out the relevant rules and outcomes accordingly.

1.1.4 Why is there a case study?

The case study is an ideal way of showing how the subject fits together. In the main part of this book, you will not be studying sentencing law until some six chapters after you have looked at legal aid and bail decisions – and yet the case study shows how interrelated the two areas are. One of the criteria for the grant of legal aid is that your client is likely to lose his liberty. One of the grounds for refusing bail is that there is a substantial likelihood that he will fail to surrender to the court if granted bail, and one of the relevant factors in this argument is that he will fail to surrender because he knows he is likely to be sent to prison once convicted. Thus, in order to make the legal aid application and the bail application you need to know something of the likely sentencing outcomes. In the case study, the lawyer checks the likely sentencing outcomes before going to court to deal with legal aid and bail.

This is a book about how law works in practice. The case study should help you to apply the principles set out in the main part of the book to the practical assessments that you will face on the LPC, and to the demands of your real clients as you enter into practice.

One final point

1.1.5 Why have we always referred to the client or defendant as "he"?

We have tried to use gender neutral language throughout the book, and not to make assumptions that lawyers, judges, or even police officers will invariably be male. This is far from the case. However, it is the case that the vast majority of those who come before the criminal courts are male. In this respect therefore the use of "he/him/his" seemed to be accurate rather than stereotypical.

[1.2] RESEARCH SOURCES

1.2.1 The Practitioner Texts

Archbold — *Criminal Pleading, Evidence and Practice*. This is a key practitioner text. It is used primarily in the Crown Court and is much beloved of barristers. It is authoritative and fairly easy to use. There is also an Archbold Magistrates Court edition.

Blackstone's — *Criminal Practice*. This is the main alternative to Archbold. It is rather more user-friendly and is easy to read. Slightly less detailed than Archbold, it is very highly recommended as a starting point for research and it covers both magistrates' court and Crown Court procedures.

Stones — *Justices Manual*. Three very dense volumes. Printed on the thinnest paper in the smallest print, it aims to cover everything that could possibly crop up in the magistrates court. Amidst the annotated legislation (covering such need-to-know subjects as the Merchant Shipping Act and the Coal Industry Act) is a very useful summary of the principal elements of Criminal Evidence and everything you need to know about magistrates' court procedure and sentencing. It is worth getting used to as it is comprehensive and, in the magistrates' court, authoritative.

Antony and Berryman — *Magistrates' Court Guide*. Small(ish) paperback with summaries of most offences and suggestions as to how they should be dealt with. Handy as a starting point if you have no idea about the offence.

Keogh, Andrew — *Blackstone's Magistrates' Court Handbook*. This is a pocket sized guide to magistrates' court practice and procedure – essentially a more portable version of Antony & Berryman with the additional coverage of evidential matters. An extremely useful book.

1.2.2 Other litigation texts

Cape — *Defending suspects at police stations* (Legal Action Group). This is a splendidly clear, comprehensive and useful book. You should take it to the police station with you when you are in practice.

Ede and Edwards — *Criminal Defence* A Law Society publication aimed at practitioners. It is terse, but clear. A guide to best practice in handling criminal defence work.

Thomas — *Current Sentencing Practice*. Recent guideline sentences: useful as a basic research tool but it can be slow to up-date. You might do better to look through recent journals and the electronic up-daters.

1.2.3 Advocacy texts

There are many skills books on basic advocacy. We particularly recommend the two books by **Keith Evans** (*Advocacy in Court, Golden Rules of Advocacy*). They are easy to read at a single sitting and contain useful general principles. Other useful texts include *The Devil's Advocate* by **Iain Morley** QC and *Effective Advocacy* by **Noel Shaw**. While Morley's text is particularly aimed at those in the higher courts, Shaw's guide to advocacy is also extremely user friendly, and incorporates sample speech templates.

1.2.4 Journals and Internet sources

The journals:

Criminal Law Review	This is a monthly publication and is essential reading, if only for the case reports. There is no better way of understanding how evidence and procedure work in practice than reading case reports and the accompanying commentaries.
Legal Action	Monthly journal of the Legal Action Group. It is useful on legal aid developments and can have summaries of cases that are not reported elsewhere.
Criminal Lawyer	A journal which is published six times per year, containing updating articles of interest to criminal lawyers.
Criminal Law & Justice Weekly	A weekly publication of particular interest to anyone working in the criminal justice system.

Internet sources:

As with all areas of law, the use of electronic sources is essential for criminal litigators. Lawtel, Westlaw and Butterworths Direct all provide daily case digest services, so that you will be e-mailed each morning with details of all relevant caselaw and legislation from the previous day. These are, of course, commercial sites and you will need passwords for access. In addition to these, there are now some useful services specifically aimed at criminal litigators:

Criminal Law Week	This is a weekly digest of relevant criminal cases and new statutes. You will find the site at www.criminal-law.co.uk. It is a commercial site and you will need a password for access. It is a superb resource, especially now that the case summaries link to the full transcript at CaseTrack.
CrimeLine	A very useful – and free – almost daily update from Andrew Keogh: available via www.crimeline.info. Andrew tries to digest some of the week's most important developments, both caselaw and statute, along with matters such as legal aid developments. Very useful as a resource for preparing for training contract interviews with criminal firms.

Other useful internet sources

Responsibility for policy on criminal justice has been passed from the Home Office to the Ministry of Justice (www.justice.gov.uk), although matters of police powers remain with the

Home Office (so that you will find the PACE Codes of Practice on the Home Office website). The Judicial Studies Board website includes the specimen directions on points of evidence for judges to use: www.judiciary.gov.uk. The "Crown Court Bench Book – Directing the Jury" contains this guidance. Sentencing Guidelines can be found at www.sentencingcouncil.judiciary.gov.uk and this will provide a full list of the definitive guidelines which apply in both the Magistrates and Crown Courts as well as details on draft guidelines and sentencing consultations. The European Court of Human Rights has a good site at www.echr.coe.int .

[1.3] CRIMINAL LITIGATION – AN OVERVIEW

An outline of the criminal process

Arrest or summons: A person suspected of an offence may be arrested, questioned and charged. They will then either be bailed to attend court or produced to court from custody. Alternatively for less serious offences a person may be summonsed to attend court. As an alternative to formal court proceedings a person may be given a formal "caution", a form of written warning, which will go on their criminal record. There is also increasing use of "fixed penalty notices" – whereby the suspect is given the option of paying a fixed fine rather than being taken to court.

Starting off the case: All cases start off in the magistrates' court. This court will consist either of lay justices (members of the community trained to sit as magistrates but not qualified as lawyers) or a single, legally qualified District Judge. The court will need to deal with issues of legal aid funding for the case, and bail issues.

Summary only offences: These are cases that are less serious. They can only be heard in the magistrates court – so called "summary trial". Trial in the magistrates will be before a bench of three lay justices, or a District Judge. The court has much more limited sentencing powers than the Crown Court. There is no jury trial in the magistrates' court. Well over 90% of cases are heard in the magistrates' courts.

Indictable only offences: These are the most serious categories of offences. They are so serious that they can only be heard in the Crown Court, and trials will almost inevitably be heard before a judge and jury. The judge rules on matters of law; the jury will decide the facts, including guilt or innocence. This category of cases would include offences such as murder, manslaughter, rape, terrorism and the like. The case will start off in the magistrates' court for the first hearing, but the magistrates will send the matter to the Crown Court at once.

"Either way" offences: These are cases that can be heard at either the magistrates' court or the Crown Court. They include many common offences, such as theft, mid-ranking assaults, and many sexual and drugs-related offences. In common with all other offences, these will start off in the magistrates' court. There is then a complex system for deciding whether they are too serious to be dealt with by the magistrates, and should therefore be sent to the Crown Court for trial. If the magistrates decide that they are prepared to hear the case, the defendant always has the power to overrule this decision and to select trial by jury in the Crown Court.

Sentencing criminal offenders: Normally a person who has been convicted in one court can expect to be sentenced by that court. There is a provision for some serious cases to be transferred from the magistrates' court to the Crown Court for sentencing if the magistrates' powers are not sufficient. Sentences that the courts can impose will include custodial sentences, punishment in the community (such as unpaid work, supervision by a probation officer, home curfews), fines, and discharges. These are all discussed in more detail in Chapter 10.

Young people: There are special rules for dealing with under-18 year olds in the criminal justice system. There are special safeguards in place at the police station stage, and young persons will normally be tried in a special Youth Court, rather than in the adult courts. The range of sentences for young people is different than that for adults. These provisions are set out in Chapter 12.

Mentally vulnerable people: As for juveniles, there are some different considerations when dealing with mentally vulnerable offenders. There are various safeguards for such persons who are detained at the police station and a number of alternative disposals available following conviction at court.

[1.4] THE CRIMINAL PROCEDURE RULES

The Criminal Procedure Rules were introduced in April 2005 and they have since been consolidated and recently amended to form the Criminal Procedure (Amendment) Rules 2011. The Criminal Procedure Rules (CrPR) do three things:

1. They consolidated all the previously scattered procedural rules into one set of rules; this makes it much easier to find the relevant law.
2. They introduced an "overriding objective" for all persons involved in the criminal justice system namely to deal with matters justly: see 7.1.
3. They introduced new powers for the courts to manage criminal cases effectively, and they require all the parties to co-operate with these case management powers.

In addition to the CrPR, however, you will also have to have regard to the Consolidated Criminal Practice Direction, which fleshes out those rules.

The text of the Rules and the Practice Directions are set out in this book where relevant. If you want to look at the full text (bearing in mind that the Rules alone are well over 350 pages long) you will find the Rules at www.justice.gov.uk, along with any accompanying Practice Directions.

Case management powers

The CrPR Part 3 contains extensive powers for courts to manage cases, and imposes duties on all the parties to comply with these requirements. The detail of the rules is discussed more fully in Chapter 7.

There is a growing body of case law where the courts are using the case management powers in the Rules to require the defence to identify at an early stage the points that it wishes to raise, and even to notify the court which witnesses it intends to call. The rules have been in place for some time now and they have brought about a huge culture change in the way in which criminal cases are managed within the justice system.

The traditional operation of the adversarial system is changing. No longer is it appropriate to play your cards close to your chest or to simply attack weaknesses in the prosecution case. Recent decisions have questioned whether putting the prosecution to "strict proof" (a principle underpinning the presumption of innocence) is within the spirit of the *CrPR: Balogun v DPP* [2010] EWHC 799 (Admin). A knowledge and understanding of the CrPR is no longer desirable – it is mandatory.

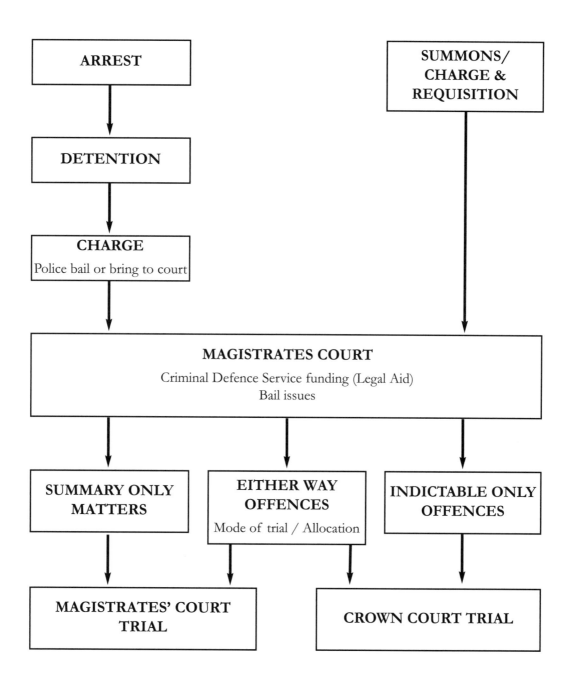

CHAPTER 2

POWERS TO STOP, SEARCH AND ARREST

> This chapter covers:
>
> The power to stop and search
>
> The power of arrest
>
> Cautioning of those suspected of involvement in offences
>
> Searches which may take place after an arrest

[2.1] THE POWER TO STOP AND SEARCH

2.1.1 The power to stop and search without arrest

There is a general police power to stop and to search a person (or his vehicle) without arresting him under s.1 of the Police and Criminal Evidence Act 1984 (PACE). The power can be exercised if a police officer has a "reasonable suspicion" that "a stolen or prohibited article" may be found. There is a detailed Code of Practice in PACE Code A which sets out how these powers should be exercised. Because the power to stop and search is such an intrusion on personal liberty, the Code stresses that the actions of the police must not be exercised in a discriminatory manner:

> *Powers to stop and search must be used fairly, responsibly, with respect for people being searched and without unlawful discrimination. The Equality Act 2010 makes it unlawful for police officers to discriminate against, harass or victimise any person on the grounds of the 'protected characteristics' of age, disability, gender reassignment, race, religion or belief, sex and sexual orientation, marriage and civil partnership, pregnancy and maternity when using their powers...if these fundamental principles are not observed the use of powers to stop and search may be drawn into question. Code A, para 1.1 and 1.3.*

If the police fail to adhere to the strict guidance set in place regarding stop and search, the lawfulness of the search can be challenged and any evidence obtained as a result of the stop and search may be excluded.

Other stop and search powers: The PACE power of stop and search is the central provision which you need to be aware of. However, in addition to their powers under PACE, the police and other agencies may have specific powers of search which are permitted under various other statutes – e.g. Firearms Act, Misuse of Drugs Act, Customs and Excise Management Act, Terrorism Act and so on.

2.1.2 What can the officer search for?

PACE s. 1(2) permits a constable to search any person or vehicle or anything in or on a vehicle for "stolen or prohibited articles". "Stolen articles" are self evident, they include items taken as a result of any dishonesty offence such as theft, handling, burglary etc. "Prohibited articles" are defined in s.1(7) PACE and include; offensive weapons (this includes obvious weapons such as knives and guns, but also articles that have been made or adapted for use as weapons, such as a makeshift knife, or a broken bottle); articles made or adapted for use (or intended for use) in the offences of burglary, theft, TWOC, fraud or criminal damage. In addition to these prohibited articles, the police are also allowed to search for certain types of fireworks.

2.1.3 When can a search take place?: the "reasonable grounds for suspicion" provision

Section 1(3) provides that the officer can only search if he has "reasonable grounds" for suspecting that he will find these articles. There must be some objective basis for the suspicion. PACE Code A 2.2–2.11 attempts to outline how this provision should be interpreted:

- *Reasonable grounds for suspicion depend on the circumstances in each case.*

- *There must be an objective basis for that suspicion based on facts, information and/or intelligence which are relevant to the likelihood of finding an article of a certain kind.*

- *Reasonable suspicion can never be supported on the basis of personal factors alone without reliable supporting intelligence ... or some specific behaviour by the person concerned.*

- *Unless there is a physical description of a suspect, a person's physical appearance, or the fact that he has previous convictions cannot be used alone or in combination with each other as the reason for searching that person.*

- *Reasonable suspicion cannot be based on generalisations or stereotypical images of certain groups or categories of people as more likely to be involved in criminal activity.*

- *Reasonable suspicion may arise from a person's behaviour – for example a person on the street at night who is trying to hide something.*

- *But reasonable suspicion should normally be linked to accurate and current intelligence.*

- *Searches are more likely to be effective, legitimate and secure public confidence where reasonable suspicion is based on a range of factors.*

The meaning of "reasonable grounds for suspicion" has been considered by the courts.

> *In O'Hara O was arrested by a policeman on suspicion of being a terrorist. The officer had been told to arrest O by a senior officer. O was later released without being charged and sued on the basis that there had never been any suspicion on the part of the arresting officer and so there had been no lawful basis for the arrest.*
>
> *The House of Lords held that the test fell in two parts: first, there must be actual suspicion on the part of the arresting officer; secondly, there must be reasonable grounds (judged objectively, rather than subjectively) for that suspicion. It was not enough simply to say that the officer was acting on instructions from his superior; he must show "reasonable grounds for suspicion". In this case there was enough evidence that the officer had formed a genuine suspicion as the result of the briefing from his superior, and that that suspicion was reasonable. O'Hara v Chief Constable RUC, [1997] Crim LR 432*

This two-stage approach to assessing reasonable grounds for suspicion was considered by the European Court of Human Rights and was held to be lawful: *O'Hara v United Kingdom*, (2002) 34 E.H.R.R. 32.

Reasonable suspicion and gangs: The above- mentioned guidance that suspicion should not be based on stereotypes is somewhat weakened however by Code A 2.6 which provides that reasonable suspicion may be based on "reliable information" about gangs who may habitually carry weapons or drugs. Where there is "reliable information" that gang members wear distinctive clothing or other means of identification, members may be identified on the basis of that clothing and this can provide reasonable grounds to stop and search.

2.1.4 What limitations are there on the search?

Where can a person be searched? The power to search may only be exercised in a public place or a place to which the public have ready access at that time: s.1(1). If a person is in the garden or the yard of a dwelling, he may be searched only if he does not live there and is not there with the occupier's consent: s.1(4) and s.1(5). The search must be carried out at or near the place where the person or vehicle was first detained: Code A 3.4. The power relates only to search of the person and/or a vehicle. For power to search premises, see later.

Information which must be given: If the officer is not in uniform, he should provide documentary evidence that he is a police officer. In any event, he must inform the suspect of his name and station, the object of the search and the grounds for the search: s.2(2) and s.2(3) PACE. Further details about what the suspect should be told are set out in Code A 3.8. In *Osman v DPP* (1999) 163 J.P. 725 Osman's conviction for assaulting a police constable was overturned on appeal because the officer had failed to give Osman details of his name and station and therefore the search had been unlawful. Note also that in *R (on the application of Michaels) v Highbury Corner Magistrates' Court*) [2009] EWHC 2938 (Admin) the fact that the suspect was known to the officer conducting the search did not relieve the officer of the obligation to provide his details.

Limiting the scope of the search: Code A 3.5 stipulates that the officer may only require the suspect to remove his outer coat, jacket and gloves. The officer is permitted to feel around the collar, socks and shoes and if appropriate, he may search the person's hair. If there are reasonable grounds for conducting a greater search, this must be done out of public view, e.g. in a police van or police station. Such a search may only be conducted by an officer of the same sex as the suspect: Code A 3.6.

s.60AA Criminal Justice and Public Order Act 1994 allows the police to remove and seize disguises and other face coverings where there is a reasonable belief that the person is wearing the item wholly or mainly for the purpose of concealing their identity. Where there are religious reasons for wearing head or face coverings then the removal should take place out of public view: Code A Notes for Guidance para 4.

Recording the search: The recording of searches is dealt with in Code A.4. A record of the search must be made at the time unless; due to exceptional circumstances it is wholly impracticable to do so. The suspect must be asked if they want a copy, and if they do, then it must be handed over immediately or alternatively they can be given a receipt which will explain how to obtain a copy. The record must note the ethnicity of the suspect, the date, time and place of the search, the object of the search, grounds for suspicion and the officer's details. There is no need to record the suspect's personal details.

Use of force: A forcible search can only take place if the person to be searched is unwilling to cooperate or otherwise resists. Reasonable force can be used if necessary: Code A 3.2.

2.1.5 Can the officer ask questions before searching?

Before carrying out the search the officer can question the person about whatever has given rise to the suspicion in order to see if there is a satisfactory explanation, see Code A 2.9. There is however no obligation to answer police questions and because the s.1 power is effective without arrest, the person remains free to leave and cannot be compelled to remain with the officer.

> *In some circumstances preparatory questioning may be unnecessary, but in general a brief conversation or exchange will be desirable, not only as a means of avoiding unsuccessful searches, but to explain the grounds for the stop/search, to gain co-operation and reduce any tension... Where a person is lawfully detained for the purpose of a search, but no search in the event takes place, the detention will not thereby have been rendered unlawful*: Code A Notes for Guidance 2 and 3.

It is worth noting that there is an additional power to require the name and address of any person who is acting in an anti-social manner: s.50 Police Reform Act 2002.

2.1.6 Searches by consent

There is no power to search a person unless it is provided for by statute: Code A1.5. An officer cannot justify a search of a person by arguing that the person consented. In order for the search to be lawful, the statutory grounds must be made out. This is somewhat undermined by the fact that if reasonable grounds for suspicion arise during "an encounter" with a person, the officer may then search the person even though no grounds existed when the encounter began, see Code A 2.11. The only exception to this rule against searching with consent, is where a person consents to be searched as a condition of entry, for example into a sports ground or music venue.

2.1.7 Other powers to stop and search prior to arrest:

s.60 Criminal Justice and Public Order Act 1994 – search in anticipation of violence:

Under s.60 Criminal Justice and Public Order Act (CJPOA)1994, the police are given authority to stop and search where it is reasonably believed that serious violence may take place in a given area and it is "expedient" to use the s.60 power to try to prevent the violence taking place. This power can also be exercised if it is reasonably believed that persons are carrying offensive weapons in any locality: s.8 Knives Act 1997.

Under s.60 a police officer, of the rank of inspector or above, must give written authorisation which specifies the locality and the time period (normally not exceeding 24 hours) within which such searches may be made. The authorisation permits officers to stop any pedestrian, vehicle, driver or passenger and to search him or anything carried by him for offensive weapons or dangerous instruments. The power of stop and search under s.60 may be exercised <u>without</u> any requirement for reasonable suspicion. For an example of the operation of this provision see *R (oao of Jane Laporte) v Chief Constable of Gloucestershire Constabulary and others* [2006] UKHL 55.

s.139B Criminal Justice Act 1988 – search for weapons on school premises:

s.139B Criminal Justice Act 1988 provides a power to search a person found on school premises for the purpose of finding bladed articles or offensive weapons. This power can only be exercised where a police constable has reasonable grounds to suspect that an offence of carrying a bladed article on school premises is being committed.

s.23(3) Misuse of Drugs Act 1971 – search for drugs:

s.23(3) Misuse of Drugs Act 1971 provides that a police constable can enter premises being used by a person in the business of producing or supplying controlled drugs in order to inspect such drugs. More importantly, an officer may also search any person who he believes to be in possession of a controlled drug (this power extends to the person's vehicle). Additionally, the police can seek a warrant to enter and search any premises where they have reasonable grounds to believe someone on the premises is in possession of a controlled drug.

ss.44–47 Terrorism Act 2000:

These sections of the Terrorism Act have recently been amended by The Protection of Freedoms Act 2012 so that police are allowed to stop and search anyone who they reasonably suspect to be a terrorist in order to find evidence that they actually are a terrorist. Under the new legislation, the police will also have power to search the suspect's vehicle and/or any passengers in the vehicle. The new legislation also allows senior officers to authorise stop and search in a specific area and for a specific time period if they reasonably suspect that an act of terrorism will take place and the authorisation to stop and search is necessary in order to prevent the act taking place. Where such an authorisation is in place, an officer can stop and search any person or vehicle, whether or not he reasonably believes there to be evidence of terrorism. Those that are arrested for terrorism may be detained for 14 days (previously it was 28 days).

[2.2] THE POWER OF ARREST

The main power of arrest is found under s.24 PACE. This is a a wide-ranging power to arrest without warrant persons for any criminal offence, no matter how minor, subject to a requirement to show that the arrest was "necessary". PACE Code G gives guidance on the likely circumstances where the necessity test will be fulfilled (we will explore this at 2.2.2). You should however be aware that there are other powers of arrest including:

- **Breach of the peace:** there remains a common law power enabling any person (not just police officers) to arrest a person where there is a danger or apprehended danger of a breach of the peace. This is a power of considerable antiquity but it is still often used to justify an arrest in circumstances where there is a risk of imminent harm to a person of his property through violence or disturbance: *Howell [1982] QB 416*

- **Arrest by warrant:** under s.1 Magistrates' Court Act 1980 a court may issue a warrant for a person's arrest. This is a rarity and will only happen where the court has received information on oath that a person is suspected to have committed an indictable or imprisonable offence and his address cannot be sufficiently established to allow for his attendance to be secured by summons. The vast majority of people are arrested without warrant under s.24 PACE or are summonsed to attend court directly.

- **Community Support Officers:** there is also a growing body of police support staff – such as community support officers – who have restricted detention powers, normally limited to detaining a person to await the arrival of a police officer.

"Indictable offences":

The term "indictable offences" is one that you will often come across, and which is particularly relevant in the context of arrest powers. A trial on indictment means a trial that takes place in the Crown Court, the indictment being the written account of the charges that the defendant faces. An "indictable offence" is therefore any offence that can be tried in the Crown Court. It will include not only the most serious range of offences, such as murder, rape and robbery, which can only be tried in Crown Court ("indictable only offence") but also the whole range of less serious "either way" offences (such as theft, drugs offences, and many sexual offences) which can be tried either in the magistrates' court or the Crown Court.

2.2.1 How to arrest:

What is an arrest? Arrest is not defined. In *Christie v Leachinsky* [1947] AC 573 arrest was said to be "the beginning of imprisonment." A person will be under arrest if it is made clear (whether by words or actions) that he is not free to go. Often an arrest will occur with a constable touching the person.

> *The case of Fiak [2005] EWCA Crim 2381 raises some difficult issues. F was charged with criminal damage to his police cell. He argued that his original arrest had been unlawful. F was seen by the police sitting in the driving seat of a stationary BMW, vomiting into the gutter. When the police spoke to him he smelt of alcohol and was unsteady on his feet. The police suspected that he was drunk in charge of a motor vehicle. F told the police that he was only sitting in the car and had left his house nearby for a few minutes to cool off after a row. The police officer told him to wait while she went to confirm his story. F refused to wait by the car and tried to force his way into his house, so that a struggle ensued. At this point he was arrested.*
>
> *F argued that because he had not been arrested by the officer before she went to confirm his story, he was acting lawfully in entering his own home. The CA held that arrest was a process, not a single event, and that it should not be "artificially compartmentalised". The officer was entitled to "postpone formal completion of the arrest" until she had checked F's story. This is a difficult decision to reconcile with authority – and it might be better to follow the court's alternative rationale – namely that the arrest was arguably completed at the point when F was told to wait with his car, even though the word "arrest" was not used.*

- **What should be said at arrest?** According to s.28 PACE, a person must be told "as soon as is practicable" that he is under arrest. No special form of words is required, but according to Code G Note 3, "An arrested person must be given sufficient information to enable them to understand they have been deprived of their liberty and the reason they have been arrested, e.g. when a person is arrested on suspicion of committing an offence they must be informed of the suspected offence's nature, when and where it was committed. The suspect must also be informed of the reason or reasons why arrest is considered necessary. Vague or technical language should be avoided". It therefore follows that a person who is arrested must know "the essential legal and factual grounds for his arrest" (*Fox, Campbell and Hartley v U.K.* (1990) 13 EHRR 157). It is not necessary to set out in detail a technical legal description that "would leave many citizens none the wiser, and might only tend to confuse them ...": *Clarke v Chief Constable of North Wales Police*, The Independent (C.S.), May 22, 2000. However this information is so important that it must be given even if the fact of arrest is obvious: PACE s.28(2) and (4).

- **Cautions:** A person who is arrested must be cautioned – that is, warned about their right to silence – unless it is not practicable to do so because of their condition or behaviour, or they were cautioned immediately prior to the arrest. For cautions generally, see below at 2.3.

Use of force: Reasonable force can be used where necessary to effect an arrest: s.117 PACE. Additionally, s.3 Criminal Law Act 1967 permits reasonable force to be used in effecting an arrest or preventing crime.

Helping the police with their enquiries? This is a meaningless phrase, originally intended to prevent actions in defamation. Either a person is under arrest or they are not. If they are not under arrest, they are free to go. If the police wish to detain them, then they must be arrested – although note the decision in *Fiak*, above.

2.2.2 Arrest by a police officer without a warrant: s.24 PACE

This section will focus on the main power of arrest contained in s.24 PACE. There are several situations giving rise to the power of arrest:

s.24(1)   A constable may arrest without a warrant:

(a) Anyone who is about to commit an offence.

(b) Anyone who is in the act of committing an offence.

(c) Anyone who he has reasonable grounds for suspecting to be about to commit an offence.

(d) Anyone who he has reasonable grounds for suspecting to be committing an offence.

2)   If a constable has reasonable grounds for suspecting that an offence has been committed, he may arrest without a warrant anyone whom he has reasonable grounds to suspect of being guilty of it.

3)   If an offence has been committed, a constable may arrest without a warrant:

(a) Anyone who is guilty of the offence.

(b) Anyone whom he has reasonable grounds for suspecting to be guilty of it.

Arrests must be "necessary", but what is the test for necessity?

Even where a power to arrest arises under one of the s.24 grounds listed above, that power will be exercisable only if the constable has reasonable grounds for believing that it is necessary to arrest that person: s.24(4).

The necessity conditions are set out in s.24(5) PACE. These are exhaustive of the circumstances where necessity can be shown – but as you will note, some of the provisions are potentially very broad.

a)   To enable the name of the person in question to be ascertained (in the case where the constable does not know, and cannot readily ascertain, the person's name, or has reasonable grounds for doubting whether a name given by the person as his name is his real name).

b)   Correspondingly as regards the person's address.

c)   To prevent the person in question:
  i) Causing physical injury to himself or to any other person.
  ii) Suffering physical injury.
  iii) Causing loss of or damage to property.
  iv) Committing an offence against public decency (subject to subsection 6).
  v) Causing an unlawful obstruction to the highway.

d)   To protect a child or other vulnerable person from the person in question.

e)   To allow the prompt and effective investigation of the offence or of the conduct of the person in question.

f)   To prevent any prosecution for the offence from being hindered by the disappearance of the person in question.

In relation to subsection c(iv) – offences against public decency – an additional provision states that this will only apply where members of the public going about their normal business cannot reasonably be expected to avoid the person in question.

What does the necessity test mean? The Code G guidance.

The "necessity conditions" are potentially very broad and without guidance, could be open to abuse. Code G therefore starts by emphasising the importance of ensuring that a power to arrest only takes place where genuine necessity can be shown.

> *The right to liberty is a key principle of the Human Rights Act 1998. The exercise of the power of arrest represents an obvious and significant interference with that right.*
>
> *The use of the power must be fully justified and officers exercising the power should consider if the necessary objectives can be met by other, less intrusive means. <u>Arrest must never be used simply because it can be used</u>. Absence of justification for exercising the powers of arrest may lead to challenges should the case proceed to court. When the power of arrest is exercised it is essential that it is exercised in a non-discriminatory and proportionate manner.* Code G, paras 1.2 and 1.3, my emphasis.

Code G does, however, go on to emphasise that ultimately it will be a matter for the "operational discretion of individual officers" whether a particular necessity condition is made out. It is therefore ultimately a judgement call for the individual officer to make in each particular situation; but in order for an officer to safely conclude that a necessity condition is made out, it is implicit that he must have considered other means of resolving the situation, for example by inviting the person to attend the police station as a volunteer, and concluded that arrest is the most practical and sensible option, see *Re Alexander [2009] NIQB 20*.

> *This question of 'necessity' was recently considered in Richardson v The Chief Constable of West Midlands Police [2011] EWHC 773 QB. In this case, a teacher, R, was accused of assaulting a pupil. R denied the allegation and maintained that the physical contact with the pupil had been accidental. During the course of the school's own investigation, the police became involved. The police suggested that the matter could be resolved by way of local resolution, but R was not prepared to accept this as it would imply an admission of guilt. It was agreed that R would voluntarily attend the police station in order to discuss the matter further. When it became clear that he was still not prepared to resolve the matter by way of resolution, he was arrested, detained and formally interviewed. R was eventually bailed and the police decided to take no further action, but he complained that the arrest had been unlawful as it had not been necessary. The police maintained that the arrest had been necessary under s.25(5)e on the basis that it was necessary for 'the prompt and effective investigation of the offence'. Although the arresting officer did not give evidence herself as to why she considered the arrest to be necessary and reasonable, the custody officer subsequently justified the decision to detain on this ground as it was a serious allegation and he did not want to run the risk of the volunteer exercising his right to leave once the interview process had commenced. The court decided that although the arresting officer did have reasonable grounds for suspecting that the teacher had committed an offence, and although it was reasonable to seek to interview him in order to question him about the incident, there were no reasonable grounds for the officer to believe that an arrest was necessary in order for that interview to take place. Looking at the facts, which were that the teacher had been entirely calm and cooperative throughout, there was nothing to suggest that the interview could not have taken place voluntarily. It was felt that the justification given by the custody officer could not cure what was at the time, an unlawful arrest. Once again, the court made reference to the decision being subject to a two-stage test; firstly, did the arresting officer believe the arrest was necessary and secondly, was that decision reasonable; the latter question being objectively decided.*

Necessary for the prompt and effective investigation of the offence: condition (e)

Most of the necessity conditions under s.24(5) are clear. There are obvious reasons why it may be necessary to arrest a person where, for example, they give what appears to be a false name or a false address, since it will then be impossible to summons the person to come to court. But what is meant by permitting an arrest under condition (e) that is, for the prompt and effective investigation of the offence or of the conduct of the offender?

Code G provides some limited assistance:

This may include cases such as:

(i) Where there are reasonable grounds to believe that the person:

- *has made false statements;*
- *has made statements which cannot be readily verified;*
- *has presented false evidence;*
- *may steal or destroy evidence;*
- *may make contact with co-suspects or conspirators;*
- *may intimidate or threaten or make contact with witnesses;*
- *where it is necessary to obtain evidence by questioning; or*

(ii) when considering arrest in connection with an indictable offence, there is a need to:

- *enter and search any premises occupied or controlled by a person*
- *search the person*
- *prevent contact with others*
- *take fingerprints, footwear impressions, samples or photographs of the suspect*

(iii) ensuring compliance with statutory drug testing provisions.

These suggestions seem to indicate that the scope of condition (e) is very broad indeed.

Necessary to prevent the disappearance of the person: condition (f)

Again, this is a rather broad necessity condition that could be abused. Clearly there may be situations where an arrest will be necessary since the suspect is otherwise thought genuinely likely to abscond, but Code G reminds officers that it is possible to grant a person street bail – that is, to arrest the person but then immediately free them on bail, subject to a requirement to attend the police station at some later date. Again, this is a reminder to the police that an arrest just to prevent the person disappearing is a serious interference with a person's liberty and should not be undertaken where an alternative method is available. Street bail is discussed below at 2.4.5.

What are "reasonable grounds"?

Both the power of arrest and the operation of the necessity conditions often refer to the officer having "reasonable grounds" to believe that a condition is made out. What will constitute reasonable grounds is not defined. The caselaw is not always clear: see, for example, *Holgate-Mohammed v Duke* (HL) [1984] AC 437. It has been suggested that there will be reasonable grounds provided the police officer actually did suspect the suspect was guilty of the offence and there were grounds that could be objectively justified as supporting that suspicion. This two part test seems to be supported by the decision in *O'Hara* [discussed above].

> In *Cumming v Chief Constable of Northumbria Police* [2003] EWCA Civ 1844 some video footage showing an offence appeared to have been tampered with. Only a small group of employees could have done this. The police arrested each member of the group. In fact they were all innocent. The Court of Appeal held that the arrests were nonetheless lawful. There was no reason why, where the offence could only have been committed by one of a small number of people, this could not amount to grounds for suspecting each of them.

2.2.3 Powers of persons other than the police: "citizen's arrest" – s.24A PACE

For persons other than constables, the power of arrest will only arise in more limited circumstances.

The power to arrest:

There will be power to arrest only where:

- A person is committing an indictable offence, or there are reasonable grounds for believing he is doing so; or

- An indictable offence has been committed and the person is guilty of committing it, or there are reasonable grounds for believing that he is guilty of committing that offence.

Note that the power is restricted to indictable offences – a term which will include all offences which can be tried in the Crown Court (i.e. all either way offences, as well as all offences which are "indictable only"). It will not therefore catch offences which are "summary only" – that is, they can only be tried in the magistrates' court. It is not clear how a member of the public can be expected to know which offences are potentially indictable.

The necessity condition for arrest:

The power of citizen's arrest is subject to two conditions:

- First, it is not reasonably practicable for a constable to make the arrest; and

- Secondly, the arrest is necessary in order to prevent the person from causing physical injury to himself or to another, or suffering from physical injury, or causing loss or damage to property, or making off before a constable can assume responsibility for him.

The importance of limitations on the citizen's power of arrest:

It is understandable that the public should have more restricted powers of arrest than police officers, but this may have significant consequences, particularly for persons such as security guards who have no additional powers of arrest beyond those given to the general public. For example, you may have noted that the power of arrest for members of the public does not arise in situations where no offence has been committed, even if there are reasonable grounds for believing that one has. This limitation can have important consequences:

S is in a store. A store detective accuses him of shoplifting. S runs off. He is chased by a passer-by who arrests him after a struggle. S is charged with theft and with assault with intent to resist arrest. At trial S argues that he is suffering from stress and lacks the mens rea for theft. The court accepts this and acquits him of the theft offence. However he is convicted of the assault offence.

On appeal the assault conviction is overturned on the basis that the arrest was unlawful. The passer-by only had a power to arrest S if an arrestable [now an indictable] offence had been committed. Because the court acquitted S of the theft offence, no offence had been committed, and the passer-by therefore never had any power of arrest. Self *[1992] 3 All ER 476*

Of course, had S been arrested after a struggle with a police officer, then the assault conviction would have been possible. In contrast to a citizen, the constable has a power to arrest where s/he has reasonable grounds for believing that an offence has been committed. The officer would therefore have been lawfully attempting to arrest S.

[2.3] CAUTIONS

A caution is a warning to a person that what they say or do not say may now have legal consequences. The terms of the caution are laid down by PACE Code C para 10.5.

> *You do not have to say anything. But it may harm your defence if you do not mention when questioned something which you later rely on in court. Anything you do say may be given in evidence.*

You will note that this caution suggests that failure to mention facts which are later relied upon in court can have adverse consequences. These "inferences" from the exercise of the right to silence are fully discussed in Chapter 15. Because inferences can only arise in certain situations, there is an alternative version of the caution which must be given when inferences cannot arise. It simply states:

> *You do not have to say anything but anything you do say may be given in evidence.* Code C, Annex C, para 2.

2.3.1 When should a suspect be cautioned?

PACE provides that a caution should be given as soon as there are "grounds" to suspect a person of an offence. The Court of Appeal has said that this means "reasonable grounds": *James* [1996] Crim L R 650. The effect of this is that no action will be necessary until a police officer has a "reasonable suspicion". At that point, he must caution the suspect, and he may also have a power to arrest him.

> *Customs officers found cocaine in a suitcase when they searched it. They let the suitcase through onto the luggage belt and then stopped two women who collected the suitcase. They first asked them routine questions about who owned the cases. Only at this point did they caution the women. It was argued that they should have cautioned before asking any questions, but the Court of Appeal held that the evidence was admissible as the questions were purely routine and there was no unfairness:* Senior *[2004] EWCA Crim 454*

Upon arrest: A suspect must also be cautioned on arrest unless it is impracticable to do so or he has been cautioned immediately beforehand.

Failure to caution? As we will see later, no inference can be drawn from the suspect's failure to put forward his defence until he has been cautioned. Where a suspect answers police questions, but has not been cautioned, it may be that the evidence of his replies will be ruled inadmissible at trial if he should have been cautioned but was not. Always look at the evidence to see if and when your client was cautioned. Ask yourself: should he have been cautioned earlier?

[2.4] POWERS AFTER ARREST

The general rule is that once a person is arrested, he should be taken to the police station as soon as is practicable: s.30 PACE. However the police may have powers to conduct searches of both the suspect and of certain premises prior to taking him to the police station. There is also a power for the police to bail an arrested person to attend the police station at some later time, a provision known as "street bail".

2.4.1 Search of the person after arrest: s.32 PACE

A constable may search the arrested person if he has reasonable grounds for believing that the suspect may present a danger to himself or others. He may also search for anything that might be used to help him escape and for anything that might be evidence relating to an offence: s.32(1) and (2). Note that the power to search is for "anything" relating to "an" offence, not necessarily the offence for which he has been arrested. This is a very wide power. It could therefore be that the person is arrested for public disorder but the officer believes it necessary and appropriate to search the person for drugs, perhaps due to his behaviour at the time of arrest. Note also that the power is limited to what is reasonably required for these purposes. The search is limited to removal of outer clothing only, but constables may search a person's mouth (e.g. in a drugs arrest). There must be reasonable grounds for suspecting the person is concealing something for which a search is permitted.

Retention of material: The constable may seize and retain material found if it might be used to cause injury, assist in escape, or is evidence of an offence or obtained as a consequence of the commission of an offence.

2.4.2 Search of premises where the arrest took place: s.32 PACE

Where a person is arrested for an indictable offence other than at a police station, there is a power to enter and search the premises in which the person was when he was arrested or immediately before the arrest. If the premises consist of two or more dwellings, the police can search the relevant dwelling and any common parts. The power is to search for evidence relating to the indictable offence. There are similar powers of seizure and retention as for searches of the person. As with search of the person, there is a condition that the officer has "reasonable" grounds to believe that there is evidence relating to the offence, therefore he cannot simply engage in a speculative, random search of the premises, it must be justified.

2.4.3 Search of premises occupied or controlled by the person: s.18 PACE

s.18 PACE permits a search of any premises "occupied or controlled" by a person who has been arrested for an indictable offence. There must be reasonable grounds for suspecting that there is evidence that relates either to the offence or to another indictable offence which is connected or is similar to it. The search can go no further than is reasonably required in looking for such evidence.

Normally written authorisation from an officer of at least the rank of inspector is required for such a search. However, an officer can search before taking the suspect to the police station, and without the authorisation, provided that "the presence of that person at a place other than a police station is necessary for the effective investigation of an offence". In such a situation, the officer would have to inform an inspector as soon as practicable after the search has been made.

2.4.4 Taking the suspect to the police station: s.30 PACE

The suspect should be taken to the police station as soon as practicable after arrest. If there is any delay, it should be recorded on the custody record. An alternative to this is the granting of "street bail" – this is discussed in the following section. There is a very general exception where the suspect's presence "elsewhere is necessary in order to carry out such investigations as it is reasonable to carry out immediately":s.30(10) PACE.

Can the police ask the suspect questions before he gets to the police station?

It is often the case that the police will have to ask a person a few basic questions post arrest and pre-police station, but normally a person may not be "interviewed" about the offence once the decision to arrest has been taken except at a police station. An "interview" is defined as the questioning of a person about his involvement or suspected involvement in a criminal offence: Code C 11.1A. The purpose of this rule is to protect a suspect's legal right to advice, as every suspect must be offered legal advice before an interview takes place. It also protects the police from any later allegation of improper questioning, as all interviews must be formally recorded.

When can questions be asked prior to arrival at the station?

Code C 11.1(a)PACE permits limited questioning to take place if delay would either:

(a) lead to

- *interference with or harm to evidence connected with an offence;*
- *interference with or physical harm to other people; or*
- *serious loss of, or damage to, property;*

(b) lead to alerting other people suspected of having committed an offence but not yet arrested for it;

(c) hinder the recovery of property obtained in consequence of the commission of an offence.

Where an interview does take place outside the police station under one of the exceptions under C11.1 it must cease as soon as the risk is gone or the necessary questions have been put to try to avert the risk.

Using the search to delay access to legal advice?

The police may want to delay taking suspects to the police station in order to conduct a s.18 search. If a search has been conducted prior to arrival at the police station, you will want to be satisfied that the search is not being used improperly as an opportunity to question the suspect before they have had access to a lawyer. If there has been improper questioning during a search, you may be able to get the evidence excluded.

> *In Raphaie [1996] Crim LR 812 the police executed a search warrant of the flat where R was staying. After they broke down the door they said they saw R in the bathroom, where he dropped a piece of rolled up cling film containing brown powder down the toilet. The package was not retrieved, but when the officers asked him what it was, he admitted it was heroin. He was then arrested. A search of the flat continued. R was asked some 43 questions and made some 34 answers during the next $1^1/_2$ hours. The incriminating replies were the backbone of the police case.*

> *Held: the questions went beyond what was reasonably needed as an adjunct to the search. The comments of Lord Taylor CJ. in <u>Khan</u> [1993] Crim LR 54 were adopted:*
>> *"... merely because the police are entitled under section 30(1) to keep the appellant in order to assist in carrying out a search or an investigation away from the police station does not mean that they have carte blanche to administer interrogation of the kind which ought properly to be reserved for the police station ..."*
>
> *The evidence of the replies should have been excluded under s.78 PACE.*

2.4.5 Street bail: s.4 Criminal Justice Act 2003 and s.30A PACE

Street bail gives officers an alternative to taking an arrested person to the police station for immediate charge or for questioning. Instead, the officers can bail the person to attend at a police station at a later time and date. Street bail is unlikely to be appropriate for serious offences, or offences where there is an ongoing risk to others.

It is possible for the police to impose conditions on a person who is granted street bail: s.30A PACE. The conditions are those that the constable considers necessary to ensure the person: (i) surrenders to custody; (ii) does not commit offences while on bail; (iii) does not interfere with the course of justice; (iv) the person's own protection. The person must be given a prescribed bail notice with full details of the offence and the ground for arrest. If the notice does not contain the details of time and place for attendance a later notice must be served with this information. Failure to answer street bail, or breaching the conditions of street bail will enable arrest without a warrant.

2.4.6 Summary justice: fixed penalty notices

It is appropriate to mention fixed penalty notices at this point as they are often issued post arrest in order to avoid attendance at the police station and formal proceedings. Fixed penalty notices (FPNs) were originally introduced in respect of minor traffic offences. Their use has been considerably expanded – at first to deal with minor nuisance offences, but now extended to include public order (s.5 Public Order Act), criminal damage under £500 and retail theft (shoplifting) under £200.

Where a police officer has reason to believe that a person has committed an offence for which a FPN is available, he may issue a FPN to the person. The person then has the option of paying the fine within 21 days, in which case no proceedings will be brought. After this period has passed the police will register the fine with the magistrates, leading to a 50% increase, or they may bring criminal proceedings in the usual way. Alternatively the person may request trial rather than paying the FPN.

FPNs appear attractive as they do not count as criminal convictions, and do not involve any admission of guilt. However, they are recorded on a person's criminal record and may be disclosed on a Criminal Records search, or used as evidence of "bad character" in any later court proceedings (see Chapter 17).

[2.5] SEARCH UNDER OTHER POWERS

2.5.1 Search with a search warrant: s.8 PACE

In addition to the powers to search premises following an arrest, the police may also search premises with a search warrant. This may be appropriate where the police are unable to contact the person they wish to arrest, or the person whose premises they wish to search. Search warrants must be obtained from a magistrate (see s.8 PACE for procedure) and can only be issued where the magistrate is satisfied that there are reasonable grounds for believing that:

(a) an indictable offence (this includes either way offences) has been committed; and

(b) that there is material on the premises which is likely to be of substantial value to the investigation of the offence; and

(c) the police are seeking evidence that is likely to be relevant and admissible; and

(d) either there is no practicable way of contacting a person who can grant entry, or entry will only be granted if there is a warrant, or the purpose of the search might be frustrated if the police were unable to gain immediate access.

2.5.2 Entry and search to effect an arrest: s.17 PACE

Police have a general power to enter and search premises under s.17 PACE. This is generally limited to situations where the police need to gain entry in order to effect an arrest under a warrant, to arrest someone for an indictable offence, or to arrest someone for certain statutory offences (See s.17 (1) c for a list of these offences). They can also enter premises in order to recapture a prisoner, and in order to "save life or limb or prevent serious damage to property". There must generally be reasonable grounds for believing the person sought is on the premises.

2.5.3 Seizure of material found during a search: s.19 PACE

The power to seize material found during a lawful search is governed by s. 19 PACE. Essentially an officer may seize anything that he has reasonable grounds for believing was obtained in the commission of an offence and where it is necessary to seize it in order to prevent it being concealed, lost, damaged or destroyed. The police are also entitled to seize anything they reasonably believe to constitute evidence in relation to the offence they are investigating or indeed any other offence, for the same reasons afore-mentioned. This power includes the power to seize a legible version of any electronic information. The police are not entitled to seize legally privileged material, nor certain other types of "excluded material". [Privilege is discussed more fully in Chapter 20.] Material that would be covered by legal professional privilege would include communications between lawyer and client which either give legal advice or are made in connection with actual or pending legal proceedings. Privilege does not cover "items held with the intention of furthering a criminal purpose": s.10(2).

Excluded material includes personal records created in the course of a business, profession or occupation. It also includes human tissue and fluid taken for medical purposes, and also journalistic material. In all cases the material must be held in confidence.

Seize and sift: Under the Criminal Justice and Police Act 2001 the police have the power to remove material to examine it elsewhere if it is not possible to examine the material properly on the premises due to constraints of time and technology. They are also given the power to seize and forensically examine an entire disk or hard drive in order to determine when individual documents have been created, amended and/or deleted, and to retain "inextricably linked" material that may be on the hard drive.

[2.6] HUMAN RIGHTS ACT ISSUES

2.6.1 Arrest and article 5

Article 5 of the European Convention guarantees the right to liberty. Exceptions to this general principle exist, including powers to arrest and detain where:

(a) the person has been convicted by a court

(b) the person has failed to comply with the lawful order of a court

(c) the purpose is to bring the person before a "competent legal authority" on reasonable suspicion of either having committed an offence, to prevent the person from committing an offence or from fleeing having committed it.

Other exceptions apply in respect of minors, of people suffering from illness and in respect of certain immigration matters.

In each case these exceptions must be narrowly construed, and there is a considerable amount of caselaw on their meaning and their extent. Note that the detention must be "lawful" and "in accordance with a procedure prescribed by law". This imports requirements that there is relevant and accessible law governing the arrest, and that the detention is proportionate and not arbitrary.

2.6.2 Stop and search without suspicion

Article 5(1)(c) provides an exception for:

> *the lawful arrest or detention of a person effected for the purpose of bringing him before the competent legal authority on a reasonable suspicion of having committed an offence ...*

However, s.60 CJPOA [see above: 2.1.7] permits detention without any requirement of reasonable suspicion.

2.6.3 "Reasonable suspicion" in ECHR cases

The European Court of Human Rights has made clear that it is possible to have a reasonable suspicion without having sufficient evidence to charge. The fact that a person is not ultimately charged does not mean that there was no original power to arrest: *Brogan v U.K.* ((1989) 11 EHRR 117. In *Fox, Campbell and Hartley* (1991) 13 EHRR 157 the court stated that reasonable suspicion "presuppose[d] the existence of fact or information which would satisfy an objective observer that the person concerned may have committed the offence in question."

STOP & SEARCH

See **PACE s.1**: police officers' power to search for offensive weapons and/or "prohibited items". Requires a "reasonable suspicion" that suspect is carrying such items.

Additional search powers conferred by other statutes: e.g. Misuse of Drugs Act.

Superficial search only. No power to search by consent unless a power of search exists.

CAUTION

"You do not have to say anything. But it may harm your defence if you do not mention when questioned something which you later rely on in court. Anything you do say may be given in evidence." **Code C 10**

Must be given:
- where there are grounds to suspect of an offence
- on arrest
- on detaining
- before (or after break in) interview
- charging

Note alternative caution if an inference is not possible.

POLICE POWERS OF ARREST

Arrest may be:
- With a court warrant; or
- For any criminal offence; s.24 PACE provided that one of the necessity conditions is made out; or
- Under common law for breach of the peace.

Duty to explain in simple language why arrested.

PACE s.24: A power for a constable to arrest:

- Anyone who is about to commit an offence; who is in the act of committing an offence; who he has reasonable grounds for suspecting is about to commit an offence; who he has reasonable grounds to suspect is committing an offence.
- Where he has reasonable grounds for suspecting an offence has been committed, anyone he has reasonable grounds for suspecting is guilty of committing it.
- Where an offence has been committed, anyone who is guilty or he has reasonable grounds for believing to be guilty.

But only if it is "necessary" to arrest. See in particular Code G para 1.3: Arrest must never be used simply because it can be used.

The necessity conditions: (a) name; (b) address; (c) preventative; (d) protect child/vulnerable person; (e) prompt and effective investigation; (f) prevent prosecution being hindered by person's disappearance.

CITIZEN'S ARREST POWERS

s.24A PACE: only where a person is committing an indictable offence – or there are reasonable grounds for believing he is; or where an indictable offence has been committed and the person is guilty of it, or there are reasonable grounds for believing he is.

Necessity test: it is not practicable for a constable to make the arrest AND necessary to prevent person harming self or another, causing loss or damage to property, or making off before a constable can assume responsibility for him.

SEARCH OF PREMISES

- With a search warrant
- To arrest for an indictable offence
- To save life, limb or serious property damage
- Premises where the suspect was arrested
- Premises occupied or controlled by suspect for evidence relating to that or similar offences.

Powers to Stop, Search and Arrest

Stop, search and arrest – test yourself questions

[The answers to these questions are set out in Appendix A at the back of this book]

[1] Which one of the following propositions is true?

(a) PACE only entitles an officer to stop and search if it is likely that he will find stolen or prohibited articles;

(b) An officer can only search for offensive weapons or bladed instruments under PACE;

(c) Before an officer can conduct a search he must arrest the suspect and caution him;

(d) The power to search under PACE applies to both persons and vehicles.

[2] At 11.30 p.m. the police observe Jim hanging around near the doors to an office building which has been burgled twice in the preceding three weeks. Jim is known to the police as he has a previous conviction for attempted burglary. Jim is aged 17. He is white and has a shaven head. He wears a combat jacket with "Free Your Mind – Live Dangerously" written across the back.

Consider the following propositions.

i. The fact that Jim has a previous conviction will be sufficient to amount to a "reasonable suspicion" that he is in possession of stolen or prohibited articles.

ii. Statistics show that most burglaries are committed by young persons: Jim's age, if considered together with his unconventional appearance, will be enough to give rise to a reasonable suspicion.

iii. The police can take into account the fact that Jim is acting warily in a place where a number of burglaries have previously taken place in deciding whether they have a reasonable suspicion.

Which of these propositions is correct?

(a) (i) only.

(b) (ii) and (iii) only.

(c) (iii) only.

(d) None of the propositions

[3] In relation to each of the following propositions, consider whether the proposition is true or false.

(a) The power under s.1 PACE is to stop and search; a police officer is not permitted to ask questions before searching.

(b) A police officer must tell the person his name and station, the object of the search, his grounds for wanting to search and the person's right to ask for a copy of the search record in due course.

(c) A person cannot be detained under the power to stop and search for longer than 15 minutes.

(d) Where the search is in a public place a person cannot be required to take off anything more than his outer coat, jacket, gloves and (under some circumstances) any face covering.

Both the following questions relate to the same scenario:

A briefcase containing a laptop computer is stolen from a pub restaurant at 12.30 p.m. Its loss is noticed very quickly, and the owner, Tariq, believes he sees a young man wearing a distinctive Liverpool Football Club shirt leaving the pub by a side door carrying something. Tariq runs out of the pub, and sees David, who is wearing a Liverpool shirt, standing by a low wall in the pub car park trying to open a briefcase.

[4] *Scenario 1:* Tariq runs across the car park and grabs David by the arm. David then punches Tariq in the face and runs off. David is later arrested by the police on suspicion of causing actual bodily harm. He argues that his actions were no more than lawful self defence since Tariq had no power to arrest him.

Which one of the following propositions is correct?

(a) Tariq was entitled to arrest David since an indictable offence (theft) had been committed and Tariq had reasonable grounds for believing that David is the perpetrator of the offence.

(b) Although Tariq had a power to arrest David in these circumstances, he could only exercise that power if he had reasonable grounds for believing that David was likely to cause physical injury to himself or another, was likely to suffer physical injury, or was likely to cause loss or damage to property.

(c) Tariq had no power to arrest David since the power of citizen's arrest is only available while the offence is being committed. Here the offence was complete once the briefcase was appropriated without consent, and therefore there is no continuing offence.

(d) None of the above is correct.

[5] *Scenario 2:* Tariq sees David trying to open a briefcase in the car park and flags down a passing police patrol car. PC O'Hare then approaches David and asks him where he got the briefcase. David throws the briefcase at PC O'Hare's head and tries to run off, but the officer manages to tackle him and brings him to the ground. David is then handcuffed and put in a police car in order to be taken to the police station for questioning.

Consider the following propositions:

(i) PC O'Hare must caution David following the arrest and must tell him the grounds for the arrest, even if it is obvious.

(ii) PC O'Hare has a power of arrest in these circumstances under s.24 PACE provided he has reasonable grounds for believing that an indictable offence (theft) has been committed and that David is the person who committed the offence.

(iii) PC O'Hare does not need to consider the issue of whether it is necessary to arrest David because it is clear that David will use violence in order to evade arrest.

(iv) PC O'Hare must still consider whether it is necessary to arrest David. On these facts it is likely that he will conclude an arrest is necessary in order to allow the prompt and effective investigation of the offence (questioning David) and in order to prevent any prosecution from being hindered by David's disappearance.

Which of these propositions are correct?

(a) (i) and (iv) only.

(b) (i), (ii) and (iv) only.

(c) (ii) and (iii) only.

(d) (i), (ii) and (iii) only.

Both the following questions relate to the same scenario:

[6] Craig is observed by the police loitering in a doorway on a side street. He is approached by a series of people. In each case there is a short conversation and then something small is exchanged. Two police officers approach Craig. As they approach, Craig is seen to move his hand towards his mouth, as if concealing something. The police officers believe that the concealed item is likely to be either crack cocaine or ecstasy – both Class A drugs.

Which one of the following propositions is true?

(a) In order to arrest Craig one of the officers must make physical contact with him and then inform him that he is under arrest and the reason for the arrest, and why the arrest was necessary, even if the reason is obvious.

(b) Following any arrest, Craig must be taken to a police station immediately.

(c) Following the arrest, the police officers will be able to search Craig's mouth, using reasonable force if he does not consent to the search.

(d) Craig must be cautioned before he can be arrested.

[7] Craig admits that he is in possession of a small amount of cannabis resin. He is arrested for possession of a Class C drug with intent to supply. Which one of the following propositions is correct?

(a) The officers have a discretion to grant Craig bail to attend the police station for questioning at a later time and date.

(b) The arrest is unlawful as there is no power to arrest Craig for possession of a Class C drug.

(c) Any power of arrest will be in breach of article 5 of the European Convention on Human Rights, and will therefore be unlawful.

(d) Craig can be granted street bail but the police are not able to impose any conditions.

CHAPTER 3

IN THE POLICE STATION

> This chapter covers:
>
> The power to detain, and the suspect's rights under PACE
>
> The right of access to legal advice
>
> Advising your client in the police station
>
> Dealing with the interview
>
> Post-interview matters, such as fingerprints and identification parades
>
> The decision to charge, and post-charge matters such as police bail

Defending at police stations is not easy. Clients may be vulnerable, nervous, apprehensive, resentful, angry, rude, or all of these things. Police officers may be uncooperative, secretive, difficult, dismissive or aggressive. The lawyer is on police territory, subject to a police agenda and is often viewed as an interloper, interfering with both the investigation and the course of justice. On top of this, it may be late at night or in the early hours of the morning, and the lawyer is alone, unsupported by professional colleagues.

Ed Cape, <u>Defending Suspects at Police Stations</u> (Fifth edition)

[3.1] DETENTION

What happens at the police station will often make or break a case. It will be your job to ensure that the suspect receives accurate and appropriate advice and that his rights are looked after. Months later, and with the benefit of hindsight, judges and advocates in the Crown Court will be looking at the actions you took and the advice which you gave alone and under pressure. It is the most important and the most demanding work that you will do.

The relevant law on detention and questioning will be found in the Police and Criminal Evidence Act 1984. These statutory provisions are then amplified by PACE Code of Practice C (Code C), which sets out in clear English what should and should not happen during detention.

3.1.1 Custody officers

Each designated police station must have a custody officer. The role and duties of the custody officer are detailed in s.37 PACE. The custody officer must be of at least the rank of sergeant and must not be connected with the investigation. The job of the custody officer is to determine whether there is sufficient evidence to charge, and if not, whether there are grounds for detention. The custody officer must keep a custody record and must ensure that the detainee is treated in accordance with PACE and the Codes of Practice. If there is a disagreement between the custody officer and a higher-ranking officer, the matter must be referred to the Superintendent for that station.

Note that under the Serious Organised Crime and Police Act 2005 there is provision for civilian police staff to act as custody officers, subject to training.

3.1.2 Custody records: Code C 2

A custody record must be opened as soon as practicable following the detainee's arrival at the police station: C2.1. All matters relating to the detainee must be recorded on this record. Where this is not complied with, there are likely to be challenges to any evidence obtained. A solicitor (or appropriate adult) is entitled to consult the custody record of a detainee as soon as practicable following their arrival at the station and at any time while the suspect is detained: C2.4. After the detainee has been released or taken to court, the detainee or solicitor are entitled to a copy of the custody record if they request it: C2.4A. [You will find an example of a custody record in the case study at Document 1.]

You should always ask to see the custody record as soon as you arrive at the police station. It will tell you:

- what your client was arrested for, and when and where the arrest took place;
- the time your client arrived at the police station;
- on what ground the custody officer authorised detention;
- whether your client was informed of, and whether he chose to exercise his rights to contact someone and to take legal advice;
- whether any interviews have already taken place;
- what other steps (for example, medical treatment) have occurred since detention: this should include a risk assessment in respect of the detainee (C 3.6); and
- whether any significant comments (or silences) from your client have been recorded.

3.1.3 Initial action: Code C 3

When the suspect is brought to the police station the custody officer will need to:

- decide whether detention should be authorised;
- inform the detainee of his rights;
- conduct an immediate risk assessment;

We will look at each of these points in turn.

Can the person be detained?

Where a person is arrested without a warrant, the first decision that the custody officer must make is whether there is sufficient evidence to charge the person. If there is enough evidence to charge then the person may be detained only so long as is necessary to enable the custody officer to charge the detainee: s.37(1) PACE.

Statutory charging: in most cases the police must consult with the Crown Prosecution Service in order to decide whether, and what, to charge. In such cases, there is a power for the custody officer to bail or detain the suspect pending such decisions: ss.37A–37D PACE. [For further details, see later 3.7.1.]

Charge, release or detain: If there is not sufficient evidence to justify a charge then a person must be released unless the officer has reasonable grounds to believe:

- that detention without charge is necessary to secure or preserve evidence relating to the offence for which they have been arrested; or
- that detention without charge is necessary in order to obtain such evidence by questioning the person.

You will find that custody officers invariably authorise detention under these provisions so as to allow the police to question the suspect.

The decision to detain is a continuing decision: Detention can only be authorised so long as one of the above-mentioned conditions apply.

Informing the detainee of his rights

The detainee must be told of his rights. At the time of detention the detainee has three rights:

- the right of intimation (i.e. having someone informed of his whereabouts): s.56 PACE
- the right to free legal advice: s.58 PACE; and
- the right to consult the PACE Codes.

Code C3.2 states that the detainee must be given a written notice setting out these rights.

The risk assessment and other actions:

The custody officer should note any comment about the arresting officer's account of events, but should not seek it. Similarly the custody officer should note any comments concerning the decision to detain. The custody officer should ask the detainee if he wants a solicitor and ask him to sign the custody record accordingly.

Additionally Code C provides that a risk assessment must take place in order to determine if the detainee is in need of medical treatment or attention, and to assess whether the detainee is a risk to staff or to himself: C3.6–3.10. Annex E to the Code provides specific guidance on dealing with mentally disordered or mentally vulnerable people. Annex G addresses the assessment of whether a detainee is fit for interview. The custody sergeant may need to consult a "health care professional" in carrying out this assessment.

What if the suspect is a "volunteer"?

A person who attends the police station voluntarily – i.e. when not under arrest – is known as a volunteer. Volunteers are dealt with in Code C 3.21. A volunteer is entitled to free legal advice. If a volunteer wishes to leave and the police want to detain him, they will need to arrest him. It is worth noting that although many of the provisions of the Codes of Practice do not apply to volunteers, the Codes make clear that volunteers should be treated with "no less consideration" than detainees.

3.1.4 Search of person and taking of initial samples:

Search of the person: Under Code C 4.1 the custody officer can authorise a search to the extent necessary to ascertain what property the detainee has. It is not always necessary to search a person or list their property, for example if they are only to be detained for a short time in the main reception area of the custody suite, rather than being placed in a cell. Property can be seized and retained if the detainee could use it to cause harm, damage property, interfere with evidence, or escape. If the detainee is not allowed to keep a particular item, then the detainee must be told the reason why. It is a matter for the custody officer as to whether he records the reason why property has been seized, but if he does, then the fact that there is a record should be noted on the custody record and the detainee should be invited to sign the record as being correct, if he refuses to do so, that refusal must be recorded: Code C.4.4.

Intimate searches: S.55 PACE provides a power to carry out intimate searches at police stations. An intimate search is one which consists of the physical examination of bodily orifices other than the mouth: Code C, Annex A 1. However, for an intimate search authorisation from an officer of at least the rank of Inspector is required, and there must be reasonable grounds for believing that an intimate search is necessary to find either Class A drugs or items that could be used to cause physical injury. Where the search is for drugs, then written consent from the detainee is needed but an inference can be drawn from any refusal, without good cause, to permit a search. Intimates searches should be conducted by a medical practitioner unless the Inspector feels this is not practicable, in which case it may be done by an officer of the same sex as the detainee. Similar same sex rules apply in relation to strip searches which allow for visual examination of the detainee stripped of clothing, but obviously touching the detainee would then cross the line into intimate searching.

Fingerprints, footwear impressions and other samples: s.61–63 PACE. There are wide powers to take fingerprints, footwear impressions and non-intimate samples from persons who are under arrest. These powers arise at the pre-charge stage provided the person is in detention for a recordable offence: s.63 PACE, as amended by s.11 CJA 2003. At the pre-charge stage, consent is required unless it is a recordable offence and such samples have not already been taken (or are of poor quality). All imprisonable offences will be recordable offences, as will many non-imprisonable offences. Post charge, fingerprints, footwear samples and non-intimate samples may be taken without consent provided it is a recordable offence and they have not already been taken. Intimate samples are discussed at 3.5.

Non-intimate samples include: hair (other than pubic hair); samples taken from nails; swab from any part of the body, including the mouth (but no other bodily orifice); saliva; or a skin impression. With both fingerprints and non-intimate samples consent is not needed and reasonable force can be used.

Drugs testing: There is a power to test for the presence of drugs in the body in some circumstances, which can then either be used to require the detainee to seek treatment, or the information about which can be passed to the court for use in making a decision about bail: see 3.5 below for further details.

Using samples and fingerprints for speculative searches: Where the police have taken a sample they will be able to conduct a speculative search against law enforcement databases to see if there is a fingerprint or DNA match with an unsolved offence. A Human Rights Act challenge to this was run in *R (Marper) v Chief Constable of South Yorkshire* [2004] 4 All ER 193. However, in that case the House of Lords held that the power was not in breach of rights to privacy under Article 8 of the ECHR. But note that in *S and Marper v The United Kingdom, S and another v The United Kingdom* (App. Nos 30562/04 and 30566/04 [2008] All ER (D) 56 (Dec) The European Court of Human Rights decided that the UK's policy of retaining such details from persons who were subsequently released without charge or not convicted did amount to a breach of Art 8 and as a result, various amendments to the power to take and retain samples have been made under The Crime and Security Act 2010 but are not as yet in force. In the meantime, the recently enacted Protection of Freedom Act 2012 has maintained a fairly generous approach to this matter. Under this legislation, DNA and fingerprint samples can be retained indefinitely in certain situations including where the suspect has a serious previous conviction. However, the samples taken from suspects who have a clean record must be destroyed after three years, albeit that the police can seek an extension of up to two years. There is also a clause permitting certain profiles/samples to be retained in the interests of national security.

3.1.5 Delaying the right of intimation: s. 56 and C 5

The right of intimation (or "the right not to be held incommunicado") is the right to have a person known to the detainee or likely to take an interest in his welfare informed of his whereabouts: C5.1. Where that person cannot be contacted, the detainee can choose up to two further people. Beyond this, further attempts to contact persons are at the discretion of the custody officer. The purpose of the provision is to ensure that detained persons do not simply disappear into police custody. There is a limited power to delay this notification. There is a separate right to make a telephone call to any person: C5.6. Both rights may be delayed. Before any telephone call is made, the detainee must be warned that his conversation may be listened to and used in evidence, this is clearly to avoid there being any "tipping off" or collusion.

When does the power to delay notification arise? The power to delay access to this right must be authorised by an officer of at least the rank of inspector. The inspector can only authorise the delay if he has reasonable grounds for believing that allowing the detainee to notify a person will either lead to interference with evidence or physical injury to other people, or lead to the alerting of suspects who are still at large, or will hinder the recovery of property obtained from the offence. This power of delay only arises if the offence is classed as an "indictable offence": Code C, Annex B.

Reminder – indictable offences: The concept of "indictable offences" cropped up in Chapter 2, as it is relevant to the exercise of certain arrest and search powers. An indictable offence is either an offence that can only be tried in the Crown Court (indictable only) or where there is a power to have the matter tried in the Crown Court (either way offences).

3.1.6 Conditions of detention: Code C 8

The custody officer is responsible for the conditions of detention. There must be adequate heat, cleanliness, ventilation and lighting in a cell. Bedding must be supplied and must be of a reasonable standard. There must be access to a toilet and washing facilities. If the detainee's clothing has been removed for any purpose, then replacement clothing of a reasonable standard must be provided. There should be two light meals and one main meal every 24 hours. The detainee should be visited every hour, and if intoxicated through drink or drugs visited and roused every half-hour. If medical treatment is needed a police surgeon or health care professional should be called: Code C 9. Where the detainee takes regular medication, the custody officer must verify this with a health care professional before allowing the detainee the opportunity to take his medication.

Allegations of mistreatment: if a person complains of ill treatment since arrest, or it comes to the attention of an officer that he may have been treated improperly, an independent officer of at least the rank of inspector must be informed. If the allegation is of assault or excessive force, the police surgeon or health care professional must be called: Code C9.2.

3.1.7 Reviews of detention: s. 40 and Code C 15

The review officer is responsible for deciding whether the suspect's detention continues to be necessary. If it is not, the suspect must be released. Where the detainee has not yet been charged, the review officer must be an inspector or above and not directly involved in the investigation. If the detainee has been charged, then the custody officer can act as the review officer. The officer must listen to any representations concerning the detention from the detainee (unless asleep) and his solicitor (if available).

When do the reviews take place? The first review must be not later than 6 hours after detention was first authorised. The second review must then take place not later than 9 hours after that. Subsequent reviews must then follow at not more than 9-hourly intervals. The review can be conducted by an inspector on the telephone, but not in those police stations where video-conferencing could be used: s.40A PACE. There is a power to delay a review if it is not practicable to conduct it, but a failure to review at the correct time will render the detention unlawful during that period: *Roberts v Chief Constable of the Cheshire Police* [1999] All ER (D) 63.

3.1.8 Detention time limits: ss.41-44

The detention time limits are complex. The general time limit on detention without charge is 24 hours. At the end of this period, if the police do not have sufficient evidence to charge a person, he must be released: s.41(7).

The "detention clock" will normally start to run as soon as the person arrives at the police station. Often an investigation may take longer than 24 hours, in which case the police can stop the clock from running by releasing the person on bail, with a date to come back to the police station (a "bail back"). When the person returns, and is re-arrested, the clock will start to run again.

The following chart sets out the conditions for detention for periods longer than 24 hours:

	Offence type	**Authorised by**	**Total maximum**
Up to 24 hours	Any offence	Custody sergeant	24 hours
An additional 12 hours	An indictable offence	Superintendent or more senior officer	36 hours
Up to an additional 36 hours	An indictable offence	Magistrates' court	72 hours
Up to an additional 36 hours, but not to exceed 96 hours.	An indictable offence	Magistrates' court	96 hours

Police authorisation for extended detention: If the person is detained for an indictable offence under s.24 PACE, then the police can detain for a further 12 hours (that is, up to 36 hours) on their own authority. This extension of detention for an additional 12 hours has to be authorised by an officer of at least the rank of superintendent (see s.42 PACE). The officer must be satisfied that there are reasonable grounds for believing that: (i) the detention is necessary to secure or preserve evidence or to obtain such evidence by questioning the suspect; and (ii) the offence is an indictable offence; and (iii) the investigation is being conducted "diligently and expeditiously".

Authorising detention beyond 36 hours: This power only arises in relation to indictable offences, and requires the police to apply to the magistrates for a warrant of further detention: s.43(1). The detainee is entitled to be represented at the hearing. The magistrates may only grant the warrant if they are satisfied that the same grounds are made out as for s.42 and that the offence is an indictable offence. The warrant may authorise detention for a further 36 hours (i.e. up to 72 hours). On a second application the court may extend the warrant for a further 36 hours, up to a maximum of 96 hours total detention on the same grounds.

Detention and terrorism offences: Note that there are special rules in relation to terrorism offences which permit longer periods of detention under the Terrorism Act 2006. Code H governs the conditions of detention for such suspects. Note that Terrorism Act extended detention powers require special consents before authorised judges, and suspects may be transferred to prison for part of the detention period since it is thought that prisons are more able to provide facilities for longer-term detention than police stations.

3.1.9 Cautioning a suspect

The caution warns a suspect that what they say may be used against them. There are essentially two forms of caution; the first type of caution will be issued where the suspect has received, or at least been offered legal advice. This caution warns the suspect that failure to mention facts when questioned may in some cases harm their defence. The wording of this caution is in the following form:

> *You do not have to say anything. But it may harm your defence if you do not mention when questioned something which you later rely on in court. Anything you do say may be given in evidence.*

The second type of caution is a slightly different version for those circumstances where failure to mention facts when questioned cannot harm any defence. This is more appropriate when the person has not yet received legal advice, or is post charge etc. The wording of this caution is in the following form:

> *You do not have to say anything. But anything you do say may be given in evidence.*

[For more information on the "inferences" from exercise of the right to silence, see Chapter 15.]

The courts take a very strict line on cautioning:

In Charles v CPS [2009] EWHC 3521, the police arrested C for being drunk in charge and, having provided a positive breath test, indicated that he would be charged with the offence. Despite this, the police then went on to interview him. C was invited to tell the police in his own words what had happened. C then went on to admit driving and was duly charged with the more serious offence of driving whilst under the influence. C complained that the police had not told him that they were investigating this more serious charge and furthermore, there had been a technical breach of PACE as according to Code C 16.5, the police cannot interview after they have indicated they are going to prosecute unless necessary for a stipulated reason (none were present in this case) and in any event, even if such an interview was necessary, the police had given the wrong caution. The High Court ruled that the magistrates had been wrong to dismiss the s.76 and s.78 arguments that had been advanced at the trial as although there had been no bad faith by the police, their error had caused unfairness. In passing judgement, Moses LJ said "These provisions are not a mere rigmarole to be recited like a mantra and then ignored. The provisions of the Police and Criminal Evidence Act and the Code relating to the caution, are designed to protect a detainee. They are important protections. They impose significant disciplines upon the police as to how they are to behave. If they can secure a conviction in breach of those provisions that is an important matter which undermines the protection of a detainee in the police station."

[3.2] ACCESS TO A SOLICITOR

A detainee is entitled to consult a solicitor privately at any time. He must be allowed to do so as soon as is practicable following his request, except to the limited extent that the police are entitled to delay that access: s.58 PACE.

3.2.1 The right to see a solicitor

PACE Code C lays down a number of requirements. First the suspect must be told of the right to consult with a solicitor, and that they can get free advice from the duty solicitor: Code C6.1. The Code makes clear that the police must not at any point do or say anything to dissuade the suspect from taking legal advice: Code C6.4. Additionally, if the suspect waives the right, they should be asked for their reasons, and those reasons should be noted on the custody record: Code C6.5.

Impact of Human Rights Act on access to a solicitor: Note the decision in *Condron v United Kingdom* (2000) 31 E.H.R.R.1 where one key consideration for the European Court of Human Rights in concluding that an inference from silence was permissible was the fact that the Condrons had had access to a solicitor:

> *The fact that an accused person who is questioned under caution is assured access to legal advice, and in the applicants' case the physical presence of a solicitor during police interview, must be considered a particularly important safeguard for dispelling any compulsion to speak which may be inherent in the terms of the caution. [para 60]*

However, although the right of access to a solicitor will be of significance in deciding whether evidence is later admissible at trial, it seems that the fact that access to a solicitor is denied will not necessarily mean that any subsequent trial is automatically unfair for the purposes of article 6: *Gourley v H.M. Advocate* 2000 J.C.93

Who is a solicitor?: "Solicitor" is defined by Code C6.12. It includes solicitors with practising certificates, but also accredited, or probationary police station representatives who are registered with the Legal Services Commission.

Defence Solicitor Call Centre and Criminal Defence Service Direct (CDS Direct): Suspects in the police station have a right to access free legal advice (see below at 3.2.3). All cases are referred to the Defence Solicitor Call Centre (DSCC). If the offence is indictable only, then the call centre will either contact a particular solicitor that the client has requested, or otherwise contact whichever solicitor is the duty solicitor for that particular police station. If the requested solicitor is not available, or cannot be contacted, then the duty solicitor will automatically be contacted. If the offence is non-indictable, then the DSCC will transfer the case to CDS Direct who will provide telephone advice only. If the matter is likely to require an interview and/or the client is particularly vulnerable, then CDS Direct will inform DSCC who will then transfer the case to either the client's own solicitor or the duty solicitor. If the case only merits CDS telephone advice but the client is not content with this, then he will have to pay privately for his own solicitor to attend.

3.2.2 The power to delay access to a lawyer

The right of access to legal advice is seen as particularly important, and where a person wants legal advice the custody sergeant must act without delay to secure provision of that advice. Access to legal advice can only be delayed if the offence is an indictable offence and if a superintendent reasonably believes that the exercise of the right of access to legal advice will lead to one of the specified consequences: Code C, Annex B. (See 3.1.5 above for details.) The provisions specifically state that access to a solicitor may not be delayed on the grounds that he might advise the person not to answer questions, or that the solicitor was originally asked to attend by a third party.

Can your client be interviewed before you arrive? The normal rule is that a person who wants legal advice may not be interviewed or continue to be interviewed until he has received it. However there are some restrictions to this. Code C6.6 provides that an interview can still go ahead if either the provisions of Annex B to Code C apply, or that the superintendent has reasonable grounds for believing that the delay might:

- lead to interference with, or harm to, evidence connected with an offence;
- lead to interference with or physical harm to other people;
- lead to serious loss of, or damage to, property;
- lead to alerting other people suspected of having committed an offence but not yet arrested for it;

- hinder the recovery of property obtained in consequence of the commission of an offence; or

- where a solicitor has said he will attend, waiting for the solicitor to arrive would cause unreasonable delay to the investigation.

What happens if a suspect no longer wants legal advice? Where a person changes his mind and decides he no longer wants legal advice, the interview can be started/continued. However, the detainee must give his agreement in writing/or on tape and an inspector must authorise the interview having checked the person's reasons for his change of mind: Code C6.6(d). Obviously, this is intended to prevent allegations that police officers have improperly attempted to persuade a suspect not to seek legal advice.

3.2.3 "Free legal advice" – who pays?

Work at the police station will generally be dealt with under the Police Station Advice and Assistance Scheme. There is no means test and no application form. It covers arrestees and volunteers. There is a locally-set fixed fee for each case.

Criminal Defence Service Direct: In straightforward cases where no solicitor is needed at the police station, the suspect will receive legal advice over the telephone from a CDS call centre. You may therefore find yourself having to contact the CDS Direct service to find out what they advised your client to do if you later have to attend the police station for interview, or if your client is charged and then comes to see you.

[3.3] ADVISING YOUR CLIENT

3.3.1 How will you be contacted?

You may be contacted via the Defence Solicitor Call Centre, by the client himself (especially if he is still at large but knows the police are looking for him) or by a third party.

What if you are contacted by a third party? Two issues arise: first, what should the police do if you contact them about a detainee in response to a third party's instructions? Secondly, what is the professional conduct position about solicitors accepting third party instructions?

Third party instructions and the police: Code C 6.15 provides that if a solicitor arrives at the police station to see a detainee, the detainee must be told of the solicitor's arrival and asked if they want legal advice. This applies even if they have earlier declined to have legal advice, and even if they are being interviewed.

Third party instructions and professional conduct: Under the new Code of Conduct, the section on client care indicates that although you may accept instructions from a third party you must ensure that the client authorises those instructions. Essentially this means that if a third party contacts you and tells you that Mr X wants you to represent him, you need to telephone/meet Mr X to ensure that he really does want you to represent him before you start to take any active steps on his case.

3.3.2 First steps on contacting the police station

When you ring the police station you will talk to the custody officer. The officer will have the custody record to hand and should be able to give you all the basic information about your client's detention. Remember, however, that the custody officer is not the investigating officer and will therefore not have full or up to date information about the investigation. Get as much information as you can – but as a minimum you need to know:

- Who are the arresting officers;
- What is the alleged offence;
- Is your client under arrest or a volunteer;
- What the time of arrest was, and the reason why arrest was necessary;
- What time did the detainee arrive at the station;
- Whether any interview has yet taken place;
- When legal advice was first requested and whether any legal advice has already been given (for example by CDS Direct);
- The result of the risk assessment.

Talking to the client on the telephone

Introduce: Introduce yourself. Explain that you are the duty solicitor's representative or a representative for his "own" solicitor where he has requested your firm in particular. Ask your client how private the telephone is – it will often be in the custody suite, but some telephones are much more liable to be overheard than others. Remind him that there is a risk of the police overhearing him, and therefore to be careful in what he says.

Inform: Tell the client whatever information you have already received from the police. Check that your client wants legal advice, and then decide whether it will be necessary to attend immediately, or perhaps at a later stage. Bear in mind that in the case of many minor offences where there is not going to be a police interview, the CDS will only fund telephone advice.

Explain: Tell the client when you will be attending the police station, whether that is immediately, or when the police are ready for interview. In the meantime, remind the client of his right to silence and advise your client not to discuss his case with anyone at the police station including custody staff, co-accuseds and medical professionals. If you do decide that it is necessary to attend for the interview, tell the custody officer that you wish to be present and that you should be informed as soon as the investigating officers are ready to interview. This should help to ensure that the police do not go ahead with an interview in your absence.

3.3.3 Should you attend for interview?

Normally you will need to attend if the police intend to interview. Advising on whether to exercise the right to silence is extremely complex, and you will need clear information from your client, as well as seeing what information the police are prepared to release to you. Because an inference can arise from silence at charge, as well as during police questioning, you may even need to attend for matters where the police simply intend to charge without interview. The CDS will expect solicitors to attend for all interviews and identification procedures, or where there are allegations of serious police misconduct. In cases where your client is not fit for interview (perhaps through intoxication or illness), you may have to wait to be informed as to when the interview will take place.

3.3.4 Attending the client at the police station

The custody officer and custody record: When you arrive at the police station you will need to speak first to the custody officer and to look at the custody record. You have a right to see this: Code C2.4. The custody record will give you the times of arrest, detention, review, any searches and their results, any delays, any interviews, any significant comments or silences, any identification procedures that have taken place, any medical issues, what the offences are and so on. Read and make careful notes. You are not entitled to a copy of it at this stage – although there is no harm in asking. The majority of police stations now keep an electronic custody record and detention log, so there should be no difficulty in the custody officer printing off a copy for you.

Talking to the officer in the case: The officer in the case will normally be the officer in charge of the investigation. He is not obliged to tell you anything at this stage. (There is a requirement to disclose original descriptions given by identification witnesses but only prior to holding an identification procedure: Code D 3.1.)

Will the police give you information about the offence?: Although not required by law to disclose information, most officers are prepared to give you some information about the offence, as they recognise you may otherwise need to keep stopping the interview to take instructions. You must press the officer for as much disclosure as possible, but you must be very wary about the information you are given. Few officers will lie to you directly (if they do, then evidence obtained as a consequence is likely to be excluded: see *Mason* 86 Cr App R 349, discussed fully in Chapter 16). However, the police will often suggest that the evidence is stronger than it later turns out to be. Additionally they will always withhold evidence for use during the interview.

Analysing the information: Once you have the basic information about the arrest and the interview, you will need to consider how much evidence there is against your client on the case that has so far been disclosed to you. You need to assess whether they already have sufficient evidence to justify bringing a charge regardless of what your client may have to say about the offence. Are there clear gaps in the case – for example, is it already clear that the police may have difficulty obtaining a statement from the alleged victim? In particular you will need to think about whether your client is alleged by the police to have made damaging admissions, whether at the scene of the crime or on his way to the police station. Any such 'significant statements' will be put to the client at the start of the interview, so you will have to check whether he is prepared to accept what he is supposed to have said. You may already be able to take a view on how likely it is that the admissibility of any such evidence at trial can be challenged because it has been obtained improperly – for example because your client was questioned prior to his arrival at the police station when he should not have been.

What if the police refuse to disclose information to you? There may be no right as such to see the witness statements that the police have taken, but if you know nothing about the case, your client may not be in a position to answer questions at interview. Inadequate disclosure of information by the police will not automatically prevent any inferences arising from failure by your client to answer questions: see Chapter 15. However, it may show that your client's failure to put forward defence facts was not unreasonable, so that no inferences can properly be drawn: see *Argent* [1997] 2 Cr App R 27, and *Roble* [1997] Crim LR 449 (both discussed more fully in Chapter 15).

3.3.5 Seeing your client

You may have the luxury of seeing your client in an interview room. Alternatively, you may have to see your client in the cells. In either event, you need to be wary. Police cells are sometimes bugged in the hope of obtaining evidence from suspects. Solicitor-client conversations will be privileged and there have been assurances that the police will turn off any listening devices. In a number of cases Lincolnshire police bugged the exercise yard at a police station in order to enable them to listen to privileged conversations between lawyers and their clients: the Court of Appeal had no hesitation in ruling that the cases should have been stayed as an abuse of process: see *Grant* [2005] EWCA Crim 1089.

By way of contrast note the decision of the Court of Appeal in *Mason* (2002) 2 Cr App R 38 where three persons suspected of conspiracy were arrested for separate offences but then placed in a bugged custody suite where damaging admissions as to the conspiracy were obtained. The court held that even if there had been a breach of the suspects' article 8 right to privacy (because the surveillance was not governed by law), the judge had correctly used his discretion under s.78 to admit the evidence and there had been no breach of the suspects' right to a fair trial. The general advice would therefore be to be careful in what is said anywhere in the police station.

Free, confidential, independent: Even with experienced clients it does no harm to remind the client of your status. In other words, you are present as their solicitor, to look out for their interests, and your advice is free, completely confidential and is independent of the police. Check that your client understands you and is feeling well enough to discuss their situation.

Tell your client what you know so far: Most solicitors will start by telling the client what they know about the case so far. This can provide a useful starting point for taking any instructions. It must also be said that this prevents clients from putting forward one version of events, then hearing what the police have told you, and immediately changing their story to fit in with it.

Professional conduct points

What if your client keeps changing his story? You are under no duty to enquire in every case whether your client is telling the truth. If your client makes statements that are inconsistent, this is not of itself a ground for refusing to act further; it is only where it is clear that the client is attempting to put forward false evidence to the court that you must cease to act.

However, while solicitors have an overriding duty not to mislead the court, (this derives from Principle 1 'the duty to uphold the law and proper administration of justice') does this duty apply at the police station stage? The answer is that even if it does not, solicitors are still subject to the criminal law: assisting a client to lie to the police would probably fall foul of s.4 Criminal Law Act 1967. It would be proper to point out to a client inconsistencies in his account, and you are not under any duty to cease acting merely because he changes his account; however, you cannot assist him in making up a defence to fit the facts. In any event, you should always remind your client that the police are likely to be withholding evidence in order to be able to test the account that he puts forward.

> *For a nice example of police practice, see the case of Rosenberg [2006] EWCA Crim 6. Here the police questioned R about drug dealing allegations without at first revealing that her next door neighbour had been covertly video recording her actions. The Court of Appeal agreed that there had been no obligation on the police to disclose the extent of the evidence against her at the start of the interview.*

What if your client tells you that he is guilty? You must still explore the facts with your client. Your client may believe that he is guilty of, for example, an assault, but it may become clear that he has a defence of self-defence. Similarly, he may be prepared to admit taking a motor vehicle, but it may become clear that he thought that he had the owner's consent.

Clients who intend to lie to the police: If a client tells you that he is guilty of the offence, but that he intends to lie to the police, you will need to explain that you cannot continue to act for him if he does so. Note that because of your duty of confidentiality (discussed in Chapter

4 of the Code of Conduct), you cannot tell the police why you are withdrawing from the matter. It is, however, perfectly proper to continue to act if the client admits his guilt, but says that he intends to remain silent in interview and at charge. You are entitled to "put the prosecution to proof", provided that you do nothing to positively assert your client's innocence. Even if your client enters a Not Guilty plea, this merely amounts to a requirement that the prosecution prove their case. Be aware that if you have agreed that your client will give a no comment interview but then, mid-interview, he ignores this advice and starts to answer questions and advance lies, then you must immediately stop the interview and withdraw for professional reasons.

What if there is a conflict of interests between clients?: Chapter 3 of the Code of Conduct deals with conflicts of interest between clients. This tells us that if there is a conflict, or a significant risk of a conflict between two or more clients, then you must not act for both of them unless the matter falls within a given exception. You will therefore need to establish whether there actually is a conflict of interests or a significant risk of a conflict, and this is not always as obvious as it may seem. It can be difficult to identify a conflict of interest and it is wise to speak to the first detainee and assess the situation before going any further. If the first detainee lays the blame at the door of the second detainee, then you should not act for the second detainee and the police should ensure that he receives separate legal advice. You then remain untainted by anything the second detainee may have wanted to tell you about the situation. Unfortunately, the conflict is not always so apparent and you may not realise there is any difficulty until you have spoken to both detainees. The difficulty then arises that you may be in possession of information from one suspect that may assist the other suspect. You are then in a quandary, as although you are under a duty to act in the best interests of your client and should therefore pass on any relevant information to the first suspect, you are also under a duty to keep that information confidential to the second suspect as he is also your client. In such a situation, you would need to withdraw from the case entirely.

There are however, situations where you can continue to act for both clients as there is no conflict of interests. In such situations, you must continue to observe the duty of confidentiality and remember not to disclose to one suspect, information that you have received from the other suspect. The only exception to this rule is where the suspects are running the same defence, the client consents to you disclosing the information, and you feel that it is in your client's best interests to pass the information on. You must however guard against unwittingly becoming the "go between" in a concocted defence. The way to do this is to ensure that each suspect is giving you unprompted instructions that are entirely independent of what the other may have said.

Advantages of an early admission of guilt: If your client tells you that he is guilty, you must always remind him of the advantages and the disadvantages of admitting the offence at this early stage. The admission, and any co-operation with the police, will often be powerful evidence of remorse, which you will refer to in your mitigation speech. An early admission will also lead to a statutory "discount" on sentence under s.144 Criminal Justice Act 2003. Indeed the guidance from the Sentencing Council suggests that in some cases the maximum discount for a guilty plea may require the defendant to make the admissions at the police station stage:

(a) the first reasonable opportunity [for the defendant to indicate willingness to plead guilty] may be the first time that a defendant appears before the court and has the opportunity to plead guilty
(b) but the court may consider that it would be reasonable to have expected an indication of willingness even earlier, perhaps while under interview.
Note: For a) and b) to apply, the Court will need to be satisfied that the defendant (and any legal adviser) would have had sufficient information about the allegations.

> Sentencing Guidelines Council: Reduction in Sentence for a Guilty Plea: Annex 2, para 3.

The disadvantage of indicating a guilty plea, however, is that the police may otherwise have had no evidence against your client, or at least insufficient evidence for them to charge him.

In such a situation, you are essentially handing over a very easy conviction to the police.

Considering your client's instructions: It is not your role to blindly accept your client's instructions. In order to give appropriate legal advice you will need to take a view on the potential strengths and weaknesses of your client's account. In particular you must consider:

- How coherent is your client's version of events?
- What gaps are there in the client's version?
- What admissions/silences have already occurred and why?
- How fit is your client to be interviewed?
- Has your client been made promises of any kind by the police?

You will need to explain to your client the legal consequences of his version of events – does it amount to an admission of guilt? Does it go some way to showing that he acted recklessly, where this is the *mens rea* of the offence (for example, with an assault)? Your client needs to understand the implications of the account that he is putting forward. Above all, however, you are going to need to consider whether your client should answer questions in interview or should exercise his right to silence.

3.3.6 Should the client exercise his right to silence?

The right to silence – and the danger of inferences: The basic principle remains that your client has an absolute right to silence. This means that he does not have to answer any police questions. He commits no offence by remaining silent. However, if your client remains silent and fails to put forward facts which he later relies on in his defence, or fails (having been given a special warning) to account for his presence, or the presence of an object, substance or mark, then inferences may be drawn at trial which will help to prove his guilt. These issues are more fully discussed in Chapter 15.

> *Juan is under arrest on suspicion of having been involved in the night time burglary of the offices where he works. The police have given you almost no disclosure, saying only that there are witnesses who place Juan at the scene of the crime. Juan tells you that he was at a restaurant with a friend during the evening and could not have been at the offices as alleged.*
> *Consider: (i) if Juan puts forward his defence (alibi: I was elsewhere), the police will immediately investigate it. If it turns out not to be true, then the lie will damage Juan's case and will make it more likely that he is charged. (ii) If Juan exercises his right to silence in interview, but is then charged with the offence, when he later raises his defence of alibi at his trial, the court may decide that the defence is less likely to be true because Juan did not mention it when he was questioned. (iii) However, if Juan does not put forward his alibi now, but the police then decide that there is insufficient evidence to charge him, no harm is done.*

Putting forward the defence account: Where your client has decided to answer police questions, remind your client that the police are likely to have withheld evidence and will use this to check the veracity of any answers.

> *I and H were arrested on suspicion of attempted robbery of a shop. The police interviewed them and noted their accounts of what had happened. Only once they had these accounts did the police reveal that they had a video of the attempted robbery which totally undermined the accounts that had been put forward. The Court of Appeal gave short shrift to the argument that the police were under a duty to disclose the fact of the video before the interview, stating: "It is totally wrong to submit that a defendant should be prevented from lying by being presented with the whole of the evidence against him prior to interview."* <u>Imran and Hussain</u> [1997] Crim LR 754

Since the police are likely to be withholding evidence, make sure you ask them before the interview, and again on tape, whether they have disclosed all relevant evidence. Make the point that if they reveal new evidence in interview, you will have to stop the interview in order to take your client's instructions. Doing this on tape is sometimes enough to trigger further disclosure as the police will not want to be seen to be deliberately withholding evidence.

If your client is going to put forward an alibi (literally: "I was elsewhere"), remind your client that the police will want to talk to any alibi witnesses at once, to prevent any chance of collusion. Your client must therefore be confident that the alibi is going to say what he expects him to say, otherwise it might make matters even worse for him. Again, remind your client that he can stop the interview at any time to take legal advice.

Character evidence and the police station interview: You will find a detailed explanation of the complex rules governing character evidence in Chapter 17. These rules deal with the circumstances where evidence of your client's "bad character" (such as previous criminal convictions) may come to be admissible at trial.

One circumstance where your client's previous convictions may be put before the court is where your client has suggested in police interview that another person is guilty of misconduct or has acted in a "reprehensible" way: s.101(1)(g) Criminal Justice Act 2003. This commonly happens when the police challenge the inconsistency between your client's account and their witnesses' account, and more often than not, the client instinctively says that as he is being truthful, the witnesses must be lying. Similarly if your client makes misleading assertions suggesting that he is of good character (when he is not) in the police interview, then this can also trigger admission of any previous bad character at trial: see s.101(1)(f) Criminal Justice Act 2003. You should therefore warn your client about the dangers of making such allegations or assertions during interview.

So should your client answer police questions? The decision is one for your client to take, but you will need to advise clearly what his options are. The basic position is simple:

- If your client talks, he may talk himself into all kinds of trouble;

- If your client puts forward his defence now, it will look terrible if he tries to change the details at a later stage (for example, when he's aware of all the evidence);

- If your client stays silent, but then puts forward a defence at trial, the prosecution and the judge can invite the jury to draw inferences from his failure to put forward his defence now;

- If your client answers the easy questions, and doesn't answer the hard ones, the tape of the interview can be played to the jury and it sounds very incriminating;

- If your client is adamant that he is guilty and wants to confess, he will get the maximum discount for co-operating with the police at this early stage. Alternatively, another advantage is that a confession at this stage could lead to a caution rather than prosecution.

Your advice will need to take account of all the factors of which you are aware, and in particular:

- How much you know of the police case and the strength of police evidence; but always remember that the police will not have disclosed everything;

- Any issues of admissibility of police evidence (if for example they are relying on comments made in response to improper questioning during a search of premises);

- The fairness of the interview and the general condition and abilities of the client (not just whether your client will be able to answer questions, but equally, will the client be able to remain silent?);

- Any advantages arising from an early statement of the client's defence;

- Any specific reasons to stay silent (for example, your client is afraid of retaliation from others);

- Whether the safest option may be to put forward a comprehensive <u>written</u> statement setting out all the relevant facts? [See the following section.]

Remember that the decision is always the client's decision. Once you have an agreed course of action, you should ask your client to sign your written notes. This will prove invaluable if he later tries to suggest that you advised a different course of action, or that he never agreed to what took place.

3.3.7 Preparing the client for interview

Tell the client what will happen: Explain that the interview will be recorded. Until recently, this would always be done by means of a cassette recording, but following recent amendments to PACE, digital recording is now being introduced throughout the UK. Where cassette tapes are still used, you must explain to your client that two tapes will be unwrapped and placed in a recorder. The police will then explain that one of the tapes will be sealed and will not be unsealed without a court order, the other will be used to make copies. Explain that because the interview is audibly recorded, at the start of the interview everyone, including the suspect, will be asked to state their name so that the various different voices can be identified. Explain the room layout – and that you will most probably be sitting beside your client, which will make it difficult to catch his eye. Above all, explain what your role is and that he can stop the interview to take legal advice.

If the interview is to be digitally recorded, you will need to explain that an audio file will be created with a unique electronic signature. This means that access to the recording can be controlled and monitored so that only those people who have specific permission to access the recording may do so. Every time someone accesses the file, this will be logged so that a clear record is kept as to who listened to the interview. The audio file will be in read only format so that it cannot be tampered with in any way. You, as the solicitor, will be able to access the recording. The remainder of the advice as to introductions, room layout etc is exactly the same as mentioned above. For further detail on the recording of interviews, see Code E of PACE.

Video-taping of interviews: s.60A PACE provides for the "visual recording" of interviews. Although this is not a routine practice, it frequently happens in very serious cases. As with audio recording, there will be a gradual transition from video cassettes to digital recording as such recordings are more secure, easier to process and require no physical storage space. Visual recording of interviews is dealt with by PACE Code F and in relation to the opening, sealing, storage of and access to video tapes; it is a very similar process to that of audio recording. If your client is going to be visually recorded, it is important to remind him of this and to point out that he needs to be aware that his body-language may be sending out unhelpful messages. Similarly you, as his legal adviser, need to bear in mind how you wish to present yourself for the recording.

Stopping the interview: If you have agreed that your client is going to give a no comment interview, explain that you may intervene if he starts to answer questions to make sure that he actually intends to do so. Remind him that "partial comment" interviews should be avoided as they sound incriminating in court, as the client appears to answer all the easy questions, but then to duck the difficult ones. In any event, remind your client that he is free to stop the interview at any point to take legal advice, and that such legal advice will be given in private.

Trick questions: Warn about standard trick questions and misleading comments, in particular suggestions that the police are somehow impartial: e.g. "We have received a complaint that we have to look into. Our job is simply to make enquiries. Obviously at the moment we only know the other side's story; this is an opportunity for you to explain your version of events. Our job is simply to gather the information and present it to the CPS." This sort of comment can induce a weak client to start talking as he may believe that there is no harm in relaying his account if the police are "just trying to find out what happened". In such a situation you must remind your client that he is under arrest and being interviewed because the police believe he has been involved in an offence and they are therefore not objective, they are looking for evidence to support their belief that he is at fault.

Police tactics in dealing with no comment interviews: Also warn your client about tactics to persuade him to start talking. The interview will almost invariably start with name, address, who is present and then a caution. If your client then intends to answer "no comment" or "no reply" or to simply say nothing, the police will often ask a series of anodyne questions about whether your client is comfortable, has he had enough time to talk to his lawyer, would he like a cup of tea and so on. This is a simple tactic designed to get the client talking. Equally, officers may start filling out the antecedents form (education, previous convictions, employment and so on). In either case, once the suspect has started to talk, he will find it difficult to stop and they will then move into the interview proper. You may need to point out to your client that this is happening.

The behaviour of your client: Warn your client to be mindful of his behaviour as the interview recording can be played at trial and if he is abusive or overly defensive, this can damage his credibility. Also remember the points on denying and alleging bad character, see para 3.3.6.

Using written statements in place of answering questions in interview: One tactic which can help to keep the interrogation process under your control, is to put forward the client's defence by way of a pre-prepared written statement. Your client will hand over the written statement at the start of the interview, or he can read it to the police; thereafter he will exercise his right to silence. If the pre-prepared statement contains all the facts on which your client will rely at any subsequent trial, then no inference can arise: *Knight* [2004] 1 Cr App R 117.

This is obviously a very useful tactic as it can protect your client from making damaging comments in interview. However there are a few issues which you need to take into account:

- By putting forward a written account, you are putting forward your client's defence. If it is inaccurate or untrue, it will undermine your client's credibility.

- Any written account must contain all the defence facts which it is reasonable to raise at this point. If your client introduces new facts at trial an inference can arise from his earlier failure to mention these when questioned.

- Assuming that the police are withholding some evidence in order to test your client's account, you may need to take further instructions when this evidence is put to your client, and then provide a further written statement to respond to it.

- Bear in mind that written statements are not infallible. The Court of Appeal in *Knight* said this:

    The making of a pre-prepared statement is not of itself an inevitable antidote to later adverse inferences. The pre-prepared statement may be incomplete in comparison with the defendant's later account at trial, or it may be, to whatever degree, inconsistent with that account. One may envisage many situations in which a pre-prepared statement in some form has been put forward, but yet there is a proper case for an adverse inference arising out of the suspect's failure "on being questioned under caution … to mention any fact relied on in his defence …" We wish to make it crystal clear that of

> *itself* the making of a pre-prepared statement gives no automatic immunity against adverse inferences under s.34. [para 13]

[3.4] THE INTERVIEW

> "The solicitor's only role in the police station is to protect and advance the legal rights of their client. On occasions this may require the solicitor to give advice which has the effect of their client avoiding giving evidence which strengthens a prosecution case. The solicitor may intervene in order to seek clarification or to challenge an improper question to their client or the manner in which it is put, or to advise their client not to reply to particular questions, or if they wish to give their client further legal advice." PACE Code C Note 6D

You need to know this pretty much off by heart. After all, what more do you need? This is your duty – and you owe that duty to your client.

3.4.1 Introductions and the problem of waiving privilege

You should always consider making a full introduction at the start of the interview, stating your name, your firm, your status, and making clear that your responsibility, as set out in PACE Code C 6D, is to protect your client's rights. You could state what information you have been given by the police, and again ask them to confirm that they have disclosed all relevant information. Not only will such an introduction inspire confidence in your client, it will also alert the police to the fact that you intend to play an active role in the interview and they are therefore less likely to be taken aback when you start making interruptions.

Waiving privilege: Essentially if information is covered by a claim of "privilege" then a person is entitled to refuse to divulge that information: see Chapter 20. One type of privilege is "lawyer/client" privilege – and this will cover situations where a lawyer and a client are communicating for the purpose of giving or obtaining legal advice. Privilege is the reason why you cannot normally be asked to divulge the contents of your consultations with your client in giving legal advice at the police station.

However the claim to privilege can be waived – that is, a person can act in such a way as to indicate that the material is not private and confidential between lawyer and client. One circumstance where this could arise is where in a public context (such as the police interview) you refer to matters that you and your client have discussed in private. The courts have decided that you can waive privilege simply by referring to what you have advised your client to do and giving the reasons for your advice. You would therefore waive privilege if you said: "I <u>have</u> advised my client to remain silent because…"

The consequence of this is that Law Society suggests that it is safe to say, "I <u>now</u> advise my client to remain silent…" since the interview is not a privileged situation and therefore no waiver of privilege can arise. But you must be very careful. If you or your client waives privilege, it is possible that the prosecution will not only be able to question you about the advice that you gave your client and the reasons for it, but also require you to produce all police station notes that you made – see the discussion of *Bowden* [2000] 2 All E.R. 418 in Chapter 20.

3.4.2 Intervening and threats of exclusion:

Code C 6D specifically states that "The solicitor may intervene in order to seek clarification, challenge an improper question to their client or the manner in which it is put, advise their client not to reply to particular questions, or if they wish to give their client further legal advice". There is therefore considerable scope to intervene. It is extremely important that you always challenge improper questions as a solicitor's silent presence can actually ratify any breaches of PACE, see *Dunn [1990] 91 Cr App R 237*.

Although you may intervene, you must be careful not to try to answer the questions on your client's behalf. Whilst doing all of this, you need to take the best notes that you can, and listen to both the questions and the answers. You should also remember that PACE requires police officers to pursue all reasonable lines of enquiry "whether these point towards or away from the suspect": see Code C Note 11B: you may like to remind the police of this if they are only focusing on the case against your client and not listening to his assertions that someonelse is responsible.

Police conduct that may warrant an intervention;

- Twisting the clients' words to suit the police account (includes situations where they try to put words into your client's mouth)
- Misrepresenting the purpose of the interview, e.g "this is your chance to tell us what happened", no, the real purpose of an interview is to obtain evidence by questioning
- Misrepresenting the law
- Disclosing new evidence
- Raising previous convictions
- Asking multiple questions
- Failing to give the client chance to respond to a question
- Oppressive behaviour, e.g. raised voices, forcing eye contact, deliberately leaving long silences, repeatedly asking the same question
- Asking irrelevant questions – this is usually a tactic to get a client talking
- Asking hypothetical questions e.g. "can you imagine what the court will think of that answer?"
- When your client starts to answer questions, despite having indicated to you that it would be a no comment interview
- When your client starts to blame others or otherwise raise bad character issues
- The officer gives his own opinion, e.g. "this is what I think of your defence."

Excluding you from the interview? Occasionally police officers may make threatening noises about excluding you from the interview. You can only be excluded if your conduct is such that "the investigating officer is unable properly to put questions": Code C 6.9. Even then the officer will need a superintendent's authorisation. Code C makes clear that removal of a solicitor is a serious step. It should be wholly exceptional. You should note the terms of your job as set out in C Note 6D (above). You can never be excluded for doing what C 6D requires you to – protecting and advancing the rights of your client.

3.4.3 How long should an interview last?

There are no specific provisions, although Code C12.2 specifies that in any period of 24 hours the detainee must be allowed a continuous period of at least 8 hours free for rest. There should also be breaks at recognised meal times and refreshment breaks every two hours (C12.8) subject to risks of delay. You will need to consider your client's state of health and state of mind. Often clients are desperate to get out of the police station and will want to be interviewed in the middle of the night, or when they are still far from well, just because it may lead to an earlier release.

When should the interview process end? Code C11.6 provides that the interview must cease when the officer in charge:

- is satisfied that all relevant questions have been put, including giving the suspect an opportunity to give an innocent explanation; and
- the officer has taken account of any other evidence; and
- the custody officer reasonably believes that there is sufficient evidence to provide a realistic prospect of conviction.

You therefore need to listen out for signs that these conditions have been met, for example "I think we've got all we need now" or "There's enough evidence to convict you, so there's no point going no comment" – if that is the case, then invite the officer to stop the interview immediately. If the officer is reluctant to stop, then it suggests that he is actually just using oppressive tactics to get your client to make admissions and you must intervene.

[3.5] Fingerprints, footwear impressions and samples

Fingerprints and non-intimate samples: The police will be able to take fingerprints, footwear impressions and non-intimate samples following arrest for a recordable offence: see 3.1.4 above for details. Assuming fingerprints and samples have not been taken at an earlier stage, they will often be taken following charge. Since consent is not required, reasonable force can be used.

Photographs: Photographs can be taken of any person who is detained at a police station, either with or without consent: s.64A PACE.

What about intimate samples? Intimate samples include blood, semen, tissue, urine, pubic hair, dental impressions and swabs from any bodily orifice other than the mouth. In order to take an intimate sample, an inspector must give authorisation. Where the suspect is detained, authorisation can only be given provided the officer has reasonable grounds for believing the suspect has been involved in a recordable offence and that the sample will tend to confirm or disprove that involvement. An intimate sample can only be taken by consent, and the suspect must be cautioned that if they refuse without good cause this may harm their case when it comes to trial. As with non-intimate samples and fingerprints, intimate samples can be used for speculative searches against samples from other investigations.

Drug testing at arrest and post-charge: s.63B PACE

The power to test a detainee for the presence of drugs is introduced into PACE by the Drugs Act 2005. It arises in relation to:

- an adult on detention (i.e. pre-charge); and
- an adult or a child aged at least 14 on charge.

The power only arises where the suspect has committed a "trigger offence" (typically theft and other acquisitive offences, as well as drugs offences, which are typically committed by persons who may have drug addiction problems). If the offence is not a trigger offence, then a test is still permissible if an officer of the rank of inspector or above authorises the test on the basis that he has reasonable grounds to suspect that the misuse of specified Class A drugs contributed to the offending.

The test takes the form of either a urine or saliva sample, and will test for the presence of heroin and cocaine/crack. Force cannot be used to take the sample, but it is a criminal offence (carrying a custodial penalty) to refuse to provide the sample without good cause.

Where the test is positive it may have two consequences:

- the information will be provided to the court for the purposes of taking a decision about bail (and may lead to a refusal of bail where the person has refused treatment – see Chapter 6 below); and
- the person may be required to attend an assessment of their drug use with a qualified person, with refusal to attend again carrying a custodial penalty.

[3.6] Identification Issues: Code D PACE

Identification is an issue that will always be raised at the police station stage. Unless your client admits his involvement in the offence, or the police have forensic evidence that shows his involvement, they will have to secure some form of identification to justify placing your client at the scene. Although this can be done by means of CCTV or other technology, it is most commonly done by means of eye witness identification, and this will be the focus of this section.

Identification cases continue to present a high degree of difficulty, both at the police station and in the courts. The law is set out in PACE, and is further detailed in PACE Code of Conduct D. Failure by the police to comply with the proper procedure can result in the defence successfully applying to have the identification evidence ruled inadmissible under s.78 PACE (see Chapter 16 for details about how this provisions operates).

3.6.1 What is the purpose of the identification process?

PACE Code D 1.2 states that:

Identification by witnesses arises, e.g., if the offender is seen committing the crime and a witness is given an opportunity to identify the suspect in a video identification, identification parade, or similar procedure. The procedures are designed to:

- *test the witness' ability to identify the person they saw on a previous occasion*
- *provide safeguards against mistaken identification.*

3.6.2 Making of a record

A record must be made of the description of the suspect "as first given" by the witness, prior to the witness taking part in identification procedures. A copy of the record must be given to the suspect or his solicitor before the identification procedures take place: Code D 3.1.

3.6.3 When must an identification procedure be held?

Code D3.12 provides that an identification procedure must be held whenever:

- A witness has identified or purported to identify a suspect before the formal identification procedures have taken place; or

- There is a witness who says they can identify the suspect; or there is a reasonable chance that they may be able to do so, and no identification procedure has taken place; and

- The suspect disputes being the person that the witness claims to have seen; unless

- The procedure is not practicable or would serve no useful probative purpose.

- A procedure may also be held if the officer in charge feels it would be useful: D3.13.

One example of where there will be no useful purpose in holding a procedure is if it is not disputed that the suspect is already well known to the witness. However this area is far from straightforward, and the police should be very cautious before turning down a defence request for an identification procedure.

> *In Haynes [2004] 148 SJ 181 a stolen vehicle was crashed into the house of the witness, W. The occupants of the car ran off. W rang the police and gave a general description of the driver. The police came round and while they were there H walked past the house. He matched W's description of the driver, so the police stopped him and W identified him as the driver. W told the police he recognised H because of H's clothing. Initially H offered to stand in a parade, then changed his mind. At trial H argued there had been a breach of Code D as he was a known suspect and a parade should have been held rather than letting W identify him at the scene. Held – this was a borderline case whether a known or unknown suspect. If there had been a breach of Code D it didn't automatically lead to the exclusion of evidence. Given that this was an identification by clothing, a parade would have a achieved little. Accordingly there had been no need to exclude the evidence.*

3.6.4 Known and unknown suspects

Where a suspect is known and available, then formal identification procedures should be used (videos, parades, groups). Where a suspect is either not known or is not available then it may be appropriate to use less formal methods – such as street identifications, the showing of photographs and so on.

What does "known" mean? According to Code D 3.4, a suspect is "known" if "there is sufficient information known to the police to justify the arrest of a particular person for suspected involvement in the offence." They will be "available" if they are available to take place in a procedure at once or in a reasonably short time. They can be treated as not being available if they refuse or obstruct a procedure: Code D 3.4. The police cannot use photographs, identikits and the like if there is a known suspect: Code D3.3.

3.6.5 Procedures to be adopted when a suspect is known and available

The hierarchy of procedures with known suspects is as follows:

1. video identification

2. identification parade

3. group identification

4. confrontation

If the suspect is known and available and it is proposed to hold an identification procedure, then the suspect must be offered a video identification unless this is not practicable or an identification parade is more suitable: Code D3.14. A video identification will normally be more suitable if it could be arranged quicker and completed sooner than a parade. Similarly a parade may not be practicable because of factors relating to the witnesses, such as the number of witnesses, their state of health, availability and travelling requirements. In practice the vast majority of identification parades now take the form of video parades, often referred to as VIPER parades.

What happens if the suspect refuses the procedure? Where the suspect refuses to co-operate, they must be asked their reason, and the identification attention officer will then consider whether it is suitable and practicable to offer an alternative procedure (such as a group identification). In some cases the officer in charge of the investigation can decide to offer a group identification first if he considers that it is more satisfactory than a video identification or an identification parade: Code D 3.16.

Rights and warnings: In any case the suspect must normally have the procedures explained to him, including his entitlement to free legal advice and to have a legal representative present during the procedure. Code D3.17 lists all of the information that must be given to a suspect prior to any identification procedure. In particular the suspect must be warned of three key points:

1. The suspect need not take part in any video identification, identification parade or group identification but evidence of refusal may be given at any subsequent trial. The suspect should be warned that the police may proceed to arrange a covert video or group identification.

2. If the police are proposing a video identification and have already obtained covert footage of the suspect which they intend to use for this purpose, the suspect must be told so that he can have the opportunity to co-operate in producing more suitable images for use in the procedure.

3. If the suspect changes his appearance prior to the identification procedure this may then mean that an alternative means of identification has to be used, and if the suspect significantly alters his appearance in between being offered an identification procedure and the holding of the procedure, the fact of this alteration may be given in evidence if the case comes to trial.

What is a video identification? Full details are provided in Code D Annex A. In a video identification the witness will be shown a set of images which will include the suspect and at least eight other people who "so far as possible resemble the suspect in age, height, general appearance and position in life". The images should, as far as possible, show the suspect and the other people in the same positions or carrying out the same sequence of movements. Normally the images must show all the people under identical conditions unless this is not possible because of a factor such as the suspect's refusal to co-operate, and even in this case any difference in the conditions must not direct the witness's attention to any individual image.

Note that no one involved in the investigation is permitted to view the material prior to it being shown to any witness. The suspect and/or his solicitor is entitled to view the compiled set of images prior to the witness viewing, and if a reasonable objection is raised, e.g. one of the participants does not resemble the suspect, then the police must take steps to remove the ground for objection, e.g. by substituting a different participant. The identification procedure is the responsibility of the identification officer – who must normally be of at least the rank of inspector and who must not be involved with the investigation. The suspect has a right to legal advice and to have his legal adviser present at the showing of the images to the witness. Only one witness at a time may view the compiled set of images and where there are multiple witnesses who need to view the compilation, there are strict procedures to be followed to ensure that there is no communication between the witnesses between the viewings, as this would clearly give rise to a risk of the identification evidence becoming contaminated.

What is an identification parade? Again there are very detailed procedures which must be followed, which are set out in Code D, Annex B. The parade is run on broadly the same basis as the video identification except that the witness will be invited to look at the suspect and at least eight other similar people, rather than at videoed images. Your client can choose his position in the line. If your client has an "unusual physical feature" (such as a scar, tattoo, hair style or hair colour) which cannot be replicated in the other members of the parade then steps can be taken to conceal that feature (such as hats, sticking plasters and so on): Code D, Annex B, 10.

A video recording should normally be taken of the parade. Sometimes witnesses at a parade may ask to see particular parade members speak or move. If this happens they should first be asked if they can identify the suspect without this and should then be warned that the parade has been organised on the basis of similar appearance only. You should normally object, although you may need to wait until the witness has left the room!

What is a group identification? A group identification involves the witness watching a random group of people, often in a public place, and seeing if they can identify the suspect who will be asked to walk through, or stand amongst the group. Group identifications are governed by Code D Annex C. Like video identifications they can take place either with the suspect's consent or covertly without his consent.

> *The place where the group identification is held should be one where other people are either passing by or waiting around informally, in groups such that the suspect is able to join them and be capable of being seen by the witness at the same time as others in the group. For example people leaving an escalator, pedestrians walking through a shopping centre, passengers on railway and bus stations, waiting in queues or groups or where people are standing or sitting in groups in other public places.*
> Code D, Annex C 4

Although clients tend to like group identifications, they can be risky if your client is of unusual appearance or for some reason is unlikely to blend in at the selected location. Annex C requires the identification officer to consider the likely general appearance and number of people likely to be present at any location, and states that a group identification need not be held if because of the suspect's unusual appearance the identification would not be fair. A photograph or video should be taken immediately after the procedure if possible so as to give a general impression of the scene. In some cases (for example a group identification in an area where there is CCTV) it may be possible to record the whole identification procedure.

What is a confrontation? A confrontation simply consists of the witness being confronted with the suspect, usually at the police station and being asked the question: "Is this the person?" It is governed by Code D Annex D. It is the least satisfactory method and the most likely to be unreliable as there is enormous psychological pressure on the witness to provide a positive identification when he is only shown one face. For this reason it appears that a confrontation should not be used if a covert identification is practicable under D 3.21.

What happens if a suspect is known but is not available or refuses to co-operate? If the suspect is known but not available or refuses to co-operate the identification officer has a discretion to make arrangements for a covert video or group identification: D 3.21–24. For the video identification the officer can make use of any suitable images of the suspect that are available or which can be obtained.

3.6.6 What happens if the suspect is not known?

Where a suspect is not "known", the first step is for the police to make a record of any description given by the witness. Only then can other steps be taken, such as taking the witness to a particular place to see whether they can identify anyone (a street identification), or showing them photographs or "composite likenesses" (such as photofits or E-fits). The use of photographs is governed by Annex E, which provides that the witness should be shown not less than twelve photographs at a time, and that these should be of a similar type so far as is possible.

Use of national and local media: Code D 3.28–29 specifically provides that nothing prevents the police from the showing of videos or photographs to the public at large through local or national media in order to trace suspects. However if this has occurred it may well undermine the evidence of identification witnesses. If there has been publication or broadcast of material in this way, witnesses should be asked after they have taken part in a procedure whether they saw any of the broadcast material.

3.6.7 One last problem – dock identifications

A dock identification occurs in court when a witness is invited to answer the question: "And can you identify that person in this court?" Answer: "Yes, that's him in the dock." Generally this is not permitted as it has little or no evidential value. In *Barnes v DPP* [1997] 2 Cr. App. R 505 the QBD said that the Justices had a discretion to allow the prosecution to identify a defendant in court where there had been no previous identification. *Karia v DPP* 166 JP 753 followed *Barnes* and held that in magistrates courts proceedings where the defence had never indicated that identification was in dispute, it was permissible for the prosecution to rely upon a dock identification – but the court said that it might be different if the prosecution were on notice that identification was in dispute.

[3.7] THE CHARGE AND AFTER

3.7.1 The charge

The decision to charge: It used to be the case that the custody officer would decide whether or not the suspect should be charged and if so, what the level of the charge should be. Unfortunately, this often resulted in the police "over charging" suspects and the prosecution would then have to withdraw the charge and replace it with something more appropriate. The Police and Justice Act 2006 addressed this problem and created a new s.37B PACE which states that this decision now rests with the CPS. The procedure is that once the police have gathered sufficient evidence to justify charging the suspect, the police will then pass the file to the CPS so that a CPS lawyer can decide precisely what the charge should be. This is known as "statutory charging". The custody officer does however retain the power to charge in minor, straightforward cases. The current government is now considering piloting a scheme to return the charging decision to the police in all but the most serious of cases. The majority of defence solicitors welcome this change as it means that they can once again make representations directly to the custody officer that may affect the level of charge.

What happens if the police are not ready to charge: Ideally there will be either a CPS employee based in the police station, or available by telephone to whom all cases can be referred for a charging decision, but where there is likely to be delay, the custody sergeant may bail the suspect to return to the police station once a decision has been taken. Equally where there is insufficient evidence to charge, and the detention clock is ticking away, the police may have to release a suspect on bail to return for further questioning once more evidence has been gathered. The clock will then re-start when the suspect returns to the police station. This form of police bail is often referred to as "bail-back".

Procedure at charge: At charge the suspect will be cautioned again, and the charge will be put to him. There is a further possibility of inferences from a failure to put forward defence facts when charged – but in many cases, suspects will either have already put forward the facts in interview or will have already failed to put forward the facts at this earlier stage. The suspect will receive a written charge sheet, with details of the offence.

Questioning after charge: The general principle is that once a person has been charged, he cannot then be further questioned. There are some limited exceptions to this. Code C 16.5 provides that questions relating to the offence cannot be put after charge unless either they are necessary for the purpose of preventing or minimising harm or loss, or they are necessary to resolve an ambiguity from an earlier answer, or it is in the interests of justice to give the accused an opportunity to comment on information that has come to light after the charge.

Ed Cape makes the point that increasingly the prosecuting agencies are looking to bring confiscation proceedings in respect of the assets of defendants with a "criminal lifestyle" or where the assets represent the benefits of criminal conduct. Questions are therefore being put to the defendant post charge concerning his assets and financial resources. It is unlikely to be in his interests to provide this information at the police station stage, and he commits no offence by declining to do so.

Drug testing after charge: See 3.5 above.

3.7.2 Formal or Police Cautions

Formal cautions are an alternative to charge and to formal court proceedings. They are not to be confused with *evidential* cautions. Formal cautions are a way of formally recording that a person admits the offence. The normal principle is that no further action will then be taken, although the House of Lords has not ruled out the possibility of private prosecutions being possible: see *Jones v Whalley* [2006] UKHL 41. A caution is not the same as a conviction but it can be referred to if your client subsequently appears before a court in relation to other offences.

When might a caution be given? A formal caution can only be given where;

1. There is sufficient evidence to justify a prosecution AND
2. The offender voluntarily admits that he has committed an offence AND
3. The offender is prepared to accept a caution AND
4. The matter is not so serious that the public interest requires the matter to be dealt with at court

The caution is often an appropriate disposal where you have a first time offender, or a very minor offence, or a vulnerable offender such as an elderly or ill client. You should not however advise your client to accept a caution lightly. Cautions in sexual matters may, for example, trigger the requirement to register on the Sex Offenders Register. For this reason, you may need disclosure of any earlier interviews that may have taken place prior to your arrival in order to be able to advise your client whether a caution should be accepted: see *D.P.P v Ara* [2001] EWHC Admin 493.

Conditional cautions: These are cautions which are conditional on your client complying with some condition imposed by the Crown Prosecution Service. The conditions can facilitate rehabilitation (conditions such as attendance at treatment programmes and the like), ensure that the detainee makes reparation (paying for the broken window; taking goods back to the store) or be punitive (paying a financial penalty). As with formal cautions, there must be sufficient evidence that the offender has committed an offence; he must be agreeable to the making of a conditional caution; and he must be aware that if he fails to comply with the conditions, then he may be prosecuted for the offence.

While conditional cautions will clearly make sense in some cases – and may encourage the police to deal with matters by way of cautions rather than formal court action – there are real concerns about ensuring that the conditions are fair and are realistic. If the police require your client to attend a treatment programme, but it is then clear that he cannot do this without giving up his job, he risks prosecution. Negotiating the conditions is likely to require an understanding of the practical consequences for your client.

3.7.3 Police bail

Bail prior to charge: The police have wide powers to release a suspect on bail to return to the police station at a later date: ss.37 and 47 PACE. This prevents the detention clock from running while investigations are carried out. There is also a power to grant bail or to detain while the file is referred to the CPS for a decision to be taken on charge: s.37(7)(a) PACE. Bail granted prior to charge can be unconditional or conditional. If the suspect breaches his bail conditions, or if he fails to attend the police station on the required date, then he may be arrested.

Bail after charge: The defendant must be released on bail unless one of the conditions under s.38 PACE (detailed below) is made out. If released on bail, the defendant will be given a date for his first appearance at the magistrates' court. In granting bail the custody officer can impose any condition that the court can, except residence at a bail hostel. If the defendant is not released he must be brought before the court as soon as is practicable, which will normally mean the following day (unless that day is Christmas, Good Friday or Sunday). In the meantime, the client will be kept in the police cells.

Making the bail decision: the s.38 conditions: Getting police bail will always be important to your client. It will also influence the magistrates when they come to decide whether to grant bail. In deciding whether to grant bail the custody officer does not have to hear representations, but will generally do so since he is required to have a reasonable belief that a s.38 condition is made out in order to refuse bail. The custody officer can only refuse bail if:

- the defendant's name/address are not known or are reasonably doubted;
- there are reasonable grounds for believing the defendant will fail to answer his bail;
- there are reasonable grounds to believe detention is needed to prevent the defendant from committing an offence (if the defendant was arrested for an imprisonable offence);
- there are reasonable grounds for believing detention is necessary in order to enable a sample to be taken;
- there are reasonable grounds to believe detention is necessary to prevent the defendant from causing harm, loss, damage;
- there are reasonable grounds to believe detention is necessary to prevent the defendant from interfering with administration of justice; or
- there are reasonable grounds to believe detention is necessary for the defendant's own protection: s.38 PACE

3.7.4 Special categories of detainee

Vulnerable suspects and appropriate adults: Vulnerable suspects would include juvenile suspects (anyone who is, or appears to be under the age of 17), but would also include other suspects who are particularly vulnerable (such as suspects with mental health problems or who are otherwise mentally vulnerable). A key element in the protection of the rights of this category of detainee is that in such cases an "appropriate adult" must be contacted as soon as practicable to attend the police station. Often the appropriate adult will be a parent or guardian. If for some reason this is not possible, the appropriate adult will normally be a social worker. A lawyer who is attending the police station in his/her professional capacity cannot act as the appropriate adult.

The appropriate adult is not simply an observer, but is there to provide support and advice to the suspect. However appropriate adults can be very unsure of their role – especially if they are the parents of the suspect. Bear in mind that while appropriate adults can help to provide support for your client, and can help to facilitate communication, they are not bound by the same duties of confidentiality as you are. For this reason the Law Society advises that you take instructions from your clients without the appropriate adult being present.

Immigration detainees: You will often find yourself dealing with immigration matters at the police station. You must bear in mind that immigration detainees are a wholly separate category of detainee. There is, for example, no question of a right of silence in an immigration investigation by the Immigration Service. Often, suspects may have been picked up on a criminal matter, but it has then become clear that there is a possible immigration offence. You are therefore having to deal with two different systems. In particular there will be different powers to detain under the Immigration Act, and some suspects may be faced with almost immediate deportation. It is particularly important that you do not try to deal with immigration matters unless you are qualified to do so. There is a chapter on immigration detainees in Cape, <u>Defending Suspects at Police Stations</u>, which sets out the basic details.

DETENTION CONDITIONS

Ground for detention: there is only one ground for detention without charge – namely that the Custody Officer reasonably thinks that such detention is necessary to secure or preserve evidence relating to an offence for which the suspect is under arrest or to obtain such evidence by questioning him: s.37(2). Once there is sufficient information the custody officer must charge or release: s.37(7)

Detention time limits:

- Reviews by C.O on arrival; after 6 hours by Inspector; then at 9 hour intervals up to 24 hours.
- If it is an indictable offence further detention of up to 36 hrs can be authorised by a Superintendent. If it is an indictable offence magistrates can authorise further detention up to total of 96 hrs.

Detention rights: (i) Access to solicitor (s.58) and (ii) Right of intimation: having told a friend or relative (s.56). Note that a limited power to delay may arise, but only where the offence is indictable.

QUESTIONING

- Must be recorded if indictable or either-way offence. May also be visually recorded.
- No rule as to maximum length of interview, but there should be breaks at meal times and every two hours. [Consider if very long interview is oppressive: s.76 PACE] 8 hours sleep, preferably at night.
- No use of oppression: C para 11.5.
- An officer should not indicate, save in answer to a question, what action will be taken by police if suspect answers questions: C para 11.5 [Consider also s.76 (2)(b) – unreliability.]
- Role of solicitor: "to protect and advance the legal rights of his client": C para 6D
- Caution at start and after breaks.
- Put significant silences or comments to suspect. [NB. effects of ss.34/36/37 CJPOA]

[NB. for a full discussion of oppression and unreliability see Chapter 16.]

IDENTIFICATION

A record must be made of the description given by the witness before any form of ID procedure. Details must be given to the suspect or his solicitor.

The identification officer (IO) should be at least an inspector who is not involved with the case.

Where the suspect is known, the IO may arrange a video identification or parade, a group identification, or a confrontation.

Video/parade: normally one of these must be held if there is a dispute and it is practicable. At least 8 others of similar appearance. If suspect refuses, consider other methods of ID including covert video and group identifications.

Where the suspect is not known: the police can use photos – see Code D Annex E.

SAMPLES

All intimate samples require the authorisation of an officer of rank of at least Superintendent with a reasonable belief that the sample will confirm or disprove the suspect's involvement. Offence must be "recordable".

Intimate: (Blood, semen, urine, pubic hair, non-oral swabs) Must get suspect's consent. Refusal to consent can give rise to adverse inference at trial.

Non-intimate (hair, nails, swabs, saliva, footprint) can be taken without consent, and can now be taken following arrest.

Fingerprints and photographs: Can be taken without consent: can use reasonable force if authorised by Superintendent.

Detention and questioning – test yourself questions

[The answers to these questions are set out in Appendix A at the back of this book]

[1] Which one of the following propositions is true?

(a) The power to detain before charge under PACE is only a power to detain in order to obtain evidence by questioning.

(b) The custody officer must be a police officer of at least the rank of sergeant and must be connected with the investigation of the offence.

(c) Where a person is arrested without a warrant and there is sufficient evidence to charge the person, the person can only be detained before charge long enough to allow the custody officer to charge them.

(d) On arrival at the police station the solicitor is entitled to a copy of the custody record but is not entitled to disclosure of any further information about the case, although the police may choose to make such disclosure.

[2] Jim is arrested on suspicion of being involved in a common assault (a summary-only offence) that followed an animal rights demonstration on Saturday afternoon. The ground given for the arrest was that it was necessary for the prompt and effective investigation of the matter. Jim was arrested at 14.25. He arrived at Kirkstone Police Station at 14.55. Detention was authorised at 15.10.

Consider the following propositions:

i. The police must either charge or release Jim by 14.25 on Sunday.

ii. The first review of Jim's detention must take place not later than 20.10 on Saturday.

iii. One further review of Jim's detention must take place, and this must be no later than 9 hours after the first review.

Which of the above are correct?

(a) i and ii only.

(b) ii only.

(c) iii only.

(d) i and iii only.

(e) None of the propositions is correct.

[3] Sarah is arrested under s.18 Offences Against the Person Act (grievous bodily harm with intent), on suspicion of having "glassed" the barman in a pub when he asked her to leave. The barman is in hospital and may lose the sight in one eye. [s.18 OAPA offences are triable only in the Crown Court, and carry a maximum sentence of life imprisonment.]

Which one of the following is correct?

a) The offence will be classed as an indictable offence, and the maximum period of detention that can be authorised by the police will be 96 hours.

b) The offence may be an indictable offence, but this will not be known until point of charge. The maximum detention period is therefore 24 hours.

- c) The offence is an indictable offence and the maximum period of detention that can be authorised by the police will be 36 hours.

- d) The offence is not indictable since it can only be tried in the Crown Court. The maximum period of police detention will therefore be 24 hours.

[4] Tony is arrested on suspicion of rape. Rape is an indictable offence.

Consider the following propositions:

- i. An extension of the detention time limit to permit detention for up to 36 hours may be granted by an officer of at least the rank of superintendent, but only if the officer has reasonable grounds for believing that the detention is necessary in order to secure or preserve evidence or to obtain evidence by questioning, and that the investigation is being conducted diligently and expeditiously.

- ii. If the police wish to detain Tony for up to a further 36 hours (i.e. up to 72 hours), they must apply to the magistrates' court for a warrant of further detention.

- iii. Tony can be detained for a maximum period of 96 hours without charge, provided the magistrates extend the warrant of further detention to cover this period.

Which of the above are correct?

(a) i only.

(b) i and ii only.

(c) iii only.

(d) All of the above.

(e) None of the above.

[5] Michael is under arrest on suspicion of having committed criminal damage. The allegation is that he smashed his ex-girlfriend's car with a hammer. The damage is tentatively estimated as being in excess of £2,000. Michael was arrested at home, and a hammer was found in his coat pocket. The hammer has been seized and will be sent for forensic examination. Otherwise, there appears to be no other evidence against Michael.

You attend the police station as a duty solicitor and speak to Michael. He readily admits that he committed the offence.

Which one of the following propositions is NOT correct?

(a) If Michael admits the offence in interview to the police he is likely to receive a substantial discount on any sentence if he then pleads Guilty at court.

(b) If Michael now tells the police in interview that he did not commit the offence, you must cease to act but you will not be able to tell the police why you can no longer act.

(c) If Michael now changes his account and says that he did not commit the offence, you will only be able to act provided you believe his explanation of why he has changed his story.

(d) If Michael says nothing in interview, you will be able to continue to act although he is refusing to admit the offence when questioned under caution.

[6] Roger has been arrested in connection with an alleged offence under the Protection from Harassment Act. At the start of an interview in the police station at which you are attending as Roger's legal adviser you make an introductory statement.

Which one of the following statements is most likely to amount to a waiver of legal professional privilege?

(a) "I have fully discussed the case with my client. I have advised him that he should not answer your questions."

(b) "You have refused to make proper disclosure of the evidence against my client. I am therefore now advising him that he should not answer your questions."

(c) "I am of the view that my client is not fit to be interviewed and that he should not therefore answer your questions. I am advising him accordingly."

(d) "I have taken full instructions from my client and I have advised him not to answer your questions on the basis that there is no case that calls for an answer."

[7] Liam is arrested on suspicion of burglary of an office block. He denies ever having been near the building but the police believe that they have witnesses who can confirm that Liam is the man who they saw climbing over a wall at the back of the building.

Liam's instructions to his solicitor are that he is not prepared to co-operate with any identification procedure since he believes that the police are attempting to frame him.

Consider the following advice which Liam's solicitor has given to him.

i. The police are now permitted to show the witnesses photographs since Liam is not available to take part in an identification procedure because he refuses to do so. They must show a minimum of twelve photographs.

ii. The police are not permitted to use force to arrange a video identification, a parade or group identification. They should therefore arrange a confrontation.

iii. The police are permitted to arrange a covert video identification, but are unlikely to do so where Liam does not consent.

Which of the above are correct?

(a) None of them.

(b) i only.

(c) ii and iii only.

(d) i and iii only.

[8] Hans has been arrested for theft. He denies that he is the person who was seen removing money from wallets in a changing room. Which one of the following is correct?

(a) An identification procedure should consist of at least nine people other than the suspect.

(b) An identification procedure should consist of at least ten people other than the suspect.

(c) An identification procedure should consist of at least eight people other than the suspect.

(d) An identification procedure should consist of at least seven people other than the suspect.

CHAPTER 4

FUNDING THE CASE

> This chapter covers:
>
> The principles of public funding
>
> How to apply for legal aid to fund your case
>
> Costs in criminal cases

Before representing any client in criminal proceedings, it is important to consider the manner in which the case will be funded. You should therefore resolve the issue of funding before appearing before the court at the clients first hearing: see ch. 5. Most criminal cases are funded publicly, by Legal Aid under a Representation Order but clients who fall outside this regime will have to fund their own case privately. This chapter is predominantly concerned with public funding and explains how the system operates.

[4.1] FUNDING CRIMINAL CASES: LEGAL AID

Criminal Legal Aid is administered by the Legal Services Commission and is the responsibility of the Criminal Defence Service (CDS). A firm can only provide a publicly funded criminal defence service if they have a contract with the Legal Services Commission. The contract dictates the way in which the criminal defence practice and its file must be managed. Under the CDS regime firms receive monthly block payments for undertaking criminal work, and submit consolidated monthly reports so that in due course the block payments can be adjusted up or down to reflect the work undertaken. The CDS then periodically audits files in order to check the claims made. Both police station work and magistrates' court work is now paid on a fixed fee basis which is calculated on the basis of the number of hours spent dealing with the case.

The Legal Aid, Sentencing and Punishment of Offenders Act 2012 contains provisions which will abolish the Legal Services Commission and transfer its responsibilities to the Lord Chancellor and a Director of Legal Aid Casework, who will work under the authority of the Lord Chancellor. The provisions are not yet in force but the idea behind them is to ensure closer accountability for legal aid spending.

Public Defender Service: The CDS funds a number of Public Defender Service projects. These are schemes where the CDS itself employs the lawyers in the projects, who then undertake publicly funded criminal work.

Price competitive tendering: The CDS is always looking for ways of restraining the criminal legal aid budget. One proposal which had been considered but subsequently shelved is to require firms to bid for certain numbers of criminal cases at a fixed price per case. The contract to do those cases will go to the lowest bidder. There are real concerns about whether this scheme is workable, and whether it will undermine the quality of publicly funded criminal work. It is possible that competitive tendering will be considered at some point in the future.

4.1.1 Advice and Assistance

The Advice and Assistance scheme enables you to undertake work in advising and assisting a client outside the police station environment but only prior to charge or summons. The scheme does not cover representation at courts or tribunals, nor does it cover work done once your client has been charged. To be eligible, the solicitor must be satisfied that there is sufficient benefit to the client to justify the work being done. There is also a means test to satisfy but persons in receipt of various state benefits, including income support and income-based job seekers' allowance will automatically fulfil the income limits.

This scheme is separate to the Police Station Advice and Assistance scheme which is available to assist clients who are detained at the police station which is not means tested and which is paid on a fixed fee basis.

4.1.2 Representation at court

A defendant who wishes to be represented by a solicitor at court can secure this in a number of ways. In order for the case to be publicly funded, he can request the assistance of the court duty solicitor or he can apply for a representation order. Alternatively, he can pay privately for a solicitor.

Court duty solicitor scheme: Defendants who do not have a solicitor can request the assistance of a duty solicitor upon their appearance at court. Most magistrates' courts will have a duty solicitor either available at the court or available to be called to court on request. The duty solicitor is restricted as to the type of work they can carry out for example, they may not represent a client at a trial or on non-imprisonable matters. The duty solicitor can however represent and advise a client who faces an imprisonable offence or a client who is already in custody therefore they will usually deal with defendants who are appearing before the court for the first time in connection with an offence. The scheme is free of charge. If the case is to progress to a subsequent hearing the duty solicitor can represent the client as his own either under a representation order (see below), or on a privately paid basis.

Applying for a representation order: Where a client has instructed a solicitor to represent him, the solicitor can make an application for a representation order on his behalf. An application for a representation order is made to the court which the defendant is due to appear before. The court administers the scheme on behalf of the Legal Services Commission. The application must initially be made in writing on the appropriate forms, usually CDS14 and CDS 15. The court will apply a two stage test to consider whether the application can be granted: a merits test (also known as the "interests of justice" test) and a means test. If granted, the representation order covers advice, assistance and representation generally by solicitor only in the magistrates' court. A representation order extends to cover representation before the Crown Court if proceedings continue there (unless the defendant's financial circumstances change). Magistrates' court cases are paid on a fixed fee basis depending on whether the defendant pleaded guilty, had a trial or was committed/allocated to the Crown Court for either trial or sentence.

Representation in the Crown Court: In the Crown Court representation will be by a barrister or by a solicitor with a higher rights qualification. The same two stage test will be applied for Crown Court cases. A Crown Court representation order will cover the cost of a solicitor undertaking preparation work, and attending with the advocate at hearings such as the plea and case management hearing, the trial and the sentencing. Crown Court cases are paid on a fixed fee basis which is determined by the number of pages of evidence, the type of offence and the type of hearing.

Authorisation for expenditure: In either court if you are faced with any unusual or expensive items of expenditure (for example, if you need medical reports, or professional transcripts), you should get approval directly from the Legal Services Commission first in order to ensure that you will be able to reclaim the cost. Such items of expenditure are not normally covered under the representation order alone.

4.1.3 Eligibility for legal aid – the interests of justice test

A representation order will be granted where a person can show that they meet both the merits and the means test. The merits test is known as the "interests of justice" criteria. These are set out in the Access to Justice Act 1999, Schedule 3, para 5 and are considered in detail below. The test will be met if your client satisfies one or more of the criteria below. The decision is made by a Clerk of the magistrates' court.

(i) whether the individual would, if any matter in the proceedings is decided against him, be likely to lose his liberty or livelihood or suffer serious damage to his reputation

Loss of liberty: The test is whether a custodial sentence is likely and not just whether custody is "possible". There is no point simply telling the court that the maximum penalty for the offence is custodial – you need to show that custody is likely to be imposed in this case.

It is useful to consider the sentencing guidelines for the offence as this will indicate the starting point for the magistrates sentencing the case. You should consider the existence of any aggravating features in the case including the client's previous convictions and whether the offence was committed while on bail.

"Likely" is said to refer to a "real and practical risk, as opposed to a theoretical one". Thus in *R (on the application of Sonn & Co.) v West London Magistrates' Court (DC, unreported, 30/10/2000)* the offender had a long history of shoplifting and had previously been imprisoned for shoplifting offences; it was therefore not reasonable to say that there was no likelihood of imprisonment where he was accused of another shoplifting matter. Similarly in *R (oao Punatar) v Horseferry Road Magistrates Court* [2002] EWHC 1196 Admin, it was held to be wrong to refuse a representation order where the public order charge had been amended to a less serious charge once the defendant arrived at court. The right time to look at the matter was when the solicitors were having to decide whether there was a real risk of imprisonment so that they needed to attend court with the client.

Loss of livelihood: You must look at the likely impact of any sentence. Is your client likely to lose their driving licence, and do they need to be able to drive for their work? If they are likely to be sent to prison, are they likely to lose their job? Is their employment such that a conviction is likely to lead to dismissal?

Serious damage to reputation: This will generally arise where your client is of previous good character. Where your client does have previous convictions, but these are very old, or where the charge he now faces is one of dishonesty and he has no previous convictions for dishonesty, it may still be possible to argue that he has a good reputation to lose. The test is whether the disgrace of the conviction would greatly exceed the direct effect of any penalty that might be imposed.

(ii) whether the determination of any matter arising in the proceedings may involve consideration of a substantial question of law

You will need to consider not only whether the charge itself involves a substantial question of law, but also whether there are difficult legal issues arising from the evidence. This will often be the case where there is a confession whose admissibility is disputed, or where there are possible inferences from failure to mention defence facts. Similarly there are complex provisions dealing with the admissibility of evidence of bad character – both that of the defendant and of other persons – and complex rules on hearsay evidence. All of these may give rise to substantial questions of law, requiring the grant of a representation order.

(iii) whether the individual may be unable to understand the proceedings or to state his own case

It is not enough to say that your client will be unable to follow the proceedings because he doesn't understand the way that the law works. It is the duty of the court to conduct its proceedings in an accessible manner. You will have to show that your client lacks sufficient command of English (perhaps because he does not speak English as a first language) or suffers from a disability which affects his ability to understand the proceedings. If your client has an alcohol or drugs problem, you may be able to argue that this is a disability which has such an effect.

(iv) whether the proceedings may involve the tracing, interviewing or expert cross-examination of witnesses on behalf of the individual

Tracing and interviewing of witnesses: In order to satisfy this criterion, you will not only need to show that you have to both trace and/or interview the witness, but also why a solicitor is needed to do this. This will normally apply to defence witnesses although it is possible that a solicitor may need to speak to a prosecution witness and it would clearly be inappropriate for the defendant to do this himself.

Expert cross-examination of witnesses: Note that this criterion is not the cross-examination of expert witnesses; it is the expert cross-examination of witnesses. In other words, why can your client, assisted by the court, not conduct his own case and cross-examine the prosecution witnesses himself? You may be able to show that the case involves putting allegations of misconduct to a professional witness, such as a police officer or a store detective, or that it involves a complex issue such as identification, where evidence needs to be carefully tested.

(v) whether it is in the interests of another person that the individual be represented

This will often be the case where the offence is sexual, and may also arise in some violence related cases, where it is in the interests of the victim that the defendant be legally represented so as not to be questioned by the defendant personally. There are evidential rules which prevent the defendant from personally cross-examining the complainant or child witnesses in certain circumstances.

(vi) any other reason

This is a catch all ground for which you may have to use your imagination. As an example, it may be relevant where you have to make careful written representations to the prosecution to discontinue a case or deal with it in a manner other than at trial.

4.1.4 The means test

The means test is intended to be a simple test, which determines whether the defendant's income is above or below the threshold levels, taking into account his household composition.

Where income falls below the threshold level, the means test will be satisfied; where it is above the top level, the defendant will not be eligible at all. Where the defendant's income falls in the middle, a more complex assessment will be applied. Applicants will automatically pass the means test if they are "passported" i.e. where the defendant is claiming income support, income based job-seekers allowance, income related employment and support allowance or guaranteed state pension credit or, where they are under 18 years old.

The applicant must disclose all income as requested on the form and must produce proof of that income. If an applicant has been remanded in custody and is not able to produce proof of income, there is a statement of truth which must be completed. The applicant's partner's income is also included for the purposes of the calculation. A partner is considered to be anyone who is living with the applicant as a couple. The applicant's partner will also be required to sign the application form. Although the means test is the responsibility of the Criminal Defence Service, the test is administered by staff in the magistrates' court on their behalf.

The income threshold is the same for means testing in both magistrates' court and Crown Court cases however the test is applied differently. If the means test is satisfied in the magistrates' court, the defendant will be granted legal aid (subject to also satisfying the merits test) and he will have free representation by his solicitor. If the defendant's income is above the threshold in the Crown Court, he will be granted the representation order but he will have to pay a contribution towards defence costs. The contributions are calculated at 90% of the defendant's monthly income and these are payable either in five monthly sums or as a lump sum payment.

One impact of the means test has been to complicate the process of getting the case started. In order to ensure that the case is not delayed for legal aid purposes, most courts deal with applications on an expedited basis on the day of the first hearing. An early cover scheme has been introduced with a fixed payment for the first court hearing where the defendant passes the interests of justice test but fails the means test. Equally, where the representation order is refused on the interests of justice, a pre-order cover scheme permits the solicitor to claim up to one hour's preparatory work towards the costs of starting the case.

4.1.5 The application process

Applications for a representation order will be on Form CDS 14 and 15.

CDS 14: This must be completed in all cases regardless of the nature of the offence or where the case is likely to be heard. It will contain details of the applicant's personal information, the offence and your explanation of why the interests of justice criteria are satisfied. The key thing to remember in filling out the application form is that it is not enough to tick the boxes; you must give reasons to show why the particular criteria are made out. (An example of a completed Form CDS 14 is provided as Document 5 in the case study.)

CDS 15: This form is submitted for the court to assess the means test. Where an applicant is "passported"(see above), where they do not own a house or if they have no savings/investments, they do not have to complete the CDS15. In most circumstances, the CDS15 must be accompanied by evidence of the client's means e.g. a wage slip.

You must complete the relevant form(s) and send the application to the court where the defendant is due to attend in connection with the charge. Alternatively, the application can be submitted directly to the court on the day of the first hearing.

Appeals against the refusal of a representation order: Where an application has been refused on the interests of justice, the client has a right to request that the decision be reviewed by the representation authority responsible for making that decision. Where the decision remains the same, there is a right to appeal to the court against the refusal of legal aid on the interests of justice test. There is no right of appeal in respect of the means test, but the defendant can ask for a hardship review (by completing form CDS16) or he can reapply if there has been a change of financial circumstances.

[4.2] DEFENDANTS AND COSTS

4.2.1 Costs orders on conviction and acquittal

Costs on conviction: If the defendant is convicted, he will generally be ordered to pay all or part of the prosecution costs according to what is just and reasonable: s.18 (1) Prosecution of Offences Act 1985. If the defendant is convicted in the Crown Court and he was ordered to pay contributions towards defence costs, he will be required to repay the defence costs from capital. Such an order will be made where the contributions already paid do not cover the full amount of defence costs or where the defendant has capital in excess of a set amount (even if the means test was initially met).

Costs on acquittal: If the defendant is acquitted and he has paid privately for a solicitor to represent him, he will generally have his costs refunded from central funds. This may be the case where, for example the client's legal aid application has been refused. Where the client is legally aided, the lawyers' costs will be claimed under the representation order, and it is unlikely that there will need to be any central funds costs order. Costs should not be refused even where the acquittal is on a technicality but only where for example, the defendant brought suspicion on himself and had misled the prosecution into thinking that the case against him was stronger than it was: *Practice Direction: Costs in criminal proceedings*. In the Crown Court, where the defendant has been making contributions towards his defence costs, these will be reimbursed with interest.

4.2.2 Wasted costs orders

As with all litigation, costs may be awarded against a legal representative for costs thrown away by an improper, unreasonable or negligent act or omission which the court considers unreasonable for the other party to pay: s.19A Prosecution of Offences Act 1985 and CrPR 76.8. The Court should only make an order where there was clearly and obviously an improper, unreasonable or negligent act or omission and not where, for example, a solicitor was following Counsel's advice: *Devas & Co, Re* [2002] EWCA Crim 1689. Solicitors must be particularly aware of this as it is being used more and more frequently in light of breaches of the Criminal Procedure Rules. As examples, see *DPP v Bury Magistrates' Court* [2007] EWHC 3256 and more recently, *R v SVS Solicitors* [2012] EWCA Crim 828.

POLICE STATION ADVICE AND ASSISTANCE

- Where the client is at the police station, whether in custody or voluntarily.
- Free legal advice and assistance, whether from the duty solicitor or from own solicitor.
- In less serious cases where there is no interview, advice may be limited to telephone advice, which will generally be provided by CDS Direct.
- No means test.

ADVICE & ASSISTANCE

- Limited legal advice on most issues of English law.
- Means-tested
- Only covers work that is done prior to charge outside the police station environment and does not cover representation at court
- Note that work must be done in accordance with CDS guidelines

REPRESENTATION ORDERS

- Representation by solicitor only in the magistrates court. In Crown Court will cover solicitor and advocate.
- The merits test: – contained in Sched 3 Access to Justice Act, but also known as the "interests of justice" criteria. Various specific factors (loss of liberty, substantial question of law, expert cross-examination etc.) are identified where the accused should be granted a representation order.
- Means test: If above threshold in the magistrates' courts, means test not satisfied. If above threshold in Crown Court, must pay contributions towards defence costs.
- Application: by completing Forms CDS 14 and CDS15 (where relevant) and submitting to the court.
- "Appeals" – if refused, you can appeal once to the court if the refusal relates to merits. There is no right of appeal in respect of the means test although a hardship application may be possible in appropriate circumstances (complete form CDS 16).

Legal aid – test yourself questions

[The answers to these questions are set out in Appendix A at the back of this book]

Rachel is arrested for the attempted theft of a book valued at £5.99 from W. H. Smiths. She is arrested by a security guard one hundred yards from the shop. The security guard says that when he challenged Rachel as she was leaving the store, she dropped the book and ran away. Rachel says that he has arrested the wrong person as she was never in the shop.

Rachel is a student. She has two previous convictions for disorderly behaviour (s.5 Public Order Act 1986), both arising from demonstrations at a controversial new by-pass. Other than these she is of good character.

The two questions below both arise from this scenario.

[1]   Consider the following "interests of justice" criteria.

   i.   Likely to lose liberty.

   ii. Serious damage to reputation.

   iii. Necessary to track and interview witnesses.

   iv. Need for expert cross-examination.

Which of the above criteria are most appropriate for you to identify when applying for criminal legal aid?

(a) All of the above.

(b) ii and iii only.

(c) iii only.

(d) ii, iii and iv only.

[2]   Rachel's application for a representation order is rejected by the court on the basis that the merits test is not satisfied.

Which of the following propositions is NOT correct?

(a) Rachel can make a fresh application to the court at any time.

(b) Rachel can make a fresh application in the Crown Court if the matter is sent to that court for trial.

(c) Rachel can apply to the Legal Services Commission to appeal the decision within 14 days of the refusal.

(d) Rachel's solicitor will still be able to claim up to one hour's preparation towards the cost of starting the case under the pre-order cover scheme.

CHAPTER 5

FIRST HEARINGS

> This chapter covers:
>
> Getting the defendant to court
>
> The first hearing
>
> Procedure on summary only offences
>
> Procedure on either way offences
>
> Procedure on indictable only offences

[5.1] GETTING THE DEFENDANT TO COURT

All cases, no matter how serious, will start in the magistrates' court. Proceedings are commenced by way of one of a number of procedures which essentially informs the defendant of the allegation against him and requires him to attend a magistrates' court to deal with the case.

The defendant's appearance can be secured at court in one of three ways:

1. **Arrest and charge:** Where there has been an arrest and the police have charged the defendant, the police have two options available to put the defendant before the court. Firstly he may be kept in police detention and physically produced before the next available court. A pilot is currently taking place in two justice areas in the UK which allows for a virtual first hearing in these circumstances. This is where a defendant who is held in custody following charge, appears before the magistrates' court by way of a video link directly from the police station. Alternatively, the defendant may be released on bail to attend the magistrates' court on a specified date. For the decision on bail, see chapter 6.

2. **Issue of a summons/warrant:** A formal document known as an information will be laid before a magistrate (or clerk) by the prosecutor. An "information" is an allegation that a person has committed an offence. It can be laid before the court either orally or in writing. This will lead to the issue of a summons requiring the defendant to attend court on a specified date. The summons must be served by personally delivering it to the person or leaving it for him with another person at his last known address or by posting it to that address. In the latter two situations, however, the service will not be proved (thus enabling the court to proceed in the defendant's absence) unless it can actually be established that the summons came to his notice.

Alternatively, the information will lead to a warrant being issued for the arrest of the defendant so that he can be brought to court in custody. The warrant can also be "backed for bail" so that when the defendant is arrested, he is released on bail to attend court on a specified date.

3. **Charge and requisition:** This is the process by which the prosecutor issues a "written charge" accompanied by a "requisition" which requires the defendant to attend court on a specified date (s.29 Criminal Justice Act 2003). This procedure is being piloted in various areas with a view to replacing the procedure of laying an information and issuing of a summons. The power of a prosecutor to obtain an arrest warrant will be retained.

5.1.1 Other preliminary matters

A magistrates' court has the jurisdiction to try any summary offence committed within England or Wales. A criminal offence is usually tried in the jurisdiction in which it was committed.

Time limits for prosecutions: There is no Statute of Limitations in English law. Where a matter is very aged the CPS may choose not to prosecute, or the defence may run an abuse of process argument, but the offence is unlikely to be statute-barred.

- *Time limits and summary offences:* There is a very important exception to this principle when dealing with a summary offence. A magistrates' court cannot try an information or hear a complaint for a summary offence unless the information was laid or the complaint made within six months from the offence being committed or the matter of complaint arose: s.127 Magistrates' Courts Act 1980. Note that this time limit does not apply to either way offences.

- *Time limits laid down by statutes:* You also need to note that some statutes contain their own time limits. In particular there is a "Notice of Intended Prosecution" procedure for certain motoring offences (such as dangerous or careless driving, or speeding). By ss.1 and 2 Road Traffic Offenders Act 1988 the driver may not be prosecuted unless he was either warned at the time that prosecution was being considered, or notified within 14 days. This does not arise if there was an accident at the same time or immediately afterwards, or if the name and address of the accused could not with reasonable diligence have been ascertained in time.

5.1.2 The decision to prosecute

The decision to prosecute will generally be a matter for the Crown Prosecution Service. They will have regard to the 'Full Code Test' set out in the Code for Crown Prosecutors. This applies a two-stage review process – an evidential test and a public interest test. The evidential test requires that there be a "realistic prospect of conviction" against each defendant. This is an objective test which means that the CPS must look critically at the admissibility and reliability of evidence as well as the defence case. If the evidential test is satisfied, the CPS must consider the public interest test. This requires that the prosecutor take into account various factors that may make it in the public interest to prosecute (seriousness, use of a weapon, breach of trust, vulnerable victim, and so on), as against those factors which may mean it is not in the public interest to proceed (long delay, minor loss or harm, reparation made, elderly or sick defendant).

You should always consider the factors in the Code. It may be possible to negotiate with the CPS for the matter to be dropped or to be dealt with otherwise than by prosecution – for example, by way of a formal caution. The Code can be found on the CPS website: www.cps.gov.uk.

Joinder – trying different defendants and different cases at the same time: Where two defendants have been jointly charged with an offence, they will normally be tried together, although the court does have a discretion to order separate trials. Where there is only one defendant, but he faces two or more charges, the matters can be tried at the same time provided that the defence and prosecution agree to this. If either party does not agree, the magistrates should only try the informations together if it is in the interests of justice to do so. The court should take into account whether the matters are related by time or by other factors, and should also take into account the convenience of the prosecution: *Re Clayton* [1983] 2 AC 473.

The rule against duplicity: An information should not charge more than one offence. However, two or more criminal acts can be contained on one information if the conduct amounted to a single activity: see *Barton* v DPP [2001] EWHC Admin 223 where 94 small thefts from a till were lawfully charged as a single count of theft during a 12 month period.

Mistakes on the charge/information: You will often have clients who come to see you waving the summons and pointing out that they are J. D. Smith rather than J. A. Smith. However such a mistake is unlikely to mean that the proceedings are invalid. The magistrates have a discretion to allow the information to be amended at any stage in the proceedings: s.123 MCA 1980. The provision specifically provides that variations between the information and the evidence at trial are not grounds for objecting to the information. However, if the defendant has been prejudiced by the error/variation then he should be granted an adjournment.

Autrefois Acquit: Autrefois acquit is a plea to a charge. The plea exists to protect a person from being charged with an offence for which they have already been tried and acquitted. The law is complex and the plea is relatively rare. It is, however, worth considering at this stage as you will need to raise the issue with the CPS so as to have proceedings discontinued once it becomes clear that the plea must succeed.

Re-trials: It is possible for certain serious offences to be brought to court a second time, even where there has been an earlier acquittal. Part 10 of the Criminal Justice Act 2003 permits the retrial of defendants acquitted of certain serious offences where new and compelling evidence comes to light and when it is in the interests of justice to order a re-trial. This is a retrospective power, and so applies to acquittals prior to the coming into effect of the provision. It will arise only in relation to "qualifying offences" which are listed in Schedule 5 to the CJA 2003 and include offences such as murder, rape, and certain Class A drugs offences. The Court of Appeal must grant leave before such a retrial can take place. In May 2011, the Court of Appeal decided to utilise this power in relation to the murder of Stephen Lawrence who was killed in 1993, the original defendant having been previously acquitted by a jury in 1996.

[5.2] THE FIRST HEARING

Solicitors and barristers have rights of audience in the magistrates' courts, as do certain categories of Crown Prosecution Service representative, and Legal Executives who have completed the requisite training. The prosecution will usually be represented by either a prosecuting solicitor or a senior caseworker who has undertaken sufficient training to undertake criminal cases before the courts. The defendant will normally be represented by his solicitor.

Generally these hearings, regardless of the type of offence, will either be in front of a District Judge (who is legally qualified) or will be in front of a Bench of lay magistrates who are advised by a court clerk on matters of law. Lay magistrates will normally sit in a bench of three, although two is possible.

The nature of the first hearing before the magistrates' court has been radically changed since the introduction of Simple Speedy Summary Criminal Justice (CJSSS) in November 2007. This scheme came into force in all magistrates' courts across England and Wales in order to simplify the conduct of criminal cases before the lower courts and to minimise the time between arrest and the conclusion of a case. Therefore, the first hearing before the court must be "effective" i.e. the court will expect the defendant to enter a plea so that the case can progress straight away, thereby reducing unnecessary adjournments. This is reiterated in Part 3 of the Criminal Procedure Rules whereby the Court must actively manage the case, identifying issues early and discouraging delay. The Senior Presiding Judge for England and Wales has issued an advice note to all magistrates on the impact of the CrPR stating that a plea should be expected at the first hearing. The CJSSS process applies to cases which have been commenced by charge rather than those instigated by summons and it does not apply to indictable only cases.

More recently, the judiciary led initiative 'Stop Delaying Justice' has reiterated this notion that cases must be moved along at the first hearing and that adjournments may only be granted in exceptional circumstances. In order to be in a position to make a decision about where the case should be tried, the defendant must have an informed choice. Part 21 of the Criminal Procedure Rules therefore requires the prosecution to provide the defence with a summary of the prosecution evidence and a copy of the defendant's previous convictions at, or before, the first hearing: see 7.5.1 for details.

5.2.1 The types of first hearing

The Crime and Disorder Act 1998 deals with the different ways in which a case can be listed for first appearance. At every hearing, if the case cannot be concluded there and then, the court must give directions so that it can be concluded at the next hearing or as soon as possible after that: CrPR3.8(1)

Early first hearings (EFH): These hearings are intended for defendants who are charged with summary or either way offences and who are likely to enter a guilty plea as soon as they get to court. These hearings operate under the CJSSS system and cases are expected to be resolved as efficiently as possible in accordance with the CrPR. Eligibility for legal aid should be resolved at this hearing.

Early administrative hearings (EAH): These hearings are an attempt to deal quickly with administrative steps in cases where a not guilty plea is likely, or where the likely plea is not known. Again, the CJSSS procedures will apply so the court will expect a plea to be entered at this hearing so that the case can proceed either to sentence or to the fixing of the next hearing date. Eligibility for legal aid should be resolved at this hearing. If the case is adjourned, a decision will also need to be taken whether the defendant should be released on bail, or remanded into custody.

Remand court: If a defendant is appearing before the magistrates' court in custody, he will appear before the remand court. CJSSS does not apply to such cases although under the CrPR the court will still be keen to take a plea and make progress. The issue of bail will usually be considered: see chapter 6. Funding should also be resolved.

[5.3] PROCEDURE ON A SUMMARY ONLY OFFENCE

This is relatively straightforward. On a summary only offence (an offence that can only be tried in the magistrates' court), the defendant will indicate his plea and if this is a guilty plea, he will be sentenced by the magistrates. In accordance with Criminal Procedure Rules, the court should try to sentence immediately where possible, but if a pre-sentence report is required, there may be a short adjournment required.

If the defendant pleads not guilty, or declines to enter a plea, then the court will move toward fixing a date for trial. This will require the parties to engage in case management, which is further explored in chapter 7. In either case, where an adjournment is required, it can either be a simple adjournment, or the court can grant bail with or without conditions. (see ch. 6).

[5.4] PROCEDURE ON AN EITHER WAY OFFENCE

Either way offences are offences that can be tried in either the magistrates' court or the Crown Court. Section 17 Magistrates' Court Act 1980 sets out a fairly expansive list of either way offences, but usually the legislation behind the offence makes it clear whether the offence falls within this category. A common example of an either way offence is theft contrary to s.1 Theft Act 1968. Clearly theft of a sandwich is more likely to be dealt with at the magistrates' court, whereas theft of a diamond encrusted watch is more likely to be dealt with at the Crown Court.

The procedure in relation to either way offences is complex and the precise detail will vary depending upon the stage of implementation of the changes made by s.41 and Schedule 3 of the Criminal Justice Act 2003. At the time of writing, the new procedure is being phased in, so for the sake of clarity, both the pre and post CJA 2003 procedures will be set out.

5.4.1   Pre CJA 2003 'Plea Before Venue, Mode of Trial and Committal Hearings'

5.4.1.1
Plea Before Venue

At the first hearing the charge will be read out, and the defendant will be asked to indicate his plea. This is known as "plea before venue". If the defendant pleads guilty, then the magistrates must accept this plea and then decide whether their sentencing powers are sufficient. If their sentencing powers are sufficient, then they must proceed to sentence, or adjourn for pre-sentence reports if required. If they feel that their sentencing powers are not sufficient, then they will commit the defendant to the Crown court for sentence under s.3 Powers of Criminal Courts (Sentencing) Act 2000 (see 5.6). Although this seems straightforward, it is not without problems. For example:

Accepting jurisdiction of serious offences If you look at the s.17 MCA list of either way offences, you will see that the list includes many very serious offences that will undoubtedly exceed the sentencing powers of the magistrates" court. For example, violent disorder (s.2 Public Order Act) will generally attract at least a two or three year custodial sentence. Possession of Class A drugs with intention to supply may attract a sentence in excess of ten years. Yet both of these are either way offences and technically this means that the magistrates could accept jurisdiction. However, in such a case it is inevitable that the magistrates are going to exercise their power under s.3 Powers of Criminal Courts (Sentencing) Act to commit your client to the Crown Court for sentence.

From your client's point of view pleading guilty at an early stage and being committed for sentence has two very negative consequences. Firstly, because he is now convicted, he will lose his prima facie right to bail and is likely to be remanded in custody. Secondly, because he is a convicted prisoner, he will lose his remand privileges and will serve his time in custody while he awaits sentencing under the stricter prison regime. Because of this most clients would prefer not to indicate a guilty plea at this stage, but would rather wait until the case got to the Crown Court. In *Rafferty [1998] Crim LR 433* the Court of Appeal has made clear that bail should normally be extended even after a guilty plea, precisely in order to help to persuade defendants to enter early pleas in this way.

What if your client still doesn't want to indicate his plea at this stage? You must warn your client that there is a clear danger that if he delays entering his guilty plea, he is going to lose some of the credit to which he is entitled under s.144 Criminal Justice Act 2003 for pleading guilty at the earliest opportunity. However, in the guidelines from the Sentencing Council it suggests that the maximum discount for pleading guilty at or prior to the mode of trial stage will be 1/3rd whereas a guilty plea immediately following committal to the Crown Court should be entitled to 30%. The difference therefore seems to be very small! Note however, that in *R v Cundell [2008] EWCA Crim 1420*, the defendant pleaded guilty at the Plea and Case Management hearing (rather than at the plea before venue stage in the magistrates' court) and it was held that because he had not indicated his plea at the earliest opportunity, he was only entitled to a 25% reduction in sentence.

If your client indicates a not guilty plea or says nothing

If the defendant indicates a not guilty plea, or says nothing, the court will then listen to representations from both prosecution and defence as to where the matter should be tried (see 5.4.1.2 below). The court will then make its decision, taking into account the representations and the relevant statutory guidance. If the court declines jurisdiction, a date will need to be fixed for a committal hearing at which the case will be sent to the Crown Court for trial.

If the magistrates accept jurisdiction, the clerk will give the defendant a formal warning. This makes it clear that the defendant has the power to elect Crown Court trial, but that even if he decides to stay in the magistrates' court, the court can still commit the matter for sentencing if he is convicted under s.3 Powers of Criminal Courts (Sentencing) Act 2000. The defendant then makes his election.

5.4.1.2
Mode of Trial

If following plea before venue, the defendant has pleaded not guilty or indicated no plea then the court will immediately deal with 'mode of trial'. A mode of trial hearing is a two stage process. Firstly, the magistrates will hear the prosecution outline of the offence and any representations that they and the defence may have as to the appropriate venue for trial. Crucially the court will not be told about any previous convictions the defendant may have. The magistrates will then decide whether they feel the case is suitable for summary trial. In making this decision, the magistrates will consider statutory guidance, particularly s.19 MCA 1980. If the magistrates decline jurisdiction, then the case will adjourn for a committal hearing and the defendant will be committed to the Crown court, regardless of where he would like the trial to be heard. If the magistrates accept jurisdiction, then we move to the second stage in the process. In the second stage, the defendant will be asked to decide whether he is content for the case to remain at the Magistrates court, or whether he would prefer the case to be tried at the Crown court. It is therefore important to examine the considerations that are taken at each stage:

The Court's decision

In accordance with s.19 MCA, the magistrates must have regard to the following matters in deciding whether an offence is more suitable for summary trial or trial on indictment:

(a)   the nature of the case;

(b)   whether the circumstances make the offence one of a serious character;

(c) whether the punishment which a magistrates' court would have power to inflict for it would be adequate;

(d) any other circumstances which appear to the court to make it more suitable for the offence to be tried in one way rather than the other;

(e) any representations made by the prosecution or the defence.

Furthermore, the National Mode of Trial Guidelines, (set out in the Consolidated Criminal Practice Direction at V.51(3) state that when making their decision:

(a) the court should never make its decision on the grounds of convenience or expedition;

(b) the court should assume for the purpose of deciding mode of trial that the prosecution version of the facts is correct;

(c) the fact that the offences are alleged to be specimens is a relevant consideration (although it has to be borne in mind that difficulties can arise in sentencing in relation to specimen counts, see *R v Clark [1996] 2 Cr App R (S) 351 and R v Canavan and others [1998] 1 Cr App R (S) 243);* the fact that the defendant will be asking for other offences to be taken into consideration, if convicted, is not;

(d) where cases involve complex questions of fact or difficult questions of law, including difficult issues of disclosure of sensitive material, the court should consider committal for trial;

(e) where two or more defendants are jointly charged with an offence each has an individual right to elect his mode of trial;

(f) in general, except where otherwise stated, either way offences should be tried summarily unless the court considers that the particular case has one or more of the features set out in paragraphs V.51.4 to V.51.18 and that its sentencing powers are insufficient;

(g) the court should also consider its power to commit an offender for sentence under sections 3 and 4 of the Powers of Criminal Courts (Sentencing) Act 2000, if information emerges during the course of the hearing which leads it to conclude that the offence is so serious, or the offender such a risk to the public, that its powers to sentence him are inadequate. This means that committal for sentence is no longer determined by reference to the character and antecedents of the offender.

Finally, the National Mode of Trial Guidelines used to provide a list of the most common either way offences together with specific guidance as to what would merit Crown Court trial rather than Magistrates trial in each case (e.g. in a case of burglary, ransacking, professional hallmarks, high value goods taken etc. would suggest Crown Court). This is what point (f) above refers to. This guidance was gradually superseded by The Magistrates Courts Sentencing Guidelines which also offered guidance as to what made particular offences more or less serious for sentencing purposes. Clearly if a case displayed elements that would mark it out as particularly serious, then that would be a case that may need to be dealt with at the Crown court.

If having considered all of this guidance, the magistrates feel that the case could not be dealt with at their court, then they would 'decline jurisdiction' and the case would adjourn for a 'committal hearing'. If however they decide that the case could be dealt with at the magistrates' court, then they 'accept jurisdiction' and the defendant then has a choice to make. The defendant can either go along with a summary trial, or he can 'elect' to have the case tried at the Crown court. If he elects trial at Crown court, then again the case will adjourn for a committal hearing. Before we examine committal hearings, let us briefly explore the defendant's decision and the factors that may help him with his choice of venue.

The Defendant's decision:

Advantages of the Crown Court

Acquittal rates: Acquittal rates are undoubtedly appreciably higher in jury trials than in the magistrates' courts. Sometimes it is suggested that magistrates tend to accept police evidence less critically than juries do. Alternatively, it may be that juries tend to be dealing with cases for the first time, and are therefore more mindful of the direction that they can only convict if they are satisfied beyond reasonable doubt of your client's guilt.

"Voir dire" procedures: One of the main advantages of electing Crown court trial is that the Crown Court can hold a voir dire to decide on admissibility of evidence. A "voir dire" is a trial within a trial. It is a process for dealing with arguments on points of law in the absence of the jury. The effect is that if you are able to persuade the judge to exclude evidence (for example, your client's confession) the jury will return to the courtroom to hear the case but will never know that the evidence existed. In contrast, while a voir dire is possible in the magistrates' court, it will be the magistrates who hear the legal arguments, and decide whether to exclude the evidence. If the magistrates rule that the evidence is inadmissible, then they need to disregard that particular piece of evidence when considering their final verdict. In this situation, there is always a risk that the inadmissible evidence will inevitably still have some bearing on the final decision and your client will thereby be at a disadvantage.

Complex legal arguments: It is sometimes argued that a judge will have a better understanding of complex legal arguments, and may be able to give succinct directions on points of law to the jury. By contrast, in the magistrates' court, points of law must be decided by the lay justices, albeit with the assistance of the legally trained clerk. It is sometimes suggested that complex points can be lost in this situation.

Committal hearings: It is sometimes argued that the committal hearing is an opportunity for further consideration of the case, to test prosecution evidence and perhaps have the case dismissed. We will explore committal hearings at 5.4.1.3.

Disadvantages of the Crown Court:

Speed: In some cases, your client will see the greater timescale involved in Crown Court matters as an advantage. The delay may ensure that witnesses forget what they saw, that police officers are transferred, and that the evil day of sentencing is put off for a while. Furthermore, the delay gives the defence more time to prepare its case. On the other hand, if your client is remanded in custody and feels that they are unlikely to be convicted, they will want their case heard as soon as possible.

Stress: Crown Court trials are undoubtedly more stressful than trials in the magistrates' court. Advocates will be robed, and if they are barristers they will wear wigs as well. There will be a judge and a jury and a great deal more formality than in a summary trial. In cases where your client is facing a serious charge, the greater likelihood of acquittal will always outweigh this factor; but in a more minor offence, the stress of the Crown Court may take on a greater importance for your client in making his decision.

Costs: There are two aspects to consider in relation to costs. Firstly, due to the differences in means testing between magistrates' and Crown court, a client who may have qualified for funding at magistrates' level, may have to pay a contribution toward his defence costs at Crown court. This will not be problematic if he is acquitted (contributions will then be refunded) but could prove extremely costly if convicted after a long, drawn out trial. Obviously if your client does not qualify at all for funding, then Crown court could be a prohibitively expensive option.

Secondly, if he is convicted, there could be an order that he pay all or part of the prosecution costs which will obviously be substantially higher in the Crown court as compared to the magistrates' court.

Powers of punishment: The Crown Court has far greater powers of punishment than the magistrates' court. Whereas the magistrates are currently limited to sentences of six months' custody (or twelve months in the case of two or more either way offences), the Crown Court can impose up to the statutory maximum for any particular offence. It also has far greater powers in imposing financial penalties.

Defence disclosure: We will consider the issue of disclosure in far more detail in Chapter 7. For the time being note that in a Crown Court case the defence have to serve a statement setting out the basic nature of their defence in advance of the trial. This means that the prosecution will be given advance notice of the defence and can therefore take steps to rebut the defence. By contrast, serving a defence statement in the magistrates' court is entirely voluntary. Although this used to be a significant advantage to remaining in the magistrates' court, this advantage is gradually being eroded as the defence are increasingly required to 'show their hand' at an early stage through case management and defence witness notices.

Publicity: It is argued that there tends to be more thorough press coverage of the Crown Courts, and thus a greater chance of publicity. This is, however, very variable. Many magistrates' courts attract local press coverage, while a major robbery or murder trial at the Crown Court may well draw all the attention from other cases taking place at the same court complex.

Advantages of the magistrates' court

Speed, informality, cost: Magistrates' court trials will tend to be listed for hearing far more quickly than trials in the Crown Court. What is more, a trial in the magistrates' court will be far quicker than its Crown Court equivalent; a trial which might take two days at Crown Court is unlikely to take more than half a day in the magistrates' court. This, and the far greater level of informality in the magistrates' court, means that your client will often find such hearings less stressful. Additionally, should your client be convicted and therefore have to pay the Prosecution costs, then, the costs of a trial in the magistrates' court will be far less than in the Crown Court.

Powers of punishment: You have already seen that the magistrates' courts are limited in their powers to imprison and to fine. On the face of it, this is therefore a huge advantage in electing summary trial. However, the magistrates have a power (under s.3 Powers of Criminal Courts (Sentencing) Act 2000) to commit your client to the Crown Court for sentence if they consider their own sentencing powers to be inadequate when dealing with an either way offence. This power to commit for sentence is discussed later in this chapter.

Disadvantages of the magistrates' court

Likelihood of conviction: There is a higher conviction rate in the magistrates' court, although it can be argued that this reflects the fact that weaker cases will tend to stay in the magistrates' court where sentencing powers are less.

Lack of proper voir dire In the magistrates' court there is no division of role between judge and jury, with the magistrates fulfilling both functions. This means that if you want to argue that your client's previous convictions should not be mentioned or that evidence should be excluded, you are going to have to do so in front of the very people who would then have to ignore this information. You should, however, be aware that increasingly, issues of admissibility are decided at pre-trial hearings which involve different magistrates to those that will be sitting on the day of the trial. This therefore undermines this particular argument.

5.4.1.3
Committal Hearings

Under the pre-CJA 2003 procedure, where magistrates had declined jurisdiction, or where the defendant had elected trial on indictment, the case would have to be 'committed' to the Crown Court. This would mean that the case would be adjourned to a 'committal' hearing and in the meantime, the Prosecution would provide the defence with a copy of all the evidence they intended to rely upon to prove the case against the defendant. There would then be either a s.6(1) MCA 1980 committal ('old style committal')or a s.6(2) committal ('new style committal'). The purpose of the committal hearing was to allow the magistrates to decide if there was a sufficiently strong case to justify sending a matter to the Crown Court for trial. The test is generally stated as being whether there is a "prima facie" case.

On an old style s.6(1) committal, the prosecution reads out the prosecution statements. No witnesses will be called. The defence can then make representations and challenges as to the admissibility of the evidence. It is usual for the defence to make a submission of "no case to answer" at a 6(1) committal, and invite the magistrates to dismiss the case. In order for the magistrates to dismiss a case, they must be satisfied that the prosecution case taken at its highest, is such that a properly directed jury could not properly convict. This is known as the 'Galbraith test' following the guidance given in the case of *R v Galbraith [1981] All ER 1060*.

Note that the prosecution may insist on having a s.6(1) committal, and the defence has no power to overrule this. A s.6(2) committal (without consideration of the evidence) can therefore only take place where all parties agree.

A 6(1) committal must be held if the defendant is unrepresented or otherwise where your client or a co-accused requests it. The only reason for asking for a 6(1) committal would be in order to argue that there is insufficient evidence on which to convict. However even if a case is thrown out at committal on the basis that there is insufficient evidence, this does not count as an acquittal, your client is merely discharged and there is therefore nothing to prevent the prosecution from prosecuting again on the same charges.

In direct contrast, a new style s.6(2) committal does not involve any consideration of the evidence at all. There are some minor formalities and the case will be committed for trial without any defence challenge. The charge will be read (although no plea will be taken from your client). The clerk will then check that all the prosecution evidence is in the correct form, and that it has been served on the defence. The evidence is not read or considered at all by the court, and there is no opportunity to make any submission of no case to answer. The case is committed to the Crown Court for trial. For a 6(2) committal your client must be legally represented and there must be no request for a 6(1) committal, whether from another defendant or from the prosecution.

So which committal should you choose? It is hard now to see any real reason for asking for a 6(1) committal in the normal run of cases. There is little or no opportunity to challenge the substance of the prosecution case, and if you point out defects in their case you are simply giving them an opportunity to correct them. There may still be some cases, however, where you take the view that if they are thrown out at committal the matter will not be pursued further. There may be other cases – especially complex public order or dishonesty offences – when you want a 6(1) committal in order to hear on what basis the prosecution is putting its case against your client.

What other matters will arise at committal hearings?

Bail: It appears that committal is not of itself a change of circumstances (thus giving rise to a right to make a new bail application). However, there is caselaw that suggests that circumstances will almost inevitably have changed, if only because after committal there may be a clearer idea of the strength of evidence, for example, than at the earlier stages.

Disclosure: By this stage, you will already have been served with the 'committal bundle', i.e. copies of the used material that the prosecution intend to rely upon in order to prove their case. The prosecution must now make disclosure of unused material (for those cases that are to be tried at Crown Court) either at committal or as soon as practicable after committal. Generally this disclosure will occur at the committal hearing.

Case Management Directions: Once the case has been committed, the magistrates will fix a date for the first Crown Court hearing (the Plea and Case Management Hearing (PCMH)) and this will ordinarily take place within seven weeks of committal. In order to ensure that the PCMH runs as smoothly as possible, the magistrates' will issue standard case management directions that provide deadlines for the provision of the defence statement, disclosure, witness notification etc. These will be looked at more closely in chapter 7.

Funding: If the defendant had the benefit of a representation order in the magistrates' court, then the defence will simply invite the court to extend that order to cover the Crown Court proceedings. If however the defendant failed the means test in the magistrates' court, he can now be granted a representation order to cover the Crown Court subject to a contribution order being made. If the defendant failed both the means and merits test in the magistrates, he will now automatically pass the interests of justice test so that he can qualify for representation at the Crown Court, again subject to there being a decision as to whether he should make any financial contribution.

5.4.2 Post CJA 2003 'Allocation and Transfer'

As previously mentioned, s.41 and Schedule 3 of the Criminal Justice Act 2003 made substantial changes to the procedure involved in dealing with either way offences. 2012 will see the steady introduction of this new procedure throughout the UK. The following section sets out the new procedure. For more detail, see Rule 9 Criminal Procedure Rules.

The initial taking of the plea is very similar to the existing plea before venue procedure. The charge will be read out and the defendant will be told that it is a charge that can be heard in either court. The defendant will be told that he is about to be asked for his plea and that if he pleads guilty, he will either be sentenced by the magistrates, or committed to the Crown Court for sentence if they do not feel that their sentencing powers are sufficient. He is also told that if he pleads not guilty, or declines to enter a plea, then the magistrates will decide on trial venue. The defendant then indicates his plea. If he pleads guilty, then in accordance with the overriding principle of the Criminal Procedure Rules to deal with cases justly, the court must expedite sentence, either at the magistrates, or commit him to the Crown. If he pleads not guilty, or withholds plea, then the magistrates must 'allocate' the trial to either the magistrates or Crown Court.

The 'allocation' procedure is similar to mode of trial. The court will invite the prosecution to make representations as to the most appropriate venue and importantly, they will invite him to reveal any previous convictions that should be taken into account. This is a major change but eminently sensible, since previous convictions inevitably will affect the decision as to whether their sentencing powers are sufficient. The court will also hear any representations from the defence. They must then allocate the case taking into consideration:

- The adequacy of their sentencing powers
- Any representations made by the parties
- Any allocation guidelines issued by the Sentencing Council

On this last point, the Sentencing Council have issued definitive guidelines on allocation that take effect from 2 June 2012. The guidelines state that the court must have regard to s.19 MCA (see above) but beyond that, either way offences should be tried summarily unless it is likely that the magistrates' sentencing powers are insufficient. The court must therefore consider the likely sentence in the light of the facts alleged by the prosecution, but also take into account all aspects of the case including those advanced by the defence. The court should also refer to sentencing guidelines to help them decide the most likely sentence.

If the case is allocated to the magistrates, then this must be explained to the defendant. He must be warned that following a trial at the magistrates, he could still be committed for sentence to the Crown Court. He will then be asked whether he wishes to consent to trial at the magistrates or whether he would prefer trial at the Crown Court. At this point, the defendant has the option of asking the magistrates to indicate whether a custodial sentence would be likely in the event of conviction on summary trial. The magistrates are not bound to give an indication, but if they do, then he must be asked again whether he would like to plead guilty. If, having received that indication, the defendant now wants to plead guilty, he can do so and the magistrates will proceed to sentence, or alternatively commit him for sentence to the Crown Court. If however he maintains his not guilty plea, he must then indicate his preferred venue. At this point, all of the factors mentioned above that weigh in favour/against each court, come into play.

If however the magistrates allocate the case to the Crown court (previously called 'declining jurisdiction') then the court will listen to any representations about ancillary matters (see above, bail, funding, case management etc) and they will then transfer the case to the Crown court for trial.

[5.5] PROCEDURE ON INDICTABLE ONLY OFFENCES

Sending under s.51 CDA:

In accordance with s.51 Crime and Disorder Act 1998, indictable only offences are sent straight to the Crown Court after the first appearance in the magistrates' court .The procedure for this is set out at Rule 9.7 Criminal Procedure Rules. The offence is read out to the defendant and it is explained to him that it is an offence that can only be dealt with by the Crown Court. The defendant is then asked if he wishes to indicate a plea, but he is not obliged to do so. Representations are then made by both parties as to ancillary matters such as bail, funding etc. This 'sending' should normally take place immediately following the first hearing, although there is provision to adjourn if necessary: s.52(5) CDA 1998.This provision for delay is rarely exercised and may include situations where there are bail issues, charging issues to be resolved, or (potentially) where a pause is needed in order to allow further offences or further defendants to be joined.

The first hearing at Crown Court will be a preliminary hearing or a PCMH, see chapter 7 for more detail.

Joinder of either way and summary offences:

Note that the sending procedure may affect your client even if he has only been charged with an either way offence. This is because s.51(3) Crime and Disorder Act 1998 provides that if a person has been jointly charged with an either way offence with another adult who has also been charged with a related indictable-only offence, the court "shall" send him to the Crown Court for trial on the either way matter.

For example, Mike and Ali are alleged to have been involved in a large scale brawl in which two club doormen have been injured. Mike is jointly charged with Ali with the either way offence of assault occasioning actual bodily harm (ABH). However, Ali has also been charged with committing grievous bodily harm with intent (GBH – an indictable only offence) on the other doorman. Ali will be sent straight to the Crown Court to be tried on the GBH matter; Mike will also be sent to the Crown Court since he is jointly charged with Ali on a related either way offence.

Therefore you cannot assume that your client will have a mode of trial/allocation hearing until you have checked whether he has been jointly charged with another person, and confirmed that any related offences are not indictable only ones.

The situation becomes more complex where – as is often the case – your client is charged with several different offences which are in some way linked. In this situation s.51 provides for the linked either way offence to be sent to the Crown Court for trial provided that it fulfils certain conditions. There is a broadly similar provision so that linked summary offences can also be sent for jury trial along with the indictable only offence.

Dieter is charged with rape of his fiancée, an indictable only offence. He must be tried in the Crown Court for this. He is also charged with assault occasioning actual bodily harm for hitting the victim's sister when she tried to comfort the victim, an either way offence. However, although the ABH matter is an either way offence, it is likely to be sent to be tried in the Crown Court alongside the rape matter because it is so closely linked to it.

In order to be sent to the Crown Court an either way offence must be "related" to the indictable only offence. This means that the either way offence arises from the same facts as the indictable only offence, or it forms part of a series of similar offences to the indictable offence and could therefore be included on the same indictment. For a summary only offence, in addition to being "related" the offence must also be punishable either with imprisonment or disqualification from driving: s.51E Crime and Disorder Act 1998.

What happens if the indictable offence disappears? It is not uncommon for the prosecution to review the case when it reaches the Crown Court and to decide that the evidence justifies a less serious charge – so that a charge of rape (an indictable only offence) might drop to a charge of sexual assault (an either way offence). Provided your client has not yet been arraigned, (indicated his plea) a mode of trial/allocation hearing will be held in the Crown Court in order to decide whether to send the either way matters back down to the magistrates for trial.

5.5.1 Transfer of fraud/complex cases to Crown Court:

There is a special regime for serious or complex fraud cases under s.4 of the Criminal Justice Act 1987. Rather than going through the committal hearing procedure, the prosecution serves a notice of transfer on the magistrates' court. The court's functions then cease (other than in respect of bail, witness orders and legal aid). The prosecution then prefers a bill of indictment. There are then provisions enabling the defence to challenge the notice by making an application to the Crown Court. This is a relatively uncommon procedure and you are unlikely to encounter it unless you are doing white collar crime work.

[5.6] COMMITTAL FOR SENTENCE

When the magistrates' court has convicted of an either way offence, if the court is of the opinion that the offence is so serious that greater punishment should be imposed than it has power to impose, it may commit the defendant to the Crown Court to be sentenced. This is the case whether the defendant has indicated a guilty plea at plea before venue/allocation or has accepted summary trial and been convicted, or has a linked matter that is to be dealt with by the Crown Court: s.3 and 4 Powers of Criminal Courts (Sentencing) Act 2000.

In deciding whether their sentencing powers are adequate, the magistrates can take into account any discount on sentence that they are likely to give for the plea of guilty: Reduction in Sentence for a Guilty Plea: para 5.5. This point is illustrated in the following hypothetical example:

Jamal is arrested on suspicion of burglary. He admits the offence in interview at the police station. He indicates his guilty plea at the first hearing in the magistrates'' court. The court is minded to impose a 9 month custodial sentence. However, the court also accepts that it will be reducing the sentence by 1/3rd to take account of Jamal's early guilty plea. The overall sentence will therefore be six months. This is within the magistrates' sentencing powers. They do not need to commit the matter to the Crown Court for sentence.

[5.7] COMMITTING/TRANSFERRING LINKED SUMMARY OFFENCES TO THE CROWN COURT

Where the defendant has been committed/transferred for trial on an indictable or either way offence and the evidence has since disclosed a summary offence which is either based on the same facts or is part of a series of offences of the same character, then the prosecution can include the summary offence on the indictment and it will be tried by the Crown Court. However, this power only applies to the summary offences of common assault, assaulting a prison warder, taking a motor vehicle without consent (TWOC), driving disqualified and criminal damage of £5,000 or less: s.40 Criminal Justice Act 1988

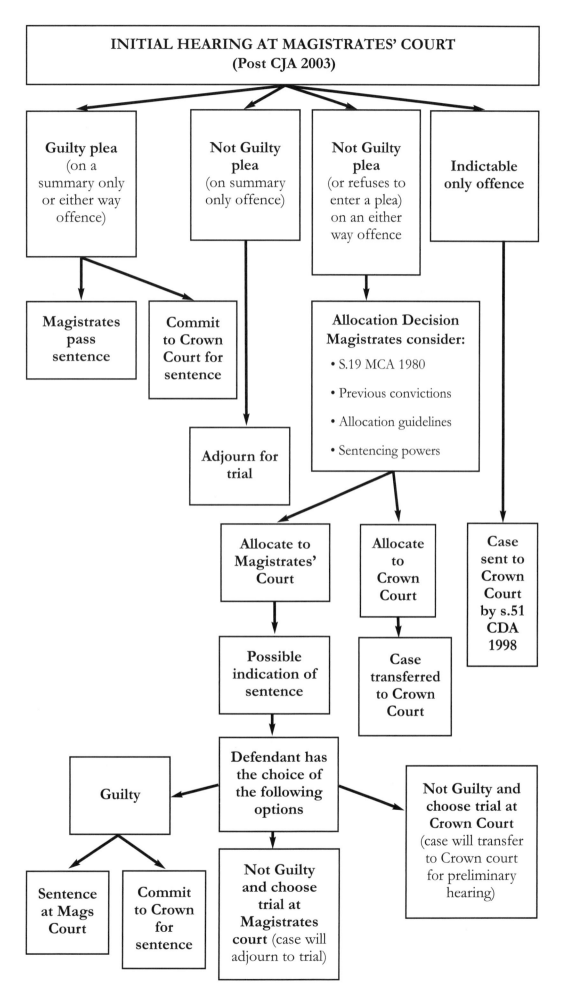

First Hearings 85

First Hearings – test yourself questions

[The answers to these questions are set out in Appendix A at the back of this book]

[2] Carl is charged with malicious wounding (s.20 OAPA). The allegation is that Carl kicked the victim in the head and body as he lay on the ground, causing serious facial injuries. You research the matter and it is clear that the likely sentence is in the region of three years' custody (see Moore (1990) 13 Cr App R (S) 130). You write to Carl to set out the position regarding mode of trial/allocation.

Which of the following explanations is most accurate?

(a) Malicious wounding is an either way offence and you will be able to decide whether it should be tried in the magistrates' or in the Crown Court.

(b) Because the likely sentence for malicious wounding exceeds 6 months, the magistrates will not accept jurisdiction of the case.

(c) If you enter a not guilty plea at the mode of trial/allocation hearing, the magistrates cannot accept jurisdiction of the case and it must be sent for jury trial.

(d) If you indicate a guilty plea at the mode of trial/allocation hearing, the magistrates will still have the power to commit you to the Crown Court for sentencing.

[3] Which one of the following propositions is correct?

(a) The magistrates can commit any offence to the Crown Court for sentencing provided that they are satisfied that their sentencing powers are inadequate.

(b) The magistrates can commit any either way offence to the Crown Court for sentencing provided that they are satisfied that their sentencing powers are inadequate.

(c) The magistrates can only commit an offence for sentence following an indication of a guilty plea.

(d) The magistrates can only commit an offence for sentence if the interests of justice test is satisfied.

[4] Andre is charged with theft of a wallet from a car and criminal damage to the car window that was caused while breaking into the vehicle. The value of the damage is £90. Andre intends to plead not guilty.

Which of the following is correct?

(a) The magistrates will have the power to commit/transfer both matters to the Crown Court for trial.

(b) The magistrates can commit/transfer the theft charge for Crown Court trial, but the criminal damage matter can only be dealt with in the Crown Court if Andre is convicted of the theft and pleads guilty to the criminal damage.

(c) The magistrates have no power to commit/transfer the criminal damage matter at all, as it is valued at less than £5,000.

(d) The matters are related and must therefore be tried together in which ever court accepts jurisdiction.

[5] Consider the following propositions about committal hearings.
   i. There can be no consideration of the evidence at a s.6 (2) committal.
   i. No live evidence can be called at a s.6 (1) committal.
   i. A s. 6(1) committal must be held if the prosecution requires it.

Which of these propositions are correct?
   (a) All of them.
   (b) i only.
   (c) i and iii only.
   (d) ii and iii only.

[6] Riaz and Morgan are student teachers. Riaz is charged with rape (an indictable only offence). He is also jointly charged with Morgan with sexual assault (an either way offence). The sexual assault is said to have taken place during a school trip to France on the coach when the party was heading out to France. The rape is said to have taken place following a party at the student hostel in Paris. Both victims were Sixth Form girls from the school.

Riaz and Morgan attend the magistrates' court for the first hearing of the matters. Which one of the following propositions is correct?

(a) Both men will be asked to indicate their plea. If they indicate a guilty plea to the sexual assault, the magistrates will have to accept jurisdiction of that offence. The rape matter, however, will be sent to Crown Court.

(b) Riaz will be sent to the Crown Court in respect of the rape matter. The sexual assault matter with which Riaz is charged will also be sent to the Crown Court since it is a related offence, because it could be tried on the same indictment. However, Morgan will remain in the magistrates' court and a date for a mode of trial hearing will be fixed to deal with the sexual assault matter with which he is charged.

(c) Both Riaz and Morgan will be sent to the Crown Court because the sexual assault is an imprisonable offence.

(d) None of the above propositions is correct.

CHAPTER 6

BAIL AND BAIL ADVOCACY

> This section covers:
>
> Remands and adjournments
>
> Applying for bail and the grounds for refusing bail
>
> Conditions that can be imposed upon bail
>
> How to make a bail application
>
> Appeals by prosecution and defence in bail cases

[6.1] REMANDS AND ADJOURNMENTS

An accused is entitled to a reasonable opportunity to prepare his case, which will often mean that he will need the opportunity to take legal advice: *R v Thames Magistrates' Court ex parte Polemis* [1974] 1 WLR 1371. Additionally, article 6(3)(b) of the European Convention on Human Rights (ECHR) guarantees a person "adequate time and facilities for the preparation of his defence". The court may adjourn a case at any stage at its discretion: ss.5 and 10 Magistrates' Courts Act 1980. Nevertheless, adjournments are becoming less and less common given the principles in the Criminal Procedure Rules which require progress to be made on each occasion a defendant appears before the court. The key considerations for the court when an advocate applies for an adjournment were set out in *CPS v Picton* [2006] EWHC 1108 (Admin) as: the need for expedition in criminal cases; the need to balance the interests of the defendant and the public, depending on the seriousness of the charge; the likely consequences of an adjournment, particularly its length; issues of who is at fault; and the history of the case in general.

6.1.1 To remand or to adjourn?

When a case is adjourned, the court has to ensure that the defendant returns on the adjournment date. They can either "remand" the defendant or simply adjourn. A remand means committing the defendant into custody (remand in custody) or placing him on bail (remand on bail) and this option has consequences for the defendant should he fail to attend at the next hearing. A simple adjournment is where the defendant is released on the trust that he will attend at the next date. With indictable offences (or with either way offences where the defendant has elected jury trial) the magistrates must remand (either in custody or on bail). Only in either way or summary cases where the defendant has appeared in answer to a summons and has not previously been remanded, may the court simply adjourn.

6.1.2 Length of remands

A magistrates' court can remand in custody for a maximum of 8 clear days. If the defendant is remanded on bail, there is no statutory maximum. There are, however, exceptions to this general rule.

1. Once a defendant has been convicted, he can be remanded for up to three weeks for enquiries (such as pre sentence reports).

2. Before conviction the court can remand for up to 28 days if the defendant has previously been remanded, and he is now before the court, and the court has fixed a date for the next effective hearing: s.128A MCA. (By "effective hearing" the statute means a hearing at which a further step will be taken in the case for example, mode of trial or trial).

3. Finally, if the defendant consents and has legal representation, he may be remanded on up to three consecutive occasions in his absence, but he must then be produced at court.

6.1.3   Custody time limits

These are laid down by s.22 Prosecution of Offences Act 1985. These are the maximum periods for which people may be kept in detention pending the completion of a particular stage in the proceedings. Once a time limit has expired the defendant will have an absolute right to bail unless the prosecution seeks an extension on the time limit (they must show "good and sufficient cause" and that they have acted with "due expedition").

In *R v Manchester Crown Court, ex parte McDonald* [1999] 1 All ER 805 the court reviewed these provisions in the light of article 5 of the ECHR – the right to liberty. The court made clear that the purpose of the provisions is to ensure that the prosecution acts with diligence and expedition. It will be for the prosecution to prove on the balance of probabilities that they have met both the conditions outlined above, even then the court is not required to grant the extension.

[6.2] THE RIGHT TO BAIL

Bail is release from the court subject to a duty to surrender to custody: s.3 Bail Act 1976. A person who fails without reasonable cause to surrender in compliance to their bail commits an offence (s.6 Bail Act) and can be fined or imprisoned. Bail can be unconditional or subject to conditions such as sureties, residence, curfews etc.

s.4 Bail Act provides a prima facie right to bail (i.e. court bail, not police bail) subject to certain exceptions set out below: see 6.2.1. This presumption in favour of bail does not arise post-conviction (unless the case has been adjourned for reports: s.4 (4)). The court must set out its reasons when granting bail if they have done so after the prosecution has opposed bail: s.5(2A) Bail Act.

The question of bail must be considered every time the defendant appears before the court: s.4(2) Bail Act 1976. Where the case is to be adjourned, the court will invite the prosecutor to make representations on bail and they will either object to bail or propose conditional or unconditional bail. The defence have an opportunity to make representations and the court will make such enquiry as is necessary from both parties to ensure that they have sufficient information to make a decision. It is always the decision of the court as to whether bail is granted irrespective of whether the prosecution and defence are in agreement.

6.2.1 Circumstances which reverse the presumption in favour of bail (exceptions to the right to bail)

There are a number of circumstances under the Bail Act 1976 when the presumption in favour of bail is reversed. These are set out below:

Those who have been convicted of a serious offence in the past: s.25 Criminal Justice and Public Order Act 1994 (CJPOA) provides that the court shall not grant bail to anyone charged with murder, manslaughter or a specified list of the most serious offences including rape (or attempts at these) if they have been convicted of any of these in the past *unless there are exceptional circumstances to justify it.*

This provision appears to conflict with the article 5 right to liberty but this has now been addressed by the courts. The House of Lords has ruled that the section simply reminds courts of the particular risks posed by defendants in this situation. If the court is unsure as to whether to grant bail, having had regard to these risks, then the provisions must be read down under s.3 Human Rights Act to provide for the grant of bail: *R (O) v Crown Court at Harrow* [2006] UKHL 42.

Those charged with murder: s.114 Coroners and Justice Act 2008 inserts para 6ZA into Schedule 1, Part 1 of the Bail Act 1976 to provide that a defendant charged with murder may not be granted bail unless the court is of the opinion that there is no significant risk that if released on bail, the defendant would commit an offence that would be likely to cause physical or mental injury to another person. It is important to note also that only a Crown Court judge can grant bail in a murder case: s.115 Coroners and Justice Act 2008. A bail decision in a murder case must be made as soon as reasonably practicable and in any event within 48 hours beginning the day after the defendant's first appearance in the magistrates' court.

Those charged with an offence which carries a maximum sentence of life imprisonment: s.14 CJA 2003 creates a second version of para 2A of the Bail Act 1976 which is currently only in force in relation to offences that carry a maximum sentence of life imprisonment. This provides that where an adult defendant (18 or over) was on police or court bail at the date of the new offence, he may not be granted bail unless he satisfies the court that there is "no significant risk" of his committing another offence if granted bail. This shifts the burden of proof onto the defendant.

s.15 CJA 2003 inserts Schedule 1, Part 1, para 6 of the Bail Act 1976 which creates a further exception to the right to bail where the defendant is charged with an offence carrying life imprisonment. It provides that if an adult defendant (aged 18 or over) who was released on police or court bail in relation to the case, failed to surrender to custody then he may not be granted bail unless the court is satisfied that there is no significant risk that if released on bail he would fail to surrender. The court may disregard this provision if it considers that the there was reasonable cause for the failure to surrender. Again, this shifts the burden on the defendant to satisfy the court.

6.2.2 Drug testing and bail

There is some evidence to indicate that certain criminal offences – particularly theft-related offences – are carried out in order to fund drug addiction. Provisions have been introduced which aim to ensure that those who are linked to the misuse of drugs are required to undergo treatment as a condition of their bail or face the refusal of bail.

The power of the police to test for the presence of specified Class A drugs at the police station, whether at arrest or charge, is set out at 3.5 above. You will recall that a person who tests positive for the presence of the specified drugs (heroin and cocaine/crack) may be required to undergo an assessment of their misuse of drugs. The result of the drugs test and of the assessment will be made available to the court when it considers whether the defendant should be bailed.

Paragraphs 6A–6C of the Bail Act 1976 Sch 1, Part 1 (inserted by s.19 Criminal Justice Act 2003), state that bail may not be granted to an adult offender where the three conditions set out in para 6B apply. The conditions are that

- there is drug test evidence that the person has a specified Class A drug (cocaine, heroin and their derivatives) in his body;
- that the offender has been charged with an offence relating to a class A drug under the Misuse of Drugs Act 1971 s.5 or there are substantial grounds for believing that misuse of a specified Class A drug caused or contributed to the offence, or the offence was motivated by it; and
- that the person does not agree to undertake an assessment into their drug dependency, and to participate in any follow-up treatment.

If the person does not agree to treatment then the court may only grant bail where it is satisfied that there is no significant risk of his committing an offence while on bail. Where an assessment or follow up is proposed and agreed to by the offender, it will become a condition of bail that the person undertakes the assessment or follow up: s.3(6D) Bail Act 1976.

[6.3] REFUSAL OF BAIL – IMPRISONABLE OFFENCES

Even in situations where your client may have a prima facie right to bail under s.4 Bail Act, this does not mean that the court has to grant bail. If your client is charged with an either way or indictable offence which carries a sentence of imprisonment, the right can be displaced on grounds which are set out in Bail Act Schedule 1, Part I.

6.3.1 The Schedule 1 "grounds"

Under Schedule 1, a defendant need not be granted bail in any of the following circumstances:

- there are substantial grounds for believing that if released on bail the defendant:
    i. would fail to surrender to custody;
    ii. would commit an offence on bail; or
    iii. would interfere with witnesses or with the course of justice. (paragraph 2)
- the defendant appears to have committed an indictable or either way offence while on bail for another matter (original paragraph 2A, as inserted by s.26 CJPOA 1994 and amended by s.14 CJA 2003)
- the defendant should be kept in custody for his own protection: (paragraph 3)
- the defendant is already serving a custodial sentence: (paragraph 4)
- it has not been practicable to obtain sufficient information to make a bail decision due to the lack of time since proceedings were commenced: (paragraph 5)
- the defendant has been released on bail (either police or court bail) and fails to surrender to bail or breaches his bail conditions (paragraph 6)

Paragraph 2A grounds: The original paragraph 2A Schedule 1, Part 1 of the Bail Act was inserted by s.26 CJPOA. This has been prospectively repealed by s.14 CJA 2003 which effectively created two versions of paragraph 2A depending on the offence charged.

Therefore, at present, where the offence committed on bail is indictable or either way, this provides grounds to refuse bail (the defendant "need not" be granted bail). Where the new offence carries life imprisonment, the right to bail is removed (the defendant "may not" be granted bail unless the court is satisfied of the matters set out at 6.2.1 above). When the amendment is fully in force (on a date yet to be set), s.14 will have the effect of creating a presumption against bail where a defendant commits an offence on bail.

Paragraph 2 grounds: The most common grounds that will arise are failure to surrender, likely to commit further offences and interfere with witnesses. Always remember that the court must be satisfied that there are "substantial" grounds for believing that one of these is likely to occur. In deciding whether this is the case, the court will consider various factors. These are set out at 6.3.2, below.

Other grounds: The other grounds crop up less commonly. The paragraph 4 ground is self-explanatory. Applications for a defendant to be kept in custody for his own protection, under paragraph 3, may arise in cases which have given rise to a high degree of public anger – especially sexual offences or offences involving children. It is important to point out in such cases that the defendant is likely to be even more vulnerable to retribution if he is remanded into custody. Often the more appropriate solution is a condition of residence outside the immediate area.

Insufficient information: Paragraph 5 will sometimes crop up, particularly where defendants are brought to court within a few hours of being arrested and charged. The provision covers situations where there has been insufficient time to obtain information that is relevant to the bail decision. It is not intended to enable bail to be refused simply because enquiries are continuing into the case generally. If the prosecution argue that the police need more time to check a name or an address, or to check for previous convictions, you will need to argue that any refusal of bail should only be for long enough to carry out these investigations. You should therefore be ready to argue that the matter could be looked at again in an hour or two, allowing the prosecution a further opportunity to complete these basic investigations.

Absconding or breaching bail conditions: Where a defendant was released on bail by either the police or by a court, and he either fails to surrender when required or breaches his bail conditions, he will be liable to arrest under s.7 Bail Act 1974. If it is proved that he absconded (an offence under s.6 BA 1974) or that he breached his bail conditions (not a criminal offence), the court "need not" re-admit him to bail. Once again, this provision has been prospectively repealed by s.15 CJA 2003. At present, this provision applies where the defendant is charged with an offence not carrying life imprisonment. Remember, where the offence that the defendant was released on bail for does carry life imprisonment, the court "may not" grant bail unless the circumstances set out at 6.2.2 above are satisfied. When the amendment comes into force (on a date yet to be set), it will effectively create a presumption against bail where the defendant absconds.

6.3.2   Is there a substantial ground? The paragraph 9 factors.

When the court is considering the grounds in paragraph 2 (failure to surrender, commit further offences, interfere with witnesses) it should consider the following factors listed in paragraph 9, Sch 1, Part 1 Bail Act 1976:

- the nature and seriousness of the offence (and the probable sentence): para 9(a)
- the defendant's character, antecedents, associations and community ties: para 9(b)
- the defendant's previous bail record: para 9(c)
- the strength of the evidence: para 9(d)

- the risk that the defendant may commit an offence on bail which would be likely to cause physical or mental injury to another person (only where the defendant is charged with an offence triable at the Crown Court and the court is satisfied that there are substantial grounds for believing that the defendant would commit an offence while on bail: para 9(e))

- any other relevant matter

Character and antecedents relates not only to whether a person has previous criminal convictions but also to include details of their education, employment and other background information. *Associations* would relate to, for example, gang membership or other people with whom the defendant associates on a regular basis. *Community ties* would cover everything from whether the defendant has a stable address, what family ties they have, any employment ties and so on. The defendant's **previous bail record** will be important if he has absconded in the past as this may be evidence that the offender will do so again. The **strength of the prosecution evidence** relates to whether an offender would rather abscond than face an inevitable conviction and/or prison sentence.

Using the factors: These factors are in fact little more than common sense. If the prosecution is going to argue that there are substantial grounds for believing that a defendant will abscond, obviously the court should look at the defendant's previous bail record. Equally, the court will want to consider the type of person that the defendant is and how close their community ties are. Above all the court will consider whether there is a motive for absconding – in other words, is it a serious offence, and is the evidence against the defendant strong, and is the defendant likely to be sent to prison? Clearly there is a far greater pressure not to attend court where a prison sentence is likely, than if the outcome is going to be a fine.

Factors – not grounds: You must distinguish between the *grounds* for refusal, and the *factors* that can be used to show the grounds are made out. This distinction is critical. It is wrong to say that because a person has absconded in the past, they should now be refused bail. However, it may be correct to say that the fact that they have absconded in the past (factor: previous bail history) shows that there are substantial grounds for believing that they will fail to surrender to custody now (ground), and therefore should be refused bail.

[6.4] BAIL FOR SUMMARY AND NON-IMPRISONABLE OFFENCES

Defendant charged with non-imprisonable offence: Where an offence is not punishable with imprisonment, it is obviously rare for remands in custody to be appropriate. The grounds for refusing bail when a defendant faces a charge which is not imprisonable are set out in Schedule 1 Part II of the Bail Act 1976 as follows:

- Where the accused absconded when he was previously granted bail and the court therefore believes that he would fail to surrender if released on bail (para 2)

- Where it is necessary for the accused's own protection (para 3)

- Where the accused is serving a custodial sentence (para 4)

- Where the accused was previously released on bail and later arrested on warrant (having absconded or breached his bail conditions) and the court therefore considers that if released on bail, the accused would fail to surrender to custody, commit an offence on bail or interfere with witnesses/obstruct the course of justice (para 5)

Defendant charged with summary offence punishable with imprisonment: Where a person is charged with a summary offence which is punishable with imprisonment, part 1A

Schedule 1, Bail Act 1976 (as inserted by Criminal Justice & Immigration Act 2008) will apply. The exceptions to the right to bail in these cases are as set out above for non-imprisonable offences with the following additions:

- Where the accused was on bail on the date of the current offence and the court is satisfied that there are substantial grounds for believing that he would commit an offence on bail if released

- Where the court is satisfied that there are substantial grounds for believing that the accused would commit an offence on bail by engaging in conduct that would cause physical/mental injury to another, or cause someone to fear such injury

- Where there has been insufficient time to obtain sufficient information to make a bail decision

[6.5] BAIL CONDITIONS

Bail conditions can be imposed to ensure the defendant surrenders to custody, does not commit further offences on bail, does not interfere with witnesses and makes himself available for reports. Conditions can also be imposed where necessary for the defendant's own protection: s.13 CJA 2003. The most common conditions will be sureties, residence, reporting, curfews, and exclusion from a particular area. An electronic monitoring condition for the purpose of ensuring that bail conditions are being adhered to can also be imposed providing certain conditions are met: s.51 & Schedule11 Criminal Justice and Immigration Act 2008. When bail conditions are imposed they can subsequently be varied providing written notice is given to the court where you intend to apply at least 24hrs in advance of the hearing: Part 19.1 CrPR.

6.5.1 Sureties

A surety is a person who guarantees that the defendant will attend court. The surety puts up a sum of money (a recognisance) which will normally be forfeited ("estreated") if the defendant absconds.

The court will not automatically accept a person as a surety but will have regard to their financial resources, whether the surety is of good character and the degree of proximity between surety and defendant. The court will not only want to ensure that the surety has the resources to pay the recognisance, they will also want to be sure that the surety is in sufficiently close contact with the defendant to be able to ensure that he attends the court. It is best if you can arrange for a surety to attend court at the bail application. You can then call them as a witness and examine them as to their suitability. If they are unable to attend court, it is possible for sureties to be taken at police stations and at prisons.

Can you stand surety for your client? The 2011 Code of Conduct is silent on this specific issue however you should remember Principle 2 requires you to act with integrity and Principle 3 states that you should not allow your independence to be compromised. Outcome 3.4 relating to conflicts of interests states you must not act if there is an own interest conflict or a significant risk of an own interest conflict (an own interest conflict is a conflict between you and a current client or clients). Standing surety for your client would create a potential for a conflict to arise between your duty to the client to keep matters confidential (outcome 4.1) and your duty as surety to the court to ensure that any information about the risk of failure to surrender is conveyed to the court. As clients can be unpredictable, standing surety for your client is likely to fall foul of these duties.

6.5.2 Residence and reporting

As with sureties, these are primarily conditions to ensure that the defendant does not abscond. They can be imposed separately or together. Residence requires the defendant to reside at a specified address. Reporting requires the defendant to report to a police station at specified times: these may vary from once a week, to twice a day, depending on the court's assessment of the risk of absconding.

6.5.3 Curfews, tagging, bail hostels and exclusion conditions

These conditions are usually directed at the prevention of further offending, and sometimes to prevent any possible interference with witnesses. A curfew requires the defendant to be home between certain hours (and is often used where the allegation is one of night-time burglary, for example). Such a "doorstep condition" requires the defendant to present himself at the door of his house when required to do so by a police officer in order to check compliance with a curfew. The Criminal Justice and Immigration Act 2008 s.51 (and Schedule 11) allows for the imposition of an electronically monitored curfew. This can only be imposed where the court is satisfied that the defendant (aged over 17 years) would not be granted bail without the electronic tag and there is provision available for the tag to be monitored. Note that time spent on an electronic curfew as part of a bail condition can be taken into account when calculating the time to be served as part of a sentence of imprisonment. You should consider asking the court to impose electronic monitoring in a situation where the court wishes to impose a curfew and your client is likely to receive a sentence of imprisonment in his case: see chapter 10.

Bail hostels are often attractive to courts because they provide a fixed address and a curfew. However, there is always pressure on bail hostel places and hostels can be reluctant to accept clients who are violent or who have problems with drink or drugs. You should therefore secure a place at a hostel before proposing this as a condition to the court.

Exclusion may be exclusion from a particular area, or a condition excluding a person from contacting particular individuals, especially the victim and other witnesses. In agreeing to an exclusion order, make sure that your client can comply with it. Does he, for example, have to come into a town centre in order to sign on?

6.5.4 Surrender of passport and the taking of a security

Both of these conditions are aimed at preventing the defendant from leaving the country. A security is where the defendant himself puts up a sum of money by way of a guarantee. You can therefore consider this where there is no suitable surety, or in addition to a surety. In contrast to a surety, with a security a sum of money is actually lodged at court.

6.5.5 Attending appointments

The court can impose a bail condition that the defendant attends an interview with his solicitor. You will need, however, to bear in mind your duty of confidentiality if asked by the court whether he has complied with this – and your duty not to mislead the court, which means that you would have to cease acting if the defendant lies to the court about attending. Because of these potential difficulties this is not a condition which is widely used.

As noted above, where the defendant has tested positive for class A drugs as a result of a mandatory test at the police station and he has been offered an assessment or follow up treatment, then if he agrees to that assessment/treatment, the court must impose attendance for this as a condition of bail: s.3(6C)-(6E) Bail Act 1976.

Equally, after conviction, the court can impose a bail condition that an offender makes himself available for the purpose of enquiries or reports to be completed: s.3(6)(d) Bail Act 1976.

6.5.6 Consequences of failure to attend

Failure to answer bail will have serious consequences for your client, and you may need to spell these out. First, failure to surrender is an imprisonable offence under s.6 of the Bail Act 1976. In *R v Evans* [2011] EWCA Crim 2842, the defendant arrived at Crown Court and presented himself to his lawyer. Later in the morning he left the court building, and he was subsequently found guilty of failing to surrender to bail. The Court held that in the absence of an arrangement peculiar to a particular court venue (e.g. a requirement to sign in at the main desk), then surrender at the Crown Court is achieved by presenting yourself to the custody officers at the dock or where you formally identify yourself in court. Surrender in the magistrates' court is likely to be the same.

The sentencing guidelines for failing to surrender suggests that the starting point for a deliberate failure to attend which causes delay will be 14 days imprisonment. Late attendance will attract a financial penalty. The sentencing of a Bail Act offence should not be delayed until the conclusion of the proceedings.

Secondly, failure to surrender will often mean that bail is not re-granted (and indeed will often lead to the refusal of bail in any later cases): see 6.2.1 in relation to defendants charged with an offence carrying life imprisonment. Finally, your client may be tried in his absence if he fails to attend: see 9.3.1.

Too sick to attend? Guidance from the Senior Presiding Judge suggests that an ordinary sick note from a doctor is unlikely to be sufficient as they normally relate to the person's ability to work. A letter to the court in advance of the hearing specifically stating that the defendant is too ill to attend court will be needed.

[6.6] HOW DO YOU APPLY FOR BAIL?

Making an application for bail is often one of the earliest pieces of advocacy in the criminal process. The client will be present, or at the other end of a video link. Bail is enormously important to most clients, and solicitors will often be judged on how successful they have been in getting bail. If so, you should also enquire on what grounds the prosecution intend to oppose bail. This will allow you to take appropriate instructions and address the court effectively.

6.6.1 Making a bail application

Bail will almost invariably need to be dealt with at the defendant's first appearance at court. You should always find the CPS representative who is dealing with your case and ask whether there is going to be any objection to bail. If so, you should also enquire on what grounds the prosecution intend to oppose bail. This will allow you to take appropriate instructions and address the court effectively.

Uncontested applications: Where the defendant has been released on police bail and subsequently attends court, it is obviously harder for the prosecution to argue that he should be refused bail. Indeed, where the defendant has been on bail in proceedings without any breaches, he should expect to be re-admitted to bail after he attends court unless one of the statutory grounds has been made out by the prosecution: *R (Fergus) v Southampton Crown Court* [2008] EWHC 3273 (Admin).

In cases where the police have refused bail, the CPS may have no objection once they have looked through the papers. In such cases, provided the prosecution agrees to the grant of bail, you will normally merely need to inform the court that bail is applied for and that the prosecution has no objections. It is possible, but unlikely, that in the absence of prosecution concerns, the court will raise any major issues.

Contested applications: In a contested application the prosecution will start by putting forward its objections. The prosecutor will need to outline briefly the facts of the case, and will then make clear on what grounds he or she objects to bail being granted. The Bench will generally have no papers relating to the case, and the prosecutor may hand up a list of your client's previous convictions. The prosecution will outline the facts of the case and point to any matters that give rise to concerns.

Evidence at bail applications: Bail hearings are not a trial and the formal rules of evidence do not apply. In some cases, especially high profile cases, the prosecutor may actually call the investigating officer to give evidence about the case. Do not indulge in a lengthy cross-examination.

The defence application: The defence will then make their application. You should focus on ensuring that you answer the prosecution objections. You may need to start by indicating which facts are agreed and where your client denies involvement at all. It is also worth identifying those cases where your client retains a prima facie right to bail. You will want to remind the court that the onus is on the prosecution to displace that right to bail.

Structuring the defence argument: You should then focus on each of the grounds put forward by the prosecution. You should not normally bother to deal with matters that have not been raised. In relation to each ground, show that the factors relied upon by the prosecution do not in fact apply (your client does have good "community ties" as he has a job and lives with his parents, for example). Where the prosecution has put forward a strong argument on one factor (your client is likely to abscond as he is facing a prison sentence) be ready to show why other factors may displace this. For example, you may argue that the evidence against him is weak, and he has already put forward a convincing defence when questioned by the police.

Deal with each prosecution ground in turn. Be thorough, but be concise. Normally, your application should not exceed three or four minutes. Make sure that you clearly identify each ground, and then show why it is not in fact a matter of concern. If no grounds are made out, then your client should be granted unconditional bail. (An example of a defence bail application is included at Document 6 in the case study.)

Should you offer the court conditions? The prima facie right to bail is a right to unconditional bail. However, it is also true to say that invariably clients are prepared to agree to almost any conditions which will ensure that they are released from custody. If you are unsure as to whether you have convinced the Bench, you may need to ask. *"That, Madam, is my application for unconditional bail. Would you and your colleagues wish me to address you further as to conditions?"*

6.6.2 How often can you apply for bail?

If the defendant makes a bail application at his first appearance, and it is refused he gets a second go at the next appearance even if he is advancing the same arguments that he put forward at the initial bail application: para 2, Part IIA, Schedule I Bail Act 1976. Unless the defendant agrees to being remanded in his absence at the next hearing, it will take place within 8 clear days: s.128(6) MCA 1980. If bail is refused at this subsequent hearing, the court may not hear any further applications for bail which are based on the same facts or law: para 3, Part IIA, Sch I, Bail Act 1976. You must therefore look for a change in circumstances to permit any further applications for bail.

If the defendant does not make an application at his first appearance, he can subsequently make one application at any later appearance. Once the defendant has had his first hearing and one further hearing, the court will only hear a further application for bail if there has been a change of circumstances. Therefore by choosing not to make a bail application at the first hearing, the defendant loses one opportunity. Note that a paragraph 5 remand (on the basis that there is insufficient information to make a decision) is not a decision not to grant bail: *R v Calder Justices ex parte Kennedy* (1992) 156 JP 716.

Any subsequent hearing will require 24 hours written notice to be submitted to both the prosecution and the court of your intention to make a bail application: Part 19, CrPR.

[6.7] REFUSAL OF BAIL – "APPEALS"

Where bail is refused following a fully argued bail application, the magistrates will issue a "certificate of full argument". There is no right of appeal against the refusal as such, however the defendant may apply for bail to the Crown Court.

6.7.1 Defence appeals to the Crown Court

An application to the Crown Court must be by way of written notice to the prosecutor at least 24 hours before the hearing on the specified form: Part 19 CrPR. You must set out the details of previous bail applications, along with the nature and grounds of the current application, details of sureties and of any previous convictions. The hearing will be in chambers (so that trainee solicitors will have rights of audience) and is a hearing *de novo*.

6.7.2 Indictable only cases where bail has been refused by the magistrates' court:

Because of the system under s.51 Crime and Disorder Act, under which "indictable only" cases are sent "forthwith" to the Crown Court after one initial appearance in the magistrates' court, there is sometimes some confusion over the status of any bail hearing at the first Crown Court appearance. Some judges are treating this as an appeal hearing – and are requiring the defence to give notice and serve relevant documents; the defence on the other hand are arguing that this is the second bail application (the first having been at the first hearing in the magistrates' court) and that they are entitled to it as of right under the Bail Act – in other words, it is not an appeal at all. This appears to be the case under s.81(1)(a) Supreme Court Act 1981 which allows the Crown court to grant bail to any person who has been sent to it in custody without a previous application having been made in the magistrates' Court. It may be safer to give notice and complete the relevant forms if you are going to have to apply for bail in the Crown Court. This application is covered by any existing representation order.

6.7.3 Crown Court powers

The Crown Court has wide powers to grant or to vary bail. Where conditional bail has been granted in the magistrates' court the Crown Court has the power to vary conditions which relate to residence, exclusion, sureties and securities, curfew and electronic monitoring.

6.7.4 Judicial Review and bail:

It is possible to apply to the Administrative Court for a judicial review of a refusal to grant bail, or in respect of bail conditions imposed, by a judge in the Crown Court. This is a relatively new development and the principles are still developing: see *R (M) v Isleworth Crown*

Court [2005] EWHC 363 (Admin). The test will be *Wednesbury* unreasonableness, and the court has indicated that its power to intervene will be exercised sparingly.

6.7.5 Prosecution appeals following the grant of bail

The prosecution has the power to appeal to the Crown Court against the grant of bail in any offence which is imprisonable, provided that the CPS have made previous representations against the grant of bail.

The procedural requirements are set out in Part 19 CrPR. The prosecution has to give immediate oral notice of its intention to appeal, and must confirm that in writing served on the defendant within 2 hours. The Crown Court must then hear the matter within 48 hours (excluding weekends and Bank holidays). Note also that the prosecution can apply for the court to "reconsider" the grant of bail in either way or indictable offences if it has fresh information: s.5B Bail Act.

The Legal Aid, Sentencing and Punishment of Offenders Act 2012 contains provisions which permit the Prosecution to appeal against a Crown Court bail decision where they believe the defendant to be dangerous or that he might flee the country. At the time of writing, these provisions were not yet in force.

[6.8] HUMAN RIGHTS ISSUES

Caselaw from the European Court of Human Rights indicates that bail is not a matter that gives rise to fair trial rights (under article 6 of the Convention). Rather, bail is a matter which concerns article 5, the right to liberty. As article 5 provides that any deprivation of liberty must be tested before a court, this has led to the importation of certain "due process" rights – most important of which is the concept of "equality of arms".

6.8.1 The HRA and the law of bail:

Convention case law makes clear that while a defendant can be refused bail on the basis that he will offend if granted bail, the prosecution must show that any likely offence would be a serious one, that the danger of the offence being committed is "plausible" and that detention is an appropriate measure to deal with the risk. Where the defendant has only minor previous convictions, or (presumably) where those convictions are particularly stale, it may be hard to show that there is a "plausible" risk, and that detention (rather than the imposition of conditional bail) is the appropriate measure.

6.8.2 The HRA and bail procedures:

A full and fair opportunity to put the case: In *R (on the application of the DPP) v Havering Magistrates Court* [2001] 2 Cr App R 2 the Divisional Court was asked to consider the effect of an allegation of breach of conditions of bail under s.7(5) Bail Act. The court made clear that Bail Act proceedings were governed by article 5. It was therefore essential that the defendant had a full and fair opportunity to comment on and to answer any material before the court.

A limited right to disclosure: *Havering Magistrates* was followed in a later custody time limits case, *Wildman v DPP* ([2001] Crim LR 565), where the court confirmed that while full pre-trial disclosure of information was not appropriate prior to a bail hearing, the prosecution would need to make such disclosure as was necessary for equality of arms at that hearing to be preserved. However, in both cases, the courts made clear that bail hearings are of their nature often emergency hearings, and it is not appropriate to import the full panoply of fair trial rights.

The right to be present at a bail hearing: In *Allen v United Kingdom 18837/06* [2010] ECHR 420 (30 March 2010), the defendant was granted bail at the magistrates' court but the prosecution exercised its right to appeal against that decision. The appeal was heard at Liverpool Crown Court and Counsel for the defendant, having arranged for his client to be produced at court, requested that she be present for the hearing. The Judge presiding refused this request. It was held by the European Court of Human Rights that this was a violation of Article 5(4) and the defendant was awarded compensation. This is an interesting decision in light of the drive towards video link courts.

BAIL – GENERAL

Bail is release from court subject to a duty to surrender to custody (Bail Act s.3). Failure to surrender at the correct time and place is an offence (BA s.6).

s.4 Bail Act gives a presumption in favour of bail. Exceptions: (i) murder-manslaughter-rape, where there is a previous conviction for murder-manslaughter-rape: bail only in exceptional circumstances; (ii) after conviction (in some circumstances): no presumption; (iii) charged with offence carrying life imprisonment and already on bail: bail only if no significant risk; (iv) If already on bail or previously failed to surrender where charged with offence carrying life imprisonment (bail only where no significant risk); (v) murder (no bail unless no significant risk of committing offence likely to cause physical or mental injury to another).

PROCEDURE

- Prosecution objections (hand up criminal record).
- Defence arguments in favour.
- Bench decides.
- Remand date set.
- Remand on bail or in custody.
- Record of decision made.

NON-IMPRISONABLE & SUMMMARY OFFENCES

Generally grant bail except in specified situations:
- Sched 1, Pt II BA – rules for non-imprisonable offences
- Sched 1, Pt IA BA – rules for summary imprisonable offences.

GROUNDS FOR REFUSING BAIL

<u>Substantial</u> grounds for believing that the defendant would:
- fail to surrender
- commit further offences
- interfere with witnesses or obstruct course of justice

Other grounds (own protection, insufficient information).

FACTORS

- Nature and seriousness of offence and likely sentence;
- Character, antecedents, community ties etc.;
- Bail record;
- Strength of evidence;
- Risk of causing physical/mental injury to another (where court satisfied of risk of further offending)
- Any other relevant matter.

CONDITIONS

- Sureties/Securities
- Reporting/Residence/Curfew/Electronic monitoring (tag)
- Others (e.g. exclusion, attending solicitor).

APPEALS

First appearance and one further application: any argument for bail. Thereafter application only if there is a new argument/change of circumstances. Court will issue certificate of full argument.

Defence can appeal to Crown Court. Chambers application. Hearing de novo. Can appeal against conditions on bail. Prosecution can appeal to Crown Court against allowing bail where the offence is punishable with imprisonment.

Possible right to apply to the High Court by way of judicial review.

Bail – test yourself questions

[The answers to these questions are set out in Appendix A at the back of this book]

[1] Consider the following cases:

   i. Paul has been arrested for theft. He has six previous convictions for robbery, and two related firearms offences. He has three previous convictions for failing to attend court when bailed. At the time of his arrest he was not on bail.

   ii. Les has been arrested for robbery. He has no previous convictions, but he is on police bail in relation to an alleged taking of a vehicle without consent.

   iii. Bob has been arrested for rape. He has a previous conviction for manslaughter. He was not on bail at the time of his arrest.

   Which of the above defendants will have a prima facie right to bail?

   (a) None of them.

   (b) Bob only.

   (c) Paul and Bob.

   (d) Paul only.

   (e) Les only.

[2] Which of the following is NOT a ground for refusing bail under Schedule 1, Part 1 Bail Act?

   (a) There are substantial grounds for believing that the defendant would commit an offence while on bail.

   (b) The defendant has previous convictions for failure to attend court when granted bail.

   (c) The defendant should be kept in custody for his own protection.

   (d) There has been insufficient time to obtain information to make a bail decision.

[3] Johnny has been charged with eight counts of burglary. All the offences relate to domestic premises which have been burgled during early hours of the morning. All the offences have taken place on a housing estate near Johnny's home. Johnny has two previous convictions, both for burglary. He also has a previous conviction for failing to attend court when bailed to do so.

   Consider the following bail conditions:

   i. A curfew.

   ii. Reporting to the police station.

   iii. A surety.

   iv. Residence at an agreed address.

   v. Not to go within 100 yards of the housing estate.

Which of the above conditions are likely to be appropriate in Johnny's case?

(a) All of them.

(b) i, ii and v only.

(c) ii, iii, iv and v only.

(d) iii and v only.

[4] Suad is charged with burglary of a dwelling house (a trigger offence for the purpose of s.19 CIA 2003). She has tested positive for the presence of Class A drugs when tested at the police station. Which one of the following propositions is correct in relation to bail?

(a) Bail can only be granted if Suad agrees to undergo any necessary assessment and then to participate in follow up treatment.

(b) Bail can only be granted if Suad agrees to undergo any necessary assessment and then to participate in follow up treatment or if the court is satisfied that there is in fact no significant risk of her committing an offence while on bail.

(c) Bail cannot be granted where there has been a trigger offence and the person has then tested positive for the presence of specified Class A drugs.

(d) None of the above is correct.

[5] Simone has been charged with fraud, an offence carrying a maximum of 10 years if tried in the Crown Court. The prosecution opposed bail on the basis that she is highly likely to abscond as they believe she has used the proceeds of her crime to buy a large house in Sri Lanka. Bail was granted by the magistrates but with a condition of residence and with an exclusion from the city centre. She wishes to appeal against the exclusion condition. The prosecution wish to appeal against the grant of bail.

Which one of the following propositions is correct?

(a) Simone may appeal as of right to the Crown Court because fraud is an either way offence.

(b) Simone may apply to the High Court by way of judicial review for leave to appeal against the refusal of bail.

(c) The prosecution can appeal to the Crown Court against the grant of bail provided that they comply with the notice requirements since the offence is imprisonable.

(d) Simone cannot appeal against the imposition of a condition; she must make a fresh application to the magistrates for the conditions to be varied.

CHAPTER 7

INTERIM HEARINGS AND DISCLOSURE

> This chapter covers:
>
> The pre-trial process after the initial hearing
>
> Case management under the Criminal Procedure Rules
>
> Interim hearings in criminal proceedings
>
> Disclosure rules

[7.1] CASE MANAGEMENT BY THE COURTS

The Criminal Procedure (Amendment) Rules 2011 came into force on 2nd April 2012, repealing the previous rules in place and introducing new changes. The Criminal Procedure Rules (CrPR) were first introduced in 2005 and they set, for the first time in the criminal process, an overriding objective that all parties to a case must comply with. The CrPR also provide detailed powers for the courts to manage cases. The rules apply to all cases in the magistrates' courts, Crown Courts and in the Criminal Division of the Court of Appeal. A duty is imposed on every person involved in a criminal case to comply with the overriding objective and each party must actively assist the court in its management of the case.

7.1.1 The overriding objective

The overriding objective of this new code is that criminal cases be dealt with justly: CrPR1.1(1)

The rules then state that dealing with the case justly includes: CrPR 1.1(2)

(a) acquitting the innocent and convicting the guilty;

(b) dealing with the prosecution and the defence fairly;

(c) recognising the rights of the defendant, particularly those under Article 6 of the European Convention on Human Rights;

(d) respecting the interests of witnesses, victims and jurors and keeping them informed of the progress of the case;

(e) dealing with the case efficiently and expeditiously;

(f) ensuring that appropriate information is available to the court when bail and sentence are considered; and

(g) dealing with the case in ways that take into account –

    i. the gravity of the offence alleged,

> ii. *the complexity of what is in issue,*
>
> iii. *the severity of the consequences for the defendant and others affected; and*
>
> iv. *the needs of other cases.*

7.1.2 Case management

Part 3 of the Rules deals with case management. By CrPR 3.2(1) there is a duty on the court to further the overriding objective by actively managing the case. Active case management is then defined as including: CrPR 3.2(2)

> *(a) The early identification of the real issues*
>
> *(b) The early identification of the needs of witnesses*
>
> *(c) Setting a timetable for the progress of the case with certainty as to who is to do what*
>
> *(d) Monitoring the progress of the case and compliance with directions*
>
> *(e) Ensuring that evidence is presented in the shortest and clearest way*
>
> *(f) Discouraging delay and avoiding unnecessary hearings*
>
> *(g) Encouraging the participants to co-operate in the progression of the case*
>
> *(h) Making use of technology*

CrPR3.3 then sets out the duty of the parties – namely that each party must actively assist the court in fulfilling its duty of active case management; and apply for a direction if needed to further the overriding objective. The duty imposed by CrPR3.3 on defence solicitors is therefore one of active assistance with the management of the case – including those matters set out in CrPR3.2, such as early identification of "the real issues" which should ordinarily be put in writing (CrPR 3.5).

A key issue is the extent to which the Criminal Procedure Rules alter the traditional adversarial nature of court proceedings by requiring the defence to give notice to the prosecution of weaknesses or flaws in the prosecution case. The defence are obviously reluctant to do this, but the appellate courts often seem to be using the case management elements of the Criminal Procedure Rules to insist that such a duty now exists.

In *Malcolm v Director of Public Prosecutions* [2007] EWHC 363 the defence advocate did not raise a point about a technical defect in the prosecution's case (failure to give evidence as to whether a warning had been given) until her closing speech. The magistrates found for her on this point, but then (even though they had retired to give their verdict) permitted the prosecution to adduce further evidence to address the point – and convicted Ms. Malcolm. On appeal the Divisional Court asserted the duty of the defence to make clear its case:

> *In my judgment, Miss Calder's submissions, which emphasised the obligation of the prosecution to prove its case in its entirety before closing its case, and certainly before end of the final speech for the defence, had an anachronistic, and obsolete, ring. Criminal trials are no longer to be treated as a game, in which each move is final and any omission by the prosecution leads to its failure. It is the duty of the defence to make its defence and the issues it raises clear to the prosecution and to the court at an early stage. That duty is implicit in rule 3.3 of the Criminal Procedure Rules, which requires the parties actively to assist the exercise by the court of its case management powers, the exercise of which requires early identification of the real issues. Even in a relatively straightforward trial such as the present, in the magistrates' court (where there is not yet any requirement of a defence statement or a pre-trial review), it is the duty of the defence to make the real issues clear at the latest before the prosecution closes its case.*

More recently, in *R v Penner* [2010] EWCA Crim 1155, the defence made a point about the absence of a warning that there would be a prosecution (in a road traffic matter requiring such a notice to be given) without giving prior notice to the Crown about that omission. While the appeal failed for different reasons, it was made clear that this was not acceptable.

Progressing the case: CrPR 3.4 requires all parties (including the defence) to appoint case progression officers who can account to the court for the progress of the case, and the court has wide powers to give directions, whether on application or of its own motion. The magistrates' court is given the power to make directions which will apply even when the case is to proceed in the Crown Court, and the reverse also applies. Finally the court is given extensive powers to require the parties to give information so as to ensure readiness for trial and the effective management of the trial.

Sanctions for non-compliance: Rule 3.5(6) gives courts a power to impose sanctions for failure, including the making of costs orders. One particular issue of concern to solicitors is that they may be wrongly criticised by the courts for failing to comply with directions when in fact the reason for the default has been some failure by their client, or some very recent change of instructions (for example) which has led to the delay. The duty of confidentiality to the client – and indeed in some circumstances legal privilege itself – will often make it impossible for the solicitor to explain that the apparent failure to comply is not their fault.

[7.2] SUMMARY TRIAL: Pre trial hearings and case management

Following a not guilty plea at the first hearing before the magistrates' court in a case to be tried summarily (i.e. a summary only or either way offence being tried at the magistrates' court), the case will immediately be adjourned to a trial date. Remember that the CJSSS process expects all contested cases in the magistrates' courts to be fully caase managed at the first hearing and disposed of at the second hearing.

In light of these case management duties, along with those imposed by the Criminal Procedure Rules (CrPR 3.2), the court will be actively managing the progress of the case in readiness for trial. This will mean that a case progression officer is appointed by the court to keep in contact with all parties (CrPR 3.4) and it may exercise any of its case management powers within the rules which include the power to make directions for disclosure (CrPR 3.5). Both prosecution and defence are under a duty to actively assist the court in fulfilling its case management duties (CrPR 3.3) and all parties must ensure that they comply with any directions made by the Court.

Case management hearings: On occasion, the court will arrange for a case management hearing to take place prior to the trial date. This is usually the case where there are matters of law or procedure which need to be considered prior to the trial which may affect the ability of the trial to go ahead on the date set. For example, the prosecution may wish to make an application prior to trial to adduce bad character evidence or hearsay evidence (see Chapters 17 and 18) or there may be witness availability issues to resolve and these matters can be dealt with at such a hearing. Where the court makes directions in order to case manage a trial, it is important that you adhere to them where possible or risk a wasted costs order being made against you: see 4.2.2.

There exists a power for the magistrates to make binding rulings on any issue relating to the admissibility of evidence or any question of law at a pre-trial hearing: s8A–8B Magistrates Court Act 1980 as inserted by Schedule 3 Courts Act 2003. Where the court makes a ruling on such issues prior to trial, the ruling will be binding on the court that hears the trial unless it is in the interests of justice to review it.

Pre- trial matters to consider: Summary trials are designed to be straightforward criminal cases therefore matters to be considered between a not guilty plea and trial are equally straightforward. Alongside the disclosure requirements (see 7.5 below), you should ensure that you take full instructions from your client, take any witness statements and consider any matters of law that may need to be dealt with before the trial takes place (e.g. bad character applications, hearsay applications etc).

[7.3] TRIAL ON INDICTMENT: Pre trial hearings and case management

Trial on indictment occurs in either way offences (either committed under committal procedures or sent to the Crown Court under the allocation process) or indictable only offences sent to Crown Court under s.51 CDA 1988. There are a number of potential pre-trial hearings that may take place prior to a trial on indictment: the plea and case management hearing (PCMH) which will take place in every case; preparatory hearings, which are confined to "long or complex" cases and preliminary hearings that assist with case management in certain cases. The choice of pre-trial hearings is determined by the way in which the case came to be before the Crown Court for trial.

7.3.1 Pre-trial hearings:

Indictable only offences and either ways offences sent under the CJA allocation procedure: Following the first hearing in the magistrates' court, the case may be listed at the Crown Court for a preliminary hearing. The preliminary hearing will be held at the Crown Court within fourteen days of the case having been sent by the magistrates' court if it is considered necessary to hold one for case management purposes. This can also be done in cases where there is expected to be a lengthy or particularly complex trial, or one involving a young defendant. In these situations, the Magistrates will direct that there be a preliminary hearing so that further directions can be given by the judge to assist with the case management. For further details see IV.41.3 Consolidated Criminal Practice Direction and Part 15 Criminal Procedure Rules. The case will progress to a Plea and Case Management Hearing (PCMH) no more than 17 weeks after the initial sending (or 14 weeks for a client in custody), and thereafter, the case will be listed for trial.

Either way offences committed to Crown Court: Any either way offence committed to Crown Court under s.6 MCA 1980 and therefore dealt with under the pre-CJA committal procedure will have a formal committal hearing that takes place at the magistrates' court before the case progresses to the Crown Court: see 5.4.1.3 for details of the committal hearing. Thereafter, the next hearing will be the Plea and Case Management Hearing which takes place at the Crown Court no more than 7 weeks after the committal. Following this, the case will be listed for trial.

Pre-trial matters to consider: In either case, as the matter is proceeding to trial on indictment, only a suitably qualified advocate may conduct the hearings in the Crown Court. With that in mind, you must ensure that you brief Counsel or a Solicitor Advocate in plenty of time so that they are prepared to deal with the case. For details on how to prepare a brief, see 7.4 below. As is the case in summary proceedings, you should also ensure that you take a proof from your client, take witness statements and consider any points of law to be raised. These matters should be seen to prior to the PCMH in all cases. Full details on preparing for trial are considered in chapter 9.

Plea and Case Management Hearings (PCMHs)

The PCMH will take place in every case to be tried on Indictment. It is an opportunity to identify how the defendant will plead to the charge ('the arraignment') and for the court to hand down detailed case management directions. The hearing should take place about 14 weeks after sending the case to the Crown Court if the defendant is in custody (17 weeks if on bail). Where there has been a committal, the period is reduced to 7 weeks, as the prosecution will have already had substantial time to prepare the case for the magistrates' court committal proceedings.

Not Guilty pleas at PCMH: Following a not guilty plea at the PCMH, the case management form must be completed by the advocates at the PCMH and submitted to the judge. The form is long and is designed to address the minds of the parties and of the court to all the potential issues in the case. It covers everything from special measures for witnesses, any need for interpreters, listing the case, evidential issues, arrangements for the provision and playing of video evidence and so on. An example of the form is set out at Document 20 in the case study. At the end of the PCMH, the judge will fix a suitable date for the trial. If for any reason a date cannot be fixed, then the trial will be placed in the "warned list" with other trials awaiting hearing. This means that when a date becomes available, the court will contact the prosecution and defence who will then secure the attendance of all parties.

The intention is that the PCMH will be attended by the advocate who will be doing the trial, or an advocate with the ability to take decisions on the case. The purpose is to reduce the number of ineffective or delayed trials.

Binding rulings at PCMH: Under s.40 CPIA 1996 there is a power for judges to make binding legal rulings at the pre trial hearing on any question as to the admissibility of evidence or any other question of law relating to the case. Note that in contrast to rulings made in preparatory hearings (see below) there is no appeal from a s.40 ruling and it will be binding at the trial.

Guilty pleas at PCMH: If your client pleads guilty at PCMH, then the judge can either immediately pass sentence, or adjourn for pre-sentence reports. If an adjournment is required, your client will either be released on bail or remanded in custody. If your client pleads guilty but disputes certain aspects of the prosecution evidence, then the case will adjourn for a "Newton hearing". At a Newton hearing, the judge will hear both the prosecution and defence version of events and decide upon which factual basis he intends to sentence.

Preparatory Hearings

Preparatory hearings are a more formal version of the PCMH. In contrast to the PCMH (which is a pre-trial hearing), the preparatory hearing is usually at the start of the trial. Preparatory hearings are available in any long or complex case where the trial judge thinks that they may be of use. The judge at the preparatory hearing can make binding rulings on matters of law and (in contrast to the normal PCMH rulings) an interlocutory appeal to the Court of Appeal is possible. Part 15 of the Criminal Procedure Rules 2011 deals with applications to hold preparatory hearings and the related procedures.

7.3.2 Compliance with directions

Pre-trial hearings will normally require directions to be made and you must comply with the standard directions set out in Part 3 of the Criminal Procedure Rules 2011 and para IV.41 of the Consolidated Criminal Practice Direction. There are also timescales to be observed under the Criminal Procedure and Investigations Act 1996. The various deadlines set by the directions will vary according to whether the case was transferred under s.51, committed under s.6 MCA 1980 or sent to the Crown Court under the CJA allocation process (considered the same as the s.51 procedure).

Getting defence witnesses to court: In addition to complying with the directions you will need to consider whether the defence needs any particular orders from the court. If you have concerns about whether a particular defence witness will attend for trial, you will normally apply to the court for a witness order. Applications for witness orders are governed by Part 28 Criminal Procedure Rules, which sets out the requirements for both oral and paper applications.

[7.4] BRIEFING COUNSEL

Solicitors have limited rights of audience in the Crown Court and unless the solicitor has a qualification for higher rights of audience, he must instruct a barrister to represent the client at any case to be heard in the Crown Court. The instructions, or "brief" as it is more commonly known, are prepared and sent immediately after the committal/transfer hearing.

Briefing an advocate to conduct the trial does not mean that you cease to be responsible for the case. The responsibility for the case remains with you, but will be shared by the advocate. You will have had the contact with the client and will understand the nature of the case and of the defence that is being put forward. The advocate may well have their own thoughts about how they feel the case should be progressed, but the solicitor and the advocate will work together and the final decisions on the case are always decisions for the client to take.

It is usual to also arrange a brief meeting (known as a conference) with the barrister at some point between sending the brief and the PCMH. Usually the conference will take place at the barrister's chambers and either the instructed solicitor or his representative will attend with the client. The conference allows an opportunity for your client to meet the barrister in more informal surroundings, rather than meeting him for the first time at the Crown Court. This is also an opportunity for general discussion about the case, and often the barrister will flag up any issues that may require work prior to the trial, e.g. obtaining further witness statements, obtaining photographs of the scene etc.

Counsel or solicitor advocate: In the following sections I have referred to briefing "counsel" (i.e. a barrister), although of course you may be briefing a solicitor advocate. The majority of Crown Court work is still done by the Bar and until there are more solicitor advocates with higher courts qualifications it is likely that you will be briefing a barrister: the points below reflect this.

Payment of counsel: In publicly funded cases, counsel will make his/her own claim for payment directly to the court, assuming that legal aid has covered the use of counsel (as inevitably it will for Crown Court matters). Remember that if you wish to use counsel in the magistrates' court, for example to have a barrister cover a particularly tricky trial, this will not normally be covered by the representation order, and you will need to make your own arrangements with counsel's clerk for the fee to be paid.

Attending counsel at court: Traditionally there has been an expectation that a solicitor or paralegal would attend Crown Court trials with the advocate. Indeed until relatively recently it was a breach of the Bar's professional conduct rules for a barrister to appear in the Crown Court without an accompanying solicitor's representative. The role of the representative was in part to keep a note of the evidence (something it is not easy to do while you are on your feet examining the witnesses), but also to liaise with defence witnesses, reassure the defendant and deal with the million unforeseen crises that crop up in the average trial.

Over the last decade changes to the legal aid rules have made it harder to fund a solicitor's representative attending court with the advocate. The new litigator graduated fee (LGF) regime means that the cost of having a representative attend court to assist Counsel will have to come out of the fixed fee that will be paid for the whole case. There is therefore a strong temptation to instruct an advocate alone to deal with the case in order to maximise profit. This will put a lot of pressure on the trial advocate and most solicitors will send someone to attend court in any event.

What goes into a brief?

The brief – always important – becomes even more so if the advocate is going to be alone at court. The brief is essentially a summary of the case, from both prosecution and defence perspective enclosing all of the relevant information that counsel will need in order to conduct the case. The brief will have numerous enclosures, often running to several lever arch files of documentation. What goes into a brief will vary from case to case but some basic guidance has been produced for solicitors firms through feedback on quality issues commissioned by the Legal Services Commission. The guidance suggests that solicitors will need to:

- Ensure that briefs contain:
    - Proofs of evidence
    - Statements from all available witnesses
    - Visits and photographs of the scene
    - Re-interviews with prosecution witnesses
    - Defence case statements
    - Chronological analysis of prosecution evidence
    - Analysis of unused materials
- Ensure that briefs do not just refer the advocate to the prosecution statements for the prosecution case and to the client's police interview for instructions. You must set out the case and relevant information in an organised, useful format. Note the headings that have been used in the sample brief that appears in the case study.
- Instruct Counsel to consider whether any enquiries are necessary and, if so, advise in writing as soon as possible.

Drafting a brief – some basic points:

Most briefs are still drafted formally and in the third person. Thus for example:

Counsel is instructed by Instructing Solicitors, Halpern Dodds and Co.

Counsel will note...

Instructing solicitors are of the view that...

If Counsel is of the opinion that... would Counsel please contact Instructing Solicitors to....

Briefs will always have a back sheet – with the case heading and solicitor details typed down the right-hand side only. The brief is then folded around the papers and tied with pink legal ribbon. Counsel uses the left-hand side of the back sheet to keep a running account of preparation, conferences and appearances at court. The brief will then be returned at the end of the case.

Please read the brief that appears at Document 21. Although each firm of solicitors will have its own unique style for drafting briefs, you will find this a useful starting point.

Always remember that it is possible that the barrister you brief – and who subsequently meets your client in conference – will turn out not to be able to do the case on the day. You will therefore need to make your brief as accessible as possible for a barrister who is picking it up at minimal notice.

Can I get Counsel to draft the defence statement? In more complex cases you may want to liaise with the trial advocate regarding the defence statement. This is because you will be identifying not only the defence but also the points of law that are to be advanced. The short deadline for the service of the defence statement may make this difficult however, and the drafting of the defence statement will normally remain the responsibility of the solicitor. For further information about defence statements, see 7.5 below.

[7.5] DISCLOSURE

Disclosure in criminal cases arises at various stages in proceedings and there are different rules depending on whether you are acting for the prosecution or for the defence. You will recall from chapter 5, that the prosecution must serve "advance disclosure" (or advance information) either prior to or at the initial hearing at the magistrates' court. This is a basic form of disclosure which normally includes a case summary, witness statements and a summary of interview. This initial disclosure provides the defence with enough information to establish whether there is sufficient evidence to prove the offence against the accused and upon which to take instructions so as to advise on plea. It is not however complete disclosure of the full prosecution case against the accused.

When a defendant enters a guilty plea, there is usually no further requirement on the prosecution to disclose any other information. The defendant has accepted the case against him and will await sentence. Where the defendant enters a not guilty plea, a trial will inevitably take place and all parties must prepare for this. Part of this process involves disclosure, both on the part of the prosecution and defence. This section will explain the rules relating to advance disclosure and then consider the pre-trial disclosure process, noting any differences for summary trial or trial on indictment as we progress.

7.5.1 Prosecution duties of disclosure

Advance disclosure

The defence must be given advance disclosure (referred to as "initial details' in the CrPR, or sometimes also known as "advance information") of evidence which has been gathered by the police in the investigation and which supports the allegations against the defendant. On the first hearing, regardless of the type of case, the defence will usually be provided with advance disclosure which normally contains a summary of the case, some of the key prosecution statements and a list of your client's previous convictions.

- **Either way and summary only cases:** Part 21 of the CrPR relates to advanced disclosure of materials in relation to both either way and summary only offences. Under these provisions, the prosecution must provide "initial details" of the prosecution case by serving them on the court and the defence at or before the day of the first hearing. The initial details must include a summary of the evidence or any statements, documents or extracts which set out the facts of the case as well as the defendant's previous convictions. Based on this information, you will be expected to advise your client as to plea and/or mode of trial in order that you can progress the case at the first hearing under the CrPR.

- **Indictable only cases:** Although part 21 CrPR does not apply to indictable only offences, in practice, the prosecution will provide the same disclosure at the initial hearing before the magistrates' court. Remember, no plea will be taken at the magistrates' court for an indictable only offence; the case is simply transferred immediately to the Crown Court for directions. A plea will be taken at the Crown Court.

Pre-trial disclosure

After a defendant enters a not guilty plea, the case will progress towards a trial (either in the magistrates' court or in the Crown Court). The prosecution are then under a duty to disclose information to the defence. Prosecution disclosure arises in relation to two classes of information and the rules are different for each:

Disclosure of *used* material

"Used material" is the evidence that the prosecution intends to raise at trial in order to prove the offence against the accused. Quite often this will be the same as the initial disclosure but statements will be typed neatly, the interview will have been transcribed and there may be some additional statements provided to support the prosecution case, e.g. forensic evidence that the defence were aware of from the initial hearing but had not seen the precise detail of. At this stage the prosecution should also disclose any evidence not previously disclosed (e.g. at the initial hearing) which might reasonably be considered capable of undermining the case for the prosecution or of assisting the case for the accused: s.3 Criminal Procedure and Investigations Act 1996. (See "disclosure of unused material" below).

- **Disclosure in summary trials:** After the initial hearing in which a not guilty plea is entered, disclosure of used material (the trial papers) should take place in "sufficient time" to enable the defence to consider the evidence before it is called: Attorney General's Guidelines on Disclosure, para 57. Given that summary trial should take place within six weeks of the initial hearing, this will have to take place fairly soon after the not guilty plea is entered. There is no set time fixed on the current Case Management Form.

- **Disclosure for trials on Indictment:** For either way offences committed for trial, disclosure of used material (committal papers) will take place before, or on the date of the committal hearing as the case cannot proceed without the magistrates' court agreeing that there is a prima facie case to commit to the Crown Court for trial. Either way offences which are sent under the CJA allocation procedure, will follow the disclosure regime for indictable only offences. In such cases, the disclosure of the documents containing the evidence upon which the charge(s) is/are based (i.e. sufficient to amount to a prima facie case) must be made within 50 days of sending the case to the Crown Court when the defendant is remanded in custody or within 70 days if the defendant is on bail: s.51 Crime and Disorder Act 1998 and Reg. 2, Crime and Disorder Act (Service of Prosecution Evidence) Regulations 2005. This will essentially contain the same sort of information that would be included in the trial papers for a magistrates' trial.

From April 2012, the CPS will be starting to work digitally, producing a digital case file for any case where a defence solicitor has been identified as representing a particular accused. This system will require defence solicitors to signup to a secure email system and Document Repository Service (DRS) where all case papers will be made available to the defence solicitor as soon as practicable after a suspect has been charged. Defence solicitors will have to ensure they have the required technology to participate in this system. Prisons and court cells have updated their systems to permit solicitors to use laptops and module devices in secure environments. It will be interesting to see how this new initiative develops as some solicitors are already expressing a resistance to the change.

Disclosure of *unused* material

Unused material is all the information which has been gathered as part of the investigation and is of relevance to the case but which the prosecution do not intend to use at trial to prove the offence. The prosecution will have control over all of the unused material, but may not intend to use it because it does not assist their case. It will often include details of witnesses who are not being called, police officers' notebooks, non-incriminating CCTV and other video footage, crime reports and radio logs. This material is not automatically disclosed to the defence, however the defence may well want to see this material in case it supports their defence or opens up new channels of enquiry.

For this reason, when the used material is served on (i.e. provided to) the defence, it will be accompanied by a schedule of "unused material". The schedule of unused material is a list of all the unused material relating to the case along with a brief description of what each item is. An example of a schedule of unused material can be found at document 16B of the case study.

The Criminal Procedure and Investigations Act disclosure regime

The rules relating to the collection and disclosure of unused material are set out in the Criminal Procedure and Investigations Act 1996 (CPIA). The basic structure of the regime is as follows:

1. *The investigators gather the material and compile a disclosure schedule*

The police officer who is investigating the offence is under a duty to record and keep all the materials which are produced in the course of the enquiry. The detailed CPIA Code of Practice sets out what material must be retained. This is basically all material that may be relevant and which either comes into police possession or is generated by them such as custody records, notebooks, statements and it may include negative information (information which does not assist the prosecution case). Material that the officer believes will not form part of the prosecution case but which is relevant (i.e. unused material) must then be listed on a schedule known as the MG6C. The schedule is given to the prosecutor who will make decisions about what unused material should be disclosed and at what stage.

2. *The prosecution then makes disclosure of unused material which might undermine the prosecution's case*

The statutory test for disclosure states that the prosecution must disclose to the defence any unused material which might reasonably be considered capable of undermining the case for the prosecution against the accused, or of assisting the case for the accused. This is an objective test. If there is no such material to disclose then the prosecutor must provide the accused with written notice to confirm this: s.3(1) CPIA 1996 as amended. This means that the prosecution must consider the MG6C Schedule of Unused Material and work out what items, if any, meet this test. If an item meets the test, it will be sent to the defence along with the used material.

The Attorney General's Guidelines attempt to give a much clearer indication of the kind of material that the defence should expect to receive:

> *Examples of material that might reasonably be considered capable of undermining the prosecution case or of assisting the case for the accused are;*
>
> i. *Any material casting doubt upon the accuracy of any prosecution evidence.*
>
> ii. *Any material which may point to another person, whether charged or not (including a co-accused) having involvement in the commission of the offence.*
>
> iii. *Any material which may cast doubt upon the reliability of a confession.*
>
> iv. *Any material that might go to the credibility of a prosecution witness.*
>
> v. *Any material that might support a defence that is either raised by the defence or apparent from the prosecution papers.*
>
> vi *Any material which may have a bearing on the admissibility of any prosecution evidence*

> *It should also be borne in mind that while items of material viewed in isolation may not be reasonably considered to be capable of undermining the prosecution case or assisting the accused, several items together can have that effect.* (AG Guidelines on Disclosure paras 12 and 13)

Material which is "neutral": There is no duty on the prosecution to disclose material which is in their possession unless it fulfils the disclosure test. There is therefore no duty to disclose to the defence material which is either neutral or which is damaging to the defence but which the prosecution are not going to rely upon: AG Guidelines, para 40.

When is prosecution disclosure made? There are no statutory time limits for disclosure of unused material despite the fact that provision has been made for a time limit to be set at some time in the future: s.12 CPIA 1996. Section 13(1) CPIA states that disclosure must be made as soon as reasonably practicable after a not guilty plea is entered for a summary trial, after committal in an either way case proceeding to Crown Court and after transfer in an indictable only case.

For a magistrates' court trial, the prosecution must make disclosure of unused material after the defendant has pleaded not guilty – it will usually accompany the trial papers. In a Crown Court matter, disclosure may be ready at the committal stage or it will be made in line with the guidelines for indictable only offences, that is that disclosure should be made at the same time as the service of the "used materials" (i.e. 50 or 70 days from the date of sending). Crown Court Protocol states that the unused material must be served in time for the defence to prepare their defence statement (see below).

Convictions of prosecution witnesses: Previous convictions of prosecution witnesses would also seem to be covered by para 12(iv) of the Guidelines, namely: *"Any material that might go to the credibility of a prosecution witness."* In *Vasiliou* [2000] 4 Archbold News 1 the Court of Appeal stated that the failure of the prosecution to disclose the convictions of prosecution witnesses was a clear breach of its duties of disclosure. Clearly it is important that this material is disclosed to the defence so that they can make any application to the court for the material to be ruled admissible under s.100 Criminal Justice Act 2003: see chapter 17.3.

Use of disclosed material: You must warn your client that the material which is disclosed may only be used for the purpose of the current proceedings and it will be a contempt of court to disclose the material for an unrelated purpose.

3. The defence may, and in the Crown Court must, serve a "defence statement"

A defence statement is a written statement which sets out the nature of your client's defence and indicates any points of fact or law that he wishes to raise at trial. Defence statements are compulsory in the Crown Court (s.5 CPIA) but voluntary in the magistrates' court (s.6 CPIA).

If serving a defence statement in summary proceedings, you should do so within 14 days of the compliance (or purported compliance) with the prosecution duty of disclosure. For a Crown Court matter, you should serve the defence statement within 28 days of prosecution disclosure. The defence statement must be served on the prosecution and the court.

Failure to serve a defence statement when required, or serving a defence statement late can lead to inferences being drawn at trial. Equally, failure to comply with the strict requirements set out in the CPIA may result in inferences being drawn by the court or comment being made by another party to the case: s.11(2) CPIA. This was made perfectly clear in the recent case of *R v Essa* [2009] EWCA Crim 43 in which the defendant failed to serve a defence statement in his robbery trial and the prosecution commented on this to the jury. It was held that where a defence statement was not served, the court was perfectly entitled to draw comment and this was not a breach of Article 6 ECHR. Failure to follow the CPIA requirements cannot however constitute contempt of court and can only be punished by the sanctions set out in s.11 CPIA: see *R v Rochford* [2010] WLR (D) 220.

As the drafting of the defence statement is so critically important it is considered in more detail at 7.1.2 below.

4. Defence must serve a defence witness notice.

An obligation has now been placed upon the defence to serve on the court and the prosecution a notice indicating whether the defendant intends to call any person other than himself as a witness at his trial: s.6C CPIA (inserted by s.34 CJA 2003). If he does intend to call such a witness, then he must disclose that witness' name, address and date of birth, or provide any information which might assist in identifying or locating that witness (where the personal details are not known to the defendant). It must be served in all cases; within 14 days of compliance or purported compliance of prosecution disclosure in the magistrates' court and within 28 days of this in the Crown Court. The notice is separate to the defence statement and an amended notice must be served if the defence intention in relation to calling witnesses changes. The same s.11 CPIA sanctions apply where the defence fail to serve such a notice, provide one late or call a witness not mentioned in the notice. The police may wish to interview the witnesses on your notice and you should be ready to attend such an interview if necessary. A code of Practice has been issued to provide guidance in such situations: *Criminal Procedure & Investigations Act 1996 (Code of Practice for Interviews of Witnesses Notified by the Accused) Order 2010.*

5. The prosecution will review the unused material in the light of any defence statement and will keep the materials under continuing review as the case progresses ("the continuing duty").

s.7A CPIA imposes a continuing duty on the prosecutor to keep the issue of disclosure under review at all times. This duty is not dependent on the service of a defence statement. However, the more comprehensive a defence statement is, the more likely it is to trigger further disclosure by drawing the prosecutor's attention to specific items of unused material that might be disclosable. If your defence statement is very terse, the prosecution may be justified in saying that it limits the disclosure that they have to make.

Can the prosecution refuse to disclose material?

Material may be "immune" from production if it is not in the public interest to reveal it. This is known as "public interest immunity" (PII). Such categories of material include some governmental and administrative matters, information that has been given for the detection of crime and other necessary public purposes and cases involving other confidential information. However, the test is always a balancing act between the interests of your client and the wider interests of society.

Under the CPIA provision is made for investigators to record any such material on a separate schedule of sensitive material. The prosecution will apply to the court for an order that such sensitive material need not be disclosed. The application can be without notice (so that the defence may never know about it) if the prosecution can persuade the court that the damage would be done if the defence were even to know about the existence of the material. This "without notice" procedure should be very rare – and may require that the court appoints independent counsel to safeguard the interests of the defence: *H and C* [2004] UKHL 3.

Early disclosure of unused material?

In some cases access to unused material might help the defence to make bail applications or to challenge the prosecution case at an early stage. This situation is covered by the Attorney General's Guidelines:

> *55. Investigators must always be alive to the potential need to reveal and prosecutors to the potential need to disclose material, in the interests of justice and fairness in the particular circumstances of any*

> *case, after the commencement of proceedings but before their duty arises under the Act. For instance, disclosure ought to be made of significant information that might affect a bail decision or that might enable the defence to contest the committal proceedings…*

Can the defence challenge deficiencies in prosecution disclosure?

The defence can make an application to the court to order disclosure provided that they can show reasonable cause to believe that there is such material which is disclosable: s.8 CPIA. However this application can only be made if the defence has served a defence statement, and the prosecution has then reviewed (or purported to review) its disclosure.

What is the effect of a prosecution failure to disclose?

There is no rule that a failure to disclose unused material will automatically result in an unfair trial or an unsafe conviction. You need to look at the effect of the non-disclosure on the ability of the defence to run its case. Where appropriate it may be possible to make an application to stay proceedings as an abuse of process or alternatively, it may result in a successful appeal against conviction: *Hadley* [2006] EWCA Crim 2544.

7.5.2 Defence Disclosure

The defence statement

s. 6 CPIA provides that where a matter is dealt with in the magistrates' court, once the prosecution has made prosecution disclosure the accused "may" give a defence statement. In the Crown Court the defence statement is mandatory: s.5 CPIA.

What is contained within a defence statement?

In your defence statement you must comply with six requirements.

- You must set out the nature of the accused's defence including any particular defences on which he intends to rely: s.6A(1)(a)

- You must indicate the matters of fact on which the acccused takes issue with the prosecution: s.6A(1)(b)

- You must set out why the accused takes issue with each of these disputed matters: s.6A(1)(c)

- You must set out particulars of the matters of fact to be relied upon in the accused's defence: s.6A(1)(ca)

- You must indicate any point of law which the accused will raise, including points relating to admissibility of evidence or to an abuse of process, and set out any authorities that will be relied upon in relation to this: s.6A(1)(d).

- If the accused intends to rely upon an alibi ("I was elsewhere") then this must be included in the defence statement along with the name, address and date of birth of any supporting alibi witnesses or as much information as possible to help identify or find such witnesses: s.6A(2)

So how do you draft a defence statement?

There is no simple answer to this. There is often a natural desire by the defence to play their cards close to their chest. The reasons for this are that:

- The defence do not want to help the prosecution to prepare their case against the defendant.

- The defence will often be concerned that if the defendant changes their account later, whether in a minor or major way, the defendant will then be prejudiced by the discrepancies between the different versions.

- The defence may not be sure what legal issues will be raised, as they will often be waiting for fuller prosecution disclosure, or for discussions with the advocate who will be representing the defendant at trial.

A defence statement which is very sparse and gives little or no meaningful details of the defence may not only risk inferences being drawn at trial, but may also mean that the prosecution gives little or no further disclosure on the basis that they do not know what the accused's case is. Note the comments on the court in *R v Bryant* [2005] EWCA Crim 2079:

> *"12. In passing we note that the defence case statement was woefully inadequate. It consisted of a general denial of the counts in the indictment, accompanied by the sentence, "The defendant takes issue with any witness purporting to give evidence contrary to his denials". That sort of observation is not worth the paper it is written on. It is not the purpose of a defence case statement."*

Who should sign the defence statement?

s.6E CPIA creates a rebuttable presumption that any defence statement is given with the authority of the defendant. As a matter of best practice you should always get the defendant to sign the statement. This prevents allegations being made that the defendant did not agree with the statement.

You have either 14 or 28 days to serve the statement – when does the clock start running?

Time runs from the date of the sending of the CPS letter, even if the disclosure schedule follows later: *DPP v Wood* [2006] EWHC 32. If it is not possible to serve the defence statement within this time, you should make a written application to the court to extend the time limit. The time limit in Crown Court cases has recently been extended to 28 days therefore any request for an extension in the Crown Court will be "rigorously scrutinised": *Ministry of Justice Circular 2011/02*

Do you have to give details of your defence witnesses?

As is noted above, there is a duty to serve a separate witness notice on both the court and the prosecution of the defendant's intention to call witnesses other than himself at trial: see 7.1.1 above. Where details of alibi witnesses are provided within the defence statement and there are no other witnesses to be called, there is no need to serve a separate witness notice: s.6C(2) CPIA.

Who do you serve the defence statement and witness notice on?

The statement and notice must be served on both the prosecution and the court.

What happens if your client changes his story at trial?

You do not have to serve a defence statement in summary cases, but once you serve the statement you are stuck with it. If your client puts forward a different defence at trial, the court or any other party (with the leave of the court) can make "such comment as appears appropriate" and the court can draw such inferences as appear to be proper: s.11 CPIA. The primary comment and inference is that your client's evidence is, at best, unreliable.

Similarly, inferences can be drawn and comment made if:

- you serve the defence statement late; or

- you fail to disclose a defence statement at all (if in Crown Court proceedings); or

- you fail to disclose details of any alibi that you are relying upon; or

- you put forward inconsistent defences in the statement (thus, you cannot draft a statement which says: I didn't take the item, and if I did take it I thought I had the owner's consent.)

- you rely on a matter of fact in your defence which is not on the defence statement

- you fail or are late in serving a defence witness notice or you call a witness which is not detailed on the defence witness notice.

Inferences can also arise from failure to identify a point of law which it is intended to take, although it is not easy to see what inference could be drawn against the defendant personally for this failure.

Can the prosecution use the defence statement as part of its case?

Prosecutors can comment on or invite inferences to be drawn only where there is a failure or inconsistency in relation to the defence statement which permits them to do so. However they can cross-examine the defendant on any differences between the defence statement and the account put forward at trial. Equally the prosecution can use the defence statement in order to advance their own enquiries and can use any evidence gained from these enquiries at trial.

Other forms of defence disclosure:

There are duties imposed by the Criminal Procedure Rules upon all parties in the criminal justice system to assist the court in its active management of the case. The impact of these duties on disclosure by the defence is discussed at 7.1 above.

The other main context where disclosure by the defence is likely to arise is in connection with expert evidence. Where the defence will be relying upon expert evidence there is a requirement for a copy of the report to be served on the court and each other party (including the prosecution) as soon as practicable: Part 33.4 CrPR.

[7.6] HUMAN RIGHTS ISSUES

A number of cases have gone to Strasbourg concerning failures to make full disclosure of unused material. The majority of these cases have related to the pre-Criminal Procedure and Investigations Act regime. In *Rowe and Davis v United Kingdom* 30 E.H.R.R. 1 the ECHR held that there had been a breach of article 6(1) in respect of the failure to disclose even to the trial judge. However, in *Jasper v United Kingdom* (2000) 30 E.H.R.R. 441) and *Fitt v United Kingdom* (2000) 30 E.H.R.R. 480 the ECHR found no breach where the information had been fully revealed to the trial judge. In the case of *Edwards and Lewis v United Kingdom* [2003] 1 WLR 3006 a breach of article 6 was found in respect of ex parte disclosure hearings, Strasbourg holding that special independent counsel should have been used to protect the interests of the defendants. The case was subsequently considered by the House of Lords in *H and C* [2004] UKHL 3, where the court ruled that the use of special counsel should be exceptional.

Note that failure by the defence solicitors to do their job properly can mean that article 6 is breached. In *Joshil Thakrar* [2001] EWCA Crim 1096 the solicitors had handed a robbery case to their office manager who had no legal qualifications and little understanding of criminal procedure. There had therefore been little review of the issues in the case with the client, until an hour before trial when the client saw his barrister. The Court held that the short conference before trial had put the defendant on notice as to the issues, and meant that he had had a fair trial. However, it will be possible for defendants to argue that if their case has not been properly prepared, a breach of article 6 may arise.

```
┌─────────────────────────────────────────────────┐
│   POLICE COLLATE EVIDENCE DURING INVESTIGATION  │
└─────────────────────────────────────────────────┘
                        │
                        ▼
┌─────────────────────────────────────────────────┐
│  SUSPECT CHARGED WITH OFFENCE AND CASE PROCEEDS │
│                    TO COURT                     │
└─────────────────────────────────────────────────┘
```

USED MATERIAL

All evidence to be used at trial to prove the case against the accused

UNUSED MATERIAL

All other evidence collected by the police but not being used to prove the case against the accused

PROSECUTION WILL SERVE

PROSECUTION WILL REVIEW UNUSED AND PREPARES SCHEDULE (LIST) OF UNUSED MATERIAL

In all cases:

Advanced Information / Initial Details provided i.e. summary of used material

This is served at/before initial hearing

After NG plea:

Trial papers served i.e. complete package of used material (statements, interview transcript etc)

- Summary only – served "insufficient time" before trial

- Either way offences committed under s.6 MCA – served on committal

- Indictable only (or either way offences transferred under CJA allocation) – served 50 days (D in custody) or 70 days (D on bail) after sending

After NG plea

Prosecution must serve:

Schedule of Unused Material

Any unused material which assists defence or undermines case for prosecution (s. 3 CPIA)

Served at same time as trial papers

After NG plea:

Prosecution keeps Schedule under review

Retains any evidence on schedule of unused which does not meet the test for disclosure (s.3 CPIA)

DEFENCE DUTIES

Defence serve Defence Statement within 14 days (Summary trial) or within 28 days (Crown Court trial)

Prosecution reviews Unused Material and serves anything now meeting test in light of defence statement

Interim Hearings & Disclosure – test yourself questions

[The answers to these questions are set out in Appendix A at the back of this book]

[1] Consider the following propositions in relation to disclosure in the magistrates' court.

   i. Prosecution disclosure of unused material must be made once the defendant has entered a not guilty plea.

   ii. The prosecutor should make available to the defence all materials in the possession of the prosecution which are not subject to public interest immunity.

   iii. In a summary trial the defendant may choose whether or not to provide a defence statement.

   Which of the above propositions are correct?

   (a) i only.

   (b) i and iii only.

   (c) ii and iii only.

   (d) All of them.

[2] Which one of the following propositions concerning the disclosure regime in Crown Court cases is correct?

   (a) In an either way case there will be no requirement on the defendant to serve a defence statement since this only arise in relation to indictable only cases.

   (b) A defence statement must include the full proof of evidence from the defendant or inferences may be drawn from service of an incomplete statement.

   (c) The defence statement must be served on both the court and the prosecution within 14 days of prosecution disclosure.

   (d) The prosecutor is only required to review disclosure of unused material where a new matter arises which changes the basis of the way in which the case is put on the indictment.

[3] Scott has been charged with theft and sent to the Crown Court for trial. He is currently remanded in custody.

   Which one of the following propositions is NOT correct?

   (a) A plea and case management hearing will be scheduled so that the judge can give directions in the case.

   (b) The judge can make binding rulings at a plea and case management hearing provided that he or she is the trial judge for the case.

   (c) The judge may hold a preparatory hearing if he or she is of the opinion that the case is long or complex and that substantial benefits are likely to accrue from the hearing.

   (d) The judge can make binding rulings at a preparatory hearing, and those rulings can be appealed to the Court of Appeal before trial commences.

CHAPTER 8

ADVOCACY

This chapter covers:

Principles of criminal advocacy

Professional Conduct and advocacy

[8.1] ADVOCACY – THE BASICS

Advocacy is the skill of preparing a case so that you can present it to the court. Advocacy is not simply the presentation. If your presentation skills are poor, the impact of your preparation will be blunted. If your preparation is inadequate, no degree of skilful presentation will conceal the fact. If you find the idea of advocacy frightening, here are two useful thoughts:

1. You are not doing this for yourself. You are doing it for your client. Ignore your own worries and concerns. Do your job: say for your client what he would properly say for himself if he had your legal training and expertise.

2. Often no one else knows how experienced you are. If you appear confident, they will assume that you know what you are doing. Make sure you don't lose this advantage.

8.1.2. Presentation

You will have your own mannerisms and your own style of presentation. These will develop as you watch other advocates and as you find out what elements are effective and which are not. There are, however, some basic principles of effective presentation.

- Don't read from a prepared text.
- Be aware of your body language: stand up straight, look the person you are talking to in the eye.
- Don't wave your arms around.
- Don't stand with the case papers in front of your face.
- Don't show emotion. (In *The Golden Rules of Advocacy* Keith Evans refers to "riding the bumps" – i.e. never showing when a witness has just made a point devastating to your case!)
- Never argue with a witness – put your points.
- Don't rush – watch the judge's/clerk's pen as they will be making a note of what is being said by the witnesses. This is also a useful way to find time to gather your thoughts!
- If you need a moment to consider matters, ask the court: "Madam, I wonder if I might have a moment to check if there are any other matters to be put."

8.1.3 Modes of address

Referring to the prosecution: Your opponent should normally be referred to by name. Alternatively, you can vary this by making the matter more impersonal: "Sir, the Crown puts its case as follows…" "Madam, the prosecution has attempted to present my client as…" You can also refer to your opposite number as "my friend", although traditionally if s/he is a barrister, s/he should be referred to as "my learned friend".

Magistrates' courts: "Sir" or "Madam" is technically correct in the magistrates' courts, but many lay benches expect to be addressed as "Your Worships". Where you have to refer to the clerk, it is customary to refer to "your learned clerk".

Crown Court: Crown Court judges will generally be referred to as "Your Honour". This is used both as an address – "I don't know if Your Honour has seen the papers." – and as a possessive – "In Your Honour's earlier ruling, Your Honour took the view that…" To a witness: "Please show His Honour where you were standing at the time."

Where the judge sitting in the Crown Court is a High Court judge, the judge should be referred to as "My Lord" or "My Lady". Here the noun and possessive is "Your Lordship/Your Ladyship". Thus: *"My Lord, in Your Lordship's earlier judgement it was suggested that …"* In the Central Criminal Courts (the Old Bailey) all judges should be addressed as "My Lord/Lady", as should the Recorders of Liverpool, Manchester and Cardiff.

8.1.4 Two fundamental principles of advocacy

The role of the advocate is not to give evidence. As an advocate, you can never give evidence. Do not give evidence yourself ("Well, officer, when I visited the scene I could clearly observe the end of the street.") and do not give the court your opinion of the evidence ("I think…", "In my opinion…").

The advocate must never mislead the court. Not only must you not mislead the court but you must not permit your client to mislead the court by putting forward a version of facts you know to be untrue: Code of Conduct Outcomes 5.1 & 5.2. Note that you are not under any duty to bring to the attention of the court facts that may undermine your case, but you should make the court aware of all relevant legislation or case law, even if it is adverse to your case: Code of Conduct IB 5.2

[8.2] EXAMINATION IN CHIEF

Examination in chief is the process of adducing evidence from your own witness. The purpose of examination in chief is two-fold:

1. to put before the court the evidence you wish to adduce from this witness

2. to anticipate any points which may be put to the witness in cross-examination.

In examination in chief you will tend to ask open questions: why, where, when, what. You are trying to get the witness to tell a story, rather than simply to respond "yes" or "no".

8.2.1 The main problem – no leading questions.

A leading question is one that assumes the answer to something that is in issue. A question such as: "Did you then keep her under observation because she seemed to be looking round in an unusual manner?" is leading: it tells the witness what to say. A question will not normally be leading if the matter is already in evidence:

> "*Mr Mohammed, you have already told the court that you were in the supermarket at 6 p.m. How long did you remain there?*"

You can avoid leading questions by using a technique called "Piggy-backing":

> *"What did you do then?"*
> *"I went out into the hall."*
> *"And when you went into the hall, what happened then?"*
> *"I opened the door."*
> *"And what happened after you opened the door?"*

Piggy-backing is a technique for guiding a witness, step by step, by using their own words to prompt them, and thus avoiding leading the witness. But it can be very monotonous, so use it sparingly.

8.2.2 Other principles of examination in chief

Let the witness tell their own story: Give your witness space to tell their own story; it will always be most convincing in their own words. However, you must still keep the witness under control. The witness will be looking to you for guidance. Don't abandon them. You can help the witness by directing your questions to their important testimony: "Could you tell the court what happened when you arrived at the house?" "How did you feel at this stage?"

Listen to the answers: It is easy to be so busy worrying about not leading your witness that you forget to listen to what they are saying.

Coaching witnesses: You are allowed to speak to witnesses before they attend court, but you must not "coach" your witness. The line between preparing and coaching can be a thin one. Remember, you must not be complicit in allowing any person to mislead or deceive the court: Code of Conduct Outcome 5.2.

Tell the witness how to behave: You should always warn witnesses that they should wait outside the court until called to give evidence. Once they have given their evidence, they may remain in the court. You will also need to warn the witness (probably as they start giving evidence) that they should keep their voice up, speak slowly enough for the court (and advocates) to make notes, and that they should try to address their answers to the Bench/judge and not to you. Keep an eye on the clerk's pen yourself; if the witness is going too fast, interrupt and slow them down.

What are the rules on witnesses using their statements? It is quite acceptable for a witness to refresh their memory from their statement before coming into court. Where the witness is in the witness box and wants to refresh their memory, they may be permitted to do so if:

- the evidence is in a document made or verified by the witness at an earlier time; and
- they state in evidence that the document records their recollection of the matter; and
- that their recollection of the matter is likely to have been significantly better at that time than at the time when they are giving evidence: s. 139 CJA 2003.

This is discussed more fully in Chapter 19.

Your mind has gone blank – what do you say next? Ask for time. "Sir, I'd be grateful if I might just have a moment." Don't worry. Count to twenty slowly. Thank the court. If you can remember what it was, continue with your questions. If you can't remember, "If we could leave that subject for the moment. I'd like to turn to…" and move on to the next matter on your skeleton plan. This applies to all advocacy – whether cross-examination or bail applications, mitigation speeches or legal submissions. Don't flounder. Don't 'um' and 'er'. Stop and ask for time.

Anticipating cross-examination: As part of your case preparation you will have identified not only the weaknesses in the prosecution case, but also the weaknesses in your own case. It is often better to deal with this evidence in your examination in chief if it is likely to come out anyway. That way you have control over the evidence and you enhance your appearance of candour before the court. Advocates sometimes speak of this as "insulating" the witness.

[8.3] CROSS-EXAMINATION

The purpose of cross-examination is also two-fold:

1. to weaken the credibility of the prosecution account

2. to "put" the defence case

In cross-examination you should try to used closed questions that prompt "yes" or "no" answers. You don't want to give the witness an opportunity to comment on evidence.

8.3.1 "Putting your case"

"Putting your case," means that where there is a witness whose account differs from the defence version of the facts, you should put that difference to the witness, thus giving the court an opportunity to assess the witness's reaction.

> *For example: the police officer says that he saw the defendant walk up the drive to a house. Your client denies ever moving off the pavement. You must put the discrepancy to the police officer when he is giving evidence or you will be taken to have accepted his version of events.*

Strictly speaking, in the magistrates' court there is no duty to put your case: *O'Connell v Adams* [1973] Crim LR 113. However you should always try to put your case anyway. It has two advantages: first, it ensures that the court is aware of the defence at the earliest stage; secondly, it prevents any suggestion that you held the material back so that the prosecution witnesses didn't have a chance to comment on it.

How to put your case: Inexperienced advocates hate "putting their case". They know that the prosecution witness is generally simply going to respond with a series of negative answers. It makes them feel that they are losing ground. You shouldn't feel like this, however. If you put your case clearly, and you keep tight control of the witness so that they don't have a chance to comment, you can often make your points in a forceful way.

One way of achieving this is simply to put your case by way of a series of direct questions. This forces the witness to respond directly.

> *You didn't see my client take the goods, did you?*
>
> > *Yes, I did.*
>
> *You didn't see my client take them, because he wasn't there, was he?*
>
> > *Yes, he was.*

> *In fact, the only person who was present was you – that's right, isn't it?*
>
> *No, that's not right.*
>
> *You were the only person there, and you took the goods, didn't you?*
>
> *No, I didn't.*
>
> *That's what happened, isn't it?*
>
> *No, it isn't.*

Note how the questions make it hard for the witness to say much more than yes or no. It is not realistic to expect the witness to break down under cross-examination and confess that they are lying, but if you do have to directly confront a witness, do it with an appearance of confidence.

8.3.2 Other aspects of cross-examination

Preparation and delivery: Do not write out every question. Use a skeleton plan of the points that need to be covered. You should make a note of what you want a witness to say in evidence as you can adapt your questions according to how the evidence is unfolding. As with examination in chief, ask one question at a time, keep the questions short and listen to the answers.

Cross-examination is not about attacking the witness: You may wish to undermine their testimony, but generally you are not going to get an admission out of them that they are wrong/mistaken/lying. The best you can hope for is to gather material for use in your closing speech.

Put your case clearly: Challenge inconsistencies but don't argue, and don't let the witness explain. Be prepared to explore ambiguities, but try not to ask questions that you don't know the answer to. Always try to be clear in your own mind what it is that you are trying to do. Do not show any reaction that you do not mean to.

Supporting the advocate: If you attend the Crown Court with an advocate, take notes for the advocate to use. The best way of keeping up with the testimony is to conflate the question and the answer. Thus: "Where were you on the night of the 25th?" "I was at Westchurch." becomes "On the night of the 25th I was at Westchurch." Keep it as legible as you can. Number your pages. Mark anything that could be useful for a closing speech.

8.3.3 Can you cross-examine the witness about someone else's evidence?

It is proper to put one witness' evidence to another witness so that they can comment on it:

> Q: *You have heard the officer say he saw you standing at the window. What do you say to this?*
>
> A: *It's not true. I wasn't there.*

One standard – and objectionable – prosecution question to your client is:

> *"You have heard the officer's evidence. Now you are saying something completely different. Why should the court believe you?"*

or

> *"Why do you think the officer would lie about this?"*

You must always leap to your feet and object. The advocate is asking your client to give their opinion about something (i.e. who the court should believe, or why an officer would lie.) Your client cannot give opinion evidence: they are there to tell the court what they saw and what they did. It is for the court to draw any inferences and to make up its mind where the truth lies.

8.3.4 "One last question"

When you have got what you need for your submission, stop. There is always a temptation to ask a final "killer" question. Don't do it. Invariably it will only end up letting the witness off the hook.

> *In one explosives case where the prosecution alleged that one defendant had been seen wearing a yellow safety helmet in his kitchen, the officer confirmed in cross-examination that a blue safety helmet had been found in the flat.*
>
> *Q: Now you've told the court, officer, that you found a helmet in my client's flat.*
>
> *A: Yes, sir.*
>
> *Q: But it was blue, wasn't it?*
>
> *A: Yes it was.*
>
> *Q: And yet you told the court you saw my client earlier in a yellow helmet?*
> *A: Yes.*
>
> *Q: And you said you were sure it was yellow.*
> *A: Yes.*
>
> *Q: But you didn't find any yellow helmet in my client's flat, did you officer?*
>
> *A: No sir. We found it in his locker at work.*

Don't ask the "question too far".

[8.4] RE-EXAMINATION

The general rule with re-examination is to avoid it unless there is some essential clarification that is necessary. For example, in cross-examination the opposing advocate has brought out part of the story – "So you saw the fight, but you did nothing?" – but has left out some crucial detail: "Mr Jones, why did you do nothing?" "I was on the other side of the river."

As with examination-in-chief, you may not lead your witness. Re-examination is confined to matters dealt with in cross-examination. You cannot raise a new matter or return to something that the other advocate has chosen not to cross-examine on. Avoid re-examination in 99% of cases. It only signals that the other side has damaged your case.

[8.5] SPEECHES

In the magistrates' court, you need in particular to focus on two key speeches, your closing speech and your mitigation speech. Remember the general principles that apply to any speech:

- Be structured – what is it you are trying to achieve?
- Be concise – no-one likes listening to another person talk at them
- Deal with the bad, don't just emphasise the good
- Avoid repetition

Listen to the prosecution opening speech and take a note of any hostages to fortune. Make a note of the basis on which the prosecution is putting its case, so that in your closing speech you can point to any inconsistencies or failures to come up to this first account. Similarly, you should listen to any closing submissions and comment on those where appropriate.

8.5.1   Making a defence closing speech:

In the Crown Court, especially in a lengthy trial, counsel will be working on their closing speeches from early on in the proceedings. In the magistrates' court, you will deliver your speech as soon as the defence case closes. You therefore need to try to prepare in advance an outline closing speech based on what you think the evidence will be, but you will always need to adapt this as you go along.

Be truthful. What is the basis on which the court should acquit your client? Keith Evans summarises this as: "Show them the way home." Try to be clear about what you are trying to say. Are you saying that there is a gap in the prosecution account (if so, did you run a no case to answer submission at the halfway point)? Are you saying that the prosecution evidence is weak and flawed – if so point to inconsistencies that you have established in cross-examination. If you are simply running a burden of proof argument, point to the elements in the prosecution case where the standard of proof (beyond reasonable doubt) has not been achieved.

While the court is risen to decide the matter, start updating your mitigation speech. You may have to launch into your mitigation immediately if the court returns and finds the matter proved.

8.5.2   Mitigation speeches

Mitigation speeches are very difficult to get right. Most mitigation speeches are rambling messes. The golden rule is to be structured. Organise your material. Keep it as short as you can. Avoid repetition. Mitigation speeches are looked at in detail in Chapter 10, which deals with sentencing.

[8.6]   TRIAL WITHIN A TRIAL: VOIR DIRE HEARINGS

A voir dire is a trial within the trial. Its purpose is to ensure that the triers of fact do not hear any evidence that may be inadmissible until the court has had an opportunity to rule on admissibility. This is a frequent occurrence at the Crown Court and is considered in more detail in chapter 9.

This procedure is problematic in the magistrates' court since the Justices are both the tribunal of fact and law thus they may be asked to rule on the admissibility of evidence, which they would then have to disregard if it was considered inadmissible. This meant that for some time there was not thought to be any point in having a voir dire procedure in summary trials. However since the magistrates are now able to make binding rulings on legal issues prior to trial, it is effectively possible to have the hearing to exclude the evidence a few weeks before the trial and in front of a different Bench of magistrates than the one that will hear the trial. This achieves the same result as a voir dire.

Where a voir dire is held during the course of a trial in the magistrates' court, bear in mind that unlike a jury, who will never know of the existence of any evidence excluded on voir dire, the magistrates will know of the existence of the evidence and you will have to reinforce in your closing speech that they must put it out of their minds.

[8.7] CONDUCT

The key chapter in the Code of Conduct is chapter 5 outlining your duties to both the client and the court in circumstances where you are acting as an advocate in proceedings or conducting litigation. This part of the rules sets out a number of outcomes which should be achieved and various indicative behaviours (non-binding) which help to illustrate when the outcomes are likely or not to be achieved.

A duty to assist the court? Outcome 5.6 requires you to comply with your duties to the court and outcome 5.3 requires you to comply with court orders which place obligations upon you. We have an adversarial system of justice whereby it remains for the prosecution to prove its case however the case management duties of the CrPR are being used to place a more active duty on the defence to assist the court in this process: see chapter 7

Never ever mislead the court. This sounds obvious, but it generally happens not because you intend to mislead the court but because you are flustered: you are asked a question, it doesn't seem like an important point, so you just answer it. If you are not sure about something, say so and if you need to take instructions from your client, ask the court for a moment to do so. The court will not object.

Outcomes 5.1 and 5.2 deal with this issue stating that you must not attempt to deceive or knowingly or recklessly mislead the court and, you must not be complicit in another person misleading or deceiving the court. It is recommended therefore that you draw the court's attention to relevant cases and statutory provisions, and any procedural irregularity (I.B 5.2). You should also inform the court immediately (with the client's consent) if you become aware that you have inadvertently misled the court or you should cease to act where the client does not give you permission to do so (I.B. 5.4).

A couple of other practical conduct points

Oaths: Do not move, talk, take instructions or anything else while the oath/affirmation is being administered (especially in the Crown Court). This is a solemn moment, and judges will be quick to voice their displeasure if you don't respect it. Similarly, you should not move around the court when a defendant is entering a plea, again particularly at the Crown Court.

Witnesses: Witnesses should wait outside the court until they are called to give evidence. You must not discuss the case with witnesses, including your client, who are in the course of giving evidence (e.g. over an adjournment). The defendant must be called before other defence witnesses, including your client, if he is giving evidence: s.79 PACE.

Advocacy – test yourself questions

[The answers to these questions are set out in Appendix A at the back of this book]

[1]   A leading question:

(a) is one that starts with the word "Did".

(b) is one that gives evidence.

(c) is not permitted in cross-examination.

(d) asks your client to comment on the evidence of other witnesses.

[2]   Consider the following forms of address in the magistrates' court. You should assume that both advocates are solicitors and that it is a lay Bench with a female Chair.

i. You may take the view, Madam, that…

ii. The Bench may take the view that …

iii. My learned friend suggests that…

iv. Your learned clerk will confirm that…

Which of the above are correct?

(a) All of them.

(b) i, ii and iv only.

(c) iii only.

(d) i, ii and iii only.

[3]   Which of the following could be correct modes of address when addressing a judge in the Crown Court?

i. Your Honour

ii. Your Worship

iii. Judge

iv. My Lord

(a) All of them.

(b) i only.

(c) iii and iv only.

(d) i and iv only.

CHAPTER 9

TRIAL PREPARATION AND TRIAL PROCEDURE

> This chapter covers:
>
> Preparing for trial - case analysis and obtaining witness statements
>
> Trial procedure in the Magistrates' court (summary trial)
>
> Trial procedure in the Crown Court (trial on indictment)

We have already considered what happens at the first hearing, how to apply for bail, and the various issues that are dealt with by way of interim hearing. We must now consider how best to prepare for the trial and how the trial process actually works.

[9.1] CASE ANALYSIS

Case analysis is a technique for organising material and focusing your attention on what is actually in issue. This is the best way to prepare for trial and ensure that nothing is overlooked.

9.1.2 A basic case analysis method

One method for identifying what facts are in issue in a criminal matter is to compare the basic prosecution and defence accounts so that you can see where they differ. The key differences will be "facts in issue". You can then focus on how the prosecution is likely to try to prove their version of each fact, and how the defence can effectively challenge this version.

1. **What are the legal elements of the charge?** Thus for example, ABH is "assault occasioning actual bodily harm contrary to s.47 OAPA 1861". The elements of the offence are:

- the defendant
- committed an assault
- which occasioned (i.e. a consequence of which is)
- actual bodily harm
- the defendant having either intended the assault or having been reckless as to the assault. [No foresight of harm is required: *Savage* [1992] 1 AC 699.]

2. **What is the prosecution account?** If the prosecution were going to outline their case in an opening speech, what would they say happened? What evidence (from which witness) is going to prove each element of the offence? Write down the piece of evidence/witness' name next to the breakdown of the elements of the offence. Are there any gaps? You need to keep your account short so that it is simply a summary of the prosecution story.

3. **What is the defence account?** If we were going to make an opening speech – and in the magistrates' court we are not going to – what do we say happened – and who is going to prove each of the elements of our account? What element of the charge do we say is not made out? Do we say that there was no assault – or that it was not our client that committed the assault – or that the injuries do not amount to actual bodily harm – or do we admit the *actus reus* but deny intention or recklessness? Alternatively, do we put forward a defence to the charge – duress, self-defence and so on? Again, you need to keep your account short; no more than a summary of the defence story.

4. **Where are the two accounts in conflict?** Sometimes referred to as the "facts in issue". This is why you need to keep the two accounts short. You need to be able to put them next to one another so that you can identify the key discrepancies. If you write three pages for each account, you won't be able to spot the issues.

5. **How is each party going to prove its version of the facts that are disputed?** Who are the relevant witnesses? What evidence is there for each side? Are there any issues of admissibility, reliability or credibility in respect of each side's witnesses?

6. **What further evidence do you need?** The number of potential defences to each offence is often in fact quite small. Thus with shoplifting the defence will often be mistake, or sometimes plant. With s.47 assault (ABH) the defences will normally either be self-defence or accident (or possibly identification). Do you need additional defence evidence to help undermine part of the prosecution account? Is there part of the defence account where further witnesses would bolster your client's story?

9.1.3 Other approaches

The "theory of the case": Many advocacy texts recommend a "theory of the case" approach. This is similar to case analysis but starts by asking what you would like to be able to say to the court/jury in your closing speech, and then asking you to focus on what it is that you need to establish in order to prove these things. This is a useful back-up technique, but you may overlook gaps in the prosecution case.

The narrative approach: Alternatively a "narrative" approach can be useful. Narrative simply means working out the story of your case. Narratives help us to make sense of motivation, and to identify gaps in the story. The narrative approach is therefore particularly useful as a presentation tool (in preparing opening and closing speeches). Stories are always more memorable and interesting than speeches.

NITA – the National Institute of Trial Advocacy: NITA tends to use a version of the theory of the case approach. Having decided what needs to be in the closing speech, the advocate brainstorms by listing all the different facts in the case as "good fact" [i.e. one that helps to establish what s/he wants to say in the closing speech] and "bad fact" [one that undermines his/her version of events]. The great advantage with this approach is that it forces you to think about how the other side's witnesses may still have "good facts" that you might want them to tell the court about. It gets rid of the idea that cross-examination is simply about attacking the other side's witnesses.

9.1.4 Which method should you use?

In practice you will often find yourself having to deal with large amounts of information in a confused state and at short notice. Use any method that you find works for you. The key requirements are that you:

- identify the elements of the charge and whether the prosecution has proved each element;
- identify any weaknesses (factual or legal) in the prosecution case that should be challenged;
- identify the line that the defence will take, and any steps that can be taken to bolster that defence.

[9.2] WITNESSES AND STATEMENTS

9.2.1 Witness statements

One often overlooked aspect of preparation for the advocate is the preparation of witness statements. You will be working closely from witness statements in leading your own witnesses through their testimony. It is therefore essential that you are able to organise material into a useable form. Your first task will generally be to prepare the defendant's proof of evidence. In any litigation practice you will find yourself taking statements from witnesses and parties to an action on a regular basis.

At the very least a statement must:

(i) be typed if possible;

(ii) be clearly laid out, preferably in numbered paragraphs;

(iii) have sufficient room for the advocate to mark up the papers;

(iv) organise material in a coherent fashion (if in doubt, try chronological order);

(v) keep paragraphs short (use headings where appropriate);

(vi) contain all the relevant information (you may not be the advocate on the day).

9.2.2 Drafting your client's proof of evidence (statement)

Do not confuse this with your client's defence statement. The proof of evidence sets out your client's instructions on the allegations in full and is read only by him and his legal team.

Content: A statement should contain everything you need to know about the client's account in order to represent him in court. However, a statement which contains too much material will become unusable because you won't be able to find relevant material. A poorly organised statement will be unusable for the same reason. You need to find a balance. You also need to bear in mind that while you may know everything about your client and his case, you may not be representing him in court. Another advocate must therefore be able to pick up the statement and find out everything he needs to know from it.

Language: In drafting the statement, use your client's language as much as you can, but edit it into comprehensible form – whether by cutting down on the slang or by using small clear sentences. Don't put legal language into your client's mouth. You need to organise your client's account, but not to change its substance.

Procedure: You should send your client two copies of his statement – one to sign and return to you with any amendments, and one to keep for his own reference. Having a signed copy of the statement is a valuable safeguard with witnesses who may not attend court. It is also valuable insurance for you where a witness, or indeed your client, later changes his account and blames you.

Comments on prosecution evidence: Most solicitors will take the client's statement in two parts. The first is a basic proof of evidence which details your client's version of the facts. The second is a separate document detailing "Comments on Prosecution Evidence". This is where your client goes through the prosecution witness statements (where these have been disclosed) and identifies points of dispute. Having a separate "comments" document is invaluable for your cross-examination, where you are under a duty to put your case.

Professional conduct: Has there been a change of instructions? You must ensure that you are not complicit in anyone deceiving or misleading the court (Code of Conduct outcome 5.2). It would be wise to refuse to continue acting for a client if you become aware they are attempting to commit perjury or to mislead the court (Code of Conduct IB 5.5) therefore you should enquire as to the reasons why the account has changed. They may be perfectly genuine in the circumstances but it is always wise to satisfy yourself.

Organising your client's statement: There is no fixed way of taking a statement for use in a criminal case. Everyone has their own way of taking statements. Subject to clarity, accuracy and above all "usability" in court, this is fine. As with case preparation, you will develop your own drafting style. Some examples of a client's proof of evidence and comments on the prosecution papers are contained at documents 10A and 10B in the case study (respectively). The suggested headings in these documents are a useful aide memoir in interview to make sure that you have not missed anything.

9.2.3 Other witnesses

The same general principles apply in drafting statements from other potential defence witnesses. Clearly you don't need the same level of background information about employment, education and so on, but you must always remember to check whether the witness has previous convictions. If they have previous convictions these may be an issue that will need to be addressed – see Chapter 17. In light of the obligations to notify the court and the prosecution of your intention to call a witness, they should be advised that their details must be provided in these circumstances and they may be contacted by the police to be interviewed under the Code of Practice for Arranging and Conducting Interviews of Witnesses Notified by the Accused. The witness may wish you or another solicitor to be present in any such interview.

What if the witness is unwilling to attend court? Think twice about using such a witness. Although it is possible to summons a witness to attend court, a reluctant witness will often be a liability. However, some witnesses will want to be summonsed simply in order to protect them from reprisals – for example, co-workers in cases where your client is charged with stealing from his employer. In other cases you may have no option; you need that witness' evidence as part of your case.

Interviewing a witness in your client's presence: It is always better to interview witnesses individually and in private. Some solicitors speed up such interviews by giving the witness a copy of the defendant's statement and asking them to comment. However, the temptation simply to confirm the defendant's account makes such statements potentially unreliable. It is always better to get the witness' account first. You can then put questions to confirm points where their account seems to vary from your client's. Don't panic about minor points of variation; everyone remembers matters differently and the courts are often rightly suspicious where a series of witnesses all give identical accounts. However, note any significant discrepancies. Note that it is not good practice to show the witnesses the prosecution statements before you take down their account: see *Halsall* [2002] 9 *Archbold* News 3, CA.

Alibi witnesses: Bear in mind that where a witness is providing your client with an alibi, you will have to reveal their identity if you are serving a defence statement. It is likely that the police will then call and take a further statement from them. They should be warned about this. They may even like you to be present at such an interview.

Photographs and plans: Photographs and plans can save huge amounts of time. You should always consider serving such evidence by way of s.9, so that it can go in by agreement. Photographs will need to be accompanied by a statement from the photographer confirming where and when they took the pictures and that the unretouched negatives remain in their possession.

Professional Conduct: can you interview prosecution witnesses?

There is no "property" in a witness. This means that the prosecution can interview your witnesses and you are equally entitled to interview theirs, including the victim, where the witness agrees to be interviewed. However, there is clearly a considerable potential for allegations that you have attempted to interfere with a witness in such circumstances.

The current Code of Conduct no longer deals with this issue. However the previous Code suggested that in order to avoid allegations of tampering with a witness' evidence it is wise, where you wish to interview a witness for the other side, to offer to interview them in the presence of the other's side's representative: Rule 11, Guidance 13 (f). This probably remains sensible advice.

[9.3] SUMMARY TRIAL PROCEDURE

Trial in the magistrates' court will either be before a Bench of lay justices (normally three in number), who will be advised on issues of law by their clerk, or before a single District Judge.

Regardless of who is hearing the evidence, the trial process will be the same, although matters tend to move faster where the hearing is before a District Judge who is legally qualified.

The normal order of proceedings: In all criminal trials the prosecution will go first and will put forward their case, with the defence then following on. There are some differences in the procedure between the Crown Court and the magistrates' courts and we will examine these later in this chapter.

In the magistrates' court, the prosecution will have an opening speech. They will then call their witnesses. Each witness will be examined-in-chief by the prosecution, and then offered for cross-examination by the defence. If necessary the prosecution will then re-examine the witness. At the close of the prosecution case the defence may make an application that there is "no case to answer" which is considered below.

Assuming that the magistrates rule that there is a case for the defendant to answer, the defence will then call their evidence. If the defendant is going to testify, he must give evidence before the rest of his witnesses do. The defence will examine in chief each of their witnesses, with the prosecution then cross-examining the witness, and the defence re-examining if necessary. At the close of the defence case, the prosecution may make closing submissions on fact or law (where the defendant is represented or where any defendant (represented or not) relies on evidence other than their own). The defence will then make a closing speech to the magistrates, who will subsequently retire to consider their decision. See CrPR 37.3.

Does the defence get an opening speech? In the magistrates' court the defence has a choice: either an opening speech or a closing one. Because of the huge tactical advantages in having the final word, few advocates are prepared to lose the chance to make a final speech and so they usually take this option. In Crown Court the defence will get an opening speech, but only if they are calling at least one witness as to fact other than the defendant.

Does the prosecution get a closing speech? It was previously the case that the Prosecution did not get a closing speech in the magistrates' court, unless the defence closing speech raised a new matter of law. In their opening speech the prosecution therefore needed to outline not only the facts of the case, but also all their legal arguments. However, a very recent change to the CrPR has changed this so that the prosecution can make closing submissions if the conditions in CrPR 37.3(3)(g) are made out (see above). Regardless, you should always take a careful note of the prosecution opening speech. At the end of the trial it is useful to be able to remind the court what the prosecution said they were going to prove, and to show where they have fallen short of this.

Reading of statements: Any witness whose evidence is to be relied upon by either the prosecution or the defence will usually provide a witness statement. If the evidence in the witness statement is agreed by the opposing party then the contents of the statement can be read to the court thus saving the need for the witness to attend the trial in person: s.9 CJA 1967. Any prejudicial information or inadmissible comments within the statement can be edited out if all parties agree to it so the court/jury does not hear these words when the statement is read out. The same weight will be attached to a witness statement which is read out at trial as if the witness had attended in person.

Agreed evidence: An alternative to reading out many agreed statements which may for example cover the same point, is to prepare a document setting out the agreed facts in the case: s.10 CJA 1967. This evidence is taken to be agreed to be true by all parties in the case and again avoids the need to call many witnesses.

Live link evidence: s.51 Criminal Justice Act 2003 enables evidence to be given by any witness (other than the defendant) by way of video link where it is in the interests of the efficient or effective administration of justice for the witness to give evidence in this way. The court will take into account various factors, including the witness' ability to attend, the importance of that witness' evidence, and the extent to which use of the video link will inhibit the testing of the witness' evidence.

Special measures for vulnerable witnesses: Various "special measures" are available for witnesses who are young or otherwise vulnerable. These include the giving of evidence by video link, the use of screens, and of pre-recorded examination in chief. For further details see Chapter 14.3.4.

What is a submission of no case to answer? This is also known as a "half time submission", because it takes place half way through the case, at the point where the prosecution closes its case. This is your opportunity to address the court and to point out where the prosecution case has fallen short of the high standard required to establish guilt. In *Galbraith* 73 Cr.App.R 124, CA the Court of Appeal set out the test to be applied in the Crown Court and this test is also used in the magistrates' court. The submission may be made and according to *Galbraith*, must be upheld in two circumstances. The first is where there has been no evidence to establish an essential element of the offence (for example, the prosecution has failed to call any evidence on the issue of dishonesty in a theft case). The second is where the prosecution evidence is so tenuous that even taken at its highest, a court could not safely convict on it. The Criminal Procedure Rules also makes reference to this submission stating that on a defendant's application or on its own initiative, the court may acquit on the ground that the prosecution evidence is insufficient for any reasonable court properly to convict but only where the prosecution has had an opportunity to make representations: CrPR 37.3(3)(c). If you succeed with this submission, the case will be concluded and your client acquitted of the charge against him.

The role of the justices' clerk: In the magistrates' court there are potential challenges to the role of the justices' clerk. In particular objection may be taken to the clerk retiring with the justices to advise on legal issues in the absence of the prosecution and defence lawyers. It is hard to justify this practice which effectively prevents the defendant from being able to challenge the legal advice that is being given. As a result, guidance was issued that confirmed that the giving of legal advice should normally take place in open court, and that where legal advice is given in private it should be repeated in open court and the parties should be given an opportunity to comment on it: see Consolidated Criminal Practice Direction part V.55.

9.3.1 Trial in your client's absence

Pleading guilty by post:

There is a power to enter a guilty plea by post on offences where the defendant has been summoned to attend court for a summary only matter: s12 Magistrates' Court Act 1980. The power is normally exercised in minor matters such as minor Road Traffic offences, TV licence non-payment and so on. Note that this is only possible where the prosecution offers the option and where the court has received written notification from the defendant stating that he wishes to plead guilty without attending court. In these circumstances, the court can proceed to dispose of the case in the absence of the accused and he will be notified in writing of the outcome of the case.

Trial in absence:

Section 11 Magistrates' Court Act 1980 (as amended by s.54 Coroners and Justice Act 2009) states that where an adult defendant fails to attend for trial, the court shall proceed in his absence unless it is contrary to the interests of justice. It goes on to state that the court shall not proceed where there is an acceptable reason for the defendant's absence although there is no onus on the court to enquire into that reason. The court can proceed in your client's absence where a summons has been served, provided that service of the summons is established to have taken place within a reasonable time before the trial or where the defendant has attended court previously in relation to the case. However, your client will be treated as being present, provided he is represented by counsel or a solicitor, unless he has been bailed and is therefore personally required to attend court to answer his bail. In such a situation, you may conduct the case exactly as you would were your client actually present. Note that where your client fails to answer his bail, while a warrant may be issued for his arrest, the court may also decide to hear the case in his absence. The court cannot sentence someone to a period of imprisonment or to a disqualification in their absence. See also CrPR37.10 and 37.11.

In the Consolidated Criminal Practice Direction, section I.13 (see above at 5.5.6), it suggests that the discretion to proceed in your client's absence should be exercised "with the utmost care and caution". It also suggests that in less serious offences it may be fairer to proceed in the defendant's absence if he is only likely to be fined for the offence, rather than landing him with the costs of an adjournment. In *Jones* [2003] 1 AC 1, it was held that while the court has a discretion to commence a trial in the defendant's absence, this power should be exercised with great caution. It was generally desirable that a defendant should be represented, even if he had voluntarily absconded and commencement of a trial in the voluntary absence of the accused did not contravene article 6 of the European Convention on Human Rights. In the case of *O'Hare* [2006] EWCA Crim 471 the Court of Appeal suggested that courts should be much more ready to proceed to trial in the absence of the defendant, and strongly urged lawyers to consider whether they should continue to represent the absent defendant in order to help mitigate any unfairness arising from his absence. See also CrPR 37.10 and 37.11.

[9.4] TRIAL IN THE CROWN COURT

Trial in the Crown Court (or 'trial on indictment' as it is often called) is in many ways very similar to summary trial, but there are some obvious differences which we need to explore as well as some different terminology.

9.4.1 The arraignment and plea bargaining

Arraignment is simply the reading of the indictment (a document that lists the offences) to the defendant and the taking of a plea on each count. However, a plea of guilty must be entered voluntarily and not as the result of any pressure to plead guilty. This has led to problems where the prosecution and defence are trying to negotiate a plea before the trial, or where the judge is asked to indicate a likely sentence.

There is no formal system of plea bargaining in the English courts – however, following the decision of the Court of Appeal in *Goodyear* [2005] EWCA Crim 888 it is possible for the defendant to request that the judge provide an indication of the likely sentence that would be imposed if he were to plead guilty. The court reiterated that the essential principle was that the defendant's plea must always be made voluntarily and free from any improper pressure but said that this would not be compromised where the defendant himself asked his advocate to ask the judge for an indication of the likely sentence in the event of a guilty plea.

Because of public concerns about cases where the prosecution appear to have accepted a guilty plea to a lesser offence rather than run the risk of losing a trial on the more serious, original offence, the Attorney General issued guidelines (*Attorney-General's Guidelines on the Acceptance of Pleas* [2001] 1 Cr.App.R. 425), which stress the importance of open justice, and provide that where any discussion takes place with the judge in chambers an independent record should be kept. The Guidelines also state that where the matter is listed for trial and either a plea is accepted to a lesser charge or a reduced number of offences, or if no evidence is to be offered on a charge, the victim and his or her family should be spoken to and their views taken into account.

In practice, where it is agreed with the prosecution that the defendant will plead guilty to some counts but not others, the pleas will be entered and the prosecution will then formally offer no evidence in relation to those latter counts. At this point, the judge will record a verdict of not guilty to those counts. Alternatively, if the evidence on the remaining counts is particularly strong, the prosecution may ask for the counts to "lie on the court file". This also results in a not guilty verdict, but technically allows the prosecution to apply to re-open the case at a later date.

9.4.2 The jury

After the arraignment the trial on indictment will begin with the empanelling of the jury. A jury will consist of twelve jurors, chosen at random from eligible members of the public. The selected jurors may be challenged "for cause" by either prosecution or defence, the primary challenge being on the basis that a juror is biased, whether because they have connections with the case or have knowledge of it which will prevent them from trying the case fairly.

Note that there is no power for the defence to select or "hand pick" a jury. There have been a number of challenges on racial and gender grounds where juries have been comprised predominantly or entirely of the opposite sex/race to the defendant, but all of these challenges have been unsuccessful.

9.4.3 The trial process

With the exception of the opening and closing speeches, there are few differences between the course of a jury trial and a summary trial.

As with a magistrates' court trial the prosecution will have an opening speech. Prosecution witnesses will then be called, with examination-in-chief, cross-examination and re-examination in the usual way. There will be the chance for the defence to make a submission of no case to answer at the close of the prosecution case. Such a submission would be made in the absence of the jury and if successful, would lead to the judge directing the jury to acquit the defendant. If however the submission is unsuccessful, the the jury return to the courtroom and the case continues in the usual way (unless of course the defendant chooses to change his plea at this stage).

At the start of the defence case the defence will normally have an opening speech (in contrast to the position in a summary trial). Defence evidence will then be called with cross-examination and re-examination. The prosecution will then make a closing speech, followed by the defence closing speech. The judge will then sum up the case for the jury, giving them directions on the law, but making clear that it is for them to decide the facts of the case. The jury will then retire to deliberate over its verdict.

Some points of difference between magistrates' and jury trials

Opening and closing speeches: The jury trial will begin with the prosecution opening speech. Unlike the magistrates' court, the prosecution will have a closing speech and therefore need not be so careful to deal with matters such as the burden and standard of proof and possible defence in the opening speech. Instead, the opening speech is likely to "set the scene" for the offence and explain to the jury what evidence the prosecution intend to call to satisfy each element of the offence. Also in contrast to the magistrates' court, the defence will have an opening speech at the start of the defence case as of right, provided that they are calling evidence as to the facts rather than simply calling the defendant himself.

Voir dire: A voir dire is a trial within a trial to rule on disputed points of law or admissibility of evidence. Its purpose is to ensure that the jury does not hear any evidence that may be inadmissible until the trial judge has had an opportunity to rule on admissibility. Thus, if the admissibility of a confession is challenged (for example, on the basis that it was obtained in circumstances that made it unreliable: s.76 PACE), a voir dire can be held and the judge, in the absence of the jury, can decide whether the confession is admissible or not. If the confession is not admissible, no further reference will be made to it, and the jury will never know of its existence. If the confession is admissible, the evidence can then be put before the jury in the normal way. By contrast, in the magistrates' courts, the Magistrates must hear the application and make a ruling. Clearly it is undesirable to have the same bench hear the evidence you wish to have excluded, because even if they do decide that it is inadmissible, they have still heard it and it could still have a bearing on the case.

The procedure for a voir dire is that the jury will be sent out of the courtroom and the advocates will make legal submissions on the issue of admissibility. Sometimes, witnesses will be called to give evidence on factual issues, for example to explain how a piece of evidence was obtained. Such witnesses give their evidence on a special voir dire oath and only give evidence on matters relevant to the admissibility of the evidence.

It may be possible to avoid a voir dire where there is agreement between prosecution and defence that evidence is inadmissible. For example, there will often be inadmissible comments or references in various witness statements or in the transcript of the police station interview. In such case the advocates will agree an "edit" which excludes the inadmissible material.

Prosecution power to appeal against evidential rulings which terminate the case: This provision permits the prosecution to appeal to the Court of Appeal against interlocutory rulings which would otherwise terminate the trial, or against "evidentiary rulings" which significantly weaken the prosecution case (for example the exclusion of a confession). This is a right to appeal while the Crown Court trial is still proceeding. If the prosecution appeals in this way and loses at the Court of Appeal, then it must terminate the prosecution.

Trial without a jury: Among the most controversial provisions in the CJA 2003 were powers to dispense with juries where either the case is a complex financial matter or there is a real and present danger of jury tampering. This provision has come into force in respect of jury tampering but is not going to be introduced for fraud trials because of Parliamentary concerns. The recently enacted Protection of Freedoms Act 2012 has repealed the CJA provision in relation to complex fraud trials.

The summing up and the verdict: In the Crown Court there is a division of roles between the judge (as determiner of law) and the jury (as finder of facts). The judge's summing-up to the jury will therefore contain directions on any issues of law, as well as a summary of the evidence that has been given. Once the jury has retired, no further evidence can be adduced. The jury can ask questions of the judge during their retirement, and the judge will invariably inform counsel and will canvass with them any proposed reply.

The jury's verdict should normally be unanimous. If, however, after at least 2 hours and 10 minutes there is no agreement, the judge can permit a majority verdict. Longer should be allowed in more complex cases. A majority verdict may be 11–1 or 10–2. If one or more jurors have been discharged, the verdict may be 10–1 or 9–1. If there are only 9 jurors, the verdict must be unanimous. If a jury cannot decide on a verdict, it will be discharged. This is not an acquittal and the defendant can, and normally will, be tried in front of a new jury.

Alternative offences: s.6(3) Criminal Law Act 1967 permits "alternative verdicts" in the Crown Court. These will arise where the offence charged in the indictment "expressly or by implication" includes an allegation of another offence.

The law on this point is often complex, but it is clear that an allegation of burglary (for example) can include an allegation of trespass and theft; it is therefore possible for the jury to find the defendant not guilty of burglary but guilty of theft. Similarly, robbery may impliedly include an allegation of common assault or theft. Causing grievous bodily harm (s.18 Offences against the Person Act 1861) can include inflicting grievous bodily harm under s.20 of that Act. Note in particular that in Public Order Act offences, it will normally be possible for a jury to convict of a lesser public order offence when trying a more serious public order offence. In cases where an alternative verdict is possible, the judge will direct the jury as to the appropriate alternative offence.

Sample offences: There is a little noticed provision in the Domestic Violence, Crime and Victims Act 2004 which permits the prosecution in a Crown Court to apply to the judge for only sample counts to be tried before a jury. The remaining counts are then tried before a judge without a jury in the event of the defendant being convicted by a jury of the sample counts: s.17 DVCVA 2004.

9.4.4 After the verdict

Once the jury has delivered its verdict it will be discharged. If the defendant has been convicted, the judge will turn to sentencing. This is considered in the following chapter.

The effect of an acquittal: If your client has been acquitted, then the general rule is that he cannot be tried again for the same matter. If an attempt is made to bring a fresh prosecution, he will be able to raise the plea of "autrefois acquit" which, if accepted, will be a bar to any further proceedings on the indictment. There are however two circumstances where a not guilty verdict may not be the end of the matter:

Tainted acquittals: Under the Criminal Procedure and Investigations Act 1996 provisions were made in respect of "tainted acquittals". These are acquittals where there has been a later conviction of a person for an administration of justice offence to do with interference with a juror or witness in the original proceedings. Subject to safeguards, including the leave of the High Court, the acquittal can be quashed and new proceedings commenced.

Retrial of serious offences: The CJA 2003 introduced controversial new provisions which permit the prosecution to apply for leave for a retrial of defendants who have been acquitted of serious offences where new and compelling evidence has come to light following the acquittal: CJA 2003, Part 10. The offences include serious offences against the person (such as murder, manslaughter and kidnapping); serious sexual offences; serious drugs importation and production offences (Class A drugs only); as well as the more serious criminal damage offences (arson endangering life, causing an explosion likely to endanger life or property).

The consent of the Director of Public Prosecutions and the Court of Appeal are required, and the prosecution must be able to show that there is new and compelling evidence. The power is retrospective and applies to acquittals prior to the commencement of the CJA. One key area where the provisions are likely to be applied is where advances in science mean that there is now strong forensic evidence against a previously acquitted defendant. The provision will also catch those who have been acquitted of an offence but later admit their guilt.

> *R v D [2006] EWCA Crim 1354 This case involved the murder of a young woman in 1989 whose body was subsequently found hidden behind a bath panel in her own home. The body was wrapped in a blanket and fibres from the defendant's rugby shirt were found on the blanket. Additionally, the defendant's fingerprints were found on a key fob that had belonged to the victim. The key fob was found hidden under the floorboards in the defendant's home address. Although the evidence appeared damning, the defendant was acquitted at trial. In 1999, whilst serving a sentence on unrelated matters, the defendant admitted to several people that he had indeed committed the murder and had lied about it at trial. He was arrested and interviewed for perjury. In the course of the interview, he admitted the murder. He was convicted of perjury. The prosecution then successfully applied for a retrial on the murder on the basis that the confessions amounted to 'new and compelling evidence' under Part 10 of the CJA. The defendant then indicated that he would never have admitted to the murder in the perjury interview if he had known it would lead to a retrial. This was rejected by the Court of Appeal, a retrial was ordered and he was duly convicted.*

OPENING SPEECHES

(Prosecution only in Magistrates' Court)

↓

PROSECUTION CALLS WITNESS(ES)

- Examination in chief (by pros)
- Cross examination (by def)
- Re-examination (by pros – if necessary)
- Questions from Bench

↓

DEFENCE SUBMISSION OF 'NO CASE TO ANSWER' (IF APPROPRIATE)

Test in *Galbraith*: no evidence to establish an element of offence or evidence is so tenuous that no court could safely convict

↓

DEFENCE CALLS WITNESSES (CLIENT GOES FIRST IF GIVING EVIDENCE)

- Examination in chief (by def)
- Cross examination (by pros)
- Re-examination (by def – if necessary)
- Questions from Bench

↓

CLOSING SPEECHES

(Defence only in Magistrates" Court unless CrPR 37.3 (3) (g) is satisfied). In Crown Court, Judge will provide summing up and jury will retire to consider their verdict, otherwise Bench will retire to consider their verdict

↓ ↓

GUILTY VERDICT

- Prosecution provides additional info for sentence (e.g. Pre cons)
- Defence plea in mitigation
- Adjourn for pre-sentence reports (if appropriate)
- Sentence is passed

NOT GUILTY VERDICT

- Case concluded (Defence may seek an order that defence costs be paid from central funds)

Trial Preparation and Trial Procedure – test yourself questions

[The answers to these questions are set out in Appendix A at the back of this book]

[1] Thomas has been charged with robbery. At the close of the case the twelve jurors are sent to begin their deliberations.

Consider the following propositions:

i. The judge must ask for a majority verdict if the jury remains deadlocked after 2 hours and 10 minutes.

ii. If the jury asks for further evidence the judge should consult with prosecution and defence advocates before agreeing to any request.

iii. The jury can find Thomas guilty of an alternative offence of criminal damage.

Which of the above are correct?

(a) All of them.

(b) i only.

(c) i and iii only.

(d) None of them.

[2] Consider the following propositions in relation to a submission of "no case to answer" in the magistrates' court.

i. A submission may be made where the prosecution has failed to call evidence on an essential element of the case.

ii. A submission may be made where the prosecution evidence is so tenuous that no reasonable court could safely convict.

iii. A submission may be made where a prosecution witness has failed to "come up to proof".

Which of the above propositions are correct?

(a) All of them.

(b) iii only.

(c) ii and iii only.

(d) i and ii only.

[3] In a summary trial, which one of the following is correct?

(a) The prosecution must give an opening speech and the defence must give a closing speech.

(b) If the matter is summary only, the defence will get a closing speech; if the matter is either way, the defence will get both an opening and closing speech.

(c) If the defence makes an opening speech, it will lose its right to a closing speech.

(d) The defence can only make an opening speech if it intends to call evidence other than the defendant and any character witnesses.

CHAPTER 10

SENTENCING

> This chapter covers:
>
> Sentencing principles: seriousness, culpability, harm and mitigation
>
> Procedures post-conviction
>
> Custodial sentences
>
> The community order
>
> Financial penalties
>
> Conditional discharges and other disposals
>
> Ancillary orders
>
> Sentencing in road traffic matters
>
> Sentencing advocacy: mitigation speeches

[10.1] SENTENCING PRINCIPLES

The Sentencing Council for England and Wales (Sentencing Council) was established in April 2010 by Part 4 of the Coroners and Justice Act 2009. It takes over from the Sentencing Guidelines Council and the Sentencing Advisory Panel, statutory bodies created by the CJA 2003, who were tasked with policy making in sentencing matters. The purpose of the Sentencing Council is to create greater consistency in sentencing with the responsibility of producing codified guidelines for sentencing and allocation to be applied by all criminal courts. In undertaking this task, it is usual for the Sentencing Council to publish a draft guideline and following a period of consultation, to produce a definitive guideline for use by the Courts. There is now a statutory duty for courts to follow any definitive guidelines available: s.172 CJA 2003.

Magistrates Court: The Magistrates' Court Sentencing Guidelines provide sentencing information for almost every offence which can be heard in the Magistrates' Court. Each guideline will indicate a starting point for the offence and then provide the court with a range of sentences within which the offender must sentenced. The Magistrates must sentence an offender within these guidelines or give reasons in open court if they find they cannot do so: s.174(2)(a) CJA 2003. The full set of definitive (and draft) guidelines are available at www.sentencingcouncil.judiciary.gov.uk.

Crown Court: Judges have historically had much more discretion when it comes to sentencing offenders in the Crown Court, tending to use previous Court of Appeal rulings to assist with finding the correct tariff. However, all Courts are now required to follow sentencing guidelines (s.174 CJA 2003) and there is now a considerable number of guidelines applicable to Crown

Court proceedings. Note that as new guidelines are introduced, they do not take effect until the set commencement date, regardless of whether the incoming guideline would positively affect the possible sentence in a particular case: *R v Boakye and Others* [2012] EWCA Crim 838.

10.1.1 Purpose of sentencing

Any court dealing with an adult offender must have regard to the purpose of sentencing. The purpose is set out in s.142 CJA 2003 as being:

- The punishment of offenders
- The reduction of crime (including reduction by deterrence)
- The reform and rehabilitation of offenders
- The protection of the public
- The making of reparation by offenders to persons affected by their offences.

10.1.2 Determining the seriousness of an offence

The court is required to take into account both the culpability of the offender and the degree of harm that was caused or might have been caused: s.143 CJA 2003. Most sentencing guidelines available will consider the various factors relevant to the seriousness of each offence but some general rules also apply.

The guidance from the Sentencing Guidelines Council (Overarching principles: seriousness, 16th December 2004 (amended on 4 April 2005) at www.sentencing council.judiciary.gov.uk) explains that the starting point should always be the culpability of the offender.

The Guidance provides that:

> *Harm must always be judged in the light of culpability. The precise level of culpability will be determined by such factors as motivation, whether the offence was planned or spontaneous or whether the offender was in a position of trust. 1.17*

Culpability is greater if:

- an offender deliberately causes more harm than is necessary for the commission of the offence, or
- where an offender targets a vulnerable victim (because of their old age or youth, disability or by virtue of the job they do).
- If unusually serious harm is caused which the offender did not intend, then culpability will be influenced by the extent to which the offender could foresee the harm.

10.1.3 Features which will make an offence more serious (aggravating factors)

Previous convictions: The CJA makes clear that if an offender has previous convictions, each previous conviction will be an aggravating factor if it is reasonable to treat it so, having regard to the nature of the offence and the time elapsed since conviction for it: s.143.

Offending on bail: Similarly the CJA provides that an offence will be more serious if it was committed while the offender was on bail. This is particularly so where the offence committed is the same as the offence for which bail was granted: *Jeffrey* [2004] 1Cr App R (S) 179.

Offences aggravated by prejudice: Offences where there is racial or religious hostility will be treated as more serious, as will offences where there is hostility on the basis of disability or of sexual orientation: ss.145/146 CJA 2003.

Factors showing higher than normal culpability: "Overarching Principles: Seriousness" sets out a list of factors in addition to those in the CJA which make an offence more culpable. These include:

- Planning of an offence
- An intention to commit more serious harm than actually resulted from the offence
- Offenders operating in groups or gangs
- 'Professional' offending
- Commission of the offence for financial gain (where this is not inherent in the offence itself)
- High level of profit from the offence
- An attempt to conceal or dispose of evidence
- Failure to respond to warnings or concerns expressed by others about the offender's behaviour
- Offence committed whilst on licence
- Deliberate targeting of vulnerable victim(s)
- Commission of an offence while under the influence of alcohol or drugs
- Use of a weapon to frighten or injure victim
- Deliberate and gratuitous violence or damage to property, over and above what is needed to carry out the offence
- Abuse of power
- Abuse of a position of trust

Factors which indicate that there is higher degree of harm: Again the guideline sets out a list of factors which indicate a higher than normal degree of harm:

- Multiple victims
- An especially serious physical or psychological effect on the victim, even if unintended
- A sustained assault or repeated assaults on the same victim
- Victim is particularly vulnerable
- Location of the offence (for example, in an isolated place)
- Offence is committed against those working in the public sector or providing a service to the public
- Presence of others e.g. relatives, especially children or partner of the victim
- Additional degradation of the victim (e.g. taking photographs of a victim as part of a sexual offence)
- In property offences, high value (including sentimental value) of property to the victim, or substantial consequential loss (e.g. where the theft of equipment causes serious disruption to a victim's life or business)

These are all matters you will need to take into account when planning how to mitigate for a client who has been convicted of a criminal offence.

10.1.4 Mitigating factors

The Guideline lists only four factors which show lower than normal culpability:

- A greater degree of provocation than normally expected
- Mental illness or disability
- Youth or age, where it affects the responsibility of the individual defendant
- The fact that the offender played only a minor role in the offence

However, the Guidance goes on to point out that the court must take into account any matters relevant to mitigation. Mitigation is therefore very fact-specific – it will necessarily vary from client to client and offence to offence. Provocation might normally provide only little mitigation but if you can show that a client is particularly vulnerable to provocation because of their personal circumstances or their previous history, it may be important mitigation.

The effect of a Guilty plea

A plea of Guilty will be relevant to mitigation in two ways. First it may evidence remorse on the part of the offender. An early admission of guilt, along with statements of apology or remorse, is important mitigation in showing that the offender genuinely regretted his actions.

Secondly, regardless of the issue of whether the offender is remorseful, a guilty plea may entitle the defendant to a reduction in his sentence because he has avoided the need for a trial. The court must take the guilty plea into account: s.144 CJA 2003.

Again this is a matter where guidance has been issued – see Reduction in Sentence for a Guilty Plea, 16th December 2004 (amended 23 July 2007). The guidelines provide that the discounts should be set at:

- **A recommended one third** where the guilty plea was entered at the first reasonable opportunity.
- **A recommended one quarter** where a plea is entered once a trial date has been set.
- **A recommended one tenth** for a guilty plea entered at the door of the court or after the trial has begun.
- **Overwhelming evidence of guilt:** there is some discretion for a lesser discount to be given where evidence of guilt is overwhelming. This is suggested to be in the region of 20%.

It is important to realise that the guilty plea may help your client in two different ways – by showing remorse and thereby reducing the core sentence, and then by entitling him to a reduction to the sentence that the court has decided on.

> *Jon is arrested on suspicion of an assault on a colleague at work. At the police station he immediately admits the offence, expresses his regrets, explaining that he simply snapped because he is under such stress at home. He enters a guilty plea at his first appearance in the magistrates' court.*
>
> *In his mitigation Jon will argue that his culpability is less than would otherwise be the case because of his immediate remorse, as evidenced by his admission of guilt at the earliest stage and his co-operation with the police. The court should decide the level of punishment in the light of this and any other mitigating or aggravating factors. Having decided the level of punishment, the court should now discount the punishment by 1/3rd to give credit for the timely guilty plea. This is separate from any credit he has been given for his remorse.*

Future developments: At present, there is no official provision for credit to be given to an offender who admits guilt at the police station. Proposals have been made for the Sentencing Council to consider whether credit should be given in such circumstances although this is currently being met with some resistance as it may place suspects under pressure to admit matters at a very early stage in the case when faced with the prospect of a much lighter sentence.

[10.2] PROCEDURE POST-CONVICTION

After your client has been found guilty of an offence or after he has pleaded guilty to an offence, the court will consider how to sentence him. In the magistrates' court this can sometimes be done on the same day but for more serious offences or for cases in the Crown court, the case may be adjourned for further information to be gathered prior to the court making its decision on sentence.

10.2.1 Are reports required?

You need to consider both whether the court will require a pre-sentence report (PSR) and whether there is any need for other reports (including medical reports). If reports are not required – for example, in a straightforward case – the court will want to proceed straight to sentence.

Pre-sentence reports:

A pre-sentence report can be either written or oral and they are provided by a probation officer (or social worker in some situations) with a view to assisting the court to arrive at the most suitable method of dealing with the defendant. A PSR must be obtained if the court is considering either a custodial or a community sentence unless the court is of the opinion that it is unnecessary to obtain one: s.156 CJA 2003. Note, however, that a sentence is not invalidated by the court's failure to obtain a report.

The court must obtain a PSR before deciding on any one of the following matters unless it is of the opinion that it is not necessary: s.156(3) & (4) CJA 2003

- whether the custody or community threshold has been passed
- what is the shortest term of custody commensurate with the seriousness of the offence
- whether the restrictions on liberty within a community order are commensurate with the seriousness of the offence
- whether certain requirements in a community order are suitable for a particular offender

What will go into a pre sentence report? PSRs are intended to assist the court by providing an objective summary and analysis of the offence, and then by analysing your client's behaviour and his attitude towards his offending. The report will consider your client's social circumstances and will specifically address the risk of his re-offending. A PSR can take one of two forms:

Fast Delivery Report (FDR): This report comprises a brief assessment of the above issues and is generally appropriate where the court indicates that a low or medium level community sentence is required. They are usually available on the same day as they are requested or within 24hrs of being requested and they can be presented either orally or in writing.

Standard Delivery Report (SDR): This comprises a full and detailed assessment of the issues above and is appropriate where the court has indicated that a custodial sentence is being considered. They are usually completed in writing within 15 days of request or within 10 days if the offender is in custody.

The defence is entitled to a copy of the report regardless of which type is prepared and in practice you will generally go to the court probation office in order to get an advance copy prior to dealing with the sentencing hearing. (You will find an example of a full pre sentence report (SDR) at Document 23 in the case study.)

Are other reports needed? You should consider whether the defence should obtain reports for example, medical reports, or an assessment on suitability for alcohol/drug rehabilitation units. Where you are obtaining such a report, always remember to get legal aid authorisation for any costs.

10.2.2 The court's power to adjourn

The magistrates' court can adjourn for enquiries for up to three weeks (two weeks if your client is in custody). The Crown Court has an inherent power to adjourn. Your client generally has no prima facie right to bail once convicted. There is a right to bail where the court adjourns to obtain reports but the Bail Act provides that even then your client need not be granted bail if it appears to the court that it would be impracticable to complete the inquiries/reports without keeping your client in custody. Bail can be made conditional on your client making himself available for reports: s.3 (6)(d) Bail Act 1976.

10.2.3 Antecedents

The prosecution will summarise the facts of the offence for the court, but it will also be their duty to adduce evidence as to your client's character and antecedents. The prosecution will provide the court with a list of your client's previous convictions which will include any warnings, reprimands, cautions and pending proceedings. The focus is normally on the details of the last few convictions and any other conviction "likely to be of interest". If the present offence was committed while subject to a community sentence (so that the court may be considering whether to revoke the community order and re-sentence), the list will contain details of the offence for which the community order was imposed.

Before the hearing, you should check the list of previous convictions very carefully with your client to make sure the details are correct – the court will often ask you to confirm this.

Professional Conduct point: should the court ask you to confirm your client's convictions?

What do you do if the list does not contain all your client's previous convictions? Bear in mind that you cannot mislead the court, nor can you breach your client's confidentiality without his consent.

10.2.4 Offences to be "taken into consideration" (TICs)

In sentencing your client, the court must only consider those offences of which your client has been found guilty (or to which he has pleaded guilty). The exception to this is where your client indicates that he is prepared to admit other offences with which he has not been charged or convicted, and that he wishes to have these "taken into consideration" at sentencing. This is a way for your client to "wipe the slate clean" and to make sure he has no further matters hanging over him.

TICs in practice:

The Sentencing Council has issued guidance on sentencing TICs, confirming that the total sentence passed should reflect all the offending behaviour. The sentence must be "just and proportionate" and must not exceed the statutory maximum for the conviction offence. A d. Schedule of Offences to be TIC'd should be prepared by the police and served on the defendant and his representatives before the sentencing hearing. The defendant should be asked in open court if he admits the offences on the schedule and wishes them to be taken into consideration on sentence. The Court should not TIC any offence where there is doubt as to whether the defendant admits it or not. TICs are a matter for the prosecution. The defence have no right to demand that outstanding matters be dealt with in this way. TICs should generally be of broadly the same kind as the offence before the court. The court may be prepared to stretch this principle provided the offences to be TIC'd are not substantially more serious than the substantive offence.

In sentencing TICs, the court should find the relevant starting point for the convicted offence and then adjust that starting point according to the aggravating and mitigating factors present. The guideline suggests that TICs will be an aggravating factor and where there are a large number of TICs, this may take the sentence outside the usual range. On the other hand, a frank admission may well be evidence of genuine remorse which can mitigate and thus adjust the starting point downwards. You should be cautious when advising your client on whether to accept TICs or not. They are capable of increasing the seriousness of the crime and thus possibly the sentence imposed

Offences to be taken into consideration and "specimen" offences: TICs are different to "specimen offences". A specimen offence is where the prosecution proceeds on, say, one count of benefit fraud out of 50 or 60 charges. Unless your client admits the outstanding charges, he can only be sentenced on the basis of the offence for which he has been convicted: *Kidd* [1998] 1 Cr App R (S) 243.

10.2.5 *Newton* hearings

Your client may plead guilty to an offence on one basis, while the prosecution is of the view that the offence was actually committed under more serious circumstances. Thus for example, your client may plead guilty to causing actual bodily harm, but may do so on the basis that he admits a single punch. The prosecution account, however, may be substantially more serious – with allegations of a number of kicks and punches. The prosecution can review its case and decide whether they accept the defendant's account of the disputed facts and in such a case, an "agreed basis of plea" can be prepared in writing. The court must consider whether it is fair and in the interests of justice to accept this and if so, the court will sentence on this basis: Consolidated Criminal Practice Direction IV 45.10–45.14; *R v Underwood* [2005] 1 Cr.App.R.13.

Where the basis of plea cannot be agreed, the court must either accept the defence account, or if the difference between the two accounts would affect the likely sentence, a Newton hearing must be held. In a Newton hearing, the judge will sit without a jury and prosecution witnesses will then be called. The strict rules of evidence apply, as will the normal burden and standard of proof. The court will then decide whether the prosecution version has been made out. Note that if a Newton hearing is held and the court does not accept your client's version of events, he may lose some or all of the credit to which he may be entitled for entering a guilty plea (see 10.1.4 above): *Stevens* (1986) 8 Cr App R (S) 291; *R v Elicin & Moore* [2009] 1 Cr.App.R.(S.)98.

10.2.6 Deferring sentencing

The court has a power to defer sentencing under s.1 PCC(S)A 2000. The purpose of the deferral is to allow the court to have regard to your client's conduct after conviction (including any reparation) or any relevant change of circumstances. The maximum period of deferral is six months and the power to defer can only be exercised where it is in the interests of justice to do so. During the period of deferral your client can be required to carry out additional requirements, and his compliance with these will be taken into account when he is sentenced at the end of the deferral period. He must consent to undertake any requirements imposed before the deferral can be ordered

[10.3] CUSTODIAL SENTENCES

10.3.1 The custody threshold

Custodial sentences are supposed to be reserved for the most serious cases where no other penalty can be justified.

> *The court must not pass a custodial sentence unless it is of the opinion that the offence, or the combination of the offence and one or more offences associated with it, was so serious that neither a fine alone nor a community sentence can be justified for the offence.* S.152(2) CJA 2003

Taking a decision whether to impose a custodial sentence: Guidance on seriousness suggests that the court must ask itself four questions:

   i.   Has the custody threshold been passed?

   ii. If so, is it unavoidable that a custodial sentence be imposed?

   iii. If so, can that sentence be suspended? (sentencers should be clear that they would have imposed a custodial sentence if the power to suspend had not been available)

   iv. If not, impose a sentence which takes immediate effect for the term commensurate with the seriousness of the offence.

The idea is very clearly that even if a custodial sentence might be justified by the seriousness of the offence, it may not be necessary to impose an immediate jail term once other measures have been considered.

Limited sentencing power in the magistrates' court: Note the magistrates' court sentencing power is limited to a maximum of six months' custody in respect of a single offence. The magistrates can impose a sentence of up to twelve months' in total when sentencing for two or more either way offences. Note two or more summary offences will attract a maximum of six months imprisonment as will a summary offence and an either way offence.

10.3.2 Applying the custody threshold

Assessing seriousness: The factors which may make an offence more or less serious are set out at 10.1 above. In addition to considering the individual seriousness indicators, you will need to have regard to any sentencing guidelines issued by the Sentencing Council.

Rose is convicted of shoplifting where she left a supermarket with a full trolley of food having made no attempt to pay for the items. The goods are valued at £95. She has three previous convictions for shoplifting. All are of low value, but all are relatively recent.

Assessing seriousness: you will obviously take into account the relatively low degree of harm intrinsic in the offence – and the aggravating factor of recent relevant convictions. If the matter is being dealt with in the Magistrates' court you should consider the Magistrates' guideline for theft which indicates that the starting point for this offence is a financial penalty – the range is anywhere from a conditional discharge to a low community order. Clearly the previous convictions will act as an aggravating factor which is likely to put this matter out of reach of a conditional discharge. In either court, you should take account of the guideline for Theft and Burglary in a Building other than a Dwelling which indicates that even where the facts of the case suggests that a fine or discharge is appropriate, where offending is "persistent" the custody or community threshold may in fact be met.

Where offences cross the custody threshold: The Sentencing Council's guidance on the imposition of custodial penalties makes clear that even if an offence is so serious that it crosses the custody threshold it does not mean that custody should be inevitable.

Passing the custody threshold does not mean that a custodial sentence should be deemed inevitable, and custody can still be avoided in the light of personal mitigation or where there is a suitable intervention in the community which provides sufficient restriction (by way of punishment) while addressing the rehabilitation of the offender to prevent future crime. For example, a prolific offender who currently could expect a short custodial sentence (which, in advance of custody plus, would have no provision for supervision on release) might more appropriately receive a suitable community sentence. <u>Overarching principles: seriousness:</u> para 1.32.

Offence prevalence: The Sentencing Council makes clear that it is not normally appropriate to penalise individual offenders more heavily simply because of prevalence. However the Sentencing Council has indicated that it may be permissible to do so in exceptional circumstances:

There may be exceptional local circumstances that arise which may lead a court to decide that prevalence should influence sentencing levels. The pivotal issue in such cases will be the harm being caused to the community. It is essential that sentencers both have supporting evidence from an external source (for example the local Criminal Justice Board) to justify claims that a particular crime is prevalent in their area and are satisfied that there is a compelling need to treat the offence more seriously than elsewhere. <u>Overarching principles: seriousness:</u> para 1.39

This approach has been confirmed by the Court of Appeal in *Oosthuizen* [2005] EWCA Crim 1978. Sentences must return to using the sentencing guidelines once the particular issue has been adequately addressed.

10.3.3 Victim Impact Statements

Statements from victims are becoming a more common feature at sentencing hearings. Their use is governed by the Consolidated Criminal Practice Direction, III.28. This provides that such statements should be considered by the court and should be served in proper form (i.e. as a s.9 statement). The defence are also entitled to a copy of the victim impact statement. However, the focus is on the effect of the offence on the victim and it is not for the victims to determine the sentence. In *Perks*, [2001] 1 Cr.App.R.(S.) 66 the Court of Appeal noted that, while a victim's forgiveness or unwillingness to press charges was not directly relevant to the sentencing exercise, it might indicate that the impact of the offence had been less that might otherwise have been expected.

10.3.4 Associated offences

In considering the seriousness of an offence, the court can have regard to associated offences in deciding whether the seriousness threshold has been crossed. An offence is "associated" if either the offender was convicted of it or sentenced for it at the same time, or it is an offence that he asks to have taken into consideration at the sentencing hearing: s.161 PCC(S)A 2000.

> *In Patterson, Jamie (2000) 165 J.P.N. 225, C.A, the indefatigable JP was seen being driven in a stolen Jaguar. He left that car, broke into a house, stole the keys to a Porsche, drove the Porsche down the motorway, stole £30 of petrol, was chased by police at 130 mph, narrowly missed mowing down motorway workers, and was finally arrested having run away when stopped at a road block. Held: the judge was right to sentence him on the basis that all the offences were "associated" "both in law and in reality". The two and a half year period of detention in a Young Offenders Institution was justified.*

10.3.5 Length of sentence

> *...the custodial sentence must be for the shortest term (not exceeding the permitted maximum) that in the opinion of the court is commensurate with the seriousness of the offence, or the combination of the offence and one or more offences associated with it.* s.153 CJA 2003

In order to get an idea of the likely sentencing outcomes you need to consider the normal range of sentences which the courts give for this type of offence – sometimes referred to as the "tariff". You can do this by looking at sentencing guidelines, and the general range of sentencing case law. A good starting point is a practitioner text like Blackstone's Criminal Practice – but sentencing law moves very quickly and you will need to check for more recent cases.

Mandatory sentences

There is a mandatory life sentence for murder. There are a number of further situations in which the court is required to impose a particular sentence.

- Certain categories of serious firearms offences: mandatory minimum five year sentence introduced by CJA 2003.

- Minimum seven year sentence for third class A drug trafficking offence, unless it would be unjust.

- A mandatory minimum sentence of three years for a third domestic burglary. In this case both the preceding burglaries must have been committed after the section came into force. There is a provision for the sentence to be disapplied if there are circumstances that would make it unjust to impose the sentence: s.111 PCC(S)A 2000.

Credit for time served: Where your client has spent time in custody on remand for an offence (or a related offence), the court must direct that the time spent in custody will count as time served towards a sentence of imprisonment: s.240 CJA 2003. The court can decline to do this in certain circumstances, one of which is where it is "just" to so decline: s.240(4) CJA 2003. S.240A CJA 2003 (inserted by s.21(4) Criminal Justice and Immigration Act 2008) allows any period on bail which was subject to an electronic monitoring (tag) condition to also count towards a sentence of imprisonment. Where the monitoring was for at least nine hours per day, one half day will be counted towards the period of imprisonment for each day spent on tag. In both cases, the amount of time has to be counted in days and must be stated in open court.

Early release: Home Detention Curfew scheme

In an attempt to reduce prison numbers a scheme called "home detention curfew" was introduced. This is a power to place selected short-term prisoners on home detention curfew – a form of tagging.

Release will be with a curfew condition of at least 9 hours a day, secured by electronic tagging. Conditions will end half way through the sentence and the prisoner moves onto the normal licence programme.

Early release: release on licence

All prisoners on fixed term sentences of over 12 months will be released from prison after they have served half of their custodial sentence: s.244 CJA 2003. They will then be "on licence" for the remainder of the custodial period, and during this period they will be subject to licence conditions – such as conditions to reside at a particular place, stay in touch with the probation services, undertake unpaid work and so on.

10.3.6 Suspended sentences: ss.189–194 CJA 2003

A sentence of imprisonment of over 28 weeks and less than 12 months can be suspended for a period of 6 months to 2 years. During this period the court will set requirements to be completed in the community under supervision. A breach of the order is likely to lead to immediate custody for the period of time stated at the outset of the order.

The courts must consider whether they can suspend a period of imprisonment where they have decided that an offence has passed the custody threshold and they can only impose an immediate prison sentence once they have decided that they cannot (see 10.3.1). As suspended sentences have been made widely available to the courts with the added "teeth" of community requirements, they are proving to be an extremely popular sentencing option with the courts and you should be alive to the possibility of asking the court to suspend a prison sentence for your client where appropriate.

10.3.7 Custody Plus and Intermittent custody: ss.181–186 CJA 2003

The Custody Plus scheme is set out in ss.181–182 CJA 2003. These sentences were due to be introduced in 2006 but now seem to have been shelved. Under the custody plus scheme the defendant will get a custodial sentence plus a period when they are on licence. The idea is that the relatively short custodial element is then followed by a much more rigorous period of community-based supervision to ensure that re-offending is minimised. Breach of the licence will lead to recall to prison.

Intermittent custody is outlined in ss.183–186 CJA 2003 and is effectively a weekend jail order. This was briefly piloted but has now been withdrawn – at least for the time being.

10.3.8 Special provisions for dangerous offenders: CJA 2003

There are special provisions for offenders where the offence which is before the court discloses that the offender is likely to present a significant risk of serious harm to the public. These "dangerous offender" provisions potentially arise wherever a person is convicted of a sexual or violent offence which is listed in Schedule 15 to the CJA 2003. This schedule lists most sexual and violent offences which are more than trivial. Following conviction for such an offence, the court must consider whether there is significant risk of serious harm to the public by the offender committing further specified offences.

In assessing dangerousness the court should have regard to the pre-sentence report, the offender's previous convictions and sometimes psychiatric reports which have been prepared specifically to address the issue of dangerousness.

What penalties are imposed on "dangerous offenders"?

Life Imprisonment or a Sentence of Imprisonment for Public Protection (IPP): If a person deemed to be a dangerous offender has committed a serious offence listed in Sch 15 CJA which carries a life sentence and the court considers that the seriousness of the offence can justify a life sentence, then the court MUST impose a life sentence. If the offence committed in Sch 15 carries life imprisonment but is not considered to be so serious or if the offence carries at least 10 years imprisonment, then the court MAY impose a sentence for public protection if one of the following two conditions is satisfied:

i. at the time that the offence was committed, the offender had a previous conviction for an offence listed in Sch 15A CJA 2003 (serious sexual or violent offences); or

ii. if the notional minimum term for the sentence is at least two years.

Under both sentences, the offender will serve a specified period in prison, but will then not be released until the Parole Board decides that the risk of harm to the public is diminished. Thereafter they will be subject to long term supervision in the community.

A fairly recent case dealt with the issue of whether IPP sentences were compatible with Articles 3 and 5(1) of the European Convention in Human Rights. As each IPP sentence was closely controlled by the law and could only be imposed under statute, it was considered that they do not offend these human rights principles: *Pedley & Others v R* [2009] EWCA Crim 840. The Legal Aid, Sentencing & Punishment of Offenders Act 2012 contains provisions to replace the IPP sentence but these are not yet in force.

Extended Sentence of Imprisonment: This is a sentence comprising of at least 12 months custody, plus an extended period of supervision on release of up to 5 years for offences of violence, and 8 years for sexual offences. A person deemed to be a "dangerous" offender who is convicted of a less serious specified offence in Sch 15 (those which carry a sentence of up to 10 years imprisonment) will be given an extended sentence if one of the two conditions below are satisfied:

i. at the time that the offence was committed, the offender had a previous conviction for an offence listed in Sch 15A CJA 2003 (serious sexual or violent offences); or

ii. if the court were to impose an extended sentence, the custodial element of that sentence would be at least 4 years imprisonment.

[10.4] THE COMMUNITY ORDER

The community based punishment that the court can impose for those aged 18 or over is known as the community order, and it offers the court a "menu" of different elements which they can require the offender to undertake in the community. These range from supervision by a probation officer to unpaid community work, and from curfew conditions to alcohol and drug treatment. Community sentences are only available for offences which are punishable by imprisonment: s.150A CJA 2003.

10.4.1 The community sentence threshold

A court must not pass a community sentence on an offender unless it is of the opinion that the offence, or the combination of the offence and one or more offences associated with it, was serious enough to warrant such a sentence. s.148 CJA 2003

In its guidance, the Sentencing Council emphasises the danger that an inappropriate community sentence can be counter-productive:

Sentencers must consider all of the disposals available (within or below the threshold passed) at the time of sentence, and reject them before reaching the provisional decision to make a community sentence, so that even where the threshold for a community sentence has been passed a financial penalty or discharge may still be an appropriate penalty. Where an offender has a low risk of reoffending, particular care needs to be taken in the light of evidence that indicates that there are circumstances where inappropriate intervention can increase the risk of re-offending rather than decrease it. New Sentences: the CJA 2003, para 1.1.9

Persistent offenders: An offender who has been fined on at least three occasions since reaching the age of sixteen can have a community sentence imposed even if the offence would not otherwise be serious enough to warrant it: s.151 CJA 2003. The court must decide that this is in the interests of justice. This provision is not yet in force.

10.4.2 The community order requirements

The maximum overall duration of the community order is 3 years. s.177(1)CJA lists the requirements which can be imposed on offenders:

(a) an unpaid work requirement: this must be between 40 and 300 hours of unpaid work, which must normally be completed within a 12 month period. The requirement is supervised by a probation officer.

(b) an activity requirement: a maximum of 60 days of directed activities, which may include activities whose purpose is reparation.

(c) a programme requirement: participation in an accredited programme which has been recommended to the court as being suitable for the offender.

(d) a prohibited activity requirement: refraining from prohibited activities.

(e) a curfew requirement: remaining in a specified place for at least 2 and no more than 12 hours per day, for no more than six months. This is due to change upon the implementation of s.71 Legal Aid, Sentencing and Punishment of Offenders Act 2012 whereby the curfew can extend up to 16 hours per day and for no more than a 12 month period.

(f) an exclusion requirement: prohibiting the offender from entering a specified location for a maximum of 2 years.

(g) a residence requirement: a requirement to reside at a specified place.

(ga) a foreign travel prohibition requirement: due to be introduced by the Legal Aid, Sentencing and Punishment of Offenders Act 2012, this prohibits travel to any country outside the British Isles on day(s) specified in the order or during a specified period. The maximum period of the order is 12 months and the day(s) specified in the order cannot be more than 12 months after the date of the order.

(h) a mental health treatment requirement: requires the consent of the offender.

This will be imposed with a view to improving an offender's mental condition.

(i) a drug rehabilitation requirement: a requirement of treatment and testing of at least six months. Again consent is required from the offender and the court must be satisfied that the offender has a propensity to use drugs and is susceptible to treatment. This requirement must be recommended to the court as being suitable for the offender and is usually subject to regular reviews so that the court can ensure progress is being made.

(j) an alcohol treatment requirement: this is the same as the drug rehabilitation requirement except that it relates to an offender's alcohol use. It will last for at least six months, with the offender's consent and must be recommended as being suitable for the offender.

(ja) an alcohol abstinence and monitoring requirement: introduced by the Legal Aid, Sentencing and Punishment of Offenders Act 2012, this requirement is currently being piloted. This requires offenders to abstain from alcohol or to refrain from consuming more than a set amount of alcohol, and to submit to monitoring (testing of blood, breath, sweat or urine). The order can last for no more than 120 days and is only available if alcohol was part of the offence committed or contributed to the commission of the offence, and where the offender is not alcohol dependant.

(k) a supervision requirement: supervision by a probation officer

(l) an attendance centre requirement: attendance at an attendance centre from 12 to 36 hours in total. The offender must be aged under 25 and they will be subject to supervised activities and instruction during their time at the centre.

10.4.3 Which menu requirements?

s.149 CJA 2003 provides that the court must impose requirements that are the most suitable for the offender, and that the restrictions on liberty are "commensurate" with the seriousness of the offence and any associated offences.

The starting point will be the seriousness of the offence: New Sentences, para 1.1.13. It should be possible to take into account the range of different options available in the local area, and to decide which are the most appropriate to meet the different purposes of sentencing – including rehabilitation and reparation as well as punishment. The Sentencing Council guidance makes clear that in relation to the community penalty seriousness must be determined by the instant offence, rather than simply increasing the penalty from whatever was previously imposed.

10.4.4 Seriousness bands for community sentences

The guidance suggests that sentencers should approach selection of the sentence by determining which of three seriousness bands the offence falls into; either low, medium or high level. The Magistrates Guidelines assists by suggesting the appropriate band of community order according to the nature of activity within the particular offence.

Low seriousness:

> *1.1.25 For offences only just crossing the community sentence threshold (such as persistent petty offending, some public order offences, some thefts from shops, or interference with a motor vehicle, where the seriousness of the offence or the nature of the offender's record means that a discharge or fine is inappropriate).*

1.1.26 Suitable requirements might include:

- *40 to 80 hours of unpaid work or*

- *a curfew requirement within the lowest range (e.g. up to 12 hours per day for a few weeks) or*

- *an exclusion requirement (where the circumstances of the case mean that this would be an appropriate disposal without electronic monitoring) lasting a few months or*

- *a prohibited activity requirement or*

- *an attendance centre requirement (where available).*

1.1.27 Since the restriction on liberty must be commensurate with the seriousness of the offence, particular care needs to be taken with this band to ensure that this obligation is complied with. In most cases, only one requirement will be appropriate and the length may be curtailed if additional requirements are necessary. New sentences

Medium seriousness:

1.1.28 For offences that obviously fall within the community sentence band such as handling stolen goods worth less than £1,000 acquired for resale or somewhat more valuable goods acquired for the handler's own use, some cases of burglary in commercial premises, some cases of taking a motor vehicle without consent, or some cases of obtaining property by deception.

1.1.29 Suitable requirements might include:

- *a greater number (e.g. 80 to 150) of hours of unpaid work or*

- *an activity requirement in the middle range (20 to 30 days) or*

- *a curfew requirement within the middle range (e.g. up to 12 hours for 2–3 months) or*

- *an exclusion requirement lasting in the region of 6 months or*

- *a prohibited activity requirement.*

1.1.30 Since the restriction on liberty must be commensurate with the seriousness of the offence, particular care needs to be taken with this band to ensure that this obligation is complied with. New sentences

High seriousness:

1.1.31 For offences that only just fall below the custody threshold or where the custody threshold is crossed but a community sentence is more appropriate in all the circumstances, for example some cases displaying the features of a standard domestic burglary committed by a first-time offender.

1.1.32 More intensive sentences which combine two or more requirements may be appropriate at this level. Suitable requirements might include an unpaid work order of between 150 and 300 hours; an activity requirement up to the maximum 60 days; an exclusion order lasting in the region of 12 months; a curfew requirement of up to 12 hours a day for 4–6 months. New sentences

10.4.5 Breach of a community order

Failure to comply with the community order without reasonable excuse will lead to a written warning at the least and potentially initiation of proceedings. A second failure within a 12 month period must lead to breach proceedings before the relevant court. If the breach of the order is proved, the court may:

- amend the order so as to impose more onerous requirements;

- revoke the order and re-sentence for the original offence; or
- revoke the order and impose a custodial penalty, even if the original offence was not imprisonable; but this may be done only in instances of wilful and persistent failure to comply with the order.

The Sentencing Council emphasises that custody should not be imposed lightly:

> *The court dealing with breach of a community sentence should have as its primary objective ensuring that the requirements of the sentence are finished, and this is important if the court is to have regard to the statutory purposes of sentencing. A court that imposes a custodial sentence for breach without giving adequate consideration to alternatives is in danger of imposing a sentence that is not commensurate with the seriousness of the original offence and is solely a punishment for breach.* New sentences, para 1.1.45.

[10.5] FINES

Fines are the most commonly imposed penalty for both summary and indictable offences. The power to impose a financial penalty is contained in ss.126–129 PCC(S)A 2000. They are suitable to punish those who have committed offences which are not sufficiently serious to justify a community or custodial sentence. The Crown Court can impose unlimited fines; the Magistrates Court is limited to a maximum of £5,000 (although they cannot impose a fine which is more than the statutory maximum set for a particular offence).

Note that there is also a power which permits the police to impose low level "on the spot" fines for anti-social behaviour. The person has a right to challenge the fine in the magistrates court. There are also various "fixed penalty" fines under the penalty notice procedure: these are for specified offences including s.5 Public Order Act (causing harassment, alarm or distress). These are set at two levels – currently £80 and £40.

10.5.1 Ability to pay

A perennial problem is the relationship between fines and the ability to pay a fine. It is entirely wrong to sentence an offender to a higher tariff penalty when a fine has been considered the appropriate sentence, simply because he lacks the means to pay it.

> *In McGowan [1975] Crim LR 113, M handled seven stolen crabs [!] and received a suspended prison sentence since he lacked the means to pay the fine. Held: if a fine was not practical, and the offence did not warrant more serious punishment, the appropriate step was to move down tariff and consider a conditional discharge.*

10.5.2 Amount of fine

Financial circumstances orders: The court can make a financial circumstances order on a convicted offender. This requires the offender to provide the court with a statement as to his financial circumstances. It is a further criminal offence to make a false statement or to fail to disclose a material fact: s.162 CJA 2003. This is not widely used.

Fixing the amount of the order: Before imposing a fine the court must always inquire into the individual's financial circumstances, even where it does not impose a financial circumstances order. The courts usually require offenders to complete a statement of means detailing their income and outgoings so that they can assess the person's means more accurately. The amount of the fine must reflect the seriousness of the offence but must also take into account all the circumstances, including the offender's means.

The Magistrates' Sentencing Guidelines will indicate whether a fine is a starting point or within the sentencing range for a particular offence. Fines within the guidelines will be within one of three bands and the choice of band is based on the aggravating and mitigating features of the offence:

- Band A fine – based on 25–75% of the offender's relevant weekly income
- Band B fine – based on 75–125% of the offender's relevant weekly income
- Band C fine – based on 125–175% of the offender's relevant weekly income

The relevant weekly income depends on the offender's means. If an offender is on state benefits or earning less than £110 per week net, the relevant weekly income figure is taken to be £110. For those who are earning over £110 per week net, the relevant weekly income is the actual weekly income (net). Anyone who fails to provide information on their financial circumstances, will be fined on the basis of £400 relevant weekly income.

Two further bands of fine have been introduced where the court feels that the seriousness of an offence warrants a community sentence or custodial sentence but where the court has decided that a financial penalty is appropriate. Band D fines (alternative to community order) are based on 200–300% of the offender's relevant weekly income and Band E fines (alternative to custody) are based on a figure of 300–500%.

Hardship and payment by instalments: A fine is intended to have a penal impact in order to remind an offender that his conduct was wrong. A degree of hardship is therefore appropriate and a fine will automatically become payable immediately on the day that it is imposed. Fines may however, with the agreement of the court, be paid in instalments. The general rule is that fines should be capable of being paid off within 12 months (see eg. *Knight* (1980) 2 Cr App R (S) 82) but it has been made clear that there is nothing wrong in principle with fines that take longer to clear: *Olliver* (1989) 11 Cr App R (S) 10. This is of particular relevance to bands D and E fines which will amount to substantially more money being owed. A fine should not be so heavy as to send the offender to prison by the back door: *Ingram* [2004] EWCA Crim 1841.

The Courts Act 2003 outlines the collection regime for financial penalties. When a fine is imposed, the court should make a collection order which means that if the offender defaults in his payments, the fines enforcement officer can take enforcement proceedings. In certain prescribed circumstances, the court can impose a period of imprisonment for failing to pay a financial penalty.

10.5.3 Fines and other penalties

Note that fines can be combined with any other sentence – including custody (although not where your client lacks the wherewithal to pay the fine or would be saddled with a significant financial burden on his release from prison) – except for a discharge.

Victim surcharges: note that where your client receives a financial penalty, the court will also impose a £15 victim surcharge. This is justified on the basis that it will go to support compensation for victims of crime.

[10.6] OTHER SENTENCES

10.6.1 Absolute and conditional discharges

Absolute and conditional discharges are available in those situations where the court takes the view that the conviction is punishment itself or where it is otherwise "inexpedient to inflict punishment": s.12 PCC(S)A 2000.

An absolute discharge is often the court's recognition that an offence has been committed but that it is purely a technical breach. A conditional discharge may be appropriate in situations where, for example, a person is convicted for the first time of a minor shoplifting offence. Provided the person does not re-offend within the period set by the sentence nothing further will happen. If they do re-offend, they will stand to be sentenced afresh for the first offence as well as being sentenced for the new offence.

10.6.2 Bind overs

Binding over to keep the peace or to be of good behaviour is an ancient power, both at common law and in statute (Justices of the Peace Act 1361), as well as under s.115 Magistrates' Courts Act 1980. A bind-over can be imposed not only where a person has been convicted but also in any case where the court believes that the person before it (including a witness in a case) is likely to cause a future breach of the peace. The court will bind a person over in an agreed sum of money that will be forfeited if there is any future breach. Where a person refuses to be bound over, they are likely to be sent to prison.

10.6.3 Disqualification from driving

Under section 146 PCC(S)A 2000 the courts can use disqualification from driving as a punishment for an offence, even if the offence is not motoring related. This is in force at last – after lengthy pilots – but anecdotal evidence suggests that it is rarely being used.

10.6.4 Additional sentencing options

The Crime and Disorder Act 1998 and the Criminal Justice and Court Services Act 2001 introduced a number of new sentencing options, especially in relation to juvenile offenders (see Chapter 12). Some provisions, however, are of relevance to adult offenders as well.

Anti-social behaviour orders

ASBOs were originally introduced as a civil procedure which imposed restrictions on the behaviour of those shown to have behaved in a seriously anti-social manner. The order was not itself a criminal penalty – but breach would give rise to a criminal prosecution and potentially the imposition of a substantial custodial penalty.

ASBOs can now be imposed as part of a criminal penalty and are available as a sentence under s.1C Crime and Disorder Act 1998. They can be imposed where the court is satisfied that the defendant has acted in a manner that caused or is likely to cause harassment, alarm or distress to others, and that the order is necessary to prevent further anti-social acts. The order can only be imposed as an addition to sentence, including conditional discharges.

> *Scott is 19. He has been convicted of criminal damage in respect of the breaking of a window on a bus shelter. He has three previous convictions for similar minor criminal damage offences. The court imposes a fine for the offence. The court also imposes an anti-social behaviour order on the basis that the order is necessary to prevent further anti-social acts. The order imposes a curfew on Scott for a two year period and forbids him from committing any act of vandalism during this period. Any breach of the order could lead to a custodial penalty of up to five years, if sentenced in the Crown Court.*

Many lawyers are extremely concerned that the effect of ASBOs is to dramatically increase the penalty for even minor, and often otherwise non-imprisonable, offences.

Drinking Banning Orders: The Violent Crime Reduction Act 2006 introduced these orders which came into force in April 2010 in a specified number of areas within the UK. Where an offender is convicted of an offence while under the influence of alcohol, the court must consider making such an order where it is necessary for the protection of others from further criminal or disorderly conduct by the offender while he is under the influence of alcohol: s.6 VCR Act 2006. It may impose a prohibition from the offender entering licensed premises or any other prohibition which the court considers necessary to achieve the purpose above. The order must be between two months and two years.

Violent Offender Order: Introduced by Part 7 of the Criminal Justice and Immigration Act 2008, the violent offender order (VOO) is designed to protect the public from the current risk of serious violent harm posed by an adult offender who has committed a specified violent offence (including murder and manslaughter (s.98(3))) and who has been sentenced to at least 12 months imprisonment: see s.99 for full list of qualifying criteria. The order will impose such conditions, restrictions or prohibitions as are "necessary" to achieve this purpose.

Orders in respect of sexual offenders

There are a number of potential orders arising where a person has been convicted of a sexual offence. The purpose of all the orders is to prevent re-offending by sexual offenders.

Notification requirements: Technically these are not an order as they arise automatically where a person is convicted or cautioned for certain sexual offences. These offences are listed in Schedule 3 of the Sexual Offences Act 2003. During the period of the notification, the person must notify the local police of his details, including his address. He must also update this information whenever he moves house.

Sexual offences restriction orders: These are effectively forms of injunction, preventing the offender from undertaking certain activities – such as going within 100 yards of a local playground, or making contact with any person under the age of 16.

Foreign travel orders: These restrict offenders convicted of sexual offences from travelling abroad, or to named countries abroad.

Disqualification Orders: These orders arise where a defendant is convicted of "an offence against a child" and receives a "qualifying sentence" (normally a custodial sentence of at least 12 months). Where these conditions arise an order disqualifying the offender from working with children must be made unless the court is satisfied that the offender is unlikely to commit any further offence against a child.

[10.7] ANCILLARY ORDERS

10.7.1 Compensation orders

Compensation orders are not the same as applications to the Criminal Injuries Compensation Scheme. Under the CICS, victims of crime can apply for compensation for personal injury suffered as a result of an offence of violence. There is no requirement that the perpetrator be caught. Quantum must be at least £1,000 for an award.

However, in addition to the CICS, in every case involving personal injury, death, loss or damage the court must consider whether to make a compensation order, and must give reasons if it decides not to do so: s.130 PCC(S)A 2000. No application by the victim is necessary, but the amount of the victim's loss should be either agreed by the defendant or established by evidence. There are Home Office guidelines as to quantum on compensation for injuries. Imposition of the order is neither a punishment for the defendant, nor does it mitigate his sentence (otherwise the defendant could "buy his way out" of punishment). If there is insufficient money for a fine and compensation, the compensation should take priority and it will reduce (or extinguish) the fine.

10.7.2 Costs orders

Recovery of prosecution costs: Costs are not a punishment, but the issue of costs will always arise at the close of the case. Where your client is convicted the prosecution will ask for costs, and you will need details of your client's financial circumstances to be able to arrange payment in instalments where appropriate. In *R v Northallerton Magistrates' Court, ex p. Dove* [2000] 1 Cr.App.R.(S.) the court held that the costs order should not be disproportionate to any fine, and that the amount of the fine should be fixed first.

Costs following an acquittal: If your client has been acquitted the normal order will be a defendant costs order – i.e. costs from central funds where the client has been paying privately. For details see 4.2.

10.7.3 Forfeiture and confiscation orders

If property in your client's possession or control has been used for committing any offence it may be subject to a forfeiture order: s.143 PCC(S)A 2000. The offence in question must be one that, if punished on indictment, could give rise to a sentence of two years' or more in custody.

Confiscation of the proceeds of crime: This is governed by the Proceeds of Crime Act 2002. This huge piece of legislation creates an Asset Recovery Agency to pursue the assets of those who have "a criminal lifestyle" and who have benefited from this "general criminal conduct". There is a rebuttable presumption that property in the defendant's possession or transferred to him or by him during the previous six years are the benefits of that "general criminal conduct". The Crown Court is given a wide range of powers, as is the Asset Recovery Agency.

The case of *Sheikh (Hafeez), Sheikh (Saqeb), Sheikh (Junaid)* [2004] EWCA Crim 492 is an important reminder to bear these provisions in mind. The defendants to pleaded guilty to relatively minor Trades Marks Act offences, only to find that the prosecution intended to seek a massive confiscation order (the sum of £11 million appears in the reports). They promptly sought to withdraw their guilty pleas, saying that they hadn't been warned that this was a possible consequence. The court held that they were stuck with their guilty pleas, and sent the matter back for the confiscation proceedings to be begun. You must make sure that you raise this with your clients – and where possible find out from the prosecution if any intended confiscation order is sought.

[10.8] ROAD TRAFFIC CASES

There is a tendency to treat motoring cases as somehow not being proper criminal cases. However, road traffic work is a complex and demanding area of law. What follows is therefore only a short summary of the main provisions.

10.8.1 The points system: endorsing a licence

In road traffic cases the general system of sentencing options is supplemented by the penalty point system, by which offenders accrue points on their licence and are disqualified once they have 12 points endorsed. Additionally there are compulsory and discretionary disqualifications for certain offences.

Where your client is convicted of a road traffic offence, he will normally receive a number of "penalty points" on his licence, in addition to any other penalty. Some offences (such as dangerous driving and careless driving) require the court to impose penalty points; in other offences this is discretionary. Additionally, some offences carry a fixed number of penalty points (disobeying traffic lights carries 3 points), while others carry a range of penalty points (so that speeding can carry between 3 and 6 points, dangerous driving between 3 and 11 points and so on). Once your client has 12 or more points on his licence, he will be disqualified from driving (see 10.7.2 below). Where a court exercises a power to disqualify a person for an offence (for example, dangerous driving, which carries an obligatory disqualification), it will not also impose penalty points.

Where your client is convicted of having committed two road traffic offences "on the same occasion" (and there is considerable case law as to the meaning of this phrase), the court will normally only impose the higher of the two sets of penalty points. However, the court does have a general discretion to penalise twice if it thinks fit to do so.

10.8.2 Disqualifications: obligatory, discretionary and points

Certain offences, including dangerous driving, carry an obligatory disqualification. Such a disqualification must normally be for at least 12 months. Other offences, including careless driving and taking motor vehicles without consent, carry a disqualification for such period as the court thinks fit. Sentencing Guidelines should be consulted for a detailed breakdown of the suggested period of disqualification for a particular road traffic offence.

An automatic disqualification for having 12 or more points on your licence will be for at least six months, but can be for much longer. Note that the court will only take into account the points that have been endorsed for the present offence(s) and those that have been endorsed for offences committed in the three years immediately before the current offence was committed. Note also that a disqualification under the points system has the effect of clearing the slate, so that the driver starts again after the disqualification period without any points. (This does not apply in the case of obligatory or discretionary disqualifications, however.)

There is a two year probationary period for newly qualified drivers. A driver who gets six or more penalty points during that period will have his licence revoked and will have to pass the test again.

10.8.3 Avoiding disqualification: mitigating in road traffic cases

Where your client is facing an *obligatory* penalty following his guilty plea or guilty verdict (whether obligatory endorsement or obligatory disqualification), you will need to show "special reasons" in order to avoid these penalties. "Special reasons" are mitigating factors that arise from the commission of the offence (i.e. not ones that are personal to your client) and they do not amount to a defence to the charge. You cannot therefore simply argue the hardship that your client faces; the special reasons must relate to the offence itself. In order to argue special reasons, you will normally be required to call evidence in support so this cannot normally be done on the day that your client enters a guilty plea. Where you intend to argue special reasons, the court will normally avoid imposing the disqualification until the special reasons argument has been decided. In contrast, where your client is facing *a discretionary* disqualification, you can mitigate on the normal basis, raising matters that are relevant to the offence and the offender, and pointing out to the court the effect of the disqualification on your client and his work, and so on.

In the case of an automatic "totting points" disqualification, there are restrictions on the matters that you will be able to raise in mitigation. You cannot argue that the present offence is trivial (since the disqualification is in respect of the totality of the three years' offending); you cannot argue hardship, unless you can show that it is "exceptional"; and you cannot rely on any mitigating circumstances which have been used to avoid a points disqualification during the last three years. If you intend to argue "exceptional" hardship, you will normally have to call your client to give evidence to the court on how the disqualification will affect him to this extent.

[10.9] SENTENCING IN REGULATORY MATTERS

This is dealt with at chapter 13.

[10.10] ADVOCACY – SPEECHES IN MITIGATION

The advocates in sentencing hearings have separate roles. *The A–G's Guidelines on the Acceptance of Pleas and the Prosecutor's Role in the Sentencing Exercise (revised 1 December 2009)* states that the prosecutor represents the public interest thus the prosecutor should be ready to assist the court in reaching its sentencing decision. Prosecutors should draw the court's attention to any victim impact statement, any statutory provisions relevant to the offender/offence, any relevant sentencing guidelines, the aggravating and mitigating factors of the offence, and any evidence of the impact of offending on the community. The prosecution may make submissions as to the relevant sentencing range. In all cases, it is the prosecution advocate's duty to apply for appropriate ancillary orders, such as anti-social behaviour orders and confiscation orders. When considering which ancillary orders to apply for, prosecution advocates must always have regard to the victim's needs, including the question of his or her future protection.

The prosecutor will therefore outline the facts of the case and any of the issues above. They are responsible for applying for a contribution towards prosecution costs and should draw the court's attention to any relevant previous convictions. The prosecutor does not make any submissions as to what particular sentence is appropriate. Prosecutors should remain impartial throughout.

The defence advocate represents the interests of the defendant and should present their client's case to the court for consideration in the sentencing exercise. Of particular importance is any mitigating factors (both in relation to the offence and the offender) which should be highlighted during the plea in mitigation. The defence advocate should be realistic in their approach to sentencing. Consider the relevant guideline and address the court on what appears to be the most sensible sentence given what the guidelines state is appropriate for the particular offence. The defence advocate should be persuasive and can suggest what sentence would be suitable in the circumstances, giving reasons to support their argument.

10.10.1 Mitigation speeches: the basics

Mitigation speeches are very difficult to do well. They are particularly prone to be disorganised, boring and full of waffle. You will make effective mitigation speeches if you concentrate on structuring your speech to make your points clearly, in a logical order, and in a way that avoids repetition. The most effective way of doing this is to relate what you are saying to the relevant sentencing law – both the statutory provisions (such as the custody and community penalty thresholds) and the relevant sentencing case law for the offence.

Be structured and be brief. In the magistrates' court your speech should normally not exceed five minutes. Repetition dulls the point you are making; it rarely improves it. But equally, if it is a complex or a serious matter, and if you need more time to do justice to your case, take your time and do the job properly.

10.10.2 Structuring your mitigation speech

In the magistrates' court, the easiest way to structure your mitigation speech is to consider the relevant sentencing guideline for the offence. You should identify the appropriate starting point and range of sentences that the Bench will be considering by looking at the examples of activity on the guideline and comparing that to the offence your client has committed. Be realistic and ensure you pitch your mitigation at the right level!

You can then follow the suggested structure below which mirrors the way in which the Magistrates will consider sentence. This structure is also suitable for use in the Crown Court. Clearly however, this is just one way of organising material – there are many other approaches.

[1] **What is the range of likely sentences?** You may know your court's policies – but also look at the Magistrates' Sentencing Guidelines, Court of Appeal tariffs, any relevant precedent cases. This gives you an idea of the likely range of sentencing outcomes. You must do this: it tells you at what level to pitch your mitigation. When dealing with a first offence of shoplifting, there is no point in addressing the court on why a custodial sentence is inappropriate since all the guidelines indicate that a first offence of shoplifting is likely to justify a fine, at the most.

[2] **Is there a pre-sentence report?** If so, has the court got a copy? Do they want time to read it? Check it with your client so that you can correct any inaccuracies.

[3] **Deal with the offence.** The prosecution will briefly outline the facts of the case to the court. Don't repeat all this material, but be prepared to bring out matters that have not been brought to the court's attention. Don't disregard any aggravating features that have been raised by the prosecution. You can deal with the bad aspects by putting them into perspective by bringing out the mitigating features of the offence. Often this will be the lack of other aggravating features – for example: yes, the offence was in a public place, however it was not racially aggravated; nor was the victim especially vulnerable.

Use the Magistrates' Sentencing Guidelines and the seriousness guidelines from the Sentencing Guidelines Council to remind yourself of the normal aggravating/mitigating features. Don't confine yourself to these: is there anything else that shows that this offence is not a particularly serious example of a burglary or an assault and so on. For example, you will often hear advocates stating that:

> *Of course x is a serious offence, and my client accepts that. However, of itself this is not an x with any substantial aggravating features. It is very much at the bottom end of the spectrum.*

[4] **Deal with the offender:** Again, aim to bring out anything positive. A clean record is unlikely, but is wonderful if you have got it. What about domestic background, employment, family, health? Why did your client actually commit the offence – is there anything positive that can be put to the court to explain how he came to offend? If there is a PSR, use the positive elements.

Make the most of anything that shows remorse or reformability – for example, co-operation with the police, any apology to victim, any attempt to make restitution. A guilty plea not only leads to a statutory discount – it also shows how much your client regrets his actions, acknowledges his guilt, and shows that he takes responsibility for putting matters right. Note that "positive good character" – in the sense of a defendant who has a history of serving the community and others, rather than the mere absence of previous convictions – should be taken into account: *Clark (Joan)* The Times 27th January 1999.

[5]   What is the appropriate sentence? This means not merely appropriate given the seriousness of the offence, but what is appropriate for this offender. Use sentencing law. What is the custody threshold – why is it not met? What is the community order threshold – has it been crossed? The sentence should not only be punitive; it should, if possible, offer opportunities for reform and rehabilitation, as well as reparation. Don't just focus on the outcome you feel is appropriate. Explain why any other likely outcome is not so ideal.

[6]   Then deal with the Guilty plea discount (if available): Remember that the guidance makes clear that the discount for pleading guilty is separate from any reduction in sentence on the basis of remorse:

> *2.1 A reduction in sentence is appropriate because a guilty plea avoids the need for a trial (thus enabling other cases to be disposed of more expeditiously), shortens the gap between charge and sentence, saves considerable cost, and, in the case of an early plea, saves victims and witnesses from the concern about having to give evidence.*
>
> *2.2 It is a separate issue from aggravation and mitigation generally.*
>
> *2.3 The sentencer should address the issue of remorse, together with any other mitigating features present, such as admissions to the police in interview, separately, when deciding the most appropriate length of sentence before calculating the reduction for the guilty plea.* Reduction in sentence for a guilty plea, paras 2.1-2.3

[You will find an example of a mitigation speech in **Document 24** in the case study.]

10.10.3 Some other points about mitigation

Don't tell the court that your client is not guilty! Never put forward anything in mitigation which amounts to an assertion that your client is not guilty. "He thought he had the victim's permission" amounts to an assertion of lack of *mens rea* in most cases (such as theft). "He didn't mean to do it" is equally unacceptable in crimes of intention, and so on. Be careful – it is easily done.

Character evidence: You are entitled to produce evidence of your client's character. Often this evidence will be put to the court in the form of written letters of support, but you may wish to call witnesses to testify to your client's otherwise unblemished character. If your client has a supportive employer, evidence from a person who is prepared to continue to place your client in a position of trust can be useful. It also has a valuable effect in reminding the court that your client is in work and makes a useful contribution to society.

Note that if in your mitigation you intend to raise the bad character of another, you should give notice of this to the prosecution.

SENTENCING – FINES/DISCHARGES

Absolute /conditional discharge: where it is "inexpedient to inflict punishment" s.12 PCC(S)A 2000.

Fines: the most common form of punishment. Available in Crown Court and magistrates', though limited to £5,000 in the latter. See s164 CJA 2003: court must inquire into the defendant's financial circumstances and must then fix a fine that "reflects the seriousness of the offence", taking into account those financial circumstances. The Magistrates' Court will fix a fine within the Band (A–C) most relevant to the seriousness of the offence. Bands D and E are available as an alternative to a community or custodial sentence if the court deems it appropriate.

THE COMMUNITY ORDER

The CJA 2003 brings together all the different community penalties and enables the court to impose a community order which selects a number of different requirements.

Requirements: these include:
- Supervision
- Unpaid work
- Activity requirement
- Exclusion requirement
- Curfew requirement
- Drug/Alcohol/mental health treatment.

Threshold requirement:
- Offence (or offence plus associated offences) must be "serious enough to warrant such a sentence": s.148 CJA 2003.
- Community order can be imposed upon a persistent offender – someone fined on three or more occasions since attaining the age of 16: s.151 CJA 2003 – not yet in force.

Type of order:
- Suitable for the offender; and
- Commensurate with the seriousness of the offence.

SGC guidance: three bands – low, medium, high seriousness.
- Foreign travel prohibition
- Alcohol abstinence & monitoring

OTHER ORDERS

Compensation: s. 130 PCC(S)A 2000: covers personal injury, loss or damage resulting from the offence. Increasingly popular. An order can be made even where the victim has not applied. Court must now give reasons if it does not make such an order. Not an alternative to sentence, but does take priority over a fine.

Note also:
- Confiscation orders
- Forfeiture orders
- Restitution orders
- Deportation
- Exclusion (e.g. pubs, sporting events.)
- Disqualification (driving; directorships)

Remember also costs as an issue – although not a punishment as such.

Proceeds of Crime Act: be very aware of possible actions for the recovery of proceeds of crime against your clients.

CUSTODIAL SENTENCES

Offence and any associated offences are: *so serious that neither a fine alone nor a community sentence can be justified for the offence.* S.152(2) CJA 2003.

Seriousness: note SGC guidelines on seriousness – consider both culpability and harm. CJA 2003 makes clear that relevant previous offences may be treated as an aggravating factor.

Sentence should be for the shortest period of time commensurate with the seriousness of the offence (s.153 CJA 2003), unless the dangerous offender provisions apply.

Note the statutory power to discount for a guilty plea: s.144 CJA 2003.

Other forms of custodial penalty:
- Suspended sentences
- Custody plus and intermittent custody – not yet in force
- Dangerousness provisions – IPP and extended sentence for dangerous offenders

Sentencing – test yourself questions

[The answers to these questions are set out in Appendix A at the back of this book]

[1] The magistrates' maximum sentencing powers for adult offenders are:

(a) a 12 month custodial sentence

(b) two six month custodial sentences, aggregated to make a 12 month sentence

(c) two six month custodial sentences, aggregated to make a 12 month sentence provided both cases are either way offences

(d) two six month custodial sentences, aggregated to make a 12 month sentence provided that at least one of the cases is an either way offence.

[2] Which one of the following propositions most accurately reflects the threshold for imposing a custodial sentence?

(a) The offence is serious enough to warrant such a sentence

(b) The offence is so serious that neither a fine alone nor a community sentence can be justified for the offence.

(c) The offence is so serious that custody should be imposed

(d) The offence is exceptionally serious and custody can therefore be justified.

[3] Derrick is convicted of assault occasioning actual bodily harm, having assaulted a woman walking her child in an isolated part of a park. In deciding whether the offence has crossed the custody threshold, which of the following factors are potentially aggravating factors?

i. The victim is particularly vulnerable because she is caring for a young child.

ii. Derrick has previous convictions.

iii. Derrick is 20 years old.

iv. The offence took place in a particularly isolated place.

(a) i. None of the above.

(b) i, ii and iv only.

(c) ii and iii only.

(d) All of the above.

[4] Sandra, who is 23, is convicted of burglary of office premises where she took property to the value of £100. She has three previous convictions for dishonesty offences, for which she has received fines. All the fines have been paid. Consider the following propositions:

i. The court could impose a community order with such requirements as are suitable for the offender provided that the restrictions on liberty are commensurate with the seriousness of the offence.

ii. If the court wishes to impose an unpaid work requirement, this cannot exceed 300 hours of unpaid work.

iii. The court can only impose a curfew requirement if it is satisfied that a curfew is necessary to prevent night time offending.

iv. If Sandra breaches a community order by failing to complete any requirement the court must impose an immediate custodial penalty.

Which of the above are correct?

(a) All of them.

(b) i and ii only.

(c) iii only.

(d) ii and iv only.

[5] Maurice is convicted of theft of £900 worth of computer equipment from a school. Maurice is of previous good character. He is currently unemployed and receives income-based Job Seeker's Allowance of roughly £114 per fortnight. He appears before the Magistrates' court and the Bench proposes to impose a fine. Consider the following propositions.

i. If Maurice cannot pay the fine immediately, the court can permit him to pay in instalments.

ii. The amount of any fine should reflect the seriousness of the offence.

iii. The court should take into account the fact that Maurice is of previous good character, but should not impose a lower fine on the basis that he is in receipt of benefits.

iv. The court will use the sum of £110 as Maurice's relevant weekly income when assessing the amount of his fine

Which of these propositions are correct?

(a) All of them.

(b) i, ii and iv only.

(c) i and iii only.

(d) ii only.

CHAPTER 11

APPEALS

> This chapter covers:
>
> Appeals from the magistrates' court to the Crown Court
>
> Appeals from the magistrates' court to the High Court, by way of Case Stated
>
> Appeals against conviction and sentence from the Crown Court to the Court of Appeal
>
> Remaining appeal routes, including appeals to the Supreme Court

[11.1] APPEALS FROM THE MAGISTRATES' COURT

In this section you will be looking at appeals in cases that have initially been heard in the magistrates' court. The section deals with:

- Appeals from the magistrates to the Crown Court
- Appeals from the magistrates to the High Court by way of Case Stated
- Applications to the High Court for judicial review

Can you avoid an appeal – the power to rehear:

Appealing a magistrates' court decision can take considerable time and effort, and in some situations, it might be more convenient to set the conviction aside and seek a rehearing at the magistrates' court. This can be done where there has been some sort of error in law or procedure in the initial hearing and it is 'in the interests of justice' for the case to be reheard. The power to set aside a conviction and reopen is contained in s.142(2) Magistrates' Courts' Act 1980. The rehearing would be in front of a different bench of magistrates. The court's discretion is a wide one but the court will look carefully at the reasons advanced for setting aside and they will not do so lightly. A common reason for seeking a rehearing is that the defendant failed to attend his trial for some legitimate reason such as failing to receive notification of the hearing, or perhaps being physically unable to attend due to sudden illness. There is no time limit for making an application under s.142(2), but any delay in making the application will be considered by the magistrates when deciding whether to allow the application, so the sooner it is made, the better.

You should also note the power of the magistrates' court to vary or rescind a sentence or an order that they have passed, again under the provisions of s.142. Again, the application will only be granted where it is in the interests of justice to do so and this mechanism can only be used where there has been some sort of error, such as a failure to take into account certain factors that would be relevant to sentence. Any such application must be made 'as soon as reasonably practicable' and the application must indicate the variation that is sought, see Rule 42.4(3) of the Criminal Procedure Rules.

11.1.1 Appeals to the Crown Court

The primary route of appeal against the decision of the magistrates' court, whether appealing the conviction itself or the sentence imposed, is to the Crown Court. Your client can appeal as of right against either conviction or sentence. For obvious reasons your client will not normally be able to appeal against conviction if he has pleaded guilty provided he was fit to plead and had received competent legal advice and representation. The power to appeal is contained in s.108 of the Magistrates' Courts Act 1980 and the procedure is dealt with in Part 63 of the Criminal Procedure Rules.

- Notice of the appeal must be sent, in writing, within 21 days from date of sentence to the clerk of the magistrates' court and the prosecution. The Crown court does have discretion to extend the 21 day deadline, but a convincing argument would have to be advanced to justify any such extension.

- There is no need to state the grounds of the appeal, although you must indicate whether the appeal is against conviction, sentence or both. Generally, if the appeal is against conviction, it is sufficient to state that the magistrates made an error of fact and/or law. If the appeal is against sentence, the ground is simply that the sentence imposed by the magistrates was excessive.

- Your client can apply for bail in the meantime, but be aware that he has no prima facie right to bail pending appeal.

- Legal aid will cover the initial advice and assistance with the appeal and either court can grant full legal aid.

- The clerk to the magistrates will then send the notice of appeal to the Crown Court and the Crown Court will then fix a date for the appeal hearing.

The appeal will be heard by a judge sitting with two lay magistrates. An appeal against conviction will involve a complete rehearing of the case and can include new evidence or points of law. On an appeal against sentence, the court is not bound to simply reconsider the sentence imposed by the magistrates; they must consider all of the issues giving rise to the sentence as well as current sentencing practice and guidance before coming to their own, independent view. The court can confirm, reverse or vary any part of the magistrates' court decision, and is not therefore limited to simply reconsidering the part which was under appeal. It should give reasons – whatever its decision: *R v Crown Court sitting at Inner London ex parte LB Lambeth* [2000] Crim L R 303. Note that its sentencing powers are limited to those available to the magistrates but there is nothing to prevent the Crown court imposing a harsher sentence than that already imposed by the magistrates. Furthermore, an unsuccessful appellant may also find that he has, in addition to a higher sentence, additional prosecution costs to pay, so the prospects of success need to be carefully considered before proceeding with an appeal.

11.1.2 Appeals to the Divisional Court by way of Case Stated

Any person who was a party to any proceeding before a magistrates' court or is aggrieved by the conviction, order, determination or other proceeding of the court may question the proceeding on the ground that it is wrong in law or is in excess of jurisdiction by applying to the justices composing the court to state a case for the opinion of the High Court on the question of law or jurisdiction involved …

s. 111 (1) MCA 1980

Case stated should be used where the allegation is that the magistrates' court decision was wrong in law, or in excess of jurisdiction. The courts have made clear that they do not feel that case stated should be used where the focus of the challenge is the facts rather than the law: see for example *Oladimeji v DPP* [2006] EWHC 1199. Common reasons for appealing by way of case stated are that the magistrates misunderstood the law, the magistrates made the wrong decision on a submission of no case to answer or perhaps they made an incorrect ruling on the admissibility of evidence.

Losing the right to appeal to the Crown Court: Your client can still appeal by way of Case Stated following an appeal to the Crown Court, provided the issue does not relate to a trial on indictment. However, if your client appeals *first* by Case Stated from the magistrates' court, he will not then later be able to appeal to the Crown Court in the normal manner if he is unsuccessful on the Case Stated.

Procedure on a Case Stated: The Case Stated procedure is governed by Rule 52 Civil Procedure Rules and Rule 64 of the Criminal Procedure Rules. The appellant (who can be either the defendant or the prosecution) must apply to the magistrates within 21 days of sentence requiring them to "state a case". The application must make clear what point of law is in issue. The court can refuse to state a case if it is of the view that the application is frivolous – although this refusal will be judicially reviewable.

A draft case is prepared by the clerk to the court and is submitted to the parties for their comments. The final version, which will include the details as to the findings of fact, the points of law, and the questions which the High Court is being asked to answer, will then be signed by the court and sent to the appellant. The appellant must lodge the statement with the Administrative Court at the High Court within 10 days after receipt of the stated case. The hearing will be before a High Court judge or judges. It is a hearing on point of law only, and no issues of fact are decided. No witnesses are therefore required. The court can affirm, reverse or vary the decision or can direct a rehearing.

11.1.3 Judicial Review

The usual criteria for judicial review will apply. In particular judicial review may be appropriate where the court has acted in excess of jurisdiction and where it has acted in breach of the rules of natural justice. An example where judicial review would be appropriate would be where the court has unreasonably failed to grant an adjournment. The remedy sought is likely to be an order quashing the magistrate's decision, or an order compelling the magistrates to act (or not act) in a particular way. There is a substantial overlap between judicial review and Case Stated procedures, and caselaw suggests that if there is a choice, generally Case Stated should be used. Bear in mind that judicial review is a discretionary remedy. Moreover, judicial review continues to be funded by the Community Legal Service, rather than the Criminal Defence Service.

The procedure for applying for judicial review is contained in Part 54 of the Civil Procedure Rules. It is essentially a two-stage process whereby leave must be sought from a single High Court judge; if leave is granted, then the matter will go to a full hearing before the Divisional Court. If the case is proven, then the High Court will make the appropriate order.

11.1.4 Further appeals?

As stated above, there may be an appeal by Case Stated from the Crown Court in its appellate capacity; but the reverse is not the case, i.e. there is no right of appeal to the Crown Court once a Case Stated has been run. The decision of the High Court in a criminal matter (i.e. on Case Stated) may be appealed to the Supreme Court, but only if the High Court certifies that the case involves a point of law of general public importance and leave is granted by either court.

[11.2] APPEALS FROM THE CROWN COURT

This section considers the right of appeal where there has been a jury trial in the Crown Court (as opposed to the situation in 11.1.1 above where we were considering an original trial in the magistrates' court and an appeal to the Crown Court). Appeal on conviction or sentence, on point of law or any matter relating to a trial on indictment, will be to the Criminal Division of the Court of Appeal.

11.2.1 Appeals against conviction

The grounds for an appeal

There is a single ground of appeal: that the conviction is "unsafe": s.2 Criminal Appeal Act 1968 (as amended by the Criminal Appeal Act 1995). Prior to the amendment brought about by the 1995 Act, it was common place for appeals to be brought on the basis of 'material irregularity' or some other shortcoming in the trial that led to the conviction being unsatisfactory. The move toward the single ground of the conviction being 'unsafe' has not swept away those types of appeal, but it has had the effect of concentrating the issue on safety, and provided the appellant can demonstrate that the technical procedural error has led to his conviction being unsafe, then such appeals can still be allowed. Whether or not a conviction is 'unsafe' is a subjective question for the Court of Appeal to consider. The test that has long been applied by the court is whether, after hearing the appeal, they are left with any 'lurking doubt' that an injustice has been done then the conviction is unsafe and must be quashed, regardless of whether or not the defendant is guilty, see *R v Cooper [1969] 1 Q.B. 267*.

There are many different factors that can give rise to a conviction being unsafe: the trial judge failing to provide an adequate direction to the jury; the trial judge wrongly admitting or excluding certain evidence; the trial judge demonstrating bias toward either prosecution or defence; new evidence coming to light that if it had been placed before the jury at the time, would have affected their decision etc.

One of the key issues is whether a breach of the right to a fair trial, under article 6 of the Convention, necessarily means that the conviction is unsafe for the purposes of the Criminal Appeal Act. There has been considerable conflicting case law and this point is discussed more fully at 11.4 below.

Procedure for an appeal: Leave to appeal against conviction is always required, see s.1 Criminal Appeal Act 1968. Either the trial judge can grant a certificate indicating the case is fit for appeal (either of his own motion, or upon application of the defendant), or the Court of Appeal can grant leave. The application for leave must be in writing, including grounds of appeal as settled by counsel, within 28 days of conviction (or sentence if the appeal is against sentence). There are standard forms for completion (see case study Doc. 25). The application is sent to the Crown Court that dealt with the trial, and the court then forwards the documentation on to the Court of Appeal. Once the Court of Appeal is seized of the application, they will request a transcript of the evidence and a copy of the summing up given at the original trial to assist them in making their decision. Advice and assistance with the initial application is covered by the original Crown Court representation order.

This initial application for leave to appeal will be considered by a single judge on the basis of the appeal papers before him. If leave to appeal is granted, the single judge will grant public funding to the defendant to cover the cost of the appeal hearing. If the single judge refuses leave to appeal, the defendant can renew his application to the full court, but if he is then unsuccessful he may be penalised with a loss of time order. This is to dissuade clients from pursuing unmeritorious appeals that take up valuable court time and resources.

Loss of time orders: These are dealt with under s.29 of the Criminal Appeal Act 1968. The court can direct that any time spent in custody after filing an application for leave to appeal (conviction and/or sentence) is not to be treated as part of the original custodial sentence. In the past loss of time orders have been little used, but the Court of Appeal has indicated that they should be used more frequently in order to discourage unmeritorious appeals: see *Hart and others* [2006] EWCA Crim 3239. This is therefore something you must take particular care to warn your client about, especially since the court has suggested that a loss of time order may arise even at the application for leave to appeal stage.

The powers of the court: If leave to appeal is granted, the appeal will be heard by the full Court of Appeal which has the power to quash the conviction and either acquit or direct a retrial, dismiss the appeal, find the defendant guilty of an alternate offence or allow part of an appeal. Upon quashing a conviction, a retrial will only take place where the court feels that it would be 'in the interests of justice', but if a retrial would be prejudicial to the defendant (perhaps the defendant has since become gravely ill) or is in some other way inappropriate (perhaps the witnesses are no longer available) then there would have to be an outright acquittal.

11.2.2 Appeals against sentence

These are dealt with by s.9 Criminal Appeal Act 1968. On an appeal against sentence, the procedure will be the same as for appeals against conviction and leave to appeal will be required. Archbold has grouped the various categories of appeal against sentence as being the following; the sentence was wrong in law; the sentence was passed on the wrong factual basis; something was wrongly taken into account on sentence; fresh information has come to light that would affect sentence; the trial judge failed to honour a legitimate expectation and where the sentence was wrong in principle or manifestly excessive. It is acknowledged that the last ground (the sentence was manifestly excessive) is by far the most widely used ground, but it is anticipated that this ground will gradually diminish in popularity as the sentencing guidelines that are used by the courts become ever more restrictive. Once the court has decide to interfere with the sentence, it can quash any sentence or order and impose any sentence that was available to the Crown Court, although the defendant should not be dealt with more severely than at Crown Court.

[11.3] FURTHER APPEALS

11.3.1 The Supreme Court

Appeal from the Court of Appeal will be to the Supreme Court with the consent of either court and provided that the Court of Appeal certifies that there is a point of law of general public importance.

11.3.2 The Criminal Cases Review Commission

The Criminal Cases Review Commission is an independent body which was set up to deal with suspected miscarriage of justice cases. The Commission has the power to refer cases to the relevant appeal court (magistrates' court convictions can be referred to the Crown court, Crown court convictions can be referred to the Court of Appeal) even where previous appeals have already been considered and dismissed. Because the Commission is a last resort, it will not usually agree to deal with a case until all normal appeal routes are exhausted. Once the case is accepted, the Commission's task is to review each case impartially. The Commission will have to decide not only if something has gone wrong during the earlier litigation process but also whether there is any realistic prospect of success if the matter was referred back to the courts.

The test that the Commission applies is:

> *In reviews of convictions: an argument or evidence which was not raised earlier in the proceedings; or some exceptional circumstances that justify referring the case without any fresh arguments or evidence.*
>
> *In reviews of sentences: a legal argument or information that was not raised earlier in the proceedings.*

If the Commission agrees to investigate a case, it may be able to decide the matter simply on the basis of the existing papers and the application form. In most cases, however, some form of further investigation will be required. The Commission's own staff will conduct the investigation, but will use experts where necessary. Once the investigation is completed, the Commission will notify the applicant as to what has been revealed. The case will then be reviewed and a decision made on whether to refer the matter to an appeal court. Once the case is referred back to the courts, the Commissioner's task is complete and the applicant and his lawyers will then argue the matter afresh in the usual way.

[11.4] HUMAN RIGHTS ISSUES

11.4.1 Article 6 and the role of appeals:

The right to a fair trial concerns the whole process, rather than focusing solely on a particular instance of unfairness in isolation.

> *A criminal charge is not really "determined" as long as the verdict of acquittal or conviction has not become final. Criminal proceedings form an entity and must, in the ordinary way, terminate in an enforceable decision... Delcourt v Belgium (1979–80) 1 EHRR 355*

The effect is that appeal proceedings may "cure" any original unfairness in the trial itself.

When unfairness at trial cannot be cured on appeal: In *Condron v United Kingdom* (2000) 31 E.H.R.R. 1, the European Court of Human Rights held that C's right to a fair trial under article 6 had been breached by the failure of the trial judge to give the appropriate direction concerning inferences from exercise of the right of silence. The Strasbourg court held that the Court of Appeal could not rectify the matter by saying that they were sure that the misdirection had had no effect on the jury's decision, since this was mere speculation; the Court of Appeal could not know on what basis the jury had arrived at its decision.

11.4.2 Does an "unfair trial" mean an "unsafe" conviction?

There remains uncertainty on the issue of whether a breach of article 6 ("unfairness") will necessarily require that a conviction be overturned under domestic law ("unsafe"). In *Rowe and Davis v United Kingdom* 30 E.H.R.R. 1 the Strasbourg court held that Rowe and Davis had not had a fair trial because of the failure of the police to disclose that a witness against the defendants was a paid informer. However, when the Court of Appeal heard the appeal against conviction following this ruling from Strasbourg, the court held that the breach of article 6 did not necessarily mean that the verdicts were unsafe. Subsequently, in the case of *Forbes* (HL) [2001] 1 AC 473, the House of Lords stated:

> *If ... it is concluded that a defendant's right to a fair trial has been infringed, a conviction will be held to be unsafe within the meaning of section 2 of the Criminal Appeal Act 1968.*

However, in the case of *Lambert* [2001] 2 Cr. App. R. 28, the House of Lords concluded that:

1. the Misuse of Drugs Act had to be interpreted as requiring the prosecution to prove that the defendant did not know that what he possessed were drugs;

2. the wrong test had therefore been applied at Lambert's trial;

3. but that Lambert's trial was prior to the commencement of the Human Rights Act which was not normally retrospective;

4. and that in any case even if the HRA had had retrospective effect, so that article 6 would have been breached at Lambert's trial, the conviction would have been "safe".

In a similar way in *Lewis* [2005] EWCA Crim 859, the Court of Appeal held that a conviction which had been held by the Strasbourg court to be unfair because of failures in the disclosure system, was nonetheless safe since it had taken place prior to the coming into force of the Human Rights Act 1998. It has therefore never been the case that "unfair" trials will automatically produce "unsafe" convictions for the purposes of appeal. More recent decisions, such as that in *McInnes (Paul) v H.M Advocate [2010] H.R.L.R. 17* have emphasised that article 6 can be offended without the whole trial being rendered unfair and that a trial would only become unfair for the purposes of appeal if there was a real possibility that the verdict could have been different had the irregularity never occurred.

```
┌─────────────────────────┐      ┌─────────────────────────┐
│   TRIAL IN              │      │   TRIAL IN CROWN        │
│   MAGISTRATES' COURT    │      │   COURT                 │
└─────────────────────────┘      └─────────────────────────┘
```

CASE STATED

Appeal to QBD. by Prosecution or Defence on grounds that there has been an error of law. Not normally appropriate for factual disputes.

Apply to original court (magistrates' court or Crown Court in its appellate capacity) within 21 days to "state a case". This outlines the facts and findings in issue and sets out the questions for the court to answer.

Hearing before a High Court judge or judges. No evidence called. Legal argument only on the questions stated. Wide powers to confirm, reverse or vary the original decision.

NB. If appealing from the magistrates, an appeal by way of Case Stated prevents any later appeal to the Crown Court – but not vice versa.

Generally use this rather than judicial review.

CROWN COURT

MCA ss108-110:

Appeal against sentence or conviction. (Defendant only.)

Notice of appeal within 21 days. No need to give detailed grounds.

Heard by judge plus at least two justices.

Hearing de novo. Wide powers to confirm, reverse or vary any element of the decision. Sentencing limited to magistrates' court.

COURT OF APPEAL

Leave to appeal will be needed in all cases unless the trial judge has certified the case as fit for appeal: s.1 CAA 1995.

Representation order covers the initial advice and drafting of grounds. Apply within 28 days.

Appeal against conviction, sentence or both. Initial filtering by single judge: where he refuses leave and the D. persists with the appeal and loses, he may lose part of his time served.

Court will hear fresh evidence in exceptional circumstances. Will overturn decisions if they are "unsafe".

SUPREME COURT

Where a point of law is certified and leave is granted.

Appeals – test yourself questions

[The answers to these questions are set out in Appendix A at the back of this book]

[1] Which of the following is NOT an available route of appeal from the magistrates' court?

(a) Appeal to the Crown Court.

(b) Appeal to the Court of Appeal Criminal Division.

(c) Appeal to the High Court by way of Case Stated.

(d) Appeal to the High Court by way of judicial review.

[2] Warren is convicted of possession of cannabis in the magistrates' court on 1st November. Sentencing is deferred to enable a pre sentence report to be prepared. On 22nd November Warren is sentenced to a community order consisting of 120 hours of unpaid work. Warren wants to appeal against the conviction only.

Consider the following propositions:

i. If Warren appeals to the Crown Court against conviction, he must do so within 21 days of conviction.

ii. The Crown Court will not have the power to increase the sentence as the appeal is against conviction only.

iii. Warren's appeal will be heard in the Crown Court by a judge sitting alone, without a jury.

Which of these propositions are correct?

(a) None of them.

(b) i only.

(c) ii and iii only.

(d) i and ii only.

[3] In which one of the following scenarios is it most appropriate to appeal by way of Case Stated?

(a) Arnold, who has been convicted of common assault. He wants to appeal on the basis that one of the lay justices is the godfather of the victim.

(b) Stacie, who has been convicted of evasion of liability by deception. She wants to appeal on the basis that she doesn't think that the identification witnesses were particularly credible.

(c) John, who has been convicted of voyeurism. He wants to argue that the acts alleged could not in law amount to voyeurism.

(d) Liz, who has been convicted of making threats to kill. She wants to appeal on the basis that the main prosecution witness was lying at trial.

[4] Rose has been convicted of conspiracy to rob, as well as various firearms offences, after a trial in the Crown Court. She was convicted on 1st November. The matter was put over for reports. She was sentenced to two years imprisonment on 1st December. Rose wishes to appeal. The trial judge has not granted a certificate of appeal.

Consider the following propositions.

i. If Rose wishes to appeal against conviction, she must apply for leave to appeal within 28 days of the date of conviction. If her application for leave is refused by the single judge, she may renew her application to the full court but will be at risk of a "loss of time" direction.

ii. If Rose wishes to appeal against sentence, she must apply for leave to appeal within 28 days of the date of sentence. If her application for leave is refused by the single judge, she may renew her application to the full court but will not be at risk of a "loss of time" direction.

iii. In hearing an appeal against conviction, the Court of Appeal must allow the appeal if they are satisfied that the conviction was unsafe or unsatisfactory.

Which of the above propositions are correct?

(a) All of them.

(b) i and ii only.

(c) i only.

(d) iii only.

CHAPTER 12

JUVENILES & MENTALLY DISORDERED OFFENDERS

> Principle Aim
>
> Juveniles at the police station
>
> Trial in the Youth court and in the adult courts
>
> Sentencing for juveniles
>
> Mentally disordered suspects at the police station
>
> Court procedure and fitness to plead
>
> Sentencing of mentally disordered offenders

[12.1] JUVENILES

The "principal aim"

Section 37 Crime and Disorder Act 1998 imposes on all of those who are involved with the youth justice system a "principal aim". The principal aim is: *"to prevent offending by children and young persons."* This statutory duty applies to defence lawyers, as well as to the courts and the prosecuting authorities. It remains your duty to act in the best interests of your client, but the Crime and Disorder Act requires you to have regard also to this "principal aim".

Presumptions of innocence

A child under the age of 10 is conclusively presumed to be incapable of committing a crime. It used to be the case that a child aged 10–13 was presumed to be incapable of telling right from wrong (*doli incapax*) unless the prosecution could bring evidence to the contrary. It has now been confirmed that both the presumption and the doctrine have been abolished: S.34 Crime and Disorder Act 1998; *R v T* [2008] EWCA Crim 815. Therefore anyone aged 10 or more is now capable of committing a criminal offence.

[12.2] JUVENILES AT THE POLICE STATION

12.2.1 Appropriate Adults

Where a person at a police station appears to be under the age of 17, they must be treated as a juvenile until there is clear evidence to the contrary. Where a juvenile is arrested, in addition to the detainee's normal right of "intimation" under s.56 PACE (i.e. to have a person informed of the arrest) the police must also try to identify the person who is responsible for the juvenile's welfare. The person must be told of the detention as soon as is practicable. Additionally an appropriate adult must also be told and must be asked to attend the police station. The appropriate adult should be either the juvenile's parent or guardian or a social worker, or another responsible adult aged at least 18 (but not a police officer): Code C 1.7.

The role of the appropriate adult is never properly explained – although Code C 11.17 says that if the adult is present at interview they should be told the purpose of their presence is to advise the interviewee, to observe whether the interview is being conducted fairly, and to facilitate communication. Note in particular that appropriate adults will not be bound by any duty of confidentiality (or indeed safeguarded by any privilege). The Law Society has therefore suggested strongly that you should initially advise your juvenile clients in the absence of the appropriate adult, so that you can warn them about possible disclosure.

The police interview: Code C, Note 11C and Code H, Note 11 C makes clear reference to the particular problems in interviewing juveniles:

> *Although juveniles or people who are mentally disordered or otherwise mentally vulnerable are often capable of providing reliable evidence, they may, without knowing or wishing to do so, be particularly prone in certain circumstances to provide information that may be unreliable, misleading or self-incriminating. Special care should always be taken when questioning such a person, and the appropriate adult should be involved if there is any doubt about a person's age, mental state or capacity.*

In *R v Stratford Youth Court ex parte DPP* [2001] EWHC Admin 615 the Divisional Court accepted that a youth of 17 might not be a juvenile for the purposes of PACE, but would be a juvenile for other purposes, and that it might therefore be necessary to provide an appropriate adult in order to protect him from the pressure of being at a police station when he had never been arrested before.

Detention period: A person arrested for an indictable offence can be detained for up to 36 hours with the authorisation of a superintendent. The Home Office guidance makes clear that the power should be used sparingly and having regard to the special vulnerability of juveniles and the alternatives to police custody.

Juveniles and bail: Where the custody officer is considering whether to bail a juvenile after charge, he or she must take into account all the criteria set out above in respect of adults (see s.38(1)(a) PACE at 37.3), but also whether the juvenile should be kept in detention on the basis that there are reasonable grounds for believing that he should be detained in his or her own interests: s.38(1)(b) PACE. Where a juvenile is refused bail they must be transferred to local authority accommodation unless it is either impracticable to do so or (provided the juvenile is 12 or over) there is no secure accommodation available and non-secure accommodation would not be adequate to protect the public from harm. If, exceptionally, the juvenile is kept in police custody, the custody officer will have to certify why this has occurred, and the certificate will have to be produced to the court.

12.2.2 Police Cautions, Reprimands and Final Warnings

Juvenile offenders are likely to be prime candidates for formal "cautioning", rather than charge and subsequent court proceedings. Police cautions for juveniles consist of a system of reprimands for first time offenders, final warnings for second time offenders, and prosecution thereafter. This system applies to all offenders under the age of 18 years (therefore includes offenders aged 17 years who will not otherwise have been treated as a juvenile at the police station). The decision will be taken by a constable where the offence alleged is summary only or either way. A Crown Prosecutor will make the decision for indictable only offences.

Before giving a reprimand or warning the officer must be satisfied that there is sufficient evidence that the juvenile has committed the offence and that the evidence is enough to provide a realistic prospect of conviction, that the young person admits to committing the offence, that s/he has no previous convictions and it is not in the public interest to prosecute: s.65(1) Crime and Disorder Act 1998. Warnings and reprimands must be given in the presence of the appropriate adult. A final warning will lead to referral to a youth offending team. They will normally provide a rehabilitation programme. If the offender is later charged and convicted with any offence, the court will not be able to consider a conditional discharge if there has been a final warning in the previous two years unless there are "exceptional circumstances" to justify such a disposal: s.66 Crime and Disorder Act 1998.

[12.3] JUVENILES AND YOUTH COURTS

For the purposes of court proceedings, a juvenile is a person under the age of 18 years old. The Youth Court is a form of magistrates' court, normally consisting of three lay, specially trained justices, although District Judges may sit alone in the Youth Court. It will be a closed court, so that only those involved in the proceedings will be present. The juvenile will be addressed by first name and will promise (rather than swear) to tell the truth. The juvenile's parents must normally attend if the juvenile is 15 or under, and may be ordered to do so if the juvenile is 16 or 17. The layout will often be less formal than an adult court. The juvenile will not sit in the dock but will sit with his parents/responsible adult in front of the magistrates.

12.3.1 Trial of the juvenile in the adult magistrates' court

The general principle is that the juvenile should normally be tried in the Youth Court. However, there are occasions when the juvenile may be tried in the adult magistrates court, and when he may be tried in the Crown Court.

The juvenile can be tried in the adult magistrates' court if he/she is charged jointly with an adult defendant in a summary only matter or where the adult offender accepts summary trial in an either way matter. This means that proceedings for a juvenile charged jointly with an adult, will always commence in the magistrates' court. If the adult defendant pleads guilty, the adult court will generally send (remit) the juvenile to the Youth Court for trial. If the juvenile pleads guilty, the adult court can sentence him but their powers are limited to fines, discharge or recognisances (for the juvenile and/or his parents), and so will generally remit the juvenile to the Youth Court for sentence: s.8 Powers of Criminal Courts (Sentencing) Act 2000.

12.3.2 Trial of the juvenile in the Crown Court

The juvenile can be tried in the Crown Court:

- If he is jointly charged with an adult and the matter is indictable only (or the adult elects jury trial in an either way offence)
- If the offence is homicide (murder or manslaughter)
- If the juvenile is charged with certain firearms offences
- Where the juvenile is charged with an offence which carries more than 14years imprisonment in the case of an adult offender or an offence specified in s.91 PCC(S)A 2000 applies – sometimes referred to as "grave crimes".
- Where the juvenile is charged with a "specified" offence under the dangerousness provisions within s.224 CJA 2003

Generally these rules are outlined in s.24(1)(a) Magistrates' Courts Act 1980.

In the above circumstances (except where jointly charged with an adult) the juvenile will appear initially before the Youth Court and a decision will be made as to where his trial is to take place. In homicide and firearms cases, the juvenile MUST be sent to Crown Court for trial. Where an offence is potentially a "grave crime", the power to send to the Crown Court is discretionary. This means that the Court will hear representations from both the prosecution and defence and details about the juvenile's previous convictions. The facts of the case will be outlined and the court can hear details of any undisputed mitigation which is available to the juvenile including an indication of the fact that he is likely to plead guilty. The test for the court, after hearing this information, is whether a sentence of more than 2 years detention would be required on conviction. If they decide that it would, then the court will send the juvenile to Crown Court for trial.

In the decision of the European Court of Human Rights in *T and V v United Kingdom* [2000] Crim L R 187, it was held that the boys tried for the killing of James Bulger had not had a fair trial in the Crown Court because their youth combined with the formality of Crown Court procedures had prevented them from being able to participate effectively. A Practice Direction was issued in response (see Consolidated Criminal Practice Direction III 30). This takes a number of steps to ensure that youths are not exposed to any avoidable intimidation, humiliation or distress as part of the trial process. It also suggests that juveniles should not normally be tried alongside adults in the Crown Court.

[12.4] SENTENCING AND JUVENILES

Under CrPR, r.37.10(7) the court must not pass sentence on a young person until his parent, guardian or supporting adult is given an opportunity to make representations and introduce evidence relevant to sentence. The court will often request a pre-sentence report (see ch.10 for more details) prior to passing sentence and it must do so (unless in certain circumstances) where it proposes to sentence to imprisonment or a Youth Rehabilitation Order. The report will be completed by an officer from the local youth offending team (youth justice team).

The Sentencing Council has developed a definitive guideline entitled "Overarching Principles – Sentencing Youths" and courts must have regard to this when sentencing any young offender: s.172 CJA 2003. In particular, the court must have regard to the principle aim of the youth justice system (to prevent offending by children and young persons) and to the welfare of the offender: para 1.1.

12.4.1 In the Youth Court

Absolute and conditional discharges: An absolute discharge is available to the youth court in respect of any offender although in reality it will be used sparingly and only in the most trivial of matters. The conditional discharge (as discussed above) is not available where the young person has received a warning within the previous two years unless there are exceptional circumstances to justify this: s.65–66 CDA 1998.

Referral orders: The referral order is aimed at first time young offenders. The court must make a referral order for a first time offender who admits their guilt to an imprisonable offence and the circumstances do not merit either a conditional discharge or a custodial sentence. In general terms, only one referral order can be ordered per offender but the court may order a second order if exceptional circumstances dictate. Under a referral order the offender will be referred to a Youth Offending Team, who will then work out a suitable programme of activities which is intended to challenge the young offender's behaviour. Reparation can be in the form of making amends to the victim (if they wish it) or to the community as a whole. A breach of the conditions of the order will result in the offender being returned to the Youth Court and they can be resentenced in another manner. The order can be for no less than 3 months in duration and no more than 12 months overall: ss.16–32 PCC(S)A 2000. The Legal Aid, Sentencing and Punishment of Offenders Act 2012 contains provisions to amend the referral order system but at the time of writing, they were not yet in force.

Reparation orders: This is a form of community order which requires the young person to make reparation for the offence otherwise than by way of compensation. It may not require more than 24 hours of reparation (to be completed within a 3 month period) by the young person and it must be with the consent of the person to which the reparation is directed. There is a statutory duty on the court to consider reparation as an element of the sentence, and the court will need to obtain a report from the Youth Offending Team to devise a suitable form of reparation: s.73 PCC(S)A 2000.

Youth Rehabilitation Orders (YRO): This is an order introduced under the Criminal Justice and Immigration Act 2008 to replace the previous system of youth community orders. A YRO can only be made if the court is of the opinion that the offence (or offences) is serious enough to warrant a YRO and the requirements of the order must reflect the seriousness. Before making a YRO, the court must obtain information about the young person before making the order (usually in the form of a PSR). The order cannot be imposed for longer than three years and it will contain one or more requirements, similar to the adult community order. The requirements can include activities, supervision, unpaid work, electronically monitored curfew (limitations on maximum periods that can be imposed), residence, exclusion or attendance at an attendance centre (to undertake specified activities). Each has its own circumstances that must be met before that requirement can be imposed: s.1 & Schedule 1 CJ&IA 2008.

Fines & Bind Overs: The juvenile can be bound over to keep the peace and be of good behaviour (and note that the juvenile's parents can similarly be bound over to take proper care of the juvenile and exercise proper control over him). The juvenile can also be fined, but where the juvenile is under 16 the parents must normally be ordered to pay the fine. Compensation orders can also be made on the same basis.

Custodial sentences: As for adults, a custodial sentence must not be imposed unless the court takes the view that the offence (or offences) is so serious that neither a fine alone nor a community sentence can be justified: s.153 CJA 2003. Detention and Training Orders are the normal custodial penalty for young offenders: ss.100, 101 PCC(S)A 2000. The sentence is half detention and training and half supervision. The supervisor will meet the offender at the start of the detention and training regime (in custody), and the supervision will then take place in the community with the aim of building on the work undertaken during the custodial stage, so that there is supervision throughout. It is supposed to have a genuine rehabilitative effect.

A Detention and Training Order is available for:

- 15–17 year olds if convicted of an imprisonable offence which is so serious that only custody can be justified (i.e. ordinary s.79 PCC(S)A 2000 test);

- 12–14 year olds if convicted of an imprisonable offence which is so serious that only custody can be justified and they are in the opinion of the court persistent offenders. [There is provision for this to be extended to certain 10- and 11-year-olds – but this is not in force.]

The Youth and Crown Courts can impose DTOs of 4, 6, 8, 10, 12, 18 and 24 months, provided they do not exceed the adult maximum. There are statutory provisions for earlier release onto supervision for good behaviour, later release for bad behaviour. Breach of supervision may lead to detention.

Parenting Orders:

These are orders requiring parents to attend guidance or counselling sessions for up to three months and/or requirements encouraging the parents to exercise control over their child (overseen by a probation officer, social worker or member of a youth offending team). Failure to comply will be a criminal offence. These orders can be made where the court has imposed a child safety order, an anti-social behaviour or sex offender order, where a young offender has been convicted; or where a parent has been convicted of permitting truancy (ss.443, 444 Education Act 1996).

12.4.2 In the adult magistrates' court

The restricted range of sentences available for juvenile offenders in the adult magistrates' court is set out in 12.3.1 above. The magistrates' will usually remit the youth for sentence in the youth court where it is possible to do so.

12.4.3 In the Crown Court

Although the Crown Court can pass any sentence appropriate for the juvenile, s.8 PCC(S)A 2000 provides that where the juvenile has been convicted on indictment the court should remit the matter to the Youth Court for sentencing unless it is undesirable to do so. Note that it is possible for young offenders to receive adult sentences in the case of certain serious offences that have been tried in the Crown Court. This provision (s. 91 PCC(S)A 2000) will only apply where the juvenile has been sent for trial under s.24 (1)(a) MCA (see 12.3.2 above). The Crown Court can also impose extended sentences or detention for public protection under the dangerous offender provisions, in which case the minimum period to be spent in custody must be two years.

[12.5] 17 TO 20 YEAR OLDS

This group are not juveniles, but are subject to a slightly different sentencing regime than adult offenders. Note that where a young offender is aged 17 years at the start of proceedings and thus attends the youth court, if he attains the age of 18 years at the point of sentencing, the court retains the powers to sentence him as if he were still 17 years old: s.29 Children & Young Persons Act 1963.

Custodial sentences: Offenders aged at least 18 but less than 21 will be detained in young offender institutions rather than prison. [This is to be abolished by s.61 Criminal Justice and Court Services Act 2000, and any offenders aged 18 or over will then serve custodial penalties in prisons. However this provision is still not in force.]

Attendance centre orders: These orders still remain available where the offender is aged under 21. The offence must be an imprisonable offence; the offender must not have served a previous custodial sentence; and there must be a place available.

[12.6] CRIME AND ANTI-SOCIAL BEHAVIOUR

The Crime and Disorder Act overhauled the entire youth justice system, with the aim of creating a system which diverts young people from starting to offend, by catching them at a stage when they may simply be acting in an anti-social manner, and by intervening effectively in the sentencing process to ensure that offenders do not re-offend.

12.6.1 Anti-social behaviour orders

A measure aimed primarily at adults (for ASBOs as a sentence of the court, see 10.6.4). However ASBOs can be used from age 10 and upwards. The order is applied for by local authority and police where a person or family is acting in "an anti-social manner". This means a manner that has caused or is likely to cause harassment, alarm or distress to one or more people not of the same household. This is a civil application to the magistrates' court, and the burden of proof is on the defendant to show that any act is reasonable. The order must be necessary to protect persons from anti-social acts. Orders must last at least two years. If the order is breached it will constitute an either way offence carrying a maximum of 5 years' custody in the Crown Court.

12.6.2 Child Safety Orders

Aimed at children under 10, this is intended to prevent them from becoming involved in criminal or anti-social behaviour. It can be applied for if a child has committed an act that would have been an offence if they'd been ten or older, where the order is necessary to prevent further offending or where the child has behaved in a manner likely to cause harassment, alarm or distress to at least one member of the same household. The order places the child under the supervision of a social worker or member of a youth offending team, and may require the child to comply with specified requirements (bedtimes, perhaps?). Breach could lead to a care order.

12.6.3 Local Child Curfew Schemes

The local authority must consult with the Home Office and can then introduce a scheme banning children of specified ages who are unsupervised by a responsible adult or parent being in a public place within specified hours (between 9 p.m. and 6 a.m). The police, if they have reasonable cause to believe that a child is in breach of the scheme, must tell the local authority and can take the child home. If there is no one at home, the child can be taken into police protection. Social services have to make enquiries following notification of any breach. No such scheme has been set up as yet and the police tend to make use of the dispersal powers set out below.

12.6.4 Dispersing groups

There is an additional power under the Anti Social Behaviour Act 2003 for the police to disperse groups of young people where a superintendent has given authorisation. The grounds for the authorisation is that there are reasonable grounds for believing that members of the public have been intimidated, harassed, alarmed or distress; that this is as a result of the presence or behaviour of two or more people in public places; and that anti-social behaviour is a persistent problem in that area. Refusal to comply with a direction is a criminal offence.

12.6.5 Removal of truants

The police can take a child or young person who they find in a public place, who they believe is of compulsory school age, and who they believe is absent from school without authority, back to school or another place designated by the local education authority.

[12.7] MENTALLY DISORDERED OFFENDERS

As for juvenile offenders, special consideration must be given to advising and representing mentally disordered offenders both at the police station and at Court. Recent government proposals suggest that those suffering from a mental disorder should be diverted from the criminal justice system where possible and it is likely that a clear agenda in this regard will be forthcoming within the next year or two.

[12.8] MENTALLY DISORDERED OFFENDERS AT THE POLICE STATION

There are provisions in Codes C, H and D in respect of the treatment of mentally vulnerable suspects at the police station. Code C Annex E provides a summary of the rules. It is the suspect's mental state at the time of detention (not at the time of the offence) which triggers the use of these rules.

12.8.1 Identifying a mentally disordered suspect

If a police officer is told in good faith or has any suspicion that a suspect may be mentally disordered or mentally vulnerable, then without clear evidence to the contrary, the person must be treated as a mentally vulnerable person for the purposes of Code C, D and H. A mentally vulnerable person is someone who "because of their mental state or capacity, may not understand the significance of what is said, of questions or of their replies" (Code C NfG 1G). Mental disorder is defined as "any disorder or disability of the mind": s.1(2) Mental Health Act 1983. This does not include anyone with learning difficulties (unless they are such that they are associated with abnormally aggressive or seriously irresponsible behaviour) or anyone who is dependent on alcohol or drugs.

Where a custody officer has any doubt about the mental state of a suspect, they must call for an appropriate adult: Code C, Code H NfG 1G. They must also conduct a risk assessment and determine whether the person requires any medical treatment or assistance to check documentation: Code C, Code H 3.5–3.10. The custody officer must ensure that a healthcare professional is called to determine whether the person is fit for interview as well as providing any medical attention required. A determination that someone is fit for interview does not negate the requirement for an appropriate adult to be called to assist a mentally vulnerable suspect. Equally, a mentally disordered offender has the same right to legal advice as any other suspect and this right should not be delayed pending the arrival of the appropriate adult.

12.8.2 The Appropriate Adult

The appropriate adult has a right to seek legal advice on behalf of the suspect he is there to assist: Code C 3.19, Code H 3.20. The appropriate adult should be either a relative, a person who is responsible for the care of the suspect, someone who has experience dealing with mentally disordered persons (but not a police officer) or some other responsible adult aged at least 18 years (not a police officer): Code C 1.7(b), Code D 2.6, Code H 1.13. Those who are not appropriate for the role are generally the same as for juveniles. The role of the appropriate adult is similar to that for juveniles: see 12.2.1. A suspect's legal representative should not take on the additional role of the appropriate adult.

Interviews: Code C warns that mentally disordered persons are prone to giving unreliable, misleading or self-incriminating information and states that the police should take special care when questioning such suspects. It is important that the suspect is fit for interview and this should be determined by a healthcare professional. A person will be fit for interview if the risk of conducting an interview will not significantly harm the suspect's physical or mental state or will not result in anything being said in interview being considered unreliable because of their physical or mental state: Code C, Code H Annex G.

Mental Health Act Assessment: s.136 Mental Health Act 1983 gives the police a power to remove a person from a place to which the public have access to a place of safety if they consider that the person is suffering from a mental disorder (under s.1 MHA) and is in immediate need of care or control. A police station can be considered a place of safety: s.135(6). The person can be detained for up to 72 hours in order to be examined by a doctor and interviewed by an Approved Mental Health Professional (AMHP) who is usually a social worker or a community psychiatric nurse. A person detained under this power has a right to legal advice. Once arrangements have been made for the person's treatment or care, the person must be released from custody. The police do not have the power to apply for the detention of a mentally vulnerable detainee under the Mental Health Act 1983 (other than under s.136) – they must call an Approved Mental Health Professional to conduct an assessment if this is considered appropriate.

12.8.3 Disposal

A mentally vulnerable suspect can be charged, cautioned or released without further action in the same way as for any other suspect. There are no special rules and the usual tests will be applied to the decision on disposal of the case from the police station. Diversion from prosecution should always be considered in the case of mentally disordered persons. A 2009 report commissioned by the Justice Secretary recommended that offenders with mental health problems should be dealt with by health services rather than prosecuted in a bid to take those with such difficulties out of the criminal justice system. Equally, there are no special rules relating to bail and those outlined in the Bail Act will apply: see chapter 5.

[12.9] MENTALLY DISORDERED OFFENDERS AT COURT

Once charged with a criminal offence, a mentally disordered offender will be subject to the same procedure before the courts as for any other offender. Equally, such offenders are entitled to bail in exactly the same way as any other suspect although conditions may be attached in order to deal with any specific concerns relating to the person's mental health problems. For example a suspect may be required to attend at a hospital or to attend medical appointments as a condition of bail. While early hearings remain the same in proceedings, there are some special considerations for such persons and there are alternative powers available to the courts on sentencing. The Consolidated Criminal Practice Direction III 30 contains some useful guidance.

12.9.1 Fitness to Plead – Crown Court Proceedings

At the stage where your client is asked how he pleads to the charge, it is normal practice him to do so however he need not enter a plea if he is mentally incapable of doing so. Whether your client is fit to plead is determined through the procedures outlined in the Criminal Procedure (Insanity) Act 1964 ss4, 4A and 5 (as amended). The test is whether the accused will be able to comprehend the course of the proceedings so as to make a proper defence: *Pritchard* (1836) 7 C & P 303. Under this test, the court must consider whether the accused can understand and reply to the charge, whether he can understand and challenge the evidence against him, and whether he can properly instruct his legal advisors and give evidence himself.

12.9.2 The procedure for determining fitness to plead

The issue of fitness to plead must be raised as soon as it arises prior to arraignment although the issue can be determined at any time up to the opening of the defence case at trial in certain circumstances: s.4 CP(I)A 1964. If the issue is raised by the prosecution then they bear the burden of proof to the criminal standard (proof beyond reasonable doubt). Where the defence raises the issue of fitness to plead, which is more likely to be the case, the burden of proof rests on the defence and the standard is on the balance of probabilities.

The issue will be dealt with at a voir dire and evidence will be called as to the fitness of the accused. The evidence must come from at least two registered medical practitioners, one of whom must be approved under s.12 of the Mental Health Act 1983. The judge decides whether the accused is fit to plead in line with the test in *Pritchard* after hearing all the evidence and any representations from both prosecution and defence.

Decision that the accused is fit to plead: In this situation, the accused will be asked to enter his plea in the normal way and the case will proceed in the usual manner. If the plea is one of not guilty, the jury will be empanelled to try the case in the usual manner. If after trial, the accused is acquitted, that is the end of the matter. On conviction, the court will have to sentence him: see 12.10 below. You should note the availability of special defences such as insanity or diminished responsibility (homicide cases only) which may assist where the accused is considered fit to plead but was suffering from mental health problems at the time of the commission of the offence.

Decision that the accused is unfit to plead: In this situation, the accused cannot be convicted of the offence in the proceedings. There will however be a trial of the facts where the issue to be decided is whether the accused did the act or made the omission charged against him i.e. the actus reus of the offence: s.4A CP(I)A 1964. A jury will be empanelled to make the decision. If the jury is not satisfied to the criminal standard that the accused committed the actus reus, then it must acquit and the case is concluded.

If the jury is satisfied that he did commit the act, they will give that verdict and the case moves to disposal. It should be noted that this verdict is not a guilty verdict in the usual sense and therefore does not constitute a conviction. Following this verdict, the judge has a limited range of statutory disposals available to him under s.5 CP(I)A 1964 as follows:

- **A hospital order:** This will authorise the accused's admission to and detention in hospital. The court must be satisfied that the mental disorder which the accused suffers from is of a nature or degree which makes the order appropriate. The order will last for at least six months but can be renewed for a further six months, and then for continuous periods of 12 months until the offender is discharged by his responsible clinician, the managers of the hospital at which he is detained, or by a Mental Health Tribunal. However, if the court considers that the nature of the offence, the antecedents of the offender and the risk of him committing further offences in the future, mean that it is necessary to protect the public from serious harm from him, they must add a restriction order (under s.41 MHA 1983) to the hospital order. In this case, the consent of the Ministry of Justice is required regarding any decisions as to the offender's transfer, leave and discharge from hospital by the responsible clinician or the hospital managers. A Mental Health Tribunal cannot discharge the order without the express consent of the Ministry of Justice..

- **A supervision order:** This requires the accused to co-operate with supervision for a period of no more than two years and usually requires the accused to undergo treatment by a doctor. Supervision is undertaken by an Approved Mental Health Professional (AMHP).

- **An absolute discharge:** imposed where no other order is necessary

12.9.3 Fitness to plead – Magistrates' Court Proceedings

There is no specific procedure for determining fitness to plead in Magistrates' Court proceedings but where this is thought to be an issue for the accused, the defence have the following options open to them:

Summary offence: The accused may enter a not guilty plea and put the prosecution to proof. Where the prosecution has to prove mens rea, evidence can be called to highlight the accused's mental condition and this may negate the mental element of the offence. The defence of insanity may be available (but note that this defence applies to the accused's state of mind at the time of the offence rather than fitness to plead which applies to his state of mind at the time of the trial): *Horseferry Road Magistrates' Court, ex parte K* [1997] QB 23

Either way offence: Your client may enter a not guilty plea or indicate no plea and elect trial on indictment. In this way, the issue can be dealt with in the Crown Court. The Magistrates may well refuse jurisdiction on the basis of any mental health issues once they are raised in any event.

Hospital Order: The court can be invited to impose such an order under s.37(3) MHA 1983 without convicting the accused. Remember that the accused must be found to be suffering from a mental disorder therefore the case is likely to be adjourned to allow evidence to be called (from two registered medical practitioners) to this effect. A hospital order made by the magistrates' court cannot have a restriction order attached and therefore can be discharged by the responsible clinician, the hospital managers or a Mental Health Tribunal.

[12.10] SENTENCING MENTALLY DISORDERED OFFENDERS

All the usual sentencing options are available to mentally disordered offenders who are convicted of a criminal offence although not all will be appropriate depending on each individual case: see chapter 10 for sentencing in general. Important guidance on the sentencing of mentally disordered offenders can be found in *R v Birch* (1989) 11 Cr App R (S)202.

Custodial Sentences: Before imposing a custodial sentence on a mentally disordered offender, the court must obtain a written or oral medical report on the person's mental condition and this should be prepared by a doctor approved under s.12 MHA 1983. The court must consider the medical report and the likely effect of a custodial sentence on the offender's condition and treatment before imposing imprisonment: s.157 CJA 2003.

In any case involving an offender with a mental disorder, the court may consider that hospital detention is more appropriate than prison. An interim hospital order (under s.38 Mental Health Act 1983) is available where there is any doubt as to the appropriate sentence. If the Court believes that a final disposal of a s.37 hospital order is appropriate, it may also consider (in the case of a Crown Court Judge only) that to protect the public from serious harm, a restriction order should be made under s.41 MHA 1983. This would mean that the release of the offender is at the discretion of the Secretary of State for Justice or the Mental Health Tribunal (i.e. responsibility for discharge is removed from the hospital itself).

If the offender is dangerous and no suitable secure hospital accommodation is available, a prison sentence may well be appropriate: *R v Birch*.

Community based disposals: Where the court considers that the threshold for a community sentence is met and it has treatment in mind for a mentally disordered offender, it may impose a community order with a mental health treatment requirement: ss.177 and 207 CJA 2003. Before imposing such a requirement, the Court must be satisfied on the evidence of a s.12

MHA approved doctor that the condition of the offender is such that requires, and would be susceptible to, treatment but it is not a case where a s.37 hospital order or a guardianship order (see below) is warranted. The offender must consent to the making of such a requirement and the treatment can be either as a resident patient in a specified hospital or care home, or treatment as a day patient at such a place. Note that a mental health treatment requirement can also be attached to a suspended sentence order although the threshold for a sentence of imprisonment must be met first: ss.189–193 CJA 2003.

Alternatively, the Court may make a guardianship order under s.37 MHA 1983. This will permit the guardian (usually the local authority social services) to require the offender to reside at a specified address, attend specified places for treatment, education or training and to permit access to an approved social worker or doctor. The court must consider that the guardianship order is the most suitable method of dealing with the offender. The order lasts for an initial period of six months which can subsequently be renewed. There is no sanction if an offender does not comply with the requirements of the guardian.

Additional considerations: When a hospital or guardianship order is made, the court can make any ancillary order including compensation. It cannot however impose a period of imprisonment or detention. It may not impose a fine, make a community order or a supervision order or require the parent of a juvenile offender to enter into a recognisance. A hospital order cannot be imposed along with a referral order (for juveniles): s.37(8) MHA 1983.

FITNESS TO PLEAD PROCEDURE – CROWN COURT

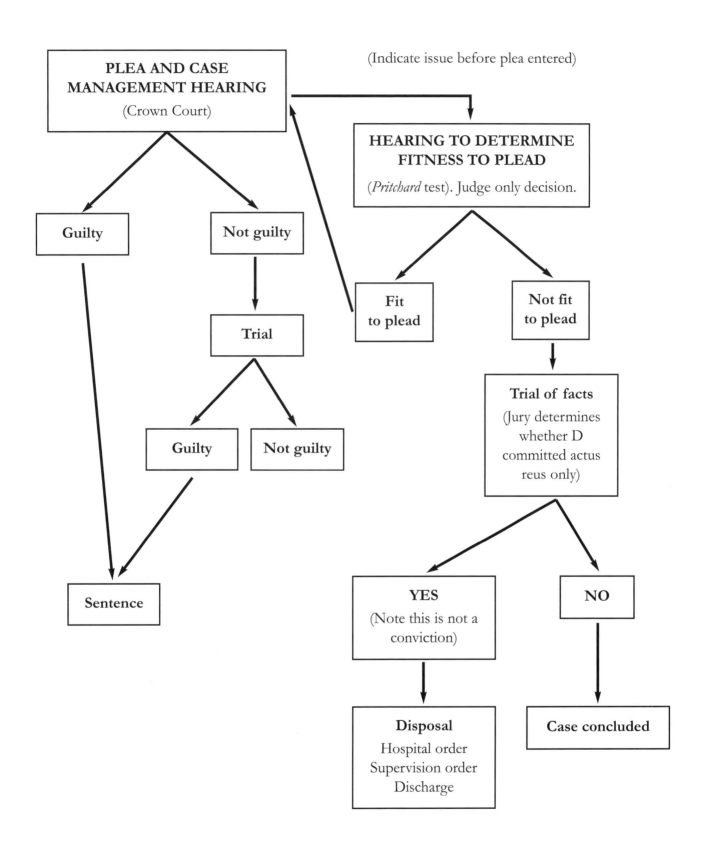

CHAPTER 13

WHITE COLLAR CRIME AND REGULATORY OFFENCES

This chapter covers:

The investigation and prosecution of white collar crime

The investigation and prosecution of regulatory offences

[13.1] THE INVESTIGATION AND PROSECUTION OF WHITE COLLAR OFFENCES

What is white collar crime?

White collar crime is a general term used to express the situation when people commit criminal offences in the course of their occupation.

Professional frauds and related offences: this includes offences such as money laundering; false accounting; credit card fraud; investment frauds (e.g. obtaining money transfers by deception, obtaining a pecuniary advantage by deception, market rigging); fraudulent trading; mortgage frauds; trading frauds; corruption and conspiracy to defraud. Such offences are usually committed by individuals taking advantage of their position within a company.

Where an offence has been committed by someone in the course of their profession, e.g. fraud by abuse of position contrary to s.4 Fraud Act 2006, then the usual course of action is for the police to conduct an investigation and for the file to be passed to the CPS for prosecution. Where the fraud is of an international nature and/or high value i.e. exceeding £1,000,000 then the case is likely to be investigated and prosecuted by the Serious Fraud Office. Serious Fraud Office investigators have extensive powers of investigation under s.2 Criminal Justice Act 1987, including the power to examine business documents that would ordinarily be privileged e.g. accounts and bank statements. The SFO will only prosecute where there is a realistic prospect of securing a conviction and where the public interest requires a prosecution. The SFO will also consider the principles set out in the Code for Crown Prosecutors when deciding whether to bring a prosecution.

13.1.1 Money laundering

Money laundering involves making money gained through criminal activity look as if it has come from a legitimate source. The term "money laundering" can be quite misleading as it actually relates to any property which constitutes a benefit from criminal conduct. Criminal property is defined in s.340 the Proceeds of Crime Act 2002 and it includes any benefit from criminal conduct committed at home or abroad. The main offences are contained within s.327–329 and they cover the wide range of involvement that individuals may have in the process of money laundering, e.g. concealing criminal property, converting property, transferring property etc. The scope of the offences is very broad and mere suspicion that laundering is taking place can be sufficient.

Although the offences are serious and can attract lengthy custodial sentences, the confiscation and civil recovery provisions contained in the Proceeds of Crime Act (POCA) 2002 may be of more concern to your client. The civil recovery procedures only require the authorities to prove to a civil standard (on the balance of probabilities) that the money/assets have come from an illegal source in order to seek recovery. We will look at the various recovery orders later in the chapter.

13.1.2 Fraudulent Trading

Section 458 Companies Act 1985 states that if any business of a company is carried on with intent to defraud creditors of the company or creditors of any other person, or for any fraudulent purpose, every person who was knowingly a party to the carrying on of the business in that manner is liable to imprisonment or a fine, or both. This applies whether or not the company has been, or is in the course of being wound up.

Within this definition, the person committing the offence needs to be someone within a managerial position who has positively acted in the fraud rather than simply turned a blind eye. Although there must be a dishonest intention to defraud, there need only be one instance of fraud to justify a charge.

Although fraudulent trading is a serious offence, the victims are creditors and this often results in it being viewed as somewhat less serious than theft or fraud which is often the preferred charge.

13.1.3 Investment frauds

Investment fraud is a generic term used to describe situations where stocks and shares are bought, mortgages or loans are obtained, deposits are made etc and a fraud has been operated in order to do so. This can include a whole range of situations from something as simple as misrepresenting the value of a property, to over-ambitious estimates of profit.

Within the term "investment fraud" there are a multitude of criminal offences including false accounting, conspiracy to defraud, obtaining services/pecuniary advantage by deception etc. The file of papers will be presented to the CPS and they will specify the most appropriate charge.

13.1.4 Corporate manslaughter

Previously, death in the workplace was prosecuted either under Health and Safety legislation or under the common law offence of gross negligence manslaughter. Unfortunately, successful prosecutions against companies were few and far between, due chiefly to the difficulties in attaching criminal liability to a corporation and the high evidential burden required of gross manslaughter. The impetus for reform came following a series of high profile public disasters including the rail accidents at Hatfield, Paddington and Southall. There was a general feeling that those responsible had to be brought to justice and that a new offence had to be created.

The Corporate Manslaughter and Corporate Homicide Act 2007 introduced a new offence of corporate manslaughter which is applicable to companies, other incorporated bodies, government departments, police forces and certain unincorporated bodies such as partnerships, trade unions or employers. Such an organisation can be prosecuted for corporate manslaughter if the way in which its activities are managed or organised causes a person's death and it amounts to a gross breach of relevant duty of care owed by the organisation to the deceased. With earlier prosecutions, there was a need to identify a 'directing mind' that was ultimately responsible for the breach of duty and this often proved problematic. Under the new legislation, all that needs to be established is that the senior management had managed the activities of the organisation in such a way that it was a substantial element in the breach of duty owed to the deceased.

If an organisation is convicted of corporate manslaughter it may face an unlimited fine, a remedial order or a publicity order under s.10 of the Act. A publicity order is intended to 'name and shame' the company and would advertise the fact of the conviction, the fine imposed and any remedial order. The level of publicity can vary but it could require advertisement by television, in local, national and trade press or in notices to be sent to customers and/or shareholders.

If the responsibility for the death clearly lies with an individual member of the corporation, then the CPS may still prosecute for gross negligence manslaughter. In such a situation, the usual sentencing powers will be available to the courts and imprisonment is almost inevitable.

The first case to be successfully prosecuted under The Corporate Manslaughter and Corporate Homicide Act 2007 was

> *R v Cotswold Geotechnical Holdings Ltd [2011] (unreported). In this case, a young geologist who had been working on a development site, died when the 3.5 metre deep pit he was working in collapsed in on him. The pit was unsupported, in contravention of standard industry guidance for pits of that depth, and in contravention of the company's own health and safety procedures. The CPS originally brought charges against the director of the company personally for gross negligence manslaughter and health and safety breaches, but these proceedings were stayed due to the ill health of the director. The CPS therefore pursued an allegation of corporate manslaughter against the company. The company pleaded not guilty on the basis that their policy of not allowing work in unsupported pits did not apply to geologists as they were expected to exercise their own professional judgment when deciding whether to enter such pits. The jury convicted the company after less than two hours of deliberation.*

Although this was a landmark decision, it is perhaps a shame that the first prosecution under this legislation involved such a small company (eight employees) where the director had actually been on site just prior to the accident and was aware of the circumstances of the dangerous working conditions. The true test of the power of this piece of legislation will surely come when there is a prosecution of a large company where the link between senior management and the breach of duy is not perhaps as obvious.

[13.2] THE INVESTIGATION AND PROSECUTION OF REGULATORY OFFENCES

Regulatory offences: Regulatory offences can occur when corporate entities or individuals commit offences in the course of their business, e.g. breaches of health and safety law; environmental law; trading standards etc. Some regulatory offences are strict liability and are committed inadvertently, but other offences can be committed wilfully.

With regulatory offences, the prosecuting agencies include the Environment Agency, the Health and Safety Executive, the Local Authority, the Department of Trade and Industry and so on. Each of these agencies has their own powers of investigation and prosecution which are found in specific regulations. Where such an agency suspects that a criminal offence has been committed, it will commence an investigation. The investigation procedure is exactly the same as it is for any other criminal offence, albeit that the interview is likely to take place in the offices of the interviewing agency. Any questioning of the suspect will amount to an interview and must be conducted in accordance with PACE 1984. The same rights will apply, including the right to legal representation. Once the case progresses to court, the case will be prosecuted either by a lawyer employed by the relevant agency, or by a solicitor/barrister instructed to act on their behalf.

Are there any alternatives to prosecution in regulatory offences? Where your client is being prosecuted by the CPS, the Code for Crown Prosecutors require that the CPS consider whether a prosecution is in the public interest. Where an offence is minor and your client is of relatively good character, the CPS may take the view that criminal proceedings are not necessary and the matter can be dealt with by way of a caution. Not only does this save your client the expense of a fine, but also the expenses associated with legal proceedings.

However, in a regulatory crime context, the prosecuting authority is likely to be someone other than the CPS and such a body may not have the power to caution your client. In such a situation, you should argue that by analogy with the CPS, they should consider whether a written warning would suffice. There is some authority for this view in the case of *R (on the application of H) v London Bus Services*, Lawtel, 17/01/02

> *H was a juvenile who assaulted a bus driver. The bus company brought a private prosecution for assault. H then sought a judicial review of the bus company's decision to prosecute on the basis that if she had been prosecuted by the CPS, she would have received a reprimand. H lost her argument on two grounds; firstly, even if the case had been prosecuted by the CPS, it was too serious to merit a reprimand; secondly, the bus company had followed its own guidance on when to prosecute which was similar to that of the Code for Crown Prosecutors. The Lawtel summary concluded: "In future, it would be wise for a prosecuting authority to be able to positively show in what respect it had taken into account the guidance, the factors that weighed one way or another, and how it had arrived at the decision to prosecute rather than issue a reprimand or warning".*

Although this case should be used with caution as it only relates to the prosecution of juveniles, it does provide a basis for arguing that non-CPS agencies should avoid arbitrary prosecutions and look to logical guidance, such as the Code for Crown Prosecutors, to justify their decision to prosecute rather than offer some form of warning.

However, note the decision in *Wandsworth London Borough Council v Rashid* [2009] EWCH 1844.

> *The defendant had left refuse bags outside of a shop and the Local Authority prosecuted him under s.34 Environmental Protection Act 1990. The defendant then successfully applied to the magistrates' court to have the proceedings stayed as an abuse of process as the Local Authority's waste management enforcement policy included alternatives to prosecution such as warnings and formal cautions and it had failed to explain why it had not preferred those options to a prosecution. Although the Magistrates were partly influenced by mitigation which the defendant had not made available to the Local Authority when it took the decision to prosecute, the finding of an abuse of process was successfully appealed. On appeal it was declared that there had been no abuse of process by the Local Authority and the decision as to whether there should be a prosecution was one for the Local Authority, not the court to make; the courts should only become involved in such a decision where there has been a clear abuse.*

The following are some of the main areas of regulatory offending:

13.2.1 Trading Standards

Trading Standards enforce a wide range of legislation in relation to consumer rights, fair trading, underage sales, food (quality, labelling, ingredients, food establishments), animal health and welfare, product safety issues such as product recall and warnings, weights and measures etc. Trading standards officers will carry out routine inspections as well as responding to allegations of relevant breaches of legislation.

Enforcement is in accordance with the Regulator's Compliance Code (which binds most regulators), the general aim of which is to keep intervention and regulation to the minimum that is required in order to maintain effectiveness. Trading standards will generally only bring a prosecution in the more serious cases, and the decision to prosecute usually takes into account the Code for Crown Prosecutors. Depending on the legislation that has been breached, alternative action can include warnings, fixed penalty notices, cautions, and seizure of goods, injunctions and improvement notices. Some offences may involve Trading Standards liaising with other regulators, such as the police on a case involving underage sales of alcohol, or liaising with the environmental health department on a case involving a breach of food safety regulations.

13.2.2 Health and Safety

The role of the Heath and Safety Executive: The primary piece of legislation governing occupational health and safety in the UK is the Health and Safety at Work Act 1974 (HASAW). The role of the Health and Safety Executive (HSE) is to enforce this, and associated legislation, in order to protect people against the various risks to health or safety that arise from work activities. A lot of their work involves issuing new regulations and providing training for employers, but they have a substantial role in inspection, investigation and enforcement. Health and Safety inspectors have wide-ranging powers that allow them to enter premises, seize property and investigate the causes of an accident.

Alternatives to prosecution: Prior to any criminal proceedings, where the HSE suspect a breach of health and safety law, they can issue an informal warning; or if the matter is more serious, issue an improvement notice or a prohibition notice.

An improvement notice will specify the breach of the law, set out what needs to be done to remedy the breach and specify a date by which this should be done. If your client feels that the notice is unfair, he has the right to appeal against it to an employment tribunal.

A prohibition notice is the next step and is only taken where work activities give rise to a risk of serious personal injury. Such a notice will require your client to refrain from a certain activity and not resume it until action has been taken to remove or control the risk. Again, the notice can be appealed to an employment tribunal. On any appeal the order may be upheld, varied or quashed. Failure to observe a notice is an offence of itself which can result in a fine or a custodial sentence, as well as leading to a prosecution for the original breach – s.33 HASAW 1974.

When, and who to prosecute: In deciding whether to prosecute, the HSE will have regard to the HSE's Enforcement Policy Statement, which reflects the principles of the Code for Crown Prosecutors. Enforcement action can be taken against anyone who is responsible for a breach, e.g. employers, owners of premises, suppliers of equipment, designers of projects and the like. Cases can be brought against individuals as well as companies, see s.37 HASAW 1974 which allows for prosecution if an offence was committed 'with the consent or connivance of, or has been attributable to neglect on the part of any director, manager or indeed any officer of the company, including secretaries'.

The Enforcement Policy recommends prosecution only where it is in the public interest and where there has (or could have been) serious harm; where there has been reckless disregard for health and safety requirements; where there have been persistent serious breaches; or where there has been deception or deliberate obstruction of an investigation.

A good example of multi-agency prosecution is the case of *R v Maurice Agis* [2009] unreported

> *The defendant was an artist who designed 'Dreamscape', a large inflatable, multi-coloured art installation which visitors could enter and walk around in whilst listening to composed music and sounds. The exhibit was first unveiled in the UK in Liverpool as the opening exhibit of the Brouhaha Street Festival. Dreamscape then undertook a national tour which included the Riverside Park in Chester-le-Street. Whilst on show at Chester-le-Street, the installation came free from its moorings and rose up into the air. The exhibit travelled some distance before colliding with a CCTV pole and crashing to the ground. Numerous people were hurt during the incident and two people died. There followed a joint investigation by the HSE and the police which resulted in the artist being charged with gross negligence manslaughter and a charge under s.3 Health and Safety at Work Act 1974 of failing to ensure the safety of persons not in his employment. It was said that he had failed to carry out proper calculations to ensure that the exhibit was equipped with a safe anchorage system*

and that he had failed to have the structure assessed by a qualified engineer. Additionally, it was alleged that the risk assessment carried out by the local Council was inadequate and it was charged with failing to ensure the safety of members of the public (not being persons in their employment) under s.3. Furthermore, the director of development services at the Council faced similar charges and the promotions company (Brouhaha International) were charged with failing to protect the safety of its employees under s.2 (1). Although the jury failed to reach a verdict on the manslaughter charge, (the prosecution declined to seek a retrial, offered no evidence and a not guilty verdict was recorded) they convicted the artist for the breach of health and safety and he was fined £10,000. This amount was subsequently reduced to £2,500 following an appeal. The promotions company and the Council pleaded guilty and were fined £4,000 and £20,000 respectively, whereas the director pleaded not guilty and the charges against him were left on file.

[13.3] SENTENCING OF WHITE COLLAR AND REGULATORY OFFENCES

There are clear limitations on sentence depending on whether your client is a corporate entity or an individual, as only individuals can be made subject to physical sentences such as imprisonment or community orders. The remainder of this chapter will consider the various issues that may arise during sentencing.

13.3.1 Proceeds of Crime

Prior to the Proceeds of Crime Act 2002 (POCA), the only way the prosecution could recover money that had been secured through criminal activity was via the Drug Trafficking Offences Act 1986 or, in limited circumstances, under the Criminal Justice Act 1988 as amended by the Proceeds of Crime Act 1995. Under POCA, wider powers were enacted to allow for the recovery of such money via civil and criminal court proceedings. The body responsible for pursuing civil recovery is the Assets Recovery Agency who can run recovery proceedings alongside criminal prosecutions, or independently if the facts do not warrant criminal proceedings. Part 8 of POCA provides for the role of 'financial investigation officers' who have their own investigative powers which are entirely distinct from those of the police.

The most common criminal court proceedings are for restraint orders, confiscation orders and receivership orders. These applications are brought where your client has benefited from his criminal conduct: s.6 POCA. Offences likely to attract POCA applications include drug trafficking, money laundering, terrorism, people trafficking and prostitution. Such applications are brought by the CPS and take place in the Crown Court. There is always provision for your client to apply to vary or discharge the order, provided he gives the required notice.

Restraint orders: These are dealt with under s.40–49 POCA. A restraint order essentially freezes the assets that may subsequently be made subject to a confiscation order. The order will prohibit any 'specified person' from dealing with realisable property. The specified person need not be the defendant; it could easily be an innocent third party that has been used to launder criminal proceeds, e.g. a bank or building society.

Once a restraint order has been made, the assets may be looked after by a 'management receiver' appointed by the court: ss.48–49 POCA. This will happen where the defendant has assets that require active management (such as a business) and the defendant is unable to attend to this himself, either because he is in custody, or because the court is unable to entrust the defendant with the assets. The receiver will preserve the assets and ensure that they retain their true value.

It is important to note that a restraint order can be sought at any time after an investigation has been started; there is no need to await charges. It is usual for the CPS to make the application on an ex parte basis, so the first your client will know of it is when he is served with a copy of the order. Breach of a restraint order is an offence of contempt punishable by imprisonment.

Confiscation orders: These are dealt with under s.6 POCA. A confiscation order can be sought following committal for sentence, or following conviction in the Crown Court. There is no form of written notice required. The CPS website contains clear guidance that the prosecution can refer to when making the decision whether to instigate confiscation proceedings. The purpose of a confiscation order is to deprive the defendant of the proceeds of his crime. These orders are becoming increasingly commonplace and vast sums of money have now been recovered. The CPS guidance refers to the case of *Sekhon* [2002] EWCA Crim 2954 wherein the Lord Chief Justice described confiscation orders as being:

> *'one of the most successful weapons, which can be used to discourage offending, committed to enrich the offender. If the evidential test is satisfied in respect of offences which allow the POCA provisions to be used by the court to best advantage, then it will generally be in the public interest to proceed on those offences'.*

Confiscation orders will be pursued where your client has a 'criminal lifestyle' as defined by s.75 POCA. This basically means that your client has made money from certain specified offences such as drugs/arms/people trafficking, money laundering, blackmail etc, or, where there has been some other form of criminal activity that has resulted in a gain of at least £5,000. Once a confiscation order has been made the defendant owes the money to the Crown. He can either pay the debt voluntarily or face enforcement proceedings in the magistrates' court. The amount becomes payable on the date of the actual order, but your client may seek an extension of up to 6 months if he needs time to pay. In exceptional cases, this can be extended for a further 6 months:s.11 POCA. The magistrates have wide powers, including the power to order that money held in your client's bank account be used to settle the debt. A confiscation order will include a default sentence which will be enforced if your client refuses to cooperate.

Although critics of POCA say that the Act is draconian, caselaw has confirmed that it is not incompatible with human rights, see *R v Rezvi* [2002] UKHL and *R v Benjafield* [2002] UKHL.

A Receivership order: If enforcement proceedings are under way in relation to a confiscation order, the CPS may apply to the Crown court for the appointment of an 'enforcement receiver': ss.50–51 POCA. This would occur in cases where the criminal proceeds included assets outside of the jurisdiction, real property or assets held in the name of third parties. The enforcement receiver will then realise these assets and the proceeds will be used to satisfy the outstanding debt. Your client should be made aware that real property can include the matrimonial home and there is a very real prospect of eviction if your client does not satisfy the confiscation order. If all of the realisable criminal property is still insufficient to satisfy the debt, then an application can be made to either vary or discharge the remaining sum: ss.23 and 24 POCA.

13.3.2 Disqualification as a punishment

If you are representing a director of a company who has committed a criminal offence, then there is always the possibility that he could be disqualified from acting as a director. Ss.1 and 2 of the Company Directors Disqualification Act 1986 provide for the making of a disqualification order against a director who has been convicted of an indictable offence (which includes either way offences) in connection with the promotion, formation, management or liquidation of a company. In *Edwards* [1998] 2 Cr App R (S) 213 the court stated that the purpose of this was:

> *The protection of the public from the activities of persons who, whether for reasons of dishonesty, or of naivety or incompetence in conjunction with the dishonesty of others, may use or abuse their role and status as a director of a limited company to the detriment of the public.*

13.3.3 Fine as a punishment

Where liability is attributable to the company rather than to an individual, the normal punishment will be a financial penalty. This is inevitable as clearly a company has no physical presence and cannot be made subject to a community order or term of imprisonment.

> *The leading case on setting the appropriate level of fine is Howe & Sons (Engineers) Ltd [1999] 2 All ER 249. In this case, a factory floor cleaner was electrocuted due to a faulty electric cable. The accident could have been avoided if the cable had been inspected and the company ended up pleading to several breaches of health and safety legislation. The initial fine was reduced on appeal, and although the court declined to lay down a tariff, they observed that the objective of the legislation was to secure a safe working environment. Any fine needs to 'bring that message home' to the company and its shareholders. The starting point is the firm's accounts. While a fine should not normally imperil the earnings of employee or lead to a risk of bankruptcy, there will be some cases where the offences are so serious that the company should not be in business.*

The decision in *Howe* has been followed in a large number of other cases which have applied the same principles to environmental offending and to other forms of regulatory offending.

The Sentencing Council has now provided guidance to assist with the sentencing of cases involving breach of health and safety legislation or corporate manslaughter. In line with the case of *Howe*, the guidance indicates that fines should be punitive, but regard must still be given to the defendant's means to pay and that any fine imposed must be capable of being paid, albeit that this may take several years. Again, in line with *Howe*, there is an acknowledgement that sometimes the amount of the fine could have the effect of putting the defendant out of business, but that "in some bad cases, this may be an acceptable consequence".

As for regulatory offences, the amount of the fine is within the discretion of the sentencing judge. An interesting argument in relation to the amount of regulatory offence fines was advanced in the following case:

> *R v New Look Retailers Ltd [2011] 1 Cr.App.R.(S.) 57 – the facts of the case were that a substantial fire broke out in the Oxford Street branch of New Look (a clothing retailer) which necessitated the evacuation of 400 people and the closure of Oxford Street for two days. New Look pleaded guilty to two regulatory offences involving failing to carry out a suitable risk assessment as to what should happen in the event of fire, and failing to ensure adequate fire safety training for its staff. Despite there being no death or injury involved, the company was fined £400,000. New Look appealed the fine on the basis that it was excessive and disproportionate when compared to the level of fines that had been ordered following health and safety convictions that had actually involved deaths. It was submitted that the judge was attempting to set an unusually high benchmark for fines imposed for breaches of fire safety regulations. The appeal was dismissed and the Court of Appeal accepted that the approach of the sentencing judge had been correct. It was acknowledged that the level of fine would always be 'fact sensitive' and that inevitably the fine would vary according to the level of culpability and harm in each case. It was felt that £400,000 was an appropriate figure given the very serious nature of the breaches which had exposed people to a very real risk or injury or death. In considering the appeal, the court once again upheld the principles set by Howe.*

13.3.4 Mitigation

Agreeing a basis of plea prior to sentencing: In the case of regulatory offending, the client is often prepared to concede that he may have inadvertently breached a regulation. In this situation, you should liaise with the prosecuting authority to see if you can agree a basis on which your client will enter a guilty plea. The guidance from the Court of Appeal is that the prosecution and defence should try to agree the aggravating and mitigating factors in a regulatory offence and where the plea is on an agreed basis, it should be put in writing in order to avoid any later disputes – *Friskies Petcare (UK) Ltd.* [2000] 2 Cr. App. R (S) 401.

Mitigation procedures: In relation to offences where the company has been convicted, your mitigation you should not only address the factors in Howe, but also the amount of fine that the company can afford. The courts have made clear that the onus is on the defence to produce up-to-date accounts to the court where the defence wish to argue about the amount of a fine. Moreover, it has also been said that in the case of corporate entities there is no objection to a company being permitted to pay a fine over a long period of time, since unlike individuals, it will be able to budget for this: *Ferrous Protection Ltd. v HSE* [2000] C.O.D. 273.

The particular focus of your mitigation should be to identify why the breach of the law occurred, especially where you can show that the breach was not done in order to increase profits, and to focus on the procedures which have been put in place in order to ensure that the breach does not occur again. This is especially important in Health and Safety cases, but is of equal relevance to all aspects of regulatory offences.

In relation to offences where you are representing an individual who has been committed, then the usual sentencing and mitigation procedures apply, see Chapter 10 for further information.

CHAPTER 14

INTRODUCTION TO EVIDENCE

> This chapter covers:
>
> Admissibility
>
> Competence and compellability
>
> The burden and standard of proof

[14.1] WHAT IS EVIDENCE?

Evidence is material put before a court so that the court may decide the truth or probability of a fact asserted before it.

Evidence is an intrinsic part of every stage of the criminal litigation process. It is not a separate "academic" subject.

- At the police station you need to be aware of the right to silence and its limits; of what may constitute oppressive conduct or may give rise to unreliability in a confession; of the rules governing the obtaining of identification evidence.

- When you take a statement you need to know what material will be admissible and what allegations (for example, attacks on a person's character) may lead to your client's criminal record being revealed to the court.

- In negotiating with the CPS at court, you need to know the strength of your case and the weaknesses in the prosecution evidence so as to have a realistic idea of what result is possible.

- In your advocacy you need to be aware of all the rules, especially the rules concerning hearsay and character evidence.

Evidence must therefore be admissible, relevant and fair. In order to give that evidence, the witness must be competent, and if the witness is reluctant to attend court, you will need to consider if they are compellable.

14.1.1 Judicial notice

Some matters are sufficiently established that they are accepted without the need to prove them by calling evidence. In these matters the court takes "judicial notice" of the issue. If a matter is of such common knowledge as to be beyond serious dispute the court will take judicial notice without further enquiry (examples include: two weeks being too short for a baby to be gestated; cats are often domestic pets etc.). Some matters may be accepted after judicial enquiry (for example, that a date fell on a particular day of the week, or matters of a political nature, such as the status of foreign countries).

Magistrates had been entitled to rely upon personal local knowledge in a trial where it was an issue of "local notoriety". The court must make the fact that local knowledge was going to be used known to the prosecution and defence so as to give those representing the parties a chance to comment upon the knowledge that the justices claimed to have. Norbrook Laboratories (GB) v Health and Safety Executive, *The Times February 23rd 1998*

Contrast: *Magistrates, who had been dealing with an allegation of breach of a Tree Preservation Order, had not been entitled to draw on their own knowledge to decide that the trees (which they had seen photographs of) must have been at least 4 years' old (and hence subject to the order). This was a matter where expert evidence should have been called.* Carter v Eastbourne Borough Council *164 J.P. 273*

14.1.2 Admissions

Note that some matters may simply be proved by admissions. In a criminal matter formal admissions are generally dealt with under s.10 Criminal Justice Act 1967; this requires that any out of court admissions must be in writing, and that if they are made by the defendant they should be made by his counsel or solicitor or approved by them.

[14.2] ADMISSIBILITY

In general evidence will be admissible provided that it is <u>relevant</u>. However this rule is subject to a number of exclusionary powers.

14.2.1 Exclusionary powers

In criminal cases there is a general common law exclusionary power – in other words, the judge has a general discretion to exclude relevant and admissible prosecution evidence in the interests of ensuring that the defendant receives a fair trial. The test is generally stated as being whether the prejudicial effect of the evidence outweighs its probative value: *Sang* [1980] AC 402.

s.76 Police and Criminal Evidence Act (PACE) also provides that confessions must be excluded if they have been obtained by oppression or in circumstances that render them unreliable. S.78 PACE provides a general statutory power to exclude prosecution evidence which would have an adverse effect on the fairness of the proceedings. [The exclusion of evidence is dealt with alongside the general issue of confession evidence in Chapter 16.]

14.2.2 Privilege and public interest immunity

As a matter of public policy, relevant and admissible evidence may be excluded because it is privileged (for example, communications between a solicitor and his client). Here the paramount interest is in the free and unhindered communication between lawyer and client, and that takes priority over other interests. Equally, as a matter of public policy, admissible evidence may be excluded if a certificate from a minister is provided certifying that its disclosure would be contrary to the public interest (such certificates are known as p.i.i. certificates). These issues are discussed more fully in Chapter 20.

14.2.3 Hearsay evidence:

English law also excludes many other forms of relevant evidence – the widest category being "hearsay" evidence. Hearsay is dealt with in detail in Chapter 18.

What is hearsay? The general principle is that evidence at trial comes from testimony from witnesses. This permits the evidence to be tested in cross-examination, and the credibility of the witness can be assessed. Hearsay evidence generally arises where the court is being asked to deal with evidence that is coming from some other source than live oral testimony.

Hearsay is often defined as "a statement other than one made by a witness in the course of giving evidence offered as evidence of the truth of its contents." In other words, hearsay tends to arise where there is documentary evidence or where witnesses want to give evidence as to what they have been told by another person, since in both these cases the original first-hand witness is not themselves in the witness box telling the court what happened.

14.2.4 Fairness

Fairness takes a number of different forms. We have general rules which prevent a defendant's previous bad character from being raised (unless he makes it an issue), and important safeguards concerning the admissibility of confessions which are alleged to have been obtained by oppression or which are unreliable. Additionally, s.78 PACE provides for the exclusion of evidence which would have an adverse effect on the fairness of proceedings.

However, do not get misled into thinking that we have a rule which excludes evidence if it has been improperly obtained. In the old case of *Leatham* (1861) 3 E&E 658, the court stated: "It matters not how you get it, if you steal it even it would be admissible in evidence." In *Sang* the House of Lords made clear that there is no general discretion to exclude relevant and admissible evidence merely on the basis that it has been obtained by improper or unfair means.

14.2.5 Relevance

> *Evidence is relevant if it is logically probative or disprobative of some matter which requires proof.*
> *DPP v Kilbourne* [1973] AC 729 at 756

To be admissible evidence must be relevant. In general, relevance is unlikely to be an issue in most mundane situations. However, on occasion it can raise difficult questions.

> *A film crew were filming a "fly on the wall" documentary, filming M. An incident then took place between M and his friends and another group of men on a minibus, as a result of which the victim got stabbed by a man wearing a beige top. The only identification evidence was that the top matched the top that M had been filmed wearing earlier. There was also evidence of phone calls from M to the film crew, which the prosecution said were made in order to persuade the crew to alter the film. There was evidence that the film had in fact been altered. And there was evidence that M had disappeared from the area and had been arrested in Holland. The Court of Appeal agreed that all this evidence was relevant and therefore admissible. The phone calls might lead the jury to conclude that a person who was mixed up in the attack would contact the film crew, and the fact that the evidence directly relating to M had been tampered with was relevant to the suggestion that he was the attacker. Equally, the evidence of flight could give rise to a logical inference about the possible causes of that flight.* Massey CA, unreported, 13th October 2000)

14.2.6 Real evidence

It is worth mentioning at this stage that while the court will normally expect to receive evidence by way of oral testimony, evidence can also be adduced as "real evidence". This category would include objects (the typical example is the murder weapon itself), but will also include intangible matters such as viewing the scene, where the court is being asked to use its own direct sensory perception of the material or location. Relevance needs to be established with real evidence, just as it will for other categories of evidence.

[14.3] COMPETENCE AND COMPELLABILITY

If a witness is competent, they can be called to give evidence. If they are compellable the court can compel them to attend and to give evidence. The basic rule is that all people are competent, and all competent witnesses can be compelled. There are a number of exceptions to this.

14.3.1 The Accused

Competence: The accused is competent for the defence, but is not competent for the prosecution: s. 53 Youth Justice and Criminal Evidence Act 1999. This makes sense because if he wished to testify for the prosecution he would presumably be pleading guilty.

Compellable: The accused is not compellable as a witness – that is, he cannot be forced to testify at his trial. However, if the accused does not testify in his own defence an inference can sometimes be drawn from his failure to do so: s.35 Criminal Justice and Public Order Act 1994, see Chapter 15.

What if there are several defendants? Since a defendant cannot testify for the prosecution, in cases where there are two or more defendants none of them can give evidence for the prosecution (i.e. turn Queen's Evidence) so long as they are a defendant. If they are going to give evidence for the prosecution, they must therefore cease to be a defendant, whether by having the charges dropped against them, by holding separate trials, or by pleading guilty. Of course this does not prevent a defendant from giving evidence in chief in his own defence against his co-accused, and the prosecution can cross-examine him in order to bring out evidence which is harmful to the co-accused.

14.3.2 Spouses

A spouse is any person whose marriage is recognised as valid under English law: *Khan* (1987) 84 Cr App R 44. A spouse will be both competent and compellable to give evidence for the defence. Although a spouse will be competent to give evidence for the prosecution (unless s/he is jointly charged and therefore a defendant herself: (s.80(4) PACE), she cannot normally be compelled to testify.

The offences where a spouse can be compelled to testify for the prosecution are:

- where the offence involves an assault, injury or threat of injury either to the spouse's wife or husband, or to a child (a person under 16);
- where the offence is a sexual offence alleged to have been committed on a child; or
- where the offence is one of secondary participation in the assault or the sexual offence: see s.80(3) PACE.

What happens where there has been a divorce? A spouse who is now divorced is not treated as a spouse: s.80(5) PACE.

What about cohabitees? Attempts to argue that the Human Rights Act requires s.80 to be interpreted so as to include cohabitees and children of the defendant were unsuccessful, and they remain compellable to give evidence for the prosecution: *Pearce* [2001] EWCA Crim 2834.

Can a witness be stopped from marrying the defendant? An attempt by the CPS to prevent a defendant from marrying a witness (with the effect that the witness would no longer be compellable to testify for the prosecution) was held to breach article 12 (the right to marry): *R v Registrar for Births, Deaths and Marriages, ex parte CPS* (2003) 1 All ER 540.

14.3.3 Other rules on competence

Competence to testify – the basic rule: s.53 YJCEA 1999: The basic rule is that anyone of any age is competent as a witness. However, a person is not competent to give evidence in criminal proceedings if it appears to the court that

- either they cannot understand questions put to them as a witness;, or
- they cannot give intelligible answers.

If a question as to competence arises, it is for the party calling the witness to satisfy the court on the balance of probabilities that their witness is competent.

Competent witnesses who will give evidence sworn: s.55 YJCEA 1999: Under the Act the assumption remains that adult witnesses will give evidence on oath. In order to be sworn in order to testify a witness must:

- be at least 14 years old and
- they must have "sufficient appreciation of the solemnity of the occasion and of the particular responsibility to tell the truth which is involved in taking an oath".

If a witness can give intelligible testimony they are assumed to comply with this test of "sufficient appreciation" unless the contrary is shown.

Competent witnesses who will give evidence unsworn: s.56 YJCEA 1999

If a witness is competent to give evidence but cannot give sworn evidence, they will give evidence unsworn. This will apply either to children who are under 14, or adults who cannot fulfil the "sufficient appreciation" test. Although the Act does not say anything about the status of unsworn evidence, the accompanying Home Office guidance states:

> *The provisions ... would therefore allow such witnesses to give evidence in future but unsworn. It will be for the jury (if there is one) to decide what weight should be placed on their evidence.*

It is clear that the test of whether a witness is competent is separate from the issue of what weight should be given to the witness's testimony.

> *In the case of MacPherson [2006] 1 Cr App R 459 (30) the witness was a six year old child who was alleged to be the victim of a sexual assault. The Court of Appeal held that the trial judge had been right to focus on the issues of whether she could understand what was being asked, and could give answers that could be understood. A young child who could speak and understand basic English with strangers would be competent. Questions of her credibility and reliability went to the weight that should be given to her testimony – rather than whether she was competent to testify at all.*

In *Barker* [2010] EWCA Crim 4 the Court of Appeal upheld the trial judge's decision that a child of 4 was competent to give evidence of sexual abuse that had occurred when she was two years old.

14.3.4 Procedural assistance for witnesses – "special measures":

The Youth Justice and Criminal Evidence Act as amended by Coroners and Justice Act 2009 provides support to certain categories of witness who might otherwise have problems testifying. These categories include: all witnesses under 18; witnesses suffering from physical or mental disorders or disabilities; witnesses who would be unable to give their best evidence to the court because of their fear and distress. Witnesses who are the alleged victims of sexual assaults would be presumed to fall into the latter category. s.99 CJA 2009 recently added witnesses to certain gun and knife crimes to this catergory.

These witnesses can be assisted by special measures such as:

- screens to hide the witness from the accused;
- giving evidence by live television link;
- removing gowns and wigs to reduce the formality;
- allowing video-recorded interviews in place of the evidence in chief, and
- allowing pre-recorded videoed cross-examination in place of live cross-examination. *[This last not yet in force.]*

Children (and witnesses with physical or mental disabilities) are also able to use an intermediary to help them give evidence, or any communication aids.

The defendant and special measures: The House of Lords has confirmed that generally special measures are aimed at protecting witnesses other than the defendant. However in *R v Camberwell Green Youth Court ex parte D* [2005] UKHL 5 Lady Hale indicated very strongly that it was likely that courts did have the jurisdiction to extend the protection of special measures to defendants where it was necessary to do so. The Consolidated Criminal Practice Direction makes provision for courts to consider whether vulnerable defendants should be permitted to give evidence by way of video link: III.30.13

Protection from cross-examination in rape cases: There have been various measures intended to protect the victim from irrelevant cross-examination on sexual issues. The rule that rape victims cannot be cross-examined as to their previous sexual history with a person other than the defendant, other than with the leave of the judge, was established by s.2 Sexual Offences (Amendment) Act 1976.

Section 41 Youth Justice and Criminal Evidence Act added a further provision which was designed to prevent the cross-examination of the defendant on any prior sexual contact with the accused, other than in very restricted circumstances. This provision was challenged as being incompatible with the defendant's right to a fair trial under article 6, and the House of Lords ruled that the provision could be read in a Convention compliant manner, so as to balance the rights of the accused and the alleged victim: *A (cross-examination in rape cases)* [2002] 1 A.C. 45.

Livelink: s.51 Criminal Justice Act 2003 gives courts the power to direct that any witness, other than the defendant, may give evidence through a live link. There is a wide discretion given to the court, which will consider issues including the availability of the witness, the need for personal attendance, the importance of the witness's evidence, the views of the witness, the suitability of any facilities, and whether permitting livelink might inhibit any party from effectively testing the witness's evidence.

[14.4] BURDEN AND STANDARD OF PROOF

14.4.1 Burden of proof

The general principle is that the prosecution has the burden of proving the guilt of the accused.

> *Throughout the web of the English criminal law one golden thread is always to be seen, that it is the duty of the prosecution to prove the prisoner's guilt.*
>
> Woolmington v DPP [1935] AC 462

There are common law exceptions (insanity under the *M'Naghten* rules) and statutory exceptions. Thus, for example, it is an offence to grow cannabis, subject to a defence that you did not know or suspect, or have any reason to suspect, some fact alleged by the prosecution in proving their case.

There is also the statutory exception contained in the Magistrates' Court Act 1980, s.101:this provides that where a defence is based on "any exception, proviso, excuse or qualification", the defendant will have the burden of proof in proving that the exception applies. Section 101 applies to summary trials only, but *Edwards* [1975] QB 27 creates a similar rule for the Crown Court. Where the defence bears this legal burden of proof, the test is the balance of probabilities (i.e. more likely than not).

There has been considerable argument whether provisions which place the burden of proof on the defendant comply with article 6(2) of the Convention, which states that in criminal matters there is a presumption of innocence. This point is considered in detail in 14.5 below. However, in cases where the defence does not bear the legal burden of proof, the defence may still bear an evidential burden: this means that the defence must ensure that there is sufficient evidence before the court to require the prosecution to disprove the defence beyond reasonable doubt.

> *Chas is charged with GBH. His defence is that he acted in self-defence. He must ensure that there is sufficient evidence before the court to raise this defence. It will then be for the prosecution to disprove the defence beyond reasonable doubt. Chas cannot simply do nothing and then ask the jury not to convict him on the basis that the prosecution have not dealt with self-defence as a potential defence!*

In *Lambert* the House of Lords considered a provision in the Misuse of Drugs Act which appeared to place the burden of proof on the defendant to show that he did not know that what he possessed were drugs. It was held that article 6 of the European Convention required that this provision be interpreted as placing only an "evidential burden" on the defendant. The effect is that the defendant must raise his defence ("I thought that it was a bag full of sports clothes; I did not know it was cocaine.") and it is then for the prosecution to prove beyond reasonable doubt that the defendant did know that he was in possession of cocaine.

14.4.2 The standard of proof

The prosecution must prove its case "beyond reasonable doubt". There have been various glosses on this including "sure" or "satisfied that you feel sure". Generally, however, judges should not attempt to explain the term. In *Walters* [1969] 2 AC 26, the Privy Council stated that it was:

> *the quality and kind of doubt which, when you are dealing with matters of importance in your own affairs, you allow to influence you one way or the other.*

Presumptions: Some matters can be taken as proved even if there is insufficient evidence because of a legal presumption. Presumptions may be presumptions of fact or of law, and may be rebuttable (i.e. in some cases they may simply shift the burden of proof).

Circumstantial inferences: Presumptions of fact are generally merely circumstantial inferences. A person is presumed to intend the natural consequences of their acts. However, s.8 Criminal Justice Act 1967 makes clear that this is not a presumption of law, and that a court is not bound to infer that a defendant intended a particular result simply because it was the natural and probable result of his actions. Rather the court should decide this based on inferences from all the evidence.

Recent possession: Some lawyers speak of a presumption of "recent possession" (i.e. that where a person is found in possession of something that has recently been stolen and they offer no reasonable explanation, it may be inferred that they have guilty knowledge). Again, this is little more than a logical inference.

> *A stolen car was found a day or two after it had disappeared in a garage to which M had access. His fingerprints were on parts of the car. M denied knowing the car was stolen. In the summing up the judge said that if the jury found M had been in recent possession of the car, then it was for M to explain that and the jury could infer guilt if they felt M had shut his eyes to the obvious. The Court of Appeal held that it was better if the formal "recent possession" direction was given to the jury but that the judge had not erred.*
>
> <u>Moulding</u> [1996] Crim LR 440

Presumptions of law include various presumptions of marriage and legitimacy, the presumption of death (no contact during a continuous period of seven years) and so on. These presumptions are all rebuttable.

14.4.3 The need for proof

It may sound obvious to say that the prosecution must prove its case, but it can be overlooked, especially as the prosecution focuses on complex rules around character evidence, for example.

> *In <u>Mills v Director of Public Prosecutions</u> (173 J.P. 157, DC) the prosecution was so intent on persuading the court to admit no less than 11 previous convictions for driving while disqualified, in order to show that the defendant had a propensity to act in this way that they forgot to produce any evidence to show that he was in fact disqualified from driving <u>on this occasion</u>. The defence called no evidence and the court purported to convict him on the basis of his silence at the police station. However as the Divisional Court pointed out, he had not relied upon any fact that could form the basis for drawing an adverse inference from his silence: what had happened was that the prosecution had neglected to prove a key element of their case.*

[14.5] HUMAN RIGHTS ISSUES

The Convention itself says nothing about specific evidential rules, and the ECtHR has always been quick to say that article 6 relates to the right to a fair trial, and that evidential issues must be considered in this context. Some caselaw has already been mentioned in earlier chapters – for example, the right not to incriminate oneself (*Saunders v United Kingdom* (1997) 23 EHRR 313); the use of inferences from silence (*Condron v United Kingdom* (2000) 31 E.H.R.R. 1) – and these and other cases will be considered in more detail in later chapters. However, there are complex issues in relation to both the burden and standard of proof which need to be considered briefly here.

14.5.1 The standard of proof – presumptions:

Since article 6(2) gives the defendant the right to be presumed innocent, are there circumstances where the state can impose a presumption of guilt, and require the defendant to prove his innocence on all or part of a charge?

The leading Strasbourg authority is *Salabiaku v. France* (1988) 13 E.H.R.R 379, where the Court was concerned with an article in the Customs Code dealing with the smuggling of prohibited goods. It was for the state to prove that the defendant had been in possession of goods; once this was established, the person was deemed guilty of smuggling. Although this provision appeared to create an irrebuttable presumption, it was found that as a matter of practice courts did not to resort automatically to the presumption but exercised their power of assessment in the light of all the evidence. The ECtHR stated that there was no breach of article 6 provided that the presumptions were kept within reasonable limits.

14.5.2 The burden of proof – reverse onus provisions:

The issue of the burden of proof is closely related to that of presumptions, in that it shifts the onus onto the defendant to show that he is not guilty of some element of an offence. Given that presumptions are permissible "if kept within reasonable limits" (*Salabiaku* – see above), it is unsurprising to find that the same test has been applied to what are known as "reverse onus" provisions – provisions which seek to shift some element of the burden of proof from the defendant.

The leading case is that of *Lambert* [2001] 2 Cr. App. R. 28. This was a prosecution under the Misuse of Drugs Act 1971, s.28(3) of which provided that it was for the defendant to prove (on the balance of probabilities) that he did not know the nature of what he possessed. Lambert was observed getting off a train, exchanging money for a sports bag with a man in a car park, and then taking the sports bag back to the station where he was arrested and found to be in possession of a significant amount of cocaine. The House of Lords held that article 6 would now require that the Misuse of Drugs Act be read so as to apply only an "evidential burden" on Lambert. In other words it was for Lambert to raise his defence that he did not know he was in possession of the drugs; it would then be for the prosecution to prove his knowledge.

Lambert has now been applied to a whole range of different offences including *Sheldrake v DPP* [2004] UKHL 43, a case concerning the burden of proof on an offence of being drunk in charge. The House of Lords held that in relation to that offence the full burden of proof lay on the defendant to prove on the balance of probabilities that he had not been going to drive the vehicle. The court held that there was no breach of the presumption of innocence because the measure pursued a legitimate aim, namely the prevention of death, injury or damage caused by unfit drivers.

EVIDENCE

All evidence must be:

1. **ADMISSIBLE:** (i.e. from a competent witness, not hearsay etc.)
2. **RELEVANT:** (i.e. generally not inexpert opinion evidence or evidence of propensity - unless founded on very similar facts)

&

3. **FAIR:** (i.e. not obtained by oppression or unfairness; generally not evidence of bad character etc.).

COMPETENCE

General rule: any person will be competent and compellable to give evidence.

Test for competence:
- Able to understand questions; and
- Able to give replies that can be understood.

Exceptions:

The accused: competent to give evidence in defence, not competent to give evidence for the Prosecution

COMPELLABILITY

In general all witnesses will be compellable.

Exceptions:

Accused: not compellable for the Prosecution.

Spouses: compellable for the defence; not compellable for the Prosecution **unless** the charge is assault involving either the spouse or a person under 16 or a sexual offence on a minor: see s.80 (3) PACE.

NB. s.80 (5) PACE: if the spouses are no longer married at the time of trial, it is as if they were never married.

CHILDREN

Does the child satisfy the competence test – i.e. able to understand and to be understood?

Can give sworn evidence if aged 14 or over, and (i) understands solemnity of occasion and (ii) particular responsibility to tell the truth.

Otherwise will give evidence unsworn.

PROOF

Facts are proved by evidence. Evidence may take the form of oral evidence from witnesses, real evidence (i.e. actual objects or places), and (where admissible) documentary evidence.

The burden of proof is on the person that asserts the facts; thus in criminal cases it is generally on the Prosecution. There are exceptions (such as insanity or diminished responsibility) where the Defendant bears the burden; generally, however, the Defendant only bears an "evidential burden" – in other words, the Defendant must ensure that there is sufficient evidence before the court for the court to be aware that the matter is a live issue.

The standard of proof for the Prosecution is "beyond reasonable doubt" – e.g. so that you are "really sure".

Formal admissions, presumptions and matters of judicial notice may be proved without evidence.

Introduction to Evidence – test yourself questions

[The answers to these questions are set out in Appendix A at the back of this book]

[1] As a general rule evidence will be admissible provided that:

i. It has been obtained lawfully

ii. It is relevant to the issues in the case

iii. It is oral testimony.

Which of these propositions are correct?

(a) None of them.

(b) i and ii only.

(c) iii only.

(d) ii only.

[2] Greg and Jenny are married. Greg is charged with affray following a brawl at a public house. Jenny was present at the scene and is a potential witness.

Which one of the following propositions is correct?

(a) Jenny is competent but not compellable for the defence; she is competent and compellable for the prosecution.

(b) Jenny is competent and compellable for the defence; she is competent but not compellable for the prosecution.

(c) Jenny is competent to give evidence for both prosecution and defence; however, she is compellable in respect of neither.

(d) Jenny is not competent as a witness for either prosecution or defence.

[3] Rowena is 7. She witnesses the death of Quentin who was knocked down by a stolen car. At the trial of the driver of the car for causing death by dangerous driving, the prosecution wish to call Rowena to give evidence.

Which one of the following is correct?

(a) Rowena must give evidence unsworn. The judge will only permit her to do so if it is in the interests of justice.

(b) Rowena can give sworn evidence only if she understands the particular solemnity of giving evidence on oath; since she is only 7, this is unlikely to be the case.

(c) Rowena must give evidence unsworn, and the court may receive the evidence provided she is capable of giving intelligible testimony.

(d) Rowena must give unsworn evidence but the court cannot receive the testimony unless it is shown that Rowena understands the duty to tell the truth.

[4] Andrew is charged with arson with intent to endanger life. Which one of the following directions from the judge to the jury correctly states the standard of proof that is required?

(a) You must be sure ...

(b) You must be sure on the balance of probabilities ...

(c) You must be satisfied ..

(d) You must be absolutely certain ...

CHAPTER 15

SILENCE AND INFERENCES

> This chapter covers:
>
> The right to silence at common law.
>
> Inferences from failure to put forward defence facts (s.34 Criminal Justice and Public Order Act 1994).
>
> Inferences from failure to explain objects, presence etc. (s.36, s.37 Criminal Justice and Public Order Act 1994).
>
> The inference from the defendant failing to give evidence at trial (s.35 Criminal Justice and Public Order Act 1994).

[15.1] SILENCE AT COMMON LAW

At common law there has generally been no duty on your client either to assist the police with enquiries (i.e. before charge) or to give evidence at his own trial.

Exceptions to the right of silence at common law

At common law no inference could be drawn from the silence of an accused either before or at charge in the face of questioning or accusations. The only exception was where the accused and accuser were on "even terms". In such a situation the failure to respond to accusations or questions could be evidentially significant.

> *In Hall [1971] 1 WLR 298, H failed to respond to a police officer who told him that a Co-Accused had implicated him. Here the Privy Council held that no inference could be drawn from the silence.*
>
> *Cf. Parkes [1976] 1 WLR 1251, where the victim's mother saw P near the body of her dead daughter holding a knife. She twice accused P of stabbing her daughter. He did not respond. When she said she was going to keep him there until the police arrived, he tried to stab her. Held: these silences/reactions could be taken into account. The parties were on "even terms".*

As a general rule, an accused will never be on "even terms" with a police officer. Obiter dictum in *Chandler* [1976] 1 WLR 585 – where the court suggested that the parties might be on even terms where the defendant was being questioned by the police provided he had a solicitor present – have never really been followed.

[15.2] FAILURE TO PUT FORWARD DEFENCE FACTS: s.34

Under ss.34–37 Criminal Justice and Public Order Act 1994 "inferences" can be drawn from your client's silence in certain specified circumstances.

Outside the particular situations dealt with by ss.34–37, the common law will still apply and no inferences will generally be possible.

Even within the ss.34–37 situations, the inferences to be drawn will be circumstantial; a person should not be found guilty simply on the basis that they failed to answer police questions. An inference is never sufficient in itself to found a conviction.

Failure to mention defence facts: Under s.34 CJPOA an inference can arise at trial if your client has failed to put forward the facts of his defence when he was being questioned under caution prior to charge or when he was charged. This is a vastly problematic provision which continues to generate a massive number of appeal cases every year. It is essential for you to understand the effect of the provision since you will be responsible for advising your client at the police station, and in particular for advising him on whether he should put forward his defence at this stage, or risk inferences being drawn later.

15.2.1 The statutory provisions

The key element is set out in s.34(1).

(1) *Where, in any proceedings against a person for an offence, evidence is given that the accused –*
  (a) *at any time before he was charged with the offence, on being questioned under caution by a constable trying to discover whether or by whom the offence had been committed, failed to mention any fact relied on in his defence in those proceedings; or*
  (b) *on being charged with the offence or officially informed that he might be prosecuted for it, failed to mention any such fact, being a fact which in the circumstances existing at the time the accused could reasonably have been expected to mention when so questioned, charged or informed, subsection (2) below applies.*

Subsection 2 then provides that if there has been a failure to mention defence facts under s.34(1) an inference may be drawn when deciding if there is a case to answer or when deciding on guilt. An additional provision states that no inferences are possible if the suspect had not been allowed an opportunity to consult a solicitor prior to being questioned. The inferences to be drawn are "such inferences as appear proper".

15.2.2 The basic principles of the s.34 inference:

(i) Your client must have been cautioned. A caution should be administered where there are "grounds" to suspect the commission of an offence: C10.1. Normally an inference will only be possible where someone is at the police station and has had the opportunity to take legal advice. In the case of *Murray v United Kingdom* (1996) 22 EHRR 29 the ECtHR stressed the importance of legal advice before an inference could arise. In consequence it is very unlikely that an inference could be drawn from silence post-caution but pre-arrival at the police station.

(ii) Questioning by constables and others The inference can only arise in the face of questioning by either the police or persons "who are either charged with the duty to investigate offences or charge offenders". This is the same wording as PACE and therefore clearly includes Customs officers, store detectives, RSPCA officials and so on. Whether a store detective is "charged with the duty to investigate offences" may depend upon the terms of their contract. A mere duty to arrest is unlikely to amount to "investigation".

If it is suggested that your client failed to put forward his facts during the interview, questions must have been asked. In *Hillard* [2004] EWCA Crim 837 the police simply read the suspect the statement of the alleged victim. The Court of Appeal held that no inferences should have been drawn since it was clear that the suspect did not understand that he was supposed to be responding to the statement by putting forward his version of events.

(iii) **s.34 is about putting forward facts – not answering questions.** The effect of s.34 is that if your client later raises a fact in his defence which he has failed to mention when questioned, an inference can be drawn. The provision does not impose any duty to answer questions and your client commits no offence by refusing to answer questions. For this reason you may recall that a pre-prepared written statement which sets out in full the defence facts will prevent any later inference from arising – regardless of whether the suspect has refused to answer questions: see 3.3.7 above and the case of *Knight*.

(iv) **The inference of itself cannot prove your client is guilty:** The judge must direct the jury that:

(i) the burden of proof stays with the prosecution;

(ii) the inference cannot prove guilt by itself;

(iii) there must be a prima facie prosecution case to answer before any inference can be drawn.

In *Doldur* [2000] Crim.L.R. 178 the Court of Appeal stated:

Acceptance of the truth and accuracy of all or part of the prosecution evidence may or may not amount to sureness of guilt. Something more may be required, which may be provided by an adverse inference from silence if they think it proper to draw one.

The Judicial Studies Board specimen direction confirms that a jury should be directed that although an inference can provide additional support for the prosecution case, a conviction should not be "wholly or mainly" based on the inference.

(v) **What are the inferences that can be drawn?** The CJPOA refers only to such inferences as appear "proper". One obvious inference is that your client didn't mention the defence fact at the time because he has made it up at a later stage ("later fabrication"). Equally another good reason for your client not telling his story in the police station is that he knows it won't stand up to close questioning at that stage (perhaps because he has yet to brief his alibi witnesses) – see for example, *Randall* [1998] 6 Archbold News 1. Alternatively your client may want to wait and see what the prosecution case is so that he can adapt his defence to fit.

In *Betts and Hall* (2001) 2 Cr App R 16, the Court of Appeal confirmed that an inference could have been drawn from B's failure to mention a defence fact in the first interview even when he mentioned this fact in a subsequent interview since:

it was open to the jury conclude that he had not thought of this line of defence until he had been picked out on the [identification] parade.

(vi) **The inference should only be drawn if it is reasonable to do so.** The Judicial Studies Board model jury direction breaks this down into three separate questions:

(i) Could he reasonably have been expected to mention these facts when questioned?

(ii) Is the only sensible explanation for his failure to do so that he had no answer at the time, or none that would stand up to scrutiny?

(iii) Is the prosecution case without the inference already so strong that it clearly calls for an answer from the suspect?

This issue of "reasonableness" needs to be broken down into a number of separate principles.

(a) **Reasonableness is a matter for the jury:** In *Argent* [1997] 2 Cr App R 27, the Court of Appeal stated that the question of whether it was reasonable for your client to have failed to answer questions was a matter purely for the jury. Nonetheless the court then stated that the jury should not look at the question restrictively:

> *"... matters such as time of day, the defendant's age, experience, mental capacity, state of health, sobriety, tiredness, knowledge, personality and legal advice are all part of the relevant circumstances; and these are only examples of what may be relevant.*
>
> *....*
>
> *Like so many other questions in criminal trials this is a question to be resolved by the jury in the exercise of their collective common sense, experience and understanding of human nature. Sometimes they may conclude that it was reasonable for the defendant to have held his peace for a host of reasons, such as that he was tired, ill, frightened, drunk, drugged, unable to understand what was going on, suspicious of the police, afraid that his answer would not be fairly recorded, worried at committing himself without legal advice, acting on legal advice, or some other reason accepted by the jury."*

You need to be aware of these principles in *Argent*. They are probably the clearest guidance on factors that the court should take into account.

(b) **Inadequate disclosure will not *of itself* justify silence:** PACE gives you no right to the disclosure of any information by the police at the police station, with the exception of the custody record and, in identification cases, the initial description by the witness. In *Argent*, the police made only partial disclosure of the evidence before questioning A about a murder. The Court of Appeal dismissed the argument that no s.34 inference should have been drawn. The court suggested that the suspect was told enough about the offence to be able to put forward his basic defence – which was that he was elsewhere at the time.

Non-disclosure where the defendant does not understand the case: Non-disclosure may, however, be a factor in showing that the failure to mention defence facts was reasonable. In *Roble* [1997] Crim LR 449 it was said that there could be case where there has been so little disclosure that the lawyer cannot usefully advise the suspect, or where your client himself does not understand the basis of the police case, or where the matter is so complex or so old that no sensible response is possible at that stage. In such circumstances the jury may conclude that your client's silence was reasonable.

(c) **There must be a situation which calls for an explanation:** In *Condron v United Kingdom*, the European Court re-iterated the proposition that it is silence in the face of "situations which clearly call for an explanation" which can be taken into account by the court. There may therefore be circumstances where so little disclosure has been made, where the situation is so confused, or where there is no significant evidence against the defendant, that it can be argued that there is no situation that clearly calls for an explanation.

(d) **Evidence being held back?** In *Imran and Hussain* [1997] Crim LR 754 (discussed in Chapter 3) I and H were videoed during an attempted robbery but the police did not reveal the existence of the tape before the interview. There the Court of Appeal took the view that this was a legitimate tactic. However, the result would probably be different if the police actually *lied* about the disclosure. You should therefore make sure that you specifically ask, preferably on tape, whether you have received full disclosure of all evidence,

(e) **Was your client too drunk, too tired, too vulnerable?** In looking at all the circumstances, the jury must look at the particular circumstances facing or affecting the defendant in question – including all his or her particular fears, illnesses and concerns. The test is not of some hypothetical reasonable man. Do note however that if a client has been certified by a doctor as fit for interview, the court may well accept the doctor's opinion, even if you (the lawyer) disagree: see *R v Condron*.

(f) **What is the effect of legal advice?** This is a very difficult area. As the Court of Appeal has recognised, if suspects can avoid an inference simply by saying that they are acting on legal advice, then every lawyer will advise silence. On the other hand suspects have a right to confidentiality (legal privilege) in their conversations with their lawyers and cannot be <u>required</u> to explain why they acted as they did.

A number of principles are clear:

- The fact that your client is acting on the legal advice that you gave him is not *of itself* enough to prevent an inference: *Condron* [1997] 1 Cr App R 185.

- The effect of legal advice is one factor for the jury to take into account: *Argent*.

- However – according to the Court of Appeal in *Howell* (2003) Crim LR 405:

    There must always be soundly based objective reasons for silence, sufficiently cogent and telling to weigh in the balance against the clear public interest in an account being given by the suspect to the police. Solicitors bearing the important responsibility of giving advice to suspects at police stations must always have that in mind.

The most recent decision on this point is *Beckles* [2004] EWCA Crim 2766 where the Lord Chief Justice summarised the issue as being *"whether the defendant <u>genuinely and reasonably</u> relied on the legal advice to remain silent."* For the time being this seems to be the applicable test.

> *Example : Doreen is under arrest for arson, having burnt down her school. She did in fact commit the offence, and she suspects the police have CCTV and maybe even eye witness evidence. You advise her at the police station and tell her that you advise her not to answer questions as you feel the police are withholding evidence. She accepts your advice. She "genuinely relies" on your advice, in the sense that she believes that it is legally correct. However her "real reason" for not putting forward her account is that she has no real defence, and she wants to make up her story later. Her reliance is genuine but is not reasonable.*

How should you advise your client? You must make clear to your client that even if you advise him not to answer particular questions, the court may later decide that his decision not to do so was not reasonable – and may decide to draw inferences from his failure to put forward his defence.

Make sure your client understands that the decision is one for him. Explain fully the possible consequences. Make sure your client signs your notes to confirm your advice.

And finally –

(vii)   The s.34 inference can also arise at charge: The s.34 inference can also arise from failure to put forward defence facts *when charged*. This is something you will need to take into account in those cases where the police have sufficient evidence to charge immediately and so do not interview your client at all. Again you could usefully consider whether a pre-prepared written statement (*per Knight*) will prevent inferences from being drawn.

> *In the case of <u>Goodsir</u> [2006] EWCA Crim 852, G was pulled over on suspicion of driving dangerously. His defence at trial was that his speeding had been the result of duress, but at the point when the police told him that he would be reported for a summons and cautioned him, he made no comment. The Court of Appeal held that an inference from his failure to mention his defence was permissible.*

15.2.3 Inferences in practice

We have looked at the basic provisions of s.34 in the preceding section. In this section we will consider some of the practical implications that flow from the inference, both in the police station and later at court.

(i) **What you say in interview can be used against your client at trial:** You will need to be very careful to agree with your client what you are going to say, especially if you intend to start the interview by making a statement.

> *In Fitzgerald [1998] 4 Archbold News 2 the defendant's solicitor made a statement at the start of the interview, explaining that he had discussed the case with his client and that he was concerned that "the possible involvement of other parties ... may prevent him from putting his case fully and frankly." By the time the matter came to trial Fitzgerald's defence was one of complete non-involvement. The trial judge concluded that the solicitor's statement was admissible, and this was upheld on appeal on the basis that the solicitor had consulted with his client and made the comments in the presence and hearing of his client expressly for the record. Thus presumably the client's consent to the admission could be assumed.*

(ii) **Can an inference arise if there was already sufficient evidence to charge?** The argument here is that there should not normally be an interview if there is sufficient evidence to support a prosecution and hence no inference should arise if the defendant is silent at any interview that does, wrongly, take place.

However, there is now a series of cases where the Court of Appeal has held that it is permissible to go ahead and interview a suspect since the suspect's account (or his silence) may affect the decision of whether to charge. The latest of this line of cases is *Elliott* [2002] EWCA Crim 931, where there was sufficient evidence to charge, but the police had not made the decision to charge *irrespective* of Elliott's account. The Court of Appeal stated that the interview was not in breach of Code C, and that s.34 inferences could therefore arise from Elliott's failure to put forward defence facts.

(iii) **If s.34 doesn't arise, the judge should direct the jury accordingly:** Where there has been a no comment interview, but all parties are clear that no inference can properly be drawn, the judge should give the jury a positive direction not to draw an inference *McGarry* [1999] 1 Cr. App. R. 377.

(iv) **Section.34 can arise before the close of the prosecution case:** The House of Lords made clear in *Webber* (2004) 1 WLR 404 that inferences could arise not just when the defendant put forward a defence fact when he was giving evidence, but also if his advocate put the fact forward as a "specific and positive" case to a prosecution witness in cross-examination.

[15.3] FAILURE TO ACCOUNT FOR OBJECTS, SUBSTANCES, MARKS OR PRESENCE: s.36 and s.37

While s.34 (failure to mention defence facts) is probably the inference which you will need to deal with most in practice, there are other inferences under sections 36 and 37 Criminal Justice and Public Order Act 1994 which apply in relation to police questioning about specific objects of marks, or about your client's presence at the scene. You need to be ready to advise your client about these where he has been found at the scene of the crime, or where he is in possession of an incriminating item, or has a potentially incriminating mark on him.

15.3.1 The statutory provisions

s.36 CJPOA 1994: accounting for objects, substances, marks:

This inference arises where:

- A person is arrested
- By a constable
- And either on his person, in or on his clothing or footwear, otherwise in his possession, or in the place where he is arrested
- There is an object, substance or mark (or mark on the object)
- The officer reasonably believes that the presence of the object/substance/mark may be because of the participation of the person in an offence
- The officer informs the person of this and asks him to explain the presence of the object/substance/mark; and
- The person fails or refuses to do so.

Before any inference can arise the officer has to give the person a special caution: see 15.3.2 below.

s.37 CJPOA 1994: accounting for presence

This inference is broadly similar to s.36 (above). The inference arises where:

- A person is arrested
- By a constable
- Having been found at a place
- At or about the time the offence for which he has been arrested is alleged to have been committed
- The officer reasonably believes that his presence at that place and at that time may be attributable to participation in the commission of the offence
- The officer informs the person of this, and asks him to account for his presence; and
- The person fails or refuses to do so.

15.3.2 The basic principles

(i)   The conditions for drawing a s.36/37 inference

Arrest: The s.36/37 inference can arise only after an arrest, in contrast to s.34, which will arise after caution.

By a constable: Note also that the s.36/37 inference applies only where the questions are asked by police and customs officers.

Failure to account: In contrast to s.34 (where an inference only arises if defence facts are raised later), the ss.36/37 inference will apply whether or not the fact is relied upon in your client's defence.

> *Donald is arrested on suspicion of conspiring to supply Class A drugs. In interview he is asked to account for a piece of paper which is found in his jacket, which lists names, quantities and prices. Donald makes no response.*

> *Provided Donald does not put forward defence facts at his trial (for example, if he simply puts the prosecution to proof), no s.34 inference can be drawn from his failure to answer police questions. However, an inference can be drawn under s.36 from his failure to explain the object found in his clothing. This inference will be part of the prosecution case against him, although alone it will not be enough to establish Donald's guilt.*

The "at the time of arrest" restriction: Note this odd restriction – the provisions are concerned with the state of the suspect, or presence of the suspect, at time of arrest. Thus the provisions don't apply, for example, to his condition at an earlier time when seen by a witness, or his presence at the scene on occasions prior to arrest.

(ii) The need for a special caution – the "ordinary language caution":

This is an additional requirement where the prosecution wish to rely upon a s.36/37 inference. The terms of the special caution are set out in PACE Code C.10.11. This special caution is only required where a s.36/37 inference is being sought; it does not arise with a s.34 inference, where only an ordinary caution is required.

Before the officer asks your client to explain an object, substance or mark, or his presence at a place, the constable must first explain in ordinary language:

1. what offence he is investigating;
2. what fact he requires your client to account for;
3. why he believes the fact may link your client to the commission of the offence;
4. that a court can draw an inference if your client fails to provide the explanation;
5. that a record is being made of the interview which can be used at trial.

Failure to give the special caution: If this "ordinary language" caution is not given, no s.36/37 inference will be possible. So, wherever you are attending your client in interview at the police station and your client is asked to explain an object/substance/mark or his presence, you must always consider whether this caution has been given first. If it hasn't you may choose to advise your client not to answer the question. (Obviously you will not tell the police why you are giving this advice: if you tell them they've missed the caution, or messed up one of its elements, they will simply put it right, and ask the question again!) You must bear in mind, however, that an inference under s.34 may still be possible if your client fails to put forward a defence fact.

(iii) Can s.36/37 inferences arise from questions asked outside the police station?

In the context of s.34 (see the preceding section), the decisions of the Strasbourg court suggest that access to legal advice is a prerequisite for the drawing of an inference. It seems likely that a similar approach would apply in relation to s.36/37.

(iv) Reasonableness

Note that, unlike s.34, there is no test of whether it was reasonable to expect your client to provide an explanation at this stage. Failure to account for the substance, object, mark or presence will give rise to an inference. However, this is probably less draconian than it appears since presumably a reasonable explanation for your client's failure might well lead the court to conclude that there are no proper inferences to be drawn.

(v) Being found at a "place": s.37

Note that "place" is defined as including buildings (or parts of buildings), vehicles, vessels, aircraft, hovercraft or any other place whatsoever! Remember too that s.37 will only arise where the suspect is found at that place (not necessarily the place where the offence has been committed) "at or about the time" of the offence. S.37 will not arise where someone else sees the suspect at a place and a constable later asks him to explain his presence.

(vi) How have the courts interpreted ss. 36 and 37?

There has been relatively little caselaw on this sections. However a nice example of the distinction between s.34 and s.36 can be seen in *Compton* (2003) 147 SJ 24, CA:

> *RC was arrested on suspicion of drug trafficking and was required to account for the presence of heroin on banknotes that were found in his safe. In interview RC said that he was a heroin addict. This too was the explanation that he gave at his trial. The Court of Appeal held that although no s.34 issue arose, because he mentioned the facts that he relied upon in his defence when questioned in interview, this did not prevent a s.36 inference from arising. The issue under s.36 was whether he had "accounted" for the presence of the heroin on the notes. A bare statement that he was a heroin user was not enough.*

[15.4] FAILURE TO TESTIFY: s.35 CJPOA

15.4.1 The terms of the s.35 inference

The inference arises:

- At trial
- At the stage when evidence can be given by the defendant
- The defendant either
    - chooses not to give evidence or
    - fails to answer any question without good cause
- Then the court may draw such inferences as are proper from the failure

Note that the defendant still cannot be <u>compelled</u> to testify. However he faces an inference if he fails to do so.

15.4.2 When can the inference be drawn?

The s.35 inference arises not simply where your client refuses to testify at all, but where he testifies but then refuses to answer any relevant questions that are put to him.

> *In <u>Ackinlose</u> [1996] Crim LR 747 A gave evidence in his own defence but refused to answer a question about the identity of a man who had escaped capture and who he alleged was in fact the drug dealer. The judge told him he had to answer the question. A again refused and was duly convicted. The Court of Appeal held that s.35 (5) applied and, although the court had an inherent discretion to excuse him from answering, the question was undoubtedly relevant. Although the judge had put the question "in a stark and undesirable way", the conviction was safe.*

The Court of Appeal handed down guidelines on s.35 in *Cowan, Gayle, Ricciardi* [1995] 4 All ER 939.

- The judge must tell the jury that the burden of proof remains on the prosecution throughout.
- The right of silence and the freedom not to testify remain.
- A s.35 inference cannot in itself prove guilt (see s.38(3) CJPOA)

- The jury must therefore be satisfied that there is a case to answer before drawing any inferences.

- Only if the jury then concludes that the defendant's silence can "only sensibly be attributed" to the defendant having no answer (or none that would stand up to cross-examination) may they draw an inference.

Finally, the court went on to point out that advocates cannot give evidence themselves as to their client's reasons for not testifying. There must be evidence called to support the reasons.

s.35 in practice

The leading guideline case, following *Cowan*, is *Friend* [1997] Crim LR 817 where the Court of Appeal had to consider the position of a mentally disabled defendant, who was aged 14 but had a mental age of 9. Medical evidence suggested that he could give a coherent account if given time, but would find it hard to concentrate. The Court of Appeal held that the trial judge had been right to permit an inference to be drawn when F did not testify.

> *The judge could make a decision on voir dire that the physical or mental condition of the defendant made it undesirable for them to give evidence, in which case the jury would be directed accordingly. Otherwise it would be for the jury to draw such inferences as appear proper to them, taking into account all the evidence about the defendant's condition. The court would be slow to interfere with the trial judge's discretion.*

More recently in the case of *Kavanagh* [2005] EWHC 820 the Divisional Court allowed an appeal against an acquittal by magistrates where the prosecution case was strong and the defendant had not given any evidence, the magistrates having decided not to draw an inference because the defendant's solicitor had warned them that his client might not testify and the defendant's mother had told the court that her son was depressed. The court emphasised that proper evidence was needed, and that the mere fact that the defendant suffered from some physical or mental condition would be taken into account in assessing his evidence rather than excusing him from testifying. In the absence of proper evidence it would be hard to justify not drawing an inference from failure to testify.

[15.5] HUMAN RIGHTS ISSUES

There are two primary issues arising in relation to the right to silence from a European Convention perspective. The first is whether the removal of the right to silence (generally in the form of a compulsion to answer questions) is a breach of Article 6. The second is whether the drawing of adverse inferences from the exercise of the right to silence is a similar breach.

Compelled questioning and the Human Rights Act

Does article 6(2) prohibit legislation which requires the defendant to answer questions? There are some legislative provisions which make it a criminal offence not to answer questions from investigating authorities. The issue is whether the use of answers obtained under this compulsion can be used at a subsequent criminal trial, or if this will offend against the presumption of innocence in article 6(2).

The leading Strasbourg authority is *Saunders v United Kingdom* (1997) 23 EHRR 213. Saunders had been interviewed by the DTI and had had to answer questions on pain of prosecution. The answers had then been used against Saunders at a subsequent criminal trial and he had been convicted. The Strasbourg court subsequently held that this had been in breach of article 6.

This issue was subsequently raised in the Scottish courts, in relation to compelled questions under Road Traffic legislation in the case of *Brown v Stott*. The case concerned suspected drink driving and shows that the HRA will impact on all sorts of criminal offences and will not simply be confined to "serious" crimes. The Privy Council held that while the right to a fair trial under article 6 was unqualified, the various elements of article 6 – including the presumption of innocence – were not absolute rights. Compelled questioning in this context was therefore permitted. This approach has been upheld by the Grand Chamber of the European Court of Human Rights: *O'Halloran and Francis v United Kingdom* (29th June 2007). The court was of the view that limited compelled questioning was acceptable in the context of regulating the use of motor vehicles.

Inferences and the Human Rights Act

Murray v United Kingdom (1996) 22 EHRR 29 considered inferences from silence under Northern Ireland legislation. The inference itself was held to be permissible (although there were dissenting views on this), primarily because it was drawn by a judge who could give reasons for drawing the inference. Murray left open the question of whether under English law, where the inference will be a matter for the non-qualified jury to decide, such an inference will be in breach of the right to a fair trial.

In *Condron v United Kingdom* (2000) 31 E.H.R.R. 1 the European Court held that the Condrons had not had a fair trial where inferences had been drawn following their silence at the police station, and the subsequent inferences left to the jury at trial. However, the basis for the court's decision was that the trial judge's direction had been defective, in that he had not told the jury that they could only draw an adverse inference if they concluded that the failure to put forward defence facts could only sensibly be attributed to the fact that the they had made up their stories later. The Court of Appeal had agreed that the trial direction had been flawed, but had held that the verdict was safe, having regard to the weight of other evidence against the Condrons. It was this point which was rejected by the Strasbourg court, who pointed out that the Court of Appeal could only guess what effect the error had had on the jury, stating that:

"It is a speculative exercise which only reinforces the crucial nature of the defect in the trial judge's direction and its implications for review of the case on appeal".

Surprisingly, the court was however prepared to hold that the drawing of the initial inference had not itself been in breach of article 6, although their judgement is hedged with qualifications.

Inferences and future challenges

The *Condron* judgment is surprising, and in many respects it sits uneasily with the European Court's extreme reluctance to permit inferences to be drawn from the exercise of the right of silence in earlier cases. The court has taken a similar approach, however, in later cases such as *Beckles v United Kingdom* (2003) 36 EHRR 13. In the light of the current caselaw on inferences where there has been legal advice to remain silent, further challenges to Strasbourg on this point are inevitable.

SILENCE AT COMMON LAW

At common law no adverse inference from exercise of the right of silence - but see *Parkes*: it was possible to draw an inference from a failure to reply where the parties were "on even terms" – i.e. a confrontation with the victim's mother. The common law right of silence was <u>qualified</u> – **not** abolished – by the CJPOA 1994.

s.34: defence facts

A court can draw "such inferences as are proper" where a suspect being questioned under caution before charge (or on being charged) fails to mention any fact relied upon his defence which it was reasonable for him to mention.

- Must be questioned <u>under caution</u>
- Questioning by constable or other person charged with the duty of investigating offences.
- Only relates to failure to mention facts which are relied on in his defence.
- Must be reasonable to expect him to mention the facts: - consider state of mind, IQ, effect of legal advice, understanding of case against him: see *Argent*.
- Beware a waiver of privilege by explaining the reason for advising silence, but simply saying "I remained silent on legal advice" is unlikely to be sufficient: *Condron*.
- "such inferences as appear proper" - *Murray*: a "commonsense approach". Presumably the main inference is that the fact wasn't mentioned because it isn't true.
- *Beckles*: if silence is on legal advice is the reliance on that advice genuine and reasonable?
- *Knight*: confirming that a pre-prepared statement which contains all defence facts will prevent an inference.

s.34 inference can be drawn at trial, but will not of itself be sufficient to commit or convict.

ss.36/37: objects & presence

Failure or refusal to account for:

- s.36: objects/substance/mark
- s.37 presence at a place

For an inference there must be:

- an arrest;
- presence of object etc. or presence at place;
- reasonable belief by police that the object/presence may be attributable to participation in offence;
- a request for the suspect to account for object/presence; and
- an explanation as to what offence and what fact the police believe to be attributable.

There must also be a special C10.11 caution.

Similar in effect to s.34.

s.35: fail to testify

- Failure to testify or failure to answer questions when testifying.
- Must be without "good cause".
- There must be a prima facie case to answer, and the inference alone cannot establish guilt.
- Inference is only possible if defendant's silence can only sensibly be attributed to having no answer or none that would stand up to x/x: *Cowan*.

Differences:

- s.34: after caution; ss.36/37; after arrest.
- s.34: defence facts only; ss.36/37: whether or not relied upon in defence.
- s.34: police or those charged with investigating offences;
- ss.36/37: police and customs only.
- s.34: ordinary caution only;
- ss.36/37: must explain the effect of failure or refusal: Code C10.11 caution.

Silence and inferences – test yourself questions

[The answers to these questions are set out in Appendix A at the back of this book]

[1] Russell is arrested on suspicion of handling stolen goods.

Consider the following propositions in relation to s.34 Criminal Justice and Public Order Act 1994.

i. s.34 inferences may arise from Russell's failure to mention defence facts when questioned following a valid stop and search under s.1 PACE.

ii. s.34 inferences may arise from Russell's failure to mention defence facts when questioned after having been cautioned.

iii. s.34 inferences may arise from Russell's failure to mention defence facts when questioned following an arrest.

iv. s.34 inferences may arise from Russell's failure to mention defence facts when cautioned and charged with an offence.

Which of the above are correct?

(a) i only.

(b) ii and iv only.

(c) iii and iv only.

(d) All of them.

[2] Vince has been arrested following large-scale public disorder at a protest rally. The custody record states that he is being detained in order to obtain evidence by questioning in relation to an offence of s.2 Public Order Act 1986 (violent disorder). John has attended the police station as duty solicitor and has advised Vince not to answer any questions in interview.

Consider the following propositions in relation to s.34 Criminal Justice and Public Order Act 1994.

i. No s.34 inference will be possible provided that Vince's failure to put forward defence facts is on legal advice.

ii. No s.34 inference will be possible provided that Vince's failure to put forward defence facts is on legal advice and he or his representative makes clear the basis for that advice.

iii. No s.34 inference will be possible provided that Vince's failure to put forward defence facts is on legal advice and John gives evidence that that advice was not given for a tactical reason.

Which of the above are correct?

(a) i only.

(b) ii only.

(c) iii only.

(d) None of them.

[3] In *Argent* the Court of Appeal considered the effect of non-disclosure of information and other factors in determining whether a s.34 inference could be drawn.

Which of the following most accurately states the proposition laid down in *Argent*?

(a) Disclosure is a matter for the police; it can never be relevant to the issue of whether an inference can be drawn.

(b) Whether an inference can be drawn is a matter for the jury and they must take into account all factors that would have affected the defendant.

(c) Whether an inference can be drawn is a matter for the judge and s/he must take into account all factors that would have affected a reasonable man in the defendant's position and direct the jury accordingly.

(d) Whether an inference can be drawn is a matter for the jury and they must take into account all factors that would have affected a reasonable man in the defendant's position.

[4] Felipe is arrested on suspicion of trading in firearms without being registered. He is questioned under caution by the police but gives a no comment interview on legal advice. At trial he gives evidence in his defence to the effect that he was not aware that the firearms were being stored in his garage as the prosecution alleges. He says that he did not give evidence in interview because he was scared that the people responsible for storing the firearms there would take revenge if he implicated them. The judge directs the jury as to the s.34 inference as follows:

i. You must consider whether the defendant's failure to put forward the facts in answer to police questions was reasonable.

ii. The inference that you may draw is any inference that is proper.

iii. The defendant was under no duty to answer police questions, but you are entitled to draw an inference from his failure to do so.

iv. Any inference can assist you in deciding that the defendant was guilty, but you cannot decide that he is guilty on the basis of the inference alone.

Felipe is convicted. You are now considering whether there are grounds for an appeal. Which of the above elements of the direction are open to challenge on appeal?

(a) i and ii are correct; but iii and iv are incorrect.

(b) ii and iii only are correct; i and iv are incorrect.

(c) i, ii and iv are correct; iii is incorrect.

(d) None of them can be challenged; all elements of the direction are correct.

[5] Roberta is stopped by a store detective as she attempts to leave a record store with three compact discs in her bag which have not been paid for. The store detective tells her that she is under arrest on suspicion of having stolen the compact discs and he takes her to the security office. While awaiting the arrival of police officers the store detective cautions her and asks her to account for the compact discs being in her bag. In due course at trial Roberta will say that the compact discs are hers and that they were in her bag when she entered the shop; however, at this stage she refuses to answer any questions.

Consider the following propositions:

i. No s.36 inference can arise from Roberta's failure to account for the compact discs as the questions are being asked by a store detective.

ii. A s.34 inference can only arise from Roberta's failure to put forward defence facts when questioned under caution if the store detective was charged with the duty of investigating offences.

iii. Inferences under s.34, s.36 or s.37 are unlikely to be arise from Roberta's silence at this stage as Roberta has not had the opportunity to take legal advice.

Which of the above propositions are correct?

(a) All of them.

(b) i only.

(c) ii only.

(d) iii only.

[6] A burglary takes place at a designer clothing warehouse at 4 a.m. Chris is arrested in a nearby street. At the police station he declines the offer of access to legal advice. In interview the police officer in charge of the investigation cautions him in the normal terms and then cautions him as follows:

I am investigating an offence of burglary at the designer warehouse in Greek Street at 4 a.m. You were seen by officers at 4.03 a.m. running round the corner of Greek Street into the High Street. You were then arrested in the High Street. I am asking you to account for your presence in Greek Street at that time, as I believe it may indicate that you were involved in the offence. I should warn you that the court may draw a proper inference if you fail or refuse to account for your presence. As you know, this interview is being recorded and the record can be used at your trial.

Chris refuses to answer the question.

Which of the following is correct?

(a) A s.37 inference may be drawn at trial. Chris is under arrest and he has been given the proper ordinary language caution.

(b) No s.37 inference can be drawn at trial. Although Chris is under arrest and he has been given the proper ordinary language caution, the inference is not possible as he has not had legal advice.

(c) A s.37 inference may be drawn at trial, provided that the arresting officers had reasonable grounds for believing that an offence had been committed and that Chris had been involved in the commission of the offence.

(d) No s.37 inference can be drawn at trial. Chris is under arrest but the ordinary language caution has not been administered in the proper form.

[7] The leading case on the effect of the s.35 inference is *Cowan*. Which of the following propositions were put forward in the Court of Appeal's decision in that case?

i. The prosecution must establish a prima facie case against the defendant, and the inference will not of itself be sufficient to prove guilt.

ii. The only inference will be that defendant remained silent because he either had no answer to the allegations against him, or none that would stand up to cross-examination.

iii. Advocates may not give evidence as to the reasons why their clients are declining to give evidence.

(a) All of the above.

(b) i and iii only.

(c) ii only.

(d) None of them.

CHAPTER 16

CONFESSIONS AND THE EXCLUSION OF EVIDENCE

> This chapter covers:
>
> Confessions.
>
> Excluding confession evidence: s.76 PACE 1984.
>
> The general discretion to exclude: s.78 PACE 1984.

[16.1] THE COMMON LAW

As you have seen from Chapter 14, the general principle of English law is that evidence will not be excluded simply because it has been improperly obtained. Thus, in *Kuruma* [1955] AC 197 the court refused to exclude evidence simply because it had been obtained as the result of an illegal search, stating:

> *The test to be applied in considering whether evidence is admissible is whether it is relevant to the matters in issue. If it is, it is admissible and the court is not concerned with how the evidence was obtained.* [*per* Lord Goddard CJ p. 203]

Confessions, however, have always been recognised as a separate category because of their high probative value. Thus in *Sang* [1980] AC 402, one of the common law grounds for excluding evidence was that it was evidence which the accused had been induced to produce as the result of unfair inducements. In particular this applied where the statement had been made in circumstances that breached the Judges Rules (which have now been replaced by PACE and its Codes). However, the general rule remains that at common law evidence will be admissible notwithstanding the circumstances in which it has been obtained. PACE explicitly preserves the common law discretion to exclude:

> *Nothing in this part of this Act shall prejudice any power of a court to exclude evidence (whether by preventing questions from being put or otherwise) at its discretion.* s.82(3)

[16.2] WHAT IS A CONFESSION?

16.2.1 The definition in PACE

> *"confession" includes any statement wholly or partly adverse to the person who made it, whether made to a person in authority or not and whether made in words or otherwise.* PACE s.82 (1)

Note therefore that a confession may not simply be a full admission ("It's a fair cop, guv. You got me bang to the rights. I did it." etc.). It also includes any statement adverse to the maker

Thus, for example, "Yes, I was in the room. But I didn't do anything." is an admission of presence. Where statements are "mixed" (that is, they are partly adverse and partly self-serving) the jury will be directed that the whole statement is evidence, but that the exculpatory elements may carry less weight than the adverse admissions: *Sharp* [1988] 1 WLR 7.

Tacit admissions? An admission need not be verbal; it may constitute a gesture, such as a nod of head. An admission may also arise where a person, by failing to object to another person's statement, acts in such a way as to adopt it.

> *In the case of* <u>Osborne</u> *[2005] EWCA Crim 3082, O hit the victim across the head with a plank of wood, killing him. O was white and his victim was Asian. There was evidence that immediately before the incident there had been a fight involving the two men. Some days after the incident a girl asked O why he had hit the victim. O's friend replied that they did not like Asian people and why did they come to the UK. O said nothing but walked away smirking. The Court of Appeal held that the trial judge had been right to leave it to the jury to decide if O had effectively adopted his friend's statement, as this might clearly go to the motivation for the assault.*

16.2.2 Statements intended to exculpate the suspect

Statements which were intended to be exculpatory, but which later turned out to be false (thus implicating the suspect in the offence) are not confessions: *Sat-Bhambra* (1988) 88 Cr. App R 55. The House of Lords has upheld this principle in *Hasan* [2005] UKHL 22.

> *P was stopped for having a defective light. The officer asked who owned the car and the electrical equipment on the back seat. P said both were his. The officer became suspicious and then arrested and cautioned him. At trial P tried to argue that the electrical equipment belonged to another. He argued that the previous inconsistent statements should be excluded as confessions. The court held that the police officer had cautioned and arrested as soon as he had had a reasonable suspicion of theft, and that the statement was not a confession since it was intended to be self-exculpatory.* <u>Park</u> [1994] Crim LR 285

16.2.3 Confessions as hearsay

Generally confessions will be placed before the court either by playing the tape-recorded interview, or by placing before the court a transcript of that interview, or a written confession. Where the statement has not been tape-recorded and the defendant has refused to sign the police officer's contemporaneous account, the officer will give evidence as to what the defendant said. This, of course, is hearsay, but confessions are admissible as an exception to the rule against hearsay.

> *In any proceedings a confession made by an accused person may be given in evidence against him in so far as it is relevant to any matter in issue in the proceedings and is not excluded by the court in pursuance of this section.* s.76(1)

Note that a confession is admissible *only against the maker*. This can cause problems where your client has confessed to an offence and has implicated a Co-Accused. The jury must then be directed that your client's confession is evidence only against your client, and should not be taken into account for other defendants. Most lawyers wonder if juries pay any real attention to this principle.

16.2.4 Excluding a confession

In some circumstances (oppression/unreliability/unfairness), the court either must or may exclude evidence of a confession. Under s.76 PACE, if it is "represented to the court" that the confession either was or might have been obtained as the result of oppression, or in circumstances that were likely to render it unreliable, the court <u>must</u> exclude the confession unless the prosecution can prove beyond reasonable doubt that it was not so obtained. Under s.78 PACE the court has a discretion to exclude any evidence, including confessions, if its admissibility might have an adverse impact on the fairness of the proceedings. Sections 76 and 78 PACE are therefore key provisions, and this chapter will now consider in more detail how these sections are applied in practice.

[16.3] OPPRESSION AND UNRELIABILITY: s.76 (2) PACE

s.76 PACE provides for the exclusion of confession evidence. The provisions are that:

- Where the prosecution is going to rely upon a confession made by the accused, and
- It is represented to the court that the confession either was or might have been obtained
    - By oppression of the accused, or
    - In consequence of anything said or done that was likely (in the circumstances at that time) to render the confession unreliable;
- The court must exclude the confession
- Unless the prosecution can prove beyond reasonable doubt that the confession was not obtained in this way.
- This applies even if the confession may be true.

16.3.1 What is "oppression"?

> *In this section "oppression" includes torture, inhuman or degrading treatment, and the use or threat of violence (whether or not amounting to torture):* s.76(8) PACE

The leading case on the meaning of oppression remains *Fulling* [1987] QB 426.

> *F was arrested. The police told her that her boyfriend had been having a long-standing affair with C, who was in the next-door cell. C confirmed this. F then made a confession, which she later contended she had made only because she was distressed and would have done anything to get out of the cells. The court held that this did not amount to oppression, stating that:*

> "...oppression in s.76(2)(a) should be given its ordinary dictionary meaning. The Oxford English Dictionary as its third definition of the word runs as follows: "Exercise of authority or power in a burdensome, harsh or wrongful manner; unjust or cruel treatment of subjects, inferiors etc.; the imposition of unreasonable or unjust burdens." One of the quotations given under that paragraph runs as follows: "There is not a word in our language which expresses more detestable wickedness than oppression."

> *We find it hard to envisage any circumstances in which such oppression would not entail some impropriety on the part of the interrogator."* [per Lord Lane, p.432]

There have been relatively few cases on oppression since most cases that approach oppression will be clearly "unreliable" (see 16.3.2 below) or excludable under s.78 (16.4 below). The case of *Paris and others* (1993) 97 Cr App R 99 is a very good example of how oppression might arise, however, even in the absence of violence.

The victim was an ex-girlfriend of Miller's. She was murdered, having been stabbed at least 50 times. The police interviewed M for 13 hours over five days, the interview filling some 19 tapes. There was no solicitor present for the first two interviews. For seven tapes, M denied participation or presence. In tapes 8 and 9 he began to admit presence. He denied involvement in excess of 300 times. M then made three adverse comments – stating "P went crazy so I started stabbing" (although the word "I" was far from clear), and agreeing with an officer that he could have been so drugged that he didn't know he was stabbing the victim, and finally stating: "I just stabbed, not stabbed her just ... thumped her in her face I mean."

On appeal the court listened to the tapes of the interviews and was appalled.

"... each member of this court was horrified. Miller was bullied and hectored. The officers ... were not questioning him so much as shouting at him what they wanted him to say. Short of physical violence it is hard to conceive of a more hostile and intimidating approach by officers to a suspect. It is impossible to convey on the printed page the pace, force and menace of the officer's delivery but a short passage may give something of the flavour:

" M: I wasn't there.
G: How you can ever...
M: I wasn't there.
G: How you ... I just don't know how you can sit there, I.
M: I wasn't...
G: Really don't
M: I was not there. I was not there.
G: Seeing that girl, your girlfriend, in that room that night like she was. I just don't know how you can sit there and say it.
M: I wasn't there.
G: You were there that night.
M: I was not there.
G: Together with all the others you were there that night.
M: I was not there. I'll tell you already ...
G: ... and you sit there and say that.
M: They can lock me up for 50 billion years, I said I was not there.
G: Cause you don't want to be there.
M: I was not there.
      .....

In our view, although we do not know what instructions he had, the solicitor appears to have been gravely at fault for sitting passively through this travesty of an interview."

The court had no hesitation in excluding the evidence under s.76 (2)(a).

16.3.2 What is "unreliability": s.76 (2)(b)

Unreliability will be much easier to show than oppression. Bear in mind that, as with oppression, once the issue of unreliability is raised, it is for the prosecution to show beyond reasonable doubt that the confession is not unreliable. If the prosecution falls short of this level of proof, the court *must* exclude the confession. Note that, as with oppression, it is immaterial that your client's confession may be true. Moreover, the test is not whether the confession is unreliable; merely whether it *might* be.

What circumstances might render a confession unreliable? "Unreliability" is not defined, but note that it must be in consequence of something said or done.

Thus in <u>Harvey</u> [1988] Crim LR 241 a woman of low intelligence with a personality disorder heard her lesbian lover confess murder in her presence. A few days later Harvey herself confessed to *the crime. Evidence from experts suggested that she might have done so in order to protect her lover. Her hearing the lover confess was something "said or done". The circumstances were her emotional state and low intelligence. As a result the confession might have been unreliable.*

In the case of *Samuel* [2005] EWCA Crim 704 the court emphasised the importance of the confession being "in consequence" of something said or done. S confessed to murder while being held in a Nigerian prison, having been told by other inmates that this would please the guards and might enable him to bribe his way out of the prison. The court held that the confession was made "in the light" of the information, but it was made in consequence of his desire to avoid extradition to stand trial in the UK.

Self induced unreliability? There is some authority that the things said or done cannot be self-induced; thus in *Goldenberg* (1988) 88 Cr App R 285:

G was an addict and confessed in order to get bail so that he could go and buy heroin. The court suggested that while the addiction might be a "circumstance", no one had "said or done" anything to give rise to the unreliability.

It can be argued that this would be otherwise if the police had known of the addiction and deliberately detained G in order to exert this pressure. Certainly in obiter comments in *Effik* (1992) 95 Cr App R 427 the Court of Appeal seemed to suggest that an interview of a person suffering from severe withdrawal symptoms might give rise to unreliability.

Inducements by the police: Improper inducements may well render a confession unreliable: note the terms of Code C11.5:

No interviewer may try to obtain answers to questions or to elicit a statement by the use of oppression. Except as provided for in paragraph 10.9, no interviewer shall indicate, except in answer to a direct question, what action will be taken on the part of the police if the person interviewed answers questions, makes a statement or refuses to do either. If the person asks directly what action will be taken if they answer questions, make a statement or refuse to do either, then the interviewer may inform them what action the police propose to take provided that action is itself proper and warranted.

Look out in interview in particular for anything that suggests that your client could be released earlier, not charged, receive a lesser sentence and so on. In the case of *Wahab* (2003) 1 Cr App R 15 the defendant asked his solicitor to find out if the rest of his family (who had also been arrested) would be freed if he made admissions. The police responded to the solicitor that they would look at the whole picture but if the evidence against the others was borderline, they would be released. The Court of Appeal held that the fact that the initiative initially came from the defendant was one important factor in finding that this was not an improper inducement.

Breaches of PACE generally; Breaches of the PACE Codes may be things done that render confessions unreliable – thus, for example, *McGovern* (1990) 92 Cr App R 229, where a pregnant 19 year old with low IQ was denied a solicitor and eventually in interview, in a distressed state, confessed to murder. The initial interview, the Court of Appeal held, should have been excluded as not having been shown not to be unreliable. However, you must always remember that it is not enough simply to find a breach of the PACE Codes or any other source of unreliability – you must go on to show that the confession may be unreliable "in consequence thereof".

Confessions and the co-Accused: The Criminal Justice Act 2003 introduces a new provision to deal with the situation where one defendant has confessed to the crime, but his confession is excluded as against the prosecution under s.76 PACE. What then is the position of the other defendant who may want to use his co-Accused's confession in his own defence. Under s.76A PACE, the co-Accused will be able to use the confession provided he can satisfy the court that it is not unreliable or has not been obtained by oppression on the balance of probabilities.

Arthur and Bernard are jointly charged with grievous bodily harm on Catherine. Arthur admitted the offence in interview but his confession has been excluded as against the prosecution at trial because the prosecution could not prove beyond reasonable doubt that it was not unreliable as a result of police inducements (offers of bail). Bernard may be able to use the confession in his own defence provided he can persuade the court on the lower standard of proof (balance of probabilities) that it is not unreliable.

16.3.3 The fruit of the poisoned tree: s.76(4) PACE

In many jurisdictions, and particularly in the United States of America, evidence will be excluded where it has been obtained as the result of information which has been wrongfully obtained. This is not the case in English law, which provides that the fact that the confession may be wholly or partly excluded does not affect the admissibility of:

> *(a) of any facts discovered as a result of the confession: or*
>
> *(b) where the confession is relevant as showing that the accused speaks, writes or expresses himself in a particular way, of so much of the confession as is necessary to show that he does so*: s.76(4) PACE.

However, the prosecution will not be able to explain that the evidence was discovered as a result of the excluded confession.

> *Maureen confesses to an assault and tells the police where to find the knife that she used. Even if the confession is later ruled to be inadmissible, this will not automatically lead to the knife being excluded from evidence. The police will simply not be able to state that they found the knife as a result of what Maureen had told them.*

What about successive interviews where the first interview is later excluded?

This is exactly the case in *McGovern* – see above – who was subsequently interviewed without impropriety and with a solicitor present. In this second interview she again made a full confession. It was argued, however, that the second interview was a direct consequence of the first. The Court of Appeal accepted this and the second interview was similarly excluded. A similar approach was taken in *Glaves* [1993] Crim. L. R. 685, although the court indicated that there was no inevitable rule that subsequent confessions would be similarly blighted. It will be a question of the facts in every case, and you will need to be ready to show that the previous oppression or unreliability fundamentally undermined your client's subsequent interview.

16.3.4 s.76 in practice

The burden of proof is on the prosecution to show beyond reasonable doubt that a confession has not been obtained by oppression or is not unreliable as a consequence of something said or done. However the defence bear the burden of first raising the issue.

The House of Lords has confirmed that even if the judge decides that the confession is admissible under s.76, the issues must still be raised for the jury to consider as part of their deliberations. The jury must be directed that they should disregard the confession if they consider that it was or might have been obtained by oppression or in consequence of anything said or done that was likely to render it unreliable: see *Mushtaq* [2005] UKHL 25

[16.4] UNFAIRNESS: s.78 PACE

Section 78 PACE is a general safety net. It gives courts a wide discretion to exclude prosecution evidence which could have an "adverse effect on the fairness of the proceedings".

> *In any proceedings the court may refuse to allow evidence on which the prosecution proposes to rely to be given if it appears to the court that, having regard to all the circumstances, including the circumstances in which the evidence was obtained, the admission of the evidence would have such an adverse effect on the fairness of the proceedings that the court ought not to admit it.* s.78 (1) PACE

16.4.1. Section 78: the basics

There are two important contrasts between s.78 and s.76. The first is that s.78 applies to all evidence, including confession evidence. In other words, a confession can be excluded under s.76 or s.78 or both. The second is that while under s.76, once the issue is raised, the prosecution must prove that the confession is admissible beyond reasonable doubt, under s.78 the matter is at the discretion of the court, which must take into account all the relevant circumstances. One of the most relevant circumstances will be a breach in the PACE Codes:

> *In all criminal and civil proceedings any such code shall be admissible in evidence, and if any provision of such a code appears to the court or tribunal conducting the proceedings to be relevant to any question arising in the proceedings it shall be taken into account in determining that question.* s.67(11):

Many cases under s.78 therefore deal with the effects of breaches of PACE, but note:

- A matter may have an adverse effect on the fairness of the proceedings even if there has been no breach of PACE.

- A breach of PACE may equally give rise to oppression/unreliability under s.76, so always consider both sections. (Equally, much of the caselaw mentioned below will be relevant to s.76 as well.)

- A breach of PACE does not of itself mean that the matter must be excluded under s.78 – you <u>must</u> go on to show that the breach has given rise to unfairness.

- s.78 applies only to prosecution evidence.

16.4.2 Tricks

While the courts generally state that they will not use s.78 as a way of disciplining the police for breaches of the Codes, there is no doubt that a deliberate trick/impropriety used to breach the Codes will give rise to exclusion.

> *In <u>Mason</u> [1988] 1 WLR 139, a very early case, the police admitted that they set about "conning" Mason by telling his solicitor that they had found M's fingerprints on glass from a bottle of inflammable liquid used in an arson attack. This was a lie. The Court of Appeal stated that such deception should never occur again and ruled out the confession.*

It is worth noting that in *Mason*, much of the court's concern was focused on the fact that the lie was to the solicitor. However, it is likely that any deliberate misinformation is likely to give rise to a similar exclusion. (Note that even innocent misinformation may give rise either to s.76 unreliability or to s.78 unfairness.)

Note also the case of *Grant* [2005] EWCA Crim 1089 (discussed at 3.3.5 above) where the police bugged an exercise area at a police station knowing that they would pick up conversations between solicitors and their clients who were having a cigarette there. The court held that the prosecution had to be stayed as an abuse of process regardless of whether there was any prejudice to the defendant – simply because the actions of the police were so reprehensible.

16.4.3 Will evidence be excluded if there has been a breach of PACE?

Possibly. But not necessarily. The test is not whether there has been a breach of PACE, but the impact on the fairness of the trial as a whole.

> *In B [2008] EWCA Crim 1524 the Court of Appeal held that a trial judge had been wrong to use s.78 to exclude identification evidence in the case. It was common ground between the parties that there had been a breach of PACE during the video identification in that the victim had not been given a warning not to make any decision on identification until he had seen the images twice. The Court of Appeal said that the judge erred by focussing on the impact of the breach, and not considering whether the consequences of the breach could be cured during the trial process, for example because of other significant evidence of involvement, or cautionary directions to the jury.*

Deliberate breaches of PACE: In *Delaney* (1988) 88 Cr App R 338, the Court of Appeal stated that s.78 would not be used simply to punish the police for breaches of PACE. However, in *Alladice*, (1988) 87 Cr App R 380 in the same year, the court stated that where the police had acted in bad faith a court would have "little difficulty in ruling any confession inadmissible under s.78": *per* Lord Lane. Where there is evidence of police malpractice, the courts seem readier to rule out the evidence. However, even an accidental breach may adversely effect the fairness of proceedings.

Significant and substantial breaches: The key proposition is contained in *Walsh* (1989) 91 Cr App R 161, at 163, and is worth setting out in full:

> *To our minds it follows that if there are significant and substantial breaches of section 58 [i.e. access to legal advice] or the provisions of the Code, then prima facie at least the standards of fairness set by Parliament have not been met. So far as a defendant is concerned, it seems to us also to follow that to admit evidence against him which has been obtained in circumstances where these standards have not been met, cannot but have an adverse effect on the fairness of the proceedings. This does not mean, of course, that in every case of a significant or substantial breach of section 58 or the Code of Practice the evidence concerned will automatically be excluded. Section 78 does not so provide. The task of the court is not merely to consider whether there would be an adverse effect on the fairness of the proceedings, but such an adverse effect that justice requires the evidence to be excluded.*

In the same case, the court stated that:

> *… although bad faith may make substantial or significant that which might not otherwise be so, the contrary does not follow. Breaches which are in themselves significant and substantial are not rendered otherwise by the good faith of the officers concerned.*

Equally, in the case of *Charles v CPS* [2009] EWHC 3521, the police not only interviewed Charles after they had told him that they were going to charge him (in breach of Code C16.5), they also failed to administer the correct caution. The Divisional Court quashed the conviction, commenting:

> *These provisions are not a mere rigmarole to be recited like a mantra and then ignored. The provisions of the Police and Criminal Evidence Act and the Code relating to caution, are designed to protect a detainee. They are important protections. They impose significant disciplines upon the police as to how they are to behave. If they can secure a serious conviction in breach of those provisions that is an*

important matter which undermines the protection of a detainee in the police station. That is not say, by any means, that every breach will lead to the exclusion of the evidence obtained in consequence of that breach; far from it. It is merely to emphasise the general importance of the breaches when exercising the judgment in Section 78. Their significance must be taken into account. There is no hint in the case stated that any of those factors were taken into account by the magistrates.

Arguing that a breach of PACE should lead to the exclusion of the evidence: A typical example of a breach of PACE is failure to allow access to a solicitor. We will look at the effect of such a breach on the admissibility of evidence.

1   Was there a breach of PACE at all? Where your client has been refused access to legal advice in interview, you must first check that the refusal of access was wrongful, and that the situation was not one where the police were permitted to delay access to legal advice. Even if the police were entitled to delay access, check that the correct authorisations were sought and granted.

2   If there was a breach of PACE was it deliberate? If the failure was wrongful, was it a deliberate flouting of the Codes? Note the dicta in *Walsh* above, which suggest that bad faith may aggravate the situation, while an honest mistake will not prevent unfairness from arising.

3   In any event, would it be unfair to admit the evidence? You must then go on to show that it would it be unfair to admit the evidence. s. 76 requires you to make a causal link between the oppression or unreliability and the confession; s.78 requires you to go on to show that, even if there has been a breach of PACE, it would be unfair to admit the evidence. The evidence will not be excluded as of right. Thus, for example, in *Alladice* (above) the evidence of A's confession was not excluded since A was experienced in dealing with the police, knew his legal rights and had been able to cope with the interview.

However, it will not generally be adequate for the prosecution to argue that unfairness can be cured by the defendant giving evidence challenging the evidence in question. In the leading case of *Keenan* (1990) 90 Cr.App.R. 1, the Court of Appeal pointed out that if Keenan had to go into the witness box to challenge the content of the admissions he was said to have made, but which had not been contemporaneously recorded, it effectively robbed him of his right not to testify, it potentially enabled the prosecution to cross-examine him on his criminal record (because he was attacking the police evidence: see Chapter 17 below), and he had lost the opportunity to correct any inaccuracies at the time.

Your presence may "cure" any breach of PACE: This is such an important principle that I have set out the leading case of *Dunn (1990)* 91 Cr App R 237 in some detail.

D was arrested for aggravated burglary. He was interviewed in the presence of a solicitor's representative, H. At the end of the interview D was asked to sign the notes of the interview. According to the police officers' evidence, the following discussion took place:

D.C. Watts says: "I said to him: "Gary, you are silly, you should have told the truth" and Gary replied: 'I was acting on what I was told.' " The officer said: "You still should have told the truth" and Gary Dunn said: "I was grassed up." The officer said: "Who by?" and Gary Dunn said: "Don't worry, I will sort him out." The officer said: "For what?" and Gary Dunn said: "If it wasn't for the watch I knew he would grass me up." The officer said: "Who were the other two?" and Gary Dunn laughed and said: "I ain't going to tell you that." The officer said: "Why did you do it?" and Gary Dunn said: "I don't know."

> *The defence denied that the conversation took place at all. The solicitor's representative, H, gave evidence that she "excluded the possibility" of the conversation having taken place. However, the judge correctly ruled that whether the conversation had taken place was a matter for the jury; his role was to determine whether it was admissible. Here the defence argued that there were three substantial breaches of PACE: (i) there was no contemporaneous note made of the conversation; (ii) the reason for the failure to make a note was not recorded in the officer's notebook; and (iii) D was never given the opportunity to read or sign the subsequent record. The trial judge however admitted the evidence on the basis that H was there to protect her client's interests.*
>
> *The Court of Appeal agreed. H could have intervened in the conversation and her mere presence would have inhibited the police from lying about a conversation, which had never taken place.*
>
>> *There were serious breaches in this case. The presence of the solicitor's clerk during the disputed conversation did not excuse those breaches. But it tipped the balance in favour of admitting the evidence. Had it not been for Mrs Hemmings' presence, the evidence would have been rightly excluded.*

If you fail to intervene to object to breaches of PACE at the police station, your presence may well be treated as effectively "curing" the breach.

Excluding evidence where there has been *no* breach of PACE: The general test is whether the admission of the evidence would have an adverse impact on the fairness of the proceedings – and not whether it has been improperly obtained. It is therefore perfectly possible to argue for the exclusion of evidence that has been entirely correctly obtained. In *Hickin* [1996] Crim. L.R. 584 there was no breach of PACE where identification witnesses had had an opportunity to collude before they were driven round the town to see if they could identify suspects, and that no initial description was taken from them first. The court held that the version of Code D which was then in force did not apply to this situation, so that the police had acted lawfully. However, the court went on to say that the evidence should have been excluded anyway since its admission would have had an adverse impact on the fairness of the trial.

16.4.4 Unfairness and undercover cases

This is an area of the law that has been subject to considerable scrutiny in the light of Strasbourg jurisprudence. The leading English cases are *Christou* (1992) 95 Cr App R 264 and *Smurthwaite* [1994] 1 All ER 898, both attempts to argue that there had been entrapment by the police. The general principle is that there is no defence of entrapment – but undercover officers are not permitted to abuse their role to circumvent PACE by asking questions which they ought properly to ask as police officers and in accordance with PACE.

Is there a defence of entrapment in domestic law? In *Teixeira v Portugal* (1999) 28 EHRR 101 the ECtHR indicated that the right to a fair trial under article 6(1) had been breached where the primary evidence against Mr Teixeira had been obtained by undercover police officers who had acted as *agents provocateurs*, in that they had instigated the offence in question by going beyond an essentially passive investigation.

The House of Lords considered the application of *Teixeira* in two linked appeals, *Loosely; Attorney General's Reference No.3 of 2000* [2001] 4 All ER 897. and held that domestic law can be applied in a manner compatible with article 6. Lord Nicholls suggested that the test was threefold:

1. Was this an "unexceptional opportunity" to commit an offence?

2. How proportionate was the conduct?

> 3. Is the conduct of the law enforcer such that it would bring the administration of justice into disrepute?

Lord Hutton laid particular stress on whether there was "persistent importunity, threats, deceit, offers of rewards or other inducements [from the undercover officers] that would not ordinarily be associated with the commission of the offence or a similar offence." In one of the appeals, where a person who had never previously dealt in heroin was induced to do so by the offer from undercover officers of smuggled cigarettes, the House of Lords agreed that the offence had been induced by the officers and the evidence was rightly excluded.

[16.5] HUMAN RIGHTS ISSUES

16.5.1 Exclusion of evidence and breaches of the Convention:

The leading case in domestic law remains the House of Lords judgment in *Khan (Sultan)* [1996] 3 WLR 162 . Khan was suspected of being involved in the importation of heroin and the police bugged the house that he was staying in. Damaging comments were obtained and Khan was arrested and charged. At trial Khan argued that the placing of the bug involved a civil trespass by the police and some damage to the property. Thus, he said, the evidence had been improperly obtained (and amounted to a breach of his right to privacy under article 8) and it must therefore be excluded under s.78. The trial judge ruled against this, and Khan pleaded guilty. The conviction was upheld by the Court of Appeal and the House of Lords.

The House of Lords considered article 8 of the Convention (the right to respect for privacy), and concluded that any breach would be a matter that could be taken into account under s.78 PACE.

> *The principles reflected in the Convention could hardly be irrelevant to the exercise of the section 78 power because they embodied so many of the familiar principles of English law and concepts of justice.*

However, even if there had been a breach of article 8 in this case, the circumstances were not such as to require the exclusion of the evidence.

Khan v United Kingdom – the Strasbourg decision ([2000] Crim.L.R. 684)

Khan applied to the European Court of Human Rights, arguing that there had been a breach of article 8, and that in consequence there had been a breach of article 6 in permitting the evidence obtained to be used at his trial.

The ECtHR agreed that there had been a breach of article 8 since there was no domestic legislation at that time which had permitted the interference with his privacy. The interference could not therefore be "in accordance with the law". However the court rejected the argument that this was a fundamental violation of the Convention and that it would be contrary to the rule of law to allow to permit his conviction to be based solely on such evidence.

The ECtHR held that the central question was the overall fairness of the proceedings. Khan had had ample opportunity to challenge both the use of the evidence and its authenticity. Exclusion under s.78 PACE had been considered fully by every domestic court, and the evidence would have been excluded if it would have given risen to substantive unfairness. There was therefore no requirement under article 6 for the evidence to be excluded.

Domestic cases following *Khan*

There have been a significant number of domestic law cases following *Khan* where the domestic courts have accepted that there may have been breaches of article 8, but have ruled that this did not of itself require the exclusion of evidence. The most striking of these cases is *Loveridge* (2001) 2 CAR 591 where the police wanted to obtain some video footage of the defendants (for the purpose of facial mapping) and so filmed the defendants in the precincts of the magistrates court where they were being produced. This was in breach of the Criminal Justice Act 1925 which prohibits such filming. The Court of Appeal took the view that the defendants could have a legitimate expectation of privacy in these circumstances, and that the interference was not in accordance with law, and so breached article 8, but still held that this did not require its exclusion under article 6. The focus is therefore not on the fact of the breach of a Convention article, but on its impact on the fairness of the trial.

16.5.2 Entrapment: see 16.4.4 above

16.5.3 Delay

What is the effect of delay on the fairness of a trial? Article 6(1) of the Convention provides that:

> *In the determination of his civil rights and obligations or of any criminal charge against him, everyone is entitled to a fair and public hearing within a reasonable time by an independent and impartial tribunal established by law...* [my emphasis]

The House of Lords confirmed that the right to a timely trial is a free-standing right which does not rely upon the defendant showing prejudice: *Porter v Magill* [2002] 2 WLR 37 (HL). In deciding whether there has been unacceptable delay the court must consider the complexity of the issues, the reasons for any delay, and the conduct of both prosecution and defence.

In *Attorney General's Reference* (No 2 of 2001) [2004] 2 W.L.R. 1 the House of Lords has said that a stay in the proceedings because of an unreasonable delay will be exceptional. It will only occur where the court is satisfied that a fair trial is no longer possible. Normally a reduction in any sentence imposed will be sufficient remedy for the delay.

UNFAIRLY OBTAINED EVIDENCE

"It matters not how you get it - if you steal it even it would be admissible in evidence." *Leatham*.

Kuruma: evidence found in an illegal search – admissible because relevant.

Sang: confirming *Kuruma*, but there is an overriding discretion to exclude evidence where the prejudicial impact outweighs the probative value. Now the courts tend to use s.78 PACE.

S.78: UNFAIRNESS

A court can exclude evidence where "having regard to all the circumstances, including the circumstances in which the evidence was obtained, the admission ... would have such an adverse effect on the fairness of the proceedings that the court ought not to admit it."

Unfairness may arise where there has been deliberate malpractice (e.g. Mason: lies to solicitor) or equally where there have been innocent errors (eg. in arranging ID's), the effect of which is unfair. Although the courts tend to say they do not use s.78 to discipline the police, deliberate malpractice or impropriety increases the likelihood of exclusion.

Walsh: if there are "significant and substantial breaches of s.58 or the provisions of the Code, then prima facie at least the standards of fairness set by Parliament have not been met." Not every breach will mean that there is such unfairness that the evidence should be excluded.

Note how the presence of a legal representative can "cure" breaches of PACE: *Dunn*.

CONFESSION EVIDENCE: S.76

S.76 relates solely to confession evidence. See s.76(2) in particular: oppression and unreliability.

Note that the burden of proof once oppression/unreliability is raised is on the Prosecution to prove beyond reasonable doubt that this is not the case. The truth or otherwise of the confession is irrelevant.

76(2)(a): Oppression

s.76(8): "includes torture, inhuman or degrading treatment, and the use or threat of violence".

Fulling ignored the statutory definition and adopted a dictionary definition – "the exercise of authority or power in a burdensome, harsh or wrongful manner etc." Court stated it was hard to imagine oppression without some form of impropriety.

Alladice suggested that improperly denying legal advice in bad faith could be oppression: *Hughes* that such a denial because of a misunderstanding was not oppression.

76(2)(b): Unreliability

No definition of unreliability.

There is no need for any impropriety by the Police: see e.g. *Harvey*.

Something must have been said or done; D's own state is not enough (see e.g. *Goldenberg* – a heroin addict desperate for a fix).

May arise because of improper inducements, failure to comply with Codes (see *Trussler*: no rest period), or because Police are e.g. unaware that D. is particularly vulnerable (*Everett*: Police unaware D had a mental age of 8).

Confessions and the Exclusion of Evidence

Confessions and improperly obtained evidence – test yourself questions

[The answers to these questions are set out in Appendix A at the back of this book]

[1] David is accused of possession of spray paint with intent to damage property, contrary to s.3 Criminal Damage Act 1971. The paint was discovered during a search of David's flat. Although the search was carried out under a search warrant, the warrant had in fact expired three days earlier and the search was therefore unlawful. At trial David argues that evidence should be excluded.

Which one of the following propositions is correct?

(a) The court should consider the effect of admitting the evidence on the fairness of the proceedings, and may take into account the circumstances under which the evidence was obtained.

(b) The fact that the breach of PACE was not deliberate means that the court should be slow to exclude the evidence.

(c) The court should not exclude the evidence; it has no power to do so as this is not a confession.

(d) The court must exclude the evidence as it has been obtained wrongfully.

[2] Suzy is accused of taking a motor vehicle without consent. When arrested she says: "Sure I took the car. But I had permission, didn't I?" The prosecution wish to adduce the comment at Suzy's trial.

Which one of the following propositions is correct?

(a) The statement is admissible since there is no suggestion that it should be excluded under either s.76 or s.78 PACE.

(b) The statement is a confession as it contains an admission against interest. However, it will be inadmissible as hearsay.

(c) The statement will be admissible as a "mixed" statement.

(d) The statement is exculpatory and therefore irrelevant except as evidence of reaction.

[3] Elaine is charged with stealing forty beagles from an experimental testing centre. In interview at the police station she was told that unless she told the police where they could find the animals, she would be kept in detention and the animals would suffer as they would have neither food nor water. Elaine then made admissions. At trial the defence indicate that they intend to make an application for the confessions to be excluded.

Consider the following propositions:

i. Once the defence has raised the allegation that the admissions were obtained under circumstances rendering them unreliable, the prosecution must show beyond reasonable doubt that they were not so obtained, or the judge must exclude the evidence.

ii. Any unreliability must be as the result of something said or done.

iii. For the purposes of s.76 PACE, it is irrelevant that Elaine's confessions were true.

Which of these propositions is correct?

(a) All of them.

(b) i only.

(c) i and ii only.

(d) ii and iii only.

[4] Consider the following propositions in relation to s.76 and s.78 PACE:

i. An application for confession evidence to be excluded may be made under either s.76 PACE or s.78 PACE but not both.

ii. Evidence will only be excluded under s.78 PACE where it has been obtained as the result of a breach of the PACE Codes, although it is not required that that breach be deliberate.

iii. In deciding whether evidence should be excluded under s.78 the court may only have regard to the issue of how the evidence was obtained.

Which of these propositions is correct?

(a) All of them.

(b) i and iii only.

(c) ii only.

(d) None of them.

CHAPTER 17

CHARACTER AND DISPOSITION

> This chapter covers:
>
> The basic rules regarding character evidence
>
> The rules in relation to the defendant's previous bad character
>
> The rules in relation to the bad character of any other person
>
> The rules for adducing the defendant's good character.

[17.1] The basic rules on character – ss.98–113 CJA 2003:

If a court is told that the defendant has previous convictions there may be a danger that the court will convict him because they regard him as a criminal, rather than considering whether there is sufficient evidence in relation to the current offence to justify a conviction. Character evidence has therefore traditionally been treated with suspicion in English criminal trials.

In December 2004 this position was changed fundamentally by the Criminal Justice Act 2003. Now it is possible for the court to be told of the defendant's previous bad character in a far wider range of situations. Moreover the court will often be able to take that information into account as showing propensity (that is, that the convictions show that the defendant is more likely to have committed the offence) rather than merely going to his credibility as a witness (by showing him to be someone who has been dishonest in the past).

Additionally the law changed to greatly restrict the circumstances in which any of the parties is entitled to raise the bad character of a non-defendant, whether a witness or any other person.

17.1.1 What is bad character?

Bad character is defined as being "*evidence of, or of a disposition towards, misconduct*" other than evidence to do with the offence charged, or its investigation/prosecution: s.98 CJA 2003. "*Misconduct*" is the commission of an offence or other reprehensible behaviour: s.112 CJA 2003.

What is misconduct? The easiest form of "bad character" to identify will be previous criminal convictions. However bad character will also include "other reprehensible behaviour". The scope of this phrase is very hard to pin down – and it seems to introduce a highly subjective element: is it reprehensible not to believe in God – or to smack your children – or to breastfeed in public (or not to breastfeed in public) – to gamble, drink or smoke – to commit a professional foul in a football match?

It is worth noting that unproven allegations will still potentially be admissible as examples of reprehensible behaviour – even where the prosecuting authorities have chosen not to charge the defendant with them.

> *In Nguyen [2008] EWCA Crim 585, N was charged with murder on the basis that he had been drunk, had smashed a glass and had used it as a weapon. The prosecution were permitted to rely on a previous similar incident which had occurred 18 days earlier, where it was alleged that N had used a glass as a weapon in this way, even though the Crown had decided not to prosecute N for those earlier offences.*

Contrast this with:

> *Braithwaite [2010] EWCA Crim 1082 where the defendant wanted to adduce evidence of bad character in relation to the group of people who were with the dead man in order to argue that they were likely to be aggressors while he was acting in self-defence. The court held that while their convictions for violence were admissible, the trial judge was correct in refusing to admit police intelligence items about complaints where the complainants had never progressed the matter. These, the court said, had no probative value at all.*

Overseas convictions: Convictions in other EU Member States can be taken into account in the same way that domestic convictions are. The offence in question must also have been an offence in England and Wales: s.144 Coroners and Justice Act 2009.

17.1.2 What is <u>not</u> bad character?

Conduct that is not "reprehensible":

Logically conduct which is not "reprehensible" and is not a criminal offence does not fall within these rules. It will therefore be admissible if it is relevant. This has led to some worrying decisions.

> *In the case of <u>Manister</u> (<u>Weir and others</u> [2005] EWCA Crim 2866), M was charged with indecent assault on a 13 year old family friend. He was of previous good character, but had had a previous relationship when he was aged 34 with a girl who was then 16. The court accepted that this relationship was perfectly legal, and indeed that it had been long-standing, but held that it since it wasn't reprehensible, it was admissible to show M's sexual interest in young girls – a decision which arguably left M with even less protection than if the behaviour had been reprehensible, where one of the Gateways under s.101 would have had to be applicable.*

Misconduct in relation to the offence charged or its investigation or prosecution: It is important to note the fact that evidence in relation to either the offence in question or its investigation is not "bad character", and therefore does not attract these rules.

> *In <u>McNeill</u> [2007] EWCA Crim 2927 M was charged with threats to kill her neighbours. Two days after the incident with which she was charged she told a local authority housing officer: "They'll come out in body bags." The court held that the trial judge was right to say that the second incident fell within s.98 and so was admissible without needing to go through a "gateway". The section embraced evidence relating to the facts of the offence or which were directly relevant because they were reasonable contemporaneous and were closely associated with it.*

Procedural restrictions: There are procedural rules relating to the admission of character evidence; these are considered in 17.2 and 17.3 below. Note that there are additional procedural steps that may also arise in this context – such as s.3 Criminal Procedure Act 1865 (which provides that you cannot attack your own witness); and s.41 Youth Justice and Criminal Evidence Act 1999 (which limits on cross-examination on a complainant's sexual history).

[17.2] BAD CHARACTER AND THE DEFENDANT

Under s.101 CJA 2003 the defendant's bad character will only be admissible if certain conditions are met. There are seven subsections, often referred to as "gateways".

The leading guidance from the Court of Appeal is the case of *Hanson* [2005] EWCA Crim 824. In that case the court stressed that the purpose of the new provisions was:

> *To assist in the evidence based conviction of the guilty, without putting those who are not guilty at risk of conviction by prejudice.*

For this reason the court stated that it hoped that prosecution applications to adduce the defendant's bad character would not be made routinely, simply because the defendant had previous convictions. Instead the prosecution had to consider the circumstances of each case. The court stressed that:

> *Evidence of bad character should not be used simply to bolster a weak case or to prejudice the minds of the jury against a defendant.*

Finally the court made the point that:

> *If there is little or no other evidence against a defendant, it is unlikely to be just to admit his previous convictions, whatever they are.*

Before addressing the grounds on which the prosecution is seeking to adduce evidence of your client's bad character, you should first consider whether the prosecution is justified in making the application at all.

17.2.1 Gateway A: Agreement: s.101(1)(a)

All the parties agree to the evidence being admissible: s.101(1)(a). This is unlikely to be problematic. This is likely to arise in situations where it is either inevitable that the evidence will be admissible under another gateway, or it actively suits the defence to put their client's bad character before the court, perhaps because it is very elderly or of a wholly different nature.

> *Jim is charged with rape. He has 30 previous convictions. All of these are for offences of dishonesty – mainly shoplifting or obtaining property by deception. The defence will rely upon Jim's record to show that while he may be a dishonest person, he has never shown any tendency to commit offences of violence or sexual offences, and he is therefore unlikely to have committed the instant offence.*

17.2.2 Gateway B: Adduced by the defendant: s.101(1)(b)

This includes situations where a witness gives evidence of the defendant's bad character, having been asked questions by the defendant, or his advocate, with the intention of adducing this evidence.

> *Frank is charged with burglary. He has some elderly previous convictions for theft but has been an upstanding member of the community ever since he got married. The prosecution made no attempt to apply to adduce his previous convictions, correctly assuming that they were unlikely to be admissible. At trial however the defence wish to present Frank as effectively being a person of good character. They know that doing this will potentially admit Frank's previous convictions (under Gateway F, for example). The defence therefore lead this evidence when they are examining-in-chief Frank, thereby hoping to show that Frank is being entirely open about his past, and enabling Frank to contrast his current law-abiding behaviour with his past misconduct.*

17.2.3 Gateway C: Important explanatory evidence: s.101(1)(c)

There may be some situations where the court needs to know the defendant's character in order to understand the case. Section 102 CJA 2003 defines "important explanatory evidence" as evidence without which the court would find it either impossible or difficult to understand other evidence in the case – and where the value of the evidence for understanding the case is "substantial".

> *Chohan was charged with robbery. There had been a robbery with an imitation firearm at the house of the elderly victim. A witness, W, saw Chohan running from the scene. Although it was a brief sighting, she recognised Chohan since she had bought drugs from him on a number of occasions. Held: the judge had been right to permit W to refer to Chohan's drug dealing under Gateway C since W's identification would not have made sense without knowing why she was likely to recognise Chohan:* Edwards and others *[2005] EWCA Crim 1813.*

Note that in the case of *Davis* [2008] EWCA Crim 1156, the Court of Appeal held that evidence admitted under this gateway could not be used as evidence of propensity, since Gateway D (see below) had much stricter admissibility requirements. This case does not sit easily with other cases.

17.2.4 Gateway D: Relevant to "an important matter in issue" between defence and prosecution: s.101(1)(d)

This provision is only available to the prosecution. For character evidence to be admissible it must be relevant to an <u>important</u> matter in issue. A matter in issue in this context is defined in s.103 as including:

- the issue of whether D has a propensity to commit offences of this kind (unless that propensity makes him no more likely to be guilty); and

- the issue of whether D has a propensity to lie (unless it is not suggested that he is lying).

"Propensity" or "propensity for untruthfulness"?

Gateway D permits the prosecution to use previous bad character to show either that the defendant has a propensity to commit offences or that they have a propensity to be untruthful.

> *Jim is charged with burglary. He has previous convictions for burglary. The prosecution may apply for these to be adduced under D to show that he has a propensity to commit burglaries – i.e. that he is more likely to have committed the offence.*
> *Doreen is charged with theft. She has a previous conviction for forgery. The prosecution may apply for this to be adduced to show that Doreen is someone who has a propensity to be untruthful since the nature of the forgery offence is the making of false representations. The effect of the conviction is to show that Doreen is not someone who should be believed.*

Propensity to commit offences: Propensity to commit offences can be established in a number of ways:

1. Is it an offence of the same description as a previous conviction?

> *Aidan is charged with possession of a Class B drug, namely amphetamines. He has a previous conviction for possession of amphetamines. This will be an offence of the same description. The previous conviction is therefore potentially admissible as to propensity.*

2. Is it an offence in the same category as a previous conviction?

> Currently there are two "categories" under the CJA: the first is Theft Act offences (for example: theft; burglary; taking of motor vehicles; handling stolen goods and so on): the second is child sex offences (rape of a child; sexual activity with a child; sexual assault on a child, and so on – but not including non-contact offences such as possession of child pornography or grooming).

> *Aidan is charged with theft. He has a previous conviction for handling stolen goods. The offences are not of the same description. However both theft and handling stolen goods are*

in the same "category" of Theft Act offences. The previous conviction is therefore potentially admissible as to propensity.

3. Is it previous bad character which is relevant to propensity even though it is not an offence of the same description/category?

In *Hanson* [2005] EWCA Crim 824 the court held that s.103(2) CJA 2003 is not exhaustive of the types of conviction which might be relied upon to show propensity to commit offences: para 8.

Aidan is charged with assault. He has a previous conviction for affray, a public order offence which involves putting others in fear of violence. The offence is not of the same description or of the same category. However these are not the only bases for the admissibility of evidence under Gateway D and it appears that the previous conviction for affray may be potentially admissible as to propensity to violence.

If an offence is in the same category or of the same description, is it automatically admissible? In *Hanson* the Court of Appeal ruled that the fact that the offence was in the same category or of the same description was not "necessarily sufficient" to show propensity.

Gateway D is not merely about propensity

The Court of Appeal has made clear that Gateway D also covers situations where there is any other evidence "which is relevant to an important issue between the prosecution and the defendant". For example, a jury may be asked to look at a whole series of allegations ("similar fact evidence") which do not necessarily show propensity (since they are unproven) but which are powerful evidence that the defendant did act as alleged: *McAllister* [2009] 1 Cr App R 129 (10).

Li is charged with a sexual assault. It is said that he rubbed his groin against a woman on the bus. He has no previous convictions, but there are five virtually identical allegations from other women. It is hard to call this evidence of propensity since nothing has been proved at any point. On the other hand the fact that six separate women have made similar allegations suggests that a defence of innocent conduct is unlikely to be the truth.

The discretion to exclude bad character evidence

Even where evidence of bad character is potentially admissible the court is entitled to refuse to admit it. There are two discretionary provisions – one in s.103(3) which specifically relates to Gateway D; one in s.101(3) which applies to both Gateways D and G.

Under s.103(3) the court must not admit evidence going to propensity under Gateway G if it satisfied that "*by reason of length of time since the conviction or any other reason*" that it would be unjust to apply the provision. The application of this test is considered at 17.2.8 below. Under s.101(3), the court must not admit evidence under gateways D or G if it appears that the admission of the evidence would have such an adverse effect on the fairness of the proceedings that the court ought not to admit it.

Gateway D in practice:

There is now quite a lot of Court of Appeal guidance. Most of it is very fact specific. The case of *Hanson, Gilmore and Pickstone* [2005] EWCA Crim 824 remains the leading case and provides guidance on a wide range issues, most in relation to Gateway D.

The general Hanson principles:

- There are no minimum number of previous convictions necessary in order to show propensity.

- However the fewer number the number of previous convictions, the weaker the evidence of propensity

- A single previous conviction will not show normally propensity.

- However a single conviction might do if it showed unusual behaviour or particular modus operandi. The court suggested that child sexual abuse or fire starting might show unusual behaviour where even a single previous conviction might be relevant.

- Old convictions with no special feature would be likely to seriously affect fairness unless they show a continuing propensity.

- The court will need to consider each individual conviction and will often need to consider the circumstances of the offence. However, in some circumstances the mere fact of convictions will be enough: for example a defendant who is charged with burglary and has a string of recent convictions for burglary.

- Propensity for untruthfulness is different from mere dishonesty. Untruthfulness relates to a defendant's behaviour when committing the offence or giving an account of it. A not guilty plea that has been disbelieved by the court might evidence untruthfulness. An offence involving the making of false representations might also show untruthfulness. The mere fact of a theft offence, however, might show dishonesty, but would without more be evidence of a propensity for untruthfulness.

    Janine is charged with benefit fraud. The prosecution wish to adduce a previous conviction for shoplifting to show that she has a propensity for untruthfulness. However, although Janine has undoubtedly behaved dishonestly in taking the goods, at no point did she lie to any person – and she pleaded guilty to the offence, and so made no attempt to mislead the court.

- The jury must be warned against placing undue reliance on any previous bad character and should not conclude guilt just because of the previous convictions. Propensity will be only one factor for the jury to take into account.

- A defendant who pleads guilty because a ruling has been made to admit his bad character is unlikely to be permitted to appeal against conviction.

Applying the Hanson principles:

Hanson *was alleged to have nipped upstairs in a pub and stolen £600 from a bedroom. He was charged with burglary. He had previous convictions for handling stolen goods, aggravated vehicle taking, robbery, burglary and theft from a dwelling. The court held that it was necessary to look at each conviction separately, even though all of these fell within the Theft Act category. Of themselves the convictions for handling and aggravated vehicle taking were not relevant to propensity to burgle. The robbery conviction might have been viewed as too prejudicial to be admissible. However the offences of burglary and theft from a dwelling were clearly admissible to show propensity and there was powerful supporting evidence.*

Gilmore *was found in the street in the early hours of the morning with a bag containing items stolen from a locked garden shed. Gilmore argued that he had found the bag and thought it was just rubbish. Gilmore had three very recent convictions for shoplifting, to which he had pleaded guilty. The judge had been right to hold that these did not show propensity for untruthfulness but did show propensity to steal, and that propensity increased the likelihood of guilt. Again, the other evidence against Gilmore was strong.*

> ***Pickstone*** *was charged with indecent assault and anal rape of a child. Pickstone denied the charge, arguing that the girl had made up the allegations in order to get him removed from the family home. There was medical evidence of injuries to her. He had a previous conviction for indecent assault on an 11 year old dating from 1993, to which he had pleaded guilty. The court agreed that this single previous conviction was still relevant to propensity even though it was comparatively old. As the judge had said: "a defendant's sexual mores and motivations are not necessarily affected by the passage of time." [Note that the convictions were also admissible under Gateway G, because the defendant was attacking the honesty of the child — see below.]*

When may previous misconduct <u>not</u> be relevant?

> ***Van Nguyen*** *was charged with being involved in the cultivation of cannabis. He lived in a shared house with his brother where the plants were found. His brother had pleaded Guilty to the offence, and Van Nguyen admitted that he knew the plants were some kind of controlled drug but denied being involved in any way with the cultivation. At trial the judge permitted the prosecution to adduce evidence that Van Nguyen was a heroin addict who had previous convictions for shoplifting, since these were said to show his familiarity with the drug scene and his need to fund his addiction. Held: this evidence should not have been admitted. Van Nguyen had admitted knowing that the plants were some form of controlled drug, what was in issue was whether he was involved in growing them. A careful jury direction was needed in order to focus on what was relevant — here there had been a disproportionate emphasis on Van Nguyen's drug addiction. The conviction was quashed.* Highton and others [2005] EWCA Crim 1985.

17.2.5 Gateway E: It has "substantial probative value" to an "important matter in issue" between the defendant and a co-accused: s.101(1)(e)

This gateway is available only to defendants and not to the prosecution. It governs the situation where there are two or more defendants, and there is an application by one defendant to rely upon the fact that one of his co-accused is of previous bad character. In order to use this provision the defendant must not only show that the previous conviction has substantial probative value, but that it relates to an "important matter in the case".

A defendant may wish to show that his co-accused is more likely to have committed the offence (propensity) or simply that the co-accused's account should be disbelieved because of a propensity for untruthfulness. If the defendant wishes to rely upon the latter, he must show that the nature or conduct of the co-accused's defence is such as to "undermine" his own defence: s. 104.

> *Chung Mae is charged with false accounting. One other member of the Accounts Department, Francine, is also charged with the offence. Mae is of good character and wholly denies any involvement in the offence. Francine, however, has two recent convictions for offences of dishonesty. Mae wishes to adduce that evidence to show:*
>
> - *That it is more likely that Francine committed the offence than that Mae did (propensity); and*
> - *That Francine's testimony, which implicates Mae, should be disbelieved because Francine has a propensity for untruthfulness.*
>
> *If Chung Mae can persuade the court that Francine's previous convictions for dishonesty amount to substantial proof in relation to an important matter in issue between the two defendants, then she will be able adduce the evidence and to argue that Francine's dishonesty in the past makes it more likely that it was her that committed this offence.*
>
> *However before Chung Mae can use Francine's bad character to argue that Francine is a person who tends to be untruthful, and that she should therefore not be believed, Chung Mae must show that*

> *Francine's defence undermines her own defence. So that if Francine's defence is simply that she knows nothing of any theft, and it in no way undermines Chung Mae's account of non-involvement, then it is unlikely that the convictions will be admissible as evidence of a propensity for untruthfulness.*

The Court of Appeal has held that applications under Gateway E should be looked at in the context of the case as a whole, rather than adopting a fine tooth comb approach: *Edwards and others (No. 2)* [2005] EWCA Crim 3244.

17.2.6 Gateway F: The evidence is admitted to *"correct a false impression"* given by the defendant: s.101(1)(f)

This is another provision only available to the prosecution. The defendant can be said to have given a false impression either in the proceedings or when being questioned by the police, or at the point of charge.

False impression is potentially a very wide concept. Would it, for example, catch someone who dresses up in a suit for court, when they would normally wear street clothes? Certainly the CJA 2003 provides that the false impression can be given by the defendant's conduct during the proceedings (other than the giving of evidence) and that this conduct includes "appearance or dress": s.105(5) CJA 2003.

Note that the provision is of relevance to the advice that you give at the police station interview stage as it catches "false impressions" which are put forward at an early stage in the investigation process.

Note also that a defendant can avoid the provision by withdrawing the misleading assertion or disassociating himself from it. The correction of the false impression will not allow the prosecution to automatically to adduce all of the defendant's bad character, but must go no further than is required to correct the false impression: s.105.

Both of these principles can be seen in play in the following case:

> *Renda was charged with robbing V in the street. In interview at the police station R told the police that he had been a soldier who had been invalided out of the army following a head injury while so employed, and that he was now in regular employment as a security guard. In fact the head injury had been sustained while on holiday, and not in the course of his duties, and although he had briefly been employed to check passes he was no longer in gainful employment. R admitted both matters while being cross-examined. Held: Gateway F was activated and the facts of a previous finding in relation to an actual bodily harm matter were correctly admitted. Note that admitting the matters while being cross-examined was not the same as making a positive withdrawal or disassociation for the purposes of Gateway F.* Renda and others [2005] EWCA Crim 2826

17.2.7 Gateway G: The defendant has made *"an attack on another person's character"*: s.101(1)(g)

This provision is available only to the prosecution – it catches an "attack" made by the defendant on any person's character. It also extends to imputations about another person made by the defendant when being questioned under caution or at point of charge.

As with Gateway D, there is discretion for the court to refuse to adduce evidence of bad character under this provision if it would have an adverse effect on the fairness of the trial: this is considered in 17.2.8 below.

Attack is defined as suggesting that the person has either committed an offence or has behaved (or is disposed to behave) in a reprehensible way: s.106(2).

What is an "attack":

In *Hanson* the court suggested that the old caselaw on the meaning of attack remained potentially relevant. If this is the case then a mere suggestion that someone is mistaken in what they are saying is unlikely to be an attack: although note *Britzman* [1983] 1 WLR 350 where allegations that in reality amounted to accusations that the police had fabricated a conversation could not be dressed up by suggesting that they were merely "mistaken" about whether the conversation took place.

Similarly in *Britzman* it was said that the court should make allowances for the strain of being in the witness box when deciding if an accused has attacked the character of another: the provision was only activated:

> *... if the judge is sure that there is no possibility of mistake, misunderstanding or confusion and that the jury will inevitably have to decide whether the prosecution witnesses have fabricated evidence. Defendants sometimes make wild allegations when giving evidence. Allowance should be made for the strain of being in the witness-box and the exaggerated use of language which sometimes results from such strain or lack of education or mental instability. Particular care should be used when a defendant is led into making allegations during cross-examination.*

Finally, under the old law a suggestion that a witness was lying was not enough to amount to an attack, but a suggestion that a witness was lying in order to obtain some benefit (such as a more lenient sentence) was an attack: *Lasseur* [1991] Crim LR 53. Post CJA authorities remain limited on this point.

Gateway G in practice:

Gateway G will often arise, since it will be very common for defendants either to blame another person, or to suggest that another person is lying about the offence. The provision has a particularly wide effect since it will apply to attacks on others that are made during the police interview.

However in the case of *Nelson* [2006] EWCA Crim 3412, the Court of Appeal suggested that it would be "most unusual" for the judge not to exclude character evidence where the attack was on a person who was not a witness and who was not the victim, since it would normally be unfair to admit such evidence. Additionally the court said that it was not appropriate for the prosecution to put the imputations in the interview before the jury simply in order to trigger Gateway G.

Propensity or propensity for untruthfulness – the effect of Gateway G:

The Criminal Justice Act 2003 is silent as to the effect of admitting convictions under Gateway G. In the case of *Highton* [2005] EWCA 1985 the Court of Appeal held that once bad character had been admitted under any one of the gateways it was potentially admissible as going to both propensity and credibility:

> *We therefore conclude that a distinction must be drawn between the <u>admissibility</u> of evidence of bad character, which depends upon it getting through one of the gateways, and the <u>use</u> to which it may be put once it is admitted. The use to which it may be put depends upon the matters to which it is relevant rather than upon the gateway through which it was admitted. ...In the case of gateway (g), for example, admissibility depends on the defendant having made an attack on another person's character, but once the evidence is admitted, it may, depending on the particular facts, be relevant not only to credibility but also to propensity to commit offences of the kind with which the defendant is charged.* <u>Highton</u>, para 10.

Note that this principal does not seem to apply to Gateway C: *Davis* (see 17.2.3 above).

17.2.8 Excluding bad character evidence – s.101(3):

There is a provision in s.101(3) for the court to refuse to admit evidence of the defendant's bad character where the prosecution seeks to admit it under either Gateways D or G. This power to refuse to admit evidence arises where its admission would have such an adverse effect on the fairness of proceedings that it ought not to be admitted – echoing the phrasing of s.78 PACE. In making this decision the court must have regard to the length of time since the incidents on which the allegation of bad character are based: s.101(4) CJA.

The test under s.101(3) to admitting previous convictions seems broadly the same as the specific Gateway D exclusion under s.103(3). In *Hanson* the court suggested that the following factors were likely to be relevant:

- How similar is the previous conviction to the offence charged – even where they are in the same description or category? The court pointed out that for example theft and assault can cover a wide spectrum of different types of conduct.

- How serious is the current offence as compared to the earlier?

- How strong is the prosecution case – the weaker the case the less likely it is to be fair to admit the previous convictions?

- The length of time since the commission of the earlier offence.

- The sentence imposed will not normally be probative or admissible. It is normally necessary to look at the facts of the previous offending.

17.2.9 Procedures for admitting evidence under s.101 CJA:

Rule 35, Criminal Procedure Rules require applications to be made pre-trial. There are prescribed forms for making the applications (for an example see **Doc 17A/B** in the case study). These are to be submitted to the court concerned and to all of the parties. It is presumably intended that there should be a binding pre-trial ruling on the admissibility of character evidence in relation both to the defendant and to any other persons whose character is in issue.

Prosecution applications to adduce the bad character of the defendant must be made:

- No more than 28 days following a not guilty plea in the magistrates' court; or

- No more than 14 days following a not guilty plea in the Crown Court

If the defence wants to oppose the application is must do so within 14 days. Part 35 CrPR states that both prosecution and defence must make clear the basis of their application or opposition on the forms.

Where it is a co-accused who is making the application (under Gateway E), they must make the application as soon as reasonably practicable and in any event within 14 days of prosecution disclosure. Again, the defence will have 14 days to oppose the application.

Power to vary time limits: Part 35.6 CrPR permits the Court to shorten or extend a time limit even after the time limit has expired. In order to request an extension of time, a party must explain the delay.

17.3 ADMITTING THE BAD CHARACTER OF OTHERS: S.100 CJA

Under the previous rules the only restriction on the admissibility of the character of persons other than the defendant was the issue of relevance. Under the CJA 2003, for the first time rules are introduced which make the "bad character" of others admissible only if it comes within one of three gateways – namely:

(a) it is important explanatory evidence;

(b) it has substantial probative value in relation to a matter in issue and is of substantial importance to the case as a whole; or

(c) all the parties agree that it is admissible.

Under the first two gateways the leave of the court will be required.

Who is caught by s.100?

This provision applies to "a person other than the defendant". It is therefore wide enough to cover both those who are witnesses, but also persons who are not involved in the proceedings.

> *Peter is charged with possession of Class A drugs with intent to supply in respect of drugs found in a flat which he shares with Victor. Peter wants to rely upon the evidence that Victor has previous convictions for drugs misuse in order to argue that it is more likely that the drugs were Victor's and not his. This will be evidence of bad character (misconduct) and therefore an application must be made under s.100 CJA 2003 to adduce this evidence. This will be case whether Victor is a witness in the case or not. Peter will need to show that one of the s.100 gateways applies.*

17.3.1 s.100 – gateway A: Important explanatory evidence: s.100(1)(a)

This is the same provision as in s.101 Gateway C – see 17.2.3 above.

Evidence will be admissible if without it the court or jury would find it impossible or difficult properly to understand the other evidence. Its value for understanding the case as a whole must be substantial.

17.3.2 s.100 – gateway B: Substantial probative value/substantial importance: s.100(1)(b)

Under this gateway the evidence must have substantial probative value to a matter in issue which is of "substantial" importance to the case as a whole. The evidence of the person's bad character will not therefore be admissible where it goes only to a peripheral issue. Note that this is a test of "enhanced relevance", so that it will be harder to argue for the admission of a non-defendant's bad character under this provision, than for a defendant's bad character under Gateway D of s.101 which only requires relevance.

In deciding whether the bad character evidence has "substantial probative value", the court must consider a number of factors set out in s.100(3) CJA 2003:

- the nature and number of things to which the evidence relates;
- when those things are alleged to have happened;
- if it is suggested that the conduct is relevant because of its similarity to the present offence; then the degree of similarity;
- the extent to which it can be shown that the same person was responsible for each instance of misconduct.

Gateway B in practice:

Gateway B was considered in the case of *Bovell* [2005] EWCA Crim 1091:

> *B was accused of wounding with intent, contrary to s.18 Offences Against the Person Act 1861. The background was a dispute with a shopkeeper, V, who refused B credit. B then returned and attacked V, stabbing him three times with a knife. B's defence was that it was V who had attacked him and that his actions were in self-defence. B said he wasn't sure where the knife had come from.*
>
> *At the time of the trial V was known to have two previous convictions. The first was for handling stolen goods and the second for robbery, both over ten years prior to the current incident. B applied to adduce these convictions, which would clearly be useful in showing both that V was a person of suspect honesty, and that he was not himself averse to violence. The judge refused to adduce either conviction. B was then convicted of the offence.*
>
> *By the time of the appeal further investigations into the background of V's offending had been undertaken and it was now known that (i) V's robbery conviction had involved the use of a knife; and (ii) three years ago V had himself been charged with a s.18 offence, but the charge had been dropped after the victim withdrew the allegation.*
>
> *The Court of Appeal held that the conviction was safe. The mere charge for s.18 was irrelevant since the matter had never been pursued. The fact that the robbery had been committed with a knife was relevant and might well have been admissible had the judge known about the use of a knife. However the other evidence against B meant that the conviction was safe.*

Remember that s.100 is equally applicable to the bad character of defence witnesses. Thus the same principles would apply if the defence are calling a witness who is of bad character.

> *In the case of <u>Yaxlev-Lennon</u> (see <u>Weir and others</u> [2005] EWCA Crim 2866) YL had a row with his girlfriend in the street which led to an off-duty police officer attempting to arrest YL, who fought back. This led to charges of ABH and assault with intent to resist arrest. YL argued that he was acting in self-defence, having been assaulted by the police officer. YL's girlfriend, W, backed up YL's account. In cross-examination at trial the prosecution asked W if she had taken drugs that evening, and when she said that she had not, she was cross-examined on a previous caution for possession of cocaine. Held: the caution was irrelevant to the matters in issue and should not have been admitted under s.100.*

17.3.3 s.100 – gateway C: by agreement between the parties: s.100(1)(c)

A self explanatory provision. There will be circumstances where a person's convictions are so clearly of substantial relevance to the issues that the parties can simply agree that they will be admissible. Remember that this will not simply consist of the defence asking the prosecution to agree to admitting this evidence; in the situation where there is a defence witness who is of bad character, the prosecution may approach the defence for their agreement.

17.3.4 Procedures for admitting evidence under s.100 CJA:

Applications in respect of a non-defendant's bad character be made by the defence, or may be made by the prosecution (most likely in respect of a person who is going to be giving evidence for the defence). Part 35.3 of the CrPR applies.

The normal rule is that any application must be made within 14 days of the prosecution making disclosure of those convictions, although the application can be made as soon as is practicable where it relates to a non-defendant who is giving evidence for the defence. Any counter-application opposing the admission of the evidence must be made within 14 days.

[17.4] OTHER PROVISIONS ON CHARACTER:

Contaminated evidence: s.107: The CJA provides that a judge in the Crown Court can either direct an acquittal or a retrial if evidence of the defendant's bad character is admitted which is "contaminated". A person's evidence is contaminated if it is false, misleading or different from what it would otherwise be as a result of an agreement with another person, or in consequence of the witness being aware of the allegations of other possible witnesses.

Exclusion of offences committed as a child: s.108: Where a person is being tried as an adult (aged 21 or over), evidence of convictions for offences committed when under the age of 14 are not admissible unless both the present and past offences were indictable only offences, and the interests of justice require the admissibility of the evidence. This effectively means that any summary or either way offences dating from before the defendant's 14th birthday will never be admissible as bad character.

Giving reasons for rulings: s.110: The CJA introduces a requirement for all rulings on the admissibility of character evidence to be given with reasons for the ruling.

[17.5] GOOD CHARACTER

Here we are looking at whether your client can call evidence of his good character at his trial. You have already seen (in Chapter 10) that he is, of course, permitted to call character evidence in his support once he has been convicted and you are seeking to mitigate his sentence.

The leading case on good character is still *Rowton* (1865) L & C 520. This established that the defendant may call evidence of his good character provided that it is couched in general terms. A witness may not be called to adduce evidence of particular creditable acts.

> *Thus, for example, your client can call evidence that he is generally well regarded in the community. However, he cannot call evidence that he once saved a person from a fire, or participated in a particular charity event.*

Under the common law if the defendant puts in his good character, the prosecution may be entitled to call evidence in rebuttal. Contrast this with s.1 (3)(ii), which merely permits the prosecution to cross-examine the defendant as to his character, and is therefore no use if the defendant does not go into the witness box.

Good character directions: Where the defendant is of good character the judge must give the jury a good character direction. The exact terms of this direction will vary from case to case and will depend on whether the defendant has testified and/or relied on exculpatory statements. If the defendant has testified then the judge must indicate to the jury that his good character is relevant to his credibility as a witness. In *Martin (Paul David)* The Times 20 December 1999 the Court of Appeal held that the judge was entitled to take into account the fact that the defendant had been cautioned by the police, and to amend the direction accordingly. However, in *Clarius* ([2000] All ER (D) 951) where C was charged with an offence of violence and had one previous caution, some six years prior to the offence, for stealing an umbrella, the Court of Appeal held that a full good character direction should have been given.

Even where the defendant has not testified, the judge should remind the jury that good character may be relevant to the issue of guilt or innocence, but is not itself a defence to the charge. The guideline case is *Vye* [1993] 1 WLR 471, and it is an area of law that is still generating a number of new guidelines.

DEFENDANT'S CHARACTER

Definition of bad character: evidence of misconduct or a disposition to misconduct, other than in relation to the offence or its investigation: s.98

Misconduct: commission of offences or other reprehensible behaviour: s.112

s.101 Gateways:

A: by agreement;

B: adduced by the defendant;

C: important explanatory evidence;

D: relevant to an important matter in issue;

E: substantial probative value to important matter in issue between defendants;

F: correcting a false impression;

G: where D has attacked the character of another.

Note that gateways D and G are prosecution-only provisions.

Hanson principles

- Prosecution should not rely upon character evidence automatically.
- One previous conviction will not normally show propensity even if in the same category/of the same description, unless some unusual behaviour.
- Propensity for untruthfulness is not the same as dishonesty.

Once evidence is admitted under any gateway, it may, depending on relevance, be admissible as going either to propensity or credibility

Discretion to exclude evidence in relation to Gateways D and G.

Good character: the defendant may call evidence as to his general good character - but not specific creditable acts. See *Vye* for the good character direction.

PROCEDURES FOR DEALING WITH CHARACTER EVIDENCE

- Pre trial paper applications made under CrPR 35.
- **Defendant character applications:** prosecution applications 28 days after NG plea (Mags) or 14 days after NG plea (Crown). 14 days to respond.
- **Non-defendant character applications:** 14 days after prosecution disclosure of those convictions, or asap if a defence witness. 14 days to respond.

CHARACTER OF PERSONS OTHER THAN THE DEFENDANT

Restrictions on adducing the bad character of a person other than the defendant. Remember that the bad character rules do no apply to the current offence: s.100 is not activated by accusing a person of being involved in the current offence.

s.100 gateways:

A: important explanatory evidence;

B: substantial probative value in relation to a matter in issue which is of substantial importance in the proceedings;

C: by agreement.

Provision applies to both prosecution and defence.

Character – test yourself questions

[The answers to these questions are set out in Appendix A at the back of this book]

[1] Graham is charged with handling stolen goods. The prosecution case against him is that other persons broke into a house and stole electrical goods which Graham then attempted to sell in his local pub. Graham gave a general denial in police interview but his defence is that he wasn't involved at all; he admits being present in the pub at the time that the goods were produced, but says that they were brought to the pub by Robert, and that it was Robert who was involved in trying to sell the goods. Graham has extensive previous convictions.

Which one of the following propositions is correct?

(a) Graham is attempting to accuse Robert of misconduct; he must therefore satisfy the court that the misconduct is admissible under s.100 CJA. If Graham is permitted to adduce Robert's conduct, this will amount to an attack for the purposes of Gateway G and Graham's own previous convictions may become admissible.

(b) Graham is attempting to accuse Robert of misconduct and he must therefore satisfy the court that the misconduct is admissible under s.100 CJA. If the court rules that the evidence of Robert's misconduct is admissible, it will not constitute an attack for the purposes of Gateway G.

(c) Graham is not attempting to accuse Robert of misconduct since Robert's conduct is in relation to the offence which is in issue at the trial. However if Graham attacks Robert in this way, this will amount to an attack for the purposes of Gateway G and Graham's own previous convictions may become admissible.

(d) None of the above is correct.

[2] Consider the following propositions:

(i) The bad character rules apply only in relation to previous convictions, whether of the defendant or of another person.

(ii) Only the prosecution is entitled to adduce evidence of the defendant's bad character under Gateway D (relevance to an important matter in issue), Gateway F (correction of a false impression) or Gateway G (attack on another's character).

(iii) Gateway F (giving a false impression) can be activated by false or misleading assertions made in the police interview, but the defendant can avoid the provision by withdrawing the assertion.

(iv) Evidence which helps a jury to understand the case will be admissible under Gateway C.

Which one of the following propositions is correct?

(a) All of them.

(b) (i) and (iv) only.

(c) (ii) and (iii) only.

(d) (i), (ii) and (iv) only.

[3] Rebecca is charged with an assault in a nightclub. She is claiming that she only acted in self defence. The victim, Tabitha, has a previous conviction.

Consider the following factors in relation to Tabitha's conviction:

(i) The conviction was for making threats to kill.

(ii) The conviction dates from ten years ago.

(iii) The threats to kill were made to social workers who were threatening to take Tabitha's child into care.

(iv) Tabitha pleaded guilty to the charge at the time.

Which of these factors are relevant to the judge's decision under s.100 CJA 2003 as to whether Rebecca should be permitted to adduce the previous conviction at her trial for assaulting Tabitha?

(a) All of them.

(b) (i) and (iii) only.

(c) (ii), (iii) and (iv) only.

(d) (ii) only.

[4] Don is charged with sexual assault on a nine year old child, X. In the police interview, when confronted with the allegations, Don tells the police that X is making up the allegations in order to get his own back on Don for barring him from the local Scout group. Don has a previous caution for indecent assault on an 11 year old. The conviction is ten years old.

Which one of the following propositions in relation to Gateway G is correct?

(a) Don has attacked the child's character in the police interview but this will not activate Gateway G provided he withdraws the attack prior to trial.

(b) The caution for indecent assault will not be admissible since it is not within the definition of bad character as it is not a conviction.

(c) The fact that the previous conviction is so old means that it is unlikely to be admissible under Gateway G, since the trial judge will be likely to exclude it as being unfair under s.101(3)

(d) None of the above is correct.

[5] Yoshi is charged with blackmail. She has four previous convictions for theft offences. No further details are known, beyond the fact that she entered guilty pleas to each offence. The prosecution wish to adduce her previous convictions to show:

(i) that Yoshi has previous offences in the same category, and these are therefore automatically admissible under Gateway D to show that Yoshi has a propensity to commit offences of this type; and

(ii) that Yoshi has a propensity for untruthfulness (and should not therefore be believed) since she has previous convictions for dishonesty offences.

Which one of the above propositions in relation to Gateway D is correct?

(a) (i) only.

(b) (ii) only.

(c) Both (i) and (ii)

(d) Neither (i) nor (ii) is correct.

CHAPTER 18

HEARSAY EVIDENCE

> This chapter covers:
>
> The general rule against hearsay.
>
> The common law exceptions to the rule.
>
> The CJA 2003 hearsay provisions.

[18.1] The general rule

18.1.1 What is hearsay?

s.114 Criminal Justice Act 2003 speaks of hearsay as evidence as being:

1. a statement

2. not made in oral evidence

3. which is adduced as evidence of any matter stated.

A statement is any representation of fact or opinion made by a person by whatever means, including a representation made in a sketch, photofit or other pictorial form: s.115(2). The statement (as defined) must not be made during court proceedings and the purpose of adducing the statement must be to prove any "matter stated". The statement will be a matter stated if the the purpose of the maker appears to be to cause another to believe the matter, or to act on the matter or to cause a machine to operate on basis of the matter: s.115(3) CJA 2003.

Some common examples of hearsay:

Reported speech: "*And then Claire told me that she had seen Roger running into the house.*" This is a statement made by a person to another person outside of court proceedings. It is likely to be hearsay evidence if the maker was trying to cause the other person to believe the statement, and the reason for adducing the reported speech in evidence is to show that Roger did indeed run into the house (i.e to prove the matter stated). You can, of course, easily avoid hearsay in these circumstances. All that needs to be done is to call Claire to give the evidence directly to the court: "*I saw Roger run into the house.*"

Documentary evidence: This is the same principle as reported speech. The original witness has recorded what they said on paper; the paper is then brought to court. In order to avoid hearsay, the advocate will need to call the original witness to tell the court what they saw, said or did.

Confessions: Confessions are generally hearsay (as they will normally consist of a witness saying what the defendant said to them). As we saw in Chapter 16, they fall within an exception to the hearsay rule, but they remain inadmissible against anyone but the maker.

> *Frank and Bernard are jointly charged with burglary and Frank has admitted the offence in interview, also implicating Bernard. Frank's confession is admissible against him. However, Frank's confession will not be admissible against Bernard and the jury must be directed to ignore it insofar as they are deciding Bernard's guilt.*

Marks on things: Just as written statements may be hearsay, so too marks or writing may be hearsay. This is often a difficult area. For an example of this principle in practice see *Brown* [1991] Crim LR 835

> *B was charged with overcharging for NHS appliances (like surgical shoes). An expert gave evidence for the prosecution that he had identified the appliances based on the patients' names on the shoes and other appliances. The patients themselves were not called to give evidence as to whether these were their appliances. There was no other method of identifying ownership of the appliances. Held: the words on the shoes were hearsay and therefore inadmissible.*

Brown follows the case of *Patel* [1965] 3 All ER 593 where the words "Produce of Morocco" stamped on bags was held to be hearsay. Contrast, however *Orrell* [1972] RTR 14 where the police were able to describe the marks that they had made on urine samples and thus give direct oral evidence identifying the samples.

18.1.2 What is not hearsay?

Non factual statements: Some statements are not factual in content. They are therefore never hearsay as the purpose of the person making the statement is not to cause someone to believe the statement etc (s.115(2)).

- A man said, "*Hello.*" – no factual content in the words.
- The crowd was shouting, "*Help him.*" – exhortation or order; again no factual content.
- A woman shouted, "*Help me.*" – similarly.

Where it is the statement itself – rather than its contents – that is in issue:

> *Why did you run away?*
>
> *Because John told me there was a fire.*

This is almost certainly not a hearsay statement – although it consists of the witness saying what someone else has told him. It would be hearsay if it was being used to prove that there was a fire. So long as it is only being used to say why the witness ran away, then what is in issue is what he was told, not whether what he was told was true.

It is very easy to get this wrong. The classic example is *Subramaniam v Public Prosecutor* [1956] 1 WLR 965

> *S was arrested and charged with unlawful possession of ammunition. His defence was duress. He wanted to tell the court what the terrorists had said to him when threatening him with immediate death. The court wrongly stated that this was hearsay and refused to admit it. In fact it was irrelevant whether the terrorists were telling the truth (i.e. whether they were really going to kill him - the factual content of the reported words), what was in issue was the effect that the words had on S. So the reported speech was not hearsay.*

18.1.3 Hearsay or real evidence?

There may be occasions when evidence contained in a document is not hearsay, simply because the document itself is "real evidence" – akin to the murder weapon, or any other physical piece of evidence.

> In *Foxley* [1995] Crim LR 636, *a corrupt Ministry of Defence official appealed on the basis that letters regarding payments into his Swiss bank accounts were hearsay and therefore inadmissible. However, when the court considered the <u>purpose</u> of adducing these letters it held that they were being produced as copies of the documents which effected the payment (i.e. as copies of the payments themselves) and not as mere records of payment. They were not therefore hearsay; they were real evidence.*

18.1.4 Hearsay and implied assertions

> *Roger's flat is raided by the police. During the next three or four hours while the police search the flat they receive ten phone calls asking to speak to Roger about drugs and seven callers arrive, also asking for Roger to supply them with drugs. Is the evidence from the police officers about the calls and visits admissible, so that the jury can infer that Roger is a dealer, or is it merely hearsay?*

s.115 CJA 2003 makes clear that this is not hearsay unless it was the purpose or one of the purposes of the person making the statement to cause another to believe it or to act as if it were true. The people are ringing to ask Roger for drugs, not with the intention of persuading the police that Roger is dealing in drugs. Accordingly these are not hearsay statements – and this leaves open the possibility that they are admissible as evidence in the case without reference the hearsay rules. This is a situation that seems to arise even more frequently in the context of text messages: see *Twist and others* [2011] EWCA Crim 1143.

18.1.5 Computers, machines and hearsay

Where a computer is simply being used as a sophisticated calculator (i.e. where the calculation could as well, if more laboriously, have been done by hand) then the resulting printout or reading is a form of real evidence. It is not hearsay. Thus, for example, a printout detailing the numbers rung on a telephone and the duration of the calls based on a machine monitoring the calls was not hearsay: *Spiby* (1990) 91 Cr App R 186.

Where the representation of fact is made by a machine but depends on input from a person then it must be shown that the information which was input was accurate: s.129 CJA 2003.

> *Selim is charged with violent disorder contrary to s.2 Public Order Act 1984 following a large brawl inside a football ground. There is CCTV footage of Selim leaving the football ground and the prosecution wish to rely upon the time shown on the footage to show that Selim left after the brawl. The CCTV footage will itself be real evidence. However the time shown on the footage will be the time which was set on the camera. This is set by the camera operating staff and checked once every three months. Because the time is the product of human input into the machine, the prosecution must show that the time on the machine is accurate.*

[18.2] COMMON LAW EXCEPTIONS

Over the years a number of exceptions to the hearsay rule were created by the common law. The Criminal Justice Act 2003 helpfully lists all the common law exceptions to the hearsay rule which it preserves. These are set below.

18.2.1 Confessions

Confessions were considered in detail in Chapter 16. You will recall that confessions are an exception to the hearsay rule, but that they are only admissible against the maker.

18.2.2 Res Gestae

The CJA defines *res gestae* as covering:

- *A statement made by person so emotionally overpowered by an event that he possibility of concoction or distortion can be disregarded; or*

- *A statement which accompanies an act which can be properly evaluated as evidence only if considered in conjunction with the statement; or*

- *The statement relates to a physical sensation or mental stage (such as an intention or emotion).* s.118(4) CJA 2003

The exception would therefore include statements that are closely associated in time and place with the event in issue. The idea is that a robber who shouts out "*Get the car, Bob.*" in the middle of a robbery is probably under sufficient pressure that the statement is likely to be instinctive and not a concoction. Similarly statements from one witness about what another witness (not giving evidence) has said about their own state of mind or physical state may be admissible as *res gestae*.

18.2.3 Other preserved exceptions

Other common law exceptions to the hearsay rule are preserved by s.118 CJA 2003. These include:

- Public information: published works containing information of a public nature, public documents and records, evidence of age or place of birth;

- Reputation as to character;

- Reputation or family tradition – for example in relation to the existence of a marriage or the identity of a person or thing;

- Admissions made the defendant's agent;

- Experts relying on the body of expertise in their field;

- Statements made as part of a common enterprise.

Most of these are relatively obscure exceptions to the hearsay rule, but it is worth noting their existence.

[18.3] ADMISSIBILTY OF HEARSAY

For the hearsay rules to take effect, the evidence to be admitted must first be considered a hearsay statement. If it does not satisfy the requirements of a hearsay statement (see 18.1 above) then the evidence is not hearsay and will be subject to the usual rule of admissibility i.e. relevance. If the evidence is hearsay, then the rules on admissibility must be followed as outlined below.

18.3.1 Admissibility of hearsay – the general rule: s.114 CJA 2003

A statement not made in oral evidence is admissible as evidence of a matter stated only if:

- The evidence falls with the CJA 2003 or some other statute: s.114(1)(a);

- It is admissible under a common law rule that is preserved: s.114(1)(b) – see above 18.2;

- All the parties agree that it should be admitted: s.114(1)(c);
- The court is satisfied that it is in the interests of justice to admit it: s.114(1)(d).

The interests of justice criteria: For the first time hearsay evidence may be admitted into criminal proceedings under a general discretion of the court to admit the evidence in the interests of justice. Guidance is provided in s.114(2) as to how the court should exercise its discretion. The guidance attempts to balance the probative value of the hearsay evidence against the potential prejudice to the parties.

The statutory factors that the court must consider are:

- Probative value of statement if true;
- What other evidence could be called;
- How important statement is to case as a whole;
- Circumstances of making of statement;
- Reliability of maker of maker of statement;
- Reliability of evidence of circumstances when made;
- Whether oral evidence could be called;
- Amount of difficulty in challenging statement;
- Extent to which difficulty prejudices the other party.

In Z [2009] EWCA Crim 20 the Court of Appeal warned that courts should be cautious in their use of s.114(1)(d), especially where a witness was available to testify and none of the s.116 exceptions applied (see immediately below), since to do otherwise would undermine the purpose of having s.116. In the Z case the impact of the hearsay evidence was made greater since it was being admitted as a way of establishing alleged previous misconduct by the defendant. The Court of Appeal overturned the conviction.

18.3.2 Witnesses who are not available: s.116 CJA 2003

The CJA widens the old statutory power to admit statements in documents where the maker could not be called. Under s.116 the hearsay statement no longer has to be in a document, but in order to ensure its reliability the maker of the statement must be identified.

A statement will be admissible under s.116 if

- oral evidence would have been admissible (i.e. it cannot contain multiple hearsay); and
- the person who made the statement is identified to court's satisfaction; and
- there is a specified reason why the person who made the statement cannot attend. These reasons are that:
    - the person who made the statement is dead;
    - the person is unfit to be a witness because of their bodily or mental condition;
    - the person is outside the United Kingdom and it is not reasonably practicable to secure their attendance;
    - the person cannot be found although such steps as it is reasonably practicable to take to find them have been taken; or
    - the person does not give (or does not continue to give) oral evidence through fear.

Witnesses who are in fear: Fear is widely construed; includes fear of death or injury to another or of financial loss. Courts should not "skew justice by accepting any procolamation of fear" but should not normally try to test the basis of the fear: *Davies (Anita)* [2006] EWCA Crim 2643. Where a witness does not attend through fear the court can only grant leave for the statement to be adduced if it considers that it is in the interests of justice to do so. The court must take into account:

- the contents of statement;
- the risk of unfairness;
- the possible use of special measures to protect the witness; and
- any other relevant circumstances.

> *Doherty [2006] EWCA Crim 2716 concerned a charge of unlawful wounding following an FA Cup final. A key witness to the assault had received odd phone calls to his home number which did not make any threats but which seemed to him to indicate that the defendant or his friends had found out where he and his family lived. He said he was in fear and therefore refused to attend the trial. The Court of Appeal held that the discretion to permit the evidence to be adduced needed to be exercised with care, particularly becaue of the veiled nature of the threats. They noted that there was other evidence against the defendant, who seemed to be admitting contact but arguing either accident or self defence, and he was able to cross-examine the victim on these points. The court held that the trial judge had acted correctly in exercising his discretion to admit the evidence.*

Applying the s.116 exception:

> *[1] Jo runs a high profile local charity. She is charged with embezzling money from it. Mark overhears a woman in a shop say that she saw Jo taking the money, but she isn't going to get involved. Can Mark give evidence of this for the prosecution?*

The statement is caught by hearsay rule as it is a statement made by a person otherwise than in oral evidence. If the maker of the statement was trying to cause the receiver to believe that Jo took the money, and as the purpose of using this evidence is to prove that Jo took the money, then it is first hand oral hearsay, and could be admissible under s.116. However, the maker of the statement cannot be identified to the satisfaction of the court. The statement will not be admissible under s.116. It is unlikely that court would use its s.114(1)(d) discretion.

> *[2] The same situation as in Example 1 above, but Mark can identify the maker of the statement as a regular customer, Doreen Giles.*

Under these circumstances the statement may be admissible – but only if there is a reason why Doreen is not available to testify: e.g. dead/unfit/abroad /lost/in fear.

18.3.3 Business documents: s.117 CJA 2003

This exception enables the use of the kinds of everyday business documents which are created in their millions ever day. These sort of documents record the first hand knowledge of a person, but then enter into a business system and are passed through a number of different hands. They are therefore clearly hearsay when they emerge at the far end.

These rules apply where a document is:

- created or received by person in the course of trade/business/profession etc.; and
- the person who supplied the information had or may reasonably be supposed to have had personal knowledge of matters dealt with in statement; and

- each person through whom information was supplied received it in course of trade/business etc.

Applying s.117:

Terry is charged with theft of two cases of spirits from the warehouse where he works. The prosecution will seek to adduce evidence that there were five cases of spirits in stock at the beginning of week commencing 12th April and that during this time a further five cases were delivered, and only two cases were sent on out to customers. The stock is now two cases short, and two cases of identical spirits have been found in Terry's garage.

Almost all of this evidence will be multiple hearsay. The original maker of the statement regarding delivery of the alcohol will be the delivery driver, but the driver will have told the warehouse delivery supervisor, who in turn will pass on the information to the warehouse stock control clerk, who will input it into a computer system, where it will then be accessed by another clerk ... and so on. So long as the statement is (i) made by a person who either had or might be supposed to have had first hand knowledge, and (ii) so long as each link in the hearsay chain is acting in the course of the business etc, and (iii) the final person who made the statement is acting in the course of the business, then the statement is prima facie admissible.

Documents prepared for criminal investigations or proceedings: If the document has been created for criminal investigation or proceedings, it will only be admissible if the supplier is unavailable or cannot reasonably be expected to remember. This protects against the possibility that business documents might be fabricated to influence the investigation or the court hearing.

Thus in <u>Kamuhuza</u> 173 J.P. 55, CA, fingerprints at a burglary were not matched until five years later. The Court of Appeal held that s.116 was unlikely to apply to the police officer, since he could easily be traced because the pension authorities were likely to have his address. However the court held that the evidence could easily be admitted under s.117 since the officer was working in public service and couldn't possibly be expected to remember anything about the scene after five years.

Excluding business documents: The court retains a general discretion to exclude hearsay evidence which might otherwise be admissible under the business documents provision. Evidence must not be allowed if it is considered unreliable in view of:

- Its content;
- The source of the information;
- The way the information was supplied or received; or
- The way the document was created or received: s.117(7) CJA 2003

18.3.4 Preserving the old common law rules: s.118 CJA 2003

See 18.2 above for some of the common law exceptions. Many of these are preserved by the CJA 2003 – including rules on reputation, res gestae, confession evidence and expert evidence.

18.3.5 Multiple hearsay: s.121 CJA 2003

s.121 CJA 2003 requires that a hearsay statement is not admissible to prove that an earlier hearsay statement was made unless:

- Either statement is admissible under s.117 (business documents), or it falls within the rule about use of prior statements (discussed in Chapter 19); or

- All parties agree; or
- Court is satisfied that the value of the evidence is so high that the interests of justice require the later statement to be admitted. The court must take into account reliability of statements.

> *Simone hears Tony say that he overheard George planning the robbery of the local bank. Simone tells her friend, Jo, but then moves house and cannot be found. The prosecution wish to rely upon Jo's statement to prove that it was George who robbed the bank.*

Jo can give oral evidence but her evidence will contain multiple hearsay. The hearsay is not in the form of a business document (s.117), nor is it a previous consistent or inconsistent statement of a witness. It is could still be admissible under the general discretion in s.114(d) but because it is multiple hearsay the court must consider s.121(1)(c) – interests of justice/reliability.

18.3.6 Capability of hearsay witnesses: s.123 CJA

This new section clarifies the rules by providing that nothing in the CJA makes admissible a statement if it was made by a person who lacked capability at the time it was made. In deciding if a person is capable to give evidence the "intelligibility" test is applied – see 14.3.3.

18.3.7 Credibility issues: s.124 CJA

Section 124 applies where the maker of the statement doesn't give oral evidence. The court can take into account any evidence relevant to credibility that would have been admissible if the person had testified. Additionally, with leave of court, the parties can give evidence of any matter that could have been put in cross-examination as relevant to credibility.

> *Wayne witnesses a car crash in which one driver is killed. The other driver, Mike, is charged with death by dangerous driving. Wayne suffers from acute schizophrenia which is partially controlled by medication. Soon after giving his statement to the police he is hospitalised and is unfit to give evidence at trial. Can the prosecution rely upon Wayne's statement? The statement is hearsay, but may be admissible under s.116. Wayne's mental health at the time of the making of the statement can be taken into account under s.123 – use the YJCEA capability test. Either party may raise issues as to Wayne's credibility if his evidence is admitted: s.124.*

18.3.8 The discretion to exclude unnecessary hearsay evidence: s.126 CJA

The court may refuse to admit a hearsay statement if the court is satisfied that the case for excluding the statement outweighs the case for admitting it. The court must balance the undue waste of time in admitting the evidence as against the value of the evidence. This applies to defence or prosecution evidence.

18.3.8 Other relevant statutory provisions:

Non-contentious evidence – s.9 Criminal Justice Act 1967: Where evidence is non-contentious both prosecution and defence can seek to admit the evidence in documentary form by agreement of the other party, provided s.9 is complied with. Commonly the prosecution will serve the defence with a number of witness statements by way of advance information and will then ask which of these can be agreed as "section 9 statements". If agreed, the statement will simply be read out in court and the witness will not be called.

Section 9 statements must be signed, must have a proper s.9 declaration (stating that the witness knows that s/he is liable to prosecution if the contents are not true), and must be served on the other party before the hearing. Once served, the statement will be admissible unless the other party objects within 7 days. Remember that the onus is on you to object to the statement being read. If in doubt, object when the statements are served on you. You can always contact the prosecution in due course and agree that some of the material in non-contentious and can be agreed under s.9.

18.3.9 Hearsay and the Criminal Procedure Rules

As with character evidence, the Criminal Procedure Rules require advance notification to the court and the other parties where hearsay evidence is to be adduced. These rules are set out in Part 34 of the Criminal Procedure Rules. The formal application process is only needed where the hearsay falls into one of the following categories:

- Hearsay admissible by virtue of s.114
- Hearsay in the absence of a witness: s.116
- Multiple hearsay: s.121.

The requirement for notification does not therefore arise in relation to hearsay under s.118 (which includes the old common law rules – such as confession evidence) or under ss.117, 119 or 120.

The notice requirements are broadly similar to those for character evidence (see 17.3.4 above), with paper applications and provision for each party to object to the applications.

[18.4] HUMAN RIGHTS ISSUES

18.4.1 Article 6 and hearsay

Article 6(3)(d) of the European Convention gives the defendant the right to "examine and have examined" the witnesses against him. The Strasbourg court has made clear that this will not always require live evidence to be called, provided that the defendant has an effective opportunity to challenge the hearsay evidence: see for example *Kostovski v Netherlands* [1990] 12 EHRR 434.

This judgement was considered by the Court of Appeal in *Thomas and Flannagan* (1998) Crim LR 887, where the court stated that the domestic hearsay provisions were Convention compliant. In particular the court considered the strength of the evidence against the defendants, and the fact that the witness's evidence had been appropriately challenged, his credibility considered, and appropriate warnings given to the jury.

Difficulty has arisen where hearsay evidence is the sole or decisive evidence against the defendant. The ECtHR in *Al-Khawaja and Tahery v UK* [2009] ECHR 26766/05 found a breach of article 6. The Supreme Court has considered the Strasbourg judgment (remember that under s.2 Human Rights Act they are not bound to follow it – only to take it into account), and has concluded that current hearsay regime in the Criminal Justice Act 2003 is compliant with Article 6: *Horncastle* [2009] UKSC 14. Meanwhile the *Al-Khawaja* judgment is being appealed to a Grand Chamber of the ECtHR.

HEARSAY

A statement which is not made in oral evidence in the proceedings which is adduced as evidence of any matter stated in it.

Hearsay will only be admissible if (s.114(1) CJA 2003): (a) it falls with a statutory exception; (b) it is an old common law exception preserved by s.118 (for example: confessions, res gestae); (c) the parties agree to admit it; or (d) the court exercises its discretion to admit it.

s.114(1)(d): the general discretion to admit hearsay even if it would otherwise not be admissible provided it is in the interests of justice to do so. See s.114(2) for the statutory tests to apply.

CONFESSIONS

s.82 PACE: any statement wholly or partly adverse to the maker.

Admissible against the maker only.

See flowchart covering ss.76/78 (following Chapter 16).

RES GESTAE

"part of the story"

Generally statements made in close association with an unusual, startling or dramatic event. Either part of the transaction or fairly contemporaneous. The spontaneity is thought to reduce the risk of the statement being concocted.

STATUTORY EXCEPTIONS

ss. 116 and 117 CJA 2003: see below. Remember also **s.9 CJA 1967:** non-controversial statements in a proper format. Must be served on other side who then have 7 days to object.

Note the **s.126** discretion to exclude hearsay evidence if the case for excluding the statement outweighs the case for admitting it.

S.116

1. First-hand hearsay only

2. oral or documentary but the maker must be identified

3. and the maker cannot attend because

- they are outside the UK and it is not reasonably practicable to secure their attendance;
- they cannot be found;
- they are dead
- they are unfit to attend
- they are in fear, but only if the court grants leave.

S.117

1. Permits multiple hearsay, provided:

2. in a document created/received by a person in course of business, trade, profession etc.

3. and any intermediaries are similarly in course of business etc.

4. and reasonable inference that original eye witness had personal knowledge.

Special rules where the document was prepared for potential criminal proceedings.

Discretion to exclude documents if reliability is doubtful.

Hearsay – test yourself questions

[The answers to these questions are set out in Appendix A at the back of this book]

[1]   Under s.116 Criminal Justice Act 2003, a reason is required why the original maker of the statement cannot be called.

Which one of the following is <u>not</u> a s.116 reason?

(a)   The witness cannot be found although all reasonably practicable steps to find them have been taken.

(b)   The witness is dead.

(c)   The witness is outside the UK and it is not reasonably practicable to secure their attendance.

(d)   The statement was given to a police officer.

[2]   Consider the following propositions concerning the Criminal Justice Act 2003.

i.   s.117 applies to records compiled as part of a business or commercial enterprise only.

ii.   Under s.117 Criminal Justice Act 2003 multiple hearsay will be permitted, but each person through whom the information is passed must be acting in the course of a trade, business, profession etc.

iii.   Documents will be inadmissible under s.117 if they have been compiled either as part of the pending criminal proceedings or as part of a criminal investigation.

Which of these propositions are correct?

(a)   All of them.

(b)   ii only.

(c)   ii and iii only.

(d)   iii only.

[3]   Westchurch Central School was the subject of an arson attack which caused serious damage. At the time Neville made an oral statement to the police confirming that he had seen Kel near the premises at the time with a petrol can. Kel has now been charged with the offence. Neville has now told the police that he is not prepared to give a written statement or to attend court to testify because his son has been threatened with serious harm if he does so. The prosecution wishes to adduce his oral statement at trial.

Consider the following propositions:

i.   The statement may be admissible under s.116(2)(e) since Neville is "in fear" and "fear" includes fear of injury to another.

ii.   Where a statement may be admissible under s.116(2)(e) the court can only grant leave for the statement to be admitted if it is in the interests of justice for it to be admitted.

iii.   Because the statement was made to a police officer by a person who might reasonably be supposed to have had personal knowledge of the facts it may also be admissible under s.117 since the officer is acting in the course of an "occupation".

Which of these propositions is correct?

(a) i only.

(b) ii and iii only.

(c) i and ii only.

(d) iii only.

[4] Zahir is arrested and charged with theft, the allegation being that he shoplifted a number of items from his local supermarket. Consider the following items of evidence:

i. A stock book compiled by the supermarket stock manager, based on stock input figures from deliveries staff in the supermarket loading bay.

ii. A bus ticket which was in Zahir's pocket when he was arrested and which indicates that a £1.30 fare for a bus journey in the town centre was paid for at the time when Zahir is alleged to have been in the supermarket two miles away.

iii. A letter from the principal of the sixth form college which Zahir attends confirming that he was teaching Zahir on the morning when the thefts are said to have taken place, but stating that the principal cannot attend trial as he intends to be on holiday at the time.

Which of the above items might be admissible under s.116 or 117 CJA 2003?

(a) i and iii only.

(b) i only.

(c) ii and iii only.

(d) i and ii only.

CHAPTER 19

RELIABILITY ISSUES

> This chapter covers:
>
> Corroboration and other forms of supporting evidence.
>
> Collateral issues and previous statements.
>
> Memory refreshing.
>
> Opinion evidence.

[19.1] CORROBORATION

Strictly speaking "corroboration" means that the evidence of a particular witness must be supported by independent testimony which affects the accused by connecting him to the crime: *Baskerville* [1916] 2 KB 658. Almost all the formal rules of corroboration were abolished some time ago, although corroboration is still required in cases of treason, perjury and speeding.

19.1.1 The old rules

Corroboration *used to be* required wherever an accomplice was giving evidence for the prosecution (an accomplice was either a participant in the offence, or a handler of stolen goods in theft cases), or in sex cases. There were also various situations where the judge might give a warning that the witness had their own purpose to serve (also known as *Prater* warnings). This was a discretionary warning that the judge could give where, e.g. a co-accused gave evidence against another defendant on his own behalf (i.e. not for the prosecution) and the jury could be warned to treat such evidence with caution.

19.1.2 *Makanjuola* warnings

The old corroboration rules were abolished by s.32 Criminal Justice and Public Order Act 1994 and the Court of Appeal moved quickly to issue guidelines to prevent the old system from being re-introduced as a matter of practice. The lead case is *Makanjuola* [1995] 1 WLR 1348 where the court laid down a number of principles:

1. *There is no need to give a warning simply because the witness is an accomplice or a complainant in a sexual offence.*

2. *Warnings are now purely at the judge's discretion. Whether he gives a warning, and in what terms he gives it, will depend on all the circumstances of the case, including the nature and quality of the witness's evidence.*

3. *In some cases it might be appropriate for a warning to be given, but there would need to be evidence to show that the witness's testimony might be unreliable.*

4. *Any discussion concerning warnings should take place in the absence of the jury.*

> 5. *Any warning would be part of the judge's general review of the evidence.*
> 6. *The terms of any warning were a matter for the judge. "The whole florid regime" of the old corroboration rules had been abolished.*
> 7. *The Court of Appeal would not interfere with the judge's discretion unless it was <u>Wednesbury</u> unreasonable.*

The court gave an example of how a judge might approach the issue:

> *Where ... the witness has been shown to be unreliable, [the judge] may consider it necessary to urge caution. In a more extreme case, if the witness is shown to have lied, to have made previous false complaints, or to bear the defendant some grudge, a stronger warning may be thought appropriate and the judge may suggest it would be wise to look for some supporting material before acting on the impugned witness's evidence.*

So we now have a simple, wholly discretionary system. You should, however, consider the need for some kind of warning where you are faced with any witness who has an ulterior motive, or any witnesses who may otherwise be unreliable (children, the sick etc.). As *Makanjuola* made clear, it will be rare for the court to intervene with a trial judge's discretion, but there will be cases where it will do so.

> *In the case of <u>Walker</u> [1996] Crim LR 742 W was accused of a number of counts of raping his cohabitee's young daughter, then aged 11/12. He completely denied the offence. The daughter subsequently went to the police with her mother, while W was awaiting trial, and withdrew the complaint, saying that she had lied. She then went back 5 days later and returned to her previous complaint. At trial this was referred to in speeches by counsel, but the judge made no reference to it in his summing-up and gave the jury no warning about the dangers of the daughter as a witness. Appeal allowed: the matter should have been dealt with in summing up, and a <u>Makanjuola</u> direction should have been considered.*

19.1.3 Disputed identification evidence: the *Turnbull* warning

Identification evidence needs to be treated with special caution. This is because a number of miscarriages of justice have shown the dangers that arise from honest witnesses who mistakenly identify an innocent person. This propensity arises from our generally poor memory for faces. The principles are laid down in the case of *Turnbull* [1977] QB 224, CA.

If the case depends wholly or substantially on identification evidence, the jury should be given a "special need for caution" warning. The judge should explain the reason why such a warning is needed (the danger of honest but mistaken identifications) and explain that testimony from honest but mistaken witnesses is particularly dangerous since the witness will generally be convincing.

The circumstances of the identification: The jury should be directed to look closely at all the circumstances of the original observation and subsequent identification: for example:

- how long did the witness see the defendant for?
- how far away was the defendant?
- what was the lighting like?
- was the observation impeded in any way?
- was the identification by recognition or of a stranger?
- how long was there between the observation and the subsequent identification to the police?

Weaknesses in the evidence: The judge should identify any discrepancies between the first description by the witness and the suspect's actual appearance. Note that Code D requires the police to preserve and subsequently provide to the defence such initial descriptions. The jury must be reminded of any weaknesses in the identification witnesses' evidence.

The quality of the identification: If the identification quality is good, the case can be left to the jury even if identification is the sole evidence – but a special need for caution warning must still be given. If the identification quality is poor (for example, a fleeting glance) the judge should withdraw the case and direct an acquittal unless there is other evidence to support the correctness of the identification. (This other evidence is sometimes referred to as "corroboration" but corroboration is a term of art and has a technical and restricted meaning. Here the jury need merely seek other evidence, which supports the identification.) The judge should indicate to the jury what other evidence there is that could be used as support in this way.

When does *Turnbull* apply? *Turnbull* applies to cases of disputed visual identification of suspects. *Turnbull* does not, for example, apply to identification of cars, or to identification of voices. *Turnbull* will not generally apply where the defendant does not dispute his presence at the scene – but a *Turnbull* warning may be appropriate if, for example, the scene is particularly crowded: see for example, *Slater* [1995] Crim. L. R. 244.

Identification from video footage: Video evidence is treated as direct evidence. The jury will watch the film and decide for themselves. In *Blenkinsop* [1995] 1 Cr App R 7 the Court of Appeal held that a general *Turnbull* warning remained appropriate in such situations.

[19.2] COLLATERAL QUESTIONS AND CROSS-EXAMINATION

Collateral questions are questions in cross-examination which are not designed to test the substance of the evidence the witness puts forward, but which go to secondary issues such as the witness's credit – i.e. whether they should be believed.

19.2.1 Collateral questions: the general rule

The general rule is that answers to questions as to credit are final and cannot be challenged.

> *In the case of Edwards [1991] 1 WLR 207 a number of the police (from the West Midlands Serious Crime Squad) had been involved in related trials where there had been acquittals of the defendants after evidence had suggested that notes of interview were inaccurate. Some appeared to have been rewritten at a later time – with added admissions (!).*
>
> *The court held that the officers could be cross-examined on whether they had given evidence at the earlier trials, and whether there had been acquittals after the fabrication of confessions had been raised as an issue. There was sufficient connection between the police evidence and the juries' decisions to justify cross-examination. However, since this went only to the officers' credit, their replies would be final and could not be contradicted by evidence in rebuttal.*

[In any event, even if this evidence were now admissible, it would presumably be subject to s.100 CJA 2003 since it would be evidence of reprehensible conduct by someone other than a defendant.]

However there are a number of exceptions to the rule against rebuttal evidence on collateral issues:

- witnesses who deny they have previous convictions;
- witnesses who deny bias;

- witnesses who deny there is a mental or physical disability affecting their reliability;
- witnesses who deny they have a reputation for untruthfulness;
- witnesses who have made previous inconsistent statements.

If the witness denies any of these matters the advocate is entitled to prove them. (Note additionally that there are special rules limiting the cross-examination of rape victims concerning their previous sexual experience with persons other than the accused.) Most of these exceptions are relatively straightforward. The law is slightly more complex where a witness is alleged to have made a previous statement which is inconsistent with their testimony at court. This needs to be looked at in more detail.

19.2.2 Previous inconsistent statements and hostile witnesses

The general rule is that you cannot cross-examine your own witnesses, whether by asking leading questions or by calling evidence to prove previous inconsistent statements, bad character or bias.

A witness who fails to come up to proof: If a witness fails to give the evidence you were expecting (an "unfavourable witness"), you cannot normally cross-examine them. They have simply "failed to come up to proof".

Where one of your witnesses fails to come up to proof, you may need to consider calling another witness (if you have one) to deal with the matter better. Alternatively you could consider untilising the memory refreshing provisions in s. 139 CJA 2003 and ask the witness to refresh their memory from their pre-prepared statement (see 19.3 below). You will only be allowed to challenge the evidence of your own witness if you apply to the court for the witness to be declared "a hostile witness".

Hostile witnesses: A hostile witness is one who is not desirous of telling the truth at the instance of the party calling them, or who displays "a hostile animus" to that party. It is for the judge to decide if a witness is hostile. Generally the advocate should not immediately apply to the judge for the witness to be declared hostile simply because they are giving evidence which contradicts their earlier statement, but should first invite the witness to refresh their memory. If the witness continues to put forward a different version of events, and the advocate is of the view that this shows the witness is not desirous of telling the truth, the advocate can then apply to the judge for the witness to be treated as hostile

Once a witness is declared "hostile", the advocate who called them may ask them leading questions and may ask them about (and prove) previous inconsistent statements: s.3 Criminal Procedure Act 1865.

Other parties' witnesses and previous inconsistent statements: The procedure here is governed by s.4 and s.5 Criminal Procedure Act 1865. s.4 provides that where a witness being cross-examined does not admit the previous inconsistent statement, they must be given details as to when they are supposed to have made it before proof can be provided that they did make it. s.5 provides that where the previous inconsistent statement is written, they can be cross-examined without showing them the statement, unless the advocate intends to put in the previous written statement as evidence. If the statement is going to be used in this way, then the witness must be shown the relevant parts first.

Effect of a previous inconsistent statement: s.119 CJA 2003: The previous statement is admissible as evidence of any matter stated of which oral evidence by the witness would be admissible.

> *In Joyce and Joyce [2005] EWCA Crim 1785 two men leapt out of a car and fired shots. Three prosecution witnesses identified the defendants to the police but at trial all three withdrew their statements and put forward unlikely explanations as to why they now believed their original statements to be wrong. The Court of Appeal held that the judge was right to direct the jury that they could (i) accept the oral evidence as true; (ii) accept the prior statements as true; or (iii) disbelieve both sets of accounts.*

The effect of a previous inconsistent statement is therefore that it undermines the credibility of the witness (because they are now saying something different to what they said before) but is also itself potentially admissible evidence as to the facts. A previous inconsistent statement made by the accused may also be admissible and this can include statements written in a court case management form (PCMH form): *R v Newell* [2012] EWCA Crim 650.

19.2.3 Previous consistent statements

Previous *consistent* statements logically prove relatively little. The fact that your client or any other witness has previously said exactly the same thing as they are now saying in court is normally irrelevant: it establishes nothing more than that they are a consistent liar. Under s.120 CJA 2003 earlier consistent statements may be admissible if any one of the following grounds is made out:

To rebut an allegation that the oral evidence is fabricated:

> *Jim is arrested on suspicion of robbery. When his wife is told about the allegation, she says that Jim was at home the whole time on the day in question. When she is giving evidence at trial, prosecution suggests that she has made up her story at a later date in order to give her husband an alibi. She would then be able to rebut this suggestion by showing that she has been giving this account since the beginning.*

Where it is a memory-refreshing document: This rule only applies where a witness uses a document to refresh their memory and is then cross-examined <u>outside</u> the passage which they have used to refresh their memory.

> *PC Smith uses her notebook to refresh her memory while testifying about a shoplifting offence. The defence advocate looks through the notebook and notices some useful material about Smith's earlier actions which he then raises with the officer in cross-examination. The result is that the whole document now becomes admissible.*

Where the earlier statement falls within one of three conditions: This is a very wide provision which permits the use of an earlier statement if the witness testifies that he made the earlier statement and that the earlier statement is true, provided either that:

- The statement identifies or confirms a person, place or thing – e.g. car number plate; or

- The statement was made when the incident was fresh and the witness cannot now reasonably be expected to remember the matter stated; or

- It is evidence of recent complaint: this provision only applies to victims, and the complaint must not have been made as a result of a threat or a promise.

> *Jemima sees two men jumping into a car and driving away at high speed after a robbery at Tesco's. She writes down the number plate of the car at the time. This is an earlier statement which is likely to be admissible under either of the first two conditions. But Jemima must testify at the trial.*
> *Rebecca is assaulted by her teacher who slaps her across the face. Rebecca immediately rings her mother to tell her what happened. This is likely to be admissible as evidence of recent complaint.*

Previous consistent statements will admissible as evidence of the truth of their contents. These provisions are potentially very wide, and seem to overlap with the memory-refreshing provisions.

[19.3] MEMORY REFRESHING DOCUMENTS

A person who is giving oral evidence may at any stage in the course of doing so refresh his memory: s. 139 Criminal Justice Act 2003. The document from which the witness refreshes their memory must be made or verified at an earlier time. The witness must:

- state in their evidence that the document records their recollection of the matter at the earlier time; and
- that their recollection of the matter is likely to have been substantially better at the earlier time than it is at the time that they are testifying.

There is no requirement that a witness must have stumbled in giving their evidence before the judge can allow them to refresh their memory. Indeed, in *Mangena* [2009] EWCA Crim 2535 the court held that it would be unusual not to be able to use a statement to refresh one's memory.

The statement must be made available for inspection: The document must be produced for the inspection of the court, and the opposing advocate may inspect it. Provided the opposing advocate in his or her cross-examination does not stray outside the passages used for refreshing the witness's memory, the document is not itself evidence. If the advocate cross-examines on parts of the document that have not been so used, then the whole document will be admissible.

Police officers and their notebooks: The most common memory-refreshing document is the police officer's notebook, and many police witnesses will automatically ask permission to refresh their memory from the notebook as soon as they enter the witness box. You should always inspect the notebook itself. You can look through the whole notebook, but you must make sure you do not accidentally make the whole notebook evidence by cross-examining "off the piste" – i.e. on matters not referred to in the memory-refreshing part. If you do cross-examine outside the scope of the relevant "memory-refreshing" part the whole document will be admitted in evidence.

[19.4] OPINIONS AND EXPERTS

Opinion evidence is generally inadmissible since the opinions of witnesses are largely irrelevant. The witness is called to give evidence as to facts perceived. It is for the court to draw its conclusions. In some circumstances the witness's opinion may simply be a convenient means of conveying what he saw. Thus a statement that someone was drunk, or was speeding, will be opinion but will generally be an acceptable way of stating the various elements of what the witness saw - or smelt.

19.4.1 Expert opinion

In some situations the court may need assistance in clarifying matters. Experts will often be used to deal with medical or scientific matters. Handwriting and video analysis by experts is also common, as is expert evidence from professionals (such as accountants). A particular problem may arise, especially in relation to psychiatric evidence, since the dividing line between matters that call for expert assistance and matters that do not is not always clear. In *Turner* [1975] QB 834 the court made clear that the mere fact that an expert has impressive qualifications does not give him any greater expertise to rule on *normal* behaviour than anyone else, and there would be a danger that the jury might feel bound to accept the expert's opinion. An expert can only therefore give evidence as to matters that call for his expertise.

The procedural rules relating to the use of experts can be found in Part 33 of the Criminal Procedure Rules.

19.4.2 Who is an expert?

An expert is someone who is suitably qualified to assist the court. The qualifications do not have to be formal, but it may be difficult to satisfy the court if they are not. Note that an expert's evidence is treated similarly to that of any other witness, and it is purely a matter for the jury as to whether they wish to accept it.

> *In Edwards [2001] EWCA Crim 2185 Edwards had been caught in possession of 29 ecstasy tablets. His defence was that he had a very heavy habit and had indeed consumed 20 tablets that day alone. He wanted to call a worker from a drugs charity to say that users could become tolerant to the drug and could consume large numbers of tablets in this way. The CPS sought to call a detective sergeant to say that this level of consumption was impossible without causing serious harm. The trial judge ruled that neither the defence nor prosecution witness could be called. Neither was an expert. Their evidence was mere hearsay. The Court of Appeal agreed.*

Part 33 of the Criminal Procedure Rules lays down rules concerning the content of expert reports, including a requirement for the expert to set out the basis of his or her expertise. There is a provision which permits the courts to require opposing experts to meet prior to trial to discuss areas of dispute, and for the court to appoint a single joint expert for two or more defendants.

19.4.3 Hearsay and experts?

Experts will often base their opinions on their experience and on information from articles and journals and the like. This information is not treated as hearsay, since it is not the evidence before the court; it is often referred to as the "secondary facts", and it is the basis for the expert's opinion, the opinion itself being the primary evidence. Note, however, that primary evidence on which the expert is basing his opinion will need to be proved in the usual way.

Under the CJA 2003 hearsay rules, the expert is permitted to rely upon the evidence of others who have a personal knowledge (for example, their lab assistants who actually carried out the tests) but there is a discretion for the court to exclude the evidence, taking into account various factors, including the possibility of calling the people with first hand knowledge: s.127 CJA 2003.

19.4.4 Disclosure of expert evidence

The prosecution will disclose expert evidence on which they rely as part of the advance information, or as part of the normal rules concerning used material. In a Crown Court case any party relying on expert evidence must give the other side notice in writing of the expert finding or opinion. Failure to give such notice may lead to the trial judge refusing to admit the evidence. Expert reports are admissible in criminal proceedings whether or not the expert attends – but if the expert is not going to give oral evidence the report is admissible only with the leave of the court: s.30 Criminal Justice Act 1988.

CORROBORATION

Corroboration is the requirement for certain types of evidence to be supported or confirmed by other, independent evidence. Most of the requirements for formal corroboration have been abolished. Even though corroboration may have been abolished, issues as to the reliability of certain types of witness still remain.

Whether a corroboration warning should be given is entirely at the discretion of the judge: *Makanjuola* [1995] 2 Cr App R 469

IDENTIFICATION

The danger of the honest but mistaken identification.

In *Turnbull*, the court provided guidelines for such cases:

(i) the judge must warn the jury of the "special need for caution" and explain why;

(ii) the jury must be told to look at all the circumstance of the identification (e.g. light, distance, time, obstructions, whether an identification by recognition, etc.);

(iii) the judge must tell the jury of any weaknesses in the evidence;

(iv) the prosecution must make the defence aware of any discrepancies;

(v) where the quality of the identification is poor, the judge should withdraw the case, unless there is other evidence to support the correctness of the identification (e.g. the defendant's subsequent behaviour etc.).

Turnbull is only relevant where identification is in issue.

PREVIOUS STATEMENTS

Consistent statements: generally not admissible but CJA introduced a number of exceptions:

- memory refreshing documents where there has been cross-examination of the document as a whole;
- to rebut allegations of recent fabrication; or
- to confirm details of person/place/thing – or made when memory better – or evidence of recent complaint.

Refreshing memory: provided document made at an earlier time when memory was better.

Inconsistent statements: From your own witness - call other evidence. You can only "impeach" your witness if you have them declared "hostile" - see below.

From other side's witness: see ss.4 and 5 Criminal Procedure Act 1865. If witness does not "distinctly admit" they made the prior (written or oral) statement, you may ask them if they made the statement and if they deny it, prove it. If the statement is in writing and you intend to contradict the witness, you must first draw their attention to those elements of it.

HOSTILE WITNESSES

A witness not desirous of telling the truth. Apply to judge for witness to be declared hostile and then s.3 Criminal Procedure Act 1865 permits the previous statement to be proved (with leave of the court), but witness must first be asked whether he has made the statement.

Reliability – test yourself questions

[The answers to these questions are set out in Appendix A at the back of this book]

[1] Consider the following situations:

　i.　A Co-Accused gives evidence against the defendant.

　ii.　The complaint relates to matters that took place over twenty years ago.

　iii.　The witness has a purpose of his own to serve in giving evidence.

In which of the above circumstances must the judge give a corroboration warning to the jury?

　(a)　All of them.

　(b)　i and ii only.

　(c)　ii and iii only.

　(d)　None of them.

[2] A *Turnbull* warning will be given where there is disputed visual identification of the suspect. Consider the following matters:

　i.　the time and circumstances of the original sighting;

　ii.　whether it is an identification by recognition;

　iii.　how long elapsed between the sighting and any subsequent identification.

Which of these propositions should be part of the *Turnbull* direction?

　(a)　All of them.

　(b)　i and ii only.

　(c)　ii and iii only.

　(d)　None of them.

[3] Which one of the following propositions is not correct?

　(a)　A previous inconsistent statement may go to the credibility of the witness and may also be evidence of the facts contained in it.

　(b)　A previous consistent statement has little or no probative value and will not normally be admissible.

　(c)　Witnesses will be permitted to refresh their memories provided that the document was made by them or verified by them at an earlier time and they state in evidence that this is the case and that their recollection is likely to have been substantially better at the earlier time.

　(d)　An advocate will not be permitted to cross-examine their own witness unless the court rules that the witness is hostile.

[4] Jerome witnessed an assault by Christine on her husband, Sean, on 5th January. On 10th January, Jerome jotted down notes about what he had seen ("the January statement"). Because of Sean's injuries the trial is then delayed, so in September Jerome writes up a statement so that he can keep his recollection fresh ("the September statement"). In any event the trial is not held until the summer of the following year (some eighteen months after the initial incident). At trial Jerome wants to refresh his memory in the witness box from his earlier statements.

Which one of the following is correct?

(a) Jerome will be able to refresh his memory from the January statement as it is substantially contemporaneous; the September statement is unlikely to be usable in this way because of the gap of time in writing down the matters.

(b) Neither statement can be used for memory refreshing as they will be hearsay.

(c) Both statements will be usable for memory refreshing provided that Jerome testifies that the statements record his earlier recollection at a time when his recollection of events was substantially better.

(d) The January statement will be usable as Jerome's recollection would have been substantially better at that time. The September statement will only be admissible if it is a previous inconsistent statement.

CHAPTER 20

PRIVILEGE

> This chapter covers:
>
> The principles and effect of privilege.
>
> Lawyer client privilege and its implications.
>
> Public Interest Immunity.

[20.1] PRIVILEGE – THE BASIC PRINCIPLES

Privilege is the principle by which certain evidence is protected from production at court. Where privilege arises, a witness cannot be compelled to answer questions on matters that are subject to privilege; a party cannot be forced to disclose privileged documents.

The two principle forms of privilege that need to be considered in a criminal context are:

   1. the privilege against self-incrimination; and

   2. lawyer-client privilege.

This chapter also briefly considers a third form of privilege – public policy immunity (PII) – which may sometimes be raised by the prosecution in refusing to provide certain information to the defence.

20.1.1 The effect of privilege

Refusal to testify or produce evidence: Once privilege has been successfully claimed, a person is entitled to refuse to divulge the information that is subject to privilege, whether in his testimony or by producing documents containing the information. The witness commits no offence by refusing to divulge privileged information, and cannot be compelled to do so. Note that in some circumstances, in particular in relation to Serious Fraud Office investigations, there may be statutory provisions, which require the suspect to answer questions (hence removing his privilege against self-incrimination).

> *In Saunders v United Kingdom (1997) 23 EHRR 313 S successfully argued at the ECHR that he had been denied a fair trial under article 6 on the basis that statements which had been obtained from him by DTI inspectors in exercise of their Companies Act powers had been used against him at trial. Note that the Youth Justice and Criminal Evidence Act 1999 now contains provisions that mean that such answers which have been obtained under such compulsion will not be admissible at trial unless first raised by the defence: s.59, Schedule 3*

Although a party may not be able to force the witness to disclose privileged information, the party is still able to adduce evidence from non-privileged sources to prove the facts in issue.

Failure to claim privilege: Privilege is a matter for the person who is entitled to claim it. A person can always waive his right to claim privilege and no other person can interfere with his decision to do so.

20.1.2 Waiver of privilege

Once privilege is waived, the evidence is no longer protected and can be adduced in the normal manner before the court. Once waived, privilege is lost in respect of the communication in issue. Indeed, in some cases the court may take the view that the witness has impliedly waived privilege in respect of other communications as well.

Severability: In some cases it may be possible to show that a person has waived privilege in respect of one part of a communication, but that the rest of the communication is "severable", so that privilege remains. For example, if you accidentally gave the first page of your client's statement to the prosecution, would privilege be waived in respect of the whole document, or simply the first page? In *Great Atlantic Insurance v Home Insurance* [1981] 1 WLR 529 the plaintiffs in a civil matter were held to have waived privilege over the whole of a document by revealing two paragraphs, as the whole document dealt with the same subject matter; the two paragraphs were not therefore "severable".

Waiver and police station advice: You will recall that the problem here arises from dicta in *Condron* [1997] 1 Cr App R 185. In the *Condron* judgement the rationale for the decision is set out very clearly:

> *Communications between an accused person and his solicitor prior to interviews by the police are subject to legal professional privilege. But the privilege can be waived by the client, though not the solicitor. If an accused person gives as a reason for not answering questions that he has been advised by his solicitor not to do so, that advice in our judgment does not amount to a waiver of privilege. But equally, for the reasons which we have given, that bare assertion is unlikely by itself to be regarded as a sufficient reason for not mentioning matters relevant to the defence. So it will be necessary, if the accused wishes to invite the court not to draw an adverse inference, to go further and state the basis or reason for the advice. Although the matter was not fully argued it seems to us that once that is done that it may well amount to a waiver of privilege, so that the accused, or if his solicitor is also called, the solicitor, can be asked whether there were any other reasons for the advice and the nature of the advice given, so as to explore whether the advice may also have been given for tactical reasons.*

Note that although the court states that only the client can waive privilege, a solicitor will often be taken to have waived privilege with his client's implied consent. *Condron* was confirmed in *Bowden* [2000] 2 All E.R. 418, where the court confirmed that a solicitor or a defendant who put forward an explanation for the advice given in an earlier privileged conversation would waive that privilege, and could therefore be called to give evidence as to the full content of the conversation.

Accidental waiver: The leading case remains *Tompkins* (1977) Cr App R 181, where a note from T to his barrister fell to the floor of the court and was mistakenly passed to the prosecuting counsel by a defence representative who picked it up. The note contradicted evidence which T had already given. The prosecution handed the note to T when he was in the witness box and asked him if he wanted to change his answer. As a result he changed his account. The Court of Appeal held that there had been no improper conduct. *Tompkins* has been followed in subsequent cases of mistaken waiver, but note always that there will still be the possibility of arguing that the evidence should be excluded as having an adverse impact on the fairness of the proceedings under s.78 PACE.

[20.2] SELF INCRIMINATION

The rule is that no one is bound to answer any question if the answer thereto would, in the opinion of the judge, have a tendency to expose the deponent to any criminal charge, penalty or forfeiture which the judge regards as reasonably likely to be preferred or sued for. [*per* Lord Goddard, in *Blunt v Park Lane Hotel* [1942] 2 All ER 187, at 188.]

Where a person in a criminal matter is at risk of being exposed to a future penalty or charge, often the judge will warn them of their privilege against self-incrimination.

Various statutes displace the privilege against self-incrimination. The Companies Act provisions have already been mentioned in connection with *Saunders v UK* (see 20.1.1 above). There are also provisions under the Children Act, in respect of proceedings where the court is dealing with the care, supervision or protection of a child. The Children Act provisions make clear that no evidence given can then be used against the witness, other than in proceedings for perjury. As has been mentioned, the Youth Justice and Criminal EvidenceAct 1999 now makes similar provision for Companies Act and other statutory exceptions. For a full discussion of the use of answers from compelled questioning see *Brown v Stott*, discussed at Chapter 15 above.

[20.3] LAWYER-CLIENT PRIVILEGE

In *R v Special Commissioner ex p Morgan Grenfell & Co Ltd* [2002] UKHL 21, Lord Hoffmann described legal professional privilege as "a fundamental human right long established in the common law". Legal professional privilege covers communications between lawyer and client for the giving or obtaining of legal advice, and also communications between lawyer or client and any third party where the dominant purpose is in relation to pending or contemplated litigation.

In the criminal context, it is lawyer-client privilege which ensures that your client cannot be required to reveal the content of any discussions between himself and his legal advisers. It therefore means that you cannot be called to give evidence and required by the prosecution to explain the content of the discussions that may have taken place in the police station. This protection is, of course, lost as soon as privilege is waived: see 20.1.2 above.

The categories of document which are protected: s.10 PACE sets out the meaning of "items subject to legal privilege", i.e. those documents that are protected from search and seizure by the police. These are:

(a) communications between a professional legal adviser and his client or any person representing his client made in connection with the giving of legal advice to the client

(b) communications between a professional legal adviser and his client or any person representing his client or between such an adviser or his client or any such representative and any other person made in connection with or in contemplation of legal proceedings and for the purposes of such proceedings and

(c) items enclosed with or referred to in such communications and made

  (i) in connection with the giving of legal advice or

  (ii) in connection with or in contemplation of legal proceedings and for the purposes of such proceedings, when they are in the possession of a person who is entitled to possession of them.

The protection of s.10(1) applies to opinions from experts which are inextricably linked to privileged information. In *Davies* [2002] EWCA Crim 85 D had obtained a psychiatric report in an attempt to establish that he had been suffering from diminished responsibility. However the psychiatrist concluded that this was not the case. The prosecution accepted that the report was privileged but sought to call the psychiatrist to give evidence as a prosecution witness. The Court of Appeal ruled that the opinion was based to a material extent on privileged communications and should not have been admitted.

Criminal purposes: s.10(2) PACE makes clear that legal professional privilege does not extend to "items held with the intention of furthering a criminal purpose". Similarly, communications from a client which are made in furtherance of "crime or fraud" fall outside the protection of legal professional privilege: *R v Derby Magistrates' Court, ex parte B* [1996] AC 487.

> *A police station representative attended the police station to see Mr Pearson who had been arrested on suspicion of involvement in drugs offences. Pearson saw the representative and told him that there was a large sum of money hidden behind the cooker in his flat. He threatened the representative and told him to dispose of the money so that the police would not find it. The representative then told the police of the request because he was worried by the threat that had been made. The court held that this information was clearly not privileged:* see R v David Octavious Pearson [2005] EWCA Crim 1412. [Note: if you look at this case you will see that the Court of Appeal suggests that it was acceptable for the police station representative to tell the police about the threat. This is surely not the case: what about your duty of confidentiality to your client?]

Information that may establish another person's innocence: Legal professional privilege exists to ensure that an accused person can openly discuss his case with his lawyer in the knowledge that the contents of the discussions cannot be used against him. What, however, is the position where the content of those discussions may show that he has admitted an offence with which another person is now charged? Do the interests of justice mean that privilege must be displaced by the need to protect the other person?

> *In* R v Derby Magistrates' Court, ex parte B *[1996] AC 487 B had been acquitted of murder. His step-father was later charged with the offence. At the committal hearing [now abolished] the defence wanted to cross-examine B to establish what instructions he had given his solicitors when charged. The magistrates ordered B and his solicitor to produce the documentary evidence on the basis that the interests of the defendant (the step-father) outweighed the public interest in protecting legal communications. The House of Lords ruled unanimously that there was no basis for breaching the right to privilege.*

> *"If the client had to be told that his communications were only confidential so long as he had 'a recognisable interest' in preserving the confidentiality, and that some court on some future occasion might decide that he no longer had any such recognisable interest, the basis of the confidence would be destroyed or at least undermined. There may be cases where the principle will work hardship on a third party seeking to assert his innocence. But in the overall interests of the administration of justice it is better that the principle should be preserved intact."* [*per* Lord Lloyd]

[20.4] PUBLIC POLICY IMMUNITY

It is not clear whether the power of the prosecution to refuse to disclose certain categories of material is a form of privilege or is a separate element of public policy. In either case it has long been accepted that there may sometimes be a conflict between the public interest that justice be done, and the need to keep material confidential where its disclosure would be harmful to the public interest.

20.4.1 Common categories of sensitive information

Sensitive information will generally fall into one of the following categories:

1. National security

2. Internal police documents

3. Information relating to informers, observation posts and the like.

National security and the security services: The courts will generally treat a PII certificate as being conclusive on any matter of national security. There has been a tendency for a similar blanket non-disclosure where security services have been involved. Here, however, the increased use of the "security services" (particularly MI5) in domestic criminal matters will mean that the defence will have to be readier to challenge any attempts at blanket non-disclosure.

Internal police documents: There is established caselaw that most internal police communications that deal with the investigation of crime will be immune from disclosure.

Informers, observation posts etc: The basic rule has traditionally been that the prosecution cannot be forced to disclose the names of informers. This immunity seeks to ensure that the "supply of information about criminal activities does not dry up": *Hennessey* (1978) 68 Cr App R 419. There is similar protection for details of the exact location of observation posts, since disclosure will either compromise the observation post or may lead to reprisals against those who allow the police to use their property. Note however that the Human Rights Act means that judges must now approach the issue of disclosure on a case-by-case basis, rather than feeling bound by earlier caselaw: *McNally v Chief Constable of Greater Manchester Police* [2002] EWCA Civ 14. The judge must consider the balance between the public interest in maintaining the anonymity of informers and the right to a fair trial.

20.4.2 Non-disclosure of information and the CPIA

The Criminal Procedure and Investigations Act 1996 (CPIA) lays down a statutory regime for the disclosure of unused material. [The details of this regime were set out in Chapter 7 above.] Under the CPIA there is a special system for dealing with the disclosure of unused "sensitive material".

> *...sensitive material is material which the disclosure officer believes, after consulting the officer in charge of the investigation, it is not in the public interest to disclose.*

The test is therefore the same as the common law test for public interest immunity.

What happens if material is "sensitive material"? Where a prosecutor takes the view that unused material is sensitive it will be listed in a special schedule of sensitive material. This will not be disclosed to the defence. Where such material would otherwise fall to be disclosed to the defence under the prosecution disclosure test, the prosecution will have to apply to court for a PII order.

Making a "PII" application: A PII application will normally be on notice, although in exceptional circumstances the prosecution need not even tell the defence that an application is being made if giving the defence such notice would have the effect of disclosing the material. The court will then hear arguments and if it makes an order for non-disclosure it must state its reasons for doing so. The House of Lords reviewed this process in *H and C* [2004] UKHL 3 and made clear the general principle that material must be provided to the defence if it falls within the CPIA disclosure test. Even PII material can only be withheld where there is a risk of serious prejudice to an important public interest – and even then it can only be withheld if the defendant's interests can be properly protected. There may be cases where disclosure is necessary in order to protect the defendant – and then the prosecution must disclose the material or drop the case.

[20.5] HUMAN RIGHTS ISSUES

20.5.1 Waiver of privilege, inferences and article 6:

You may think that there is an argument that article 6 (right to a fair trial) may be breached since a defendant cannot prevent an inference simply by saying he has acted on legal advice, but if he explains the legal advice, he effectively waives privilege. This would appear to undermine the provision of the legal advice. However, this argument was briskly dismissed by the ECHR in *Condron v United Kingdom* (2000) 31 E.H.R.R. 1, where the court stated:

> *The Court would observe at this juncture that the fact that the applicants were subjected to cross-examination on the content of their solicitor's advice cannot be said to raise an issue of fairness under article 6 of the Convention. They were under no compulsion to disclose the advice given, other than the indirect compulsion to avoid the reason for their silence remaining at the level of a bare explanation. The applicants chose to make the content of their solicitor's advice a live issue as part of their defence. For that reason they cannot complain that the scheme of section 34 of the 1994 Act is such as to override the confidentiality of their discussions with their solicitor.*

20.5.2 The disclosure regime and article 6:

Article 6 requires "equality of arms" between the parties. This will particularly be an issue where the prosecution has access to information which is denied to the defence. The cases that have so far been to Strasbourg concern the earlier common law regime(s) for dealing with the disclosure or non-disclosure of sensitive information and these are discussed at 7.5.1 above. In the case of *Edwards and Lewis v United Kingdom* (2003) 1 WLR 3006 the ECtHR suggested that use of independent counsel might be necessary to protect the interests of defendants where material is being withheld; the position in domestic law is set out in *H and C* (see 20.4.2 above).

Privilege – test yourself questions

[The answers to these questions are set out in Appendix A at the back of this book]

[1] Which one of the following propositions about privilege is not correct?

    (a) Where evidence falls within a category protected by privilege, it need not be produced at court.

    (b) Privilege can only be waived by the person entitled to claim it, or by a person authorised by them to do so.

    (c) Privilege will only arise if there is a real possibility that the production of the evidence will lead to self-incrimination.

    (d) Once privilege is waived the protection provided by privilege is lost.

[2] Mario is charged with fraud. The offence alleged arises from Mario's activities as the director of a small family company. Mario consults with solicitors to prepare his defence, and Counsel is briefed for trial.

Consider the following categories of documents:

    i. The minutes of the company meetings.

    ii. Draft statements taken by the solicitors.

    iii. Briefs to Counsel

Which of the above categories are likely to be privileged?

    (a) All of them.

    (b) i and iii only.

    (c) ii and iii only.

    (d) ii only.

[3] Which of the following categories of information possessed by the police is likely to attract public interest immunity?

    i. The name of an informer.

    ii. The previous convictions of witnesses.

    iii. A police covert surveillance tactical manual.

    (a) All of the above.

    (b) i and iii only.

    (c) ii and iii only.

    (d) ii only.

Appendix A

Test Yourself Answers

Appendix A
Test yourself questions – the answers

Chapter 2: Stop Search and Arrest

[1] The correct answer is (d). Section 1(2) of PACE entitles an officer to search any person or vehicle and anything which is in or on a vehicle.

(a) is incorrect because it suggests that the test is whether an officer is "likely" to find a stolen of prohibited article; in fact the test is whether the officer has "reasonable grounds for suspecting" that he will find stolen or prohibited articles. This is different, since "likely" suggests that the test is objective, whereas the test of "reasonable grounds for suspicion" is in part a subjective test.

(b) is wrong: it is right to say that offensive weapons and bladed instruments would be included in the "prohibited articles", but so are articles made or adapted for use in various dishonesty offences, and articles made, adapted or intended for use in criminal damage offences. In some circumstances it is also possible to search for fireworks.

(c) is also wrong: the power under s.1 is to stop and search; there is no requirement to arrest the person first.

[2] The correct answer is (c). Code A 2.3 provides that reasonable suspicion may exist where a person is seen on the street at night obviously trying to hide something. Here Jim is not carrying an item but his actions at that place and that time may give rise to a reasonable suspicion that he is in possession of a stolen or prohibited article.

Both (a) and (b) are incorrect because propositions (i) and (ii) are wrong. Code A 2.2 states that "reasonable suspicion can never be supported on the basis of personal factors alone without reliable supporting intelligence or information or some specific behaviour by the person concerned." A 2.2 specifically refers to a person's previous convictions, their age and their appearance as matters that <u>cannot</u> be used "alone or in combination" as the sole basis for a search. (d) is incorrect as proposition (iii) was correct.

[3] (a) is false: an officer may question the person before carrying out a search in order to see if there is a satisfactory explanation which may make a search unnecessary: A 2.9.

(b) is correct: see s.2(3) PACE.

(c) is false. There is no time limit as such. A 3.3 states that the length of time must be reasonable and must not extend beyond the time taken for the search. Code A provides that the time must be "kept to a minimum".

(d) is true: see A 3.5. If on reasonable grounds a more thorough search is required it must be done out of the public view.

[4] ((d) is correct – propositions (a), (b) and (c) are all incorrect.

(a) is correct as far as it goes – but fails to deal with the "necessity" test for any citizen's arrest under s.24A – it is therefore incomplete. (b) is wrong since it notes only part of the necessity test – but fails to deal with two further factors – namely that it may also be necessary to arrest a person in order to prevent them from making off before a constable can assume responsibility for them – and also that in all cases of citizen's arrest, there is a condition that it appears to the person making the arrest that it was not reasonably practicable for a constable to make the arrest instead.

(c) is incorrect – since the power of arrest under s.24A arises both where a person is in the acting of committing an indictable offence (or where there are reasonable grounds for believing that he is), but also where an indictable offence "has been committed". On these facts, it is clear that an indictable offence – namely, theft – has been committed.

[5] (b) is correct – since propositions (i), (ii) and (iv) are all correct. (i) is correct since there is a duty to caution the person and to tell them the reasons for arrest, even where those reasons may be obvious. (ii) is correct since a power of arrest clearly arises on these facts since there is a reasonable suspicion that there has been a theft, and that David is involved with it. (iii) is incorrect: the necessity test always applies – and in every case the officer must consider whether the arrest is necessary. (iv) is correct – on these facts it is likely that the office will wish to arrest David, and he will be able to justify this by reference to s.24(5) (e) and (f).

[6] The correct answer is (c). s.32(4) permits a search of the mouth of an arrested person to the extent that search is reasonably required for the purpose of discovering evidence and where the arresting officer has reasonable grounds for the search. s.117 permits reasonable force to be used.

(a) is incorrect since no physical contact is required for an arrest; an arrest can arise once a person makes clear that the arrested person is no longer free to go where he wants to go. (b) is incorrect: s.30 requires Craig to be taken to a police station as soon as practicable, but there are permitted exceptions – for example, if a s.18 search of premises is required. Additionally the police can consider granting street bail. (d) is wrong; both an arrest and a caution can be triggered as soon as there are reasonable grounds to believe Craig is committing an offence. The police are entitled to arrest immediately, although Craig must then be cautioned at once.

[7] The correct answer is (a): the police now have a power to grant "street bail". (d) is wrong since the police do have the power to grant street bail with conditions on it.

(b) is wrong in principle since police officers have the power to arrest a person for any offence, no matter how trivial, provided it is necessary to do so. The legality of any arrest in this situation will therefore depend on whether the police can show that they had reasonable grounds for believing that one of the necessity conditions under s.24(5) was made out.

Finally (c) is wrong: article 5 is certainly engaged by the arrest, since it is an interference with Craig's liberty, but that interference will be permissible under article 5(1)(c) – see section 2.6.2.

Chapter 3: Detention and Interrogation

[1] The correct answer is (c): see s.37 (1) PACE. (a) is incorrect as the custody officer <u>also</u> has a power to detain a suspect if he has reasonable grounds for believing that his detention without being charged is necessary to secure or preserve evidence relating to an offence for which he is under arrest: s.37 (2). (b) is incorrect as a custody officer must not be connected with the investigation. (d) is incorrect, as a solicitor is entitled to see the custody record on arrival at the police station (C 2.4) but is not entitled to a copy of it at this stage (although of course you can always ask).

[2] (e): none of the propositions is correct. (i) is wrong: although the time limit on detention is 24 hours, this will run from the time of arrival at the police station rather than of arrest: s. 41(2)(d). [Note that because the offence is not indictable – that is, it is not an either way offence, nor one that can only be tried at Crown Court, the limit on the detention period is 24 hours. There is no power to extend this period.]

(ii) is incorrect: the first review must be not later than six hours after detention is authorised – here this would be 21.10: s.40(3)(a). (iii) is incorrect: although the second review should follow not later than nine hours after the first review, there must be continuing reviews of detention at no more than nine-hourly intervals thereafter.: s.40(3)(c).

[3] The correct answer is (c). Any offence that can be tried in the Crown Court will be an "indictable offence". The normal detention period is 24 hours, but in the case of indictable offences this can be extended by a officer of at least the rank of superintendent to a total of 36 hours. Thereafter the detention can be extended to a total of 96 hours by warrants of further detention issued by the magistrates' court.

(a) is therefore incorrect since the police can only extend detention to 36 hours. (b) is wrong since the test will be whether the offence for which Sarah has been detained is classed as indictable. (d) is incorrect since it suggests that offences that are tried in the Crown Court are not indictable; they are.

[4] (d) is correct. All of the propositions are correct: see ss.42–44 PACE.

[5] (c) is the proposition which is not correct. As a solicitor for the defence if a client makes inconsistent statements either before or during the course of proceedings, this is not of itself a ground for refusing to act further. It is for the court and not for you to assess the truth of your client's account. Only if it is "clear" that your client is attempting to put forward false evidence should you cease to act.

Propositions (a), (b) and (d) are all correct.

[6] (d) is most likely to amount to a waiver of privilege because you are referring back to the contents of a privileged discussion (your earlier lawyer-client discussion with Roger) and you are now revealing the advice.

(a) is unlikely to waive privilege as you do not go beyond saying that you have advised him to remain silent; *Condron* suggests that simply stating the fact of the advice will not of itself be enough to waive privilege. It would be otherwise if you went on to explain the reasons for your advice.

Neither (b) nor (c) risks waiving privilege as in both statements the advice is couched in the present tense, and does not therefore refer back to any earlier privileged conversation.

[7] (a) is correct: all the propositions are wrong. (i) is wrong since the police are not permitted to show photographs where there is a "known" suspect such as Liam. (ii) is wrong since it presumes that a confrontation is the appropriate option rather than considering whether a covert video identification or a covert group identification might be more successful. (iii) is wrong since a covert identification procedure is intended for those situations where the suspect's consent is not forthcoming or is unlikely to be forthcoming.

[8] (c): Code D, Annex B, paragraph 9: an identification procedure should consist of at least eight people in addition to the suspect.

Chapter 4: First appearances and Legal Aid

[1] The answer is (d): ii, iii and iv only.

This is a minor case of shoplifting. If found guilty Rachel is unlikely to face more than a fine. There is no likelihood that Rachel will be sent to prison. Criterion i is therefore inappropriate.

There are good reasons for ticking the remaining three criteria. Even though Rachel has two previous convictions, both are for minor public order matters, both arising from demonstrations. There is no previous suggestion of dishonesty, and a conviction for shoplifting will carry a far greater stigma than the minor public order convictions could ever do. There will also be a need to track and interview witnesses in a case such as this where there are likely to be members of the public who may have observed what happened at the store and who can therefore back up Rachel's account. Similarly, there will be a need for expert cross-examination of the store detective as this is a case where identification is disputed, and it will call for careful cross-examination to test the reliability of the store detective's identification.

[Incidentally, in an identification case such as this, it would normally also be appropriate to tick the box stating that there is a "complex issue of law". As you will see later, identification evidence needs to be treated with particular caution because of the danger of an honest but mistaken identification; the court will need a careful direction about the need for caution, and hence the matter gives rise to a complex legal issue.]

[2] (c) is incorrect. Under the old criminal legal aid scheme there was a right of appeal against the refusal of legal aid in some circumstances. This is no longer the case. Any "appeal" now would be by way of a judicial review. (a), (b) and (d) are all correct.

Chapter 5: First Hearings

[1] (c) is not an either way offence. See s.22(1) Magistrates' Courts Act 1980: criminal damage (unless caused by fire or with intent to endanger life) is triable only summarily where it appears that the value involved does not exceed £5,000. All the other offences, although they appear to be for less serious matters, are either way offences.

[2] (d) is correct. If Carl indicates a guilty plea, the court must proceed to accept jurisdiction of the case and to convict of the offence. However, the court will still be able to commit Carl to the Crown Court for sentencing (s.4 PCC(S)A 2000), and are likely to do so.

(a) is incorrect, as it is not true to say that Carl will be able to decide the venue. If, as is likely, the magistrates decline jurisdiction, Carl will not be able to prevent the matter from being sent to the Crown Court for trial. Only if the magistrates accept the case, can Carl overrule them. (b) is incorrect as sentencing powers are only one factor for the court to take into account. The magistrates should not decline jurisdiction unless there is a specified reason why the matter should be committed to Crown Court for trial and their sentencing powers are inadequate. (c) is incorrect as a not guilty plea will merely mean that the magistrates will have to consider mode of trial/allocation, in contrast to an indication of a guilty plea which would force them to accept jurisdiction.

[3] The correct answer is (b): the power to commit for sentence arises in relation to either way offences only: see s.3 PCC(S)A 2000. (a) is therefore incorrect. (c) is wrong as it suggests that the power only arises following an indication of a guilty plea; although the power to commit for sentence does arise then, it also arises in other either way offences where the defendant has accepted the jurisdiction of the court. It is for that reason that the court clerk gives him a warning before he makes his election. Finally, (d) is incorrect: there is no "interests of justice" test as such that applies at this stage.

[4] (a) is correct. Theft is an either way offence, and criminal damage of £5,000 or less is one of the matters listed in s.40 Criminal Justice Act 1988 that may be included on the indictment and tried in the Crown Court. (b) is therefore incorrect as it deals with matters that would effectively be committed for sentence only under s.41 CJA 1988. (c) is wrong as s.40 specifically lists criminal damage of £5,000 or less as one of the offences that can be committed for trial. (d) is incorrect as the conditions are laid down by s.40, and are narrower than simply stating that the offences are "related".

[5] The answer is (a) – all the propositions are correct

[6] The answer is (d): none of the propositions is correct. Rape is an indictable only offence, so that it must be sent to Crown Court forthwith. The either way offence is related since it could be joined on the same indictment as the rape; this is because it clearly forms part of a series of offences of the same character. (It also fulfils the alternate limb of the test: it is "founded on the same facts.") In respect of Morgan, he will be sent to the Crown Court because he is brought before the same court charged jointly with the related either way offence.

Chapter 6: Bail

[1] The correct answer is (d): only Paul has a prima facie right to bail under the Bail Act. It is likely that the prosecution will raise substantial grounds to oppose the granting of bail, not least that he is unlikely to surrender to custody and that he is likely to commit further offences and that, given the offence is one of violence and he has extensive previous convictions for violence, he is likely to interfere with witnesses or with the course of justice. Nonetheless, the burden of proof is on the prosecution.

Les has lost his prima facie right to bail by virtue of paragraph 2A, Schedule 1, Part 1 Bail Act as inserted by s.14 CJA 2003. This provides that the court need not grant bail where a person is alleged to have committed an offence carrying life imprisonment while on bail.

Bob can only be granted bail if there are exceptional circumstances. s.25 CJPOA once applied an absolute bar on the grant of bail to persons who were charged with murder, manslaughter, rape, and attempted murder or rape, if they had ever previously been convicted of any of these offences. The Crime and Disorder Act amended this so that bail is now available, but only if there are exceptional circumstances.

[2] (b) is the correct answer: *previous* failures to answer bail will be a relevant "factor" under paragraph 9 (bail history), but they are not of themselves a ground for refusing bail. The ground would presumably be that there are substantial grounds for believing that the defendant would fail to surrender to custody. (a), (c) and (d) are all grounds on which bail can be refused.

[3] (a) is the correct answer. All of these conditions are likely to be appropriate in this case. The curfew would address suggestions that Johnny is likely to commit further offences if granted bail; all his offences have been at night, and a curfew would therefore ensure that this did not occur. Equally, an exclusion order (v) would be appropriate where, as here, the offending has all taken place in a particular geographical area.

The prosecution is also likely to argue that Johnny will fail to attend court; he has a previous breach of bail, and domestic burglary is a serious offence that is likely to attract a custodial sentence (increasing his motivation for absconding). Reporting to the police station (ii) and a surety (iii) are both appropriate as means of ensuring that Johnny does not abscond. Residence at an agreed address (iv) should also help allay prosecution concerns that Johnny may abscond, as it will enable the police to keep track of him.

[4] The correct answer is (b) – the court must either require an assessment with any follow up treatment, or grant bail only if satisfied that there is no significant risk of offending – something which in these circumstances will be very difficult for the defendant to convince the court of. (a) is therefore not correct since strictly speaking bail is still possible – albeit subject to the "no significant risk" test. (c) is not correct since it assumes that bail cannot be granted at all.

[5] The correct answer is (c): the prosecution are able to appeal to the Crown Court in respect of any offence that is imprisonable.

(a) is incorrect since it is irrelevant that the offence is either way – the defence would still have a right of appeal in a summary only offence. (b) is incorrect – a judicial review is unlikely to be permitted since here there is a statutory appeal route to the Crown Court. (d) is incorrect as the Crown Court has a power to vary conditions of bail – a power introduced by s.13 CJA 2003.

Chapter 7: Interim Hearings & Disclosure

[1]   (b) is correct: (i) and (iii) are correct propositions. (ii) is incorrect because the prosecution duty is to disclose only those materials which undermine the prosecution case or assist the defence case. The Attorney General's Guidelines make very clear that the prosecution should not simply make available all materials on an unrestricted basis.

[2]   (c) is correct – the defence statement must be served on both the prosecution and the court within the 14 day period. (a) is wrong since the defence disclosure duty arises in relation to any case which is heard in the Crown Court – not simply indictable only cases. (b) is incorrect because is confuses the concept of the defence disclosure statement with the statement given to you by your client (his proof of evidence): the requirements for a defence disclosure statement are set out in s.6A CPIA 1996. Finally (d) is wrong: there is a continuing duty of review on the prosecutor throughout the case.

[3]   (b) is incorrect: under s.40 Criminal Procedure and Investigations Act 1996 the judge at a plea and case management hearing will have power to make binding rulings on the admissibility of evidence and any other issue of law. This will be the case whether or not they are the trial judge. All the other propositions are correct. Note that (d) is correct because while there is normally no power to appeal pre-trial rulings, preliminary hearings are treated as if they are part of the trial itself, and there is an interlocutory right of appeal.

Chapter 8: Advocacy

[1] (b) is correct: a leading question is one that gives evidence itself, rather than drawing the evidence from the person who is testifying. (a) is incorrect: not all questions that start with the word "did" will be leading questions, although the word is a danger sign and often will indicate a leading question. However there will be some circumstances where what appears to be a leading question – "Did you then see her hit the victim twice in the face?" – will not be leading because the witness has already given this evidence earlier in their testimony.

(c) is incorrect as leading questions are permitted in cross-examination. Indeed, you will want to keep your questions in cross-examination "closed" so that they force the witness only to deal with the matters that you raise, rather than the kind of "open" questions you will use in examination in chief to avoid leading. Finally, (d) is incorrect. Asking a witness to comment on the evidence of other witnesses may be permissible provided they are not giving opinion evidence; in any event it will not be a "leading" question.

[2] (b) is correct: (i), (ii) and (iv) are all correct modes of address in the magistrates' court, assuming a lay Bench with a woman Chair. iii is incorrect as the term "my learned friend" is reserved for barristers! All the more reason to refer to the other advocate by name.

[3] (d) is correct: most Crown Court judges will be addressed as "Your Honour"; some will be addressed as "My Lord" if they are High Court judges or senior Recorders in Liverpool, Manchester or Cardiff, or if they are sitting in the Old Bailey. "Your Worship" would only ever be appropriate in the magistrates' court. "Judge" is an informal mode of address to be used when speaking to a judge at a social occasion.

Chapter 9: Trial Preparation and Trial Procedure

[1] The correct answer is (d): none of the propositions is correct. (i) is wrong in that it suggests the judge is required to ask for a majority verdict at this stage; this is not the case: the judge may ask for a majority verdict once 2 hours and 10 minutes has passed, but in many cases the judge will choose to wait a lot longer to allow the jury to arrive at a unanimous verdict.

ii is incorrect as there is a strict rule that no further evidence will be adduced once the jury has retired. If the jury has <u>questions</u>, the judge will generally discuss any proposed response with the advocates. iii is wrong as criminal damage is neither explicitly nor impliedly part of the robbery count; robbery is theft with violence and alternative verdicts of theft or of violence-related offences may be possible, but not criminal damage.

[2] (d) is correct: propositions i and ii reflect the test laid down in the case of Galbraith (1981) 73 Cr. App. R. 124. There is no basis for proposition iii. When a witness does not "come up to proof", we mean that their evidence falls short of the account given in their witness statement or "proof of evidence". However, the prosecution may still be able to establish a prima facie case on the basis of that witness's evidence or on the basis of the evidence of other witnesses therefore iii is incorrect.

[3] (c) is correct. The defence is entitled to one speech either before or after the evidence. (a) is incorrect in that it suggests that the defence "must" have a closing speech: obviously advocates would rather have the last word and therefore tend to choose to have a closing speech, but it is not compulsory. (b) is incorrect as there is no distinction between the position of summary only and either way offences when tried in the magistrates' court. (d) is wrong as it represents the rule in the Crown Court, but does not apply to the magistrates' court.

Chapter 10: Sentencing

[1] The magistrates are limited to a sentence of six months' custody in respect of any one offence, or where imposing two or more terms of imprisonment to run consecutively: s.78 PCC(S)A 2000. Where the terms are in respect of offences triable either way, the aggregate can exceed six months, but must not exceed 12 months. (c) is therefore the correct proposition.

[2] (b) is correct.

[3] (b) is correct as all the factors are potentially aggravating (according to the Sentencing Guidelines Council) other than the fact of Derrick's age, which does not seem to be relevant. The Sentencing Council refers only to a particularly vulnerable victim: it seems likely that this is applicable in this case. Derrick's previous convictions are potentially aggravating factors. Finally the fact that the offence took place in an isolated place is also potentially aggravating.

[4] The correct answer is (b): both (i) and (ii) are correct. (iii) is incorrect since curfew requirements are not limited to night time offending: they are a general penalty. (iv) is incorrect since the court has a wide discretion in sentencing for breach of a community order and is not required to impose a custodial penalty.

[5] (b) is correct. Proposition (i) is correct: the court will generally permit the payment of fines in instalments. (ii) is correct as s.164 CJA 2003 requires the court to ensure that the fine reflects the seriousness of the offence. (iii) is correct to the extent that s.164 also requires the court to take into account all the circumstances of the case: Maurice's previous good character is potentially relevant.

However, (iii) is incorrect in suggesting that the court should not impose a lower fine because Maurice is in receipt of benefits. s.164 requires the defendant's financial circumstances to be taken into account: s.164 explicitly permits the sentencing court to increase or reduce the fine as a result of taking into account the defendant's financial circumstances. (iv) is correct. Maurice is claiming £114 per fortnight in state benefits which amounts to £57 per week. The relevant weekly income in his case is therefore deemed to be £110.

Chapter 11: Appeals

[1] (b) is incorrect. There is no appeal from the magistrates' court to the Court of Appeal, except in some categories of case where the sentencing or re-sentencing has taken place in the Crown Court: s. 10 Criminal Appeal Act 1968. The Court of Appeal is the route for appeals from the Crown Court.

[2] (a) – all of the propositions are wrong. i is incorrect as it suggests that the time limit runs from the date of conviction. This would be the case in the Crown Court (although there the time limit is 28 days). In the magistrates' court the time for appeal (which is 21 days) runs from the date of sentencing.

ii is incorrect as the Crown Court will hear the matter *de novo*. It therefore has the powers to confirm, reverse or vary any part of the decision. This includes the power to increase the sentence of the lower court, even if the appeal was against conviction only: s.45 Supreme Court Act 1981. However the sentence must not exceed the sentence that could have been imposed by the magistrates.

iii is incorrect as the judge will sit without a jury, but will not sit alone; he or she will sit with two lay justices.

[3] (c) is most appropriate for an appeal by way of case stated. The appeal is a matter of law, rather than a re-canvassing of the facts of the case. It should be possible to agree a summary of the facts and to formulate questions of law for the High Court to consider.

(a) would most appropriately be dealt with by way of judicial review. The allegation is one of bias, and the allegation would be that the conduct of the trial was in breach of the principles of natural justice.

Both (b) and (d) are probably best appealed to the Crown Court. In each case the appeal appears to be based on a factual dispute – who is telling the truth? – rather than on a particular question of law. In any event, if the appeal to the Crown Court is unsuccessful, both Stacie and Liz will still have preserved their right of appeal by way of Case Stated. If they appeal first by way of Case Stated and are unsuccessful, they will not then be able to launch a Crown Court appeal.

[4] (c) is correct as only proposition i is correct. ii is wrong because, although the time limits and procedural information are correct, Rose will be at risk of a loss of time order even if her appeal is against sentence alone. iii is incorrect because it partially restates the old test applied by the Court of Appeal; the new test is simply whether a conviction is "unsafe".

Chapter 14: Introduction to Evidence

[1] (d) is correct: (ii) is the only correct proposition. It is not true to say that evidence will generally be admissible provided that it has been obtained lawfully. Evidence will generally be admissible notwithstanding the circumstances under which it has been obtained provided that it is relevant. (iii) is also incorrect; it is not merely oral testimony that will be admissible evidence; real evidence will also be admissible, as will documentary evidence and other evidence where it falls as an exception to the rule against hearsay.

[2] (b) is correct. Jenny is not jointly charged; therefore s.80 (4) PACE does not apply, and she is competent for both prosecution and defence. As s.80 (4) does not apply, she is also compellable for the defence. However, the proceedings do not fall within s.80 (3) and Jenny is not therefore compellable for the prosecution.

[3] (c) is correct: the test is as set out in the Youth Justice and Criminal Evidence Act.

[4] (a) is correct: the test is that the jury must feel satisfied beyond reasonable doubt. The phrase "so that you are sure" has been judicially approved, as has "satisfied so that you feel sure". (b) is incorrect because it introduces a balance of probabilities test; while (c) is incorrect because it does not make clear to what standard a jury should be satisfied. (d) is incorrect as it puts the standard too high. In general, caselaw suggests that judges should not attempt to further define the standard of proof.

Chapter 15: Silence and Inferences

[1] The correct is answer is (b) as (ii) and (iv) are correct. s.34 inferences may arise from failure to mention defence facts when questioned after caution, or when charged under caution. In both cases, the Youth Justice and Criminal Evidence Act makes it a requirement that Russell must have had an opportunity to take legal advice before any such inference can be drawn.

(i) and (iii) are both incorrect as the inference will only arise following a caution. While a caution may follow an arrest, it is the caution and not the arrest that triggers the potential inference.

[2] (d) is correct: none of the propositions is correct. (i) and (ii) are both wrong. *Condron* makes clear that legal advice of itself will not prevent an inference from arising. Where the basis for the legal advice is explained (with the side effect that privilege will be waived) the jury may take the view that Vince's silence is reasonable, and that no inference is proper, but that is a matter for them: it is certainly not true to say that no inference is possible. There is of course now a line of cases which suggests that the jury should look at whether the reliance on the legal advice was "genuine and reasonable" (*Beckles*). But it remains the case that legal advice *per se* will not prevent an inference from arising.

(iii) is incorrect – although it was a proposition which was argued in *Condron*; the court in *Condron* specifically rejected it, pointing out how hard it would be to establish whether the advice was bona fide.

[3] (b) is correct. *Argent* makes clear that the question is for the jury "in the exercise of their collective common sense, experience and understanding", and that they are to have regard to the factors that related to this particular defendant, rather than a hypothetical "reasonable man". (a) is incorrect as disclosure may be a relevant factor in deciding whether the defendant could reasonably have been expected to put forward his defence facts. (c) is incorrect in that it suggests the matter is one for the judge, rather than the jury.

[4] (c) is correct. All of the elements of the jury direction are correct – apart from (iii). The statutory provision itself provides that, for an inference to arise from failure to mention a fact, the fact must be one that "in the circumstances existing at the time the accused could reasonably have been expected to mention": s.34 (1). It also provides that the jury may draw "such inferences as appear proper": s.34 (2). s.38 (3) makes clear that Felipe cannot be convicted solely on the basis of the inference, so that (iv) is also correct.

(iii) is incorrect as it is suggests that the jury are automatically entitled to draw an inference from Felipe's failure to answer the police questions. This is wrong in two respects. First, the inference arises from a failure to put forward defence facts, rather than simply failing to answer questions. Secondly, the jury will only be entitled to draw an inference if, as was set out in (i), they consider that Felipe's failure to put forward the facts was not reasonable.

[5] (a) – all of the propositions are correct. (i) is correct as s.36 and 37 only arise where the questioning is by police or customs officers, and so will not arise in relation to questioning by a store detective. In contrast, s.34 inferences will be possible where the questioning is by a person "charged with the duty of investigating offences…": s.34 (4). Finally, (iii) is correct. The Youth Justice and Criminal Evidence Act makes clear that no inference can be drawn at the police station prior to the opportunity to take legal advice. *Murray v United Kingdom* and *Condron v United Kingdom* make it clear that

legal advice is an essential element safeguarding the article 6 rights of a suspect before any inference is possible, and the Human Rights Act requires ss.34/36/37 to be read in compliance with the Convention and in the light of the Strasbourg caselaw.

[6] (a) is correct. A s.37 inference will be possible. Chris is under arrest. The questions are being asked by police officers. He is being asked to account for his presence having been found by a constable at a place at or about the time that the offence was committed. The caution complies with the requirements of Code C 10.11 PACE.

(b) is incorrect as the inference will be possible once Chris has had an opportunity to take legal advice. Chris can't avoid the inference simply be refusing to take legal advice. (c) is incorrect as it does not state the test that applies in relation to the s.37 inference, but instead one of the circumstances where a power of arrest under s.24 PACE may arise. (d) is incorrect as it suggests that the ordinary language caution is defective; there is no basis for saying this.

[7] (a) is correct – all of the propositions are drawn from the decision in *Cowan*.

Chapter 16: Confessions

[1] (a) is correct: see s.78 PACE, which effectively alters the traditional position at common law that the lawfulness of the obtaining of the evidence is irrelevant. s.78 specifically provides that the circumstances under which the evidence is obtained should be taken into account.

(b) wrongfully suggests that because the breach is accidental this should mean the court will be slow in excluding the evidence. In some cases the courts have suggested that where there is evidence of a deliberate breach of PACE the court may be faster to conclude that the breach of PACE is "significant and substantial", but it has also been said that the fact that a breach is accidental does not prevent it from being significant or substantial. Indeed, evidence can of course be excluded even if there has been no breach at all.

(c) is wrong as s.78 is not confined to confession evidence (in contrast to s.76). (d) is also incorrect.

[2] (c) is correct: the statement is "mixed" in that it contains an admission (that Suzy drove the car) and an exculpatory element (she thought she had permission). The whole statement will therefore be admissible. (a) assumes that the statement is admissible and simply considers the basis on which it might be excluded – but you need first to consider on what basis is could be admissible. (b) correctly identifies the element that is a confession (a statement against interest), but overlooks the fact that, confessions are, of course, an exception to the hearsay rule when adduced against the maker. (d) wrongly suggests that the statement is largely irrelevant.

[3] (a) – all of the propositions are correct. Once the issue of unreliability is raised, s.76 makes clear that it is for the prosecution to show to the criminal standard of proof that the confessions are not unreliable. If the prosecution falls short, the confessions must be excluded. It is irrelevant that the confessions are true. Under s.76, the unreliability must be in consequence of something said or done.

[4] The answer is (d); all of these propositions are incorrect. A confession may be excluded under s.76 or s.78, and the defence may apply on both basis. Of course, since the judge must exclude the confession under s.76 unless the prosecution can show beyond reasonable doubt that the confession was not obtained by oppression or under circumstances that render it unreliable, you will always begin such an application with s.76. If the s.76 application is unsuccessful, an application to exclude the confession on the basis that it will have an adverse impact on the fairness of the proceedings may still succeed.

(ii) is wrong as s.78 is not confined to breaches of PACE; indeed evidence may be excluded under s.78 even where it has been entirely correctly obtained (see, for example, *Hickin*). (iii) is wrong: s.78 states that the court must have regard to all the circumstances, including the circumstances under which the evidence was obtained.

Chapter 17: Character

[1] (c) is correct. s.98 CJA 2003 provides that the restrictions on raising a person's bad character do not arise where the allegation of bad character is in relation to the current offence (or its investigation). Here Graham is clearly suggesting Robert is involved in the current offence. However it is also correct that this suggestion will be an attack for the purposes of Gateway G, and that the prosecution will be able to apply to the court to adduce Graham's previous convictions.

[2] (c) is correct, since propositions ii and iii are correct. Proposition i is incorrect as bad character also includes reprehensible behaviour and is not confined solely to previous convictions. Proposition iv is wrong since Gateway C requires the evidence is evidence without which the court would find it either impossible or difficult to understand the case – and where the value in relation to the case as a whole is substantial: it is not enough for the evidence simply to "help" the jury.

[3] The correct answer is (a): all of the factors are relevant. It is relevant that the conviction is for an offence of violence (or threatened violence), since similarity between the previous misconduct and that in issue in the trial is one issue for the judge to consider under s.100(3). Similarly the judge must consider the time lapse since the previous conviction: the long lapse of time here may mean that the judge is unlikely to permit Rebecca to adduce this evidence. The judge will also consider the very different circumstances of the former offence – and again this may make it less likely that the previous conviction will be admissible. Finally, the fact that Tabitha pleaded guilty will be relevant since it shows that she is highly likely to have been responsible for the earlier misconduct – another issue that the judge must consider under s.100(3).

[4] (d) is correct: none of the propositions is correct. (a) is wrong since an attack made during a police interview under caution may well activate Gateway G; although the Nelson case suggests that it would be wrong for the prosecution to admit the interview simply in order to trigger the provision. It is also wrong to suggest (as (b) does) that a caution would not constitute misconduct; it clearly can do. Finally (c) is incorrect on these particular facts: if you look at the decision in Hanson, the court suggests that the trial judge (in Pickstone) was correct to find that abnormal sexual motivations were unlikely to change with time, so that even old convictions for child sex offences might be admissible.

[5] (d) is correct as neither proposition is right. It is correct that the blackmail offence is in the same category for the purposes of s.103(2) CJA as the previous theft offences, but Hanson confirms that the previous convictions are not automatically admissible just because they are in the same category. It is also wrong to suggest that simply because they are offences of dishonesty, the previous theft convictions must show "propensity to dishonesty"; again in Hanson the court made clear that propensity to untruthfulness would involve situations where the person had put forward an account that had been disbelieved at trial, or where the circumstances of the offences clearly showed the making of untruthful representations. Since we know nothing about the facts of the earlier theft matters, and since we know that Yoshi pleaded guilty to the offences, they cannot show that she has a propensity to untruthfulness.

Chapter 18: Hearsay

[1] (d) is not a s.116 reason. Under s.116(2) it makes no difference if the statement was made to a police officer or not.

[2] (b) is correct: only proposition (ii) is correct. Proposition (ii) is an accurate summary of s.117(2)(c) CJA 2003. (i) is incorrect as s.117 applies to documents created or received by a person in the course of a trade, business, profession or other occupation or as the holder of a paid or unpaid office: it is therefore not confined to records compiled as part of a business or commercial enterprise. Proposition (iii) is wrong in suggesting that such documents must be excluded: under s.117(4)/(5) there will be an additional requirement that either there is a s.116 reason for not calling the maker of the document, or they cannot now be reasonably expected to remember the facts.

[3] (c) is correct: both propositions i and ii are correct in relation to s.116(2)(e) – the "in fear" provision. Note that this provision applies even where the statement is oral hearsay (as here) provided that the maker of the statement can be identified to the satisfaction of the court. s.116 contains a special leave provision to which the court must have regard before admitting evidence under this provision. Proposition iii is wrong since s.117 applies only to business <u>documents</u>.

Note however that even if the hearsay evidence had been in written form, so that s.117 prima facie applied, s.117(4) makes clear that since the statement was prepared as part of a criminal investigation the prosecution would need to show either that a s.116(2) reason applied so that Neville could not be called, or that Neville could no longer be expected to remember the facts.

[4] The correct answer is (d) – propositions i and ii are correct. i is clearly a "business document" for the purposes of s.117: it was not prepared for the trial and there seems no reason to doubt its authenticity. It is therefore likely to be admissible under s.117 CJA 2003. Similarly ii is likely be admissible as a business document for exactly the same reasons: the bus ticket is effectively a written statement confirming that a person paid £1.30 at a particular time on a particular bus. Obviously it doesn't prove that Zahir was a passenger on the bus at this time; but given that it was found in Zahir's possession it is useful circumstantial evidence.

Proposition (iii) is incorrect: the letter is unlikely to be admissible whether under s.116 since there is no reason under s.116(2) why the witness cannot attend court to give oral testimony. The principal may wish to be on holiday at the time, but he is not at present on holiday and he can therefore be witness summonsed and his attendance required. Given the importance of his testimony this would probably be advisable in any event: live evidence is always more convincing than hearsay evidence. Note that the letter will not be admissible under s.117 since it was prepared for the forthcoming trial, and a s.116 reason is therefore required (or the court must be satisfied that it is no longer reasonable to expect the person to remember the matter).

Chapter 19: Reliability

[1] (d) is correct: the judge is not required to give a corroboration warning in any of these situations. The *Makanjuola* warning itself is not a corroboration warning. Under *Makanjuola* it is a matter for the judge both whether he gives a warning and the terms under which he gives it.

[2] (a) is correct: these are all matters that should be dealt with in a *Turnbull* direction. First the judge will explain the special need for caution in cases of disputed visual identification. Then the judge will direct the jury on the circumstances of the identification: all of these propositions are matters to which the judge should direct the jury's attention. Finally the judge will point to any specific weaknesses in the evidence.

[3] (b) is wrong: a previous consistent statement will now be admissible in a wide range of different circumstances under s.120 CJA 2003: for example, rebutting an allegation of recent fabrication; where it is evidence of recent complaint; where it is evidence of a person, object or place; etc.

All the other propositions are correct.

[4] The correct answer is (c): this is the CJA position regarding memory-refreshing documents. (a) is incorrect as it is the old rule about memory refreshing (which required substantial contemporaneity) and this was abolished by the CJA 2003. (b) is incorrect as the question does not concern the admissibility of the statements into evidence (in which case it is right to say that they are hearsay, and would only be admissible if permitted by the hearsay rules); rather the issue in this scenario is the use of the statements to refresh memory – and the hearsay rules are therefore irrelevant. (d) is incorrect as the issue is not the admissible of the statement, but its use as a memory refreshing document.

Chapter 20: Privilege

[1]   (c) is not correct because it sets out the test for the privilege against self-incrimination. A person may still, however, be able to claim lawyer-client or litigation privilege.

        All the other propositions are correct.

[2]   (c) is correct: the draft statements and the Briefs to Counsel are both likely to be covered by lawyer-client privilege as they have been generated either as part of the litigation or with a view to the litigation. There is no reason to believe that the company minutes fall within this category, or within the privilege against self-incrimination.

[3]   (b) is correct: the name of the informer and the police internal operations manual are both likely to be covered by public interest immunity. The previous convictions of witnesses will not be so protected. Note, however, that there is no rule that such convictions must be automatically disclosed to the defence. However, the decision of the Court of Appeal in *Vasiliou* (see 7.5.1) and the AG guidelines on Disclosure both suggest that they should be disclosed.

Appendix B

Criminal Case study
R v Butcher

List of documents

Document 1	Custody Record
Document 2	Transcript of Interview
Document 3	Charge Sheet
Document 4	Criminal Record: Peter Butcher
Document 5	Representation Order application: CDS 14
Document 6	Application for Bail
Document 7	Letter to client: client care
Document 8A–H	Advance Information
Document 9	Attendance Note: Character evidence
Document 10	Proof of Evidence and Comments: Peter Butcher
Document 11	Letter to client: Mode of Trial
Document 12A–B	Statements: defence witnesses
Document 13A–C	CPS letter and draft indictment
Document 14	Magistrates' court case directions
Document 15	CDS 11: magistrates' court fixed fee claim
Document 16A–B	Prosecution Disclosure Letter enclosing Schedule of Unused Material (MG6C)
Document 17A	Prosecution s.101 bad character application
Document 17B	Defence s.101 bad character response
Document 18A–C	Letter enclosing Defence statement (B) and Defence Witness Notice (C)
Document 19A–B	Prosecution Disclosure of witness convictions
Document 20	Plea and Case Management Hearing Questionnaire
Document 21	Brief to Counsel
Document 22	Cross-examination of Arthur King (extract)
Document 23	Pre Sentence Report
Document 24	Mitigation speech
Document 25	Form NG 2 & 3: appeal to Court of Appeal

> **Saturday 15th February – the initial contact**

00.05 The first telephone call

Jim Kettle, an assistant solicitor at Halpern Dodds, is on the firm's internal duty rota for the evening of 14th/15th February. At 00.05 on Saturday 15th February he receives a telephone call to inform him that Peter Butcher has been arrested, is being held at Westchurch Central Police Station and is requesting legal advice.

Jim rings the police station and speaks to the Custody Officer, Sergeant Evans. The custody officer tells him that Butcher has been arrested on suspicion of s.20 wounding, following a brawl at a wedding reception, during the course of which one man was hit in the face by a glass. Butcher was the groom and the injured party is his father-in-law. Butcher was named at the scene by the victim as the person who assaulted him. The victim has been taken to hospital for treatment and the officers are waiting to interview him. Butcher has cuts on his hand and is clearly somewhat intoxicated. The doctor has been called out.

Jim gets information about the time of arrest, the time of arrival at the police station and the grounds for detention. It is clear to him that this is still a very early stage in the investigation, and that the investigating officers are unlikely to be ready to interview the suspect until they have statements from the victim and from any witnesses. Jim asks the custody officer if he can speak to the OIC (the officer in the case) but is told that he is at the hospital waiting to speak to the injured party.

Peter Butcher is brought from his cell to the custody suite telephone. Jim introduces himself, and immediately reminds Peter that the telephone is not in a private place. Jim then tells Peter all the information that he has obtained from the custody officer. He explains to Peter that he will come down to the police station to give him legal advice, but that it seems more sensible to wait until they know when the police are likely to be ready to interview. Jim tells Peter that the doctor has been called out and will be coming to look at his hands.

Peter tells Jim that he wants to be released at once and that he has done nothing wrong. He states that it is his father-in-law's fault and that he does not want to be banged up in a police station on his wedding night. Jim gets the impression that Peter is still fairly drunk. He tells Peter he will come down to the station now, but Peter must not talk to the police or say anything further in the meantime. This seems to calm Peter down, and Peter then agrees that Jim should not attend until the police are ready to proceed.

Peter is then taken back to his cell. Jim speaks to the custody officer and asks him to note on the record that he wishes to attend for interview and should be informed as soon as the police are ready to interview. This ensures that the custody officer is aware of what is going on, but also prevents any suggestion that Peter has now had his "independent legal advice" under s.58 PACE.

05.43 The second telephone call

At 05.43 Jim is contacted by the custody sergeant who tells him that the officers have taken a statement from the injured party and that Butcher has now woken up and wishes to be interviewed. The doctor has certified Butcher as fit for interview. Jim tells the custody officer that he will attend.

06.10 Attending the police station

Jim arrives at the police station at 06.10. He introduces himself to the custody officer and produces proof of identity. There has been a shift change and the new custody officer does not know much about the case. Jim asks to see the custody record (see Document 1 – although note that at this stage the record would clearly only be completed up to 06.10). In this case, the custody record adds little to what Jim has already been told.

Jim then asks to speak to the officer in the case, PC Stanley. In talking to the police officer it becomes clear that there has been a large-scale disturbance at the reception following Peter Butcher's wedding. The injured party is Arthur King, Peter Butcher's new father-in-law. Eight other guests were arrested. Five have been released without charge. Three others have been detained on minor public order matters, including Steven Fiddler, who seems to have been the best man. They have already been charged and will be produced at court later on in the day.

The delay in interviewing Peter Butcher has arisen from the need to take a statement from Arthur King. Mr King has been undergoing surgery at Westchurch General Hospital in order to remove glass fragments from his face, and in particular from around his left eye. He has only recently been sufficiently recovered to give a full statement to the officers. Butcher is currently arrested on suspicion of s.20 OAPA (malicious wounding), but the charge could ultimately be one of grievous bodily harm with intent (s.18 OAPA).

Jim asks for fuller details of what each witness to the incident says happened. PC Stanley makes clear that he is under no obligation to go into this level of detail and states that he wants an initial account from Peter Butcher. He tells Jim that King's allegation is that Butcher took offence to his speech and left the room. Fiddler, the best man, then started abusing King. Everyone started shouting at one another and then Butcher reappeared and grabbed the bride by the arm. King shouted at him not to hurt her, at which point Butcher punched King in the face with a glass that he was holding. The glass broke and cut King, who fell to the floor. When King got up, Butcher and his wife had left the room.

Jim is extremely concerned about the police officer's refusal to make fuller disclosure. In particular he is concerned that the police officer is withholding damaging information from other witnesses, which will then be used to ambush his client, Peter Butcher, if Butcher starts giving his account in interview. He therefore tries to persuade PC Stanley to go into more detail about the incident, but the officer refuses. Jim makes representations to the custody officer, and asks for the officer's refusal to be noted on the custody record.

DOCUMENT 1

Westchurch Police
CUSTODY RECORD

		Number	—/020607
		Station	W1
		OIC	487
Surname	BUTCHER	**DOB**	26/2/–(29)
First name(s)	PETER MICHAEL		

Address	FLAT 4, JAMES PARK EAST BUILDINGS PARK STREET, WESTCHURCH
Arrested for	SUS. S.20 WOUNDING

Time/Date **Arrival at Station**	(23.15) 14.02.—	**Arrest**	(22.55) 14.02.—
Condition on arrival	MAY BE INTOXICATED. CUT PALM AND FINGERS R HAND.	**Relevant time**	23.15 14.02.—

A notice setting out my rights has been read to me and I have been provided with a copy. I have been provided with a written notice setting out my entitlements whiles in custody.

I <u>WANT</u> a solicitor as soon as practicable

Named solicitor: HALPERN DODDS & Co
Signature of detained person: *Peter Butcher*
Time: 23.20   Date: 14.02.—

NO I do <u>NOT WANT</u> a solicitor at this time

Signature of detained person:
Time: Date:

Notification of detention to named person: [Not requested]
Time: **Date**: 14.02.—

Detention Authorisation	Secure/preserve evidence relating to the offence, interview to obtain evidence by questioning including the opportunity to say what you want about this offence

Officer opening record: 3456   **Time**: 23.20   **Date**: 14.02.—

Last review of detention at: Next review of detention due before: 05.15		Name: BUTCHER, Peter M.
Date	**Time**	**Full details of any action/occurrence involving the detained person.** *Include full particulars of all visits/officers* **All entries to be signed by the writer (include rank/number)**
14/02	23.20	Detention authorised for questioning. Duty Solicitor Call Centre Contacted. Own solicitor Halpern Dodds requested. Ref no 1402112320A.
		Risk assessment: alcohol consumption – injury to hand. FME Dr James contacted and will attend. Sgt. 3456 Evans
14/02	23.20	Search prisoner. Cash, keys and laces retained. Risk assessment: no likely harm to self or others. To cell. 1 Sgt. 3456 Evans
15/02	00.05	Telephone call from Halpern Dodds representative – James Kettle. Prisoner from cell to custody suite telephone for legal advice. Sgt. 3456 Evans
15/02	00.15	Prisoner to cell. 1. Solicitor informed that FME is on call. Unlikely to interview before morning as officer in case is at hospital to take statement from injured party. Solicitor requests that I note that he wishes to attend for any interview and should be notified as soon as the interview is ready to proceed. Sgt. 3456 Evans
15/02	00.20	In cell – awake.
15/02	00.40	FME James attending prisoner. Sgt. 3456 Evans
15/02	00.45	Antiseptic cream to cuts on palm and fingers R hand. 2 paracetomol prescribed. Prisoner given two paracetomol and glass water. Prisoner certified fit for interview. Dr. James
15/02	01.20	In cell asleep. Sgt. 3456 Evans
15/02	02.20	In cell asleep. Sgt. 3456 Evans
15/02	03.20	In cell asleep. Sgt. 3456 Evans
15/02	04.20	In cell asleep. Sgt. 3456 Evans
15/02	05.15	Detention reviewed: detention authorised to secure evidence by way of questioning. Prisoner is being allowed a rest period. Asleep at time of review. Will be informed of review at first opportunity. Insp. 781 Laidford.
15/02	05.40	In cell, awake. Given cup of tea. Informed of the review. Wishes to be interviewed now. Informed that Solicitor will be contacted to attend. Sgt. 3456 Evans
15/02	05.43	Solicitor representative contacted. Will attend. Sgt. 3456 Evans
15/02	06.00	Custody transferred to Sgt. 287 Baker. Sgt. 3456 Evans
15.02	06.10	Solicitor arrives. Given view of custody record. Solicitor to custody room B. Sgt 287 Baker
15.02	06.12	Prisoner from cell to custody room B for private consultation with solicitor. Sgt 287 Baker
15.02	06.40	Solicitor requests fuller disclosure regarding the incident from OIC. OIC states that he has made sufficient disclosure for prisoner to know the case against him. Solicitor requests that I note the response on the custody record. Sgt 287 Baker
15.02	06.42	Custody to PC 487 Stanley for interviewing. Sgt 287 Baker
15.02	07.11	The interview with the prisoner is concluded. The prisoner has been interviewed in accordance with the provisions of the Police and Criminal Evidence Act 1984 and of the Codes of Practice. Stanley, PC 487.

15.02	07.25	Matter referred to CPS for charging decision – decision relayed to charge. Butcher to cell for consultation with solicitor while charge is prepared. Sgt 287 Baker
15.02	08.10	Prisoner charged. Response to caution: I told you. It wasn't me. Solicitor makes representation re bail. Bail refused: likely to abscond and to interfere with witnesses. Prisoner to cell. Solicitor leaves. Sgt 287 Baker
15.02	08.30	Meal in cell.
15.02	09.10	Into custody of PC Selborne for transport to Market Street Magistrates' Court. Sgt 287 Baker

PROPERTY

Withheld by police	Retained by prisoner
Seal number **Cash**: £63.10 **Items withheld**: 1 set keys, 1 pr. shoe laces	

Reason for withholding property (if applicable):
to prevent harm or loss to self or property

I agree that the property listed above is correct:
Name: Peter Butcher   Witnessed by: Terry Munford

Signature: *Peter Butcher*   Signature: *Terry Munford*

Date: 14.02.—   Time: 23.20

AMENDMENTS

Withheld by police	Retained by prisoner
Seal number **Cash**: **Items withheld**:	

Reason for withholding property (if applicable):
I agree that the property listed above is correct:

Name: Witnessed by:

Signature: Signature:

Date: Time:

DISPOSAL

How disposed of: Returned to prisoner

Signature: *Peter Butcher*

Witness: *WPC 6564 Gordon*

Date: 15.02.—

06.12 Advising Peter Butcher

When Jim sees Peter Butcher in the interview room, he first checks with Peter that he is feeling well enough to be interviewed. He also makes his own assessment, and decides that Peter is clearly sober now, and that he has at least had some rest.

Jim outlines the police account of what has happened, but stresses that the police may well be withholding evidence. Peter is furious about what Arthur King is saying. He makes clear that King has always hated him, that there is a long history of ill-feeling between the two men, and that he only came back into the room because he heard a lot of shouting and yelling and was worried about the safety of his bride, Joanne, who is pregnant. He explains that he pushed into the crowd to try to get Joanne to safety, and Arthur King went for him. He stumbled as Arthur lunged at him. The beer glass that he was holding hit a chair or table and smashed. He dropped the glass and grabbed Joanne by the arm to leave. Meanwhile Arthur King stumbled and fell over. Peter is not clear how King came to be injured. He presumes that the injury arose from King falling on the dropped glass.

Advice on whether to answer questions in interview

A lengthy discussion then takes place. It is clear that Peter Butcher is prepared to put his account forward in interview. He is not clear on the exact sequence of events leading up to King's injury, but Jim takes the view that this is entirely explicable in the context of a confused melee of this kind.

Jim, however, is very concerned that the inadequate disclosure means that the police could well be hoping to pin Peter Butcher down to one account, so that they can then produce evidence from other witnesses to discredit his version of events. Jim therefore advises Peter in the strongest possible terms that he should not answer questions in interview, notwithstanding the possible inferences. Peter reluctantly accepts this advice.

Is Jim's advice correct?

With the benefit of hindsight, it is probably not good advice. As you will see, in fact the police do not seem to have been withholding any hugely incriminating information. The effect of Peter's refusal to answer questions is therefore that there will be potential inferences under s.34 (failure to mention defence facts) and s.36 (failure to account for the cuts on his hands). Potentially, the "no comment interview" could dramatically undermine the credibility of Peter's account when it is put forward at trial.

Although as a general rule it is not a good idea for a client to give a "partial comment" interview – i.e. answering some questions and not others – in this case, this would have been one possible solution. Peter could have put forward his basic response to King's allegations – "He was drunk. He fell over. I never hit him." – and could then have refused to answer further questions until fuller disclosure was made. Alternatively, Jim could have handed in a prepared statement at the start of the interview to set out his defence and thereafter he could have remained silent. Again, this would put his case forward in anticipation of fuller details being disclosed by the police during the interview.

Advice on identification procedures

Jim and Peter agree that there is no point in requesting an identification procedure if the witness is Arthur King. Obviously King is identifying Peter by name as the person who attacked him. If there are other witnesses, a parade may be appropriate, although all of them will presumably know who Peter is since he was the groom.

Jim then notifies the police that his client is ready for interview.

DOCUMENT 2

[Note that this is a copy of the police transcript of the interview which is served on the defence as Advance Disclosure, along with other prosecution material, prior to the initial hearing. It is included at this early stage so that you can see how the interview progressed.]

WESTCHURCH POLICE

RECORD OF TAPE RECORDED INTERVIEW

PLACE OF INTERVIEW: *WESTCHURCH POLICE STATION*

TIME OF INTERVIEW:

    START: *06.43*

    FINISH: *07.10*

DATE OF INTERVIEW: *15th February —*

TAPE REFERENCE NUMBER(S): *JSP/190/008/SB/9*

EXHIBIT REF: *ES/1*

FULL NAME OF INTERVIEWEE: *Peter Michael BUTCHER*

DATE OF BIRTH: *26/2/— (29 years old)*

ADDRESS: *Flat 4, James Park East Buildings, Park Street, Westchurch*

INTERVIEWING OFFICERS: *PC STANLEY 487*
WPC HERBERT 621

OTHER PERSONS PRESENT: *Jim KETTLE - solicitor*

****

CONTENT OF INTERVIEW

TAPE TIME/

NUMBER
00.00

STANLEY	Introductions and caution. Do you understand?
A	Yes.
STANLEY	Peter, you have a legal representative present. I'm sure he will have explained to you how important this interview is. Serious allegations have been made against you by Mr King ...
A	He's a drunk.
STANLEY	Just let me finish, Peter. Serious allegations have been made. This is your opportunity to respond to them. As I have said, you do not have to say anything. If, however, you don't tell us about things now, and you later want to put forward these explanations in your defence at court, the court can draw inferences from your not having mentioned them at this stage. Do you appreciate that?
KETTLE	Officer, before this interview began I have made representations both to

	you and to the Custody Sergeant that my client cannot possibly respond to the allegations that are being made if you will not disclose what the other witnesses in this case have said about the incident. A number of arrests were made. This appears to have been a confused melee. My client cannot reasonably respond to a case without more details. I am therefore now advising my client not to answer questions at this stage.
STANLEY	Well, although I am under no obligation to disclose any matters to you, as you know I have told you about the allegation made by Mr King against your client. The allegation is that there was a brawl at the reception in which your client punched Mr King once in the face with a glass. The glass broke and caused extensive injuries to Mr King's face.
KETTLE	But you agree, officer, that you have not disclosed any further details concerning this offence?
STANLEY	As I have said, your client has sufficient information to know what the victim is alleging. If your client has an answer, now is the time to put it forward.
KETTLE	I do not accept that it is reasonable for my client to be expected to answer questions when he does not know the detail of the case against him. Accordingly I am now advising my client to remain silent.
STANLEY	As you wish. You will appreciate, however, that I am entitled to put questions to Mr Butcher in any event.
KETTLE	Yes.
STANLEY	Peter, you have heard what your legal representative and I have been saying, is there anything at this stage that you wish to say?
A	[Silence]
STANLEY	Very well. Before I put any questions to you I wish first to put to you the statement that you made on being cautioned at the North Cliffe Castle Hotel. I told you that Mr King had said you had attacked him. Your response was to say: "He's a drunken fool. He ruined our wedding." Do you agree that those were your words?
A	[Silence]
STANLEY	Peter, Mr King alleges that during the course of the brawl at the wedding, you punched him in the face with a glass. Is this what happened?
A	[Silence]
STANLEY	Mr King alleges that the brawl began as the result of your taking exception to something he'd said in his speech. He says that you stormed out of the room and that your Best Man then came over and threatened him. He says that what I suppose could be described as a shouting match ensued and that you pushed your way into the group and grabbed Mr King's daughter, your wife. He says that he remonstrated with you, at which point you deliberately punched him in the face.
A	[Suspect makes a sound of disgust and shakes his head]
STANLEY	Very well, Peter. But if you don't agree, if you have something to say, then now is the time to say it.
A	I'm saying nothing on legal advice. That's all I've got to say.
STANLEY	Well do you agree that you punched him in the face?
A	[Silence]
HERBERT	Was it an accident, Peter?
STANLEY	Or did you have to do it in self-defence?
A	[Silence]

HERBERT	There must be some explanation, Peter. How do you think your father-in-law got hurt?
KETTLE	I think my client has made clear that he does not intend to answer questions on my legal advice.
STANLEY	Very well. Let's move on. Peter, the FME has put some cream on your right hand but I noticed earlier that you have several cuts to the palm and to the inside of the fingers of your right hand. You are being questioned concerning an alleged wounding in which a glass was smashed in the victim's face. I believe that these cuts may have been caused by your assaulting Mr King with a glass. I am therefore asking you to provide an explanation for the mark. The court may draw a proper inference from a failure by you to account for the mark, and as you know this interview is being recorded and can be used at evidence at trial. Would you therefore please explain how your hand got cut?
A	[Silence]
HERBERT	All right then Peter, what about where you were when Mr King was assaulted. Do you agree that you were present at the scene?
STANLEY	Again, Peter, you were in the corridor outside the room when you were arrested. You are alleged to have assaulted Mr King. Do you agree that you were present in the room when he was assaulted, and if so, what were you doing there? If you fail to account for your presence, again the court may draw a proper inference from your failure.
A	[Silence]
STANLEY	Mr Kettle, are you sure you don't want to advise Mr Butcher to answer these questions? If he wasn't involved or if there is some other good explanation he is only hurting his defence by his refusal to answer questions.
KETTLE	I have nothing further to add to what was said at the start of the interview.
HERBERT	Would your client be prepared to co-operate with an identification procedure?
KETTLE	Are you going to have a video i/d parade? I thought we agreed that since everyone present knew Mr Butcher and would recognise him, there was no merit in having an identification procedure unless you had a witness who said that they did not recognise the alleged assailant. Have you got such a witness?
STANLEY	I agree. At present a parade doesn't resolve anything. Mr Butcher, is there anything that you wish to say at this stage?
A	[Silence]

Interview terminated.

Matters arising in the interview

Only one matter was raised that had not previously been disclosed. This is the comment: "He's a drunken fool. He ruined our wedding." The police are under a duty to put any significant comments or silences to the suspect at the start of the interview (C 11.4 & 11.4A). Peter explains to Jim after the interview that he did make the comment, but he simply meant that King had ruined his wedding; it isn't an admission that he assaulted King in any way.

Note, however, that the interview has given Peter an opportunity to put forward all relevant defence facts, and he has now failed to do so. The police have also complied with the duty to give an "ordinary language caution" (C 10.11), and thus there will be a potential inference under s.36 from Peter's failure to explain the cuts on his hand.

After the interview

Once the interview has been terminated, the officers indicate that they intend to contact the CPS with a view to taking a charging decision. Peter is returned to his cell and Jim accompanies him to discuss what will happen next.

Jim discusses with Peter the possibility of making a statement at charge. Peter, however, is fed up and concerned only with whether he will be granted bail. He reminds Jim that he has just spent his wedding night in custody and he wants to be released. Jim discusses Peter's previous convictions with him, and in particular the convictions for failing to attend court. He advises Peter that it is likely that the custody officer will refuse to grant bail, but that Peter will be brought to court that morning.

Jim completes the Criminal Defence Service forms so that an application for a representation order can be submitted to the court at the hearing. Jim checks Peter's employment status and Peter states that he is currently unemployed and is receiving income-based Job Seekers' Allowance. He signs the representation order application that Jim has completed (see Document 5), [Note that the financial information form (CDS 15) does not need to be completed. Peter is automatically eligible because he is in receipt of income-based Job Seekers Allowance.] He also tries to make as comprehensive notes as possible on all material which may be relevant to bail, as whoever represents Peter will to need to make a bail application in a few hours' time and will not have the opportunity to take detailed instructions before then.

08.10: Peter Butcher is charged with s.20 wounding

The CPS instruct the police to charge Peter and he is charged with the malicious wounding of Arthur King. As Jim anticipated bail is refused, despite his representations, on the basis that Peter is likely to fail to answer his bail and is likely to interfere with prosecution witnesses. Peter will be produced at court later that morning. Jim confirms that someone from the firm will be at court to represent him.

DOCUMENT 3

WESTCHURCH POLICE
NOTICE OF OFFENCES CHARGED

Sheet No.......1.........of.......1....
Custody Record No: —/020607
JSP 190008/XB/9

AREA COMMAND: WESTCHURCH
SECTION: Westchurch Central

COURT: WESTCHURCH MAGISTRATES COURT
Market Street
Westchurch

at........10 a.m.......on.......Saturday 15/2/—

PERSON CHARGED: Peter Michael BUTCHER
ADDRESS:

Flat 4,
James Park East Buildings
Park Street
Westchurch

D.O.B. 26/2/- (29 years old)
OCCUPATION:
Unemployed Marine Welder

You are charged with the offences shown below. You do not have to say anything but it may harm your defence if you do not mention now something which you later rely on in court. Anything you do say may be given in evidence.

CHARGE

That on the 14th day of February —— you did unlawfully and maliciously wound Arthur King

<u>Contrary to section 20 of the Offences against the Person Act 1861</u>.

REPLY: *I told you. It wasn't me.*
OFFICER IN THE CASE: P.C. Stanley 487
OFFICER CHARGING: P.C. Stanley 487
TIME/DATE: 15/2/—
08.10
OFFICER ACCEPTING CHARGE: J. Baker Sgt.

NOTICE OF BAIL

The above named has this day been released on bail in accordance with s.38 (1) of the Police And Criminal Evidence Act 1984 and the Bail Act 1976 in connection with the alleged offence(s) outlined above, and is required to surrender to custody at the Magistrates' Court sitting at the place and time shown above to answer the charge(s).

Bail: ~~Yes~~/No   *Copy of charge:* Yes/~~No~~

I have been informed that unless I surrender to custody as shown above I may be liable to a fine or imprisonment or both.

Signature of person: …………………………………………..
Time: *Date:*   *No:*   *Signature:*

09.00 Briefing the advocate

On leaving the police station, Jim immediately contacts Edwina Halpern, who is the senior criminal litigator at Halpern Dodds. She knows Peter, having represented him on a number of prior occasions. She therefore arranges to meet Jim at the office, so that she can collect his police station notes on her way to the Saturday court.

Edwina is concerned when Jim explains what has happened at the police station. She already anticipates problems from the no comment interview. However, there is nothing that can be done about this for the time being and she concentrates on making sure that she has the material ready for the hearing. Edwina starts her preparation by having a quick glance at Blackstone's Criminal Practice. The section dealing with s.20 OAPA provides the sentencing guidelines on s.20 offences involving "glassing". Edwina can see that the "going rate" for the offence is likely to be a significant custodial penalty. The use of a weapon – the glass – and the serious injury will be taken into account when deciding the most appropriate venue for trial and, given the likely sentence, it is unlikely that the magistrates will in due course accept jurisdiction.

This information is central both to the representation order application and the bail application. For legal aid purposes, Edwina can confidently indicate that it is a serious offence and the sentence is likely to involve loss of liberty. For bail purposes, the seriousness and the likely custodial outcome give some indication of the likely prosecution objections. The fact that the case is likely to be sent to Crown Court for trial gives Edwina an indication that a refusal of bail is likely to result in Peter being remanded in custody for three or four months awaiting trial.

Edwina is confident that the seriousness of the matter means that the court is almost certain to grant a representation order. She rightly anticipates that there is likely to be more argument about the grant of bail.

Saturday 15th February The first hearing: Westchurch Magistrates' Court

Edwina arrives at court. She asks to be notified as soon as the police van arrives with Peter Butcher and the other police station detainees. She submits her legal aid application to the clerk of the court who indicates that it is granted subject to the financial information being confirmed as correct.

She finds the CPS representative, who is still reading the summary of the case. The representative gives her a copy of the summary along with a copy of Peter Butcher's criminal convictions to confirm with her client. These will be relevant to the bail application. Although the prosecution should have the full advance disclosure package available, as it is a Saturday court, they are not fully prepared so there are no prosecution statements to hand. It is agreed that the case will have to be adjourned for plea and mode of trial until this material can be considered, subject of course to the Magistrates' discretion. They will be anxious to make progress straight away under the Criminal Procedure Rules.

When Peter arrives at court, Edwina goes down to the cells to let him know that she is here and to briefly discuss the case. Edwina shows him the previous convictions form. He agrees that it is accurate, to the best of his recollection. In particular Edwina finds out why Peter failed to attend court last year. It turns out that he was working on a North Sea oil rig at the time, and was unable to get to the mainland. This explains the otherwise very lenient conditional discharge that was imposed.

They briefly discuss the court hearing. Edwina asks if Peter has anyone who can stand surety for him, but the only person is his wife, Joanne, and he does not want her called to court as she is six months' pregnant and he is worried that she will find the experience too upsetting. Edwina advises Peter that due to the lack of disclosure at this stage, the case is likely to be adjourned. She will make a bail application on his behalf in the meantime. The bail application is set out at **Document 6**.

DOCUMENT 4

WESTCHURCH POLICE

NAME: Peter Michael BUTCHER   **ref:** CRO 49393/—

DATE OF BIRTH: 26/2/-

RECORD OF CONVICTIONS OR FINDINGS OF GUILT

December — [10 years ago]	Minster Magistrates	s.4 Public Order Act	Fine - £150
May — [9 years ago]	Westchurch Magistrates	s.47 OAPA - ABH	Community Service Order - 100 hours
January — [8 years ago]	Westchurch Magistrates	Common Assault	Fine - £90
		Breach of the Peace	Bind over to keep peace - 12 months
		Failure to surrender to Bail	Fine - £130
June — [7 years ago]	East Minster Magistrates	Taking a motor vehicle without consent	Community Order Supervision Requirement 12 months.
		Going equipped	Fine £120
January — [6 years ago]	Westchurch Magistrates	Burglary (non-residential) x 4	Custodial sentence - 15 weeks.
July — [last year]	East Harham Magistrates	Careless driving	Fine - £300 6 penalty points
		Failure to surrender to Bail	Conditional discharge 6 months

Form CDS14

Application for Legal Aid in Criminal Proceedings

Protect – Personal

MAAT Reference

If the case is an **Appeal to the Crown Court** and there is no change in circumstances, answer **1** and then go to question **23**.

Case type
- Summary ☐
- Either way ☑
- Indictable ☐
- Committal for sentence ☐
- Appeal to Crown Court ☐
- Trial now in Crown Court ☐
- Appeal to Crown Court and no changes ☐

Priority case
- Custody ☑
- Vulnerable ☐
- Youth ☐
- Late application in the Crown Court for trial ☐
- Date of trial

ⓘ Please use the Guidance
If you do not complete the form correctly, we will return it. You will find Guidance to help you fill in the form correctly, at: www.legalservices.gov.uk/criminal/forms/7573.asp
If you need more help or advice, please contact a solicitor.

If you have a partner
If you answer Yes to a question which asks about you **or** your partner, and that answer is true for both of you, give details for you **and** your partner, not for one of you only.

About you: 1

1

Mr ☑ Mrs ☐ Miss ☐ Ms ☐ Other title ☐

Your forenames or other names (in BLOCK LETTERS)
PETER | MICHAEL

ⓘ **Guidance** National Insurance Number and ARC Number: give one of these only.

Your surname or family name (in BLOCK LETTERS)
BUTCHER

Your date of birth
26 / 2 / 1983

National Insurance Number
X X 4 4 4 4 4 4 X

Application Registration Card (ARC) Number

Contacting you

2

Do you have a usual home address?
No ☐ Yes ☑ → Your usual home address
FLAT 4, JAMES PARK EAST BUILDINGS, PARK STREET, WESTCHURCH

3

✓ your solicitor's address **only**, if you are of 'No Fixed Abode', or not at your usual address because you are on bail or remand.

To what address should we write to you?
Your usual home address ☑
Your solicitor's address ☐ (see the side panel)
This address

4

Your email address

CDS14 Version 9 ©Crown copyright 2012

338 Appendix B

5 Your telephone number (landline): 02332 470470
Mobile phone number: N/A
Work phone number: N/A

About you: 2

6 ✓ one box

Your usual home address is:
- a Tenancy (rented) ✓
- Temporary ☐
- Your parent's home ☐ (you live with them)
- Owned by you ☐
- Owned by your partner ☐
- Owned jointly by you and your partner ☐

7 Are you under 18 years old?
No ✓   Yes ☐ → Are you charged with an adult? No ☐ Go to **23** Yes ☐ Go to **23**

8 Guidance
Do you have a partner?
No ☐   Yes ✓ Go to **10**

9 ✓ one box / Guidance
You are: Single ☐ Go to **14**   Widowed ☐ Go to **14**   Divorced ☐ Go to **14**
Married but separated ☐ Date of separation [ ] Go to **14**

10 ✓ one box
You and your partner are:
Married ☐   In a Civil Partnership ☐   Living together ✓

About your partner

11 Your partner's details

Mr ☐ Mrs ☐ Miss ✓ Ms ☐ Other title [ ]
Your forenames or other names (in BLOCK LETTERS): JOANNE

Guidance
National Insurance Number and ARC Number: give one of these only.

Surname or family name (in BLOCK LETTERS): KING
Date of birth: 21 / 12 / 1983

National Insurance Number: X X 5 5 5 5 5 5 X
Application Registration Card (ARC) Number: [ ]

12 If you ✓ Yes, and your partner is a victim, prosecution witness, or co-defendant with a conflict of interest, do not give your partner's details for questions **13** to **22**

Is your partner a victim, prosecution witness or a co-defendant in the case for which you require legal aid?
No ✓   Yes ☐ → Victim ☐ Go to **14**
Prosecution witness ☐ Go to **14**
Co-defendant ☐ Does your partner have a conflict of interest? No ☐ Go to **13** Yes ☐ Go to **14**

CDS14 Version 9   2   ©Crown copyright 2012

13 Is your partner's usual home address different from yours (the address at question 2)?

No ✓   Yes ☐ → Your partner's usual home address

Your income and your partner's income

14 Do you or your partner receive any of the benefits listed here?

⚠ Guidance

No ☐   Yes ✓ →

	You	Your Partner
Income Support	☐ Go to **23**	☐ Go to **23**
Income-Related Employment and Support Allowance (ESA)	☐ Go to **23**	☐ Go to **23**
Income-Based Jobseeker's Allowance (JSA)	✓ When did you last sign on? 10 / 2 / 2012 Go to **23**	✓ When did you last sign on? 10 / 2 / 2012 Go to **23**
Guarantee State Pension Credit	☐ Go to **23**	☐ Go to **23**

15 Do you or your partner, together, in a year have a total income from all sources before tax or any other deduction, of more than £12, 475?

⚠ Guidance

No ✓   Yes ☐ → You will need to **complete form CDS15**. Go to **23**

16 Sources of income for you and your partner. Please give details in the table

⚠ Evidence

⚠ Guidance, for:
- Employment
- Total of other benefits
- Other source of income

For all parts of this question:
- If you do not receive income from a source, put **NIL** after the '£'.
- After '**every**' put either:
  week,
  2 weeks,
  4 weeks,
  month,
  or year.

	You		Your Partner	
Employment (wage or salary)	£ every	Before tax ☐ After tax ☐	£ every	Before tax ☐ After tax ☐
Child Benefit	£ every		£ every	
Working Tax Credits and Child Tax credits	£ every		£ every	
Total of other benefits	£ every		£ every	
Maintenance income	£ every		£ every	
Pensions	£ every		£ every	
Any other source of income such as: - a student grant or loan - board or rent from a family, lodger or tenant. - rent from a property - financial support from friends and family	£ every Source:		£ every Source:	

CDS14 Version 9   ©Crown copyright 2012

17 ⓘGuidance Are you or your partner self-employed, in a business partnership, or either a company director or a shareholder in a private company?
No ✓   Yes ☐ → You will need to **complete form CDS15**. Go to **23**

18 Do you or your partner have any income, savings or assets which are under a restraint order or a freezing order?
No ✓   Yes ☐ → You will need to **complete form CDS15**. Go to **23**

19 ⓘGuidance Are you charged with a Summary offence, only?
No ✓   Yes ☐ Go to **22**

20 Do you or your partner own or part-own any land or property of any kind, including your own home, in the United Kingdom or overseas?
No ✓   Yes ☐ → You will need to **complete form CDS15**. Go to **23**

21 ⓘGuidance Do you or your partner have any savings or investments, in the United Kingdom or overseas?
No ✓   Yes ☐ → You will need to **complete form CDS15**. Go to **23**

22 Do your answers to the previous questions tell us that you have no income from any of the sources which we have asked about?
No ☐   Yes ✓ → How do you and your partner pay your bills and daily expenses?

BENEFITS

Information for the Interests of Justice test

23 ⓘGuidance

Describe the charge briefly: for instance, 'Assault on a neighbour'.

What charges have been brought against you?

Charge	Date of offence
1 S.20 OFFENCES AGAINST THE PERSON ACT 1861	15 / 2 / 2012
2	
3	
4	

24 ⓘGuidance
✓ one box only: if you are charged with more than one offence, ✓ the most serious.

The type of offence with which you are charged

Class A ☐   Homicide and related grave offences
Class B ✓   Offences involving serious violence or damage, and serious drugs offences
Class C ☐   Lesser offences involving violence or damage, and less serious drugs offences
Class D ☐   Sexual offences and offences against children →

CDS14   Version 9   4   ©Crown copyright 2012

Class E ☐ Burglary etc

Class F ☐ Other offences of dishonesty (specified offences and offences where the value is £30,000 or less)

Class G ☐ Other offences of dishonesty (specified offences and offences where the value involved exceeds £30,000 but does not exceed £100,000)

Class H ☐ Miscellaneous other offences

Class I ☐ Offences against public justice and similar offences

Class J ☐ Serious sexual offences

Class K ☐ Other offences of dishonesty (high value: if the value involved exceeds £100,000)

25 Do you have any co-defendants in this case?

No ☑ Go to 27   Yes ☐ → Their names

26 Is there any reason why you and your co-defendants cannot be represented by the same solicitor?

No ☑   Yes ☐ → The reason(s)

27 Are there any other criminal cases or charges against you or your partner which are still in progress?

No ☑   Yes ☐ → You   Your Partner

The charges

The Court hearing the case

Date of the next hearing

28 Which Court is hearing the case for which you need legal aid?

The Court hearing the case   Date of the hearing

CDS14 Version 9   5   ©Crown copyright 2012

342   Appendix B

29 Why do you want legal aid?

Guidance

1 to **9** are possible reasons.

We suggest you choose one or more reasons with the help of a solicitor.

For each reason you choose, say why you have chosen it.

Mention any evidence that supports your choice of a reason.

If you need more space to answer, please use a separate sheet of paper and put your full name, date of birth and 'Question 29' at the top of the sheet. Please make sure you show which part of the question (**1** to **10**) your writing refers to.

1 It is likely that I will lose my liberty if any matter in the proceedings is decided against me.

> THIS IS A SERIOUS OFFENCE AND THE SENTENCING GUIDELINES MAKE CLEAR THAT A CUSTODIAL SENTENCE WILL BE INEVITABLE IF I AM FOUND GUILTY

2 I have been given a sentence that is suspended or non-custodial. If I break this, the court may be able to deal with me for the original offence.

3 It is likely that I will lose my livelihood.

4 It is likely that I will suffer serious damage to my reputation.

5 A substantial question of law may be involved (whether arising from legislation, judicial authority or other source of law).

> I HAVE PREVIOUS CONVICTIONS WHICH MAY BE THE SUBJECT OF A BAD CHARACTER APPLICATION BY THE PROSECUTION. THERE ARE LIKELY S.34 AND S.36 INFERENCES FROM MY FAILURE TO PUT FORWARD DEFENCE FACTS IN INTERVIEW.

6 I may not be able to understand the court proceedings or present my own case.

7 Witnesses may need to be traced or interviewed on my behalf.

> THIS WAS A LARGE AND CONFUSED BRAWL. MANY WITNESSES ARE FAMILY MEMBERS. I WILL NEED A SOLICITOR TO TRACE AND INTERVIEW THEM ALL.

8 The proceedings may involve expert cross-examination of a prosecution witness (whether an expert or not).

> THE MAIN PROSECUTION WITNESS IS MY FATHER IN LAW. EXPERT CROSS EXAMINATION IS NEEDED TO AVOID INADVERTENTLY RAISING ISSUES IN RELATION TO BAD CHARACTER.

9 It is in the interests of another person (such as the person making a complaint or other witness) that I am represented.

> MY PARTNER WOULD FIND IT DISTRESSING IF I HAD TO CROSS EXAMINE HER FATHER (MY FATHER IN LAW) MYSELF. IT IS NOT APPROPRIATE THAT I CROSS EXAMINE THE MAIN PROSECUTION WITNESS AS IT MAY BE SEEN AS INTIMIDATING IN A VIOLENCE CASE.

10 Any other reason

Legal representation

30

ⓘ Guidance

You must tell the solicitor that you have said in this form that you want them to act for you.

The solicitor who you want to act for you

Mr ☐ Mrs ☐ Miss ☐ Ms ✓ Other title ☐

Solicitor's initials, surname or family name (in BLOCK LETTERS)

EDWINA HALPERN

Name and address of the solicitor's firm

HALPERN DODDS, 29 CHESTERFIELD PLACE, WESTCHURCH

Telephone (land line): 0071 229 228

Mobile phone:

Document Exchange (DX):

Fax: 0071 229 229

email address:

31

✓ **1** or **2**

If you choose **2**, ✓ one of the two other options to show whether you have been instructed by a firm with an LSC contract, or by a solicitor employed by the LSC.

Examples of an LSC contract are the 2010 Standard Crime Contract or an Individual Case Contract.

Declaration by the legal representative

1 ✓ I represent the applicant. I confirm that I am authorised to provide representation under a contract issued by the Legal Services Commission (LSC).

2 ☐ I represent the applicant. I confirm that I have been instructed to provide representation by:

☐ a firm which holds a contract issued by the Legal Services Commission (LSC)

☐ a solicitor employed by the Legal Services Commission (LSC) in a Public Defender Office who is authorised to provide representation.

Signed: *E. Halpern*

Date: 15 / 2 / 2012

Legal Service Provider's LSC Account Number: X X 1 2 3 H

Full name (in BLOCK LETTERS): E. HALPERN

About the information which you have provided and its protection

32

ⓘ Guidance

Data Protection

You will find more information about data protection in the Guidance for this question.

- We will process the information in this form according to the principles of the Data Protection Act 1998 and relevant provisions about confidentiality.

- We or HM Courts and Tribunals Service, may use the information on this form and on forms CDS15 and CDS15C, to produce management or research information. To help us do this, we need extra information about you. **Question 1, and questions 2 and 3 on page 8, ask you for this extra information.** The information we publish will not identify you or anyone else.

1 Are you male or female?

Male ✓   Female ☐   I prefer not to say ☐

CDS14 Version 9   7   ©Crown copyright 2012

344   Appendix B

2 Do you consider that you have a disability?

No ☑   Yes ☐ → The best definition: I prefer not to say ☐

✓ one box in the table to show the best definition of your disability.

The Equality Act 2010 defines disability as a physical or mental impairment which has a substantial and long-term adverse effect on a person's ability to carry out normal day-to-day activities.

Physical impairment ☐   Cognitive impairment ☐
Sensory impairment ☐   Long-Standing Illness ☐
Mental Health Condition ☐   Health Condition ☐
Learning Disability or Difficulty ☐   Other ☐

3 Which of the options in the table best describes you?   I prefer not to say ☐

✓ one box in the table of ethnic groups.

White	Mixed	Asian or Asian British	Black or Black British	Chinese	Other ethnic group
British ☑	White and Black Caribbean ☐	Indian ☐	Black Caribbean ☐	Chinese ☐	Other ☐
Irish ☐	White and Black African ☐	Pakistani ☐	Black African ☐		
White other ☐	White and Asian ☐	Bangladeshi ☐	Black other ☐		
	Mixed other ☐	Asian other ☐			

Evidence to support the information which you have given

33 Have you have been directed to complete a form CDS15 (see questions 15, 17, 18, 20 and 21)?

No ☑   Yes ☐ → If you have a partner, now go to **38**. If not, go to **39**.

34 Has a court remanded you in custody?

No ☑ Go to **36**   Yes ☐ Go to **35**

35 Will your case be heard in a magistrates' court?

No ☑   Yes ☐ → If you have a partner, now go to **38**. If not, go to **39**.

36 Are you employed?

⚠ Evidence

No ☑   Yes ☐ →

- **If your case will be heard in a magistrates' court**
  We need a copy of your wage slip or salary advice. You must provide it with this form: see the guidance about evidence.

⚠ Evidence

- **If your case will be heard in the Crown Court**
  We need a copy of your wage slip or salary advice. You must provide it with this form or within 14 days of the date of your application: see the guidance about evidence.

37 If you have a partner, now go to **38**. If you do not have a partner, go to **39**.

CDS14   Version 9   ©Crown copyright 2012

Declaration by your partner

38

⚠ Guidance

If your partner is not able to sign this declaration, you must give the reason at the end of question **39**.

I declare that this form and any form CDS15 and CDS15C is a true statement of all my financial circumstances to the best of my knowledge and belief. I agree to the Legal Services Commission and HM Courts and Tribunals Service, or my partner's solicitor, checking the information I have given, with the Department for Work and Pensions, HM Revenue and Customs or other people and organisations. I authorise those people and organisations to provide the information for which the Legal Services Commission, HM Courts and Tribunals Service or my partner's solicitor may ask.

Signed: *[signature]*

Date: 15 / 2 / 2012

Full name (in BLOCK LETTERS): JOANNE KING

Declaration by you

39

When you read this declaration, please keep in mind that some parts of it may not apply to you because the declaration is designed to cover several types of court case.

I apply for the right to representation for the purposes of criminal proceedings under the Access to Justice Act 1999.

I declare that this form and any form CDS15 and CDS15C is a true statement of my financial circumstances and those of my partner to the best of my knowledge and belief. I understand that this form must be fully completed before a Representation Order can be issued. I understand that if I tell you anything that is not true on this form or the documents I send with it, or leave anything out:

- I may be prosecuted for fraud. I understand that if I am convicted, I may be sent to prison or pay a fine.
- My legal aid may be stopped and I may be asked to pay back my costs in full to the Legal Services Commission.
- If my case is in the Crown Court, the Legal Services Commission may change the amount of the contribution which I must pay.

Crown Court I understand that in Crown Court proceedings the information I have given in this form will be used to determine whether I am liable to contribute to the costs of my defence under an Income Contribution Order during my case, or if I am convicted, under a Final Contribution Order at the end of my case, or both.

I understand that if I am ordered to pay towards my legal aid under an Income Contribution Order, or if I am convicted and ordered to pay under a Final Contribution Order, but fail to pay as an Order instructs me, interest may be charged or enforcement proceedings may be brought against me, or both.

I understand that I may have to pay the costs of the enforcement proceedings in addition to the payments required under the Contribution Order, and that the enforcement proceedings could result in a charge being placed on my home.

Evidence I agree to provide, when asked, further details and evidence of my finances and those of my partner, to the Legal Services Commission, its agents, or HM Courts & Tribunals Service to help them decide whether an Order should be made and the terms of any Order.

Changes I agree to tell Legal Services Commission or HM Courts & Tribunals Service if my income or capital or those of my partner, change. These changes include the sale of property, change of address, change in employment and change in capital. →

CDS14 Version 9 ©Crown copyright 2012

It is important that you understand that by signing this declaration you agree to the Legal Services Commission, the courts, or your solicitor, contacting your partner to check the information you have given in this form, and in forms CDS15 and CDS15C if you complete them.

Enquiries I authorise such enquiries as are considered necessary to enable Legal Services Commission, its agents, HM Courts & Tribunals Service, or my solicitor to find out my income and capital, and those of my partner. This includes my consent for parties such as my bank, building society, the Department for Work and Pensions or HM Revenue and Customs to provide information to assist the Legal Services Commission, its agents or HM Courts & Tribunals Service with their enquiries.

I consent to the Legal Services Commission or my solicitor contacting my partner for information and evidence about my partner's means. This includes circumstances where my partner is unable to sign or complete the form.

I understand that if the information which my partner provides is incorrect or if my partner refuses to provide information then: if my case is in the magistrates' court, my legal aid may be withdrawn or, if my case is in the Crown Court, I may be liable to sanctions. I understand that the sanctions may result in me paying towards the cost of my legal aid or, if I already pay, paying more towards the cost of my legal aid, or paying my legal aid costs in full.

Ending legal aid I understand that I must tell my solicitor and write to the court if I no longer want public representation. I understand that if I decline representation I may be liable for costs incurred to the date when my solicitor and the court receive my letter.

Signed *[signature]*

Date 15 / 2 / 2012

Full name (in BLOCK LETTERS)

PETER MICHAEL BUTCHER

If your partner has not signed the declaration at 38, please explain:

Official use

To perform the test, consider all the available details of all the charges, against the Interests of Justice criteria.

Mention issues here which you considered when you decided the application. Include information given orally.

I have performed the Interests of Justice test and the application is

Passed ☐ Refused ☐ My reason(s):

Financial eligibility for:

Magistrates' Court Passed ☐ Refused ☐

Crown Court No income contribution ☐ Contribution due ☐

Signed

Date / /

Name of the appropriate officer

Case Number

CDS14 Version 9

DOCUMENT 6

At court the CPS representative indicates that he objects to the grant of bail. It is clear to Edwina that he has been influenced by the custody officer's earlier refusal of bail.

The grounds put forward by the prosecution are that:

- Peter Butcher is likely to abscond: it is a serious offence that is likely to carry a custodial sentence; he has a relatively recent conviction for failing to attend court and a second conviction for the same offence.

- Peter Butcher is likely to interfere with prosecution witnesses – and in particular his father in law, the injured party, Arthur King.

In Edwina's application she makes sure that she responds directly to these issues.

Application for bail

Sir, my name is Edwina Halpern and I appear this morning for Mr Butcher. I can confirm that this is a case where Mr Butcher retains his prima facie right to bail under the Bail Act.

The grounds raised by the prosecution were that my client was either likely to abscond if he were granted bail, or that he was likely to interfere with the prosecution witnesses.

The prosecution has outlined the facts of this matter to the court. This is said to be an assault on my client's father in law, Mr King, arising from disorder at my client's wedding. In relation to the suggestion that Mr Butcher is likely to interfere with witnesses, the prosecution's case seems to be simply that in the light of the allegation of assault and its familial context, there is likely to be contact between the two parties and that this is a matter of concern to the prosecution. But that is it, sir. That is the sole basis for this objection.

Sir, Peter Butcher denies any involvement in the offence. He does not know how his father-in-law came to harm. At the time of the incident Mr Butcher was concerned only with shepherding his pregnant wife to safety. Indeed, the prosecution concedes that if there was an assault it is one that took place in the context of a general melee. They admit that a number of other people were arrested for related offences. From what little information the police have disclosed it appears that the allegation is of a single blow, delivered by someone in the midst of this confusion. So not only does my client deny any involvement, but there seems, at least at this stage, to be very little evidence to the contrary.

I mention this, sir, because it clearly goes to the issue of whether there is any substantial ground for believing that Mr Butcher would seek to interfere with a prosecution witness. Not only is there no motive in a case where Mr Butcher can confidently expect to clear his name, there is also no real evidence that Mr Butcher has any intention of approaching his father-in-law for any reason at all. Mr Butcher has a young wife, with a baby on the way. You can imagine his distress at having to deal with this incident. He has no desire to make matters worse. He wants only for the court to resolve this matter as soon as possible so that he can get on with his life.

The prosecution did refer you, to two previous convictions: one for common assault, one for s.47 assault. My friend accepts that these are matters that took place eight and nine years ago respectively. There has been no repetition of this type of behaviour. Indeed, other than a solitary driving offence last year, you will, I am sure, have noted that my client has avoided any trouble at all during the last six years. Under the circumstances, I would respectfully suggest that they have no bearing at all on this matter.

Turning to the suggestion that Peter Butcher would abscond if granted bail. I accept, sir, that this is a serious allegation. The prosecution in particular draws your attention to my client's two previous failures to attend court when granted bail. They argue that there must therefore be a substantial concern that if bail is granted today, my client will again fail to attend.

The first of these two breaches of bail took place over eight years ago. Although my client clearly had a somewhat troubled youth, you will note that this was the sole breach of this kind at that time. Since putting his past behind him, my client has only appeared once before the court, and this was last year in relation to a motoring matter. Here the prosecution directs you to a second Bail Act offence.

I understand that at the time of the offence in question, my client, whose normal employment is as a marine welder, was employed on a North Sea oil rig. He accepts that he failed to attend court. However, because of his employment, it is perhaps not entirely surprising that he was simply unable to get to court on the day in question. You and your colleagues will note, sir, that the court at the time felt it appropriate to impose no more than a conditional discharge in respect of that offence. I would suggest that this is a clear indication that the court regarded my client's failure to attend as carrying little culpability.

But equally importantly, sir, can I draw your attention to other relevant factors, which I would argue support the defence's position that there is no substantial likelihood that my client will fail to attend court. The first, and the most important, is that, as I have said, my client denies any involvement in this matter. He actively wants his name cleared. He has every reason to want to attend court to ensure that this happens. He has also just got married. He lives with his new wife. They have a baby on the way. This is where he has always lived. He could not have closer ties with this community. Not only has he no reason to want to leave, he has every reason to want to stay.

Sir, the prosecution raised these matters, as matters that show such a substantial likelihood that my client will abscond, such a substantial likelihood that he will interfere with witnesses that you can treat this as an exception to my client's right to be remanded on bail, pending the resolution of what may be a drawn out affair. I hope I have been able to show the court that there are in fact no grounds for concern, and certainly no substantial grounds for these concerns. I hope that I have persuaded you and your colleagues, sir, that this is a case where you should grant unconditional bail.

If you are not with me as to granting my client bail unconditionally, I know that my client would be prepared to undertake not to contact any specified prosecution witness, whether directly or indirectly. I know he would also be prepared to comply with any other conditions that might meet any other residual concerns that you might have. But my application this morning is for unconditional bail, and I am happy to address the court if there are any matters that are continuing to cause concern to yourself or to your colleagues. Otherwise, that, sir, is my submission.

Outcome of Hearing

Case is adjourned until Wednesday 26th February 20_ [note that this adjournment was an exception rather than the rule]

Bail is granted subject to conditions:

> (i) not to contact Arthur King directly or indirectly;
>
> (ii) to reside at Flat 4, James Park East Buildings, Park Street;
>
> (iii) to report to Westchurch Central Police station at 6.00 p.m. on Mondays and Thursdays.

DOCUMENT 7

Halpern Dodds
for all your legal needs

29 Chesterfield Place,
WESTCHURCH
Telephone (24 hours): 0071 229 228
Fax: 0071 229 229
e mail: HalpernDoddsX@germail.co.uk
17th February –

Dear Peter,

Westchurch Magistrates' Court matter: 26th February 20_ at 10am

I am writing to confirm what was arranged at court on Saturday morning, and to discuss the future progress of your case.

Funding your case

The court has granted a representation order in your case. This order will cover your legal costs in the magistrates' court. If in due course the case goes to the Crown Court for trial, I will apply for the order to be extended to cover those costs as well.

If you were to be convicted of the offence, then at the end of the trial the prosecution would probably apply for an order that you pay a contribution towards the costs of the proceedings. It is also possible that you could be required to pay some or all of the costs of your defence, although since you are at present on benefits, this is not likely. If, on the other hand, the case against you is dropped or is unsuccessful, we will make an application for your personal out of pocket expenses to be paid. It would therefore be a good idea if you could keep a record of any travel or other expenses that you incur.

Bail

The court granted you bail on Saturday. The bail was subject to three conditions: that you reside at your current address; that you report to Westchurch Police Station at 6 p.m. on Mondays and Thursdays; and that you do not contact Arthur King, whether directly or indirectly. When we discussed these conditions, you felt that you would have no problem in complying with them. It is important that you do so, as any suggestion that there has been a breach of the conditions may well lead to loss of bail. If there are any problems, please let me know at once.

HALPERN DODDS Partners: Edwina Halpern, LLB, LLM, Dip Crim. John Dodds, BA. Associate: Mike Levin

Client Care

I am one of the partners at Halpern Dodds, and I will be taking primary responsibility for the day to day handling of your case. Rachel Smith, a trainee solicitor at this firm, will also be involved in helping to prepare your case, and she will be working under my supervision.

If there is anything that you are unhappy or unsure about, please do not hesitate to contact me so that I can deal with the matter. If you feel that your complaint has not been resolved by discussing the matter with me, you should contact John Dodds, who is the partner who deals with client care issues. If for some reason we are unable to resolve the matter for you, we will then refer you to the Legal Ombudsman who may be able to help.

What will happen next?

The offence that you have been charged with can be tried either in the Crown Court or in the magistrates' court. This is a decision that we will have to take in due course. However, before we can decide on this we will need more information about the case against you. The Crown Prosecution Service will be serving us with this "advance information" in the next few days. As soon as we have this information I will send you a copy and ask you and Joanne to come in and see me so that I can take statements from both of you.

Is there anything that you should do now?

Please make sure that you remember to attend the Police Station at the required times. You and Joanne might also want to write down your own recollections of what happened on Friday night while the memories are still fairly fresh in your head. This will be very useful when we have the prosecution information and can take a formal statement from both of you. If you know of anyone else who might have witnessed the incident, please note down their name, address and telephone number so that we can decide whether we should ask them for a statement in due course.

Your case has now be adjourned until 10.00 on Wednesday 26th February. I will meet you at the entrance hall to Westchurch Magistrates' Court at 9.55.

Yours sincerely,

Edwina Halpern

Edwina Halpern

Progressing the case

There is relatively little that can be done while waiting for the advance information. Edwina has made a deliberate decision not to seek more detailed instructions until Peter has had a chance to look at the prosecution material. She does, however, write to the prosecution requesting a copy of the custody record and copies of the tapes of interview as well as the full advance disclosure package.

Service of the Advance Information

The advance information arrives in the post a day or two after the last hearing. The advance information can be found at **Documents 8A–H**. It contains witness statements from Arthur King, and from his wife Maureen. It also contains witness statements from the two police officers, a statement confirming that the fingerprints on the glass belong to Peter Butcher, and a short statement confirming the extent of Arthur King's injuries. A copy of the interview tapes and the custody record is also available. Edwina needs to ensure that she is prepared for the next hearing so immediately contacts Peter Butcher and arranges an appointment with him.

Preparing for the decision on venue for trial

Taking a client statement

Edwina sends a copy of the advance information to Peter Butcher and when he attends his appointment, she takes a statement from him. Peter's statement (sometimes known as a "proof of evidence") and comments on the prosecution statements are set out in **Document 10**.

Advice on venue for trial

The next hearing, on 26th February, the court will determine venue for trial. Although some courts have implemented the CJA 2003 allocation procedures, they are not yet in force at Westchurch magistrates' Court therefore Edwina prepares for the usual plea before venue and mode of trial hearing. Although Edwina has discussed the issues with Peter when she took his statement, she also writes to confirm her advice. This letter is provided at Document 11.

As you will see, Edwina remains of the view that this is a serious case, carrying a likely sentence in excess of the magistrates' own sentencing powers, and with aggravating features (use of a weapon, serious injury). She expects the magistrates to decline jurisdiction. However, she and Peter still need to decide where they want the case to be heard. If they decide that it would be better to keep the case in the magistrates' court, Edwina will make representations at the mode of trial hearing in an attempt to persuade the magistrates to accept jurisdiction.

What is the best option in the unlikely event that the magistrates do accept jurisdiction? It is true that proceedings would be quicker and less stressful in the magistrates' court, and if convicted Peter would face a far smaller costs order. The biggest advantage is that the magistrates' sentencing powers would be limited to 6 months custody. However Edwina's view is that, although the magistrates have restricted sentencing powers, if they did accept jurisdiction of the case, they would be likely to commit it to Crown Court for sentencing under s.38 Powers of Criminal Courts (Sentencing) Act. This is because the guideline sentences all suggest a significant period in custody.

In favour of trial in the Crown Court is the fact that the acquittal rate at Crown Court is far higher. This is a case where the jury might have some sympathy with Peter, and certainly where they might take a view that it is not reasonable to draw an inference from his failure to put forward his defence facts when he had been so strongly advised not to do so. Edwina also bears in mind the voir dire procedure at Crown Court.

What about Peter's previous convictions? Edwina notes that Peter has extensive previous convictions. She prepares a short attendance note setting out her views: **Document 9**.

DOCUMENT 8

Crown Prosecution Service,
North Chambers,
Waterville Street,
WESTCHURCH

Halpern Dodds,
29 Chesterfield Place,
WESTCHURCH

Yr ref:
Our ref: JMB/211

Dear Sirs,

re: R v BUTCHER
      Westchurch Magistrates Court

In accordance with R21 of the Criminal Procedure (Amendment) Rules 2011 I enclose copies of the following documents:

(a)   ~~copy summary of the prosecution case~~
(b)   copy record of tape recorded interview
(c)   statements of witnesses
(d)   other relevant information: criminal record – *Peter Michael Butcher*

Please confirm that the record of interview is accepted by your client. Tape playing facilities are not available in court unless specifically required.
Yours faithfully,

R. Dixon

R. Dixon
Crown Prosecution Service

DOCUMENT 8A

WITNESS STATEMENT
(Criminal Justice Act 1967, s.9; Criminal Procedure Rules 2011, Rule 27)

STATEMENT OF: Arthur John KING

AGE IF UNDER 18: Over 18

OCCUPATION:

This statement (consisting of 2 page(s) each signed by me) is true to the best of my knowledge and belief and I make it knowing that if it is tendered in evidence, I shall be liable to prosecution if I have wilfully stated anything which I know to be false or do not believe to be true.

DATED: 15th February —

I am a 56 year old Building Services Manager for a major commercial property company. My responsibilities are to organise and to co-ordinate repair and refurbishment works on the company's rental property stock.

On the 14th February — my daughter Joanne married a man called Peter Butcher. The wedding and the reception took place at the North Cliffe Castle Hotel. There were about fifty or sixty guests, some of them members of our family, and the rest were Peter Butcher's friends. I don't think that any members of his family had bothered to come. Joanne knew Peter Butcher at school, but she had not seen him for a long time until they ran into one another last year. I have always disapproved of him because he and his family have always been trouble. I knew he had spent time in prison when he was younger and I was very upset when Joanne announced that she was going to marry him. What made it worse was that it was all happening very fast, and I felt she was only doing it because she was pregnant.

In order to make the best of a bad job, I agreed to a full-scale wedding celebration, with all the trimmings. The wedding itself took place at the hotel, and we all gathered in the bar while we waited for the rest of the party to arrive for the reception. I did my best to be polite to the groom and to his friends, most of whom had not even bothered to dress up for the reception, for my daughter's sake. I was worried, however, when I saw how much they were drinking at the bar and I thought there might be trouble.

Throughout the meal Peter Butcher and his best man, who was called Steve something, were making offensive remarks about members of Joanne's family and sniggering and carrying on in a way which was clearly upsetting my wife and Joanne as well. I didn't say anything at he time because I was determined that

---

Signed: Arthur King   Witnessed: *Patricia Herbert*

Joanne's wedding should not be spoilt. However, when it came to the speeches, Steve stood up and just started saying this filth. It was all jokes about sex and rude remarks about the other guests. I think he meant it to be funny, but clearly no-one thought it was.

I then stood up and made my speech. I just said what a splendid wedding it was and in order to show that I had no hard feelings I made a few jokes about how Peter was now a reformed character. I may have made a jibe or to at the Best Man, but nothing serious. However, I could hear Peter muttering something to Joanne, and I could see she was getting upset, so I finished the speech as quickly as I could and the band started up and people started dancing.

I tried to say something friendly to Peter, but he just stood up and pushed past me and stormed out of the room. Joanne started crying. I leant over to pat her hand and say that it would all be all right, and suddenly Steve stood up from his chair and came over and started abusing me, saying that I was drunk and I'd ruined the wedding and my daughter was ashamed of me. I wasn't having that, so I stood up and told him what I thought of him and his friends in no uncertain terms. Some of my family came over and started telling Steve what they thought, and his and Peter's friends came over to see if they could make trouble. They were shouting and jostling, using all sorts of swear words and obscenities. I lost my rag and asked them what the hell they thought they were doing ruining a young girl's wedding.

The next thing I knew was Peter Butcher came barging into the middle of the crowd. He just grabbed my daughter by the arm and started to yank her up. I wasn't having that, not with her in her condition, and I shouted at him not to hurt her. He turned round and swung at me. He just swung round with his right hand and punched me hard in the face. He had a pint glass in his hand which must have broke when the punch landed and the glass cut my face. He did it quite deliberately. I heard him say: "You stupid old bastard, you deserve it," or something like that.

I fell over and when I got up, Peter and Joanne had gone. The people around me were still shouting and scuffling – not fighting as such, but pushing and yelling at one another. I sat down on a chair. I didn't know what else to do. Then I felt the blood trickling down my face and I realised that I had been cut quite badly. My wife, I think it was, handed me a napkin which I pressed to my face. Soon afterwards the police arrived and started arresting everyone.

One of the officers asked me what had happened and I told them that Peter Butcher had hit me in the face with a glass. They asked me to point Peter out but he wasn't in the room. One of them said he'd call an ambulance to get me to hospital to get my face looked at, and as we left the room I saw Peter in the corridor with Joanne and I pointed him out to the police.

At the hospital I had to wait for two hours before they could deal with the cut. I had eleven stitches and three injections. The cut went from just next to my left eye, all the way down to my jawbone. The doctors aren't yet sure if there is permanent nerve damage to the area below my eye, but they say I will have a permanent scar.

Signed: Arthur King   Witnessed: *Patricia Herbert*

DOCUMENT 8B

WITNESS STATEMENT
(Criminal Justice Act 1967, s.9; Criminal Procedure Rules 2011, Rule 27)

STATEMENT OF: Maureen King

AGE IF UNDER 18: Over 18

OCCUPATION: Administrator

This statement (consisting of 2 page(s) each signed by me) is true to the best of my knowledge and belief and I make it knowing that if it is tendered in evidence, I shall be liable to prosecution if I have wilfully stated anything which I know to be false or do not believe to be true.

DATED: 15th February —

My daughter Joanne King got married on the 14th February —. I organised the wedding and attended both the wedding and the reception with my husband, Arthur.

Joanne was marrying Peter Butcher, a boy who she has known for a long time. He and my husband have never got on at all well. Both Arthur and I had also been very upset because Joanne told us that she was pregnant before the wedding. This was not something that we wanted our family to know about; many of them are still very traditional and I knew that they would be very shocked at the news.

I was therefore very dismayed when at the reception the young man who was Peter's Best Man made a speech which was full of rather crude jokes about why my daughter was getting married. I could see that some of the family members were very concerned, but I was also worried because I could see that Arthur was getting very angry. Arthur has been responsible for running a substantial part of a major property company for some years and he can be very forceful when he feels that something is not right.

When Arthur stood up to make his speech it was obvious that he was still upset but he was doing his best to smooth matters over. He made a few pointed remarks about the behaviour of some of Peter's friends, but sensibly he kept his speech short and sat down as soon as he could. I was shocked, therefore, when Peter just got up from his chair and stormed out of the room. I don't know if he said anything to Joanne but I could see that she was on the verge of tears. Arthur was just reaching out to take her hand when the young man who had been Best Man suddenly appeared and started shouting these awful things at Arthur. I can't remember exactly what he was saying but he did say that Arthur must be drunk, which was nonsense.

Signed: *Maureen King* Witnessed: *Patricia Herbert*

Arthur had had quite a bit to drink but it was obvious that it was this young man who was the drunk one. Arthur wasn't going to put up with that and so he stood up and started telling the man to behave, and then some of my family came over to see if they could help calm things down. However, more of Peter's friends came pushing up and there was a lot of shouting going on.

I'm not sure exactly when Peter arrived but when I looked up I saw him standing next to Joanne, who was sitting crying in her chair. He was shouting something at Arthur. Someone must have got in front of me then, because the next thing I saw was Arthur falling down and hitting his head on one of the wooden chairs behind him. I think I screamed. Arthur is a big man and I'm always worried about him having a heart attack at his age. I knelt down to try and help him get up and I saw his face was bleeding very badly. As I helped him up he said: "That little thug is going to pay for this." I looked round at once but both Joanne and Peter had disappeared. So I got Arthur sat on a chair with a napkin to his face and within about ten minutes the police had arrived.

Signed: *Maureen King*   Witnessed: *Patricia Herbert*

DOCUMENT 8C

WITNESS STATEMENT
(Criminal Justice Act 1967, s.9; Criminal Procedure Rules 2011, Rule 27)

STATEMENT OF: Edward Stanley

AGE IF UNDER 18:   Over 18

OCCUPATION: Police Constable

This statement (consisting of 2 page(s) each signed by me) is true to the best of my knowledge and belief and I make it knowing that if it is tendered in evidence, I shall be liable to prosecution if I have wilfully stated anything which I know to be false or do not believe to be true.

DATED: 15th February —

On 14th February — at about 22.35, acting upon information received, I attended the North Cliffe Castle Hotel with three other officers. On entering into the Banqueting Suite I saw what appeared to be a large-scale disturbance, with about fifteen to twenty adults, mainly males, shouting and pushing one another. The other officers and I approached the crowd and began separating the participants. There was a wedding cake on a nearby table and from the formal attire of those in the room it was clear that this had been a wedding party. A number of those involved in the disturbance smelt strongly of alcohol. Eight arrests for breach of the peace and minor public order matters were made.

When order was restored, I was made aware of an older gentleman who was sat on a chair with a cloth of some kind pressed to his face. I now know the gentleman to be Arthur King, the father of the bride. I asked him what the matter was and he removed the cloth to show a long gash across the left of his face which was bleeding profusely. One of the other officers checked that an ambulance had been called.

I asked Mr King how he had come by his injury. Mr King replied that he had been punched in the face with a glass. I asked him who had done this. He replied that he had been punched by the groom, a Mr Peter Butcher. I asked Mr King to point out Peter Butcher, but Mr King told me that Mr Butcher was no longer in the room. However, as I escorted Mr King from the room to the waiting ambulance, Mr King pointed to a man and a woman who were sitting in the corridor outside. He informed me that the man was Peter Butcher.

I approached Mr Butcher and said to him: "Are you Peter Butcher?" He replied: "Yes." I then cautioned him and told him that I had reason to believe that he had assaulted Mr King.

Signed: *Edward Stanley*   Witnessed: *Patricia Herbert*

Mr Butcher replied: "He's a drunken fool. He ruined our wedding." I noted that Mr Butcher smelt very strongly of alcohol and that there were cuts on his right hand. I then informed Mr Butcher that he was under arrest. He shrugged. The young woman who was with him, who I now know to be Joanne Butcher (nee King) started weeping. I heard her say: "Oh, Peter, you should have stayed out of it."

In the police car on the way to the station I made a note of the comments made and asked Mr Butcher to sign these as a true record. This he declined to do.

Mr Butcher was then detained for questioning on suspicion of having been involved in a s.20 malicious wounding. Mr Butcher was seen by a Force Medical Examiner in order to bandage the cuts on his hand and to confirm that Mr Butcher was fit for interview. However, there was a delay while other arrests from the party were being processed and while statements were being taken.

Mr Butcher subsequently saw his solicitor. Mr Butcher was then interviewed in accordance with the Police and Criminal Evidence Act with his legal representative present. During the interview Mr Butcher declined to answer any questions. A summary of the interview is attached marked ES/1. After the interview Mr Butcher was charged with the s.20 offence.

Signed: *Edward Stanley*   Witnessed: *Patricia Herbert*

DOCUMENT 8D

WITNESS STATEMENT
(Criminal Justice Act 1967, s.9; Criminal Procedure Rules 2011, Rule 27)

STATEMENT OF: Patricia Herbert

AGE IF UNDER 18: Over 18

OCCUPATION: Police Constable

This statement (consisting of 1 page(s) each signed by me) is true to the best of my knowledge and belief and I make it knowing that if it is tendered in evidence, I shall be liable to prosecution if I have wilfully stated anything which I know to be false or do not believe to be true.

DATED: 15th February —

On 14th February — at about 22.35, acting upon information received, I attended the North Cliffe Castle Hotel with a number of other officers. On our arrival we were directed to the Banqueting Suite. Inside the room a disturbance was taking place. Some fifteen adults, mainly males, were shouting at one another. There was some pushing and scuffling. A number of arrests for breach of the peace and minor public order matters were made.

With PC Stanley, my attention was directed to an older man who was sitting on a chair. He had an improvised bandage across the left side of his face. I now know the gentleman to be Arthur King, the father of the bride. Mr King removed the cloth to show PC Stanley and myself a long and deep incision that had been made across the left side of his face of his face. I immediately radioed to check that an ambulance had been called.

While PC Stanley spoke to Mr King, I looked around the floor near the table where Mr King was sitting. I immediately saw a broken straight-sided beer glass, which had what appeared to be blood on the broken edges at the top of the glass. I directed Mr King's attention to the glass, and he confirmed that he had been standing in that area when he had been attacked. I then placed the glass in an evidence bag in order to forward the glass for fingerprinting. I exhibit the glass as exhibit PH/1.

Acting on information received, Peter Butcher was then arrested by PC Stanley and was taken to Westchurch Police Station where I later attended with PC Stanley at an interview with Mr Butcher. Following the interview Mr Butcher was charged and fingerprinted. I exhibit Mr Butcher's fingerprints, exhibit PH/2.
I later forwarded the glass, exhibit PH/1, and the fingerprints of Mr Butcher, exhibit PH/2 for analysis.

Signed: *Patricia Herbert*   Witnessed: *Edward Stanley*

DOCUMENT 8E

WITNESS STATEMENT
(Criminal Justice Act 1967, s.9; Criminal Procedure Rules 2011, Rule 27)

STATEMENT OF: Jacqueline Ashfield

AGE IF UNDER 18: Over 18

OCCUPATION: Fingerprint Officer

This statement (consisting of 1 page(s) each signed by me) is true to the best of my knowledge and belief and I make it knowing that if it is tendered in evidence, I shall be liable to prosecution if I have wilfully stated anything which I know to be false or do not believe to be true.

DATED: 19th February —

I am a fingerprint officer employed by Westchurch Constabulary. I have been engaged in the identification of persons by means of finger and palm prints for over five years. I am enrolled on the national Register of Fingerprints experts. It has never been known for the ridge characteristics of the finger or palm prints from different persons to agree in sequence.

On 15th February — I received exhibits PH/1 (a broken glass) and PH/2 (one set of impressions on fingerprint form). The glass had contained alcohol and there had been some spillage, which had affected the surface of the glass. I was, however, able to detect one clear thumb print and one complete fingerprint, along with a number of incomplete fingerprints.

I have compared the impressions on the glass (exhibit PH/1) with impressions on the fingerprint form in the name of Peter Butcher (PH/2) and I have no doubt that these impressions were made by the same person. The impressions identified achieve the current National Fingerprint Standard of a minimum ten ridge characteristics in agreement for two or more impressions.

The fingerprint impressions and fingerprint form mentioned in this statement have been retained in the Westchurch Constabulary Fingerprint Bureau and may be examined by prior appointment with the Officer in Charge.

Signed: *Jacqueline Ashfield*   Witnessed: Tim James

DOCUMENT 8F

WITNESS STATEMENT
(Criminal Justice Act 1967, s.9; Criminal Procedure Rules 2011, Rule 27)

STATEMENT OF: Michael Gifford

AGE IF UNDER 18: Over 18

OCCUPATION: Surgeon

This statement (consisting of 1 page(s) each signed by me) is true to the best of my knowledge and belief and I make it knowing that if it is tendered in evidence, I shall be liable to prosecution if I have wilfully stated anything which I know to be false or do not believe to be true.

DATED: 18th February —

I am a surgeon employed by the Westchurch Health Trust and based primarily at Westchurch General Hospital. I have been qualified as a surgeon for twenty-three years.

In the early hours of 15th February — I was called to Westchurch Hospital to treat a Mr Arthur King, who had suffered severe facial lacerations. There was concern that there was potential damage to Mr King's sight, and potential extensive facial scarring.

The primary incision was 5.3 centimetres in length and ran from just below Mr King's left eye across the left side of his face, slanting forward towards the mouth. The incision was jagged and uneven in depth, at one point reaching down to the cheekbone itself.

There were six further deep lacerations around Mr King's left eye, some primarily puncture wounds, others of greater extent. One incision in particular had partially severed the muscles below the eye itself.

Mr King received immediate treatment in order to remove a number of large glass fragments from the wounds, some of which were potentially threatening to the left eye. Extensive suturing was then required. All steps were taken to repair muscle damage and to minimise facial scarring.

At this early stage it is difficult to predict the longer term prognosis. There will inevitably be some scarring, and there is likely to be some residual loss of muscle control around the left eye.

During my work as a surgeon, I have treated a regrettably large number of incidents where damage has been caused by beer glasses and other glasses that have been used as weapons. I can confirm that the injuries sustained by Mr King are entirely compatible with an agent of this kind having been used to inflict the harm.

Signed: *Michael Gifford*   Witnessed: *Simone Shaw*

DOCUMENT 8G

WESTCHURCH POLICE

RECORD OF TAPE RECORDED INTERVIEW

[This document has already been provided as Document 2, the record of the police station interview.]

DOCUMENT 8H

WESTCHURCH POLICE

NAME: Peter Michael BUTCHER   **ref:** CRO 49393/—

DATE OF BIRTH: 26/2/-

RECORD OF CONVICTIONS OR FINDINGS OF GUILT

Date	Court	Offence	Sentence
December — [10 years ago]	Minster Magistrates	s.4 Public Order Act	Fine - £150
May — [9 years ago]	Westchurch Magistrates	s.47 OAPA - ABH	Community Service Order - 100 hours
January — [8 years ago]	Westchurch Magistrates	Common Assault	Fine - £90
		Breach of the Peace	Bind over to keep peace - 12 months
		Failure to surrender to Bail	Fine - £130
June — [7 years ago]	East Minster Magistrates	Taking a motor vehicle without consent	Community Order Supervision Requirement 12 months.
		Going equipped	Fine £120
January — [6 years ago]	Westchurch Magistrates	Burglary (non-residential) x 4	Custodial sentence - 15 weeks.
July — [last year]	East Harham Magistrates	Careless driving	Fine - £300 6 penalty points
		Failure to surrender to Bail	Conditional discharge 6 months

[This concludes the advance information.]

DOCUMENT 9

ATTENDANCE NOTE

Case Name: Butcher
Action: Reviewing previous convictions
Date:` 21st February
Time start:
Time finish:
Total time: 2 units

Client precons – admissibility issues:

Two likely circumstances in which those previous convictions might be raised at trial.

Gateway D:

- Does PB have a propensity to be violent?
    - Note previous convictions for public order offences, for common assault and for actual bodily harm.
    - None of these are in the same category or of the same description as the current offence, but these are not exclusive categories – *Hanson*.
    - All of them at least 8 years old – likely to be treated as stale.
    - Client can't remember circumstances of convictions clearly – note: unlikely that prosecution have any details either.
- propensity for untruthfulness?
    - Some dishonesty convictions – but elderly.
    - Limited client information – burglaries all empty office buildings – client says all matters dealt with on a G plea basis – strong argument that there is no evidence of a propensity for untruthfulness.
- Initial conclusion? Unlikely to be permitted in.

Gateway G:

- Client's account is that IP (injured party) was drunk and fell over/injured self/author of his own troubles.
- Is this an attack for the purposes of s.106 – i.e. behave in a reprehensible way?
- Conclusion: seems unlikely to be admissible without more.
- **Further action: check IP's precons with initial prosecution disclosure.**

DOCUMENT 10A   Proof of Evidence of Peter Butcher

Statement of: Peter BUTCHER

Address: Flat 4, James Park East Buildings

Park Street,

WESTCHURCH

Telephone: -

Date of birth: 26/2/- (age: 30)

Charge: s.20 OAPA 1861 - unlawful wounding - 14th February —

Education/Employment:

[1]   I left school at 18 with one A level and went to work at the shipyards on a training scheme. I stayed there for three years until I had my trades certificates and then I went freelance, working as a specialist welder out on North Sea rigs. I've been doing that off and on ever since. When there is work it pays very well, but you can have long periods looking for work. I was in work on a job all last year and earned around £34,000 before tax. The job ended before Christmas and I've been looking for work since then. I am currently receiving Income-Based Job Seekers Allowance because my wife Joanne was recently made redundant.

Family:

[2]   I got married to Joanne on 14th February this year, which was when this incident happened. We have no children but Joanne is six months pregnant. We live in a rented flat in Park Street.

Previous convictions:

[3]   I have quite a few previous convictions, but apart from a driving conviction last year, they all relate to my early twenties, when I admit I was a bit of a handful. I used to hang out with a bunch of lads that I knew from the shipyard and we used to egg one another on to get into trouble. I have a couple of convictions for brawling, as well as convictions for joy-riding and for four burglaries. It was the burglaries that were the last straw. They were all of empty office buildings one weekend, but I ended up getting a three month prison sentence. It really shook me up and when I came out I decided to stay out of trouble. I had a probation officer who really helped me, and apart from the driving I've kept my nose clean ever since. I have pleaded guilty in every instance that I have been before the court.

Present charge:

[4]   Like I said, Joanne and I got married on 14th February. It was Valentine's Day and we thought it would be romantic to have the wedding then. We had the wedding and the reception as a package up at North Cliffe Castle Hotel. We had all the trimmings and about fifty guests, with a sit down dinner for the reception after the wedding.

[5]   The problem is Joanne's father, Arthur King. I've known Joanne since school and Arthur's never liked me. When I was getting into trouble he actually forbade Joanne to see me, and I can understand that. So anyway, I didn't see her for ages – not until I was back last summer from a job in the North Sea and we ran into one another in a pub. We really hit it off and we soon started going out. When she told her dad about it, he really hit the roof and said he wasn't having her seeing a criminal and all that sort of stuff. He was giving her a really hard time. In the end she had to tell him that she was an adult herself and that she was going to do what she wanted. He quietened down a bit after that. Anyway, Joanne found out she was

pregnant just before Christmas, and we decided we wanted to get married anyway. So she told her parents at Christmas that we were doing it, and he hit the roof again.

[6]   I thought things had got better after he and I had a talk and I explained that all my troubles had been when I was younger and that I'd turned over a new leaf ages ago. I even offered to pay for half the cost of the wedding out of what I'd saved from work and I thought this had convinced him that I'd be able to look after Joanne properly. He did calm down a lot, and I think Maureen, his wife, helped to persuade him that since Joanne and I were going to do it anyway he had better make the best of the situation. He still used to make comments about marrying into a criminal family (my brother, Chris, is serving three years for an insurance scam), and about Joanne being pregnant, and about how neither of us had jobs, but I didn't mind that so long as he left Joanne alone.

[7]   Anyway, at the wedding I thought we'd put all this behind us. Everything went fine during the service itself. Then there was a delay while they got the dinner on the tables and we were all drinking at the bar for over an hour. There were a lot of Joanne's family there, most of whom I hadn't met, and Joanne and I had invited a lot of our old school friends. Everyone was having a good time and although it was getting pretty rowdy by the time we all got sat down for dinner, it was all good-natured and everyone was just having fun.

[8]   I think the trouble started with Steve's speech. Steve was my Best Man and is one of my oldest friends. He was just being funny about me and Joanne, and her being pregnant, and all the trouble we used to get into. Everyone was laughing, even Joanne and I. I mean, we were both embarrassed by it but that's the point of these speeches, isn't it. They're supposed to be funny. Arthur looked furious though, and when he stood up to make his speech and I could see he'd had far too much to drink.

[9]   He was very red in the face and he was having to hold himself up on the table. He just launched into this attack on me, and how I and all my friends were criminals, and how he didn't understand how Joanne could want to have anything to do with me. He tried to make out that it was all a big joke, but the way he was saying it, it was clear that he meant every word. A few people were laughing, but I think they were just laughing because they were embarrassed. I didn't know where to look, so I just sat there. I could see that Joanne was looking at the table and trying not to cry. Thank God he shut up after about five minutes. He just sat down. He didn't propose a toast or anything.

[10]   Then the band started up and people started dancing. We were all in this huge room, with the head table at one end, where Joanne and I had been sitting with her parents and close family, along with Steve and a few other mates of mine. The rest of the tables were around the edges of the room, so that people could dance in the dance floor in the middle. I went outside into the garden to get a breath of fresh air and to get away from Arthur and cool down a bit. I was pretty angry with him for ruining our wedding, and especially for getting Joanne so upset. One of the waiters was sneaking a quick cigarette out there and he gave me a light. You could still hear the music – it was pretty loud – but then I also heard the noise of plates and glasses breaking. At first I thought it was just a waiter dropping a tray, but I went back in and there was this brawl going on.

[11]   I didn't know how it had started, but Joanne says that her dad and Steve had words and before she knew it everyone was shouting at one another. By the time I got there most of her family and a lot of our friends had joined in and there was a lot of pushing and shoving and people punching other people, all of it up round the head table. I ran up there and shoved my way through the people. I was obviously very worried about Joanne, especially with her being pregnant and everything. She was right in the middle of it, crying and trying to calm everyone down. I pushed in front of her, in between her and Arthur and Steve and some other people I don't know. I still had a pint glass of beer in my hand which I'd been drinking outside.

It was all happening so fast that I didn't really realise it was still in my hand, although I can remember thinking at the time that the beer was slopping all over my suit and that I'd have to have it dry-cleaned.

[12] Arthur was obviously very drunk. He was yelling all sorts of obscenities and when he saw me he just went for me. I was half-turned away, trying to shield Joanne and with the glass in my right hand and I must have stumbled as Arthur lunged forward. The glass hit a chair or the table and smashed. I dropped it and turned away to make sure Joanne was out of the way. Arthur must have knocked into a chair because he fell over and I just grabbed Joanne by the arm and tried to push our way out of the scrum of people.

[13] It all happened very quickly and I got Joanne out of the room and into the corridor. She was very upset and I was trying to calm her down and make sure she was all right when the police arrived.

[14] It took ages to get it all sorted out, and I saw them arrest about fifteen people and take them away. Arthur was brought out with a big cut under his left eye and when he saw me and Joanne he pointed to me and said something to a police officer and the policeman came over and arrested me. I can't remember exactly what he said because I was just trying to keep Joanne from losing it again. Joanne's mum came out and started to look after Joanne, and the police officer put me in the back of the police car and drove me off to the station.

[15] At the station they kept me in a cell for the rest of the night. I was pretty frantic by the time they were ready to interview me. I stank of alcohol from all the beer that had spilt on me and I was really worried about Joanne – I thought she might have a miscarriage or something. The police officers were really understanding. They told me I should have a solicitor. This lad came down from the firm and he started going on about how I shouldn't say anything to the police because they wouldn't tell him what the other people were saying. I told him I didn't mind giving the police my version, but he said I shouldn't say anything at this stage until we knew more about the case.

[16] During the interview I just kept my mouth shut like the lawyer told me to do. They asked all these questions about whether I had hit Arthur. I kept shaking my head, but I didn't say anything because I'd been told not to. I was gob-smacked when they said they were going to charge me with malicious wounding and I completely lost it and told them that I hadn't done it. By then, though, I was just really depressed about the whole thing. Our wedding night was completely ruined and I thought Joanne would think it was all my fault. Then I was taken to court.

[17] I want to tell the court that I did nothing wrong. I never touched Arthur, no matter what he says.

Bail:

[18] I have two convictions for failure to attend court, one of them from when I got into trouble when I was younger. I agree that I did fail to attend court last year on the driving offence, but that was because I was out on the rigs when the court date came up and I wrote to the court to explain that there was no way I could make it back from the middle of the North Sea just to come to court and asking them to hold the case a month later. I went straight to the police station when I got back and they arrested me and took me to court. I pleaded guilty both to the driving and the fail to attend, but I don't know how they expected me to get to court from the North Sea.

DOCUMENT 10B

COMMENTS ON PROSECUTION STATEMENTS

Comments of: Peter BUTCHER

Address: Flat 4, James Park East Buildings

Park Street,

WESTCHURCH

Telephone: -

Date of birth: 26/2/- (age: 30)

Charge: s.20 OAPA 1861 - unlawful wounding - 14th February —

Statement of Arthur King

I don't know what to say. The statement shows how much Arthur dislikes me. He says he was worried that there might be trouble but all the trouble was caused by him and his drinking. He says that Steve's speech was offensive, but no-one else there thought it was. Everyone was laughing. The Best Man's speech is supposed to be funny.

I see that Arthur admits that he went out of his way to make "jibes" in his speech. That was what started the trouble. As he says, I left the room afterwards. I admit I was furious. I don't agree that he tried to say anything "friendly" to me at that point.

He says that when I came back in I "grabbed" Joanne by the arm. That is not true. I was really worried about her in the middle of a fight. I tried to get between her and the brawl. I could hear Arthur yelling obscenities. He never said anything about not hurting Joanne; there was no reason to; there was no question of my hurting her. Nor did I swing round and punch him in the face. As I have said, I may have stumbled and I agree that I had a glass in my hand and that got smashed. But I never touched Arthur. I certainly never said "You stupid old bastard, you deserve it," or anything like that.

Statement of Maureen King

Again, I can only say that Maureen's statement supports my case that Arthur was the one who started everything. He was the angry one. I note that Maureen did not see why Arthur fell over. I also note Arthur's comment that he was going to make me "pay for this" (I assume I am the little thug referred to; I am certainly a good three or four inches shorter than Arthur).

Statement of Edward Stanley

I have no comments about this statement. I agree that I may have told the police officer that Arthur was a drunken fool. It was not an admission that I had punched him or been involved in any way.

Statement of Jacqueline Ashfield

I accept that they are likely to be my fingerprints on the glass. It was my glass. But I didn't punch Arthur with it.

Statement of Michael Gifforth

I accept this statement. I would simply say that the glass wasn't used as a weapon. Arthur must have fallen on it.

Record of taped interview

This record seems correct. I wanted to put forward my version of events but the solicitor kept telling me that I shouldn't do this until the police had told us what the witnesses were saying. I was very upset and I wasn't thinking very clearly. I just wanted to get out of the police station and back to Joanne. I just did what the lawyer told me to do.

Record of Previous Convictions

I confirm that the list of my criminal convictions is correct.

DOCUMENT 11

Halpern Dodds
for all your legal needs

29 Chesterfield Place,
WESTCHURCH
Telephone (24 hours): 0071 229 228
Fax: 0071 229 229
e mail: HalpernDoddsX@germail.co.uk
21st February

Dear Peter,

Westchurch Magistrates' Court: 26th February 20__ at 10am

I am writing to confirm our discussion this afternoon. As you know, we have now received the advance information from the prosecution and I have been able to take a statement from you setting out your account of what happened on 14th February. I enclose two copies of your statement for you to look at. Please make any changes or corrections on the statement, sign it and return it to me. The other copy is for your own reference.

What will happen at the next court hearing?

At the next hearing the court will decide whether this is a matter that can be tried in the magistrates' court, or whether it is sufficiently serious that it should be tried in the Crown Court.

At the hearing, the clerk will ask you to give your name and address to the court. The clerk will then ask you whether you intend to plead Guilty to this offence. You should tell the clerk that you intend to plead Not Guilty. The court will then listen to submissions from myself and from the prosecution, before making up its mind whether it can hear the case.

If the magistrates decide to decline jurisdiction and to send the matter to Crown Court, you cannot overrule their decision. However, if they decide that they can hear the case, you will still have the power to require that they send the matter to be heard in front of a jury in the Crown Court. The clerk will also warn you that, even if you decide that the magistrates can hear your case, they will still be able to send the matter to the Crown Court for sentencing if the court feels that its sentencing powers are not adequate.

What decision is the court likely to make?

My experience is that the court is likely to decide that it should not hear the case. It is a serious offence, and the court may take the view that the allegation that a weapon was used and serious injuries were caused makes the matter more serious. However, if you decide that you do want to try to keep the case in the magistrates' court, I can certainly try to persuade them to do so.

HALPERN DODDS Partners: Edwina Halpern, LLB, LLM, Dip Crim. John Dodds, BA. Associate: Mike Levin

Which court should you choose?

My own view, as you know, is that you would be far better off with the Crown Court. Most lawyers feel that a jury can be far more open-minded than the magistrates, perhaps because juries tend to be hearing cases for the first time and so are more careful. It is true that the Crown Court has greater sentencing powers, but if you were convicted I suspect that the magistrates' court would send this matter to the Crown Court for sentencing in any event.

There are some disadvantages with the Crown Court. It is certainly a slower process, and it is very formal which can make it more stressful: I know that, with a baby on the way, you would like to get this matter sorted out as quickly as possible. In some cases it can be a disadvantage to be in the Crown Court because we will have to disclose our defence before trial; however, your defence is very clear, and I think it will do no harm to reveal it at an early stage. It is also the case that if the case is heard in the Crown Court the court can require you to repay some or all of the defence costs if you are convicted. Since you are not currently in work, however, this does not seem applicable to your case.

Finally, I should add that in the Crown Court it would be possible for a jury to convict you of a lesser offence – for example, actual bodily harm. In the magistrates' court, this is not possible; they must either find you guilty or not guilty. However, in this case I think there is little doubt that the injuries Arthur King suffered amount to a s.20 offence. The issue is whether you caused those injuries, which of course you deny. I do not think that this factor is therefore very relevant for your decision.

My advice

I would advise you to have this case dealt with in the Crown Court. However, this is a decision that you must make for yourself. If you decide that you do want me to try to persuade the magistrates to try the matter, please let me know as soon as possible, so that I can prepare my arguments for the next hearing. In any event, I will meet you at court on Wednesday 26th February at 9.55am.

Yours sincerely,

Edwina Halpern

Edwina Halpern

> **Wednesday 26th February: Mode of Trial hearing**

Peter has contacted Edwina and confirmed that he wants the case to be heard before a jury in the Crown Court.

At the mode of trial hearing, Peter indicates a Not Guilty plea. The prosecution makes representations to the court that this is a case that is suitable for summary disposal. Edwina makes no representations against this although she disagrees with the prosecutor's opinion.

The magistrates decide to accept jurisdiction which means that Peter gets the choice as to where his case is heard. He elects trial by jury. A date for committal is fixed for five weeks' time. Bail is extended to the committal hearing.

When Edwina gets back to the office she sends a letter to Peter confirming the outcome of the hearing and his next court date. She also considers any further preparation necessary for the case.

Taking statements from witnesses

Edwina has discussed the situation with Peter. The only witnesses that are likely to be of any help are Joanne Butcher, nee King, and Steven Fiddler, his best man. Edwina arranges for these two witnesses to come in so that she can take statements from them.

DOCUMENT 12A

Statement of: Joanne BUTCHER – nee King

Address: Flat 4, James Park East Buildings

Park Street,

WESTCHURCH

Telephone: -

Date of birth: 21/12/- (27 years old)

I got married to Peter on 14th February —. I have known Peter since we were at school, and we used to see one another a lot after we'd left school. But Peter was a bit of a tearaway in those days, and I stopped seeing him after a while. I heard from friends that he'd got himself sorted out and had started working on the rigs, and when I ran into him again last year everything clicked and we started going out together.

We got engaged just before Christmas. We knew we wanted to get married anyway, but I supposed we hurried things a bit more because I had found out that I was pregnant. My mother was very good about it, but my father has always disliked Peter and has never accepted that he has put his old ways behind him. My father is very old-fashioned, although he would never admit it, and I think he was very shocked that I was pregnant, and he was also offended when Peter offered to pay half the cost of the wedding.

I thought everything had been smoothed over and the wedding itself was beautiful. During the reception everyone was really celebrating and having a good time. Steve, who is one of Peter's friends, made this really risqué speech, which everyone was laughing at. I was a bit worried, because I knew my father wouldn't approve, and I was also concerned that he had been drinking quite a lot, which can make him very argumentative.

When my father stood up and made his speech I was horrified. He just kept making all these digs about how Peter was some sort of criminal. None of my family knows Peter, and they must have thought I was marrying some sort of thief or something. Peter stormed off when the speech finished and I just sat there staring at the table. I didn't know what to do. I was very upset. Then I heard raised voices, and when I looked up, Steve was arguing with my dad, telling him that he'd ruined the wedding. My dad started arguing back and soon there was a crowd of people shouting and pushing one another. I started crying. I was pulling at people's sleeves, trying to get everyone to stop fighting

All of a sudden Peter reappeared. He looked very upset. He reached out to take my hand. I couldn't hear what he was saying because of all the row. I saw him look round at my dad, who was shouting something. I started to get up and looked down to make sure I wasn't stepping on the hem of my dress. As I got up Peter fell over. When he got up I saw that his hand was bleeding. I took him by the arm and we left the room to get away from all the noise and confusion. I was amazed when the police arrived and arrested Peter. I couldn't understand what he was supposed to have done. I didn't even know that my father was hurt. I certainly didn't see Peter punch him, and I can say that it is absolutely not the sort of thing that Peter would ever do. If anyone punched anyone it would be the other way round; my father has a very short temper and he was the one who was shouting and carrying on.

DOCUMENT 12B

Statement of: Steven Fiddler

Address: 92 Gormley Gardens

West Passage,

MINSTER

Telephone: -

Date of birth: 6/6/- (29 years old)

I am a sales representative for an agricultural machinery company. I have worked for the company for four years. Before that I was a sales assistant in a large sports retail outlet.

I have known Peter Butcher since we were at school. We both worked together briefly at the shipyards after we left school, but I didn't like the work and so moved into retail sales work.

I have seen a fair amount of Peter over the last few years, although with him working out on the rigs, sometimes months can go by. But whenever he's back in town we got out for a drink. I knew he'd started seeing Joanne again, and I was over the moon when he told me that they were going to get married. I've always thought that they were right for one another, and even though I know her father can be a pain, I told Peter that he should just stay out of the old man's way.

The wedding should have been brilliant. It was a really classy do, and all the old school crowd were there. We were all drinking at the bar and having a good time before the reception started, and even though there were a fair number of Joanne's family there, everyone seemed to be having a good time. Even Arthur, Joanne's father, was putting the drink away. I stood up and did my speech, which seemed to go down really well. I agree I made a few comments about Peter's old girlfriends, and I may have made a few jokes about the wedding being only just in time with Joanne being in her condition, but people were laughing; it was just good humoured stuff.

I was appalled when Arthur King just stood up and started laying in to Peter and me and all the others there. He was calling us all sorts, like we were all criminals and we had ruined his daughter's life and stuff. No-one said anything. He went on like this for a while and then sat down. I turned to Peter to tell him to ignore it, that Arthur was just drunk, but Peter got up and walked out of the room. I wasn't sure if I should follow him so I looked across at Joanne and I could see she was really upset. I admit that I did lose it a little then. I got up and went over to Arthur and told him exactly what I thought of a man who ruins his daughter's wedding like that. I couldn't believe his behaviour.

Anyway, Arthur stood up and started shouting at me. He wasn't making any sense. He was very red in the face. He'd clearly had far too much to drink. Before I knew it, other people had come up and some of them were shouting back at Arthur, and some older people were shouting at us. There was some shoving and jostling, but mainly it was people screaming abuse.

I'm not sure when Peter turned up. I heard some other old fool call Joanne a slag, and I really lost it at that stage and grabbed him and told him what I was going to do to him. I wasn't paying attention to what was going on around me. It was turning into a bit of a brawl. It was around that time that the police turned up. They just grabbed everyone in sight and hustled us off into the vans, the way they do. I didn't even know Peter had been arrested until the following day. I was amazed when they said he'd smashed a glass into Arthur's face. There's no way Peter would have done that. I didn't see exactly what happened, but Arthur was the one who was looking for a fight. He was the one that would have punched Peter, not the other way round.

Most of us were kept in the cells for the night and released the next day. A couple of us were charged with threatening words and behaviour (s.4 POA) but at court we all got off with breach of the peace and bind-overs.

I have been in trouble with the police in the past. I was involved with Peter in the office burglaries back in — (six years ago) and I got a suspended prison sentence for them. Last year I was convicted of fiddling the gas meter, and I got a £200 fine.

I am happy to go to court for Peter. I am sure he didn't do this.

DOCUMENT 13A

Crown Prosecution Service,
North Chambers,
Waterville Street,
WESTCHURCH

Halpern Dodds,
29 Chesterfield Place,
WESTCHURCH

Yr ref:
Our ref: JMB/211

Dear Sirs,

R v PETER BUTCHER
WESTCHURCH MAGISTRATES COURT
2ND APRIL --

I enclose by way of service in accordance with section 5B Magistrates' Courts Act 1980 committal papers for the above.

Committal papers have been prepared in accordance with the Consolidated Criminal Practice Direction. I enclose one copy of the committal volumes for your client, together with a further copy for your own use.

If no depositions are taken, and there are no alterations to the Crown Court case papers now served, no further copies will be served on you. It will be for you to prepare any further papers for your own counsel and your client. If there are any alterations, the Crown Prosecution Service will supply you with copies of depositions and an amended list of witnesses and/or exhibits. These arrangements will ensure that the judge and all parties at the trial will work from identically indexed volumes.

The written statements contained in the committal volumes will be tendered in evidence before the magistrates unless you object to any statement being tendered under section 5B Magistrates' Courts Act 1980 and Criminal Procedure Rules 2010. If you object to any statement being tendered in evidence, you should inform me as soon as possible. Delay and expense may be caused if you fail to act promptly upon this letter in this regard. It is however for the prosecution to decide what evidence to bring in support of the charge at committal stage.

Unless I hear to the contrary I will assume that the committal will be in accordance with the provisions of section 6(2) Magistrates' Courts Act 1980.

Yours faithfully,

Maureen Docherty

Maureen Docherty,
Principal Crown Prosecutor

DOCUMENT 13B

Draft

INDICTMENT

THE CROWN COURT AT WESTCHURCH

THE QUEEN
-V-
PETER MICHAEL BUTCHER

PETER BUTCHER is charged as follows:

STATEMENT OF OFFENCE

UNLAWFUL WOUNDING contrary to section 20 of the Offences against the Person Act 1861.

PARTICULARS OF OFFENCE

PETER BUTCHER on the 14th day of February -- unlawfully and maliciously wounded Arthur King.

[Note that, other than the draft indictment and a bundle of photographs of Arthur King's injury, the committal bundle is identical to the advance information that has already been served. Its contents are not therefore duplicated.]

DOCUMENT 13C

Notice to defendant: proof by written statement

(Criminal Procedure Rules, r 27.1(2);
s.9 Criminal Justice Act 1967)

To Peter Butcher of Flat 4, James Park East Buildings, Park Street, Westchurch

On the 2nd .. day of April , 200-. , the Magistrates Court
sitting at .. Westchurch will hear evidence relating to the following charge(s) against you.

    Unlawful wounding contrary to s.20 Offences Against the Person Act 1861

This offence (or these offences) may be tried before a jury or by the Magistrates' Court).

Written statements have been made by the witnesses named below and copies of their statements are enclosed. [If the offence is (or the offences are) tried by the Magistrates Court]. Each of these statements will be tendered in evidence before the magistrates unless you want the witness to give oral evidence. If you want any of these witnesses to give oral evidence you should inform me as soon as possible. If you do not do so within 7 days of receiving this notice you will lose your right to prevent the statement being tendered in evidence and you will be able to require the attendance of the witness only with the leave of the Court.
. . .

If you intend to consult a solicitor about your case you should do so at once and hand this notice and the statements to him so that he may deal with them.)

Names of witnesses whose statements are enclosed

    King, Arthur;
    King, Maureen;
    Stanley, Edward;
    Herbert, Patricia;
    Ashfield, Jacqueline;
    Gifford, Michael

Address any reply to: address on letter head

Maureen Docherty.. (Signed)
.. .. (On behalf of the Prosecutor.)

> **Case preparation**

Edwina has now received the committal bundle, but has seen the material before since it was disclosed as Advance Information. She has asked Peter to talk to other friends who were present at the wedding, but so far no other witnesses have been found. She has also contacted the hotel and spoken to the duty manager from the night in question, but it appears that none of the staff was present in the room at the time that the brawl began.

The tapes and the custody record have both been received from the police. Edwina checks the custody record, but it reveals nothing new. She also listens to the tapes to check that the police summary is a fair and accurate one. It is.

What kind of committal?

It is clear from the committal bundle that there is a prima facie case against Peter Butcher. Arthur King clearly states that Peter Butcher smashed a glass into his face and then told him that he deserved it. Whether the committal is "with consideration of the evidence" (s.6 (1)) or "without consideration of the evidence" (s.6 (2)), Arthur King's statement will simply go before the court on paper. There is no possibility of Arthur King being called to give evidence at committal.

As there is a prima facie case, and the basis on which the prosecution is putting its case seems clear, there is no reason for asking for a s.6 (1) committal. Edwina tells the CPS that she will agree to a s.6 (2) committal on 2nd April.

Case Analysis

In the short period following the committal Edwina will need to contact the CPS about witness arrangements, wait for prosecution disclosure and then serve a defence statement and a defence witness notice on the CPS and the court. She will also brief counsel, arrange a conference, and make decisions about the plea and case management hearing. She therefore needs to be clear about the strengths and weaknesses of the prosecution's case and of her own.

[1] Elements of the offence:

Peter is charged with s.20 OAPA – wounding or inflicting grievous bodily harm. The indictment indicates that the prosecution is proceeding on the basis of wounding Arthur King (rather than GBH). Edwina checks the elements of the offence.

The actus reus:

The prosecution must show that Peter unlawfully and maliciously wounded Arthur King. Wounding simply requires the breaking of the continuity of the whole skin – which has clearly occurred here. The requirement that the wounding is unlawful merely establishes potential defences such as self-defence, which do not arise here.

The mens rea:

"Maliciously" requires either an intent to do some kind of bodily harm or recklessness as to whether such harm might be caused. The prosecution do not need to show that Peter intended or foresaw that he would wound Arthur King; an intention to cause a minor injury would be enough: *Mowatt* [1968] 1 QB 421. Peter will lack the mens rea if he was not aware that his conduct could cause any injury at all (*Savage* [1992] 1 AC 699), although he cannot argue simply that he lacked intention because he was drunk.

Arthur King will give evidence that Peter assaulted him. He, his wife, the police officers and the doctor can all confirm that he was wounded. The comment: "You stupid old bastard, you deserve it," which Arthur King says Peter said, will clearly go to mens rea.

[2] Prosecution narrative:

There is a history of ill feeling between Butcher and King. At the wedding reception Butcher takes offence to King's speech. Butcher leaves the room. Butcher's best man starts shouting at King, and other guests join in the disturbance. Butcher reappears and grabs his pregnant wife by the arm. King shouts at Butcher not to hurt her. Butcher turns and punches King in the face with his right hand, which contains a glass. The glass breaks, cutting King's face. Butcher says: "You stupid old bastard, you deserve it." King falls over. Butcher leaves the room. When arrested Butcher has clearly been drinking and says: "He's a drunken fool. He ruined our wedding." In interview Butcher refuses to answer any questions; he fails to account for the cuts on his right hand.

[3] Defence narrative:

There is a history of ill-feeling between Butcher and King. At the wedding reception, King takes offence at the best man's speech. He makes an offensive speech in reply. Butcher leaves the room. A disturbance begins in his absence. He returns and, concerned for his wife's safety, tries to interpose himself. King goes for him. Butcher attempts to shield his wife, but stumbles. The glass in his hand hits a chair or table and smashes. King falls over. Butcher grabs his wife and leads her to safety. At the police station Butcher refuses to answer questions on the strong advice of his solicitor.

[4] Key factual disputes

There are a number of factual discrepancies, comparing the defence and prosecution narratives. In the list below, Edwina is focusing on what she sees as important or key disputes of fact ("the facts in issue"). Subsidiary factual disputes are put in square brackets.

- [Did King make an offensive speech?]
- Was Peter Butcher drunk?
- Was Arthur King drunk?
- Was Peter Butcher trying to protect his wife, Joanne?
- Did Peter Butcher punch Arthur King?
- Did the glass smash when it hit the furniture or because it hit Arthur King's face?
- Did Peter Butcher say: "You stupid old bastard, you deserve it"?

[5] How will each side prove its account?

(i) Who are the main witnesses?

It is very clear that the two main witnesses will be King and Butcher themselves. No-one else sees exactly what happens between the two men. Both Maureen King (Arthur's wife) and Joanne were looking elsewhere at the crucial moment.

Note that in respect of the facts in issue, Maureen King, although a prosecution witness, can be very useful to the defence. She can give evidence confirming (a) her husband's long standing dislike of the defendant; (b) that her husband is a "forceful man" and that he had been drinking and was already angry; and (c) that King said that "That little thug is going to pay for this." She is a useful reminder that cross-examination is not simply about attacking the prosecution's witnesses, but is also about eliciting useful evidence from them. She can also confirm that Arthur King fell over.

The evidence of the police officers and of the other prosecution witnesses generally adds little of substance to the case, although of course it does establish Peter's silence at the police station when questioned under caution. [For inferences, see below.]

It may be worth calling Joanne Butcher. She confirms that Arthur King is wrong when he says Butcher "grabbed" her by the arm and "yanked" her up. She also does not hear the comment to Arthur King alleges Peter Butcher made to him. However, as Peter's wife, her credibility is limited.

Steven Fiddler is clearly going to do more harm than good. Edwina takes the view that his previous convictions are unlikely to be admissible under s.100 CJA 2003, but her instinct is that he will not come over well to the jury. Moreover, his statement in fact proves very little.

(ii) The role of alcohol – whose case does it damage?

It is also common ground that the two men had been drinking. As the prosecution case is that Butcher intentionally hit King in the face – see the evidence of King himself – there is no suggestion that this is a case of drunken recklessness. Drunkenness cuts both ways. It may make it more likely that Peter Butcher lost his self-control and punched King. It also makes it more likely that King is confused and has got his recollections muddled.

(iii) Butcher's previous convictions:

Edwina has another look at her earlier attendance note (Document 8) on this issue. She concludes that her earlier analysis is still good. The convictions are unlikely to be admissible to show either propensity for violence (too old) or for untruthfulness (all are guilty pleas) for the purpose of Gateway D. They might be admissible under Gateway G if the defence attacks King's testimony, but in her view they are not going to do this.

Her instinct is that the prosecution will make an application to adduce the precons, but she is fairly confident that the application will not succeed.

(iv) Inferences from Butcher's earlier silence:

Here there is a real problem. Unless the jury accepts that it was not reasonable to expect Butcher to put forward defence facts when questioned under caution, s.34 inferences will be drawn from Butcher's earlier silence if he now puts forward his defence. *Argent* of course makes clear that the police non-disclosure is unlikely of itself to avoid an inference. However, again relying on *Argent*, Butcher will clearly want to argue that his silence was reasonable given the effect of the legal advice he had received. *Beckles* now suggests that the reliance on the advice has to be both genuine and reasonable. Arguably the advice was not particularly good, but Butcher will also point to the fact that it was his wedding night that he was drunk; that he was hurt; and above all that he was extremely worried for pregnant wife.

Similar arguments will arise in respect of the s.36 inference.

Wednesday 2nd April   Committal

The s.6 (2) committal takes place at Westchurch Magistrates' Court and the case is committed to Westchurch Crown Court for trial. The court issues standard directions set a timetable for various stages in the case (**Document 14**).

Disclosure of unused material: The prosecutor at the hearing serves the schedule of unused material (see **Document 16A–B**). This triggers the start of the 28 day period within which to serve the defence statement and defence witness notice.

Character evidence: the prosecutor serves the defence with a prosecution application to adduce the defendant's previous convictions: see **Document 17A**

The plea and case management hearing is listed for 30th April, and Peter Butcher's bail is extended on the same conditions as before.

Post committal matters

Edwina now reviews the file and takes the following actions:

- Billing the magistrates' court file. **(Document 15)**
- Considering prosecution disclosure and serving the defence disclosure statement. **(Documents 16 and 18)**
- Dealing with character evidence applications. **(Document 17)**
- Completing the PCMH questionnaire. **(Document 20)**
- Briefing Counsel. **(Document 21)**

Costs:

The magistrates' court stage of the case is now completed, and Edwina updates the CDS 11, Claim Cost Summary Sheet, which is kept on the file so that it is available for any future audit by the Criminal Defence Service. The costs payable are purely a lower standard fee which takes account of all work done on the file, but the rest of the form must be completed to record the times spent on the case preparation, travel and waiting.

Disclosure:

Edwina has now been served with the prosecution disclosure schedule. Clearly the most interesting item is Item 4 – the criminal record of Arthur King. There may be helpful material in officers' notebooks or from the other witnesses listed, but having talked to Peter, Joanne and Steven about the fracas, Edwina suspects that it is unlikely that any of these saw anything significant. Anxious to have a look at King's previous convictions, Edwina speaks to the prosecutor and suggests that these should be disclosed under the Attorney General's Guidelines as material which potentially goes to the credibility of a prosecution witness. The prosecutor agrees to review this.

Edwina uses her analysis of case as the basis of the defence statement (**Document 18**). For the principles of drafting a defence statement, see Chapter 7.5.2. The statement provided in Document 18 is simply one way of drafting the statement. Edwina also drafts and serves the defence witness notice on the prosecution and the court (**Document 18C**).

Edwina subsequently receives further prosecution disclosure of Arthur King's criminal record (**Document 19**) but of no other material.

PCMH:

Edwina completes as much of the Plea and Case Management form (**Document 20**) as she can. She then briefs Counsel (**Document 21**). She does this early so that a conference can be arranged before the hearing. There three particular concerns which she has with the case:

> *[1]* *Character evidence:* Edwina drafts and serves on prosecution and court a defence counter-application to the prosecution application to adduce Mr Butcher's previous convictions: **Document 17B**.
>
> At this point she decides not to serve a notice for permission to adduce the bad character of Arthur King, the injured party. This is a difficult tactical decision. King has a recent conviction for defrauding the VAT. This is probably going to be admissible if an application is made under s.100 because it is substantially probative to an important matter in issue – namely whether Mr King is an honest witness. On the other hand, if this conviction is put to Mr King, it will clearly activate Gateway G since it will be an attack on his character. This would enable the prosecution to raise Mr Butcher's previous convictions.
>
> There is no right answer to this dilemma, and different practitioners might take different views. Edwina's instinct is that the best way to run the case is on the basis that Mr King had had too much to drink and was simply mistaken about what happened. This avoids any need to suggest active dishonesty on his part – and it avoids activating Gateway G.
>
> *[2]* *Inferences from the police station:* There is nothing that can be done about this now. The advice to Peter Butcher at the police station was not good, and there is a clear risk of a s.34 inference being drawn from his failure to put forward his account.
>
> *[3]* *Dangerous offender provisions:* Finally, as part of her general preparation Edwina considers the likely sentencing outcomes. She notes that if Peter is convicted of the s.20 OAPA offence (a Sched. 15 CJA 2003 offence) this may trigger the dangerous offender provisions. The court will consider whether Peter is a dangerous offender (is there a significant risk of serious harm to the public by the offender committing further specified offences?). If this is the case the judge can consider imposing an extended sentence – so that Peter will receive a minimum of 12 months in prison, followed by a up to 4 years on licence.
>
> Edwina takes the view that the gap between offences, and the wholly different nature of this offence, makes it unlikely that the judge will take the view that there is a significant risk of serious harm. Furthermore the conditions for imposing an extended sentence set out in Part V CJA 2003 do not appear to apply so the risk is relatively low but it is one more thing to worry about.

DOCUMENT 14

Submit by Email

MAGISTRATES' COURT

DIRECTIONS FOR CASE COMMITTED TO THE CROWN COURT

Westchurch.Magistrates' Court
Date committed 2nd April.

The Plea and Case Management Hearing will take place

on 30th April at Westchurch Crown Court

Name of defendant	Case no	Remand status	Youth jointly charged with adult?	Represented by:
D1 Peter Butcher		Bail		
D2		Bail/cust/COM		
D3		Bail/cust/COM		
D4		Bail/cust/COM		

COM= in custody on other matters

Defence telephone numbers:
D1..(home)..(mobile)   D1   solicitor   (office)
D2....(home).(mobile)   D2   solicitor   (office)
D3...(home)..(mobile)   D3 solicitor (office)
D4..(home)..(mobile)   D4 solicitor (office)

Prosecution telephone number

CASE DETAILS

1. Has the defendant been advised that the case may proceed in his or her absence?

D1: Y ☐ N ☐   D2: Y ☐ N ☐

D3: Y ☐ N ☐   D4: Y ☐ N ☐

2. Has the defendant been advised about credit for pleading guilty?

D1: Y ☐ N ☐   D2: Y ☐ N ☐

D3: Y ☐ N ☐   D4: Y ☐ N ☐

3. What pleas, if any, are indicated?
D1:**Not guilty**
D2:.
D3:
D4:.

NOTE: If the defendant decides to plead guilty after committal, the Crown Court must be notified immediately. The Crown Court will then list the case for a hearing as soon as possible.

4. Does the defence intend to make an application under section 41 of the Youth Justice and Criminal Evidence Act 1999 to cross-examine the complainant about his or her sexual history? **No** (to be served within 28 days of primary/initial disclosure)

5. Please give details of any other matters which should be dealt with at the same time as these proceedings (e.g. other offences, offences to be taken into consideration)?
D1:**None**

DOCUMENT 14

Insert committal date in blank box:
2nd April 200-

ACTION	TIME LIMITS	DIRECTIONS
1	**Date committed**	• Prosecution to serve provisional draft indictment, if not already done.
2	14 days after Action 1	• Prosecution to serve primary or initial disclosure • Defence to notify prosecution of witness requirements • Prosecution to serve any application for hearsay or defendant's bad character
3	28 days after Action 1	• Prosecution to serve final draft indictment and any special measures applications • Defence to serve any application under section 41 of the Youth Justice and Criminal Evidence Act 1999
4	14 days after Action 2	• Defence to serve: • (i) Defence statement* (including any alibi details) OR notification of guilty plea (ii) Any application for hearsay/bad character (iii) Response to hearsay/bad character application by prosecution
5	14 days after Action 3	• Defence to serve response to any prosecution application for special measures • Prosecution and defence to notify Crown Court of names of trial advocate and time estimate • Defence to notify Crown Court of non-availability of expert witnesses, with reasons • Witness Care Unit to notify Crown Court and prosecution of dates when witnesses required by defence are unavailable, with reasons.
6	14 days after Action 4	• Prosecution to serve responses to hearsay/bad character

NOTE: if any party seeks a subsequent variation in the timetable or further direction, a written application must be made to the Crown Court within 14 days of committal, and copies served on all other parties. A Crown Court judge may make directions as appropriate. If at any time either party is unable to comply with any direction, it must notify the case progression officer immediately and apply to the Crown Court for a variation.

* indicates those time limits which cannot be varied by a magistrates' court.

Please record any further directions here:

Received. .(defence signature) **(prosecution signature)**

DOCUMENT 15

Claim Cost Summary Sheet — CDS11

Class (delete where appropriate) - ~~Criminal Investigations~~ / Criminal Proceedings / ~~Appeals and Reviews~~ / ~~Prison Law~~ / ~~Associated CLS~~

- One form should be completed for each claim you make
- Where this claim relates to a Lower Standard Fee, do not complete Profit / Core Cost information
- Where this claim relates to the Associated CLS Class of Work, only Legal Help claims should be recorded on this form. Where Investigative Help and Legal Representation are being claimed the appropriate CLS claim form should be used.

Client surname and initial: BUTCHER, P

UFN: _____/_4_/___

Our reference: _____

Profit Costs

Description	Rate £	Hours / Mins	Net Total £	VAT £	Gross Total
ADVOCACY	62.35	/6	68.59		
PREP	49.70	/	124.25		
CORRESPON.	3.90	X3	11.70		
		Total	204.54	35.79	240.33

Disbursements

Description	Rate £	Total	VAT	Gross Total
Mileage	@ p			

Travel

Description	Rate (£)	Hours / Mins	Total £	VAT £	Gross Total
TRAVEL X2	26.30	0/24	10.52		
		Total	10.52	1.84	12.36

Waiting

Description	Rate (£)	Hours / Mins	Total £	VAT £	Gross Total
WAIT AT CRT	26.30	0/30	13.15		
		Total	13.15	2.30	15.45

Where the claim is in the Proceedings Class and a Representation Order has been granted, where applicable indicate level of standard fee claimed i.e. lower or higher standard fee category.

Pre-order work? [N]   Standard Fee   £ 276.50

Date order granted 15 / 2 / --   Total Core Costs   £ 204.54

DOCUMENT 16A

Crown Prosecution Service,
North Chambers,
Waterville Street,
WESTCHURCH

Halpern Dodds,
29 Chesterfield Place,
WESTCHURCH
Yr ref:
Our ref: JMB/211

2nd April 20 —

Dear Sirs,

Re: R v BUTCHER - Westchurch Magistrates Court
<u>Disclosure of Prosecution Material under section 3 Criminal Procedure and Investigations Act 1996</u>

I am required by section 3 Criminal Procedure and Investigations Act 1996 (CPIA) to disclose to you any prosecution material which has not previously been disclosed and which in my opinion might undermine the case for the prosecution against you or assist your case.

Attached to this letter is a copy of a schedule of non-sensitive unused material prepared by the police in compliance with their duty under Part II CPIA and the provisions of the Code of Practice. The schedule has been prepared by the police Disclosure Officer.

Unless the word "evidence" appears alongside any item, all the items listed on the schedule are not intended to be used as part of the prosecution case. You will receive a written notice should the position change.

Where indicated, copies of the items listed are attached. Material marked as available for inspection can be viewed by arrangement with myself.

This material is disclosed to you in accordance with the provisions of the CPIA, and you must not use or disclose it, or any information recorded in it, for any purpose other than in connection with these criminal proceedings. If you do so without permission of the court, you may commit an offence.

If you supply a written defence statement to me and to the court within 28 days of the date of receipt of this letter, material which has not been disclosed at this stage will be further reviewed in the light of that statement.

A defence statement is required by section 5 CPIA in Crown Court cases. In magistrates' court cases, section 6 CPIA makes a defence statement optional. Please bear in mind that we will rely upon the information you provide in the statement to identify any remaining material which has not already been disclosed but which might reasonably assist the defence case as you have described it. The statement will also be relied on by the court if you later make an application under section 8 CPIA.

If you do not make a defence statement where one is required, or provide one late, the court may permit comment and/or draw an adverse inference.

If you request access to any item which marked for disclosure by inspection, it essential that you preserve this schedule in its present form, as access will only be granted upon production of the schedule to the person supervising access.

If you have a query in connection with this letter, please contact myself.

Yours faithfully,

R. Dixon

R. Dixon
Crown Prosecution Service

DOCUMENT 16B

Form MC 6C

POLICE SCHEDULE OF NON-SENSITIVE UNUSED MATERIAL

R v BUTCHER

The Disclosure Officer believes that the following material which does not form part of the Prosecution case is NOT SENSITIVE

Item No	DESCRIPTION	LOCATION		FOR CPS USE
1	Notebooks of PCs Stanley, Herbert, Ross, Jones, Roberts.	Westchurch Police Station	*	**COMMENTS**
2	Witness statements: Sarah KING Lawrence DONALD Conor SCOTT Debbie COWAN David EMMIN-SMITH	"		
3	Custody record: BUTCHER			*Disclosed*
4	Criminal Record: Arthur KING			
5	Tape of interview: BUTCHER			*Disclosed*

DATE:	CONTINUATION SHEET:	REVIEWING
2nd April 20 —	none	**LAWYER**
		Thomas Burton

* Enter D=disclose to defence I= Defence may inspect

DOCUMENT 17A

NOTICE TO INTRODUCE EVIDENCE OF A DEFENDANT'S BAD CHARACTER

(Criminal Procedure Rules, rule 35.4(2))

Case details

Name of defendant: Peter Butcher

Court: Westchurch Crown Court

Case reference number:

Charge(s): s. 20 Offences Against the Person Act 1861

This notice is given by the prosecutor

[~~.. (name of co-defendant)~~]

I want to introduce evidence of the bad character of Peter Butcher (defendant's name) **on the following ground(s) in the Criminal Justice Act 2003:**

☐ it is important explanatory evidence: s.101(1)(c).

☒ **it is relevant to an important matter in issue between that defendant and the prosecution: s.101(1)(d).**

☐ it has substantial probative value in relation to an important matter in issue between that defendant and a co-defendant: s.101(1)(e).

☐ it is evidence to correct a false impression given by that defendant: s.101(1)(f).

☐ that defendant has made an attack on another person's character: s.101(1)(g).

How to use this form

1. Complete the boxes above and give the details required in the boxes below. If you use an electronic version of this form, the boxes will expand. If you use a paper version and need more space, you may attach extra sheets.

2. Sign and date the completed form.

3. Send a copy of the completed form to:
 (a) the court, and
 (b) each other party to the case.

Notes:

1. You must send this form so as to reach the recipients within the time prescribed by Criminal Procedure Rule 35.4(3) or (4). The court may extend that time limit, **but if you are late you must explain why.**

2. A party who objects to the introduction of the evidence must apply to the court under Criminal Procedure Rule 35.4(5) **not more than 14 days after service of this notice.**

DOCUMENT 17A

1) Facts of the misconduct. If the misconduct is a previous conviction, explain whether you rely on (a) the fact of that conviction, or (b) the circumstances of that offence. If (b), set out the facts on which you rely.

The defendant has previous convictions as set out in the attached PNC printout. In particular the prosecution points to:

10 years ago – s.4 Public Order Act
9 years ago – s.47 OAPA (ABH)
8 years ago – common assault and breach of the peace
7 years ago – taking a motor vehicle without consent and going equipped to steal
6 years ago – four burglaries of non-residential premises

No fuller information is currently available about the circumstances of the above offences

The prosecution rely on the fact of the conviction

---

2) How you will prove those facts, if in dispute. A party who objects to the introduction of the evidence must explain which, if any, of the facts set out above are in dispute. Explain in outline on what you will then rely to prove those facts, e.g. whether you rely on (a) a certificate of conviction, (b) another official record (and if so, which), or (c) other evidence (and if so, what).

These will be proved by a certificate of conviction for each offence.

---

3) Reasons why the evidence is admissible. Explain why the evidence is admissible, by reference to the provision(s) of the Criminal Justice Act 2003 on which you rely.

The Crown applies to adduce the defendant's previous convictions as being relevant to an important matter in issue between the prosecution and defence (s.101(1)(d)). The important matters in issue are that:

(i) the defendant has a propensity to commit offences of violence – the prosecution relies on the previous convictions under s.4 POA, s.47 OAPA and common assault. These convictions are not in the same category or of the same description but s.103 is not exhaustive of the circumstances under which the convictions may be admissible: see *Hanson*. There are multiple convictions of varying levels of severity. These show a propensity to violence and make it more likely that the defendant has committed the instant offence.

(ii) the defendant has a propensity for untruthfulness – the prosecution rely upon the convictions for dishonesty, and in particular for burglary to demonstrate this.

---

4) Reasons for any extension of time required. If this notice is served late, explain why. N/A

DOCUMENT 17A

Signed: *Maureen Doherty*... **[prosecutor]** ~~[co-defendant / co-defendant's solicitor]~~ **Date**: 2nd April 20--.............................

DOCUMENT 17B

APPLICATION TO EXCLUDE EVIDENCE OF A DEFENDANT'S BAD CHARACTER

(Criminal Procedure Rules, rule 35.4(5))

Case details

Name of defendant: Peter Butcher

Court: Westchurch Crown Court

Case reference number:

Charge(s): s. 20 Offences Against the Person Act 1861

This is an application by [the prosecutor]

                          Peter Butcher…………………… (name of defendant)

I object to the introduction of the evidence of which the prosecutor [……………………… (name of co-defendant)] served notice on 2nd April 20-- (date) **because:**

☐ that evidence is not admissible.

☒ I am the defendant named in that notice and it would be unfair to admit that evidence.

☐ I object to the notice for the other reason(s) explained below.

How to use this form

1. Complete the boxes above and give the details required in the boxes below.
If you use an electronic version of this form, the boxes will expand. If you use a paper version and need more space, you may attach extra sheets.

2. Sign and date the completed form.

3. Send a copy of the completed form to:

    (a) the court, and

    (b) each other party to the case.

Note:
You must send this form so as to reach the recipients not more than 14 days after service of the notice to which you object. The court may extend that time limit, **but if you are late you must explain why.**

DOCUMENT 17B

1) **Facts of the misconduct in dispute.** Whatever reasons you have for objecting to the notice, explain (a) which, if any, facts of the misconduct set out in it you dispute, and (b) what, if any, facts you admit instead.

I admit the facts of the previous convictions subject to the application.

2) **Reasons for objecting to the notice.** Explain, as applicable:

(a) why the bad character evidence is not admissible, by reference to the provision(s) of the Criminal Justice Act 2003 relied on in the notice.

(b) if you are the defendant named in the notice, why it would be unfair to admit the evidence. (You can object on this ground under section 101(3) of the Criminal Justice Act 2003 only if the notice gives as grounds for admitting the evidence (i) that it is relevant to an important matter in issue between you and the prosecution, or (ii) that you have made an attack on another person's character.)

(c) what other objection you have to the notice.

(i) the defendant has a propensity to commit offences of violence

I have no previous convictions which are in the same category or of the same description as the offence charged. The convictions relied upon are less serious offences and the prosecution is unable to show any common features to the alleged offence which make the earlier convictions probative of any propensity to violence. The previous convictions all date from a number of years ago when I was significantly younger. I have since reformed myself in the intervening period. Accordingly the prosecution fails to show that the convictions are admissible under s.103 as having any probative value at all.

(ii) the defendant has a propensity for untruthfulness

I assert that there is no evidence of propensity for untruthfulness in the convictions that are relied upon by the prosecution. In particular I pleaded guilty in each case and a dishonesty offence in itself does not indicate untruthfulness.

3) **Reasons for any extension of time required.** If this application is served late, explain why.

N/A

Signed: Peter Butcher .... [prosecutor]
[defendant / defendant's solicitor]

Date: 12th April 20--..............................

DOCUMENT 18A

Halpern Dodds
for all your legal needs

29 Chesterfield Place,
WESTCHURCH
Telephone (24 hours): 0071 229 228
Fax: 0071 229 229
e mail: HalpernDoddsX@germail.co.uk

12th April 20__

Crown Prosecution Service,
North Chambers,
Waterville Street,
WESTCHURCH

Dear Sirs,

Re: R v Butcher, Westchurch Crown Court

Please find attached the defence statement under s.5, Criminal Procedure and Investigations Act 1996 in respect of Peter Butcher. We also enclose the defence witness notice.

We look forward to hearing from you accordingly.

Yours faithfully,

Halpern Dodds

Halpern Dodds

HALPERN DODDS Partners: Edwina Halpern, LLB, LLM, Dip Crim. John Dodds, BA. Associate: Mike Levin

DOCUMENT 18B

DEFENCE STATEMENT
s.5, Criminal Procedure and Investigations Act 1996

To the Prosecutor:	CPS, North Chambers, Waterville Street.
To the Court:	Westchurch Crown Court.
Defendant:	Peter BUTCHER
Charge:	s.20 Offences against the Person Act
Date of next hearing:	Plea and Case Management Hearing, 30th April
Defendant's solicitors:	Halpern Dodds, 29 Chesterfield Place, WESTCHURCH

1. The nature of the accused's defence including any particular defence on which he intends to rely is:

    I did not assault Mr King as alleged or at all.

2. The accused takes issue with the prosecution in relation to the following matters:

    I disagree with any statement that suggests that I hit Mr King or assaulted him in any way. I also disagree with any statement that suggests I said to Mr King: "You stupid old bastard, you deserve it."

3. The accused takes issues with the prosecution about these matters for the following reasons:

    I take issue with these matters because I did not hit Mr King and I did not say these words.

4. The accused intends to raise the following points of law:

    There may be future issues in respect of character evidence and possible inferences. However this will only be clear once the defence is told of the basis on which the prosecution puts its case.

5. The accused will raise the following facts in his defence:

    Mr King is confused about his account due to his alcohol intake. The glass did not smash in Mr King's face. It smashed on the furniture.

6. The accused requests disclosure of the following material as it might undermine the prosecution case or might reasonably be expected to assist the defence disclosed in this statement:

    Item 4 – criminal record: Arthur King

    Items 1 and 2 – notebooks and witness statements

Signed: Peter Butcher   Date: 12th April 20 —

DOCUMENT 18C

DEFENCE WITNESS NOTICE
s.6C, Criminal Procedure and Investigations Act 1996

To the Prosecutor: **CPS, North Chambers, Waterville Street.**
To the Court: **Westchurch Crown Court.**
Defendant: **Peter BUTCHER**
Charge: **s.20 Offences against the Person Act**
Date of next hearing: **Plea and Case Management Hearing, 30th April**
Defendant's solicitors: **Halpern Dodds, 29 Chesterfield Place,**

The accused hereby gives notice of his intention to call the following witnesses at his trial:

1.   Joanne Butcher (DOB 21/12/19__)
Flat 4, James Park East Buildings, Park Street, Westchurch

Signed: Peter Butcher   Date: 12th April 20__

DOCUMENT 19A

DEFENCE STATEMENT

(Criminal Procedure and Investigations Act 1996, section 5 & 6; Criminal Procedure and Investigations Act 1996 (Defence Disclosure Time Limits) Regulations 2011; Criminal Procedure Rules, rule 22.4)

Case details

Name of defendant: Peter Butcher

Court: Westchurch Crown Court

Case reference number:

Charge(s): s.20 Offences Against the Person Act 1861

When to use this form

If you are a defendant pleading not guilty:

(a) in a Crown Court case, you **must** give the information listed in Part 2 of this form;

(b) in a magistrates' court case, you **may** give that information but you do not have to do so.

The time limit for giving the information is:

14 days (in a magistrates' court case)

28 days (in a Crown Court case)

after initial prosecution disclosure (or notice from the prosecutor that there is no material to disclose).

How to use this form

1. **Complete the case details box above, and Part 1 below.**

2. **Attach as many sheets as you need to give the information listed in Part 2.**

3. **Sign and date the completed form.**

4. **Send a copy of the completed form to:**

   (a) **the court, and**

   (b) **the prosecutor**

   before the time limit expires.

If you need more time, you **must** apply to the court **before** the time limit expires. You should apply in writing, but no special form is needed.

DOCUMENT 19A

Part 1: Plea

I confirm that I intend to plead not guilty to [all the charges] the following charge against me:

s.20 Offences Against the Person Act 1861

Part 2: Nature of the defence

Attach as many sheets as you need to give the information required.

Under section 6A of the Criminal Procedure and Investigations Act 1996, you must:

(a) set out the nature of your defence, including any particular defences on which you intend to rely;

I did not assault Mr King as alleged or at all.

(b) indicate the matters of fact on which you take issue with the prosecutor, and in respect of each explain why;

I disagree with any statement that suggests that I hit Mr King or assaulted him in any way. I also disagree with any statement that suggests I said to Mr King: "You stupid old bastard, you deserve it."

I take issue with these matters because I did not hit Mr King and I did not say these words.

(c) set out particulars of the matters of fact on which you intend to rely for the purposes of your defence;

Mr King is confused about his account due to his alcohol intake. The glass did not smash in Mr King's face. It smashed on the furniture.

(d) indicate any point of law that you wish to take, including any point about the admissibility of evidence or about abuse of process, and any authority relied on; and

There may be future issues in respect of character evidence and possible inferences. However this will only be clear once the defence is told of the basis on which the prosecution puts its case.

(e) if your defence statement includes an alibi (i.e. an assertion that you were in a place, at a time, inconsistent with you having committed the offence), give particulars, including –

(i) the name, address and date of birth of any witness who you believe can give evidence in support of that alibi,

WARNING: Under section 11 of the Criminal Procedure and Investigations Act 1996, **if you (a) do not disclose what the Act requires; (b) do not give a defence statement before the time limit expires; (c) at trial, rely on a defence, or facts, that you have not disclosed; or (d) at trial, call an alibi witness whom you have not identified in advance, then the court, the prosecutor or another defendant may comment on that, and the court may draw such inferences as it thinks proper in deciding whether you are guilty.**

2

DOCUMENT 19A

> (ii) if you do not know all of those details, any information that might help identify or find that witness.
>
> Not applicable
>
> The accused requests disclosure of the following material as it might undermine the prosecution case or might reasonably be expected to assist the defence disclosed in this statement:
>
> Item 4 – criminal record: Arthur King
>
> Items 1 and 2 – notebooks and witness statements

Signed: *Peter Butcher*............................. defendant / ~~defendant's solicitor~~

Date: 12th April 20__.............................

WARNING: Under section 11 of the Criminal Procedure and Investigations Act 1996, **if you (a) do not disclose what the Act requires; (b) do not give a defence statement before the time limit expires; (c) at trial, rely on a defence, or facts, that you have not disclosed; or (d) at trial, call an alibi witness whom you have not identified in advance, then the court, the prosecutor or another defendant may comment on that, and the court may draw such inferences as it thinks proper in deciding whether you are guilty.**

DOCUMENT 19B

DEFENCE WITNESS NOTICE

(Criminal Procedure and Investigations Act 1996, section 6C; Criminal Procedure and Investigations Act 1996 (Defence Disclosure Time Limits) Regulations 2011; Criminal Procedure Rules, rule 22.4)

Case details

Name of defendant: Peter Butcher

Court: Westchurch Crown Court

Case reference number: Not known

Charge(s): s.20 Offences Against the Person Act 1861

When to use this form

Under section 6C of the Criminal Procedure and Investigations Act 1996, if you are a defendant pleading not guilty you must:

(a) let the court and the prosecutor know **whether you intend to call anyone other than yourself as a witness at your trial**;

(b) do so **not more than -**

14 days (in a magistrates' court case)

28 days (in a Crown Court case)

after initial prosecution disclosure (or notice from the prosecutor that there is no material to disclose);

(c) give as many details of each witness as you can (see the list below);

(d) let the court and the prosecutor know if you later -

(i) decide to call a witness, other than yourself, whom you have not already identified in a defence witness notice,

(ii) decide not to call a witness you have listed in a notice, or

(iii) discover information which you should have included in a notice if you had known it then.

How to use this form

1. Complete the case details box above and give the details required below.
2. Sign and date the completed form.
3. Send a copy of the completed form to:
   (a) the court, and
   (b) the prosecutor
   before the time limit expires.

If you need more time, you **must** apply to the court **before** the time limit expires. You should apply in writing, but no special form is needed.

DOCUMENT 19B

List of intended defence witness(es)

1. Do you intend to call anyone other than yourself as a witness at your trial? No ☐ Yes ☐ If yes, give details below. If you use an electronic version of this form, the boxes will expand. If you use a paper version and need more space, you may attach extra sheets.

Name	Date of birth (if known)	Address, or any other contact or identifying details
Joanne Butcher	21/12/19--	Flat 4, James Park East Buildings, Park Street, Westchurch

2. Have you given a defence witness notice in this case before?
No X   Yes ☐   If yes, give the date(s).

Signed: Peter Butcher...[defendant / ~~defendant's solicitor~~]

Date: 12th April 20___

WARNING: Under section 11 of the Criminal Procedure and Investigations Act 1996, if you (a) do not give a defence witness notice before the time limit expires, or (b) at trial, call a witness whom you have not identified in a witness notice then the court, the prosecutor or another defendant may comment on that, and the court may draw such inferences as it thinks proper in deciding whether you are guilty.

2

DOCUMENT 20

Plea and Case Management Hearing

Advocates' Questionnaire

The Crown Court

CC Case Number D1 [   ]

Date of trial [   ]

Fixed ☐
Warned ☐

■ Parties must complete this form.
■ This form is to be used at all Crown Court Centres, without local variation.
There is an electronic version of the form on the Ministry of Justice website, at:
http://www.justice.gov.uk/guidance/courts-and-tribunals/courts/procedure-rules/criminal/formspage.htm

PART ONE
(Questions 1 to 15 are to be completed in all cases, together with question 37 'Witness List')

1 Date of trial and custody time limits

1.1 Date of PCMH: 30th April 20--
     Judge: HHJ Mayfield
     PTI URN: xy/yx
     Estimated length of trial: 2 days

1.2 What are the custody time limit expiry dates as agreed between the parties? *(If different custody time limits attach to different offences or defendants, please give details.)*

n/a

1.3 Can an application to extend any custody time limit be made today? ☐ No ☐ Yes

2 Parties

	Parties' names	Age	Remand status	Instructed Advocate	PCMH Advocate (if not the Instructed Advocate)
P	CPS			Bayfield	Rands-Morven
D1	Peter Butcher	29	C ☐ B ☒	Lee	Lee

Plea and Case Management Hearing, Criminal Procedure Rules 2011 – July 2011

Criminal Case Study – *R v Butcher* **405**

DOCUMENT 20

3 Contact details

3.1 Parties

P — Office

Name	Dixon	Phone	0071 229 4444
Email	dixon@cprs.gsi.gov.uk		

Advocate

Name	Ike Bayfield	Phone	0071243432
Email	chambersadmin@cedricstreetchambersx.co.uk		

D1 — Solicitor

Name	Edwina Halpern	Phone	0071229228
Email	Halperndoddsx@germail.co.uk		

Advocate

Name	Eva Lee	Phone	0071 229 7666
Email	LeeE@cedricstreetchambersx.co.uk		

3.2 Case progression officers

P

Name	R. Dixon – details as above	Phone	
Email			

D1

Name	E Halpern – details as above	Phone	
Email			

Court

Name	Xan Yiang	Phone	0071222991
Email	YiangX@westchurchcc.courtservice.gov.uk		

4 Which, if any, of the orders made at the magistrates' court have not been complied with?

5

D1 Has the defendant been advised that he or she will receive credit for a guilty plea? ☐ No ☒ Yes

6

D1 Has the defendant been warned that the case may proceed in his or her absence? ☐ No ☒ Yes

7 What plea(s) is / are the defendant(s) offering?

D1 Not Guilty

8 Should the case be referred to the Resident Judge for a trial judge to be allocated? ☒ No ☐ Yes

Plea and Case Management Hearing, Criminal Procedure Rules 2011 – July 2011

DOCUMENT 20

9 Give details of any issues relating to the fitness to plead or to stand trial.

D1 none

10 Disclosure, the defence statement and notification of defence witnesses

10.1 Has the prosecution made statutory disclosure?

P Yes

D1 As far as is known

10.2 Has a defence statement been served?

D1 Yes

10.3 Does it comply with the statutory requirements?

P Yes

10.4 If not clear from the defence statement, what are the real issues?

D1 This is clear from the defence statement – defendant denies being involved in any assault on the victim

10.5
D1 Has / will the defence made / make an application in writing under section 8 of the Criminal Procedure and Investigations Act 1996?   X☐ No ☐ Yes

10.6
D1 Has the time limit for the notification of defence witnesses expired?   X☐ No ☐ Yes

If yes, give particulars (preferably on the relevant from of Notice).

If no, can any orders be made even at this stage?   X☐ No ☐ Yes

Details of any proposed order(s)
Defence witness notice served

11 Further evidence

What further evidence is to be served by the prosecution? By when is it reasonably practicable to serve this?

P None

DOCUMENT 20

12 Expert evidence

12.1 Give details of any expert evidence likely to be relied upon, including why it is required and by when it is reasonably practicable to serve this.

P | There is an outstanding issue in relation to analysis of blood sample on the glass said to have been used as the weapon. It is hoped that the final report will be served by the time of the PCMH. It is not anticipated that this will be contested material.

D1 | None

12.2 Is a note of agreement / disagreement required?

No

13 Witnesses

13.1 Have the parties completed the Witness List (see **37**)? ☐ No X☐ Yes

13.2 Are the parties satisfied that all the listed witnesses are needed (see **37**)? ☐ No X☐ Yes
If 'no', give details.

13.3 Are the parties satisfied that the time estimates for questioning witnesses are realistic (see **37**)? ☐ No X☐ Yes
If 'no', give details.

13.4 Is any witness summons necessary? X☐ No ☐ Yes
If 'yes', give particulars:

13.5 Can a timetable be fixed now for the calling of witnesses? ☐ No X☐ Yes
If 'no', why not?

14 Timetabling of the trial

14.1 Are there matters which need to be determined at the start of the trial, which may affect the timetable? ☐ No X☐ Yes

DOCUMENT 20

> If so, when will (1) the jury and (2) the witnesses be required?
>
> Bad character application – will take approximately half an hour therefore jury can be empanelled on day one immediately after this

14.2 What timetable can now be set for the conduct of the trial (see rule 3.10)?

> All prosecution evidence to be called on day 1. Defence case to start on day 1 and possibly run into day 2. Closing speeches and verdict on day two.

15 The indictment

15.1 Has the indictment been signed and dated as required by Part 14 of the CrimPR? ☐ No ☒ Yes

15.2 Is any amendment of the indictment required? ☒ No ☐ Yes

PART TWO question 37 (Witness list) is to be completed in every case

Answer the remaining questions only where relevant

16 Admissions and agreed facts

What matters can usefully be admitted or put into schedules, diagrams, visual aids etc.?

> Dates and times admitted.

17 Case summary

P Is it proposed to serve a case summary or note of opening? ☒ No ☐ Yes

18 Measures to assist witnesses and defendants in giving evidence

18A Measures to assist a witness in giving evidence.

> *Each of these issues must be addressed separately in respect of each young vulnerable or intimidated witness who is or may be required to give evidence in person. (If completed electronically, the form will expand to deal with each separate witness separately. If completed manually, attach separate sheets if necessary.)*
>
> Name and age of witness:
>
> name: age:

DOCUMENT 20

What arrangements have been made for a pre-trial visit?		
What arrangements have been made to ensure that the witness sees the video of their evidence BEFORE the trial (i.e. not immediately before giving their evidence over the live link)?		
Has the witness been offered a 'supporter'? If 'yes', give particulars:	☐ No	☐ Yes
Does the witness need an intermediary? If 'yes', give particulars:	☐ No	☐ Yes
What arrangements have been made for the witness to access the court building other than by the main public entrance?		
What are the arrangements to ensure that this witness can give evidence without waiting or at least by reducing waiting to a minimum *(e.g. by ensuring that the opening and any preliminary points will be finished before the time appointed for the witness to attend or by agreeing and fixing a timed witness order in advance)*?		
Have the views of the witness been sought and, if so, has s/he expressed any particular view or concerns? If 'yes', give particulars: If views not sought, why not? What material (if any) needs to be available to the witness in the video suite?	☐ No	☐ Yes

18B   **Defendant's evidence direction**

Is any defendant's evidence direction to be sought?	X☐ No	☐ Yes
If so, has the necessary application been made, complying with Section 4 of CrimPR Part 29?	☐ No	☐ Yes

Plea and Case Management Hearing, Criminal Procedure Rules 2011 – July 2011

DOCUMENT 20

If so, give details

18C **Witness anonymity order**

Is any witness anonymity order sought / to be made?	X☐ No ☐ Yes
If so, has an application been made, complying with Section 5 of CrimPR Part 29?	☐ No ☐ Yes
If so give details (subject to the restrictions in Section 5 of CrimPR Part 29).	

19 Young or vulnerable defendants

Are any other arrangements needed for any young or vulnerable defendants?

D1

20 Reporting restrictions

State type and grounds of any reporting restriction sought.

P

D1

21 Third party material

21. Is any application to be made for the production of third party material? X☐ No ☐ Yes

22 Defendant's interview(s)

22.1 Specify any issue relating to the admissibility of all or any part of the defendant's interview(s). Can the issue be resolved now? If not, when? Are skeleton arguments needed and, if so, when?

No issues

22.2 By how much can the interview(s) be shortened by editing / summary for trial? Give a timetable for the service of any proposed summary by the prosecution and agreement / counter-proposal by the defence.

DOCUMENT 20

22.3 Specify any other issues concerning the defendant's interview(s).

23 Witnesses giving evidence by video or DVD interview

23.1 Is there video or DVD evidence of any young / vulnerable / intimidated witness yet to be served?

> No

23.2 Has each video been transcribed?

23.3 Is there an issue in relation to the accuracy / admissibility / quality / length of any video or transcript?

24 Witness interview(s)

24.1 Are there any videos / audio tapes of witness interviews which, if they meet the disclosure test, are yet to be disclosed as unused material?

> No

24.2 If so, is any application made for that video / audio tape to be transcribed and, if so, why?

25 CCTV evidence

25.1 Are there any outstanding issues in relation to service or disclosure of CCTV footage? *If the material is in the possession of a third party, complete 21 instead.*

DOCUMENT 20

25.2 Is an edited version to be served / used?

26 Electronic equipment

26.1 Give details of any special equipment (e.g. CCTV, live link, audio recordings, DVD) required in the trial courtroom.

P | N/A

D1 | N/A

26.2 Is the evidence in its present form compatible with the equipment in court?

N/A

27 Cross-examination on sexual history

If an application has not already been made, does the defence intend to make an application under section 41 of the Youth Justice and Criminal Evidence Act 1999 to cross-examine a witness about his or her sexual history?

D1 | N/A

28 Bad character

Are any directions necessary in relation to bad character applications? Are there to be any further applications?

P | Yes – an opposed prosecution application to adduce the defendant's bad character needs to be heard

D1 | No directions necessary – all papers served

DOCUMENT 20

29 Hearsay
Are any directions necessary in relation to hearsay applications? Are there to be any further applications?

P | No

D1 |

30 Admissibility and legal issues
What points on admissibility / other legal issues are to be taken? Is it necessary for any to be resolved before trial?

P | Possible inferences from silence in interview – not necessary to resolve before trial.

D1 |

31 Public interest immunity
Is any 'on notice' public interest immunity application to be made?

P | No

32 Jury bundle
What proposals do the prosecution make for a jury bundle?

P | These are in hand.

33 Concurrent family proceedings
Give details of any concurrent family proceedings.

None

DOCUMENT 20

34 **Other special arrangements**

Give details of any special arrangements (e.g., interpreter, intermediary, wheelchair access, hearing loop system, breaks) needed for anyone attending the trial.

> None required

35 **Linked criminal proceedings**

Are there other criminal proceedings against the defendant or otherwise linked?

> No

36 **Additional orders**

Are any additional orders required?

> No

37 **Witness List** (see table for completion, over page)

DOCUMENT 20

37 Witness List

The parties should indicate here which prosecution witnesses are required to give evidence at trial. The attendance of any witness is subject to the judge's direction.

Name of witness	Page No.	Required by	What is the relevant, disputed issue?	Estimated time for questioning	
				Chief	X - exam
Arthur King		P	Who hit King – self defence?	45	45
Maureen King		D	Who hit King	30	30
Edward Stanley		P	Covers arrest and interview – OIC	30	30

Plea and Case Management Hearing, Criminal Procedure Rules 2011 – July 2011

DOCUMENT 21

WESTCHURCH CROWN COURT
PLEA AND CASE MANAGEMENT HEARING
30th April

Indictment No:
LEGAL AID

R
v
BUTCHER

BRIEF TO COUNSEL FOR PCMH AND TRIAL

Counsel has herewith;

1. Draft Indictment

2. Committal bundle, including

   a) Statement Arthur King

   b) Statement Maureen King

   c) Statement Edward Stanley

   d) Statement Patricia Herbert

   e) Statement Jacqueline Ashfield

   f) Statement Michael Gifford

   g) Transcript of police station interview

   h) Previous convictions: Peter Butcher

   j) Exhibit list and copy photographs

3. Defence statements:

   a) Statement Peter Butcher and Comments

   b) Statement Joanne Butcher

   c) Statement Steven Fiddler

4. Custody Record

5. Tapes of interview

6. Representation Order

7. Prosecution Disclosure Schedule

8. Defence Statement

9. Defence Witness Notice

10. Prosecution Disclosure: Criminal convictions, Arthur King.

11. Copy prosecution bad character application, and defence response

12. PCMH Questionnaire

Counsel is instructed by Edwina Halpern of Halpern Dodds on behalf of the defendant, Peter Butcher. Mr Butcher is charged with a single count of s.20 wounding arising from an alleged assault on his father-in-law, Arthur King, at Mr Butcher's wedding reception on the evening of 14th February. A glass is alleged to have been used and Mr King suffered facial wounds.

Mr Butcher will plead Not Guilty to this offence.

Case History:

Mr Butcher has the benefit of a representation order. At mode of trial on 26th February in Westchurch Magistrates' Court, the justices declined jurisdiction of the matter. Committal on 19th March was by way of s.6 (2). The prosecution has been notified that all prosecution witnesses are currently required to attend trial. A defence statement was served within the specified time on 31st March, and prosecution disclosure of the criminal convictions of the victim, Mr King, has been made.

Prosecution and defence accounts:

Counsel will note that the prosecution case is straightforward. A heated argument broke out at the wedding reception following Mr King's speech. Although Mr Butcher had left the room, he returned, intervened in the argument and punched Mr King once in the face. He was holding a glass at the time. Mr Butcher then told Mr King he deserved it. He then left the room with his bride, was subsequently arrested and refused to answer questions in interview. A glass with blood on it and Mr Butcher's fingerprints was found on the ground at the scene of the incident.

The defence case is similarly simple. Mr Butcher, hearing the noise of the argument, returned to the room as a result of his concern for his pregnant bride. Mr King launched himself at the defendant. Mr Butcher stumbled. The glass in his hand hit the furniture and broke. Mr Butcher turned away and pushed his way out of the crowd with his wife. Mr King fell over, and presumably cut his face on the glass on the ground. There was no punch. Mr Butcher denies having made any comment to Mr King.

Clearly the primary fact in issue is simply whether Mr Butcher punched Mr King. Other than the victim and the defendant, there do not seem to be any witnesses for either prosecution or defence who were looking at the crucial time. Indeed, it may be that, as no witnesses other than Mr King saw the punch, it supports the defendant's suggestion that no punch took place.

Prosecution evidence:

Counsel will note that there is general agreement that there had been drinking taking place, and indeed that there was a general melee involving other members of the wedding party. Instructing Solicitors note that Mr King's wife, Maureen, will confirm that her husband was angry, is a "very forceful" man, and that he "had had quite a bit to drink". She will also say that she heard her husband say: "That little thug is going to pay for this." Instructing Solicitors are of the view that, although a prosecution witness, Mrs King's evidence would in many respects assist the defence account.

Counsel will further note that Mr King's testimony is itself open to attack on a number of grounds: that he had been drinking and either mistook the situation or has misremembered it; that he has a long-standing dislike for the defendant, exacerbated by his daughter's pregnancy, and that his testimony is coloured by this bias; and that he is not a credible witness in any event, having two previous convictions, one of them very recent, for dishonesty offences.

Instructing Solicitors are of the view that a mere suggestion of drunkenness is unlikely to activate s.101(1)(g) in these circumstances, and that general suggestions of bias are also unlikely to amount to suggestions of reprehensible behaviour. Clearly, however, any attempt to bring in Mr King's convictions is extremely likely to lay open the defendant to cross-examination on his own (extensive) previous convictions. Instructing Solicitors are therefore currently of the view that no defence application should be made under s.100 to adduce the bad character of Mr King, useful though his recent dishonesty conviction might be, because the Gateway G consequences would be worse.

Instructing Solicitors are of the view that there is little of relevance to be produced by the remaining prosecution witnesses. It may be that PC Stanley could be usefully cross-examined as to his refusal to make any meaningful disclosure prior to interview. Instructing Solicitors understand that the Crown Prosecution Service intend to adduce further evidence in relation to the blood on the glass. Assuming that there is such forensic evidence to further link the glass to the injury to Mr King, Instructing Solicitors are minded merely to make an admission on this point, and would be grateful for Counsel's view of the matter.

Defence evidence:

Mr Butcher is a pleasant and intelligent man, who would come across generally well in the witness box. Clearly there are potential problems in relation to his previous convictions. If Counsel takes the view that Mr King should be discredited as a witness, and a s.100 application made to adduce his bad character, it would certainly be possible to bring out the fact that Mr Butcher's own previous convictions almost all relate to a period in his early twenties, and that he is a reformed character. However, the jury may take the view that his previous convictions show a clear disposition towards violence, and it may be hard to displace this in the jury's mind.

Counsel will note that a prosecution application to adduce Mr Butcher's previous convictions has been made, and it is likely that binding rulings will be made on this at the PCMH. Instructing Solicitors are of the view that it is unlikely that the court will admit the previous convictions under either Gateway D or G. Should the court do so, then the position vis-à-vis Mr King's character will be simpler and an application should be made to adduce his previous conviction from last year.

The other key problem, which Counsel will have noted, is that Mr Butcher gave a No Comment interview at the police station. Instructing Solicitors are of the view that inferences under s.34 and 36 are both possible and indeed likely as a consequence. With the benefit of hindsight it is clear that the advice from Jim Kettle at the police station that Mr Butcher should remain silent was flawed. There is some similarity with the situation in Argent, in that the court could well take the view that Mr Butcher at least knew the basics of the case against him; and could be expected to respond with the basics of his defence.

It is clear that Mr Butcher did put these facts forward to Mr Kettle in the police station. If therefore the prosecution suggests later fabrication, this can be countered without waiving privilege. However, an equally likely inference is that Mr Butcher did not put forward his defence because he was concerned it would not stand up to closer scrutiny.

As against this, it can clearly be argued – again drawing on the dicta in Argent – that Mr Butcher was reasonable in not answering questions: it was his wedding night; he had been drinking; he was hurt; he was extremely concerned for the safety of his pregnant wife, Joanne. On top of this his legal representative, rightly or wrongly, was telling him in the strongest possible terms that he should exercise his right of silence. All of these, it can be argued, show that it was reasonable for Mr Butcher to remain silent.

There are two other possible defence witnesses. Joanne Butcher has relatively little useful to say – although it may be significant that she does not hear the alleged comment "You stupid old bastard etc." – but it is a moot question as to whether the jury will see her as being a credible witness. Steven Fiddler, the defendant's best man, would in Instructing Solicitors' opinion do more harm than good. He has previous convictions he clearly regards the incident with no great remorse and it does the defendant little good to be associated with him.

Doubtless Counsel will advise if there are further witnesses who Counsel would like called. The PCMH form is enclosed.

Mitigation:

If Mr Butcher is convicted, a custodial sentence seems an inevitable outcome, although some positive material can be drawn from Mr Butcher's newly married state and his pending fatherhood. There are potential dangerous offender issues. However Instructing Solicitors are of the view that the court is unlikely to find that Mr Butcher constitutes a significant risk of serious harm to the public.

A financial penalty seems out of the question, although the court might be minded to make a compensation order. If so, it will need to be borne in mind that the family is currently in receipt of state benefits, and what little spare income there is will doubtless be spent on the new baby. The only realistic alternative to custody would be a substantial community penalty, perhaps combined with a compensation order. This would, in any event, be dependent on a supportive pre sentence report.

Counsel is accordingly briefed to represent Mr Butcher at PCMH and then at trial. Counsel will doubtless wish to see the defendant in conference and Instructing Solicitors will contact Counsel's clerk to make the necessary arrangements. Counsel should contact Instructing Solicitors if there are any pressing steps that need to be taken in the interim.

WESTCHURCH CROWN COURT
Indictment No:

PLEA AND CASE MANAGEMENT
30th April

R
v
BUTCHER

BRIEF TO COUNSEL

Eva Lee,
Westchurch Chambers
WESTCHURCH

Halpern Dodds
29 Chesterfield Place,
WESTCHURCH

[0071 229 228]

Ref: EH/BUTC

A conference is arranged, and, following the conference, Counsel decides that it would be worth exploring whether expert evidence could be obtained to show that it is possible that Arthur King's injuries arose from falling on the glass. Edwina talks informally to two possible experts. Both of them indicate that, at this late stage, based only on photographs and the limited medical reports, it would now be impossible to be categorical one way or the other.

At the conference Counsel also indicates that she agrees with Edwina's approach to the character evidence issue. It is tempting to seek permission to raise Arthur King's previous conviction for dishonesty, but the defence case is more one of mistake by King than an active attempt to dishonestly frame the defendant. Counsel also agrees that the harm done by activating Gateway G and permitting Butcher's previous convictions to go before the jury is too great a risk.

30th April – The Plea and Case Management Hearing

Character evidence: The PCMH is heard before the trial judge. The prosecution applies to adduce evidence of Mr Butcher's previous convictions as per their application form – see Document 17. As Edwina anticipated the judge concludes that the previous convictions are not admissible as going to propensity under Gateway D, nor is there any evidence of propensity for untruthfulness. The prosecution application is therefore dismissed. The defence makes no application in respect of Mr King at this stage.

Other issues: Counsel discusses the issue of causation of the injuries with the prosecution advocate at the plea and case management hearing and the prosecution agree to make an admission under s.10 that there is no evidence as to whether the injuries arose from a blow with the glass, or through passive contact with the glass.

Additional evidence: The prosecution serves additional forensic evidence linking the blood on the glass to Mr King. Having discussed the matter with Counsel, Edwina agrees to this evidence being given by way of s.9 statement, along with the evidence of Ashfield (fingerprint evidence) and Gifford (surgeon).

Trial date: The trial date is fixed for 28th June with a three day time estimate and Peter is released on bail on the same conditions as before until that date.

28th June – Trial Westchurch Crown Court:

Edwina attends on the first day of the trial to sit behind Counsel and take a full note of the evidence.

Eva Lee, the barrister briefed on the case, intends to cross-examine on the basis that Mr King was angry, had been drinking, was involved in a confusing melee, and has simply got his facts muddled. It is obviously a less strong approach than a direct assault on Arthur King's credibility – on the basis that he is a liar, and a convicted liar at that, who has always hated his son-in-law, and is now framing him for the assault. On the other hand, if Eva can raise reasonable doubt as to King's reliability without Peter's previous bad character being exposed, she takes the view that the jury should be prepared to acquit.

Mr King's evidence in chief is broadly in line with the account in his witness statement. He is categorical that Peter Butcher punched him in the face with a glass, and then told him he deserved it.

An extract from the cross-examination follows.

DOCUMENT 22

Mr King, do you regret making the speech that you did?

How do you mean?

It's a simple question, Mr King. Do you regret making the speech that you did?

Why should I regret it?

You don't regret it?

I don't see why I should.

You've told the court that in your speech you may have made a few "jibes" at Mr Butcher's party?

Yes. Nothing serious though.

And you said that you had yourself been offended by the best man's speech.

It was filth. It simply wasn't funny, but that doesn't ..

I'd be grateful if you could simply answer my questions. You said that you noticed that perhaps Mr Butcher wasn't very pleased with your speech.

Well, I could see him muttering to Joanne. And I could see her getting upset.

But when you finished your speech, it wasn't Mr Butcher that came over was it?

No.

It was Mr Fiddler, the best man.

Yes. He came over and started saying all sorts of stuff.

You told the court he said that you'd ruined the wedding. That Joanne was ashamed of you. And I think you told us that he'd said that you were drunk.

He was saying all sorts of nonsense. It was very unpleasant.

You'd accept that there had been a degree of drinking. It was a wedding reception after all.

Mainly Peter Butcher and his friends. I thought there would be trouble.

But you yourself had not had anything to drink?

I'd had a bit to drink. Obviously. You do. But not much.

There had been a delay I think, before the reception, and you'd all had to wait at the bar.

Yes.

And while you were waiting you all had a few drinks.

One drink, I think.

And then there was the meal, before the speeches.

Yes.

And, again, I assume that you along with everyone else had had something to drink with the meal.

Yes.

And there were toasts to the happy couple?

Yes.

So it would be fair to say, that most of the people present, including yourself, Mr King, had been drinking before the speeches began.

Well, yes. To a degree.

To a degree. Thank you. But Mr Fiddler was simply being abusive, to your mind, when he said you were drunk.

Yes. I wasn't drunk.

But you weren't entirely sober either, I would suggest.

I was sober enough.

Sober enough to decide to make a speech in which you made jibes at the wedding party?

Judge: Mrs Lee, I'm not entirely clear where this is going?

Your Honour, the injury to Mr King appears to have occurred during a melee at the wedding reception. I want to explore with Mr King the circumstances that gave rise to the fracas.

    Judge: Very well.

Now, Mr King, you delivered your speech. You could see that it wasn't going down well. So you then finished and sat down.

    Yes.

And who was it that then approached you?

    The best man.

Mr Fiddler.

    If that's his name, yes. He came over and started shouting.

So it was Mr Fiddler that had taken offence. Mr Fiddler came over to you.

    Yes.

And did you see where Mr Butcher was at this time.

    Well, as I said, he'd just stormed out of the room.

He'd left the room.

    Yes.

So, let me get this straight. It is Mr Fiddler that comes over to you.

    He came over to me, yes.

It is Mr Fiddler, the best man, that starts, as you put it, abusing you.

    Well he did. He abused me.

So when your friends come over, they are coming over to confront Mr Fiddler, aren't they?

    I wouldn't say it was confronting him.

And when Fiddler's friends come over and the trouble starts to break out, the argument is still between yourself and Mr Fiddler. That's right, isn't it?

    I wouldn't call it an argument. He was screaming at me.

But you've told the court that, and I think these are the words you used, you lost your rag. Isn't that what you said? You "lost your rag" and asked them "what the hell they were doing ruining a young girl's wedding".

    Well, I wasn't just going to stand there.

But when you lost your rag, when this "shouting and jostling" began, Mr Butcher wasn't there?

    No, but ..

He wasn't there. He'd left the room. He wasn't the one who was confronting you at all?

    No, but ..

And when Mr Butcher came back into the room, when you next saw him, what did he do?

    He hit me.

No, Mr King. What did he do before this alleged blow took place?

    I don't know what you mean.

Mr King, you've already told the court that Mr Butcher pushed his way back into the crowd, and, well this is your account, he grabbed your daughter by the arm and started to "yank" her up, although that is not what my client or your daughter will tell the court.

    Well, he did.

He did push his way into this mass of shouting people, but he didn't say anything to you, did he? He was returning for Joanne.

    [Silence]

He was returning for his pregnant wife, and it was you, Mr King, that said you weren't "having that", and you shouted at him.

I shouted at him because of the way he was treating Joanne.

Then you'd accept that because of your concern you shouted at Peter Butcher and moved towards him.

No. He turned and punched me.

He turned away from you, Mr King. He turned away and stumbled. And you fell over in the confusion.

He hit me in the face with a glass.

Mr King, it was a confused and distressing incident. You accept that you had – "to a degree" – been drinking, and that there was a lot of pushing and shoving going on around you. Mr Butcher wasn't there to pick a fight with you, he was there to get his wife away, wasn't he?

No, that's nonsense.

And that's what he did, isn't it. He was escorting your daughter out of this scrum of people and in the confusion you fell over.

He smashed a glass in my face.

No, Mr King. I accept that there was a lot going on, but cast your mind back. That's not what happened is it? You shouted at Peter Butcher. He remembers turning away. He thinks that, because he stumbled in the confusion, his glass got smashed on the furniture and he dropped it. You stumbled too, didn't you? You stumbled and fell over?

No. I fell over because he hit me.

Now, you've told the court that you didn't like my client.

Yes.

In fact, I think you made very clear that you were not happy that he was marrying your daughter.

No, I wasn't.

And the fact that your daughter was pregnant at the time of the wedding, that was a further source of contention.

I wasn't pleased, no. I thought it would break her mother's heart.

Let me suggest, Mr King, that your dislike for Peter Butcher is colouring your recollection of the incident. You've accepted that you had been drinking at the time of the incident.

(Silence)

And what you've said, Mr King, is that the argument was between yourself and Steven Fiddler, and various other members of the party. My client was even in the room at the time, was he? And when Peter Butcher did come back into the room, he did so in order to look after his wife.

I wouldn't say "look after".

Mr King, this was a confused situation. But you have made a mistake, haven't you? My client didn't hit you at all. He was turned away to deal with his wife.

He might have been at one point.

In the confusion, you slipped, you fell over, and you injured yourself on the broken glass on the floor.

Nonsense. He hit me with the glass.

And having been injured, you immediately leapt to the wrong conclusion, that my client must have been involved in some way.

No.

Which is why you then turned to your wife. Can you remember what you said to her?

Not exactly.

Roughly then?

I said something about Peter Butcher being punished for what he'd done to me.

You said: "That little thug is going to pay for this."

Yes, I might have said something like that.

The rest of the cross-examination

Eva Lee then turns to the alleged comment: "You stupid old bastard, you deserve it." She points out that Arthur King is the only person to have heard these words. Again, she suggests that he is confused in his recollection, and that if the words were spoken they were much more likely to be spoken by one of the other people involved in the fracas. She concludes her cross-examination by again suggesting that King's mistaken recollection is the result of his dislike for Peter Butcher.

Re-examination

In re-examination, prosecuting counsel simply confirms with Mr King that he is sure that Mr Butcher punched him, and that he did so with a glass in his hand. He also asks Mr King to confirm that he is sure that Peter Butcher called him a "stupid old bastard" who deserved it.

Eva Lee is not too concerned about this. Her own view is that she has got confirmation of Mr King's ill feeling towards her client. His denial of any heavy drinking can usefully be explored with Maureen King, whose witness statement suggests that she is likely to say that Arthur had had "quite a bit to drink". Arthur King has also confirmed that there was a single punch in the context of a very confused melee.

Gateway G: the judge's ruling

Eva is taken aback when, in the absence of the jury, the judge then tells prosecuting counsel that, in his view, the defence have attacked Arthur King, by suggesting that he is biased and that he was drunk. Eva argues hard that neither amounts to reprehensible behaviour in this context, and that there has been no attack for the purpose of Gateway G. When it is clear that she cannot persuade the judge of this, she then argues that in any event he should exercise his discretion under s.101(3) to refuse to admit the previous convictions. She argues that the convictions are generally elderly, they are potentially very prejudicial and that if there was an attack on Mr King's character, it was marginal and cannot justify such great prejudice to her client's case. Again, the judge is against her.

Eva then applies for permission to adduce Mr King's previous convictions. The judge points out that the application should have been made prior to trial, however he exercises his discretion and tells Eva that the conviction for VAT fraud from last year can be admitted under s.100 CJA 2003.

Eva asks for Arthur King to be recalled so that she can put his previous convictions to him. The judge tells her that it is too late for this; she will have to content herself with asking one of the police officers to confirm Arthur King's conviction. Eva points out that this is far short of being able to cross-examine Arthur King on the issue of his dishonest behaviour. The judge tells her that she is an experienced advocate, she chose to attack Mr King's character in cross-examination, and now she and her client must stand by the consequences.

The rest of the case

All the witnesses give evidence more or less in line with their witness statements. PC Stanley confirms Arthur King's previous conviction. Peter Butcher does well in the witness box, but Eva has no choice but to lead his previous convictions in her examination in chief, and to make the point that he is a reformed character. This is a point that she reiterates in her closing speech.

The judge gives an accurate and fair summing up of the evidence. In particular he tells the jury that Peter's previous convictions are generally elderly, and they may consider that they have less probative value because of this. The judge also gives an accurate direction on the possible inferences, drawing out all the factors which the jury might take into account in deciding whether Peter Butcher could have reasonably been expected to put forward his defence when questioned at the police station.

The verdict

The jury is out for four hours. After three hours the judge gives a majority verdict direction. The jury then convicts Peter Butcher on an 11–1 majority. The judge adjourns the matter for two weeks for a pre sentence report to be compiled. He makes clear that it is to cover all possible sentencing options.

Post conviction

Peter Butcher is remanded in custody despite Eva's arguments that he has a young baby and has complied with his bail throughout the proceedings.

The pre sentence report is set out in **Document 23**. It is followed by Eva Lee's mitigation speech; **Document 24**.

DOCUMENT 23

Confidential

Westchurch Probation Service

This is a pre-sentence report, as defined in s.158) of the Criminal Justice Act 2003. It has been prepared in accordance with the requirements of the National Standard for pre-sentence reports. This report is a confidential document.

FULL NAME Peter Michael BUTCHER **DOB** 26/2/— (30 years old)

ADDRESS Flat 4, James Park East Buildings, Park Street, Westchurch

OFFENCE(S) DEALT WITH IN PSR: s.20 Offences Against the Person Act

OFFENCE DATES: 14th February —

COURT: Westchurch Crown Court

HEARING DATE: 10th July —

DATE REPORT REQUESTED: 30th June —

IS PSR EXPEDITED?: No

PSR WRITER: Sam Adamson

OFFICIAL TITLE: Probation Officer

OFFICE LOCATION: Westchurch Probation Service, Narey House, Westchurch

TELEPHONE NUMBER: 0071 229 213

DATE REPORT COMPLETED AND SIGNED: 5th July —

INTRODUCTION:

This report is based on information from the following sources:

1. One interview with Peter Butcher while in custody on 2nd June.

2. One office meeting with Joanne Butcher, Mr Butcher's wife.

3. Mr Butcher has had no recent contact with the Probation Service.

4. I have been informed that the Court indicated that the report should consider all sentencing options.

OFFENCE ANALYSIS:

1. I have been provided with the Prosecution witness statements in this matter. I have also had the opportunity to speak to Mr Butcher concerning his version of events.

2. It appears to be common ground that the offence occurred at the reception following Peter Butcher's marriage to Joanne King. It appears also to be common ground that a certain amount of drinking took place both before and at the reception and that tensions between the bride's family and the groom's friends were exacerbated. Mr Butcher is said to have left the room in anger following his father-in-law's speech, and to have returned and struck Mr King once in the face while holding a glass.

3. In analysing the circumstances of the offence and considering the information provided, this incident could be viewed as an aberration. At trial Mr Butcher denied that this incident took place and he has continued to deny the offence, making it impossible to discuss the causes of his offending. I have had sight of his Police antecedent history, and while Mr Butcher has a history of offending in the past, there is nothing to suggest that this offence is part of an established pattern of behaviour. The court may take the view that it can, however, draw some conclusions from the circumstances surrounding the assault that this was an offence that arose from the very particular stresses of the familial occasion, and that it was fuelled by alcohol consumption at that event.

RELEVANT INFORMATION ABOUT THE OFFENDER:

4. Mr Butcher was born and brought up in the Westchurch area. He was one of four children and describes his childhood as happy. He remained at school to obtain an A level at 18. At this point he left in order to attend an apprenticeship scheme in the shipyards, before leaving to work as a self-employed welder on the North Sea oil platforms. Although this work is of its nature sporadic, Mr Butcher is well paid when he is in work and shows clear enthusiasm for his chosen career.

5. Mr Butcher has a number of previous convictions, all bar one dating from a period in his early twenties when, as he himself concedes, he was "a handful". The convictions start with public order and assault matters, and move on to dishonesty offences. In January six years ago, Mr Butcher received a short custodial sentence and the shock of this seems to have helped him to review his behaviour and to adopt a more mature and responsible life-style. Since that time, Mr Butcher has appeared only once before the courts. This was last year and was in relation to a road traffic offence, for which he was fined. The fine has been paid.

6. In discussion with Mr Butcher, it is clear that he regards his earlier offending as belonging to a wholly different stage in his life, and I would support the suggestion that the instant offence be seen in its particular context rather than as part of a pattern of offending. Support for this view was increased by Mr Butcher's clear commitment

to his new status as a married man, and indeed now a father. Mr Butcher spoke with enthusiasm about married life and fatherhood, and was clearly extremely upset at being separated from his six week old daughter, Natalie. Mrs Butcher also referred to his excitement at the birth of his daughter and the evidence of his desire to be an active and involved parent.

7. Financially, the couple remain reliant on state benefits, but Mr Butcher has made clear his desire to find work in his field. The criminal proceedings have made it impossible for him to accept work on oil rigs, his normal occupation, during the last four months, but it is clear that he expects to find work as a marine welder in the near future. Before Mr Butcher was remanded in custody, the family were in receipt of £115.33 per week Job Seekers Allowance, including a housing costs element in respect of the outstanding mortgage on the current accommodation. Outgoings were estimated as follows:

Food	£50
Fuel costs	£18
Baby costs	£27
Water	£5
Telephone	£4
Credit Card	£8
Incidentals	£3

The couple also have store card debts of about £400.

RISK TO THE PUBLIC OF RE-OFFENDING:

8. The nature of this offence indicates that on this occasion Mr Butcher clearly presented a risk of harm to the public. The fact that Mr. Butcher continues to deny responsibility for the offence is clearly a matter of concern. However, the particular circumstances of the offence suggest that it arose from an unfortunate combination of events, including a formal social gathering, with feelings running high between the bride and groom's parties, and with alcohol playing a significant role in fuelling the ill will that already existed. I feel that there is little likelihood of repetition, and on this basis that there is a **low risk of further offending**.

9. While recognising the violent nature of this offence and the fact that Mr Butcher's criminal record discloses a previous conviction for a Schedule 15 offence (namely, s.47 assault), I note the very different circumstances of the instant offence, and the gap in time between the offences. In my view there is no information available to me that suggests that this offence is part of an established pattern of violent or dangerous behaviour. I therefore conclude that Mr. Butcher does not present a significant risk of serious harm to the public from committing further Schedule 15 offences.

CONCLUSION

10. Clearly this is a serious matter and I note that the court has requested an all options report. In considering a custodial sentence, the court may be concerned that the pattern of earlier offending indicates a more basic and unresolved problem for Mr Butcher in exercising appropriate self-control. While a custodial sentence would serve as punishment, there must be doubt as to whether it would address this underlying issue. The court may also wish to have regard to Mr. Butcher's family circumstances, and the fact that Mr Butcher shows a clear commitment to his family life, and is clearly distressed to be separated from his young daughter. The court may take the view that the stability offered by family life offers an opportunity for Mr Butcher to develop a number of important life skills which may help to ensure that there is no future repetition of this offending.

11. Should the court feel able to consider a community-based disposal I have considered the options available and discussed them with Mr. Butcher. Both supervision

requirements and unpaid work requirements are available to the court. I can confirm that Mr Butcher would in my view react well to a community order with these requirements. He continues to speak very positively of the discussions with his probation officer although this is now some seven years ago, and it may be that this form of support would enable Mr Butcher to attain a greater insight into the root causes for his offending behaviour. I can also confirm that Mr Butcher would be suitable were the court to wish to impose an unpaid work requirement. I note Mr Butcher's earlier compliance with such an order. I have no doubt that he would continue to respond positively.

Sam Adamson
Senior Probation Officer

DOCUMENT 24

10th July   Westchurch Crown Court

Your Honour, I appear this morning for Mr Butcher. Your Honour will recall that Mr Butcher was convicted in this court of a s.20 wounding, the victim being my client's father in law. Might I ask if Your Honour has a copy of the pre sentence report of Mr Adamson.

> I have, yes.

I am grateful. I don't know if Your Honour has had an opportunity to read the report?

> Yes. Mrs Lee, it may be of assistance to indicate that I am of the view – in the light of the contents of the report – that your client does not present a significant risk of serious harm to the public. So, in my view the dangerous offender provisions do not arise in this case.

Your Honour, I am extremely grateful for that indication. In relation to the report, Your Honour will have noted that the report speaks very favourably of Mr Butcher's suitability for a community disposal. I know that Your Honour will be very mindful of the caselaw on wounding where a glass has been used, where the courts have taken the view that a wounding of this sort will generally cross the custody threshold. I don't seek to persuade Your Honour that those cases – and I have them to hand if Your Honour wishes me to refer further to them – I don't seek to persuade Your Honour that these are not relevant, but I will seek to argue that Mr Butcher's case is very different from these cases for a number of reasons.

My first point, Your Honour, is that it is common ground in this case that we are dealing with a single punch. Moreover, we are dealing with a punch by someone who had a glass in his hand, and a punch that was delivered in the midst of a confused melee, which again, it is accepted, was not of my client's making. Mr King himself told this court that my client had originally returned to the melee not in order to pick a fight with him, but to be with his pregnant bride. Even in Mr King's account, it was Mr King who then intervened and thus precipitated the incident. So my client is not in the same position as some young man in a public house who, following heated words, then deliberately picks up a bottle or glass, often smashing it to make it into a weapon, and who then assaults the victim. This is a case, I would suggest, where, even on the prosecution's account, we are talking about an unpremeditated punch, a punch which might have amounted to no more than common assault, or at worst actual bodily harm, but for the fact that Mr Butcher was holding a glass at the time.

> I can't see how you can say that. Does your client admit this offence, Mrs Lee? Otherwise it seems to me that you are simply making assumptions.

Clearly Your Honour I accept that it would be wholly wrong for me to seek to go behind the jury's verdict. But Your Honour, I don't seek to suggest that my client has a defence; I accept that this is a matter that the jury has determined. However, what I do say is that, even on the prosecution account, the account that went before the jury, I can point to a number of matters that set this particular offence aside from the more run-of-the-mill woundings. Taken together, I would argue, Your Honour, that the picture the prosecution presented was of a single punch in a confused melee, with my client holding a beer glass at the time of the punch, the glass then shattering and causing injury to Mr King. What I say is that this can be properly distinguished from the more common situation where the glass is used deliberately and with a degree of pre-meditation as a weapon.

> He used a glass, Mrs Lee. I can't see how you can seek to say that he didn't use it as a weapon.

Your Honour, I seek only to say that the prosecution alleges a punch with glass in hand – intact glass in hand. That, I say, must be less serious than those cases involving the deliberate initial smashing of a glass and then the use of the glass as a weapon. Certainly, this was the view of the Court of Appeal in <u>McLoughlin</u> (1985) 7 Cr App R (S) 67 and confirmed in <u>Stewart</u> (1990) 12 Cr App R (S) 15, although it is right to say that in those cases custodial sentences were nonetheless imposed.

And that, Your Honour, takes me to my second point. Again, Your Honour, it is often the case with s.20 cases involving the use of glasses as weapons that the seriousness of these assaults is aggravated by their public nature – whether in the streets or in the public houses – as well as by the element of assaults on strangers. Your

Honour, I simply point out that, again even on the prosecution's account, this is very much a family matter. Mr King conceded that there was a history of ill feeling between himself and my client. Both parties properly conceded that the incident may well have been fuelled by alcohol, but Your Honour will take into account that this was of course Mr Butcher's wedding reception, and therefore, I would respectfully suggest, a gathering where a certain amount of drinking might reasonably take place.

So if it's my party, I can assault my friends, Mrs Lee, that's all right is it?

No, Your Honour. I don't seek to argue that Mr Butcher's behaviour can be excused. But, I am sure that Your Honour would agree with the proposition that an assault on a stranger in a public place will necessarily aggravate the seriousness of the assault. It will be particularly frightening for the victim; it will further frighten bystanders and the public at large. The converse is the case here, Your Honour, and I would argue that, while it does not excuse the offence, again it permits Your Honour properly to distinguish it from offences that are very much at the other end of the seriousness scale.

Your Honour, those two points can be taken together with other factors that help to show that this was not a deliberate, unprovoked, assault, but rather a single unpremeditated blow, under circumstances where there had been considerable provocation. Again, I respectfully remind Your Honour that Mr King himself accepted that his speech had been to some extent deliberately inflammatory, and Mrs King of course went somewhat further. The circumstances included a confused fracas, which was not of my client's making, and my client's understandable concern for his pregnant wife, caught in the middle of this situation.

What, I would suggest, is most relevant in this matter is the personal mitigation which my client is able to put before the court. And it is that personal mitigation that I would argue enables Your Honour to take the view that this is a case which is not so serious that only a custodial sentence can properly be imposed.

The pre sentence report makes clear that Mr Butcher stands very much at a turning point in his life. I do not say that, Your Honour, on the basis that he is someone who has been offending, but now has the opportunity for reform. Indeed, Your Honour will have noted that that particular turning point took place some years ago. That Mr Butcher, having had a troubled youth, successfully made the transition away from offending behaviour, that he found a job, that he got qualifications, and that he stayed out of trouble and put his old ways behind him. There is of course a single road traffic matter last year, but I would suggest, Your Honour, that that is of little relevance to today's decision.

Yes. I accept that.

I'm grateful. It is of course the case that Your Honour may take into account my client's previous convictions. But this, I would suggest, Your Honour is a case where if you choose to take them into account they can be taken into account in his favour, as showing a clear indication of his will to reform and of his ability to do so. I cannot come before you today and argue that Mr Butcher is of previous good character…

No. Not by a long chalk!

But Your Honour, I can say that until this incident, which involved a single blow, which involved provocation and a history of ill feeling, which seems to have been unpremeditated and unplanned, my client had successfully put his past behind him and had managed, under very difficult circumstances, to make something of his life. He managed to do that, and that is the particular tragedy of this conviction. However, Your Honour, it does provide Your Honour with powerful evidence of my client's will to reform and his capacity to do so.

In addition, I would ask Your Honour to have regard to his current circumstances. This incident took place just as my client was seeking to make that transition, the turning point I spoke of earlier, from being a single man with no responsibilities to becoming a married man, with a small child. Your Honour will have noted how positively the pre sentence report speaks of Mr Butcher's involvement with his six-week-old daughter, Natalie, and with family life as a whole. Your Honour will know the extent of the commitment that Mr Butcher was taking on, and I ask Your Honour to take it into account, and to take into account the benefits of ensuring that Mr Butcher continues to be able to contribute to his new family life.

Your Honour is looking today at a single offence, a one-off matter, which arose in the context of a particular social gathering. There is no suggestion that Mr Butcher presents a danger to the public at large, no suggestion that there is likely to be any repetition of this offence. What will concern Your Honour is whether Mr Butcher is capable of learning to restrain his temper, to deal with his anger. Mr Butcher's previous record shows his capacity for reform. The pre sentence report refers to how positively Mr Butcher speaks of his previous experience of community rehabilitation, and to his ability to complete a period of community punishment. This is a case, I would respectfully suggest, where the need for punishment can properly be balanced with the need to ensure reform.

Your Honour, with this in mind, I would urge Your Honour to take account of the strong recommendation in the pre sentence report that a community order will meet both objectives of punishment and reform. It will enable Mr Butcher to make reparation and to take responsibility for this offence. It will enable Mr Butcher to meet his family responsibilities and at the same time to take steps to learn to deal with the loss of self-control that led to the incident.

Your Honour, I would respectfully suggest that a community order with requirements for supervision and for unpaid work, requiring Mr Butcher to make reparation and to face his punishment, but combining the community punishment element with the guidance that the probation service can provide, the assistance in dealing with his loss of self-control – Your Honour, this, I would respectfully suggest, is a disposal which can properly address the seriousness of the offence and the needs of the offender. It is an order which, Your Honour, should ensure that Mr Butcher does not find his way before this court or any court in future. Alternatively, in view of Mr Butcher's family responsibilities, Your Honour might take the view that a curfew order would place significant constraints upon Mr Butcher's liberty while ensuring that he was able to undertake his responsibilities within the family.

If Your Honour is not with me on this point, and takes the view that this is a case which must cross the custody threshold, I would urge upon the court the imposition of a suspended custodial penalty. This would, in my respectful submission, enable the court to impose the forms of community requirements proposed by the pre-sentence report while also ensuring that Mr Butcher has hanging over him the threat of an immediate custodial term in the event of non-compliance or of further offending.

That, Your Honour, is my submission.

> And what about compensation, Mrs Lee. This is a case where I'm going to have to consider compensation.

Indeed, Your Honour. And Your Honour might take the view that the payment of compensation, which would of course not be possible were a custodial sentence to be imposed, would be a further means of ensuring that Mr Butcher made direct reparation for his actions..

> Very well.

10th July – The sentencing hearing

The judge imposed an immediate 24 month custodial sentence, stating that the matter was so serious that only a custodial sentence could be justified. The dangerousness provisions were not activated in this case.

Peter Butcher can expect to be released onto home detention curfew after about 7? months (? less 135 days); he will then be on licence from 12 months (? way) until the end of the sentence.

The appeal

Counsel advises Peter to appeal against sentence and conviction.

The papers are set out in **Document 25**, although Counsel's Advice and Draft Grounds for Appeal are not reproduced.

The grounds on the appeal against conviction are that the judge erred in law in concluding that Gateway G had been activated by the cross-examination, and that the judge was wrong in concluding that the admission of the previous convictions could be fair for the purposes of s.101(3) CJA 2003.

The ground for the appeal against sentence is that the sentence is too long, having regard to statutory requirement in s.153(2) CJA 2003 that the sentence must be for the shortest term that is commensurate with the seriousness of the offence.

The result of the appeal

The appeal against conviction is successful on the basis that the judge erred in concluding that Gateway G had been activated, the court holding that even if it had been activated, the elderly nature of the previous convictions meant that they should not have been admitted under s.101(3) CJA 2003. As a result, the conviction was unsafe.

The prosecution indicates that it does not seek a retrial and Peter Butcher is released from prison.

DOCUMENT 25

FOR OFFICIAL USE -   CAO No.   /   /

NOTICE and GROUNDS of appeal or application for permission to appeal against conviction or sentence to **THE COURT OF APPEAL CRIMINAL DIVISION** *(Criminal Procedure Rules, rr 68.3(1),(2))*

Form **NG**

*Please ensure that you have read the notes for guidance attached **before** completing this form. Write in **BLACK INK** and use **BLOCK CAPITALS***

The Appellant		
Surname	_BUTCHER_	Prison Index No __XX 3987__
Forenames	_PETER_	Prison _HMP WESTCHURCH_
Address (if not in custody)		
postcode		Date of birth ___26/02/19___

The Court where tried Or sentenced	
The Crown Court at _WESTCHURCH_	Name of Judge __HHJ MAYFIELD__
Date Trial started _28th JUNE 20--_	Date of conviction _30th JUNE 20--_
Date of sentence __10th JULY 20--__	
Total period of remand in custody prior to sentence _10 days_	

The Conviction(s) and/or sentence(s)	Crown Court Case number(s)	Count No.	Offence(s)	Sentence
	WC/3214/--	1	s.20 Offences Against the Person Act 1861	24 months imprisonment
			Total sentence	24 months

Applications The appellant is applying for: Please tick (√) as appropriate Please also see the attached guidance notes			
	☐	Extension of time in which to make any of the following application(s) (not to be applied for separately – see Note 7))	
	☒	Permission to appeal against conviction	☒ Representation Order
	☒	Permission to appeal against sentence	☒ Bail
	☐	Permission to appeal against a confiscation order	☐ Permission to call witness

436   Appendix B

DOCUMENT 25

Legal Representation (please use BLOCK CAPITALS)	Name of **Counsel** ___MS EVA LEE_____
	Address _WESTCHURCH CHAMBERS_____
	Post Code _____ DX No _____
	Telephone No _____ Reference _____

Name of **Solicitor** _MS EDWINA HALPERN_____

Address __HALPERN DODDS SOLICITORS, 29 CHESTERFIELD PLACE,

WESTCHURCH_____

Post Code _____ DX No _____

Telephone No _____ Reference _____

Prosecuting Authority _____

Address _____

Post Code _____ DX No _____

Telephone No _____ Reference _____

IMPORTANT NOTES

Grounds of Appeal (r.68.3 (2))

Please also see the attached guidance notes, particularly note 8

The grounds of appeal must be attached to this notice of application, and should be listed separately for conviction, sentence, or other order, under appropriate headings.

The grounds of appeal **must**:

1) Identify each ground of appeal on which the appellant relies, numbering them consecutively (if there is more than one) and concisely outlining each argument in support;
2) Identify the transcript that the appellant thinks the court will need, if the appellant wants to appeal against conviction (see notes on Transcripts below);
3) Identify the relevant sentencing powers of the Crown Court, if sentence is in issue;
4) Where the Criminal Cases Review Commission has referred a case to the court, explain how each ground of appeal relates (if it does) to the reasons for the reference;
5) Summarise the relevant facts;
6) Identify any relevant authorities;
7) Identify any other document or thing that the appellant thinks the court will need to decide the appeal (Please Note: any report relied upon and which was not retained by the Crown Court must be copied and attached to this application form).

NB:
(1) Where grounds have been settled by counsel they must be signed by counsel with the name of counsel printed underneath.
(2) If an extension of time is needed, the detailed reasons for the delay must be attached to the grounds of appeal, preferably under a separate heading – grounds for extension of time.

Other Applications (r.68.3(2)(h))

Any other application **must** be made in accordance with rule 68.3(2)(h) of the Criminal Procedure Rules, and be attached, together with reasons, preferably under a separate heading for each such application, together with Form B (Bail) or Form W (Witness) duly completed if appropriate. (Please also see the attached guidance notes, particularly note 7).

Transcripts	On an application for **permission to appeal against conviction** a transcript of the trial judge's summing up is obtained by the Registrar as a matter of course. On an application for **permission to appeal against sentence** the Registrar will obtain a transcript of the sentencing judge's remarks, and on a plea of Guilty, the prosecution opening of facts.
	If ADDITIONAL transcript is sought, this **must** be specified within the grounds of appeal, **giving specific dates and times** of the part of the proceedings for which the transcript is requested. **Failure to give such details could result in unnecessary delay and prejudice the appellant**.
	Please note that transcript obtained by means other than through the Registrar may result in the cost of the transcript not being allowed upon taxation in cases subject to a Representation Order.

Reminder	Have You:		*delete as appropriate
	a)	included reasons in support of any application for extension of time?	Yes/No*
	b)	included Form B if applying for bail?	Yes/No*
	c)	included Form W and witness statement (conviction cases only) if seeking to call a witness	Yes/No*
	d) (i)	attached your grounds of appeal?	Yes/No*
	(ii)	are the grounds of appeal signed by counsel/solicitor?	Yes/No*
	e) (i)	attached your request for additional transcript?	Yes/No*
	(ii)	specified the dates and times of transcript requested?	Yes/No*

Signature	**APPELLANTS *IN CUSTODY ONLY***
	I understand that if the single judge and/or the Court is of the opinion that the application for permission to appeal is plainly without merit, an order may be made that time spent in custody as an appellant shall not count towards sentence.
	***ALL* APPELLANTS**
	I understand that if the court dismisses my appeal or application it may make an order for payment of costs against me, including the cost of any transcript obtained.
	[This form should be signed by the appellant but may be signed by his/her legal representative provided the WARNINGS set out above have been explained to him/her. NB if signed by a legal representative, the appellant will be given the opportunity to request a copy of the form.]
	Signature *Edwina Halpern* Date 20/07/20--
	(of appellant or legal representative signing on *behalf* of the appellant)

NOW PLEASE SEND THIS FORM TO THE CROWN COURT WHERE TRIED OR SENTENCED UNLESS IT RELATES TO A REFERENCE BY THE CRIMINAL CASES REVIEW COMMISSION, IN WHICH CASE IT SHOULD BE SENT TO THE REGISTRAR OF CRIMINAL APPEALS DIRECTLY.

DOCUMENT 25

For Prison Use	This notice was handed to me by appellant today.	Appellant's Index No _____
	Signed _____ Prison Officer	EDR _____
	Date _____	PED _____

For Crown Court Use

Immediately upon receipt of Form NG the Crown Court must complete and send tear-off slips 1-3 overleaf as applicable. These tear-off slips **must** be used so that the correct notifications are sent out.

Slip 1 (Acknowledgement)

☐ Sent to _____ Date sent _____

Slip 2 (Notification to Prosecution / Statements)

☐ Sent to _____
(Prosecuting Authority (e.g CPS, RCPO, H&S Executive))

Address _____
_____
_____ DX Number _____

Date sent _____

Slip 3 (Monetary penalty / order)

☐ Sent to _____ Mag. Court   Date sent _____

Form NG received in Crown Court:	Sent to the Criminal Appeal Office
Signed _____	Signed _____
Date Received _____	Date Sent _____

Criminal Case Study – *R v Butcher*

DOCUMENT 25

Slip 3   Notification to Magistrates of appeal in cases involving monetary penalty or order (to be sent in all cases involving monetary penalty or order)

To: Clerk to the Justices   From: Court Manager
                    Magistrates Court   Crown Court at

Dear Sir / Madam,   Date

R -v-   Crown Court Ref:

I write to inform you that in this case, in which you are responsible for enforcing the monetary penalty or order, the above-named has lodged notice of appeal to the Court of Appeal Criminal Division.

Yours faithfully,

Slip 2   Notification from the Crown Court to Prosecuting Authority of receipt of Application for permission to appeal to the Court of Appeal (to be sent in all cases)

To: From: Crown Court at

                                                                 Date:

Dear Sir / Madam,

R -v-   Crown Court Ref:

Please note that an application for permission to appeal has been received in the above matter. All exhibits must be retained in safe custody pending the determination of the appeal. Please ensure you are aware of the location of your case file since you will be contacted if this matter is to proceed to a hearing by the full Court of Appeal and if, therefore, any victim or their family needs to be informed about the appeal. If the matter involves a committal for sentence, please forward forthwith witness statements / statements of facts, enclosing this slip for reference purposes to:

The Registrar, Criminal Appeal Office   Telephone 020 7947 6011/6014   Yours faithfully
Royal Courts of Justice   DX: RCJ 44450 STRAND
Strand, London WC2A 2LL   FAX: 020 7947 6900

Slip 1   Acknowledgement of Form NG (to be sent in all cases to sender of Form NG)

                                    From: Court Manager
                                          Crown Court at
                                          Crown Court Ref:
                                          Date:

To

                                    Your Ref:

R -v-

Dear Sir / Madam,

I acknowledge receipt of form(s) NG (B* W*) which have been forwarded to the Registrar of Criminal Appeals for attention. All further communications should be addressed to:

The Registrar, Criminal Appeal Office
Royal Courts of Justice   Yours faithfully,
Strand, London WC2A 2LL
(Tel: 020 7947 6011/6014: DX: RCJ 44450 Strand: Fax: 020 7947 6900)

*Delete as appropriate

DOCUMENT 25

Notes for guidance on the completion of this form

1. Everyone who is convicted or sentenced in the Crown Court in circumstances where the appeal is to the Court of Appeal Criminal Division is entitled to have advice or assistance on appeal. Provision for this is included in a trial Representation Order.

2. Solicitors and Counsel are expected to be familiar with "A Guide to Proceedings in the Court of Appeal Criminal Division" copies of which are available from any Crown Court Centre. The Guide is also available on the Court Service Internet site **(www.hmcourts-service.gov.uk)**, as are all necessary forms.

3. Separate application forms should be submitted for convictions or sentences that do not arise in the same proceedings.

4. This notice will be treated as a notice of appeal where permission to appeal is not required.

5. **In the initial stages the Court is reliant upon the information that you provide. It is in your own interests to assist by providing accurate and complete information in the form. Please indicate if you or your legal advisers have already been in correspondence with the Criminal Appeal Office.**

6. Please give details of the appellant's full name; if in custody give the prison index number and address where detained. If not in custody give details of address at which residing and to which correspondence should be sent.

7. **Applications**

   This application form should be served on the appropriate Crown Court Officer, not more than 28 days after the conviction, sentence, verdict or finding appealed against. If the appellant is in custody the form should be handed to the prison authority (or other person having custody) for forwarding to the Crown Court, and the date of handing in should be recorded on the form.

   - **Extension of time** The period of 28 days cannot be extended except with permission of the Court of Appeal Criminal Division and detailed reasons for the delay must be attached to this form. **An application for an extension of time will not be considered before an application for permission to appeal conviction or sentence has been lodged on Form NG, whether or not the 28 day period has already expired.**
   Please Note: the time for applying for permission to appeal runs from the date of verdict, finding or order. For permission to appeal against conviction, time runs from the date of conviction even where sentence is passed on a later date.

   - **Permission to appeal against conviction.**

   - **Permission to appeal against sentence.**

   See Note 8 below

   - **Representation Order** (ie. legal assistance) A Representation Order made in the Crown Court does not provide for oral argument before the Court of Appeal. If a Representation Order is sought for this purpose it should be applied for.

   - **Bail** Where bail is applied for Form B (CAO) must also be completed. If Form B (CAO) accompanies Form NG it should be submitted to the Crown Court but if submitted later should be sent to:- *The Registrar, Criminal Appeal Office, Royal Courts of Justice, Strand, London WC2A 2LL.*

   - **Permission to call a witness (<u>conviction cases only</u>)** Where permission is sought to call a witness in support of an application for permission to appeal against **conviction** an application should be made on **Form W (CAO).** A separate form is required for each witness. A signed statement from the witness should be appended to Form W (CAO) and, if it is said that the witness was not available at trial, an affidavit, sworn by the appellant's solicitor, should also be lodged, describing the circumstances in which the witness came forward and the circumstances in which the statement was made. If Form W (CAO) accompanies Form NG it should be sent to the Crown Court but if submitted later should be sent to:-*The Registrar* at the address given above.

8. **Grounds of appeal** If a positive advice on appeal is given it should always be incorporated into the same document as the grounds of appeal, as a single document. **Grounds must be settled in accordance with the requirements of r.68.3(2) as set out on page 2 hereof.** Wording such as "the conviction is unsafe" or "the sentence is in all the circumstances too severe" will be ineffective as grounds unless accompanied by detailed reasons. Ineffective applications will be rejected, thus causing delay and possibly making it necessary for an extension of time to be sought (see note 7 above). Unsigned grounds will be returned, again with resulting delay to the application.

An appeal against **conviction** is <u>not</u> another trial which looks again at the facts of the case in the way the jury did to decide if the appellant is guilty or innocent. The Court of Appeal will only be concerned with whether the conviction is unsafe and will consider issues such as: whether the trial as a whole was fair; whether the trial Judge made the correct legal rulings during the course of the trial (for example, in relation to disclosure of evidence, the admissibility of evidence or a submission of no case to answer); whether the trial Judge fairly summed up the case to the jury with the appropriate legal directions; "fresh evidence" that was not presented at trial.

An appeal against **sentence** will only succeed if the sentence was **"manifestly excessive"** (i.e. the sentence was too high given the facts of the offence or in light of any available personal mitigation) and/or **"wrong in principle"** (i.e. the sentencing Judge made some mistake when imposing the sentence. For example, there was no power to pass the particular sentence imposed or the sentence was passed on some incorrect factual or legal basis). Grounds should therefore explain <u>why</u> the sentence was "manifestly excessive" and/or "wrong in principle".

9. Where a certificate that the case is fit for appeal is granted by the trial judge this should be stated (and see generally paragraph 17 of "A Guide to proceedings in the Court of Appeal Criminal Division").

10. Where an appellant has been **granted** permission to appeal s/he is entitled to be present on the hearing of the appeal only. If the appellant is in custody and wishes to be present at any hearing for which permission to be present is required s/he must apply for permission in writing.

11. Where the Criminal Cases Review Commission refers a case to the Court, the Court must treat that reference as the appeal notice if the appellant does not serve such a notice of appeal under rule 68.2 of the Criminal Procedure Rules.

INDEX

[note: references marked "Doc." are to documents in the case study in Appendix B to this book]

A

Absence, trial in	9.3.1
Absolute discharge	10.6.1
Accomplice	
warning where witness	19.1.2
Acquittals	
autrefois acquit	5.1.2
tainted	9.4.4
Adjournments	
see also Remands	
generally	6.1.1
post-conviction	10.2.2
Admissibility, of evidence,	
generally	Chapter 14
challenging, *see* voir dire	
compellability *see* Witness	
competence *see* Witness	
confessions, *see* Confessions	
improperly obtained evidence,	
see Unfair evidence	
opinion, *see* Opinion	
privilege, *see* Privilege	
relevance *see* Relevance	
unfair, *see* Unfair evidence	
Admissions	
confessions, *see* Confessions	
formal	14.1.2
Advance Information	
right to in either way offences	5.2
Advice and Assistance	
extent of	4.1.1
police station scheme	3.2.3
Advising,	
in the police station,	
see Legal Advice at Police Station	
Advocacy	
basic principles	Chapter 8
cross examination	8.3
bar on, rape cases	14.3.4
collateral questions	19.2, 19.2.1
discrediting the witness	8.3
one last question	8.3.4
previous inconsistent statements	19.2.2
putting your case	8.3.1
examination in chief	8.2
hostile witnesses	19.2.2
leading questions	8.2.1
other principles	8.2.2
mitigation	10.10
mode of address	8.1.3
no case to answer	9.3
preparation for,	
see Case Analysis	
putting your case	8.3.1
re-examination	8.4
speeches	8.5
closing speech, defence	8.5.1
mitigation, *see* Mitigation	
opening	9.3
Aggravating factor	
sentencing, and	10.1.3
Alibi	
disclosure of	7.5.2
Allocation	5.4.2
Alternative offences	9.4.3
Ancillary matters, at the police station	3.5
Ancillary orders	10.7
Antecedents	10.2.3
Anti-social behaviour orders	10.6.4, 12.6.1
Antony and Berryman,	
Magistrates' Courts Guide	1.2.1
Appeals, generally	Chapter 11
case stated	11.1.2
Criminal Cases Review Commission	11.3.2
Crown Court, from	11.2
conviction, against	11.2.1
sentence, against	11.2.2
judicial review	11.1.3
legal aid, and	11.1.1, 11.2.1
magistrates' court, from	11.1
Crown Court, to	11.1.1
Divisional Court, to	11.1.2
further appeals	11.1.4
notice of	Doc. 25
prosecution termination appeals	9.4.3
Supreme Court, to	11.3.1, 11.1.4
Appropriate adult	3.7.4, 12.2.1
Archbold *Criminal Pleading,*	
Evidence and Practice	1.2.1
Arrest	
see also Detention, Questioning, Inferences	
bail, failure to surrender and	6.5.6
caution	2.3.1
citizen's arrest	2.2.3
detention, *see* Detention	
force, use of and	2.2.1
human rights	2.6
necessity test	2.2.2
power of	
police	
with/without warrant	2.2.2
removal to police station	2.4.4

search after	
of the person	2.4.1
of premises controlled etc.	2.4.3
of premises where arrested	2.4.2
street bail	2.4.5
volunteer, of	3.1.3
Associated offences	10.3.4
Attendance Centre Order	12.5
Attendance Note	Doc.9
Audience,	
trainees, and	6.7.1
Autrefois acquit, plea of	5.1.2, 9.4.4

B

Bail	
appeals	
Crown Court	6.7.1
Judicial Review	6.7.4
prosecution, by	6.7.5
application	6.6, 6.6.1
example of application	Doc.6
breach of	
failure to surrender	6.5.6
conditions	6.5
conviction, *see* post-conviction	
curfews	6.5.3
decision, record of	6.7
drugs testing and	6.2.2
exclusion	6.5.3
factors	6.3.2
fail to attend	6.5.6
full argument, certificate of	6.7
further applications	6.6.2
grounds for refusal	6.3.1
hostel	6.5.3
juveniles	12.2.1
legal adviser, condition to attend	6.5.5
meaning	6.1
non-imprisonable offences, and	6.4
offence committed on,	
loss of right to bail	6.2.1
passport, surrender of	6.5.4
police bail	
before charge	3.7.3
after charge	3.7.3
post-conviction	10.2.2
refusal of	
factors	6.3.2
grounds for	6.3.1
reporting	6.5.2
residence	6.5.2
right to	6.2
loss of right to	6.2.1
right of audience in Crown Court	6.7.1
securities	6.5.4
street bail	2.4.5
sureties	6.5.1

Barrister,	
see Counsel, Brief	
Bias,	
collateral questions, and	19.2.1
Bind overs	10.6.2
Blackstone *Criminal Practice*	1.2.1
Blood,	
see Sample	
Brief,	7.4, Doc. 21
to Counsel,	
contents of	7.4
example of	Doc. 21
Burden of Proof,	
see Proof, burden of	

C

Cape, Ed, *Defending Suspects in the police station*	1.2.2, 3, 3.7.1
Case Analysis	
techniques of	9.1
Case management	1.4, 7.1, 7.1.2, 7.3
Case Stated	11.1.2
Caution	
for Conditional cautions see Police Caution	
failure to caution	2.3.1
formal or police caution, *see* Police Caution	
meaning and significance	2.3
ordinary language	15.3.2
questioning under, *see* Police Interview	
special, *see* ordinary language (*above*)	
terms of and requirement for	2.3, 2.3.1
what kind of caution	3.1.9
when required	2.3.1
CCTV, *see* Video	
CDS Direct,	
see Criminal Defence Service Direct	
Central Funds, costs from	4.2.1
Character, evidence of	Chapter 17
attacking character of another	17.2.7
bad character,	
meaning of	17.1.1
of defendant	17.2
bail	6.3.2
of non-defendant	17.3
co-Accused, and	17.2.5
false impression	17.2.6
gateways	17.2
general rule	17.1, 17.2
exceptions	17.2
good character	
putting in at trial	17.5
at sentencing	10.10.3
mitigation, and	
good character	10.10.3
previous convictions	10.1.3

police interview	3.3.6
procedure	17.2.9, 17.3.4
propensity generally	17.2.4
propensity for untruthfulness	17.2.4

Charge
bail after	3.7.3
bail before	3.7.3
detention without, *see* Detention	
inferences at	3.7.1
questioning after	3.7.1
requirement to,	3.7.1
sheet	Doc. 3
statement at	3.7.1
statutory charging	3.1.3, 3.7.1

Child
see also Juveniles, Youth Court
witness, as	14.3.3

Child Safety Orders	12.6.2
Citizen's Arrest	2.2.3

Clerk to Justices
mode of address	8.1.3
role	9.3

Client, *see* Defendant

Co-Accused *see* Defendant

Codes of Practice
for PACE Codes, see Table of Statutory Instruments etc.
Crown Prosecutors
disclosure	7.5.1

Collateral questions	19.2, 19.2.1

Commencement of proceedings
charge, by	5.1
decision to prosecute	5.1.2
information, laying	5.1
magistrates' courts, in	5.1
requisition, by	5.1
summons, by	5.1
time-limits	5.1.1
Notice of Intended Prosecution	5.1.1

Committal Proceedings, generally	Chapter 5

Community order 10.4
breach	10.4.5
curfew, *see* Curfew requirement	
persistent offenders	10.4.1
pre-sentence report	10.2.1
probation, *see* Supervision requirement	
requirements	10.4.2
seriousness bands	10.4.4
threshold for	10.4.1

Community support officer	2.2

Compellability,
see Witness

Compensation order	10.7.1

Competence
see Witness

Computers	18.1.5
Conditional caution	3.7.2
Conditional discharge	10.6.1

Conduct
see Professional Conduct

Confession
admissibility	16.1, 18.2.1
breach of PACE	
curing a breach, presence of	
a solicitor	16.4.3
unfairness, and	16.4.3
unreliability, and	16.2.4
co-Accused, admissibility of	16.2.3
definition of	16.2.1
excluding	16.2.4, 16.3, 16.4
exculpatory statements	16.2.2
hearsay, as	16.2.3, 18.2.1
mixed statements	16.2.2
oppression, obtained by	16.3.1
tricks	16.4.2
unfairness and	16.4, 16.4.1, 16.4.2, 16.4.3, 16.4.4
unreliability	16.3.2

Confiscation order	10.7.3
Conflict of Interest	3.3.5

Conviction *see* Criminal record; Sentencing

Corporate manslaughter	13.1.4

Corroboration
abolition	19.1
Makanjuola warning	19.1.2
meaning of	19.1

Costs
central funds, from	4.2.1
order	10.7.2

Counsel
attending at trial	7.4
briefing of	7.4
example of brief	Doc. 21

Court of Appeal
appeals to
conviction, against	11.2.1
sentence, against	11.2.2

Criminal Cases Review Commission	11.3.2

Criminal Defence Service
see generally	4.1

see also Advice and Assistance, Advocacy Assistance, Representation Order

Criminal Defence Service Direct	3.2.3

Criminal Litigation
see under specific entries
Outline of,	1.3.1
Overview of,	1.3

Criminal offence, *see* Offence

Criminal Procedure Rules
   Generally   1.4
   For specific Rules, see Table of Statutory Instruments in Introductory material.

Criminal record
   see Previous convictions

Cross examination, *see* Advocacy

Crown Court,
   appeals
      from the Crown Court   11.2.1, 11.2.2
      to the Crown Court   11.1.1
   bail, appeals to   6.7.1
   committal for sentence to,   5.6
   plea and case management hearing, *see* Plea and Case Management Hearing
   sentencing, *see* Sentencing
   trial in, *see* Trial on indictment
   voir dire, in, *see* Voir dire

Crown Prosecution Service
   Code for Crown Prosecutors   5.1.2

Culpability   10.1.2, 10.1.3

Curfew
   bail and   6.5.3
   early release and   10.3.5
   requirement   10.4.2

Custodial sentence   10.3
   dangerous offenders   10.3.8
   intermittent   10.3.7
   length of   10.3.5
   suspended   10.3.6
   threshold   10.3.1, 10.3.2

Custody *see also*
Arrest; Detention, Custodial sentence, Sentencing
   record, *see* Custody record
   release on bail, *see* Bail
   remand in   6.1.2
   time limits   6.1.3

Custody officer
   contacting   3.3.2
   duties of   3.1.1
      decision to detain   3.1.3
      entries in record   3.1.2
      requirement to charge   3.7.1
   information from   3.3.2

Custody plus   10.3.7

Custody record
   entries in   3.1.2
   example of   Doc.1
   failure to record   3.1.2
   inspection by solicitor   3.1.2

Custody time limits   6.1.3

D

Dangerous offenders   10.3.8

Defence
   alibi *see* alibi
   disclosure *see* Disclosure
   financing of, *see* Legal aid
   statement, *see* Disclosure

Defence solicitor call centre   3.2.1, 3.3.1

Defence statement
   contents of,   7.5.2
   Crown Court trial, in   7.5.1
   example of   Doc.18B
   inferences from   7.5.2
   summary trial, in   7.5.1, 7.5.2
   time-limit   7.5.2
   use by prosecution   7.5.2

Defendant
   character   *see* Character
   co-accused
      evidence against   16.3.2
      prosecution witness as   14.3.1
   compellability   14.3.1
   competence   14.3.1
   confession, *see* Confession
   failure to testify, *see* Inferences
   interview with police, by, *see* Police Interview
   previous convictions, *see* Character
   prosecution witness, as   14.3.1
   silence, right to, *see* Silence, Inferences
   statement, taking of
      comments on prosecution evidence   9.2.2
      example of   Doc. 10A and 10B
      taking the statement   9.2.2
spouse of, as witness   14.3.2
witness, defendant giving evidence before   9.3

Deferred sentence   10.2.6

Delay
   police station, at
      right of intimation   3.1.5
      right to legal advice   3.2.1
   prosecution in, 4.1.3

Detention, generally *see* **Chapter 3**
   appropriate adults, *see* Appropriate Adults
   Code of practice C, *see* **Chapter 3**
   conditions   3.1.6
   custody record, inspection of   3.1.2
   decision to detain   3.1.3
   intimation, right to   3.1.5
   juveniles, *see* Juveniles
   legal advice, *see* Legal advice (at Police Station)
   maximum periods   3.1.8
   obtaining evidence by questioning, for   3.1.3
   rest periods   3.1.6, 3.4.3
   reviews of   3.1.7
   search of person   3.1.4
   time limits, without charge   3.1.8
   warrant of further detention   3.1.8

Detention and Training Order   12.4.1

Directions hearing,
see Plea and Case Management

Discharge	
absolute	10.6.1
conditional	10.6.1

Disclosure
advance information	5.2
Attorney General's guidelines	7.5.1
code of practice	7.5.1
CPIA regime	7.5.1, 7.5.2

Crown Court, in
defence case, statement of
see also Defence statement
contents of,	7.5.2
example of,	Doc. 18B
prosecution, use by	7.5.2

expert evidence *see* Expert evidence
non-disclosure
police station, at	3.3.4
used material, in summary trial	7.5.1
police station, at	3.3.4
prosecution	7.5.1

summary trial, in
defence disclosure, in	7.5.2
prosecution unused material	7.5.1
prosecution used material	7.5.1

unused material
prosecution	7.5.1
Disqualification orders	10.6.4, 13.3.2

Disqualification from driving
see driving offences
as sentencing option	10.6.3

Divisional Court, *see* High Court

Dock Identification	3.6.7

Document, *see* Disclosure, Hearsay

Drinking Banning Orders	10.6.4

Driving offences
prosecution, warning of	5.1.1
sentencing and	10.8
disqualification	10.6.3, 10.8.2
mitigation and	10.8.3
points system	10.8.1

Drug testing
at the police station	3.1.4, 3.5
bail and	6.2.2

Duty solicitor scheme
court	4.1.2
police station	3.2.3, 3.3.1

E

Early Administrative Hearings	5.2.1
Early First Hearings	5.2.1
Either way offence, *see also* Mode of Trial	5.4

Ethics, *see* Professional conduct

European Convention on the Protection of Human Rights, *see* Table of Statutory Instruments etc. *for details. See also* Liberty, Fair Trial, Expression

Evans, Keith	1.2.3, 8.1.2, 8.5.1

Evidence
See: Alibi, Character, Confessions, Corroboration, Expert, Hearsay, Inferences, Opinion, Privilege, Proof, Relevance, Res gestae, Similar fact, Unfair evidence
fairness	14.2.4
general principles of	Chapter 14

hearsay, *see* Hearsay
improperly obtained
see generally	Chapter 16

see also confessions, unfair evidence
judicial notice	14.1.1

previous convictions, *see* Character, Previous convictions
proof, burden and standard	14.4.2
real	14.2.6
recent possession	14.4.2

relevance, *see* Relevance
res gestae, *see* Hearsay, Res gestae
silence, *see* Silence, Inferences
similar fact, *see* Similar Fact

Examination in chief, *see* Advocacy

Expert witness
disclosure of evidence	7.5.2
hearsay and	19.4.3
notice of evidence	7.5.2, 19.4.4
opinion evidence	19.4.1
who is	19.4.2

Expression, freedom of
see article 10 ECHR (Table of Stat. Inst. etc.)

F

Fair trial,
see article 6 ECHR (Table of Stat. Inst. etc.)

Fines, generally	10.5
ability to pay	10.5.1
against companies	13.3.3
amount of	10.5.2
other penalties, with	10.5.3

Fingerprints	3.5
Fixed penalty notices	2.4.6
Forfeiture order	10.7.3
Footwear impressions	3.5
Fraudulent trading	13.1.2
Fruit of the poisoned tree	16.3.3

G

Gangs
reasonable suspicion and,	2.1.3

Guilty plea
    either way offence, *see* mode of trial
    early guilty plea
        discount   **3.3.5, 5.4, 10.1.4**
        Newton hearings, and   **10.2.5**
    At PCMH   **7.3**

H

Health and Safety   **13.2.2**

Hearsay evidence   **Chapter 18**
    admissibility,
        generally   **Chapter 18**
        judicial discretion   **18.3.1**
    business document in   **18.3.3**
    capability   **18.3.6**
    common law exceptions   **18.3.4**
    computers, and   **18.1.5**
    confessions,   **16.2.3**
    credibility   **18.3.7**
    definition   **18.1.1**
    discretion   **18.3.1**
    exceptions
        common law, *see* res gestae,
        statutory, *see* first hand, multiple,
        business document
    excluding   **18.3.8**
    first-hand (s.116)   **18.3.2**
    human rights challenges   **18.4.1**
    implied assertions   **18.1.4**
    judicial discretion   **18.3.1**
    multiple   **18.3.5**
    non factual statements   **18.1.2**
    res gestae   **18.2.2**
    section 9 statement   **18.3.8**
    weight   **18.3.5**

High Court
see also Queen's Bench Division
    appeal, by case stated   **11.1.2**

Home Detention Curfew   **10.3.5**

Human Rights Act, *see also the* Table of Statutes.

I

Identification   **3.6**
    confrontation   **3.6.5**
    disputed   **19.1.3**
    dock   **3.6.7**
    evidence of
        admissibility   **16.4.3, 19.1.3**
        disputed   **19.1.3**
    group   **3.6.5**
    known suspect   **3.6.4**
    methods of   **3.6.5**
    parade
        record of   **3.6.5**
        refusal to stand in   **3.6.5**
    PACE Code D, *see* **3.6.**, *see also* Table of Statutes
    Photographs   **3.6.6**
    Turnbull guidelines   **19.1.3**

    unknown suspect   **3.6.4, 3.6.6**
    video   **3.6.5**

Immigration detainees   **3.7.4**

Improperly obtained evidence,
see Unfair evidence.

Imprisonment, *see also* Custodial
sentence; Sentencing

Improvement notice   **13.2.2**

Indictment
see also Trial on indictment
    meaning

Indictable offences – definition   **2.2**

Inferences
    defence facts, failure to mention (s.34)
        3.3.6, 15,2, 15.2.1, 15.2.2, 15.2.3
    defence statement, and   **7.5.2**
    defendant's silence, at common law   **15.1**
    disclosure, by police and   **3.3.4**
    effect of inference
        matter for jury   **15.2.2**
        not enough to prove guilt   **15.2.2**
    failure to provide intimate sample   **3.5**
    failure to testify (s.35)   **15.4, 15.4.1**
    identification, and   **3.6.**
    non-disclosure by police, and   **3.3.4**
    object, substance, mark, failure to account for (s.36)
        15.3, 15.3.1, 15.3.2
    ordinary language caution   **15.3.2**
    presence, failure to account for (s.37)
        15.3, 15.3.1, 15.3.2
    privilege, waiver of   **3.4.1, 15.2.2, 15.2.3**
    solicitor's advice, silence on   **15.2.2**

Information
    duplicity   **5.1.2**
    joinder, *see* Joinder
    laying   **5.1**

Intermittent custody   **10.3.7**

Internet
    sources   **1.2.4**

Interview
see Police Interview
    at police station
        client, with
        3.3.5, 3.3.6, 3.3.7, 3.4, 3.4.1, 3.4.2, 3.4.3
    definition of, PACE   **2.4.4**
    to take statement
        client, with   **9.2.2**
        witness, with   **9.2.3**

Intimate Sample
    see Sample

Intimation, right to   **3.1.5**

Investment frauds   **13.1.3**

Investigating officer,
    see Officer in the Case

Investigation, *see also* Detention;

J

Joinder
- offences, of   5.1.2
- offenders, of   5.1.2

Judge
- mode of address   8.1.3

Judicial notice   14.1.1

Judicial review   6.7.4, 11.1.3

Jury, *see also* Inference
- arraignment   9.4.1

Juveniles, generally   **Chapter 12**
- appropriate adult   3.7.4, 12.2.1
- arrest   12.2.1
- bail   3.7.3, 12.2.1
- Crime and Disorder Act, and
  - anti social behaviour orders   12.6.1
  - child curfew schemes   12.6.3
  - child safety orders   12.6.2
  - detention and training orders   12.4.1
  - parenting orders   12.4.1
  - principal aim   12.4
  - reparation orders   12.4.1
  - reprimands and warnings   12.2.2
  - truants   12.6.5
- Crown Court, trial in   12.3.2
- *doli incapax*, abolition of   12.1
- magistrates' court, trial in   12.3.1
- police reprimand, and   12.2.2
- sentencing, and   12.4
  - Crown Court, in   12.4.3
  - magistrates' court, in   12.4.2
  - Youth Court, in   12.4.1
- seventeen to twenty year olds
  - attendance centre orders   12.5
  - custodial sentences   12.5
- Youth Court, and   12.3

K

Knives.
- bladed instruments, search for   2.1.2

L

Leading questions   8.2.1

Legal advice at Police Station
- advising your client   3.3, 3.3.5, 3.3.6, 3.3.7, 3.4, 3.4.2,
- CDS Direct   3.2.3
- delaying access to
  - permitted delays   3.2.2
- disclosure, refusal of   3.3.4
- exclusion, threats of   3.4.2
- intervening to give   3.4.2
- interviews with police, and   2.4.4, 3.3.6, 3.3.7, 3.4, 3.4.1
- no longer required   3.2.2
- payment for,   3.2.3
- right to   3.2, 3.2.1, 3.2.2,
- silence, whether to exercise right to   3.3.6
- telephone contact   3.3.2
- volunteer detainee, of

Legal aid
generally, see Chapter 4
see also Advice and Assistance, Advocacy Assistance, Criminal Defence Service, Representation Order

Legal professional privilege   20.3

Liberty, right to
see article 5 ECHR (Table of Stat. Inst. etc.)

Local Child Curfew Schemes   12.6.3

M

Magistrates,
- district judge   5.2
- lay justices   5.2

Magistrates' Association
Sentencing Guidelines   10.1, 10.10.2

Magistrates' court
- adjournments
  - generally   5.1
  - mistake, to correct   5.1.2
- appeals from
  - Crown Court, to   11.1.1
  - Divisional Court, to   11.1.2
- bail, *see* Bail
- clerk,
  - mode of address   8.1.3
- commencement of proceedings *see* Commencement of proceedings
- committal
  - sentence, for   5.6
- disclosure in, *see* Summary trial, Disclosure
- duty solicitor scheme   4.1.2
- first appearance in
  - Early Administrative Hearings   5.2.1
- Early First Hearings   5.2.1
- legal aid in   4.1.2
- remands   6.1.1, 6.1.2
- sentencing, *see* Sentencing
  - powers   10.3.1
- trial, *see* Summary trial

Mandatory sentences   10.3.5

Memory refreshing, *see* Witness

Mentally disordered offenders Chapter 12
- Appropriate adult   12.8.2
- Fitness to plead   12.9.1
- Identification of   12.8.1
- Interview   12.8.2
- Police station   12.8
- Sentencing   12.10

Mistakes,
- in magistrates' court
  - summons or charge   5.1.2

Mitigation
    driving offences, and   10.8.3
    factors,
        aggravating and mitigating   **10.1.2, 10.1.3, 10.1.4**
guilty plea, discount, *see* Guilty plea
speech   **8.5.2, 10.10**
    basics   10.10.1.
    example of   **Doc. 24**
    organisation   10.10.2
    white collar and regulatory offence   13.3.4

Mode of address, *see* Advocacy

Mode of trial hearing
    generally   5.4
    letter to client   **Doc.11**

Motoring, *see* Driving offences

Money laundering   13.1.1

N

Newton hearing   10.2.5, 7.3.1

No case to answer
    submission of,   9.3

Non-disclosure, *see* Disclosure

Notice of appeal   **Doc.25**

Notice of Intended Prosecution   5.1.1

O

Offence
    classification of   1.3
    driving, *see* Driving;
    either way, list of   1.3
    indictable   1.3
    joinder, *see* Joinder
    summary, trial of   9.3
    taken into consideration (TIC)   10.2.4
    triable either way, *see* Either way offence

Offence triable either way,
    see Either Way Offence, mode of trial

Officer in the case
    disclosure by   3.3.4

Opinion evidence   19.4, 19.4.1
    experts, opinion of
        disclosure of evidence   7.5.2
        hearsay and   19.4.3

Overriding objective   1.4

P

PACE, Codes of Practice
    for individual sections, see Table of Statutory Instruments etc.
    effect of breach   16.3, 16.4

Parenting Orders   12.4.1

Penalty notice procedure   10.5

Photograph
    documentary evidence, as
    police station, at
        using for identification   3.6
        of the detainee   3.5
    use in court   9.2.3

Plea
    fitness to plead – Crown Court   **12.9.1, 12.9.2**
        – Magistrates Court   **12.9.3**
    guilty, see Guilty plea
    not guilty
        plea before venue   5.4.1

Plea and case management hearing   **7.3, Doc. 20**

Plea bargaining   9.4.1

Plea before venue
    mode of trial hearing, at   5.4.1

Police
see Custody officer; Officer in the case
    arrest and detention, powers of*see* **Chapters 2 and 3** generally
    caution, *see* Caution
    questioning, see Interviewing suspect (police)

Police Bail   3.7.3

Police Caution   **3.7.2, 12.2.2**

Police Interview
    see also Inferences, Silence, right to
    advising the client   **3.3, 3.3.5, 3.3.6, 3.3.7, 3.4, 3.4.2**
    character evidence   3.3.6
    definition of,   2.4.4
    exclusion, threats of   3.4.2
    intervening during   3.4.2
    introductions   3.4.1
        waiver of privilege, and   3.4.1
    legal advice, *see* Legal Advice at Police Station
    length of   3.4.3
    mentally disordered   12.8.2
    no comment, *see* Silence, Inferences
    partial comment   3.3.7
    preparing the client for   3.3.7
    prior to legal advice   2.4.4
    silence, whether to exercise right to   3.3.6
    see also Silence, Inferences
    stopping the interview   3.3.7

Police and Criminal Evidence Act, *see* PACE
Police Powers
    see; Arrest; Detention, Search

Police station	
see especially **Chapter 3**	
attendance, decision to	3.3.3
detention at, *see* Detention	
interview at,	
see Inferences; Police Interview; Silence,	
legal advice at, *see* Legal advice at Police Station	
procedure at	
3.3.2, 3.3.3, 3.3.4, 3.3.5, 3.3.7, 3.4.1, 3.4.2	
removal to, post-arrest	2.4.4
Preliminary hearing	7.3
Preparatory hearing	7.3
Pre-sentence report	10.2.1
Presumptions,	14.4.2, 14.5.1
Pre-trial hearings	7.2, 7.3
Previous convictions	
collateral questions,	
exception to rule	19.2.1
defendant, of	
bail, and	6.2.1, 6.3.2
cross-examination, on, *see also* Character	
generally	**Chapter 17**
professional conduct and,	
see Professional Conduct	
sentencing, and	10.1.3
witness, of	17.1.2
Previous inconsistent statements,	
see Statements	
Prison , *see also* Custodial sentence; Sentencing	
Privilege, generally	14.2.2, **Chapter 20**
effect of	20.1.1
inferences, waiver of, and	3.4.1, 15.2.2, 20.1.2
lawyer client	20.3
legal and professional, *see* lawyer client (*above*)	
police station, waiver of	3.4.1
public policy immunity	20.4
search and	2.5.3, 20.3
self incrimination	20.2
waiver,	
see also inferences and waiver (*above*)	20.1.2
accidental	20.1.2
severability	20.1.2
Probation *see* Supervision requirement	
Proceeds of crime	13.3.1
assets recovery agency	13.3.1
confiscation order	13.3.1
financial investigation officer	13.3.1
receivership order	13.3.1
restraint order	13.3.1
Proceedings, *see* Commencement of proceedings;	
Professional conduct	
advocacy, and	8.1.4, 8.7
advocate as witness	8.1.4, 8.7
mitigation	10.10.3
unhelpful law	8.1.4, 8.7
convictions, confirming client's	10.2.3

counsel	
attending	7.4
paying	7.4
defence	
duty to client	1.1.3
guilty, client who says he is	3.3.5, 8.7
inconsistent instructions	3.3.5
misleading the court	8.7
prosecution witnesses, interviewing	9.2.3
standing surety	6.5.1
Prohibition notice	13.2.2
Proof	
burden of	14.4.1, 14.5
defence, on	14.4.1, 14.5
generally	14.4.1
prosecution, on	14.4.1
presumptions	14.4.2, 14.5.1
standard of	14.4.2
Proof of evidence	9.2.1, 9.2.2
Prosecution	
burden of proof, *see* Proof	
Code for prosecutors	
commencement of	
see Commencement of proceedings; Summons	
disclosure	
advance information	5.2
unused material	7.5.1, 7.5.2
magistrates' court	7.5.1
standard of proof, *see* Proof	
Public policy immunity	14.2.2, 20.4
categories of sensitive information	20.4.1
non-disclosure and the CPIA	20.4.2
Publicity order	13.1.4
Putting your case	8.3.1

Q

Queen's Bench Division Divisional Court
see High Court

Questioning, see Police Interview, Inferences

R

Real evidence	14.2.6
Receivership order	13.3.1
Record	
custody, *see* Custody record	
Re-examination, *see* Advocacy	
Referral orders	12.4.1
Regulatory offences	**Chapter 13**
health and safety	13.2.2
trading standards	13.2.1
sentencing	13.3

Relative
    detainee's right to inform, *see* Intimation

Relevance   14.2.5

Remand
    adjournment, or   6.1.1
    length of   6.1.2

Remedial order   13.1.4

Reparation Orders   12.4.1

Report
    expert, of   *see* Expert witness
    pre-sentence   *see* Pre sentence report

Representation Order
    application form
        example of   Doc.5
        how to complete   4.1.2, 4.1.3
        applying for   4.1.2, 4.1.3
        criteria   4.1.2, 4.1.3
        interests of justice test   4.1.2, 4.1.3
        means test   4.1.4
        scope   4.1.2

Res gestae   18.3.4

Restraint orders   13.3.1

Residence
    bail condition   6.5.2

Retrial   5.1.2, 9.4.4

Reverse onus provisions, *see* Proof, burden of

Rights of audience, *see* Advocacy

Road traffic case
see Driving offences

S

Samples
    suspect, from   3.5
    intimate   3.5
    non-intimate   3.1.4, 3.5

Search, police power of
    persons
        2.1, 2.1.1, 2.1.2, 2.1.3, 2.1.5, 2.1.6, 2.1.7
        arrest, after   2.4.1
        consent   2.1.6
        detention, after   3.1.4
        identification, to establish **3.1.4**
        limitations,   2.1.4
        police station, at
        questions before search   2.1.5
        reasonable grounds for suspicion,   2.1.3
        stolen or prohibited articles   2.1.2
        terrorism, anticipation of   2.1.7
        violence, anticipation of   2.1.7
    premises
        after arrest   2.4
        to delay access to lawyer   2.4.4
        of premises controlled etc.   2.4.3
        of premises where arrested   2.4.2
        general power   2.5.2

search warrant, *see* Search warrant
seizure, *see* Seizure

Search warrant   2.5.1

Security
    bail, condition of   6.5.4

Seizure
    material, of   2.5.3
    privilege, and   2.5.3, 20.3

Self-incrimination
    privilege, and   20.2

Sentencing, generally   Chapter 10
    absolute discharge   10.6.1
    adjournment, power to   10.2.2
    aggravating factor   10.1.3
    ancillary orders   10.7
    antecedents   10.2.3
    appeal against sentence, *see* Appeals
    associated offences   10.3.4
    bind overs   10.6.2
    committal for   5.6
    community penalty   10.4
        breach   10.4.5
        threshold for   10.4.1
    compensation order   10.7.1
    conditional discharge   10.6.1
    confiscation order   10.7.3
    costs orders   10.7.2
    curfew requirement   10.4.2
    custodial sentence   10.3
        criteria for   10.3.1, 10.3.2
        custody plus   10.3.7
        early release   10.3.5
        length   10.3.5
        mandatory   10.3.5
    custody threshold   10.3.1, 10.3.2
    dangerous offenders   10.3.8
    deferred   10.2.6
    discount, see Guilty plea
    discharge,   10.6.1
        absolute   10.6.1, 12.9.2
        conditional   10.6.1
    dispute as to facts, *see Newton* hearing
    disqualification from driving
        see Driving offences
        as sentencing option   10.6.3
    driving offences, *see* Driving offences
    early release   10.3.5
    fines, generally   10.5
        ability to pay   10.5.1
        amount of   10.5.2
        other penalties, with   10.5.3
    forfeiture order   10.7.3
    guilty plea, discount for
                                     3.3.5, 5.4.1, 10.1.4
    hospital order   12.9.2
    imprisonment, *see* custodial sentence
    juveniles, *see* Juveniles
    mandatory   10.3.5
    maximum sentence at
        magistrates' court   10.3.1
    mentally disordered   12.10

mitigation and, *see* Mitigation	
motoring cases, *see* Driving offences	
Newton hearings	**10.2.5**
pre-sentence reports	**10.2.1**
example of	**Doc. 23**
previous convictions, and	**10.1.3**
procedure, post-conviction	**10.2**
reports, need for	**10.2.1**
Sentencing Guidelines Council	
See Table of *Stat. Inst.*	
seriousness tests	
custody	**10.3.1**
community penalty	**10.4.1**
specimen	**10.2.4**
suspended sentence	**10.3.6**
taken into consideration, offences	**10.2.4**
Youth Court, in	*see* Juvenile

Serious Fraud Office   **13.1**

Sex Offender Orders   **10.6.4**

Shaw, Noel, *Effective Advocacy*   **1.2.3**

Silence, *see also* Inferences
advising client on	**3.3.6**
inferences, *see* Inferences, Police Interview	
at charge	**3.7.1**
interviews, and	**3.3.6**
right to	**15.1**
solicitor's advice, silence on	**3.3.6, 15.2.2, 15.2.3**
trial, at	

Solicitor
see also Legal advice (at Police Station)	
conduct, *see* Professional Conduct	
duty solicitor schemes	
court	**4.1.2**
police station	**3.2.3**
ethics, *see* Professional conduct	
interview	
see Interview, Police Interview	
police station, at	**3.3, 3.4**
see also Police Interview	
advising suspect	
3.3, 3.3.5, 3.3.6, 3.3.7, 3.4, 3.4.2	
attendance at	**3.3.3**
duties of	**3.4**
privilege, and	**3.4.1**
remuneration	
legal aid order, *see* Legal Aid	
police station	**3.2.3, Doc.9**
representation by, *see* audience, rights of (*above*)	
statements, taking	
client	**9.2.2**
example	**Doc.10**
defence witnesses	**9.2.3**
generally	**9.2.1**

Special measures, for witnesses   **14.3.4**

Speech,
closing, *see* Advocacy
mitigation, *see* Mitigation
opening, *see* Advocacy

Spouse
as witness	**14.3.2**

Statements
consistent	**19.2.3**
recent fabrication, and	**19.2.3**
defence, by, *see* Defence statement, Disclosure	
inconsistent	**19.2.2**
hostile witnesses	**19.2.2**
taking statements	
client	**9.2.2**
example	**Doc.10**
defence witnesses	**9.2.3**
generally	**9.2.1**

Street bail   **2.4.5**

Stones *Justices Manual*   **1.2.1**

Stop and Search
see Search

Summary offence *see also* Magistrates' court;

Summary trial
disclosure	**7.5, 7.5.1, 7.5.2**
see also Disclosure	
costs	**4.2.1**
electing,	
see mode of trial	
joinder	**5.1.2**
jurisdiction	**5.1.1**
mistake in summons etc.	**5.1.2**
preparation for,	
generally	**Chapter 9**
case analysis	**9.1**
witness statements	**9.2**
disclosure	**7.5, 7.5.1, 7.5.2**
procedure	**9.3**

Supervision requirement   **10.4.2**

Surety   **6.5.1**

Suspended sentence   **10.3.6**

Suspicion, reasonable   **2.1.3**

T

Taken into consideration, *see* Sentencing

Tape-recording
documentary evidence, as

Third party, contact from
right to see detainee	**3.3.1**
right to take instructions from	**3.3.1**

Thomas,
Encyclopaedia of Sentencing Practice   **1.2.2**

Trading Standards   **13.2.1**

Trial
Crown Court, in, *see* Trial on indictment
indictment, *see* Trial on indictment
magistrates, in, *see* Summary trial
summary, *see* Summary trial

Trial on indictment *see also* Crown Court
    counsel, briefing   **7.4, Doc. 21**
    jury   9.4.2
    listing for   7.3
    preparation   **Chapter 9**
    procedure   9.4.3
    sentence, see Sentencing

Turnbull guidelines   19.1.3

U

Unfair evidence   **Chapter 16**
    adverse impact on fairness
        16.4, 16.4.1, 16.4.2, 16.4.3, 16.4.4
    breach of PACE, and   16.3.2, 16.4.3
    curing a breach, presence of a solicitor
        3.4.2, 16.4.3
    common law, at   16.1
    discretion, judge's   16.4.3
    fruit of the poisoned tree   16.3.3
    oppression   16.3.1
    tricks   16.4.2
    undercover policing   16.4.4
    unfairness where no breach of PACE   16.4.3
    unreliability   16.3.2

Unreliability,
    confessions and   16.3.2

V

Victim Impact Statements   10.3.3
Victim surcharge   10.5.3
Video evidence   14.3.4
Video identification   3.6.5
Violent offender order   10.6.4
Voir Dire   8.6
    crown court, in   9.4.3
Volunteer
    police station, at   3.1.3

W

Warned list   7.3
Warrants
    arrest   2.2.2
    further detention   3.1.8
    search   2.5.1
Wasted costs orders   4.2.2
White collar crime   **Chapter 13**
    Corporate manslaughter   13.1.4
    Fraudulent trading   13.1.2
    Investment frauds   13.1.3
    Money laundering   13.1.1
    Proceeds of crime   13.3.1
    Sentencing   13.3

Witness
    alibi   9.2.3
    afraid   18.3.2
    attendance
    unwilling witness   9.2.3, 7.3.2
    child,   14.3.3
    compellability   14.3
    defendant   14.3.1
    competence   14.3
    child   14.3.3
    Co-Accused   14.3.1
    defendant   14.3.1
    spouse   14.3.2
    dead   18.3.2
    document, contemporaneous, use of   8.2.2
    expert
    hostile   19.2.2
    ill   18.3.2
    insane   18.3.2
    interference, bail and   6.3.1
    interviewing, *see* statement, taking (*below*)
    lost,   18.3.2
    memory, refreshing   8.2.2, 19.3
    reliability   **Chapter 19**
    special measures   14.3.4
    statement,
    taking   9.2
    summons   7.3.2
    unfavourable   19.2.2
    waiting outside court   8.7

Y

Youth Court
    see Juvenile